The Mass Media:

Aspen Institute
Guide to Communication
Industry Trends

Christopher H. Sterling Professor, Department of
Radio-TV-Film
Temple University

Timothy R. Haight Institute for Communication
Research, Stanford University

Published with the
Aspen Institute for
Humanistic Studies

The Praeger Special Studies program,
through a selective worldwide distribution
network, makes available to the academic,
government, and business communities significant and timely research in U.S. and
international economic, social, and political issues.

→ # The Mass Media: #b

Aspen Institute
Guide to Communication
Industry Trends

PRAEGER SPECIAL STUDIES IN U.S. ECONOMIC, SOCIAL, AND POLITICAL ISSUES

Praeger Publishers   New York   London

Library of Congress Cataloging in Publication Data

Sterling, Christopher H. 1943-
  The mass media.

  (Praeger Special Studies in U. S. Economic, Social,
and Political Issues)
  (Published with the Aspen Institute Program on
Communications and Society)
  1. Mass media—United States. I. Timothy R. Haight.
II. Aspen Institute Program on Communications and Society.
III. Title.
P92.U5S68   301.16'1'0973   76-24370
ISBN 0-275-24020-7

  **The publishers have obtained permission to reprint copyrighted tabular and other materials
from the following individuals, publishers, and organizations:** Advertising Research Foundation,
New York; Agency for Instructional Television, Bloomington, Ind.; American Film Institute,
Washington, D.C.; American Library Association, Chicago; American Newspaper Publishers Asso-
ciation, Washington, D.C.; Annenberg School of Communications, University of Pennsylvania;
The Arbitron Company, New York; Arno Press Inc., New York; Associated Publications,Kansas
City, Mo.; Association of American Publishers, New York; Audit Bureau of Circulations, Chicago;
Ayer Press, Philadelphia; Ben H. Bagdikian, University of California, Berkeley; Ted Bates and
Company, New York; Batten Barton Durstine and Osborn, Inc., New York; *Billboard*, Los Angeles;
John Blair & Company, New York; Robert T. Bower, Bureau of Social Science Research, Washing-
ton, D.C.: R. R. Bowker Company,[1] New York; *Boxoffice*, Kansas City, Mo.; Broadcasting Publi-
cations, Inc., Washington, D.C.; University of California Press,[2] Berkeley; Children's Television
Workshop (CTW), New York; Mrs. John Cogley, Santa Barbara, Calif.; Communications Resource
Center, Washington, D.C.; The Conference Board, New York; Corporation for Public Broadcasting,
Washington, D.C.; John P. Dessauer, Darien, Conn.; Duke University,[3] Chapel Hill, N.C.; *Editor
and Publisher*, New York; Electronic Industries Association, Washington, D.C.; Fearon-Pitman
Publishers, Inc., Belmont, Calif.; The Ford Foundation, New York; *Foreign Service Journal*, Wash-
ington, D.C.; *Fortune*, New York; Freedom of Information (FOI) Center, Columbia, Mo.; W. H.

PRAEGER PUBLISHERS

200 Park Avenue, New York, N.Y. 10017, U.S.A.

Published in the United States of America in 1978
by Praeger Publishers, A Division of
Holt, Rinehart and Winston, CBS, Inc.

© 1978 by the Aspen Institute for Humanistic Studies
ISBN: 0-275-24020-7

Printed in the United States of America

Book design and composition by Teresa Mallen
Typesetting by Diane M. Willis

Freeman and Company Publishers, San Francisco; The R. Russell Hall Company, Greenwich, Conn.; Harvard University Program on Information Technologies and Public Policies, Cambridge, Mass.; Hastings House, Publishers, Inc., New York; David Hatcher, University of Wisconsin-Madison; Hope Reports, Inc., Rochester, N.Y.; University of Illinois Press, Urbana; *Journal of Broadcasting*, University of Georgia, Athens; *Journalism Quarterly*, Ohio University, Athens; Paul Kagan Associates, Inc., Rockville Centre, N.Y.; Alfred A. Knopf, Inc., New York; Knowledge Industry Publications, Inc., White Plains, N.Y.; James Larson, Stanford University, Stanford, Calif.; Timothy L. Larson, University of Utah, Salt Lake City; Lexington Books,[4] Lexington, Mass.; Lawrence W. Lichty, University of Wisconsin-Madison; A. D. Little Company, Cambridge, Mass.; Macmillan Publishing Company Inc.,[5] New York; Magazine Publishers Association, Inc., New York; Marketing World, Ltd., Baldwin, N.Y.; McCann-Erickson, Inc., New York; *Merchandising*, New York; Michigan State University Press, East Lansing; Moody's Investor's Service, Inc., New York; Motion Picture Association of America, Inc., New York; National Association of Broadcasters, Washington, D.C.; National Association of Educational Broadcasters, Washington, D.C.; National Association of Record Merchandisers, Cherry Hill, N.J.; National Association of Theater Owners, New York; National Broadcasting Company, New York; *The New York Times*; New York University Press; The Newspaper Advertising Bureau, New York; Nielsen Television Index, A. C. Nielsen Company, Northbrook, Ill.; University of North Carolina Press,[6] Chapel Hill; Christine L. Ogan, Bloomington, Ind.; Paul Peterson, Ohio State University, Columbus; Overseas Press Club of America, Inc., New York; Jerome Ozer Publications, Englewood, N.J.; Pennsylvania State University Press, University Park; Prentice-Hall, Inc., Englewood Cliffs, N.J.; Publishers Information Bureau, New York; *Publishers Weekly*,[7] New York; Radio Advertising Bureau, New York; The Rand Corporation, Santa Monica, Calif.; Random House, Inc., New York; Recording Industry Association of America, Inc., New York; Fernando Reyes Matta, Instituto Latinoamericano de Estudios Transnacionales, Mexico City; Screen Actors Guild, Hollywood; James N. Rosse, Stanford University, Stanford, Calif.; Donald L. Shaw, University of North Carolina, Chapel Hill; W. R. Simmons and Associates, New York; Southern Illinois University Press,[8] Carbondale; Standard Rate and Data Service, Inc., Skokie, Ill.; *Television Digest*, Inc., Washington, D.C.; Television Information Office, New York; Tucker Anthony and R. L. Day, Inc., New York; UNESCO Publications,[9] Paris; United Church of Christ, Office of Communication, New York; *Variety* Newspaper, New York; Wadsworth Publishing Company, Inc., Belmont, Calif.; Bureau of Research and Service, University of Wisconsin-Madison; Writers Guild of America West, Inc., Los Angeles; Book Industry Study Group, Inc.

Contents

SECTION 1
GROWTH OF THE MEDIA INDUSTRIES

**SECTION 2
OWNERSHIP AND CONTROL OF THE MEDIA INDUSTRIES**

SECTION 3

SECTION 4
EMPLOYMENT AND TRAINING IN THE MEDIA INDUSTRIES

SECTION 5
CONTENT TRENDS IN THE MEDIA

SECTION 6
SIZE AND CHARACTERISTICS OF MEDIA AUDIENCES

SECTION 7
U.S. MEDIA INDUSTRIES ABROAD

Preface

This book is a collection and assessment of the currently available quantitative descriptive information on the mass media industries of the United States. The core of the book is its more than 300 tables of data. These data are supplemented by a brief interpretative text, an analysis of source reliability and validity, and a listing of several sources of further information in each subject area.

The purpose of the book is to provide a single reference source for the most significant statistics describing communication industry trends in the United States since 1900. In compiling this information, the editors and their sponsors have endeavored to create something of a census or benchmark of currently available data which will allow researchers and media-industry professionals to focus on subject areas for which statistical information has been either unavailable or insufficient or widely scattered. It is hoped that this volume will support the eventual development of a series of statistical indicators through which communication industry trends can be more readily identified and understood.

This book can be approached in many different ways, depending on what the reader is seeking. There is a strong historical tone to the book; for wherever possible, the editors have traced the development of given segments of the media over as many years as data are available. The editors have also purposely divided the book into seven general subject areas (ownership, economics, content, audience, etc.), rather than by media industries, in order to encourage the reader to think of the media in relation to one another. Within each subject area, the units are arranged and numbered according to the following media categories:

00-09	general background data describing two or more media
10-19	books
20-29	newspapers
30-39	magazines
40-49	recordings
50-59	motion pictures
60-69	broadcasting in general
70-79	radio
80-89	television
90-99	cable television

The editors have gathered data from all available sources—government, business and trade, academic, and private correspondence. In all cases, the intention has been to compile as much primary data as possible—to use figures based on either a thorough census or a carefully constructed sample survey. Nevertheless, the reliability and validity of the data printed here vary widely; for in some subject areas, the available information is either meager or somewhat suspect or both. The usefulness and validity of the data are assessed by the editors in the "Sources" section of the text of each unit.

As is often the case with complex reference books, what you are reading here is not what the editors and sponsors originally intended to publish. A bit of background on the development of the book will help to explain much of what the reader does or does not see in these pages.

The project began early in 1975 as the brainchild of Douglass Cater, the founding director of the Aspen Institute's Program on Communication and Society. Cater presented the idea to the editors, who undertook the development of a detailed proposal. The book was initially conceived as a small reference work of perhaps 100 tables with a brief supporting text. The guiding principle was to gather existing data, rather than to generate new information, and to employ these data in the development of some cogent communication industry indicators.

As work on the project progressed, the editors found both too little and too much material for the kind of book that was first envisioned. The abundance of interesting and useful data in some subject areas doubled and then tripled the original projection for the length of the book.

On the other hand, the editors discovered that much of the available data was still too limited, and communication theory too underdeveloped, to permit acceptable statistical indicators to be developed. In many subject areas, these limitations resulted mainly from insufficient research. In other areas, the problem appeared to be obfuscation or careless record-keeping by the industries themselves.

Thus, by necessity, this book has become a longer, more ambitious statistical abstract of the communication industries. There was a good deal of coordination and cooperative writing on the Introduction and on the more general units of this book, but Haight had final responsibility for the material on books, newspapers, and magazines, while Sterling was responsible for motion pictures, recordings, radio-television, and cable systems.

If there is sufficient interest in *The Mass Media*, the editors and sponsors intend to continue the work of gathering, analyzing, and generalizing these data for a revised and more comprehensive edition in 1982. Work is also beginning on a companion volume—*Point-to-Point Communications: An Aspen Institute Guide to Communication Industry Trends*. With these two goals in mind, we welcome and encourage comments and suggestions on all aspects of this book.

Palo Alto, California   Christopher H. Sterling
March 1978   Timothy R. Haight

Acknowledgements

First of all, the editors would like to acknowledge those who provided inspiration for *The Mass Media*. Douglass Cater should be mentioned at the top of the list; for it was he who initiated the project in 1975, when he was serving as Director of the Aspen Institute Program on Communications and Society. As a White House Special Assistant working on the Public Broadcasting Act of 1967, Mr. Cater had first-hand experience with the hardships of discussing and planning communications policy without a comprehensive source book of readily comparable data.

Also due a special mention is Richard Chapin, of Michigan State University, whose *Mass Communications: A Statistical Analysis* (1957) is clearly a direct ancestor of this book, in intent if not in form. Chapin's pioneering work was the first published attempt to gather and assess the state of communications industry statistics. Professor Chapin also reviewed a draft of *The Mass Media* manuscript and generously provided many useful suggestions and additions.

The editors also took several useful ideas on approach and treatment from Fritz Machlup's *The Production and Distribution of Knowledge in the United States* (1962), a sophisticated analysis which encompasses far more than the mass media. Special thanks is due as well to William S. Lofquist, of the Printing and Publishing Industries Division of the U.S. Department of Commerce, who reviewed the manuscript and provided much helpful advice.

We would like to express our gratitude to those who attended a planning conference for *The Mass Media* at the Markle Foundation in New York in 1976: Anthony G. Oettinger, Director of the Program on Information Resources Policy at Harvard University; Lloyd N. Morrisett, President of the Markle Foundation; Fritz Machlup and Bruce Kagan of Princeton University; and Marc U. Porat, Forrest Chisman, and Roland S. Homet of the Aspen Institute Program on Communications and Society.

Creating a book such as *The Mass Media* is as much an exercise in information-gathering as it is in writing. Although the editors spent a considerable amount of time gathering data themselves, they frequently turned to others for help. Thus, we would like to offer our special thanks to Douglas Ferguson of the Stanford University Libraries and to Kathryn de Garza of Temple University, both of whom provided invaluable advice in locating sources of information and many helpful suggestions on approach and organization. Our thanks, too, to Conrad Smith, Michael Woal, Juliet Lushbough, and Daniel Appelman of Temple University for their assistance. We are especially grateful to John P. Dessauer, of John P. Dessauer, Inc., for his help in locating and understanding book industry statistics.

Many other individuals and organizations were generous in providing us with data. Among them are Herbert Alexander, Director, Citizens Research Foundation; American Film Institute; Arbitron Television; John F. Baker, Paul D. Doebler, and Chandler B. Grannis, *Publishers Weekly*; Edward I. Barz, W. R. Simmons and Associates Research; John Blair and Company; Henry S. Breitrose, Stanford University; George Brightbill, Paley Library, Temple University; Market Research Department, CBS Records; Robert J. Coen, McCann-Erickson; Office of Communication Research, Corporation for Public Broadcasting; Benjamin Compaine, Knowledge Industry Publications; Charles R. Cook, Printing and Publishing Industries Division, Bureau of Domestic Commerce, U.S. Department of Commerce; Kenneth Costa, Radio Advertising Bureau; the office of Representative Robert Edgar (D-Pennsylvania); Electronic Industries Association; Lawrence Frerk, Nielsen Television Index, A. C. Nielsen Co.; George Gerbner, University of Pennsylvania; R. Russell Hall, R. Russell Hall Co.; William Hart, GOP National Committee; Rebecca Hayden, Wadsworth Publishing Co.; Susan Hill and John Dimling, National Association of Broadcasters; Thomas W. Hope, Hope Reports, Inc.; Robert C. Hornik, Stanford University; Herbert Howard, University of Tennessee; Paul Kagan, Paul Kagan Associates; James F. Larson, Stanford University; Timothy Larson, University of Utah; Lawrence W. Lichty, University of Wisconsin; Joan Loftus, Government Documents Division, Stanford University Libraries; Nathan Maccoby, Stanford University; Thomas D. McKee and Sharon Murov, Association of American Publishers; Margaret Myers, American Library Association; National Association of Educational Broadcasters; National Association of Record Merchandisers; National Association of Theater Owners; National Cable Television Association; The Newspaper Fund; Harold Niven, Broadcast Education Association; Michael Nyhan, Institute for the Future; William J. Paisley, Stanford University; Edwin B. Parker, Stanford University; Paul Peterson, Ohio State University; Mary Picinski, *Folio: The Magazine for Magazine Management*; Katheryn Powers, Magazine Publishers Association; Recording Industry Association of America; William L. Rivers, Stanford University; Frank L. Schick, Chief, Learning Resources Branch, Division of Multilevel Education Statistics, National Center for Education Statistics, U.S. Department of Health, Education and Welfare; Karen Shapiro, Institute for Communication Research, Stanford University; William Suter, Merrill Lynch, Pierce, Fenner & Smith; *Television Digest* and *Television Factbook*; B. Stuart Tolley, Newspaper Advertising Bureau; Jack Valenti and Michael Linden, Motion Picture Association of America; Wharton Econometric Forecasting Associates, University of Pennsylvania; Writers Guild of America West. Our sincere apologies to any individual or organization we may have inadvertantly overlooked in this list.

Under the direction of Aspen Institute publishing consultant Richard Kuhn, the final job of putting the book together was undertaken by the Aspen Institute Publishing Office in Palo Alto, which handled the work of editing, permissions, design, and typesetting—and the general problem of coordinating a very complex project in a too-brief space of time—with admirable dedication, efficiency, and good humor. Among those who contributed are James Arntz, Gertrud Browatzki, Teresa Mallen, Susan Rumsey, Wally Thompson, and Diane Willis. We are also grateful to the members of the Aspen Institute Communications Policy Clearinghouse, 90 of whom responded to our queries and provided helpful advice at various stages of this project.

Finally, extraordinary thanks are due to Ellen Sterling and Jan Maltby, without whose patience and understanding this book would never have been written.

C. S. and T. H.
March 1978

Introduction: The State of Mass Media Statistics

The Mass Media: Aspen Institute Guide to Communication Industry Trends is primarily a reference work which brings together, in a single volume, a wide variety of information developed by scholarly researchers, libraries, government offices, businesses, and trade associations around the country. But this book is also an examination of the state of mass media statistics in the United States, leading, we hope, to better systems of understanding and reporting communications data in the future. The scope of this book was defined by our idea of what kinds of statistics are necessary for adequate communications policymaking and research. Our search, then, was a test of the statistical status quo.

The Statistical Needs of Communications Policymaking

Recent trends in policymaking and research have indicated the urgent need for development of a coordinated, comprehensive national program of communications policymaking and planning. It is no longer possible, as it was 20 or perhaps even 10 years ago, to treat various communication industries separately and to allow the cumulative process of litigation and regulation to decide government policy toward these industries on essentially an ad hoc basis. The increasing importance of communications to the way in which the people of this nation conduct their business, pursue their international interests, and maintain their democracy has made this kind of policymaking obsolete. Further, when one also considers those technological advances which are bringing most communication modes crashing together over the same work, it becomes clear that "the ad hoc method of policy formulation is not only obsolete but dangerous" (Domestic Council Committee on the Right of Privacy, 1976, p. 183).

Internationally, the need for nations to plan communications systems for national development has led to plans for collecting communications statistics. An international panel of consultants to UNESCO made this recommendation:

> The production of an inventory of the present communication resources within the country, in order to build a complete picture of the communication streams in society, is the starting point to all further studies of the various factors governing the processes of communication. The inventory provides the static background for investigations into the dynamics of the system. Without such an overall map, individual pieces of research will lose their perspectives and policy decisions will be based on inadequate evaluation of the status quo (UNESCO, 1971, p. 8).

But what kinds of communications statistics are most informative for policymaking? The UNESCO panel recommended that all of the following be covered by empirical data in both statistical and descriptive terms:

1. Institutions of production and distribution measured in money, personnel, equipment, circulation, and coverage, and then divided according to medium (radio, TV, press, etc.), form of control (public, private, etc.), and form of income (license, advertising, etc.).
2. The production of these institutions measured in space/time, and divided according to broad categories of content (news, entertainment, education, advertising, etc.).
3. Consumption measured in "time devoted to the media" and divided according to the demographic background variables of the society (UNESCO, 1971, p. 8).

To understand why these kinds of statistics are considered the most useful for policymakers, one must consider two structural limitations which affect policymaking. First, for those concerned with national policymaking, aggregations at the national level are most appropriate. Disaggregations may be investigated only along policy-relevent lines, as in the case of employment of minorities and women. Second, the usual level of analysis for policymakers is the *industry*. Specific industries become the focus of legal or economic pressure, and policymakers must settle questions involving not video versus print, but television versus cable or books versus photocopies.

And there is another trend in communications policymaking which may also determine what information is useful: Policymaking has become a public issue. Before 1966, private citizens and public interest groups did not have standing in cases involving broadcasting regulation. Now, increasing numbers of citizens are involved not only in regulatory proceedings, but in other phases of communications policymaking as well. This citizen involvement has led to new demands for readily available information which can be understood by informed lay people.

At the same time that new forces have been changing the needs of communications policymaking, events have been transforming the communications research which supplies data to the policymakers. One notable development is the emergence of "communications policy research" (Pool, 1974, and Schiller, 1976), as scholars attempt to tailor their work to the multi-disciplinary approaches, political agendas, and funding priorities of government. But beyond this, something within the communications research discipline itself has occurred which Rogers and Agarwala-Rogers (1976, pp. 17-23) have called an "intellectual revolt." They mention three conceptual/methodological biases of previous research which are now being questioned:

1. Lack of a process orientation.
2. Neglect of mutual casuality among the elements in the communications process.
3. Psychological orientation which leads to the shortchanging of structure in the communications process.

To some extent, the lack of a process orientation may be due as much to a relative absence of time-series data, as it is to conceptual limitations. Collecting time-series data is expensive; repeated questioning in survey research leads to problems of respondent sensitization; and various career pressures in academic life militate against the careful collection of information over extended periods. But regardless of the cause, "communication thus becomes, in prevailing communication research, an artificially halted 'snapshot' rather than a continuous 'film' or moving picture" (Rogers and Agarwala-Rogers, 1976, p. 19).

This absence of time-series data has also contributed to the relatively unsophisticated examination of causality in communications research. One-shot survey designs do not allow consideration of time-order. Moreover, the selection of a narrow set of variables—perhaps for easier measurement—makes analysis of the data problematic for anyone whose approach emphasizes "a *system* of variables in mutual interaction."

Communications research in social psychology and audience studies has traditionally selected the individual as the basic level for study. An extreme result of this is *person blame*, in which an individual subject is held responsible for problems which really involve society at different levels. Overcoming this bias requires an expansion of our search for data beyond the individual to the firm, the industry, and the nation.

The Role of Indicators

At these broader levels, communications research and policymaking needs argue for collecting statistics which might be called "communications indicators," a subclass of "social indicators." Social indicators have been defined as "statistics which reflect directly on some matter of public concern." They are "time-series that allow comparisons over an extended period and which permit one to grasp long-term trends as well as unusually sharp fluctuations in rates." In addition, they can be "disaggregated by relevant attributes of either the persons or conditions measured" (DeNeufville, 1975, p. 7; Sheldon and Freeman, 1970, p. 97). There is, however, a debate concerning social indicators which keeps us from proposing that the data collected here be assigned such a role.

Briefly, problems with indicators develop when special attention is given to one statistic while another is ignored. The question is: On what basis does one decide which data to collect and how to transform them for presentation? Either implicitly or explicitly, some idea of the behavior of the communications system will influence one's choices. In its most explicit form, this idea would be a theory of communications, similar to generally accepted economic theories which identify such major economic indicators as the gross national product or the unemployment rate.

Some critics of social indicators maintain that, without such a theory to guide the selection of statistics, one risks time, money, and clarity collecting indicators which later analysis may prove irrelevant. Others reply that unless some data are collected, no one will have anything on which to test hypotheses flowing from potential theories.

Beyond this chicken-and-egg controversy is the fact that without consensus about the importance of an indicator, its value for policymaking is limited; for the debatable qualities of the indicator will muddle the policy debate. There is no doubt that current communications theory and policymaking lack a firm consensus about anything. Yet, while this state of affairs continues, statistics are quoted and policy decisions are made. Industries are basing plans on trends and projections, and consumers are boycotting television advertisers after reading about the number of violent acts shown during programs.

Certainly, the reader who comes to this book to examine a particular trend wants information and cares little about whether the data are based on a developed theory or a vague idea. Our own position is that it is better to know what information is "out there," since such knowledge may eventually lead to good theory. Of course, we have not reported everything "out-there."

Our Approach to Data Selection

Our approach to collecting communications statistics was both intuitive and empirical. It was intuitive in that we chose the kind of statistics to collect, and the areas in which to search for them, on the basis of our general knowledge of the major policy-relevent questions in the field. It was empirical in that we collected what was there, within broad guidelines, rather than explicitly formulating a collection design on the basis of theory.

The kind of material we sought was specified in a number of ways. We chose the communication industries to be included—books, newspapers, magazines, film, recordings, radio, television, and cable television. And we decided to search first for data involving long time-series—hopefully from as far back as 1900, if the industry in question had started by then. This time-series requirement eliminated the results of most communications research studies from our consideration. The only exceptions to this rule were made with regard to subjects for which no time-series data were forthcoming. Here, we substituted "snapshot" findings for one point in time to provide a possible model for subsequent collection of information.

We excluded figures for specific local areas, such as market-by-market listings of advertising rates, circulation, and so forth. Instead, we concentrated on national statistics, with some attention to disaggregation by region, population density, and demographic characteristics of audiences.

Next, we picked seven topic areas, according to what data we knew to exist and what issues we thought should be examined. These topic areas included: (1) growth of the media industries, (2) ownership and control of the media industries, (3) economics of the media industries, (4) employment and training in the media industries, (5) content trends in the media, (6) size and characteristics of media audiences, and (7) U.S. media industries abroad. Putting all of these requirements together, we created a list of sections similar to the table of contents of this volume. We then circulated this preliminary list among a large number of communications scholars, asking them to make additions, deletions, and corrections. We took considerable advice from their responses.

At that point, we began our search for data with which to fill our projected tables, plus some indication of how valid and reliable the numbers were in each case. Finally, we collected related information and citations useful to a reader interested in a given topic.

Sufficient information was not available to fill all of our tables with good data. Almost every series in this volume has some limitations, and a number of tables are severely flawed. In most cases, the data were taken from so many sources that comparisons can only be made at the national level. Further, comparisons were often limited by the fact that definitions of the collected information varied greatly among sources—even among those within the same industry. In short, we do not have a coherent, comprehensive system of communications statistics in the United States.

We do, however, have a large number of interesting statistics, and possibilities exist for improving the total system with some relatively minor changes in collection procedures. Some industries, such as book publishing, have made major strides in their statistical efforts in recent years. Others, such as the motion picture industry, seem to be less informative now than they were 20 years ago.

The Limits of Media Statistics

To help the reader understand the various kinds of limitations affecting our statistics, we will review each major section of this volume and illustrate the particular constraints on each kind of information presented.

Growth of the Media Industries. This section includes tallies of the basic units of production and distribution in each industry—for example, the number of newspapers and magazines and the number of book publishers; the number of books, libraries, and bookstores; the number of motion pictures and theatres; and the number of radio and television stations and cable television systems. Such data are fairly plentiful. In fact, with the exception of the extensive section on economic information, this first section on media growth and size is the largest section of this book. Yet in many ways the data are not what we might wish them to be.

As is so often the case, the same process which makes the information in this section plentiful also makes it incomplete. The problem is money. Collecting comprehensive national figures for an industry each year is expensive. The process will take place only if the market for this information pays for it. There are two principal markets for data about producing and distributing units—government and private enterprise—and both want to know who is doing business in each media industry. The government wants to know for purposes of taxation, regulation, social security, and the general monitoring of the state of the economy; while private enterprise requires knowledge of suppliers, markets, and advertising. For these reasons, lists of individual companies are compiled, and these lists can be added up.

Such lists are the primary source of information about the number of newspapers, magazines, bookstores, record stores, broadcast stations, libraries, and other units, and they are usually published as directories. In these directories, a prospective seller or advertiser finds his market, or a channel of advertising to his desired market. Basic information about the number of book and record titles comes from additional lists, either of trade magazines notifying prospective buyers of a title's existence or of copyright registrations to protect a creator's financial interest in his product.

Government alone requires extensive counts of the number of regulated firms (such as radio and television stations) and data about overall industrial production (such as the number of establishments primarily producing books). Without this information, the basic economic tasks of government would not be possible. And when the needs of government are taken along with those of the private sector, it is clear there is adequate demand for expensive information of this sort to be collected.

But while the information itself is plentiful, there are also basic problems in compiling data— and some particular ones flowing from the economics of data collection—which make the situation less than ideal. A primary problem with all data collection is how to classify what is to be counted. Book publishing statistics suffer from lack of comparability over time because of changing answers to the question, "What is a book?" Distinguishing between a pamphlet and a book is a little like deciding when a girl becomes a woman. And the book publishing industry's response has varied from time to time. At present, an international definition sanctioned by UNESCO is accepted, and books are "all non-periodical publications of 49 or more pages exclusive of the covers, bound by any methods." But the major definitional changes which occurred in 1947 and 1958 affect the historical series; and before 1939, the definition was left up to the individual book publisher.

Yet the book industry is fortunate by comparison. For we still have no universal definitions of such apparently simple objects as a daily newspaper, a feature film, a magazine, or a radio station affiliated with a network. Each collector of data selects whatever characteristics are to be included in a definition, according to his own purposes, and we are left with imperfect choices. For example, while *Editor and Publisher* includes English-language newspapers of general circulation in its annual tally, the *Ayer Directory of Publications* includes both general circulation and some trade dailies, plus foreign-language dailies. So anyone looking for a count of general circulation dailies, in any language, is out of luck. The *Census of Manufactures* has such a definition, but it doesn't count newspapers—only newspaper-producing establishments.

The limits of commercial motives for collecting data become clear when we ask how many new book titles appeared last year. Books from private publishers are relatively well-recorded—either by *Publishers Weekly,* where they are announced, or by the copyright office. But what if a researcher wishes to caluclate all nonperiodical units of intellectual output in print, including dissertations, masters' theses, and government documents?

Dissertation Abstracts counts doctoral dissertations submitted to University Microfilms (where virtually all are sent), and the U.S. Government Printing Office can give figures on federal document production. But to our knowledge, no one has adequately counted master's theses or added up the number of publications produced by state government printing offices. And when one also considers the great number of private reports published by business and academia each year, it is clear there is a tremendous gap between what is produced and what is recorded. When it comes to documents outside usual trade channels, the economic motivation to count them is less than the effort required to do it.

Another problem with lists and directories is that there is no dependable way of establishing whether they include every business "out there." Not every bookstore or record shop belongs to a trade association, or advertises in the telephone directory, or gets on somebody's mailing list. Paradoxically, a directory's ability to improve its detection procedures from year to year places the value of its statistics over time in question: Is the larger number of entries in the directory due to growth of the trade or better reporting by the directory?

Government statistics should not suffer from this problem. Government agencies can, and do, use tax and social insurance records to locate those firms to whom they send their questionnaires. And answering the surveys is required by law. But in many cases, government is plagued by definitional problems which do not bother private industry.

Bookstores are a good example. A directory of stores which buy books need not distinguish between a book department in a department store and a store that sells only books. But since the government must measure the entire retail trade sector, without double-counting, it must make distinctions. As a result, a large number of bookselling establishments are not counted under the government's strict definition of "bookstore." The very scope of the government's counting, which could allow establishment of the universe of bookstores, is limited by itself because of the need to serve broad purposes.

Both government and private statistics share another limitation. After awhile, the search for data reaches a point of diminishing returns. Getting that next store recorded is just too expensive. The usual method of limiting the search is to go after the big money and let the small fry go. Thus, minimum levels of reporting are established, and firms below a certain level of employment or earnings go unreported. For example, large discrepancies appear between public and private counts of weekly newspapers, since the great number of small operations in existence allows much room for different definitions and different counts.

Generally, regulation improves basic counts of a firm's existence. If there is some bottleneck—such as a licensing procedure—through which a business must go, that business stands a good chance of being counted. To the extent that the size of an industry is relevant to the overall regulatory process—as is definitely the case with the FCC—the statistics involved also stand a good chance of being reported. Thus, the figures given in this first section for the number of broadcasting stations are quite reliable and valid. On the other hand, the procedures regarding cable television systems are not as advanced as those for broadcasting, and the information in this area is less complete.

Even in the relatively simple process of counting, then, information is limited in a number of ways. When we ask what other data would help us to understand trends in the number of producers and distributors, the situation becomes even more discouraging. Government regulation has obviously affected the growth of a number of media industries, but very few quantitative measures of regulation exist over a measurable period of time. The introduction of new technology obviously influences industry growth, but businesses do not report changes in the ability of their machines to produce. Moreover, sales counts of such machinery are usually placed in categories which were designed years before and are so general that most important, media-related distinctions are overlooked.

Finally, much of the information one would wish to gather is private property. The government collects information about industries only with the understanding that it will not release data concerning individual firms. Consequently, the kind of information we would like to obtain on specific entities or areas is often unavailable. Moreover, competitive pressures may keep the industries themselves from voluntarily producing information.

Ownership and Control of the Media Industries. Characteristics of statistics about chain ownership and industry concentration—the usual focus points for analysis of ownership and control—can only be discussed intelligently if we assume the validity of the kind of data on media growth we have just examined. For example, if we are to discover what percentage of sales is attributable to the top four firms in an industry, we must have adequate definitions of firms, a good count of the number of firms in the industry, and information on the sales of each. Statistics on concentration, then, depend on the accuracy of the more basic numbers upon which the percentages are based.

But since studies of ownership and control depend on information about individual companies, the problem of gathering figures is more difficult than it would be if we were simply trying to measure overall industry growth. Often, we cannot resort to the lists we used in measuring the numbers of firms in an industry, because these lists do not usually mention whether the company is an independent firm or a subsidiary. And so we must depend on other lists for fields in which concentration or chain ownership has been identified as either a problem (as in the case of newspapers) or a regulatory concern (as in the case of broadcasting and cable). In other fields, such as books, magazines, or film theaters, systematic collections of time-series information about concentration, and especially chain ownership, are rare.

An exception to the above complaint is the government's tabulation of the percentage of sales attributable to the top four, eight, twenty, and fifty companies in an industry. The government has been publishing these tabulations since 1958 with its censuses of manufactures and business, and we have relied heavily on these sources in our analysis of ownership and control. But even government tabulations have limitations. First, the analysis of nationally aggregated percentages of sales is not always the most appropriate measure of communications monopoly. In the case of the daily newspaper industry, for example, the geographic distribution of papers in an increasingly one-to-a-city pattern leads to local information monopolies which do not show up in national totals. To some extent, the same problem affects analyses of information control in broadcasting.

Chain ownership is not studied by the government at all in these surveys. Although concentration of sales is recorded by company, chain owners are not separated from large individual firms in the calculations. Nor do these surveys offer such data as the number or the circulation of newspapers per firm. And, of course, information about individual firms, which would allow comparisons with lists from other sources, is confidential.

However, some new sources of information help in this area of study. Books of corporate descriptions, which list subsidiaries, are available for companies which sell stock. Also, there are some special tallies of chain ownership in one industry which present related information about other media. Such lists were of considerable help to us in our examination of cross-media ownership in Unit 201.

When we turn from concentration and examine ownership in terms of the characteristics of the owner, as in a study of minority ownership, data-gathering becomes even more difficult. Commercial sources are virtually useless. Lists of media aimed at minority audiences exist, since they allow advertisers to decide where to advertise. But knowing the demographics of ownership does not have a parallel economic value. Data collection has been left to the government in this field, and serious work began to show results only in 1969. Although the *Survey of Minority-Owned Businesses* is a great step forward in collecting statistics of this kind, it still has problems. Most significantly, it is not strictly comparable to figures collected about the rest of the economy in the major economic censuses. Again, differing definitions of what to count are the basis of the problem.

In the field of equal employment and ownership opportunity, however, the federal government has made at least one important step toward standardizing its information across agencies collecting data. The Office of Management and Budget has recently established uniform definitions of ethnic and racial groups for use by all agencies. Hopefully, the same care for standardizing definitions will be applied to other categories as well.

The overall question of "Who controls the media and to what degree?" cannot really be answered with available statistics. For many communication industries, information is scarce. The industries which represent virtually virgin territory for studies of this sort include books, magazines, motion pictures—especially the theaters—and recordings. Broadcasting, in which concentration and chain ownership are regulatory concerns, has the best statistics, with newspapers and cable coming next in quality.

Anyone who attempts to examine ownership patterns across all the media listed in this book will soon discover that virtually nothing on this subject has been compiled. What studies have been done have focused on the large publicly owned conglomerates, drawing largely on corporate descriptions without any attempt to map the entire terrain. And, to our knowledge, no time-series studies of this type of ownership have ever been done.

Finally, we must note that, to some extent, ownership is not the only question relevant to a study of information control. One has merely to relect on the influence of television networks and international "wire services" to be aware that traditional approaches to industrial concentration are not adequate for discussing control of communications. New measures, based on new paradigms, are needed, and research in this area has barely begun.

Economics of the Media Industries. More information is available about mass media finances than about any other subject covered in this book, and consequently, the best time-series are found here, too. Not only are government and industries concerned with financial matters and willing to pay for such information, but the dollar is a widely used device for expressing different activities in common terms.

Yet the ease with which so many industry activities can be converted into dollars does create some problems. Although we can compare book publishing production with broadcasting production in terms of the revenues generated by these respective industries, we may thus be tempted to make misleading statements concerning the relative impact of the two industries. On a more mundane level, the ease with which we can add the sales of "apples and oranges," if not the units themselves, leads to some dismaying ways of counting things. Perhaps the most maddening aggregation of this kind is the listing of consumer expenditures in the categories of "books and maps," "newspapers, periodicals, and sheet music," and "broadcast receivers, recordings, and musical instruments" (see Unit 301). Whoever designed those categories certainly helped frustrate studies of the mass media.

The power of economic indicators sometimes leads to further errors. The Consumer Price Index is a recognized indicator of inflation. The general index is compiled carefully, by sampling prices in a fairly large number of cities, at the retail level. Therefore, when one sees a Consumer Price Index (CPI) for a particular product—such as magazines—one grants that statistic some credence. In some cases, however—such as magazines—that credibility may not be deserved.

As of this writing, the CPI for magazines is based on prices reported nationally by the Audit Bureau of Circulations for 13 general circulation magazines. This sample is neither large enough nor inclusive of enough kinds of periodicals to represent all magazines. (Discovering this fact involved innumerable telephone calls to Washington, D.C.) The basis of the detailed CPI is not presented with the figures, or even in the Bureau of Labor Statistics' otherwise excellent *Handbook of Methods.* The Bureau of Labor Statistics is currently revising the Consumer Price Index, however, and by the time these words see print, the problem may well be corrected (see Unit 300).

The problems created by government-collected financial statistics often pale in comparison with those created by the industries themselves. The most common industry practice is to report what is easy to collect, and to use the result as an estimate of something harder to examine. In theory, this might seem a sensible practice; in actuality, one often forgets what one is looking for and takes an indicator as validly representing something it does not, in fact, represent.

A classic example of this misleading practice occurs in both the recording and book industries, in which the list prices of records and books are used to illustrate costs of these items to the consumer. Yet records are usually sold at something below list price; and with books, the problem is more subtle. Although some books are discounted, many others are sold at list price. And cheaper books sell more copies than expensive ones. One must know the number of copies at each price, then, to get a good overall figure of retail prices. But this information is not available; and so for years, the trade has been using the prices which are reported for each title in the "Weekly Record" of *Publishers Weekly.* John Dessauer, the leading statistician for the book industry, has recently produced some estimates to correct for this error, but the situation still illustrates how a lack of attention to questions of validity in trade circles can lead to important mistakes.

This problem is compounded because of secrecy on the part of many trade statisticians about how they arrive at their estimates. Their attitude is understandable. Providing statistics for businesses is a competitive undertaking, unlike the cumulative scholarship of academia. Full publication of a business's tediously developed methods would give the competition an advantage. But it is difficult to judge the validity of statisitics without knowing the methods by which they were obtained. The reputation of the statistician is all we have to go by.

To make matters worse, some industry associations release their statistics and methods with what we suspect is a desire to present their affairs in the best possible light, even if that presentation is not entirely accurate. Some associations, such as the Motion Picture Association of America, happily sent glossy summaries of audience figures which show the bright side of theatrical attendance. But when we asked for the rest of their survey—to compare present summaries with figures released in previous years—or for the methods employed during the study, the MPAA refused our requests.

The Association of American Publishers, on the other hand, is an example of an organization that is going "public" with its statistics. Over the last few years, the AAP has been increasingly willing to provide figures to analysts and to the press for study, with much supporting methodological information. As a result of the AAP's openness, plus the efforts of *Publishers Weekly* and the Book Industry Study Group, the book industry has made tremendous strides in its statistical program which other industries could emulate.

Still, because industry surveys are voluntary, there is a tendency toward self-selection by respondents—that is, firms in the red may not answer the questionnaires as often as others. In the newspaper industry, this kind of bias shows up in *Editor and Publisher* reports of the balance sheets of a "typical" newspaper. Although a single newspaper cannot be considered representative of an entire industry, such balance sheets would seem to be informative. A few years ago, however, we noticed that one "typical" paper which had been reporting its statistics for several years suddenly stopped providing them, after a couple of years in the red. Since industry insiders can often decipher a company's identity from its balance sheet figures, we began thinking about which firms would want to publicize—and which would prefer to conceal from public view—extensive reports of their financial conditions. "Typical" newspaper studies have lost some of their appeal for us.

On a larger scale, the general problem posed by financial reporting concerns the value of statistics gained from censuses versus inferences about an entire industry drawn from a survey of a selected sample. If the sampling procedures and other methods are sound—and if the standard errors are reported, as they are in the *Annual Survey of Manufactures*—sample survey data can be quite valuable. In fact, the resultant savings in data-gathering costs make the sample survey the best method in most cases. But many survey reports, especially those done by the private sector, neglect to fully describe confidence intervals or other measures of accuracy. While this information may be available on demand, it would be more helpful to provide it with the basic figures.

The problem becomes more serious as time passes. For example, during the 1960s the Department of Commerce did a very interesting study of American ownership of periodicals overseas. The Department of Commerce usually is quite good about saving its analysts' work sheets. But when we sought to replicate the study, we found that its analyst was no longer with the department and that the work sheets for the study had been thrown out when the department moved to a new building. If only the original report had contained a fuller description of its author's methods, the value of the study would be far greater.

Employment and Training in the Media Industries. In this fourth section, the FCC's figures on broadcasting employment best suggest those forces which limit the value of current data about the mass media. At this writing, the FCC has issued a notice of proposed rulemaking concerning the way in which it collects broadcasting employment statistics (Federal Communications Commission, 1977). How these statistics are compiled is decided by the Commission in what is essentially a regulatory proceeding, complete with the testimony of adversaries. And decision-making at the FCC is a political process, as many studies have made clear (Krasnow and Longley, 1973; Noll, Peck, and McGowan, 1973; and Cole and Oettinger, 1978). Knowing this is important to understand some of the limitations of current FCC broadcasting employment statistics.

One simple problem has to do with the fact that although the FCC collects statistics on the percentage of minorities and of women employed, it does not break down these categories by both race and sex. As a result, "double counting" takes place, and a female member of a minority group is tallied twice—once in the "minorities" column, and again in the column "for women."

A more subtle statistical problem is created by the FCC's requirement that information about employment in specific job categories be reported. These categories include: officials and managers; professional; technicians; sales; office and clerical; craftsmen (skilled); operatives (semiskilled); laborers (unskilled); and service workers. They follow the categories suggested by the Equal Employment Opportunity Commission and are used throughout a number of industries. However, according to critics, these categories do not fit the normal radio-television job classifications. Moreover, they are just vague enough to allow manipulation of employee classifications, with the result that counts of women and minority-group members in high-ranking jobs become inflated. A number of studies have shown evidence of such inflation by comparing FCC statistics with those from different sources (Federal Communications Commission, 1977, pp. 3-5).

Another point of confusion in FCC statistics has to do with the way in which the racial or ethnic background of employees is determined. In most cases, broadcasters are asked to make a determination without consulting their employees. Although it can be argued that this method protects individuals who do not wish to identify their ethnic origins, such a guessing game allows considerable opportunity for error on the part of employers.

While allowing employers to report figures leads to bias in some instances, letting employees do the reporting can also cause problems. The *Census of Population* collects data about people in various occupations by asking them what their jobs are. Analysis of their responses indicated that people tend to place themselves in more prestigous job categories than others would put them in. For example, library assistants tend to call themselves "librarians," thus causing census statistics for these two jobs to differ from other counts. Such double-bind situations suggest the need for some duplication of measurement, so that comparisons between statistics compiled in various ways are possible. Streamlining and efficiency in compiling statistics may have their limits.

A general deficiency of employment and training data is that most detailed examinations of these areas are very recent. Most of the figures we were able to obtain were either for very short periods or at relatively high levels of aggregation. Employment by small industries is frequently not covered at all, because surveys classify these industries as subcategories of larger industrial groupings. Moreover, beyond some statistics for journalism, virtually nothing is available on media training. The kind of interesting data on the characteristics of media workers presented in Unit 404 is the result of a single academic study. Still, this one study makes routinely collected statistics about media employment look sketchy by comparison.

Content Trends in the Media. Research about mass media content trends is uneven. Some industries, such as book and magazine publishing, have collected considerable data on content. Books have long been announced to the trade in subject categories, and studying "editorial mix" continues to be an element in magazine management planning. In the newspaper industry, however, the usual practice is to make occasional studies of the relationship between content and sales, rather than to monitor that relationship continuously, as *Hall's Magazine Editorial Reports* has done.

Other media have been even less systematic in their approaches to content trends. Perhaps the recording industry presents the greatest difficulty, since the names of music categories, such as "middle of the road," change as rapidly as new programming formats are developed. In general, it is easier to study content trends in print media than content trends in electronic media. For print media, there are at least many original books, newspapers, and magazines from which retrospective content studies can be done. But with the electronic media, such archives are less likely to exist, and the need to institutionalize some practice for measuring content trends is more urgent.

The most difficult methodological problem affecting content studies is category construction. Even the best available studies allow only rough comparisons across media, because the content categories for each medium have been drawn with just that medium in mind. And in the worst studies, content categories are designed on an entirely ad hoc basis and never replicated. Any comparison of such information with other statistics is risky.

There is great need for a standardized set of content categories which can be applied to the products of several industries over time. However, we fear that a major theoretical breakthrough may be necessary to convince researchers to abandon their current practices and adhere to a new system. Research in this area is gaining popularity, and most studies now reflect attempts at new theoretical formulations, rather than large-scale attempts to record trends.

Content may be the most important aspect of communications. But though much is written about trends and cycles in media entertainment, there is a vast gap between simple criticism and a presentation of quantitative information supporting such statements. In some areas, such as political campaign communications (see Unit 502), we have access to detailed information gathered over many years. Ironically, though, this compilation has been stopped recently as a result of the transfer in authority over this area from the FCC to the Federal Elections Commission. At present, information is being collected, but not compiled.

Hopefully, more attention will be given to content on a large-scale continuing basis. Certainly, it is not difficult to list a few of the content questions which concern policymakers. For example, where does most news media content come from? Although much comes from the two major news agencies, Associated Press and United Press International, we have little reliable statistical information on these organizations. Also, to what degree are the entertainment formats and news broadcasts provided by this country's thousands of radio stations very much alike or different? An answer to this question could provide valuable insights to the discussion of radio deregulation.

Size and Characteristics of Media Audiences. The expenses of data collection about mass media audiences produce some interesting differences in available statistics across media. Because of advertisers' needs for rating and circulation statistics, data on audiences are available for every publication and for commercial broadcasting. The problem in adapting this information for our use is that there is little reason for anyone to pay for all these magazine circulation figures to be added up into a meaningful total, or for aggregation of the demographic characteristics of the entire magazine audience. Advertisers limit their advertisements to particular publications, and, therefore, information is plentiful only on the single-publication level. Similarly, there is an abundance of information on commercial network television audiences and a scarcity of information on public television audiences.

For some industries for which major trade associations exist, total national circulation figures are compiled and enlisted in the debate over which is the best medium for national advertising. Information on specialized magazines or weekly newspapers is much harder to come by. And in addition to economically based limitations, there are methodological problems which also affect the usefulness of these data. Much of the available demographic information is based on surveys which have asked such questions as: "How many books have you read in the last six months?" Beyond the obvious problem of inflated estimates from such a question, there is the more difficult problem of the differences in the way questions are worded for different studies. As opinion researchers have learned, even apparently minor variations in the wording of a survey question can lead to a wide discrepancies in the distribution of responses. For this reason, we cannot join the results of two studies with apparently similar findings in the same table without qualifying the results as gross estimates. In many cases, we have avoided this practice entirely, preferring to let the reader draw his own conclusions from the various sets of data.

Even demographic categories can change over time. A simple example of such change involves levels of income—for example, "more than $5,000 but less than $10,000." Obviously, salaries in this range had a different value 20 years ago than they do today. Moreover, expressing these categories in constant dollars does not help, since they rarely correspond to later divisions without overlapping.

Finally, we might add that academic studies have not been very useful in the area of audience size and characteristics. Because of the expenses involved, most academic studies have been locally focused at one point or two points in time. Further, because they have been designed to test hypotheses rather than to provide broad descriptions, the special construction of most such studies limits their comparability.

U.S. Media Industries Abroad. We lack statistics about almost every aspect of American communications activity abroad. We have a large amount of import-export data, and we can name those countries which are important importers and exporters of communications hardware. But we know far less about the software, the content, that is sent abroad.

Moreover, what import and export information we do have is limited in its usefulness. Book trade experts believe that exports for this industry are underestimated by 50 percent or more (Grannis, 1972, p. 128). This underestimation is due to exclusion of sales by foreign subsidiaries and to the existence of a $250 bottom limit on the reporting of exports. Furthermore, this bottom limit has changed three times in the past 30 years, threatening the historical comparability of the figures. Rights, royalties, and translation payments from abroad are also not included in book import-export totals.

In general, very little information is available on American ownership of media abroad, or on the extent of their sales. We cannot determine the degree to which (to quote the title of a recent book) "the media are American" (Tunstall, 1977). And it is difficult to obtain proper statistics even in the area of the international communications hardware trade—though negotiations with Japan over television set imports are just one example of how our international relations are being affected by the development of new communications technologies.

Finally, much more light should be shed on the role of our international news agencies, which many people still call "wire services" despite the extent to which satellites have replaced "wires." When we attempted to get information from Associated Press and United Press International, we found that our letters were not answered. And a personal visit to AP headquarters in New York yielded only press releases and apologies.

The Progress of Media Statistics: A Comparison of 1957 and 1977

While this introduction has focused primarily on the limitations of our present system of communications statistics, it is also worth noting the progress that has been made in the past several years. Back in 1957, Richard Chapin provided the first cohesive analysis of mass media statistics in his *Mass Communications: A Statistical Analysis.* He concluded that study with a chart which summarized what was known about mass communications at that time. We have composed a similar chart to illustrate the changes in the field in the past 20 years. We have added the categories of "media content" and "U.S. media abroad" to Chapin's analysis, but all of the other categories are his.

Chapin concluded 20 years ago, that:

for all of the mass media of communications ... more information is available about the number of producers than any other aspect of the industries involved ... In regard to the other ... questions in the table, the statistics range from mostly acceptable to very poor. The preceding compilation [the body of Chapin's book] does give an indication of the size of the audience and some isolated facts on the finances of the media. At the other end of the scale, however, one can see that little is known about the total use of the media. When the media are considered individually, the radio and television industries ... have more industry-side data than the other media.

Even taking into consideration the great improvements which have been made in book industry statistics, these conclusions still ring true two decades later.

Chapin also stated that "where there are good statistics, one can usually see either a governmental agency or a strong, centralized trade association or a good publication." Again, we agree. More information is now available; Chapin's study totaled only 148 pages. But new demands on our knowledge of American mass communications require that we do more. We cannot wait for new trade associations or publications to be created for communications industries which currently lack them, and we cannot wait for those that exist but hold back information to spontaneously change their ways. Neither can we continue to be frustrated by the fragmented practices of the many government agencies which are collecting relevant information. We must begin to develop a coherent picture of our communications system.

The Availability of Statistics on the U.S. Communication Industries: A Comparison of the Coverage of Chapin (1957) and This Book (1978)

Subject Matter	Placement of Subject Matter in This Book	Books 1957	Books 1978	Newspapers 1957	Newspapers 1978	Magazines 1957	Magazines 1978	Recordings[a] 1978	Motion Pictures 1957	Motion Pictures 1978	Radio 1957	Radio 1978	Television 1957	Television 1978	Cable[a] 1978
Consumers
Numbers	Section 6	3	2	3	4	0	2	1	1	2	3	3	3	3	2
Consumption	Section 6	0	2	0	0	0	2	1	0	2	3	3	1	3	1
Expenditures	Sections 3 and 6	3	4	0	0	0	0	2	4	4	2	3	2	3	2
Producers
Numbers	Section 1	4	3	4	4	2	2	2	3	3	4	4	4	4	3
Revenues	Section 3	2	3	2	2	2	2	2	1	2	3	4	3	4	2
Employment	Section 4	2	3	3	4	1	3	2	3	3	2	3	2	3	2
Expenses	Section 3	2	2	3	3	1	2	0	0	1	3	3	3	3	1
Income	Section 3	0	2	1	1	0	0	1	3	3	3	4	3	4	2
Investment	Section 3	0	0	0	0	0	0	1	1	1	3	3	3	3	1
Ownership/ Competition	Section 2	3	3	2	4	0	2	3	0	2	3	4	3	4	2
Media Content[a]	Section 5	--	3	--	2	--	2	2	--	1	--	2	--	3	3
U. S. Media Abroad[a]	Section 7	--	1	--	1	--	1	1	--	2	--	3	--	3	0

Ratings key:
4 – statistical data are plentiful and reliable.
3 – statistical data are available and acceptably reliable.
2 – statistical data are available but too limited for general uses.
1 – statistical data are unacceptable.
0 – statistical data are unavailable.

Note: (a) These subjects were not included in the Chapin study.

The Future of Media Statistics

Having concluded this somewhat gloomy survey of the problems of mass media statistics, what suggestions can we offer for their improvement? The first is a general plea for openness and cooperation among those individuals and organizations collecting communications statistics. While we understand the importance of protecting the confidentiality of statistics reported by individual firms, we also must emphasize the important contribution that would be made to communications research and policymaking if there could be a company-by-company listing of statistics and characteristics across all of the major subject categories in this volume. That is, if we could study how ownership concentrations affected finances, how size of firm was related to content, how content was related to the demographics of the audience, and so forth, we would be in a much better position to build the kind of communications theory necessary to the development of useful communications indicators. Perhaps data could be sorted and compared without the release of any protected information. Perhaps a listing of company-by-company data could be made available for research and various computer runs while the integrity of the data remains preserved.

We realize that this suggestion will probably be ignored, unless some agency, such as the new National Telecommunications and Information Administration, decides to take responsibility for bringing people together to work out the problem and the possibilities. Assuming that such a meeting could come to pass, we suggest the following items on the agenda:

1. *Define the universe of American mass media firms and their foreign subsidiaries.* We need to go beyond the approximations developed by counting lists.
2. *Develop uniform definitions of terms and data-collection categories.* These definitions should be decided among government agencies and with private industry statisticians.
3. *Provide full technical information or references.* This information should accompany each major presentation of industry statistics, public or private.
4. *Collect adequate information for all of the mass media, regardless of size.* For example, data for recordings and cable systems should not be aggregated with larger industrial classifications.
5. *Support national, industry-wide studies of content and audiences on a continuing basis.*
6. *Compile information now supplied to government but not analyzed.* This compilation could include such sources of information as reports to the Federal Elections Commission and the annual publishers' statements to the United States Postal Service.
7. *Use sampling techniques to estimate sales below the minimum amount for which government reports are required.* This is especially important in the foreign trade area.
8. *Expand the information available for data analysis on a company-by-company basis.*
9. *Create new measures to be incorporated into government data collection.* A good start would be a continuing measure of the impact of new technologies on production.
10. *Protect companies' legitimate rights to confidentiality, while providing the best possible overall analysis.*

This list could be a starting point for cooperative efforts that would benefit government, industry, and the public by providing systematic knowledge about communication industries for policy, planning, and research. While the American tradition of decentralization in policymaking has much to recommend it, coordination at least at the information-gathering level may be essential if our communication industries are to remain competitive and to serve the public interest. Other nations are making much more coordinated efforts to develop their information sectors.

As for this book, it will have served a major purpose if it demonstrates the great potential for the use of communications statistics and if it stimulates efforts to improve our quantitative knowledge about how our communication industries operate. We invite the reader to use our work in this spirit.

References

Caplan, Nathan. "Social Research and National Policy: What Gets Used, by Whom, for What Purposes, and with What Effects," *International Social Science Journal* 28 (1):186-194 (1976).

DeNeufville, Judith Innes. *Social Indicators and Public Policy*. New York: American Elsevier Publishing Company, 1975.

Domestic Council Committee on the Right of Privacy. *National Information Policy: Report to the President of the United States*. Washington: National Commission on Libraries and Information Science, 1976.

Federal Communications Commission. *Broadcast Annual Employment Report Form*. Docket No. 21474 (Mimeo No. 83668). Washington: FCC 77-779, 1977.

Grannis, Chandler B. "Statistics—More or Less," *Publishers Weekly* (September 18, 1972), p. 128.

Krasnow, Erwin G., and Lawrence D. Longley. *The Politics of Broadcast Regulation*. New York: St. Martin's Press, 1973.

Noll, Roger, Morton Peck, and John McGowan. *Economic Aspects of Television Regulation*. Washington: The Brookings Institution, 1973.

Pool, Ithiel de Sola. "The Rise of Communications Policy Research," *Journal of Communication*, *24* (2):31-42 (1974).

Rogers, Everett M., and Rehka Agarwala-Rogers. *Communication in Organizations*. New York: The Free Press, 1976.

Schiller, Herbert I. *Communication and Cultural Domination*. White Plains, N.Y.: International Arts and Sciences Press, 1976.

Sheldon, Eleanor B., and Howard E. Freeman. "Notes on Social Indicators: Promises and Potential," *Policy Sciences* 1:97-111 (1970).

Tunstall, Jeremy. *The Media Are American*. New York: Columbia University Press, 1977.

UNESCO. "Proposals for an International Programme of Communication Research," COM/MD/20. Paris: UNESCO (September 10, 1971).

SECTION 1

Growth of the Media Industries

Table 100–A.
U. S. Population by Community Size, Region, Households, Median Age, and Education, 1900–1975

Year	Total Population	% of Population by Community Size			% of Population by Region				Total Households	Median Age of Population	% of High School Graduates among Population over 17
		Urban	Suburban	Rural	North-east	North Central	South	West			
	(millions)								(millions)		
1900	76.1	19%	21%	60%	28%	35%	32%	6%	16.0	22.9	6%
1905	83.8	- -	- -	- -	- -	- -	- -	- -	17.9	- -	7
1910	92.4	22	24	54	28	32	32	8	20.2	24.1	9
1915	100.5	- -	- -	- -	- -	- -	- -	- -	22.5	- -	13
1920	106.5	26	26	48	28	32	31	9	24.5	25.3	16
1925	115.8	- -	- -	- -	- -	- -	- -	- -	27.5	- -	24
1930	123.2	30	27	44	28	31	31	10	30.0	26.5	29
1935	127.4	- -	- -	- -	- -	- -	- -	- -	31.9	- -	41
1940	132.1	29	28	43	27	30	32	11	35.2	29.0	49
1945	139.9	- -	- -	- -	- -	- -	- -	- -	37.5	- -	47
1950	151.7	29	35	36	26	29	31	13	43.5	30.2	57
1955	165.3	- -	- -	- -	- -	- -	- -	- -	47.8	- -	63
1960	180.7	28	41	30	25	29	31	16	52.8	29.4	63
1965	194.3	- -	- -	- -	24	28	31	17	57.3	28.1	76
1970	204.9	28	45	26	24	28	31	17	62.9	27.9	76
1975	213.6	- -	- -	- -	23	27	32	18	71.1	28.8	74

Sources: U. S. Bureau of the Census data reprinted in *Historical Statistics* (1975) and *Statistical Abstract.*

Note: Definitions for ''community size'' are as follows: ''urban''—100,000 or more population; ''suburban''—2,500 to 99,000; ''rural''—under 2,500.

Table 100–B.
Growth of U. S. Population and Number of Households
over Five-Year Periods, 1900–1974

Five-Year Period	Average Population (add 000)	Percent of Population Growth	Average Number of Households (add 000)	Percent of Household Growth
1900-1904	79,128	9.6%	16,736	- -
1905-1909	87,096	9.4	18,844	11.2%
1910-1914	95,588	8.8	21,118	10.8
1915-1919	102,699	6.9	23,228	9.1
1920-1924	110,220	7.3	25,702	9.6
1925-1929	118,907	7.9	28,596	10.1
1930-1934	124,782	4.9	30,563	6.4
1935-1939	128,967	3.4	33,105	7.7
1940-1944	135,104	4.8	36,295	8.7
1945-1949	144,252	6.3	39,539	8.2
1950-1954	156,976	8.1	45,422	13.0
1955-1959	171,197	8.3	49,672	8.5
1960-1964	186,406	8.1	54,420	8.7
1965-1969	198,592	6.1	59,287	8.2
1970-1974	208,618	4.8	66,637	11.0

Sources: U. S. Bureau of the Census data, reprinted in *Historical Statistics* (1975) and *Statistical Abstract.*

Interpretation of Tables

The media industries require minimum levels and concentrations of population for their products and services. Without these minimums, the industry costs for creation/transmission would outweigh the prospects for profit. Consequently, the growth of the U.S. media industries, which is detailed in the units of Section 1, has generally occurred first in cities, then in suburban communities, and only most recently in rural areas. Three other population characteristics have a significant effect on media use by the public: (1) family size (the number of households compared to the total population); (2) the median age of the population; and (3) the educational level of the population.

Regarding family size, the data in **Table 100-A** reveal that the average U.S. household has become smaller, shrinking from 4.76 persons in 1900 to 2.94 persons in 1975. This trend is accelerating as the birth rate continues to drop. Correspondingly, the median age has generally increased since 1900, though this trend was interrupted temporarily by the post-World War II "baby boom." Finally, today's smaller household, made up of older persons, is better educated than the average household of past years, in that a majority of the population over age 17 has graduated from high school, and an increasing proportion has also attended at least some college.

Other population characteristics found in **Table 100-A** are the trend from a suburban to a more urbanized population, and the recent, very substantial growth of the suburban areas. The American media audience is also increasingly Western- and Southern-based because of the continuing migration of the population from older sections of the country to the sun-belt states.

Table 100-B provides five-year averages of the population growth in the United States since 1900. These are the base-line figures against which the rates of media growth or decline are compared in later units.

Sources

Both **Tables 100-A** and **100-B** are based on Census Bureau information reprinted in *Historical Statistics* (1975) and updated in annual issues of *Statistical Abstract*. In **Table 100-A**, the percentages for population by place size (columns 3, 4, 5) were calculated by the editors from raw population totals found in Series 57-69 of *Historical Statistics*. However, the eleven urban categories used in *Historical Statistics* were condensed by the editors into two groups: urban and suburban. The editors also combined the three rural categories into one total.

Figures for regional location of the U.S. population (columns 6, 7, 8, 9) were figured by the editors from raw population totals for the four sections of the country in Series A-172 of *Historical Statistics*. The regional categories used by the Census Bureau are as follows:

Northeast (9 states): Maine, New Hampshire, Vermont, Massachusetts, Connecticut, Rhode Island, New York, New Jersey, and Pennsylvania.

North Central (12 states): North Dakota, South Dakota, Nebraska, Kansas, Missouri, Iowa, Minnesota, Wisconsin, Illinois, Indiana, Ohio, and Michigan.

South (16 states): Texas, Oklahoma, Arkansas, Louisiana, Mississippi, Alabama, Georgia, Florida, South Carolina, North Carolina, Tennessee, Kentucky, West Virginia, Virginia, Maryland, and Delaware.

West (11 states): Montana, Wyoming, Colorado, New Mexico, Arizona, Utah, Idaho, Nevada, Washington, Oregon, and California. (Hawaii and Alaska are not included in the listings.)

The figures for educational levels in **Table 100-A** are taken from Series H-599 of *Historical Statistics*. As noted on the table, the information for 1965 and 1975 is only for persons age 18 or older, and the figures for 1945 and 1955 actually represent data for the years 1946 and 1956.

In **Table 100-B**, the five-year population averages (column 2) were adapted by the editors from Series A-23 of *Historical Statistics*. The editors simply totaled each five-year group of population figures and then divided these totals by five. The percentage rates of growth (columns 3, 5) were calculated by the editors from these averaged figures. Household averages (column 4) were figured in the same way from Series A-350 of *Historical Statistics*.

Further Information

For national, regional, and state-by-state information on vital statistics, migration, and education, see Chapters A, B, C, and H of *Historical Statistics* (1975). The most recent data on these topics are found in annual issues of *Statistical Abstract*. The standard data-base for U.S. population information is the U.S. Census Bureau's multi-volume reports from each decennial census. These reports are available in most large university or research libraries.

For a more analytical discussion of population data, as well as an excellent series of summary charts and graphs, see *Social Indicators* (both the 1973 and 1976 editions). Kahn (1975) provides a popular discussion of the meaning of the 1970 census results, as compared to those of earlier years.

Copyright and Patent Registrations 101

Interpretation of Tables

Copyrights and patents are administered by the federal government to protect the creators of artistic, literary, or technical works by preserving for them the right and the benefits of any financial exploitation of their works. Because artists and inventors will generally rely on the legal protection provided by copyrights and patents, the records of copyright and patent registrations should serve as valuable indicators of the vigor of the country's cultural and technological development.

The 1909 Copyright Act, as amended, controlled the copyright registration process for most of the period covered in **Table 101-A**. This act granted protection to the creator for a period of 26 years, with an option to renew once in the 26th year, giving a total of 52 years' protection. Although the data in **Table 101-A** extends only to 1975, it is worth noting that, late in 1976, Congress passed a new and heavily revised copyright act which became effective on January 1,

Table 101–A.
Number of Copyright Registrations in U.S., 1900–1976

Years	Total Copyright Registrations	Average Registrations per Year	Average Copyrights per Year: Books/ Pamphlets	Periodicals	Musical Compositions	Motion Pictures	Average Registrations per 10,000 Population
1900-1904	481,236	96,247	- -	- -	- -	- -	12.2
1905-1909	594,780	118,956	30,544	22,487	27,432	- -	13.7
1910-1914	587,852	117,570	28,491	22,943	26,286	- -	17.3
1915-1919	562,329	112,465	33,940	25,772	22,044	2,435	11.0
1920-1924	712,115	142,423	48,837	35,078	27,844	1,534	12.9
1925-1929	883,356	176,671	56,212	43,009	26,046	1,985	14.6
1930-1934	765,640	153,128	44,406	39,362	29,346	1,756	12.3
1935-1939	792,800	158,560	47,072	38,075	33,767	1,760	12.3
1940-1944	869,269	173,988	42,832	42,976	47,513	1,853	12.9
1945-1949	1,050,518	210,103	44,760	53,250	62,090	1,847	14.7
1950-1954	1,055,794	211,158	48,897	57,422	53,936	2,170	13.4
1955-1959	1,156,117	231,223	55,103	60,137	62,538	3,158	13.5
1960-1964	1,289,548	257,910	65,816	68,454	69,301	3,815	13.8
1965-1969	1,479,598	295,919	80,620	80,025	80,212	2,924	14.9
1970-1974	1,717,217	343,443	99,423	86,763	96,288	2,815	16.5
Average: (1900-1974)	- -	186,650	51,925	48,268	47,475	2,338	13.4

Sources: Copyright Office, Library of Congress. "Averages" were calculated by the editors from base data listed in *Historical Statistics* (1975), Series W-82, 83, 85, 88, and 93.

1978. The new law brings American copyright practices into line with international standards by extending copyright protection to cover the life of the author, plus 50 years. There were several other significant changes as well.

To illustrate copyright trends since 1900, **Table 101-A** provides both five-year totals and five-year averages of U.S. copyright registrations, as well as a breakdown of the categories of the registrations. Note that average registrations per 10,000 population have changed little since 1900, except for an appreciable climb during the last decade. Regarding the categories of copyright registrations, the following comments will be of use to the reader:

1. Pamphlets are defined by the U.S. Copyright Office as "any collection, to be offered for sale, of at least 8 but less than 64 paperbound pages."

2. Periodicals are defined as publications "issued at regular intervals of less than a year."

3. The listing in **Table 101-A** includes both issue copyrights and title copyrights.

Motion pictures are covered in **Table 101-A** only after 1912, and many unregistered shorter films are excluded. The increases in film registrations after 1950 are due mainly to filmed television programming and commercials, while more recent decreases probably reflect a continuing decline in the number of feature films produced.

Table 101-B illustrates the trends in U.S. patent registrations. Whether issued as a result of research and development by government, industry, or individuals, a patent provides protection to the creator for 17 years, is nonrenewable, and can be obtained for "any new and useful machine, manufacture, composition of matter or process, or any new and useful improvement thereof, if it is lawful and operative." In addition, patent laws stipulate that the subject matter of a patent

Table 101–B.
Number of Patents Issued in U.S., 1900–1974

Years	Total Patents Issued	Average Patent Issues per Year	Percent of Yearly Issues to Individuals	Percent of Yearly Issues to Corporations	Average Patent Issues per 10,000 Population
1900-1904	140,596	28,119	N/A	N/A	3.6
1905-1909	166,100	33,220	N/A	N/A	3.8
1910-1914	178,004	35,601	N/A	N/A	3.7
1915-1919	203,194	40,639	N/A	N/A	4.0
1920-1924	194,417	38,883	70%[a]	30%[a]	3.5
1925-1929	220,506	44,101	60	40	3.7
1930-1934	243,634	48,727	49	51	3.9
1935-1939	199,217	39,843	43	57	3.1
1940-1944	180,903	36,181	39	61	2.7
1945-1949	126,731	25,346	38	62	1.8
1950-1954	205,259	41,052	42	58	2.6
1955-1959	220,731	44,146	34	66	2.6
1960-1964	244,284	48,857	27	73	2.6
1965-1969	323,574	64,714	24	76	3.3
1970-1974	367,960	73,592	23	77	3.5
Averages, 1900-1974	- -	42,868	41%	59%	3.2

Sources: "Total patents issued" from U. S. Patent Office; percentage figures calculated by editors from data in *Historical Statistics* (1975), Series W-99, 100, and 101.

Note: (a) These data are based on four- instead of five-year averages, since there were no population breakdowns of patent registrations before 1921.

must be sufficiently new or original as not to be obvious to one skilled in the field to which the patent relates. Thus, a patent request requires an investigative procedure which often produces at least a three-year lag between the application and the granting or denial of a patent.

Because of this lag, the peak of patent grants during the years 1930-1934 represents the numerous patent applications which were filed in the boom period of the 1920s. Similarly, the 1935-1949 decline in issued patents reflects both the Great Depression and the World War II period. Only since 1965 have the figures for patents per 10,000 population begun to approach pre-Depression levels. **Table 101**-B also illustrates the gradual decline of the individual inventor in the face of corporate-supported research efforts.

Sources

The copyright information summarized in **Table 101**-A is based on data in the annual Reports by the Copyright Office of the Library of Congress. The figures for the first three "averages" columns in this table were calculated by the editors by dividing the five-year totals by five. Figures for the final column were derived by dividing the U.S. population averages listed in Unit 100 into the average copyright registrations per year.

The patent information in **Table 101**-B is based on information from the Patent Office, U.S. Department of Commerce. "Percents of individual and corporation patents" were calculated by the editors from raw data found in *Historical Statistics* (1975), Series W-99, 100, and 101. (As noted on the table, the data for 1920-1924 are based on four-year averages for population and patents, since no breakdown for 1920 patent registrations was available.) The editors calculated "average patents per 10,000 population" by the same method outlined above for "copyrights per 10,000 population."

Further Information

Specific information on U.S. copyright and patent registrations, as well as more specific historical statistical information, is best obtained from the responsible government offices. Machlup (1962) presents an interesting economically oriented discussion of both indicators, while Schmookler (1966) provides an excellent analysis of patent information.

Book Publication and Publishers

110

Table 110–A.
U. S. Book Title Output, 1900–1975

Year	New Books	New Editions	Total
1900	4490	1866	6356
1901	5496	2645	8141
1902	5485	2348	7833
1903	5793	2072	7865
1904	6971	1320	8291
1905	7514	598	8112
1906	6724	415	7139
1907	8925	695	9620
1908	8745	509	9254
1909	10193	708	10901
1910	11671	1799	13470
1911	10440	783	11223
1912	10135	768	10903
1913[a]	10607	1623	12230
1914	10175	1835	12010
1915	8349	1385	9734
1916	9160	1285	10445
1917	8849	1211	10060
1918	8085	1152	9237
1919	7625	969	8594
1920	5101	1086	6187
1921	5438	1008	6446
1922	5998	865	6863
1923	6257	921	7178
1924	6380	1158	7538
1925	6680	1493	8173
1926	6832	1527	8359
1927	7450	1449	8899
1928	7614	1562	9176
1929	8342	1845	10187
1930	8134	1893	10027
1931	8506	1801	10307
1932	7556	1479	9035
1933	6813	1279	8092
1934	6788	1410	8198
1935	6914	1852	8766
1936	8584	1852	10436
1937	9273	1639	10912
1938	9464	1603	11067
1939	9015	1625	10640

Table 110-A. (Cont'd.)

Year	New Books	New Editions	Total
1940	9515	1813	11328
1941	9337	1775	11112
1942	7786	1739	9525
1943	6764	1561	8325
1944	5807	1163	6970
1945	5386	1162	6548
1946	6170	1565	7735
1947	7243	1939	9182
1948	7807	2090	9897
1949	8460	2432	10892
1950	8634	2388	11022
1951	8765	2490	11255
1952	9399	2441	11840
1953	9724	2326	12050
1954	9690	2211	11901
1955	10226	2363	12589
1956	10007	2531	12538
1957	10561	2581	13142
1958	11012	2450	13462
1959	12017	2859	14876
1960	12069	2943	15012
1961	14238	3822	18060
1962	16448	5456	21904
1963	19057	6727	25784
1964	20542	7909	28451
1965	20234	8361	28595
1966	21819	8231	30050
1967[b]	21877	6885	28762
1968	23321	7066	30387
1969	21787	7792	29579
1970	24288	11783	36071
1971	25526	12166	37692
1972	26868	11185	38053
1973	28140	11811	39951
1974	30575	10271	40846
1975	30004	9368	39372
1976	26983	8158	35141

Source: *Publishers Weekly*.

Notes: (a) These data do not include pamphlets after 1912. From 1900 to 1912, pamphlets are included. (b) The decline in title output from 1966 to 1967 indicated in this table does not mean a decline in American book production as such; rather it reflects a revision which was made in the method of counting at the beginning of 1967 (see text).

Interpretation of Tables

Table 110-A lists the number of new book titles published each year in the United States, from 1900 to 1976. This is but one way of looking at the growth of the American book industry in this century. For a more complete picture of book production trends, the reader should compare these figures for book title output with such other statistics as the number of books in print each year (see **Table 110-B**) and the annual sales of book publishing companies (see **Table 110-C** and all of Unit 310). The reader should also note that the figures for **Table 110-A** do not include government publications or Ph.D. theses, both of which represent a considerable volume of new

Table 110–B.
U. S. and World Book Publication, including U. S. University Theses, 1965–1973

Note: All production figures are in thousands.

Year	U.S. Books In Print	U.S. Private New Titles	U.S. Federal New Titles	U.S. University Theses	U.S. Total New Titles	World Total New Titles	U.S. % Of World Total
1965	185	28.3	13.1	13.0	54.4	450	12%
1966	190	30.1	12.3	16.2	58.5	460	13
1967	245	26.6	12.1	20.2	58.9	478	12
1968	250	26.4	12.4	20.4	59.2	487	12
1969	275	23.4	11.9	26.8	62.1	496	13
1970	305	35.4	13.2	30.9	79.5	546	15
1971	330	34.8	13.3	31.3	80.6	548	15
1972	345	37.6	12.4	32.5	82.4	561	15
1973	398	38.4	13.3	32.1	83.7	580	14

Source: Books in print—*Books in Print*, annual, 1965-1973. All others—*UNESCO Statistical Yearbook*, 1968, 1971, 1974.

Table 110–C.
Number of Book Copies Sold in U. S., 1925–1972

Year	Copies Sold (millions)	Year	Copies Sold (millions)
1925	201.0	1945	428.8
1927	219.3	1947	487.2
1929	214.3	1951	659.3
1931	150.2	1954	747.3
1933	108.6	1958	1040.1
1935	138.9	1963	1172.5
1937	193.1	1967	1434.3
1939	174.6	1972	1337.1
1942	457.7		

Sources: 1925-1939: *U. S. Census of Manufactures*, quoted in Lofquist (1970). 1942, 1945, 1951: Chapin (1957). 1947, 1954-1967: *U. S. Census of Manufactures*, quoted in Lofquist (1970). 1972: *U. S. Census of Manufactures*.

titles (not to mention intellectual output) every year. (**Table 110-B** remedies these omissions.)

It is interesting to observe in **Table 110-A** that the peak production level achieved by the U.S. book industry in 1913 was not surpassed until the late 1950s. In the more than 40 intervening years, the effects of various cataclysmic world events—World War I, the Great Depression, and World War II—rolled back any advances made by the book industry during the brief periods of prosperity and peace. From the late 1950s to the early 1970s, book title output began to rise again at a steady rate. This growth has leveled off only recently, due mainly to decreases in the school-age population and the resultant drop in the demand for textbooks and in federal educational funding.

Table 110-B represents national book title output as estimated by the UNESCO method. The UNESCO tabulation of new titles includes U.S. federal government documents and university theses (presumably, both Master's theses and Ed.D. and Ph.D. dissertations). During the nine-year

Table 110–D.
Number of Book Publishing Establishments and Companies in U. S., 1909–1972

Year	Establishments	Companies
1909	1007	- -
1914	999	- -
1919	989	- -
1921	644	- -
1923	603	- -
1925	613	- -
1927	679	- -
1929	721	- -
1931	638	- -
1933	410	- -
1935	505	- -
1937	530	- -
1939	706	- -
1947	648	635
1954	814	804
1958	903	883
1963	993	936
1967	1024	963
1972	1205	1120

Sources: Number of establishments, 1909-1967: *U. S. Census of Manufactures*, quoted in Lofquist (1970), pp. 13-25. Number of companies, 1947-1972; number of establishments, 1972: *U. S. Census of Manufactures*, quoted in Lofquist (1976), pp. 12-27.

period covered in this table, book production by the federal government remained relatively constant, but the output of university theses in the United States more than doubled.

Also included in **Table 110-B** is the number of titles in print each year in the U.S.—a computation which may be more useful than annual production figures in providing an accurate indication of the cumulative number of titles available in the United States. Finally, this table provides a comparison of U.S. book title output with that of the rest of the world. The figures show a small relative increase of U.S. output in recent years.

Table 110-C is a measurement of the number of book copies sold by U.S. publishers in various years. (Again, these figures do not include pamphlets, theses, or government publications.) In general, we see a pattern similar to that for title production: a severe decline during the Depression, a dramatic rise following World War II, and indications of a recent slowing down in the growth rate.

Table 110-D lists the number of book publishing establishments and companies in the United States from 1909 to 1972. A book publishing "establishment" is defined by the Census Bureau as a place where books are published. The meaning is close to "factory." A "company," as the term is used in the *Census of Manufactures*, is a business organization consisting of one or more establishments under common ownership or control. **Table 110-D** makes it clear that most book publishing establishments are single-company enterprises, although there has been a very slight overall tendency toward multiple-establishment ownership since 1958.

Interestingly, the number of book publishing establishments declined from 1909 until 1935, possibly due to the changing methods of production and distribution which allowed larger firms to exploit the resulting economies of scale. There was another downward movement during World War II, but since that period, the number of book publishing establishments has moved steadily upward. Between 1954 and 1972, the number of establishments increased by 48 percent. (The sharp decline from 1919 to 1921 is primarily a reflection of changes in census-reporting requirements.)

Sources

The information included in **Table 110-**A is based upon reports from private book publishers to the "Weekly Record" of *Publishers Weekly*, the industry's primary trade magazine. Each year, these publishers' reports are compared with the records of new books received by the Library of Congress. This information is not always comprehensive, since certain types of books—some textbooks, some mass-market paperbacks, and many of the publications by small private presses—tend not to be reported. However, this number is small and relatively unimportant in measuring trends.

A more important factor in the accuracy of these book title figures is the change in accounting procedures over the years. Up until 1913, pamphlets were included with books in the title output figures; and until 1940, there was no clear line of demarcation between "books" and "pamphlets." Since then, the definitions have been changed twice. The latest, developed by UNESCO and in use by Bowker since 1959, defines a book as any publication of 49 pages or more (compare the U.S. Copyright Office definition in Unit 101).

Table 110-A figures prior to 1940 may also be confused somewhat by the publishers' practice of including in their reports of new titles any books which were printed with plates imported from abroad. Since 1940, however, the definition of new titles includes only those books manufactured and published by U.S. companies. Another change in counting procedure was made in 1967. Before that time, separate volumes in multi-volume sets were counted as if sold separately. After 1967, multi-volume sets were counted in this manner only if each volume had a different title and formed a distinct unit complete in itself. (For example, multi-volume reference works could no longer be counted as separate titles.)

Thus, the drop in title output in 1967 is mainly the result of this changed procedure rather than of an actual decline in industry production. For all of these reasons, the title output figures can be regarded as good indexes of broad trends. However, year-to-year changes, especially prior to 1940, should be regarded with caution.

The data in **Table 110-**B are from the appropriate issues of *Books in Print*, for the "Books in Print" column, and from the *UNESCO Statistical Yearbook* for all other columns in the table. UNESCO takes its commercial book figures from R.R. Bowker Company sources. The editors were not able to learn how UNESCO arrives at its university theses figures. The best available source of information on the output of Ph.D. dissertations in the United States is *Dissertation Abstracts*, which is published by University Microfilms, Inc. University Microfilms does not provide data on the number of Master's theses produced in the United States.

The data in **Tables 110-**C and **110-**D come from the *Census of Manufactures*, a survey which the U.S. Census Bureau has been conducting in various forms since the mid-nineteenth century. Until the 1909 census, book publishing information was recorded together with commercial printing; and until 1925, books and pamphlets were not counted separately. Between 1925 and 1940, the Census Bureau allowed publishers to use their own definitions in distinguishing books and pamphlets. Therefore, the statistics for these periods must be considered somewhat inaccurate.

In 1947, the Census Bureau issued its own strict definition of a "book," and this definition was then changed again in 1958 to conform with the UNESCO procedures for recording such data. These changes undoubtedly affect the precision of the figures, but the overall trends remain clear and valid. Moreover, the *Census of Manufactures* presents the most reliable information available for the publishing industry.

Further Information

The most useful discussions of book title output and book sales appear in *The Bowker Annual of Library and Book Trade Information* (R.R. Bowker Co., annual); in *Publishers Weekly* (especially its annual statistical issue, which usually appears in late January or early February); and in *Printing and Publishing*, a quarterly publication of the U.S. Department of Commerce. Two excellent articles from this last source are Hokkanen (1970) and Lofquist (1970). Chapin (1957) also discusses these data.

Table 111–A.
Number of Bookstores in U. S., by Type of Store, 1958–1975

	1958	1961	1963	1965	1967	1969	1971	1973	1975	Percent Change 1958-1975
Antiquarian	1,008	947	1,048	1,052	954	953	911	902	886	-12%
College	1,240	1,394	1,623	1,566	1,815	1,946	2,265	2,538	2,559	106
Department Store	682	628	735	882	858	894	901	1,012	451[a]	- -[b]
Drug Store	116	106	75	62	44	57	53	40	61	-52
Educational	97	117	116	143	129	133	100	106	77	-21
Export-Import	12[c]	10[c]	13[c]	14[c]	51	51	51	48	34	- -[b]
Foreign Language	76	67	73	88	80	70	65	61	60	-21
General	1,941	1,961	1,937	2,062	2,081	2,306	2,468	3,065	3,498	80
Gift Shop	174	190	187	196	219	221	201	153	142	-18
Juvenile	57	46	51	48	33	32	47	50	55	-4
Law	57	47	42	40	38	40	38	48	48	-16
Mail Order	34	194	226	85	162	132	114	108	100	194
Medical	41	53	61	68	72	85	83	97	82	100
Museum	- -	- -	- -	- -	- -	102	100	115	121	- -[b]
News Dealer	42	45	33	40	80	70	63	62	128	205
Office Supply	57	76	85	84	80	84	100	98	97	70
Paperback	23	84	352	484	564	578	591	609	598	2,500
Religious	1,976	1,671	1,840	1,820	1,702	1,640	1,638	1,698	1,421	-28
Rental	90	55	46	34	31	29	23	17	10	-89
Science/Technology	48	26	36	52	50	63	50	57	43	-10
Special	297	255	277	304	370	428	583	648	866	192
Stationer	292	311	304	320	315	338	297	254	253	-13
Total	8,360	8,286[d]	9,160	9,444	9,728	10,252	10,742	11,786	11,717[d,e]	40
Census of Business Totals	2,885		3,154		4,479[f]			7,830[g]		171[h]

Sources: Census of Business Total: *U. S. Census of Business* 1958, 1967; *U. S. Census of Retail Trade* 1972. All other data from *American Book Trade Directory*, 1958-1975.

Notes: (a) "Main" department stores only. (b) Change cannot be computed because series is not historically comparable. (c) "Exporter" only. (d) Total includes stores not accounted for in type breakdown, 1961 (3), 1975 (7). (e) Total includes 120 "used" bookstores. (f) Estimate derived by authors based on proportional change in stores "with payroll" for the same period. (g) 1972 figure. (h) 1958-1972 percent change.

Interpretation of Tables

Table 111-A lists the number of bookstores in the United States from 1958 to 1975, as compiled by R.R. Bowker's *American Book Trade Directory* and the U.S. Census Bureau's *Census of Retail Trade*. (See **Table 310-B** for Census Bureau data for the years 1929 to 1972.) It is evident that the figures from these two sources do not match; and the discrepancies are further complicated by the fact that yet another source—a recent U.S. Department of Commerce estimate—puts the total number of bookstores in 1976 at around 12,000.

Table 111–B.
Number of Book Clubs in U. S., 1958–1975

Year	Number
1958	56
1961	55
1963	57
1965	62
1967	127
1969	138
1971	156
1973	161
1975	198

Sources: 1958-1973: *American Book Trade Directory*, appropriate biennial volumes. 1975: *The Bowker Annual* (1977), based on data from *Literary Market Place, 1976-1977.*

It is probable that these differences can be explained by the variations in each source's definition of "bookstore." For example, the Census Bureau definition of "bookstore" is "an establishment primarily selling new books and periodicals." This definition excludes a number of the bookselling establishments which are counted in the *American Book Trade Directory*, such as department stores, drug stores, gift shops, mail-order houses, museums, news dealers, office-supply stores, and stationers. The Census Bureau totals also exclude nonprofit establishments, which eliminates a number of college and religious stores.

The differences in the growth trends represented by each set of statistics are not so readily explained. For example, according to the *American Book Trade Directory* count, the number of bookstores in the United States increased by 40 percent from 1958 to 1975. The *Census of Retail Trade* shows a 171 percent increase for the shorter period of 1958-1972. And the Department of Commerce estimate of 12,000 bookstores in 1976 would put the increase of stores since 1958 at 316 percent. The editors are unable to reconcile the sharp differences here.

Despite this problem, the reader may gain some insights into current trends in the field of book-selling establishments by looking at the relative increases in numbers of certain categories of stores. The most spectacular growth has been in the "paperback" category, which is defined as "stores with stock consisting of more than 80 percent paperbacks." Since 1958, the number of these stores has grown from 23 to 598, an increase of 2,500 percent. No other category of bookstore comes even close to matching this growth. It is interesting to note, however, that most of this growth had taken place by 1967. Since that time, the number of paperback booksellers has increased by only six percent.

The other big increases are among news dealers (205 percent), among that catch-all category of "special" stores (192 percent), and among college stores (106 percent), medical-text stores (100 percent), and general bookstores (80 percent). The 194 percent increase shown for mail-order houses is probably meaningless, because this increase is computed with the very low 1958 figures as a base. If the editors had chosen 1961 as the base year for the calculation, mail-order houses would show a decline of 47 percent.

Table 111-B lists the changes in the number of book clubs in the United States between 1958 and 1975. Since 1958, according to these figures, the number of book clubs has increased by 253 percent.

Sources

The *American Book Trade Directory*, the primary source of **Tables 111**-A and **111**-B, gets most of its information directly from stores and companies through the use of questionnaires. R.R. Bowker Company, the publisher of the directory, asserts that its information is gathered from secondary sources only when it is unattainable through the survey method. Also, any secondary-source information is always verified as to the "active status" of the listing. However, these secondary sources may include lists of subscribers to various Bowker Company services, the membership roles of book trade organizations, and "other available sources." The editors can therefore imagine a number of ways in which some book outlets might be excluded from this tally. The editors also have good reason to suspect *over*estimates from a statistical procedure which allows gift shops, news dealers, and drug stores to be counted as bookstores.

The U.S. Census Bureau's *Census of Retail Trade*, another source of data in **Table 111**-A, is generally considered very reliable. But in this particular case, the Bureau's strict definition of "bookstore" makes the validity of its information somewhat problematic. Thus, in an overall assessment of the available information on bookstores in the United States, the editors would agree with Chapin (1957, p. 52), who concluded in an early analysis of mass media statistics: "To determine the number of book outlets in the United States is extremely difficult."

Further Information

Some discussion of U.S. bookstores is included in Vanier's (1973) work on the book publishing market structure. Interesting interpretations of the Census Bureau data are found in two recent articles by Lofquist (1976/77, 1977). The figures from the *American Book Trade Directory*, sometimes supplemented by data from other sources, are usually reprinted in *The Bowker Annual*.

Libraries   112

Table 112–A.
Number of Libraries in U. S., 1927–1976

Year	Number of Libraries Listed in *American Library Directory*	Adjusted Totals
1927	10812	8322
1930	11999	9109
1935	9212	9212
1939	9166	9355
1945	11380	11380
1948	11334	11334
1951	11034	13398
1954	12748	16078
1957	12852	18140
1960	13676	19076
1962	13019	18813
1964	14240	19764
1967	21344	21344
1970	23998	23998
1972	24069	24069
1974	25934	25934
1976	29345	29345

Source: R. R. Bowker Co., *American Library Directory*, for years listed.

Note: Adjusted totals were computed by the editors to account for changes in accounting procedures. In 1927 and 1930, high school libraries were deleted from adjusted total. In 1939, 1951-1964, branch and subsidiary department libraries were included in adjusted total.

Table 112–B.
Number of Libraries in U. S., by Type of Library, 1962–1976

	1962	1970	1976	Change 1962-1976
Main Public Libraries	6463	7190	8504	32%
Branch Public Libraries	4028	4855	5477	36%
Public Libraries on Armed Forces Installations, Including Veterans' Hospitals	N.A.	481	559	N.A.[a]
University and College Libraries	1379	1896	1696	23%
Junior College Libraries	645	1072	1129	75%
Special Libraries	3473	4277	6563	89%
Within University, College Systems	951	1216	1252	32%
Within Armed Forces Installations	438	274	85	-81%
Law Libraries	434	477	806	86%
Within University, College Systems	109	115	147	35%
Medical Libraries	755	1315	1955	164%
Within University, College Systems	138	181	157	14%
Religious Libraries	N.A.	600	996	N.A.[a]
Within University, College Systems	N.A.	49	19	N.A.[a]
Total Number of Libraries Listed in *American Library Directory*	13019	23998	29345	125%
Adjusted Totals[a]	18813	23998	29345	56%

Source: R. R. Bowker Co., *American Library Directory, 1962-63, 1970-71, 1976-77.*

Note: (a) The 1962 total is adjusted to account for changes in the Bowker counting procedure. Until 1967, the *American Library Directory* did not include branch, special, medical, law, or recreational libraries in its total count, although the disaggregated data were listed. Recreational libraries have been included in the "Public Library" category here, following Bowker's later procedure.

Interpretation of Tables

As major distributors of knowledge in the United States, libraries represent important markets for the industries that produce books, periodicals, and audio-visual materials. Only recently, however, have the libraries in this country begun to provide adequate statistical descriptions of their operations. A number of professional associations and trade services, as well as the National Center for Education Statistics (NCES), are now involved in the task of collecting data on libraries, but the analytical process is far from complete. We have only rough estimates of the number and other characteristics of certain categories of libraries, such as business and national trade association libraries.

Table 112-A presents information from one of the oldest continuing sources of knowledge about the number of libraries in the U.S., the *American Library Directory*, which is published by the R.R. Bowker Company. According to the directory, the number of libraries in the United States has grown from 10,812 in 1927 to 29,345 in 1976. Until 1935, however, the directory counted high school libraries in its totals. Thus, the real growth since 1927 is from 8,322 nonschool libraries to 29,345, an increase of more than 250 percent in 49 years.

This total and growth rate are further modified by the fact that the directory does not include public libraries or law libraries with less than 10,000 volumes. (The small libraries are excluded, according to Bowker [1977, p. 259], because of their minimal purchasing power.) In 1976, Bowker claimed knowledge of 2,511 public libraries and 170 law libraries which had been excluded from

Table 112–C.
Number, Size of Collections, and Annual Operating Expenditures of Libraries in U. S., by Type of Library, 1972–1977

Type of Library	Number of Libraries	Number of Volumes[a]	Annual Operating Expenses	Date of Data
All College and University Libraries	3,026	612,000,000	$1,071,000,000	1975
Major Academic Libraries	81	217,000,000	291,000,000	1972-73
Library of Congress	1	85,200,757	74,352,187	1972
National Agricultural Library	1	1,523,000[b]	4,251,842	1972
National Library of Medicine	1	1,428,360	16,974,354	1972
All Federal Libraries	2,313	59,283,718[c]	191,825,882[d]	1972
Public Libraries	8,307	397,053,559	1,018,893,522	1974
Elementary and Secondary School Libraries and Media Centers	74,625	574,988,512	1,182,284,107	1973-74
Special Industry Libraries	14,000	N/A	N/A	1973
State Libraries	2,400[e]	N/A	N/A	1977
National Professional/Business/ Trade Association Libraries	2,000[e]	N/A	N/A	1977

Sources: College and university libraries: Ladd (1977), pp. 15-17. Major academic libraries and special industry libraries: Oettinger (1976), pp. 22-23. All federal libraries: Olson (1975), pp. 2, 10, 11, 22. Public libraries: National Center for Education Statistics (1976). Elementary and secondary school libraries: National Center for Education Statistics (1976). State and national association libraries: Schick (1977).

Notes: (a) Collection figures include all books, periodical titles, microforms, audiovisual materials, and other print or nonprint materials. (b) Includes total volumes and periodical titles received only. (c) Based on questionnaire responses from approximately 1,845 federal libraries. (d) Based on questionnaire responses from about 1,673 federal libraries. (e) These figures are rough estimates.

the directory because of their size. Therefore, the grand total of libraries in the United States in 1976 is 32,026.

Table 112-B, which shows the growth trends for particular types of libraries, is also from the *American Library Directory*. With minor exceptions, the categories of libraries have remained the same since 1962, which is why the editors began the table with the data for that year. The greatest percentage increases have been in the number of medical libraries (164 percent), followed by special libraries (89 percent), law libraries (86 percent), and junior college libraries (75 percent). Note that the editors adjusted the 1962 total upward in order to account for branch libraries, which were excluded in the count of the *American Library Directory* until the 1966-67 edition.

Table 112-C estimates the number of libraries and the collections and annual operating expenditures of libraries in the United States by putting together data from a number of diverse sources. The largest number of libraries are those associated with elementary and secondary schools, nearly 75,000 (including those designated as "media centers") in the 1973-74 school year. These school libraries are not included in most counts, such as those of the book industry, because the school district, rather than the individual libraries, are usually responsible for the purchase of books.

If these school libraries and media centers are excluded from the total number of libraries represented in **Table 112-C**, the sum of 32,049 libraries in the United States is quite close to the 32,026 sum listed by Bowker. Of course, **Table 112-C** is made up of survey data from various years and includes some very rough estimates, so to some extent the similarity of the figures may be misleading.

Regarding the annual operating expenditures of U.S. libraries, **Table 112-C** shows a total exceeding $2 billion in the early 1970s, with more than another billion dollars being spent for school libraries and media centers. Note that association, state, and industry libraries are excluded here due to the absence of budgetary data in these categories. Unit 314 provides a detailed examination of the available data on library finances.

Sources

The R.R. Bowker Company's *American Library Directory*, the source of information for **Tables 112-A** and **112-B**, locates its entries by scanning other library directories, state library service lists, library association lists, telephone directories, college and university library lists, and other similar sources. The publisher of the *Library Directory* then sends two sets of questionnaires to each library located. For libraries that do not respond to the questionnaires, the *Library Directory* uses information from secondary sources and then marks these entries accordingly.

Because of this procedure, there is no guarantee that all libraries in the United States are included in the Bowker Company directory. As noted above, small public libraries (with annual expenditures of less than $2,000 or book funds of less than $500) and small law libraries (with collections of less than 10,000 volumes) are excluded from the listings. Nevertheless, it is very likely that this search of lists and directories discovers most of the libraries in America. As a result, the directory has been a trade standard for many years.

Table 112-C presents figures from a variety of sources. The information about public and college and university libraries comes from two different surveys of university and public libraries—one performed by the U.S. Office of Education in 1962, the other by the National Center for Education Statistics in 1974. In the 1962 survey, questionnaires were sent to most of the libraries listed by state library agencies. There were responses from around 6,500 libraries in this group. In 1975, the estimates were based upon information gathered in a stratified random sample of 1,460 libraries. The information for public school libraries and media centers are drawn from a NCES sample survey of 3,500 public school libraries and media centers in the 1973-1974 school year. The stratification for the random sample was based on size of school. Detailed information about the validity and reliability of this information can be found in the NCES reports on these surveys (National Center for Education Statistics, 1977a, 1977b).

The data for all federal libraries, including the Library of Congress, the National Agricultural Library, and the National Library of Medicine, were furnished to the National Center for Education Statistics in response to a NCES survey in 1972 (see Olson, 1975). The number of libraries actually surveyed was somewhat less than the total, due to the deletion for various reasons of some libraries in the Executive Office of the President, the U.S. Information Agency, and the U.S. Army. Of the 1,908 libraries surveyed by the NCES, 1,744 (91 percent) provided all or substantial amounts of the data requested in the survey. Given this procedure and the high response rate, the editors regard these figures as valid.

In contrast, the figures for special industry libraries, for state libraries, and for national association libraries can be regarded only as rough estimates. The estimate for industry libraries includes those in Canada, and the validity of the definitions for the inclusion of libraries in this category could be questioned (see Oettinger, 1976, p. 23). The estimates for the number of state and association libraries are by Dr. Frank L. Schick, chief of the Learning Resources Branch, Division of Multi-level Education Statistics, at the National Center for Education Statistics. Dr. Schick has labeled these estimates "approximate."

Further Information

Reports of the NCES and reports and publications of the Association of Research Libraries, the Medical Library Association, the American Library Association, and other such associations are filled with detailed information about their member libraries. Considerable summary information about libraries, including bibliographic references, can also be found in the *Bowker Annual* and in such periodicals as Bowker's *Library Journal*.

One very interesting aspect of the interpretation of library statistics is the opportunity to compare what we know about the various characteristics of libraries with some measures of the nation's needs for library services. A recent report to the National Commission on Libraries and Information Science (Ladd, 1977) makes such a comparison by contrasting NCES library statistics with various indicators of public needs. The purpose of this study was to assess the adequacy of current resources among academic, public, and school libraries.

Table 120–A.
Number of Daily and Sunday Newspapers in U. S., 1900–1976

| | DAILIES | | | MORNING DAILIES | EVENING DAILIES | SUNDAY | |
	Census of Manufactures	Ayer Directory[a]	Editor and Publisher	Editor and Publisher	Editor and Publisher	Editor and Publisher	Census of Manufactures
1900	2226[b]	2154	- -	- -	- -	- -	- -
1901	- -	2170	- -	- -	- -	- -	- -
1902	- -	- -	- -	- -	- -	- -	- -
1903	- -	- -	- -	- -	- -	- -	- -
1904	2452	2283	- -	- -	- -	- -	494
1905	- -	2262	- -	- -	- -	- -	- -
1906	- -	- -	- -	- -	- -	- -	- -
1907	- -	- -	- -	- -	- -	- -	- -
1908	- -	- -	, - -	- -	- -	- -	- -
1909	2600	- -	- -	- -	- -	- -	520
1910	- -	2433	- -	- -	- -	- -	- -
1911	- -	2418	- -	- -	- -	- -	- -
1912	- -	- -	- -	- -	- -	- -	- -
1913	- -	2442	- -	- -	- -	- -	- -
1914	2580	2457	- -	- -	- -	- -	571
1915	- -	2447	- -	- -	- -	- -	- -
1916	- -	2461	- -	- -	- -	- -	- -
1917	- -	2410	- -	- -	- -	- -	- -
1918	- -	2371	2166	519	1647	- -	- -
1919	2441	2343	2078	457	1621	- -	604
1920	- -	2324	2042	437	1605	522	- -
1921	2334	2331	2028	427	1601	545	538
1922	- -	2313	2033	426	1607	546	- -
1923	2271	2310	2036	426	1610	547	602
1924	- -	2293	2014	429	1585	539	- -
1925	2116	2283	2008	427	1581	548	597
1926	- -	2281	2001	425	1576	545	- -
1927	2091	2222	1949	411	1538	526	511
1928	- -	2215	1939	397	1542	522	- -
1929	2086	2248	1944	381	1563	528	578
1930	- -	2219	1942	388	1554	521	- -
1931	2044	- -	1923	384	1539	513	555
1932	- -	2008	1913	380	1533	518	- -
1933	1903	1902	1911	378	1533	506	489
1934	- -	2032	1929	385	1544	505	- -
1935	2037	2027	1950	390	1560	518	523
1936	- -	2107	1989	405	1584	520	- -
1937	2065	2084	1983	406	1577	539	528
1938	- -	2056	1936	398	1538	523	- -
1939	2040	2015	1888	383	1505	524	542
1940	- -	1998	1878	380	1498	525	- -
1941	- -	1974	1857	377	1480	510	- -
1942	- -	1894	1787	345	1442	474	- -
1943	- -	1859	1754	333	1421	467	- -
1944	- -	1857	1744	338	1406	481	- -

Table 120-A. (Cont'd.)

	DAILIES			MORNING DAILIES	EVENING DAILIES	SUNDAY	
	Census of Manufactures	Ayer Directory	Editor and Publisher[c]	Editor and Publisher	Editor and Publisher	Editor and Publisher	Census of Manufactures
1945	- -	1850	1749	330	1419	485	- -
1946	- -	1872	1763	334	1429	497	- -
1947	1854	1873	1769	328	1441	511	416
1948	- -	1887	1781	328	1453	530	- -
1949	- -	1894	1780	329	1451	546	- -
1950	- -	1890	1772	322	1450	549	- -
1951	- -	1873	1773	319	1454	543	- -
1952	- -	1887	1786	327	1459	545	- -
1953	- -	1875	1785	327	1458	544	- -
1954	1820	1860	1765	317	1448	544	510
1955	- -	1841	1760	316	1454	541	- -
1956	- -	1824	1761	314	1454	546	- -
1957	- -	1844	1755	309	1453	544	- -
1958	1778	1855	1751	307	1456	556	552
1959	- -	1854	1755	306	1455	564	- -
1960	- -	1850	1763	312	1459	563	- -
1961	- -	1850	1761	312	1458	558	- -
1962	- -	1854	1760	318	1451	558	- -
1963	1766	1844	1754	311	1453	550	560
1964	- -	1843	1763	323	1452	561	- -
1965	- -	1846	1751	320	1444	562	- -
1966	- -	1844	1754	324	1444	578	- -
1967	- -	1833	1749	327	1438	573	- -
1968	- -	1833	1752	328	1443	578	- -
1969	- -	1838	1758	333	1443	585	- -
1970	- -	1818	1748	334	1429	586	- -
1971	- -	1809	1749	339	1425	590	- -
1972	- -	1792	1761	337	1441	603	- -
1973	- -	1806	1774	343	1451	634	- -
1974	- -	1819	1756	339	1436	639	- -
1975	- -	1813	1768	340	1449	641	- -
1976	- -	1811	1762	346	1435	650	- -

Sources: *Census of Manufactures* data: *Historical Statistics of the U. S.* (1976). *Ayer Directory* data: *Ayer Directory of Publications*, annual issues. *Editor and Publisher* data: 1918, 1919: Chapin (1957), p. 9; 1920-1970: *Historical Statistics of the U. S.* (1976); 1971-1976: *Editor and Publisher International Yearbook*, annual issues.

Notes: (a) Figures are listed for the year when the data was collected not the year listed in the *Ayer Directory*, which is the year after the count. (b) Includes "other" newspapers. (c) 1954-1976 totals adjusted to account for "all day" papers listed in both morning and evening categories.

Interpretation of Tables

Table 120-A presents several different counts of daily newspapers (both morning and evening) and Sunday newspapers in the United States. Generally, the number of U.S. dailies increased until about 1910, then declined steadily until the end of World War II. Since that time, the total number of daily newspapers has remained relatively constant. However, when this total is broken down by city size (see Unit 121), it becomes apparent that significant changes have taken place in the newspaper industry.

Table 120-B presents the number of weekly and semiweekly or triweekly newspapers in the United States. Although weekly newspaper figures reached a peak between 1910 and 1915, and have shown some small temporary increases since then, the general pattern has been one of decline. The effects of the Great Depression were especially felt in the weekly newspaper field. However,

Table 120-B.

Number of Weekly and Semiweekly/Triweekly Newspapers in U. S., 1900-1976

Year	Weeklies	Semiweeklies and Triweeklies
1900	15,813	574
1905	16,136	640
1910	16,227	672
1915	16,043	668
1918	14,724	544
1919	13,964	565
1920	13,847	558
1921	13,608	569
1922	13,482	563
1923	13,267	550
1924	13,383	540
1925	13,121	551
1926	12,862	550
1927	11,112	477
1928	11,387	461
1929	11,159	470
1930	10,972	435
1931	10,702	420
1932	10,711	392
1933	10,543	382
1934	10,626	385
1935	10,505	382
1936	10,805	412
1937	10,629	397
1938	10,728	411
1939	10,860	406
1940	10,796	412
1941	10,682	408
1942	10,196	364
1943	9,763	324
1944	9,692	300
1945	9,661	301
1946	9,749	301
1947	9,736	320
1948	9,625	336
1949	9,794	364
1950	9,727	376
1951	9,591	354
1952	9,408	359
1953	9,184	343
1954	9,126	355
1955	9,030	351
1956	9,032	368
1957	8,959	356
1958	9,006	371
1959	8,979	363

the greatest drop occurred during World War II, and again during the Korean War. Rucker (1968) attributes these wartime declines to disruptions of supplies and manpower, which were felt most sharply by small operations. From the mid-1950s to the mid-1960s, the number of weeklies remained relatively constant. But since 1965, figures have declined an additional five percent.

Semi- and triweekly papers, now primarily suburban publications, are faring considerably better than the weeklies. In the earlier years of this century, the semiweekly and triweekly publications declined from a high of 672 in 1910 to a low of 300 in 1940. Since that time, their num-

Table 120–B. (Cont'd.)

Year	Weeklies	Semiweeklies and Triweeklies
1960	8,953	372
1961	8,954	386
1962	8,915	404
1963	8,941	406
1964	8,989	402
1965	8,958	402
1966	8,915	408
1967	8,858	446
1968	8,855	474
1969	8,903	476
1970	8,888	469
1971	8,682	448
1972	8,804	516
1973	8,711	593
1974	8,824	572
1975	8,735	578
1976	8,506	621

Sources: *Ayer Directory of Publications*, annual issues. 1900-1934 data cited by Chapin (1957), p. 13.

Note: Listings in the annual *Ayer Directory* are as of January of each year, hence the figures are always more representative of the previous year than of the publication year of the Ayer volume. For this reason, the editors have listed the data in this table for the year preceeding the one for which they are listed in the *Ayer Directory*.

bers have more than doubled to a 1976 level of 621, a figure which approaches the peak achieved nearly 70 years earlier. Growth has been especially pronounced in the last 10 years—52 percent since 1966.

Sources

The reader will note discrepancies in the figures for daily newspapers among the three sources presented in **Table 120-A**. These discrepancies are probably due to differences in the definition of a daily newspaper and to differing guidelines as to the type and the size of the newspaper establishments to be included in a survey. The *Editor and Publisher International Yearbook* includes only English-language dailies of general circulation. Foreign language dailies and specialized papers, such as the daily business press, are excluded. Before the *Census of Manufactures* stopped reporting the number of newspapers in 1967, it included foreign language papers but *not* trade dailies. In addition, the *Census of Manufactures* limited its efforts to those newspaper publishing establishments with at least one paid employee. The *Ayer Directory of Publications* is more inclusive and less precise in its definition of what constitutes a daily newspaper. Thus, foreign language dailies and some trade publications are probably included.

Table 120-B information comes from the *Ayer Directory of Publications*. The data up to 1934 were taken from Chapin (1957); subsequent data were compiled by the editors directly from the *Ayer Directory*. The editors followed Chapin's procedure by reporting figures for one year earlier than they are listed in *Ayer*. Chapin initiated this procedure because the *Ayer Directory* comes out each January with its figures listed for the year of publication. It seems obvious, then, that the figures given by *Ayer Directory* for a particular year are actually more reflective of the previous year.

As of 1927, the *Ayer Directory* began to differentiate between trade and general circulation newspapers. This explains the drop in the number of weeklies between 1926 and 1927. It also suggests that figures for the early part of the century are somewhat inflated. Since 1927, however, the data have been collected in a consistent way and should be historically comparable, though the editors suspect that some trade and other specialized newspapers may have slipped into the totals. *Ayer* does not have a strict definition of a newspaper of general circulation and states simply that "all publications, regardless of editorial accent or orientation, may qualify for listing, except those which are published by primary or secondary schools or houses of worship." House organs are also generally excluded.

Further Information

Further discussions of growth trends in daily newspapers can be found in Bagdikian (1971), Rucker (1968), and Rosse et al. (1975). For additional information on nondaily newspapers, the reader should check the National Newspaper Association's (NNA) annual publication, *National Directory of Weekly Newspapers*. This volume contains specific data on most weekly newspapers of general circulation in the country. The NNA also provides, upon request, some general statistics on overall trends in this field.

For discussions of trends in weekly newspapers during the earlier parts of this century, the reader should see Willey and Rice (1933), Lee (1937), and Chapin (1957). Chapin drew his *Ayer Directory* data from Lee for the period up to 1927. Rucker (1968) is a more recent source for a general analysis of the nondaily press.

Newspaper Publishing by Community Size   121

Table 121–A.
Number of Daily Newspaper Firms in U. S., by Size of City, 1948–1973

	1948	1958	1968	1973	% Changes 1948-1973
Total Number of Firms in U. S.	1,536	1,545	1,547	1,566	2.0%
Number of Firms in Cities of:					
Less than 10,000	451	409	365	333	-26.2
10,001-99,000	881	927	975	1,030	10.9
100,000-500,000	137	137	151	149	8.8
500,000-1,000,000	37	44	34	33	-10.8
More than 1 Million	30	28	22	21	-33.3

Sources: Rosse et al. (1975), p. 40, using data from *Editor and Publisher International Yearbook*.

Interpretation of Tables

Table 121-A offers a breakdown, by city size, of the number of daily newspaper firms operating in the United States in 1948, 1958, 1968, and 1973. A newspaper "firm" is defined by the authors of the study (Rosse et al., 1975) as a single company which publishes one or more newspapers in a given city. Thus, each individual city newspaper company in a chain of newspaper companies would be counted as one firm. Also, a single company which publishes more than one newspaper within the city—or several newspapers which share printing, advertising, or editorial facilities—would be counted as only one firm. This definition of "firm" is the basis of the difference between these figures and the counts of daily newspapers in **Table 121-C**.

The size of city in which a newspaper operates appears to have some effect upon that newspaper's fortunes. As **Table 121-A** shows, the total number of newspaper firms throughout the

	Less than 100,000	100,000 to 250,000	250,000 to 500,000	500,000 to 1,000,000	1 Million and over	All Daily Newspapers
1953						
Paper tons	819,018	687,530	932,275	1,153,084	1,694,910	5,286,817
% of Increase	15.5%	13.0%	17.6%	21.8%	32.1%	100.0%
1964						
Paper tons	1,336,407	785,619	1,061,609	1,547,288	1,972,815	6,703,738
% of Increase	19.9%	11.7%	15.8%	23.1%	29.4%	100.0%
1969						
Paper tons	1,582,541	1,115,733	1,498,680	1,730,283	2,364,480	8,291,717
% of Increase	19.1%	13.5%	18.1%	20.9%	28.5%	100.0%
1974						
Paper tons	2,000,847	987,444	1,331,106	1,786,220	2,044,849	8,150,466
% of Increase	25.0%	12.1%	16.3%	21.9%	25.1%	100.0%
1975						
Paper tons	1,876,489	923,816	1,174,316	1,555,044	1,839,787	7,369,452
% of Increase	25.5%	12.5%	15.9%	21.1%	25.0%	100.0%
% Changes 1953-1964	63.0%	14.0%	14.0%	34.0%	16.0%	27.0%
% Changes 1964-1975	40.0%	18.0%	11.0%	1.0%	-7.0%	10.0%

Sources: 1953, 1969 data: Udell (1970), p. 19. 1964, 1974 data: Udell (1976), p. 10. 1975 data: Udell (1977), p. 7, using data from the American Newspaper Publishers Association.

Note: Percentages may not add to 100% because of rounding.

country increased during the 25-year period from 1948 to 1973. However, this growth was primarily due to increases in the number of newspapers in mid-sized cities. In cities with populations of either less than 10,000 or more than 1 million, the number of dailies declined. Bagdikian (1976/ 1977) found a similar trend in a study of newspaper failures between 1961 and 1970: Small-town papers were most likely to fail, while suburban papers showed the lowest failure rates.

Another dimension of this situation becomes apparent when newsprint consumption by daily newspapers is broken down by city size and then examined as an indicator of newspaper growth. As **Table 121-B** reveals, newsprint consumption in smaller cities with populations of less than 1 million has increased most significantly over the past 20 years, while newsprint consumption in larger cities (populations over 1 million) has shown the greatest relative decrease.

An exact comparison of **Table 121-B** with **Table 121-A** is impossible, because the categories in **Table 121-B** are broader at the low end of the population distribution. However, the figures in

Table 121–C.
Number of Daily and Sunday Newspapers in U. S., by Size of City, 1955–1975

TOTAL NUMBER OF DAILIES

Size of City	1955	1960	1965	1970	1975	% Changes 1955-1975
More than 1 Million	34	33	29	27	25	-26%
500,001 to 1,000,000	45	48	48	50	49	9
100,001 to 500,000	181	201	203	219	213	18
50,001 to 100,000	181	218	221	238	238	31
25,001 to 50,000	287	308	294	302	308	7
Less than 25,000	1048	955	956	912	923	-12
TOTAL	1760	1763	1751	1748	1756	-0

NUMBER OF MORNING DAILIES[a]

Size of City	1955	1960	1965	1970	1975	% Changes 1955-1975
More than 1 Million	16	16	12	15	14	-13%
500,001 to 1,000,000	20	22	23	26	25	25
100,001 to 500,000	78	85	86	91	89	14
50,001 to 100,000	61	64	64	65	69	13
25,001 to 50,000	58	54	54	59	67	16
Less than 25,000	86	71	81	78	75	-13
TOTAL	316	312	320	334	339	7

Tables **121**-A and **121**-B do bear some relationship to one another. For example, since newspapers in large cities have large press runs, their numerical decline would certainly tend to decrease newsprint consumption. On the other hand, when several firms fail in smaller cities, the ones that remain may tend to increase their size and newsprint consumption.

Table **121**-C reports the actual number of daily and Sunday newspapers by city size for the last 20 years. The same patterns of decline in the lowest and highest population categories of Table **121**-A are evident in Table **121**-C. It is also interesting to note the total figures for evening, morning, and Sunday newspapers: Only the evening dailies show an overall decline, while morning and Sunday newspapers actually increased in number.

Sources

Table **121**-C was compiled by the editors directly from information in the *Editor and Publisher International Yearbook*. This source was also used for raw data for the Rosse et al. study (1975), from which Table **121**-A was derived. The information in the *Editor and Publisher International Yearbook* is based on data supplied by the Audit Bureau of Circulations—the leading monitor of circulation figures in the newspaper and magazine industry—plus publishers' statements

Table 121–C. (Cont'd.)

NUMBER OF EVENING DAILIES[a]

	1955	1960	1965	1970	1975	% Changes 1955-1975
Size of City						
More than 1 Million	18	17	17	12	12	-33%
500,001 to 1,000,000	25	26	25	24	24	-4
100,001 to 500,000	103	116	118	129	127	23
50,001 to 100,000	120	158	162	178	175	46
25,001 to 50,000	229	256	244	250	248	8
Less than 25,000	962	886	878	836	850	-12
TOTAL	1454	1459	1444	1429	1436	-1

TOTAL NUMBER OF SUNDAY PAPERS

	1955	1960	1965	1970	1975	% Changes 1955-1975
Size of City						
More than 1 Million	17	18	15	15	16	-6%
500,001 to 1,000,000	24	28	27	30	30	25
100,001 to 500,000	103	113	110	119	119	16
50,001 to 100,000	79	95	102	115	126	59
25,001 to 50,000	101	120	121	126	146	45
Less than 25,000	220	189	187	181	202	-8
TOTAL	541	563	562	586	639	18

Source: *Editor and Publisher International Yearbook, 1956, 1961, 1966, 1971, 1976.*

Note: (a) Figures for morning and evening dailies include several "all day" newspapers (19 in 1975). The double counting has been eliminated from the adjusted figures for "Total Number of Dailies."

furnished to the U.S. Post Office. In addition, *Editor and Publisher* sent individual questionnaires to each newspaper, and this survey information was then cross-checked. The results of this thorough procedure should be quite reliable. Only general circulation English-language dailies are included in the *Editor and Publisher International Yearbook* listings.

Table 121-B was taken from Udell (1970, 1976, 1977), who used statistics supplied by the American Newspaper Publishers Association (ANPA). The ANPA provides such information to the newspaper industry itself, and its figures are generally regarded as accurate.

Further Information

The ANPA publishes current statistics on newsprint consumption at least once each year in its series of newsprint and traffic bulletins. Information updating Table 121-C appears annually in the *Editor and Publisher International Yearbook.*

Table 130-A.
Number of Periodicals in U. S., by Publication Schedule, 1932–1976

	Total	Weekly	Semi-Monthly	Monthly	Bi-Monthly	Quarterly	Other
1932	6215[b]	--	--	--	--	--	--
1933	6345[b]	--	--	--	--	--	--
1934	6274[b]	--	--	--	--	--	--
1935	5901[b]	1374	335	3170	186	462	374
1936	6021[b]	1426	356	3194	187	466	392
1937	5680	1148	387	3096	184	494	371
1938	5771	1134	354	3224	207	495	357
1939	6155	1313	374	3353	234	528	353
1940	6432	1399	427	3466	241	538	361
1941	6468	1366	406	3501	261	564	370
1942	6709	1531	427	3525	271	566	389
1943	6354	1401	408	3346	256	551	392
1944	5982	1363	411	3021	264	555	368
1945	5880	1269	428	3025	284	545	329
1946	5985	1251	435	3097	319	564	319
1947	6429	1315	463	3357	372	574	348
1948	6669	1412	462	3509	385	538	363
1949	6883	1451	427	3600	433	593	379
1950	6960	1443	416	3694	436	604	367
1951	6977	1434	427	3655	487	594	380
1952	7050	1421	426	3643	532	625	403
1953	7142	1440	424	3640	570	635	432
1954	7382	1520	456	3711	574	650	471
1955	7648	1602	503	3782	608	674	479
1956	7907	1665	494	3904	573	768	503
1957	7907	1610	498	3907	594	776	522
1958	8074	1619	524	3925	632	841	533
1959	8136	1514	530	4001	663	866	562
1960	8422	1580	527	4113	743	895	564
1961	8411	1571	521	4063	753	915	588
1962	8616	1656	527	4135	769	945	584
1963	8758	1709	543	4166	801	939	600
1964	8900	1640	550	4273	846	979	612
1965	8990	1716	550	4195	876	1030	623
1966	9102	1799	557	4230	848	1036	632
1967	9238	1808	573	4296	859	1051	651
1968	9400	1796	606	4331	899	1078	690
1969	9434	1787	587	4353	899	1084	724
1970	9573	1856	589	4314	957	1108	749
1971	9657	1873	544	4277	1005	1124	834
1972	9062	1606	493	4093	852	1106	912
1973	9630	2022	506	4107	925	1148	922
1974	9755	2027	529	4123	942	1164	970
1975	9657	1918	537	4087	1009	1093	1013
1976	9872	1915	557	4144	1058	1161	1037

Sources: *Ayer Directory of Publications*, appropriate years. 1932-1956 data cited by Chapin (1957), p. 62.

Notes: (a) Figures are listed by the year of the *Ayer Directory* from which they are taken. However, they actually represent the number of periodicals counted during the previous year. Hence, the figures given for 1976, taken from the 1976 edition, in fact are figures for 1975; (b) Breakdown of totals for 1932-1936 is not comparable to breakdown for 1937-1976.

Table 130–B.
Number of Periodical Publishing Establishments and Companies
in U. S., 1939–1974

Year	Number of Establishments	Number of Companies	Number of Reporting Units[a]
1939	2,337	N/A	N/A
1947	2,166	2,106	N/A
1954	2,045	2,012	N/A
1958	2,332	2,246	N/A
1959	N/A	N/A	2,399
1962	N/A	N/A	2,599
1963	2,630	2,562	N/A
1964	N/A	N/A	2,562
1965	N/A	N/A	2,552
1966	N/A	N/A	2,504
1967	2,510	2,430	2,479
1968	N/A	N/A	2,401
1969	N/A	N/A	2,431
1970	N/A	N/A	2,424
1971	N/A	N/A	2,357
1972	2,535	2,451	2,306
1973	N/A	N/A	2,312
1974	N/A	N/A	2,394

Sources: Number of establishments and companies, 1939-1963: *1963 Census of Manufactures*; 1967-1972: *1972 Census of Manufactures*. Number of reporting units: *County Business Patterns*, appropriate annual issues.

Note: (a) A "reporting unit" in the periodicals industry is equivalent to an "establishment" in the *Census of Manufactures*. See text for further explanation.

Interpretation of Tables

A primary problem with all statistics on periodicals is that the various compilers of data in the field tend to work from different definitions of the terms "periodical" and "magazine." Thus, published figures which purport to describe the number of periodicals in the United States will vary widely from source to source. **Table 130-A** presents data from the *Ayer Directory of Publications*, which is the most widely quoted source in the field. Since 1963, the *Ayer Directory* is also the only source offering a tally of American periodicals. (Before 1963, the *Census of Manufactures* also published such figures—see **Table 630-B**.)

Another major problem with any analysis of statistics on periodicals is that small periodicals are not easily located by the compiler of such data. It is therefore difficult for the analyst of **Table 130-A** to say whether the slow, steady growth of periodicals represents growth in the industry, or whether it is simply the result of yearly improvements in *Ayer's* ability to locate obscure periodicals.

Table 130-B shows U.S. Census Bureau figures for the number of periodical publishing establishments, companies, and reporting units in the United States. The Census Bureau defines a "periodical publishing establishment" as a place where periodicals are published—the meaning is close to "factory." A "company" is a business organization consisting of one or more *establishments* under common ownership or control. A "reporting unit," as used by the Census Bureau's *County Business Patterns* survey, is equivalent to the *Census of Manufacture's* use of the term "establishment."

In comparing the **Table 130-B** figures for the number of periodical *publishers* with the *Ayer Directory* figures (**Table 130-A**) for the number of *periodicals*, the reader will note a considerable difference. A number of explanations can be offered for this difference—perhaps so many, in fact, as to render any one of them unsatisfactory. One explanation is that some periodical publishers publish several magazines. Also, many periodicals included by the *Ayer* company are published by nonprofit organizations, which fall outside the scope of Census Bureau surveys. Further, only those firms primarily involved in the publication of periodicals are included in the Census Bureau figures in **Table 130-B**. For example, periodicals published by newspaper companies or book publishers are not included in this table, even though some huge magazine chains are owned by such firms.

What we can conclude from the data in **Table 130-B** is that the number of periodical publishing establishments, companies, and reporting units has remained fairly constant over time. The relationship of number of periodicals to number of periodical publishers must remain unclear.

Sources

The *Ayer Directory of Publications*, the source of **Table 130-A**, compiles its listings by scanning other directories of periodical names and then contacting a "responsible spokesperson for the original source" who can provide specific information about the newspaper or magazine. The scope of inclusion in the *Ayer Directory* is fairly broad: "All publications, regardless of editorial accent or orientation, may qualify for listing, except those which are published by primary or secondary schools or houses of worship." House organs are also generally excluded.

It is likely that some small, local publications escape inclusion in the *Ayer* tally. Most house organs are consciously excluded (the latter are estimated by one source [Penkert, 1971] to include more than 50,000 distinct publications). However, with these omissions, the *Ayer* listing remains the most inclusive directory available. The *Ayer Directory* has always turned up a larger number of periodicals than any other source, including the U.S. Census Bureau.

The information in **Table 130-B** comes from two Census Bureau surveys, the *Census of Manufactures* and *County Business Patterns*. The data for both surveys are based upon the results of questionnaires sent by the Census Bureau to publishing firms. Some of the information in *County Business Patterns* is also taken from Internal Revenue Service or Social Security filings. The *Census of Manufactures* data are the more valid of the two, but the information from *County Business Patterns* is very similar, and it is available on an annual basis.

Further Information

There is no recent, comprehensive history of periodical publication. Peterson (1964) still represents the best single source. Another useful volume is Schacht's (1972) bibliography for the study of magazines. In addition, two recent studies on the publication of journals— King et al. (1976), and Fry and White (1976)—provide some insights into this category of periodicals.

Motion Picture Production and Distribution 140

Interpretation of Tables

There are at least three ways to judge the physical scope of the motion picture industry: (1) the number of films it produces, (2) the number of theaters being used to show those films (see Unit 141); and (3) the size of the motion picture audience (see Unit 640). Unfortunately, it is difficult to trace even one of these basic indicators, because the American film industry has a strong dislike for specific statistics. In many cases, the industry is unwilling to give out whatever data do exist.

Table 140-A illustrates this problem with a comparison of two markedly different tabulations of the number of feature films released in the United States over the past 60 years. One set of figures come from the *Film Daily Yearbook* (*FDY*), the other from the National Association of Theater Owners (NATO). (For data on imported films and their proportion of the U.S. market, see Unit 740.) The *FDY* totals apparently included many "shorts" (films shorter than feature length) for the period up to the 1930s. The reader should also be aware that the "majors"—the

Table 140-A.
Number of Feature Films Released in U. S. Market, 1917–1975

	Film Daily Yearbook Data			National Association of Theater Owners Data		
	Films Released by Major Distributors	Films Released by Independent Distributors	Total Releases	Total Releases	New Releases	Re-Releases
1917	- -	- -	687	- -	- -	- -
1918	- -	- -	841	- -	- -	- -
1919	- -	- -	646	- -	- -	- -
1920	- -	- -	796	- -	- -	- -
1921	- -	- -	854	- -	- -	- -
1922	- -	- -	743	- -	- -	- -
1923	432	144	576	- -	- -	- -
1924	426	153	579	- -	- -	- -
1925	442	137	579	- -	- -	- -
1926	477	293	740	- -	- -	- -
1927	510	233	743	- -	- -	- -
1928	462	372	884	- -	- -	- -
1929	393	314	707	- -	- -	- -
1930	362	233	595	355	- -	- -
1931	324	298	622	345	344	1
1932	318	367	685	358	357	1
1933	338	306	644	379	376	3
1934	361	301	662	389	389	0
1935	356	410	766	391	388	3
1936	362	373	735	423	413	10
1937	408	370	778	497	487	10
1938	362	407	769	468	448	20
1939	388	373	761	483	468	15
1940	363	310	673	475	472	3
1941	379	219	598	504	497	7
1942	358	175	533	492	484	8
1943	289	138	427	432	426	6
1944	270	172	442	415	409	6
1945	234	143	377	375	367	8
1946	252	215	467	400	383	17
1947	249	237	486	426	371	55
1948	248	211	459	448	398	50
1949	234	245	479	491	406	85
1950	263	359	622	473	425	48
1951	320	334	654	439	411	28
1952	278	185	463	386	353	33
1953	301	233	534	414	378	36
1954	225	202	427	369	294	75
1955	215	177	392	319	281	38
1956	237	242	479	346	311	35
1957	268	265	533	382	363	19
1958	237	270	507	352	327	25
1959	189	250	439	254	236	18
1960	184	203	387	248	233	15
1961	167	295	462	240	225	15
1962	162	265	427	237	213	24
1963	142	278	420	223	203	20
1964	144	358	502	242	227	15
1965	167	285	452	279	257	22
1966	149	302	451	257	231	26
1967	157	305	462	264	229	35
1968	177	277	454	258	241	17
1969	- -	- -	- -	251	241	10
1970	- -	- -	- -	306	267	39
1971	- -	- -	- -	313	281	32
1972	- -	- -	- -	312	273	39
1973	- -	- -	- -	267	229	38
1974	- -	- -	- -	268	223	45
1975	- -	- -	- -	222	182	40

Sources: *Film Daily Yearbook* (1969), p. 98. National Association of Theatre Owners (1976), pp. 48, 50.

Note: The *Film Daily* figures include both foreigh- and U. S.-made features.

Table 140-B.
Number of Feature Films Released by the Eight Major Distribution Companies in U. S., 1930–1976

Year	Columbia	M-G-M	Paramount	RKO	20th Century	United Artists	Universal	Warner Bros.	Total
1930-31	27	43	58	32	48	13	22	69	312
1931-32	31	40	56	48	46	14	32	56	323
1932-33	36	37	51	45	41	16	28	53	307
1933-34	44	44	55	40	46	20	38	63	350
1934-35	39	42	44	40	40	19	39	51	314
1935-36	36	43	50	43	52	17	27	58	326
1936-37	38	40	41	39	52	19	40	58	327
1937	61	49	62	51	59	10	51	60	403
1938	54	41	55	45	60	9	47	51	362
1939	51	51	63	48	45	16	51	51	376
1940	51	48	48	53	49	20	49	45	363
1941	61	47	45	44	50	26	58	48	379
1942	59	49	44	39	51	26	56	34	358
1943	47	33	30	44	33	28	53	21	289
1944	51	30	32	31	26	20	53	19	262
1945	38	31	23	33	27	17	46	19	234
1946	51	25	22	40	32	20	42	20	252
1947	49	29	29	36	27	26	33	20	249
1948	39	24	25	31	45	26	35	23	248
1949	52	30	21	25	31	21	29	25	234
1950	59	38	23	32	32	18	33	28	263
1951	63	41	29	36	39	46	39	27	320
1952	48	38	24	32	37	34	39	26	278
1953	47	44	26	25	39	49	43	28	310
1954	35	24	17	16	29	52	32	20	225
1955	38	23	20	13	29	35	34	23	215
1956	40	24	17	20	32	48	33	23	237
1957	46	29	20	1	50	54	39	29	268
1958	38	29	25	--	42	44	35	24	237
1959	36	25	18	--	34	40	18	18	189
1960	35	18	22	--	49	23	20	17	184
1961	28	21	15	--	35	33	19	16	167
1962	30	21	17	--	25	36	18	15	162
1963	19	35	17	--	18	23	17	13	142
1964	19	30	16	--	18	18	25	18	144
1965	29	28	24	--	26	19	26	15	167
1966	29	24	22	--	21	18	23	12	149
1967	22	21	30	--	19	19	25	21	157
1968	20	27	33	--	21	23	30	23	177
1969	N/A	N/A	N/A	N/A	N/A	N/A	N/A	N/A	N/A
1970	28	21	16	--	14	40	17	15	151
1971	37	20	21	--	16	26	16	17	153
1972	27	22	14	--	25	20	16	18	142
1973	16	16	26	--	14	18	19	22	131
1974	21	--	23	--	18	21	11	15	109
1975	15	--	11	--	19	21	10	19	95
1976	15	--	15	--	19	18	13	12	92

Sources: 1930-1937: Temporary National Economic Committee (1941), p. 9. 1937-1939: Huettig (1944), p. 86. 1940-1952: Conant (1960), p. 123. 1953-1968: *Film Daily Yearbook* (1969). 1970-1976: National Association of Theatre Owners (1976), pp. 49-50.

Table 140–C.
Number of Nontheatrical Motion Pictures Produced in U. S., by
Type of Producing Organization, 1958–1976

Year	Business/ Industry	Government	Education	Religion	Community Agencies	Medicine/ Health	Independent	Total
1958	4,500	1,500	940	200	200	300	100	7,740
1959	5,400	1,500	1,260	220	210	400	100	9,100
1960	5,000	1,500	1,020	190	210	300	100	8,320
1961	5,100	1,550	1,100	190	200	250	110	8,500
1962	5,600	1,700	1,150	180	190	270	110	9,350
1963	5,900	1,800	1,180	180	180	300	140	9,670
1964	6,200	1,850	1,200	200	190	290	150	10,080
1965	6,400	1,900	1,370	210	210	390	190	10,670
1966	7,400	2,000	1,500	200	300	400	250	12,070
1967	7,500	2,200	1,700	180	320	370	300	12,570
1968	8,900	2,000	1,950	170	200	380	400	14,010
1969	9,400	1,900	2,400	150	310	510	500	15,170
1970	9,000	1,410	2,140	150	305	570	600	14,175
1971	9,630	1,700	2,430	190	160	460	550	15,120
1972	10,170	1,755	2,450	225	240	550	600	15,990
1973	11,565	1,740	2,175	255	150	700	600	17,185
1974	10,655	2,060	2,590	220	150	935	800	17,410
1975	9,940	2,315	2,740	170	140	640	660	16,605
1976	8,550	2,650	2,350	150	120	530	700	15,050

Source: Data supplied to editors by Hope Reports, Inc., Rochester, N.Y.

major production and/or distribution companies—have varied from period to period, though usually they have consisted of the eight firms listed in **Table 140-B**: Columbia, M-G-M, Paramount, RKO, 20th Century-Fox, United Artists, Universal, and Warner Brothers. All other firms are included in the category of "independents."

Table 140-B summarizes the feature-film output of the eight major studios and traces the drastic declines in annual levels of production from the heyday of Hollywood in the 1930s. The slight overlap in figures for 1937 is due to a change in the sources of the information.

Table 140-C provides estimates for the biggest film "market" of all: the large number of nontheatrical films produced annually by government agencies, businesses, industries, educational institutions, and other organizations. Most of these films never reach the public eye, since they are produced for internal, often training, uses. Nevertheless, the nontheatrical film products provide considerably greater opportunities for employment and investment within the motion picture industry. The "independent" category in **Table 140-C** includes student experimental films. The increases in this category in recent years is undoubtedly due, at least in part, to the growing numbers of university students who are studying the film medium.

Table 140-D addresses the film-television interrelationship by showing the number of theatrical and, after 1966, "made-for-television" films shown on network television. The reader should particularly note the decline in the median number of months between first theatrical showing and first network television showing—a drop from 8.5 years in the early 1960s to 4.5 years in the late 1960s. Moreover, as Hollywood theatrical production levels have dropped, network reliance on the "made-for-television" movie has increased. Many of these "made-for-television" films have been designed specifically as pilots for possible television series, and the unexpected popularity of other such films has led to their becoming the basis of a series (see Unit 582). The growth of this special product only adds to the irony that the motion picture industry's nemesis of the 1950s has become its chief employer in the 1960s and 1970s.

The film industry is still completing the transition from its pre-television mass-medium role to its present status as a more specialized entertainment medium. However, the overall trend in motion pictures is clear: a smaller annual output of the traditional Hollywood product and continued emphasis on products which cater to smaller, more specific audiences (see Unit 640).

Table 140–D.
Number and Frequency of Theatrical and Made-For-TV Feature Films on U. S. Network Television, 1961–1974

| Season | Theatrical Films | | | Made-for-TV Films | | Total Number of Films Shown on Network TV |
	Number of Films Shown on Network TV	Months Since First Theatrical Release of Film	Percent of All Films Shown on Network TV	Number of Films Shown	Percent of All Films Shown on Network TV	
1961-62	45	103	100%	--	--	45
1962-63	72	67	100	--	--	72
1963-64	60	97	100	--	--	60
1964-65	85	82	100	--	--	85
1965-66	120	71	99	1	--[a]	121
1966-67	142	62	93	11	7%	153
1967-68	138	51	97	4	3	142
1968-69	141	43	89	17	11	158
1969-70	140	45	77	43	23	183
1970-71	113	50	68	53	32	166
1971-72	133	51	51	94	49	227
1972-73	107	53	42	149	58	256
1973-74	118	54	40	180	60	298

Source: McAlpine (1975), pp. 14-15.

Note: (a) The figure for this season is less than 1%.

Sources

The figures in **Table 140-A** are taken from the *Film Daily Yearbook* (1969) and from reports of the National Association of Theater Owners (1976). Unfortunately, the *Film Daily Yearbook* has been out of business since 1969, and there is no way of reconstructing the approach and definitions used by its staff. Nor can the origins of the *FDY* and NATO figures be identified. Figures from both sources must be taken as estimates and as indications of the degree of variation to be expected in even basic statistics regarding the motion picture industry in the United States.

Figures in **Table 140-B** present similar problems, since none of the sources relate how their information was developed. The "seasonal" 1930-31 through 1936-37 data are taken from the Temporary National Economic Committee (1941); the 1937-39 data from Huettig (1944); the 1940-52 data from Conant (1960); the 1953-68 data from *Film Daily Yearbook* (1969); and the 1970-76 data from the National Association of Theater Owners (1976). These figures must all be considered estimations. Indeed, in one case in which the sources overlap—for the year 1939, which is covered by both Huettig (1944) and Conant (1960)—there is a difference between the two sources in both specific company figures and aggregate figures. Despite such inconsistencies and uncertainties, the information in **Table 140-B** is likely to be accurate as to overall trends in the industry.

Table 140-C, from Hope (1969), is labeled by the author as an estimation. The rounded, even figures are evidence that these statistics are only very approximate indications of output in the highly diverse field of nontheatrical film production.

Table 140-D is taken from McAlpine (1975). The data are based on unpublished industry research which was provided by television program suppliers to the FCC during the commission's hearings on pay-television. All broadcast time-periods (not just prime-time) are covered by the table, but only network-originated films are represented by the figures. Films broadcast by local and/or independent stations are excluded. Given the specific nature and limited scope of the information in **Table 140-D**, it can be taken as nearly exact.

Further Information

Despite the difficulty of obtaining consistent information on the U.S. motion picture industry, current pieces of the puzzle may be found in *Variety* and other trade periodicals, as well as the *International Motion Picture Almanac* (annual). The reader may also wish to contact the Motion Picture Association of America. The editors recommend Conant (1960), Jowett (1976), Jarvie (1970), and Bluem and Squire (1972) for general information and useful statistics on the industry.

Motion Picture Theaters 141

Table 141–A.
Number and Capacities of U. S. Motion Picture Theaters, 1923–1972

Year	Four-Wall Theaters Number	Four-Wall Theaters Total Seats	Outdoor Theaters Number	Outdoor Theaters Total Spaces	Total Number of Theaters	Index: Theaters[a]	Total Theater Capacities	Index: Capacities[a]
1923	15,000	7,605,000	- -	- -	15,000	81	7,605,000	65
1931	22,100	12,143,761	- -	- -	22,100	119	12,143,761	104
1935	18,263	11,132,595	- -	- -	18,263	98	11,132,595	95
1939	N/A	N/A	N/A	N/A	15,115	81	N/A	N/A
1948	17,811	N/A	820	N/A	18,631	100	11,701,300	100
1954	14,716	7,775,300	3,775	1,142,300	18,491	99	8,917,600	76
1958	12,291	6,994,800	4,063	1,428,600	16,354	87	8,423,400	72
1963	9,150	6,389,100	3,502	1,652,200	12,652	68	8,041,300	69
1967	8,803	4,787,400	3,384	1,402,500	12,187	65	6,189,900	53
1972	9,209	6,063,800	3,490	1,921,900	12,699	68	7,985,700	68

Sources: 1923 data: *Film Daily*, January 23, 1923. 1931-35 data: Bertrand (1935), pp. 38-39. 1939-72 data: U. S. Census Bureau, *Census of Selected Service Industries*, appropriate issues.

Note: (a) For these indices, the base figure of 100 is used for the year 1948.

Interpretation of Tables

Though many films are now shown on television, the motion picture theater is still an important outlet for the film medium. Unfortunately, there is little consistent information on the number of movie theaters in the United States. This is partly because owners, especially those of large chains, appear reluctant to give out detailed figures on the number of theaters they control (see Unit 241).

Table 141-A lists the most detailed and accurate data available on the number of "four-wall" (indoor) and drive-in (outdoor) movie theaters in the United States. The table also notes the aggregate number of seats or car spaces these theaters offer to the American moviegoer. The reader will note that while drive-in units have generally increased since World War II (the first drive-in was built in the late 1930s), the number of indoor theaters had declined until a new spurt of construction in the early 1970s began to reverse this downward trend (see **Table 141**-**C**).

Table 141-B shows the most commonly reproduced, year-by-year estimates of the number of motion picture theaters in the United States. However, these data present certain problems. For example, a comparison of figures listed for 1956 and 1957, and again for 1961 and 1962,

Table 141–B.
Number of Motion Picture Theaters in U. S., 1926–1975

Year	Four-Wall Theaters		Outdoor Theaters	Total
	Silent	Sound		
1926	19,489	- -	- -	19,489
1927	21,644	20	- -	21,664
1928	22,204	100	- -	22,304
1929	22,544	800	- -	23,344
1930	14,140	8,860	- -	23,000
1931	8,865	13,128	- -	21,993
1932	4,835	13,880	- -	18,715
1933	4,128	14,405	- -	18,533
1934	2,504	14,381	- -	16,885
1935	- -	15,273	- -	15,273
1936	- -	15,858	- -	15,858
1937	- -	18,192	- -	18,192
1938	- -	18,182	- -	18,182
1939	- -	17,829	- -	17,829
1940	- -	19,032	- -	19,032
1941	- -	19,645	95	19,740
1942	- -	20,281	99	20,380
1943	- -	20,196	97	20,293
1944	- -	20,277	96	20,373
1945	- -	20,355	102	20,457
1946	- -	18,719	300	19,019
1947	- -	18,059	548	18,607
1948	- -	17,575	820	18,395
1949	- -	17,367	1,203	18,570
1950	- -	16,904	2,202	19,106
1951	- -	16,150	2,830	18,980
1952	- -	15,347	3,276	18,623
1953	- -	14,174	3,791	17,965
1954	- -	15,039	4,062	19,101
1955	- -	14,613	4,587	19,200
1956	- -	14,509	4,494	19,003
1957	- -	14,509	4,494	19,003
1958	- -	11,300	4,700	16,000
1959	- -	11,335	4,768	16,103
1960	- -	12,291	4,700	16,991
1961	- -	15,000	6,000	21,000
1962	- -	15,000	6,000	21,000
1963	- -	9,250	3,550	12,800
1964	- -	9,650	4,100	13,750
1965	- -	9,850	4,150	14,000
1966	- -	10,150	4,200	14,350
1967	- -	13,000	4,900	17,900
1968	- -	13,600	4,975	18,575
1969	- -	9,750	3,730	13,480

will reveal that the data are identical for both years—a highly improbable situation. The sharp declines shown for 1963 are also most unlikely. (Another sudden decline in 1969 is the result of a change in source material—see the discussion below and in the Sources section.)

Similar anomalies can be seen elsewhere on the table. Some data are given as odd numbers and therefore appear to be exact counts. Other data are rounded even numbers, which one would assume to be mere estimations. Some sequences of data rise and dip in a plausible fashion; other sequences change far too drastically from year to year. The Motion Picture Association of America (MPAA) estimates, which are listed in the notes of **Table 141-B** and in the body of the table for the years 1969-73, seem to be more plausible and, therefore, reliable, in that they are not as high as the earlier figures and they do not change radically from year to year.

Table 141–B. (Cont'd.)

Year	Four-Wall Theaters		Outdoor Theaters	Total
	Silent	Sound		
1970	- -	10,000	3,750	13,750
1971	- -	10,300	3,770	14,070
1972	- -	10,580	3,790	14,370
1973	- -	10,850	3,800	14,650
1974	- -	11,612	3,772	15,384
1975	- -	12,168	3,801	15,969

Sources: 1926-1968 figures: *Film Daily Yearbook 1969*. 1969-1973 figures: Jowett (1976), p. 482, reprinting Motion Picture Association of America (MPAA) estimates which were based on census figures. 1974-1975 figures: National Association of Theater Owners (NATO) (1976), p. 43.

Note: Jowett (1976) also provides MPAA estimates for the years 1963-1968. These slightly differing figures are as follows:

Year	Four-Wall Theaters	Outdoor Theaters	Total
1963	9,150	3,502	12,652
1964	9,200	3,540	12,740
1965	9,240	3,585	12,825
1966	9,290	3,640	12,930
1967	9,330	3,670	13,000
1968	9,500	3,690	13,190

Table 141-C focuses on new motion picture theater construction over a 12-year period from 1963 to 1975. The figures indicate that most such construction has been of either outdoor (drive-in) theaters or indoor theaters in shopping centers. According to *Boxoffice*, a majority of the indoor theaters constructed during the 1970s have been "mini-theaters" (350 seats or less). The "Total, All New Theaters" columns include a category of "other new theaters" which presumably are newly constructed (or announced) theaters *not* located in shopping centers. Not represented on this table are the large number of older theaters which have been adapted to multiple-screen units. (The MPAA estimates that the roughly 14,000 sites operating in 1975 had close to 16,000 screens. Most of those additional 2,000 screens were housed in two-screen units.)

One important factor on which little consistent information is available is the average number of seats in theaters. A very rough approximation can be made using data in Table 141-A (dividing theater capacities by number of theaters), but these figures show little change (an average of 507 seats in 1923 to 629 in 1972 for all theaters, with outdoor establishments having smaller capacities than indoor units). There has always been a substantial difference in the capacities of chain or circuit-owned theaters and independently owned theaters. In 1939, for example, MPAA reported that circuit theaters averaged 1,445 seats in major urban areas, whereas independent theaters averaged only 515 seats (Heuttig, 1944, p. 74). In 1945, 35 percent of all theaters seated 350 or less, 23 percent seated 351-500, 16 percent seated 501-750, and 11 percent seated 750-1,000. The remaining 14 percent of theaters could seat more than 1,000 persons (Conant, 1945, p. 48, quoting *Variety*). By 1975, 85 percent of indoor circuit-owned theaters had a capacity of 400 or more, but only half that proportion of independent theaters (44 percent) could match that capacity (IMPA, 1975, p. 35A).

Sources

There is no single published source which provides information on the specific number of movie theaters in the country at a given point in time. Consequently, the editors found it necessary to construct Tables 141-A, 141-B, and 141-C from a variety of limited sources.

Table 141-A drawn mainly from the *Census of Selected Service Industries*, gives a detailed count, but includes only those businesses with a payroll. Table 141-B, from the *Film Daily Yearbook* (1969), contains very approximate estimates. As noted above, the fluctuations from year to year are too great and sudden to be considered accurate, and the figures for the late 1960s are

Table 141–C.
Construction of New Motion Picture Theaters in U. S., by Type of Theater, 1963–1975

Year	Shopping Center Theaters Only			Outdoor Theaters Only			Total, All New Theaters		
	Completed	Announced/ Started	Total	Completed	Announced/ Started	Total	Completed	Announced/ Started	Total
1963	46	97	143	34	46	80	127	193	320
1964	74	147	221	35	66	101	153	297	450
1965	100	138	238	47	55	102	208	246	454
1966	103	101	204	55	44	99	223	221	444
1967	98	92	190	31	40	71	212	235	447
1968	90	108	198	20	59	79	191	280	471
1969	92	133	225	39	59	98	287	344	631
1970	96	84	180	24	27	51	275	278	553
1971	111	100	211	18	25	43	321	294	615
1972	140	138	278	21	15	36	299	282	581
1973	112	83	195	14	21	35	291	181	472
1974	N/A	N/A	N/A	N/A	N/A	N/A	144	240	384
1975	174	52	226	16	- -	16	228	63	291

Source: The figures were provided to the editors by the Motion Picture Association (MPAA), which gathered the information from issues of *Boxoffice*.

clearly inflated. the MPAA data in **Table 141-B** are also estimates but the figures are based on 1963 census figures and are therefore likely to be far more accurate.

Finally, although the MPAA/*Boxoffice* figures presented in **Table 141-C** appear to be based on actual counts, they should nevertheless be viewed by the reader as no more than close estimates. Many of the theaters listed as "announced/started" may in fact never have opened. Moreover, *Boxoffice* notes that well over one-third of the indoor theaters built in the 1970s have been "multi-mini" theaters housing two or more screens in one complex.

Further Information

The *Census of Selected Service Industries* provides detailed regional, state, and city break-downs of motion picture theater data. *Boxoffice* magazine regularly reports on new theater construction and planning, and similar data often appear in *Variety* as well. In Hall (1961), the reader will find an accounting of American motion picture theaters in their heyday in the 1920s and 1930s.

Table 150–A.
Number of Recordings Manufactured in U. S., 1899–1972

Note: All figures are in thousands.

Year	Cylinder Recordings	Disc Recordings 78 rpm	Disc Recordings 45 rpm	Disc Recordings 33 rpm	Tape Recordings	Total Number of Recordings
1899	2,763.3	- -	- -	- -	- -	2,763.3
1909	18,611.2	8,572.8	- -	- -	- -	27,184.0
1914	3,907.1	23,314.2	- -	- -	- -	27,221.3
1919	5,911.6	101,085.0	- -	- -	- -	106,996.6
1921	1,755.2	103,436.7	- -	- -	- -	105,191.9
1923	5,249.2	92,855.1	- -	- -	- -	98,104.3
1925	- -	82,125.1	- -	- -	- -	82,125.1
1927	- -	104,766.2	- -	- -	- -	104,766.2
1931	- -	30,851.0	- -	- -	- -	30,851.0
1939	- -	349,900.0	- -	- -	- -	349,900.0
1947	- -	332,000.0	- -	- -	- -	332,000.0
1954	- -	127,600.0	76,200.0	24,000.0	- -	227,800.0
1958	- -	23,326.0	185,000.0	108,900.0	.3	317,226.3
1963	- -	- -	182,000.0	159,200.0	1.4	341,201.4
1967	- -	- -	358,900.0	217,500.0	13.5	576,413.5
1972	- -	- -	531,600.0	437,100.0	128.5	968,828.5

Source: *Census of Manufactures*, appropriate issues.

Interpretation of Tables

Consistent statistics are few and far between in the recording business. **Table 150-A** offers statistics on the number of recordings—cylinder, disc, and tape—manufactured during census years from 1899 to 1972. The most obvious trend is the ever-changing recording formats—from cylinders, to 78rpm discs, to the long-playing modes, and, finally, to various forms of tapes. It is also interesting to identify the clear cycles in this industry's production levels and to speculate about their underlying causes.

The decline in the 1920s, for example, was due primarily to the initial competition from radio. The reason for the drastic dip during the Great Depression is obvious. The temporary decline of 1954 was probably due to the industry's shift from 78rpm to 45rpm and 33rpm discs. However, with statistics available only for the census years 1954 and 1958, it is difficult to quantitatively judge the battle between 45rpm and 33rpm speeds during the early 1950s. One curious and unexpected figure in **Table 150-A** is the sudden, sharp rise in the number of cylinder recordings produced in 1923, just before the ultimate demise of that mode in the face of competition from discs.

Table 150-B provides more detailed, though unofficial, information from *Billboard* magazine on the generally increasing number of single recordings and albums released annually. While such specific information is not available for the period after 1972, it is continued in a sense by the U.S. Copyright Office statistics for the total number of single and LP titles registered each year. (Recordings were added to the national copyright laws in 1972, after the record industry demanded relief from the serious problem of the "bootlegged"—illegally duplicated—recordings which were appearing on the market.)

Since 1971, the Record Industry Association of America (RIAA) has issued estimated sales figures for records and tapes in the United States. **Table 150-C** uses these figures to outline the number of disc (singles and LPs) and tape recordings sold in retail establishments from 1971

Table 150-B.
Number of New Titles (Singles and LPs) Released by U. S. Recording Industry,
1955–1976

Year	New Singles (45 rpm)			New LPs (33 rpm)			Total Titles Released	
	Number of Titles	% Change from Previous Year	% of Total Releases	Number of Titles	% Change from Previous Year	% of Total Releases	Number of Titles	% Change from Previous Year
1955	4,542	- -	73%	1,615	- -	27%	6,157	- -
1956	4,451	-2%	64	2,500	+55%	36	6,951	+13%
1957	4,649	+4	61	3,000	+20	39	7,649	+10
1958	4,576	-2	57	3,471	+16	43	8,047	+5
1959	5,812	+27	63	3,480	- -	37	9,292	+15
1960	5,797	- -	65	3,112	-11	35	8,909	-4
1961	6,036	+4	67	2,939	-6	33	8,975	+1
1962	6,700	+11	65	3,655	+25	35	10,355	+15
1963	6,543	-2	64	3,686	+1	36	10,229	-1
1964	6,503	- -	65	3,543	-4	35	10,046	-2
1965	7,116	+9	67	3,548	- -	33	10,664	+6
1966	7,086	- -	65	3,752	+6	35	10,838	+2
1967	7,231	+2	63	4,328	+15	37	11,559	+7
1968	6,523	-10	62	4,054	-6	38	10,577	-8
1969	6,261	-3	59	4,368	+8	41	10,629	- -
1970	5,685	-9	59	4,016	-8	41	9,701	-9
1971	5,372	-6	56	4,227	+7	44	9,599	-1
1972	5,132	-5	56	4,056	-5	44	9,188	-4
1973	N/A[a]	N/A	N/A	N/A	N/A	N/A	6,718[b]	- -[c]
1974	N/A	N/A	N/A	N/A	N/A	N/A	9,362	- -
1975	N/A	N/A	N/A	N/A	N/A	N/A	8,938	-5
1976	N/A	N/A	N/A	N/A	N/A	N/A	9,048	+1

Sources: 1955-1972 data: *Billboard Directory and Buyers' Guide*, appropriate issues. 1973-1976: U. S. Copyright Office, *Annual Report.*

Notes: (a) *Billboard* ceased providing the categorical breakdown of new titles in 1973. (b) This figure represents the total number of titles copyrighted. The copyright laws were extended to recordings in 1973. (c) Percentage-change figures are not included for the transitional years of 1973-74, because the change in the copyright law and in the reporting of new titles would make the percentage figures misleading.

through 1976. The listing reveals the slow growth experienced by the recording industry during this period (especially when compared to the **Table 150-B** *Billboard* "new titles" figures for the early (1960s). *Standard and Poor's Industry Surveys: Amusements* (1956), p. A64, estimated total unit sales for earlier years: 325 million in 1947, 184 million in 1950, 200 million in 1955.

As another point of comparison, **Table 150-C** also lists the number of "Gold Records" awarded during this 1971-76 period. These awards were established in 1958 to honor singles or albums with sales of one million dollars or more at factory prices. The increasing numbers of "Gold Record" albums during the 1971-76 period provide a rough indication of the rising popularity and sales of LP recordings.

Table 150-D lists the RIAA sales figures for record clubs and other mail-order outlets during the 1971-76 period. There is a marked decline in this market, except for tape sales. The growth of the latter from 1971 to 1976 can probably be explained by the newness of the tape format (cassettes and eight-track cartridges are relatively recent innovations in the industry) and the increasing numbers of American consumers who have cassette and/or eight-track tapedecks. The conveniently small size of the tapes may also make them more desirable for mail-order purchases.

Late in 1977, the recording industry was reported operating at capacity, paced by a demand for recordings of Bing Crosby and Elvis Presley, both of whom died that year. The *New York Times* (December 29, 1977) reported that the 4 million LP records produced each day were insufficient to meet the overall consumer demand for popular instrumental and vocal recordings. Production bottlenecks were such that many companies were farming out production, and new titles were being delayed in release. Record sales were reported to be rising rapidly and balancing

Table 150–C.
Number of Recordings Sold in U. S. Retail Establishments, 1971–1976

Note: All figures in millions.

	1971	1972	1973	1974	1975	1976
Number of Discs Sold	386	408	432	415	377	425
Singles	204	216	228	204	164	190
LPs	182	192	204	211	213	235
Number of Tapes Sold	67	75	70	72	74	89
Total Discs/Tapes Sold in Retail Stores	453	483	502	487	451	514
Total Discs/Tapes Sold in U. S. Market (includes club/mail order sales)	560	596	617	592	555	611
"Gold Record" Awards						
Singles	54	66	70	68	48	55
LPs	92	125	116	127	125	149

Source: Figures provided to the editors by CBS Records, Market Research Department.

Table 150–D.
Number of Disc and Tape Recordings Sold by Mail in U. S., 1971–1976

Note: All figures are in millions.

	1971	1972	1973	1974	1975	1976
LP Discs:						
Record-Club Sales	47	37	24	23	22	20
Mail Order Sales	40	50	52	42	37	31
Tapes:						
Record-Club Sales	19	24	29	30	32	34
Mail Order Sales	1	2	10	11	13	12
Total Sales:						
Record Clubs	66	61	53	53	54	54
Percent of All Recordings Sold	12%	10%	9%	9%	10%	9%
Mail Order	41	52	62	52	50	43
Percent of All Recordings Sold	7%	9%	10%	9%	9%	7%

Source: Figures provided to the editors by CBS Records, Market Research Department.

Note: Each disc/tape included in multiple-set packages was counted as one unit in calculating these figures.

out the seasonal sales slumps of earlier years. As a result, the pessimism of the early 1970s about the prospects for the industry seemed to be fading.

Sources

The figures in **Table 150-A** were taken from the *Census of Manufactures*. Although the *Census of Manufactures* gathers data on a more regular basis than **Table 150-A** would indicate, the Census Bureau publication did not provide recording manufacturing information for the years 1904, 1933, 1935, and 1937.

The data in **Table 150-B** through 1972 represent those recordings reviewed by *Billboard*, which claims to review every recording it receives. Industry professionals estimate that *Billboard* receives well over 90 percent of all records produced in this country. The totals after 1972 come from the U.S. Copyright Office's *Annual Report* and show the number of single and LP titles which have been copyrighted each year. Since some recordings are not copyrighted, neither the Copyright Office figures nor *Billboard's* measures can be said to represent the exact situation.

The data in **Tables 150-C** and **150-D** are estimates, originally supplied to the editors by the CBS Records Market Research Department. A comparison of figures in **Tables 150-A** and **150-C** for 1972 (the only year covered by both sources) shows substantial differences. Clearly, the industry itself does not know how many recordings it actually sells.

Further Information

The best background information on the popular recording industry can be found in Denisoff (1975), which offers both statistical information and sociological analysis, and in Chapple and Garofolo (1977), which details the history, economics, and politics of the popular record industry. Although *Variety* reports on the recording industry, the most important trade periodical is *Billboard*. *Billboard's* annual *Directory and Buyer's Guide*, published in August or September, contains a number of useful summary statistics. For background on the historical development of disc recordings and the recording industry, see Gelatt (1976).

Retail Outlets for Recordings

151

Table 151–A.
Types of Retail Record/Tape Outlets and Their Percentage Shares of U. S. Market, 1964–1976

Type of Retail Outlet	1964	1965	1969	1970	1971	1972	1973	1975	1976
			Percent of Dollar Volume (in retail prices)						
Department and Discount Stores	8%	11%	54%	54%	55%	61%	62%	71%	72%
Variety Stores	37	35	18	15	15	13	7	2	3
Record Stores	- -	3	7	12	14	13	17	18	16
Drug Stores	21	20	10	8	8	5	6	4	5
Supermarkets	25	24	4	4	3	3	2	- -	- -
Military Base PX Outlets	1	1	4	3	2	4	3	3	3
Miscellaneous Stores	7	6	4	4	3	1	2	1	2

Source: National Association of Record Merchandisers. For the retail proportion of *total* sales of recordings, see Table 150-C.

Table 151–B.
Number of Establishments Selling Recordings in U. S., 1929-1972

Year	Music Stores	Record Shops	Total, All Outlets for Recordings
1929	2,232	- -	- -
1939	2,930	- -	- -
1948	6,120	- -	- -
1954	5,810	- -	- -
1958	7,974	2,889	10,863
1963	8,075	2,571	10,646
1967	6,020	1,760	7,780
1972	7,529	2,590	10,119

Source: *Census of Manufactures*, appropriate issues.

Note: The figures for 1967 and 1972 include only those establishments with a payroll.

Interpretation of Tables

In 1976, the National Association of Record Merchandisers (NARM) arranged for a nation-wide telephone survey of "buyers" to discover where people get their records and tapes. A "buyer" was defined as anyone who had purchased at least one tape or record in the previous year. The results of this survey indicated that 22 percent of all buyers obtained their records or tapes from department stores, 25 percent from discount stores, 33 percent from record shops, 12 percent from mail-order houses, 4 percent from variety stores, and 5 percent from all other sources—mainly drug stores and supermarkets.

Table 151-A measures the shifting popularity of these retail outlets over the past decade, using a percentage breakdown of the total dollar volume of tape and record sales. Mail-order sources are excluded from this tabulation, and traditional variety stores which have grown into the super-variety type (such as Woolco and K-Mart) have been included in the department and discount stores category. The table clearly indicates that department stores (probably the discount stores primarily) and retail record outlets have become the two leading sources of records and tapes, taking over the business once carried by supermarkets, drug stores, and variety stores. Table 151-B confirms this trend by showing the growth of two specialized types of record outlets: the general music store and the record shop.

Sources

The reader should note that the National Association of Record Merchandisers, which supplied the data for Table 151-A, reports only on the sales figures of its members. In 1964, that membership included only about one-half of the recording retail industry. By 1975, that membership figure had risen to perhaps 90 percent of the retail firms in the United States. Thus, the validity of Table 151-A increases with more recent years.

While based on *Census of Manufactures* information, Table 151-B must be taken as a very sketchy profile of outlets for recorded music. First of all, the table figures do not take into account the many other kinds of stores which sell records as a part of their larger concerns. Secondly, for the years 1967 and 1972, the table lists only those firms having a payroll, thereby excluding the several thousand other establishments which sold records during those two years.

Further Information

Except for data concerning record clubs and other direct order-by-mail services (see Table 150-D), the basic source for information on retail outlets for recordings is NARM. The reader may find it useful to compare the data in Table 151-B with that for radio and television receivers in Table 660-C. Employment levels for the establishments listed in Table 151-B are given in Unit 450.

Table 170-A.
Number of Radio Stations in U. S., 1921–1977

Year	AM Total	FM Commercial	FM Educational	FM Total	Total Radio Stations	Average Number of Stations: per 5-year Period	Average Number of Stations: per 10,000 Population
1921	5	- -	- -	- -	5		
1922	30	- -	- -	- -	30	- -	- -
1923	556	- -	- -	- -	556		
1924	530	- -	- -	- -	530		
1925	571	- -	- -	- -	571		
1926	528	- -	- -	- -	528		
1927	681	- -	- -	- -	681	613	.005
1928	677	- -	- -	- -	677		
1929	606	- -	- -	- -	606		
1930	618	- -	- -	- -	618		
1931	612	- -	- -	- -	612		
1932	604	- -	- -	- -	604	603	.004
1933	599	- -	- -	- -	599		
1934	583	- -	- -	- -	583		
1935	585	- -	- -	- -	585		
1936	616	- -	- -	- -	616		
1937	646	- -	- -	- -	646	652	.005
1938	689	- -	- -	- -	689		
1939	722	- -	- -	- -	722		
1940	765	- -	- -	- -	765		
1941	831	18	2	20	851		
1942	887	36	7	43	930	893	.006
1943	910	41	8	49	959		
1944	910	44	8	52	962		
1945	919	46	8	54	973		
1946	948	48	9	57	1005		
1947	1062	140	10	150	1212	1585	.011
1948	1621	458	15	473	2094		
1949	1912	700	27	727	2639		
1950	2086	733	48	781	2867		
1951	2232	676	73	749	2981		
1952	2331	637	85	722	3053	3033	.019
1953	2391	580	98	678	3069		
1954	2521	560	112	672	3193		
1955	2669	552	122	674	3343		
1956	2824	540	123	663	3487		
1957	3008	530	125	655	3663	3684	.022
1958	3196	537	141	678	3874		
1959	3326	578	151	729	4055		
1960	3456	688	162	850	4306		
1961	3547	815	175	990	4537		
1962	3618	960	194	1154	4772	4780	.026
1963	3760	1081	209	1290	5050		
1964	3854	1146	237	1383	5237		
1965	4044	1270	255	1525	5569		
1966	4065	1446	268	1714	5779		
1967	4121	1643	296	1939	6060	6048	.030
1968	4190	1753	326	2079	6269		
1969	4265	1938	362	2300	6565		

Table 170–A. (Cont'd.)

Year	AM Total	Commercial	FM Educational	Total	Total Radio Stations	Average Number of Stations: per 5-year Period	Average Number of Stations: per 10,000 Population
1970	4292	2184	413	2597	6889		
1971	4343	2196	472	2668	7011		
1972	4374	2304	511	2815	7189	7206	.035
1973	4395	2411	573	2984	7379		
1974	4407	2502	652	3154	7561		
1975	4432	2636	717	3353	7785		
1976	4463	2767	804	3571	8034	- -	- -
1977	4497	2837	839	3676	8173		

Sources: 1921-1926 data: U. S. Department of Commerce. 1927-1934 data: Federal Radio Commission. 1935-1977 data: Federal Communications Commission, as reprinted in Sterling and Kittross (1978), p. 511, which details the secondary sources used for the official data.

Interpretation of Tables

Prior to World War I, AM broadcasting stations appeared on the air experimentally both in the United States and abroad. However, regularly scheduled and continuing AM broadcasting began with station KDKA in Pittsburgh in November 1920. FM experimental stations did not appear until the late 1930s and were not subject to regular licensing until January 1, 1941. Since few radio stations sold much advertising time in these early years (see Unit 370), the "commercial" designation is a misnomer for AM radio up to 1930, and for FM well into the 1960s. Perhaps the designation is best viewed as a declaration of intent.

The numerical supremacy of AM over FM radio is clearly evident in **Table 170-A**. This dominance by AM has been due to a number of factors, including: (1) AM's well-developed network structure, which predated FM's inception; (2) the lack of separate programming on most FM stations until the late 1960s; and (3) the greater expense of FM receivers. These conditions and others led to AM's larger audiences and, thus, to greater advertiser interest. Only in the 1970s did the gap between AM and FM radio begin to close.

The early growth of AM radio was sudden and unregulated. The combination of a government allocation policy and the Great Depression finally checked this growth and led to a decline in the number of radio stations from 1928 through 1935. A construction freeze during World War II also held down any notable increase in stations, but the number of AM stations rose dramatically after 1945—a result of increasing demand for local radio service in suburban and rural communities. Indeed, so many new stations were established that, by the 1970s, the FCC was imposing power limitations and daytime-only operations on about half the stations in order to reduce interference. Twice since 1962, the FCC has placed freezes on the processing of applications for AM stations, and the commission now encourages, as much as possible, the expansion of FM stations.

The last column on **Table 170-A** represents the proportion of broadcast stations—both AM and FM—to 10,000 population. Though this proportion increased regularly through the late 1960s, the declining rate of new stations going on the air led to a slowing of that growth in the 1970s. Now, with the end in sight not only for AM growth but also for FM expansion (as FM's allocations are gradually filled), the number of stations per 10,000 population will level off. And it is reasonable to expect that, by the 1980s, this figure will begin to decline as population growth outstrips any increases in the number of stations.

Table 170-B traces changes in: (1) the number of AM radio stations per U.S. community; (2) the number of AM stations by station class designation; and (3) the percentage of AM stations with daytime-only operations. The reader will note that for educational AM stations, no separate category exists under "number of stations by station class." The reason for this omission is that no specific AM educational allocation was ever created, and only sporadic information is available on educational AM broadcasting. The bits and pieces of information on this subject indicate that the number of nonprofit AM licensees reached a peak in the early and mid-1920s, then declined in the late 1920s and throughout the 1930s, and finally leveled off to a plateau of approximately 30 stations by 1940. About the same number are operating today.

Prior to 1960, FM radio also had a checkered career. Some of FM's difficulties have already been mentioned. Another difficulty—perhaps the most damaging—was that, in 1945, FM had to cope with the problem of having to begin anew on a higher frequency allocation which was in competition with both expanding AM stations and the newly developing television stations (see Unit 180). Congress and the FCC did their best to encourage FM expansion during these post-war

Table 170-B.
Characteristics of AM Radio Stations in U. S., 1935-1975

	1935	1945	1950	1960	1970	1975
Number of Stations per Community						
4 or more	--	43	113	143	202	N/A
3	--	31	68	120	106	N/A
2	--	57	174	319	321	N/A
1	--	435	897	1660	1611	N/A
Total Number of Radio Communities	--	566	1252	2242	2240	N/A
Number of Stations, by Station Classification[a] and Percentage of Total Number						
Dominant Clear Channels (I-A and I-B Stations)	44	68	N/A	63	56	56
% of Total	7%	7%	N/A	2%	1%	1%
Secondary Clear Channels (II Stations)	50	74	N/A	754	1151	1264
% of Total	8%	8%	N/A	21%	27%	28%
Regional (III Stations)	280	345	N/A	1748	2088	2117
% of Total	44%	36%	N/A	50%	49%	48%
Local (IV Stations)	260	474	N/A	944	1005	1005
% of Total	41%	49%	N/A	27%	23%	23%
Total Number of Stations	636	961	N/A	3509	4300	4442
Daytime-Only AM Stations						
% of Total	12%	8%	29%	47%	49%	--

Source: Compilations based on figures listed in *Broadcasting Yearbooks* (1936, 1945, 1960, 1971, 1976) by L. W. Lichty of the University of Wisconsin.

Note: (a) For background information on AM station classifications, see Emery (1971), pp. 110-125.

years, but as **Table 170-A** shows, FM experienced a sharp decline throughout the 1950s until 1958, when AM reached urban saturation and the first spurt of television expansion was complete.

The subsequent growth of FM radio was aided by the development of (1) the federal government's program of Subsidiary Communications Authorizations (1955), which allowed nonbroadcast services to be transmitted by FM stations, thus increasing their income potential; (2) the achievement of a technology for stereo broadcasting in 1961; and (3) the FCC's nonduplication programming requirements after 1965, which separated FM station content from the content of co-owned AM stations, thereby providing for more FM diversity. As a result of these developments, FM has firmly established its own identity since the early 1960s and has won sufficient audience acceptance to become the fastest growing broadcast medium in the United States. Even educational FM stations have steadily increased in number, though many operate with merely 10 watts and cover an area of only three to five miles. (There has been a special educational FM allocation—the lowest 20 channels on the FM band—since 1945.)

Sources

All information given in **Table 170-A** was drawn from various FCC reports. With the exception of data for the years 1927 through 1947, the figures in this table refer to stations actually on the air, regardless of license status. Information for 1927-1947 includes stations which were listed as "authorized" and/or "licensed," but not necessarily "on the air." All of the figures are as of January 1, with the following exceptions for AM stations: March 1 for 1923, October 1 for 1924, June 20 for 1925, and June 30 for 1926-1932. The last column of **Table 170-A** is based upon the population figures given in **Table 100-B**. These figures are subject to variations due to averaging and rounding of both station and population data.

Table 170-B data were hand-counted from secondary sources (*Broadcasting Yearbook*). Consequently, the figures must be considered approximate.

Further Information

The FCC and its predecessor organizations, the Federal Radio Commission (1927-1934) and the Department of Commerce (prior to 1927), are the official sources for station counts. Historical discussion and statistics appear in the FCC's *Annual Report* (1935 to date), while summary statistics appear in *Broadcasting Yearbook* (annual) and *Television Factbook*. These statistics are updated monthly in *Broadcasting* and weekly in *Television Digest*. Additional historical analysis and descriptive statistics may be found in Lichty and Topping (1975), and in Sterling and Kittross (1978). Wood and Wylie (1977) offer a discussion of the rise and decline of educational AM stations.

The reader with an interest in radio in the 1970s, and in projections of its growth in the near future, should consult the National Association of Broadcasters' *Radio in 1985* (1977). Further or more specific information may be obtained by contacting the National Association of Broadcasters, the National Radio Broadcasters Association, the Radio Advertising Bureau, National Public Radio, and the Corporation for Public Broadcasting.

Network-Affiliate Radio Stations 17

Interpretation of Tables

Table 171-A offers a statistical profile of the number and percentage of affiliates held by each of America's four radio networks: NBC, CBS, ABC, and Mutual. The National Broadcasting Company (NBC), a subsidiary of Radio Corporation of America (RCA) throughout its history, was the first to broadcast in September 1926. In January 1927, NBC added a second parallel network, and the two systems became known as NBC Red (not only the first, but financially the more important) and NBC Blue.

The Columbia Broadcasting System (CBS) went through 18 months of name changes and uncertainty before the Paley family took control in 1928. At that point, however, the network quickly became a strong competitor for NBC. The competition was ensured in 1941, when an FCC ruling, upheld by a landmark 1943 Supreme Court case (*National Broadcasting Co., Inc., et al. v. United States et al.* 319 U.S. 190—May 10, 1943), forced RCA to divest itself of one of its two networks. RCA therefore sold off the Blue Network, and it became the American Broadcasting Company (ABC) in 1945.

Unlike NBC, CBS, and ABC, Mutual began as a program cooperative rather than a centralized network operation. For many years—until ABC's ascendency in the past decade—Mutual was numerically the largest radio network. However, its affiliates have always held less broadcast power and drawn smaller audiences than any of the other three networks.

After a network-affiliation peak during the years immediately following World War II, the radio networks declined in importance as hundreds of new nonaffiliated stations went on the air and the competition from television began. The radio networks today are little more than general news services with a few features added for seasoning.

In recent years, there have been a few attempts to revive radio networking. In 1968, for example, the ABC network split into the four specialized-format networks shown in **Table 171-B**. At this point, ABC became the biggest of the radio "webs." The recent increase in ABC affiliate stations is also due to this four-way split. NBC experimented with a network-level, all-news service in 1975-77, but that experiment failed due to lack of affiliates.

Sources

The affiliation figures in **Tables 171-A** and **171-B** were obtained by the editors in correspondence with the networks and supplemented by data in *Broadcasting Yearbook*. The figures vary because radio stations sometimes hold affiliations with more than one network. Also, the number of affiliates in each network will vary according to how many stations an advertiser wants and is willing to pay for. Thus, the statistics for any given network might change dramatically in a single day. The data given here are basically averages of the number of affiliates as of January 1 of each year. The percentage breakdowns were calculated by the editors.

Table 171–A.
Radio Network Affiliates in U. S., 1927–1977

	NBC Affiliates		CBS Affiliates		Mutual Affiliates		ABC Affiliates		Total Stations	Total Network Stations	
	Number	Percent	Number	Percent	Number	Percent	Number	Percent		Number	Percent
1927	28	4.1%	16	2.3 %	- -	- -	- -	- -	681	44	6 %
1928	52	7.6	17	2.5	- -	- -	- -	- -	677	69	10
1929	58	9.6	49	8.1	- -	- -	- -	- -	696	107	18
1930	71	11.5	60	9.7	- -	- -	- -	- -	618	131	21
1931	75	12.3	76	12.4	- -	- -	- -	- -	612	159	26
1932	86	14.2	84	13.9	- -	- -	- -	- -	604	170	28
1933	88	14.7	91	15.2	- -	- -	- -	- -	599	179	30
1934	88	15.1	92	15.8	4	.7 %	- -	- -	583	184	32
1935	88	15.0	97	16.6	3	.5	- -	- -	585	188	32
1936	89	14.4	98	15.9	39	6.3	- -	- -	616	226	37
1937	111	17.2	105	16.3	80	12.4	- -	- -	646	296	46
1938	142	20.6	110	16.0	107	15.5	- -	- -	689	359	52
1939	167	23.1	113	15.7	116	16.1	- -	- -	722	396	55
1940	182	23.8	112	14.6	160	20.9	- -	- -	765	454	59
1941	225	27.1	118	14.2	166	20.0	- -	- -	831	509	61
1942	136	15.3	115	13.0	191	21.5	116	13.1 %	887	558	63
1943	142	15.6	116	12.7	219	24.1	143	15.7	910	620	68
1944	143	15.7	133	14.6	245	26.9	173	19.0	910	694	76
1945	150	16.3	145	15.8	384	41.8	195	21.2	919	874	95
1946	155	16.4	147	15.5	384	40.5	195	20.6	948	881	93
1947	162	15.2	157	14.8	488	46.0	222	20.9	1062	1028	97
1948	167	10.3	162	10.0	519	32.0	256	15.8	1621	1104	68
1949	170	8.9	167	8.7	526	27.5	269	14.1	1912	1132	59
1950	172	8.2	173	8.3	543	26.0	282	13.5	2086	1170	56
1951	180	8.1	183	8.2	552	24.7	295	13.2	2232	1210	54
1952	191	8.2	194	8.3	560	24.0	302	13.0	2331	1247	53
1953	207	8.7	203	8.5	560	23.4	348	14.6	2391	1318	55
1954	212	8.4	205	8.1	560	22.2	360	14.3	2521	1337	53
1955	208	7.8	207	7.8	563	21.1	357	13.4	2669	1335	30
1956	205	7.3	204	7.2	558	19.8	342	12.1	2824	1309	46
1957	199	6.6	201	6.7	525	17.5	334	11.1	3008	1259	42
1958	203	6.4	200	6.3	431	13.5	299	9.4	3195	1133	35
1959	209	6.3	198	6.0	441	13.3	286	8.6	3326	1134	34
1960	202	5.8	198	5.7	443	12.8	310	9.0	3456	1153	33
1961	201	5.7	195	5.5	428	12.1	339	9.6	3547	1163	33
1962	200	5.4	206	5.6	510	13.8	342	9.3	3618	1258	35
1963	200	5.4	207	5.6	510	13.9	366	10.0	3760	1283	34
1964	202	5.2	227	5.8	500	12.8	353	9.1	3854	1282	33
1965	209	5.2	237	5.9	501	12.5	355	8.9	4044	1302	32
1966	215	5.3	239	5.9	520	12.8	361	8.9	4065	1275	31
1967	216	5.2	240	5.8	N/A	N/A	337	8.1	4121	N/A	N/A
1968	217	5.1	243	5.7	515	12.1	500	11.8	4170	1475	35
1969	222	5.2	245	5.7	492	11.4	1013	23.6	4265	1972	46
1970	220	5.1	247	5.7	523	12.0	1175	27.0	4292	2165	50
1971	230	5.2	249	5.7	538	12.3	1074	24.5	4343	2091	48
1972	231	5.2	242	5.5	545	12.4	1169	26.5	4374	2187	50
1973	233	5.3	243	5.5	568	12.8	1246	28.1	4395	2290	52
1974	230	5.2	248	5.6	632	14.3	1293	29.2	4407	2403	55
1975	232	5.2	247	5.6	657	14.8	1322	29.8	4463	2458	55
1976	223	5.0	257	5.8	684	15.3	1353	30.3	4463	2517	56
1977	236	5.2	266	5.9	755	16.8	1546	34.4	4497	2803	62

Sources: Sterling and Kittross (1978), pp. 512-13. Total stations: FCC. Number of affiliates: the four networks. Mutual affiliates 1941-1944: *Broadcasting Yearbook*.

	Entertainment	Contemporary	Information	FM Stations	Total
1968	132	76	200	92	500
1969	251	224	362	176	1013
1970	298	262	425	190	1175
1971	275	242	348	209	1074
1972	306	276	387	200	1169
1973	322	300	414	210	1246
1974	347	319	412	215	1293
1975	365	329	419	209	1322
1976	382	334	442	195	1353
1977	423	372	557	194	1546

Source: ABC, Inc.

Further Information

Additional historical information on the radio networks appears in the FCC's *Chain Broadcasting* (1941) and *Network Broadcasting* (1958). Chapter 13 of the latter source is especially useful. Lists of radio network affiliates, along with the names and addresses of their officers, appear in annually updated editions of *Broadcasting Yearbook*. Readers seeking information on a specific network should contact that network.

Television Stations and Markets

180

Interpretation of Tables

After many years of experimental operation with both mechanical and electronic systems of television, the FCC finally approved regular television station operation on July 1, 1941. A handful of stations got on the air before the war, but manpower and equipment shortages closed down most of them for the duration.

As **Table 180-A** reveals, television did not experience an immediate spurt of growth after the war. Several factors held television back during these early years, including the high cost of station construction and operation (as compared with radio); the limited number of VHF-only channels available in major cities, and some serious allocation problems in 1947-1948. Finally, in the Fall of 1948, the FCC placed a six-month freeze on the processing of station applications while it dealt with such problems as limited channels, educational allocation, and color TV standards. However, as it turned out, the freeze did not end until 1952—which explains the flat rate of growth for those four years. It was in April of 1952 that the FCC's *Sixth Report and Order* added the UHF channels 14-83 to its system of allocations.

The following six years saw substantial growth on the more desirable VHF channels, which had greater range (and thus larger audiences) and simpler tuning mechanisms. After that period, commercial television growth slowed down. Less than 80 new commercial VHF stations have appeared in the past 15 years.

Like FM radio, commercial UHF television enjoyed an initial burst, but then declined for several years. UHF's problems were even more complex than those of VHF. The relatively limited range of UHF, combined with the problem of getting television sets equipped for UHF reception,

Table 180–A.
Number of VHF and UHF Commercial
and Educational (Public) Television Stations in U. S., 1941–1977

| | VHF | | | UHF | | | Total | | |
	Commer-cial	Educa-tional	Total	Commer-cial	Educa-tional	Total	Commer-cial	Educa-tional	Total Number of Stations
1941	2	--	2	--	--	--	2	--	2
1942	4	--	4	--	--	--	4	--	4
1943	8	--	8	--	--	--	8	--	8
1944	8	--	8	--	--	--	8	--	8
1945	8	--	8	--	--	--	8	--	8
1946	6	--	6	--	--	--	6	--	6
1947	12	--	12	--	--	--	12	--	12
1948	16	--	16	--	--	--	16	--	16
1949	51	--	51	--	--	--	51	--	51
1950	98	--	98	--	--	--	98	--	98
1951	107	--	107	--	--	--	107	--	107
1952	108	--	108	--	--	--	108	--	108
1953	120	--	120	6	--	6	126	--	126
1954	233	1	234	121	1	122	354	2	356
1955	297	8	305	114	3	117	411	11	422
1956	344	13	357	97	5	102	441	18	459
1957	381	17	398	90	6	96	471	23	494
1958	411	22	433	84	6	90	495	28	523
1959	433	28	462	77	7	84	510	35	545
1960	440	34	474	75	10	85	515	44	559
1961	451	37	488	76	15	91	527	52	579
1962	458	43	501	83	19	102	541	62	603
1963	466	46	512	91	22	113	557	68	625
1964	476	53	529	88	32	120	564	85	649
1965	481	58	539	88	41	129	569	99	668
1966	486	65	551	99	49	148	585	114	699
1967	492	71	563	118	56	174	610	127	737
1968	499	75	574	136	75	211	635	150	785
1969	499	78	577	163	97	260	662	175	837
1970	501	80	581	176	105	281	677	185	862
1971	503	86	589	179	113	292	682	199	881
1972	508	90	598	185	123	308	693	213	906
1973	510	93	603	187	137	324	697	230	927
1974	513	92	605	184	149	333	697	241	938
1975	513	95	608	198	146	344	711	241	952
1976	513	97	610	197	155	352	710	252	962
1977	517	101	618	211	155	366	728	256	984

Sources: FCC figures for January 1st of each year, as reprinted in *Television Factbook*, and (for 1977 data) in *Television Digest*.

resulted in small audiences and, thus, in limited advertiser interest in the UHF stations. Finally, the scarcity of VHF channels forced TV expansion to the UHF channels.

Even so, UHF stations clearly could not compete with VHF network affiliates. Only in the late 1960s, after passage of an all-channel receiver law (see Unit 680) did the number of UHF commercial allocations increase. **Table 180-B** sketches UHF's varied pattern of development, with statistics showing the number of stations on the air for four selected years and the number of unassigned channels as of 1975.

Noncommercial television began in 1952, when the FCC ended its freeze and promulgated an allocation for nonprofit educational television stations. As with commercial television, the growth in educational television stations was slow at first—the result of high operating costs—and came first to VHF channels. **Table 180-C** provides an outline of educational/public station increases

Table 180–B.
Number of VHF and UHF Commercial Television Stations in U. S.,
by Market Group, 1958–1975

	UHF Stations					VHF Stations				
	1958	1965	1968	On-air in 1975	Unassigned Channels in 1975	1958	1965	1968	On-air in 1975	Unassigned Channels in 1975
Markets 1-10	1	6	23	} 60	} 83	40	41	41	} 160	none
Markets 11-50	11	11	31			114	124	126		
Markets 51-100	37	38	42	51	83	102	110	112	111	none
Markets 101-200	18	23	37	} 75	} 119	131	151	160	} 215	13
Markets 201 and up	10	8	21			15	20	23		
Total Stations in All Markets	77	86	154	186	285	402	446	462	486	13

Source: 1958-1968: A. D. Little Co. (1969), p. 143, table 57; 1975: FCC figures as reprinted in *Broadcasting* (September 1, 1975), p. 29.

Notes: The 1958-1968 information is for February (1958, 1965) and December (1968), while the 1975 data is as of July 1st. The A. D. Little information was gathered from issues of *Television Factbook*, with the market rankings based on number of prime-time TV households. Thus, there may be (and likely are) some differences in market groups between the 1958-68 information and the 1975 data, though the basic comparisons are still valid.

Table 180-C.
Number of VHF and UHF Educational (Public) Television Stations in U. S., by Market Group, 1958–1976

	UHF Stations					VHF Stations				
	1958	1965	1968	On-air in 1975	Unassigned Channels in 1975	1958	1965	1968	On-air in 1976	Unassigned Channels in 1976
Markets 1-10	2	6	10	⎱ 52	⎱ 34	4	5	5	⎱ 26	3
Markets 11-50	3	16	24	⎰	⎰	11	19	19	⎰	
Markets 51-100	2	7	14	26	38	4	10	16	19	none
Markets 101-200	0	2	10	⎱ 74	⎱ 103	1	8	10	⎱ 41	
Markets 201 and up	0	7	39	⎰	⎰	3	16	26	⎰	9
Total Stations in All Markets	7	38	97	152	175	23	58	76	86	12

Sources: 1958-1968: A. D. Little Co. (1969), p. 143, table 57. 1976: "Use of Television Channels as of July 1, 1976," FCC Mimeo 72188, September 23, 1976, p. 2.

Table 180–D.
Reception of Television Stations in U. S. Communities, 1964–1976

Number of Stations Receivable in a Community	Percent of All Communities				
	1964	1968	1970	1972	1976
1 to 3 Stations	22%	7%	10%	6%	4%
4 Stations	19	11	11	11	8
5 Stations	14	13	13	12	11
6 Stations	19	9	9	10 .	12
7 Stations	12	20	20	18	18
8 Stations	6	11	11	12	9
9 Stations	4	9	9	11	11
10 and more Stations	4	17	17	20	27

Sources: 1968-1970 data: Nielsen Television Index information as printed in *Broadcasting*, August 19, 1971, p. 31. 1964, 1972-1976 data: Nielsen Television Index (1976), p. 13.

for 1958, 1965, and 1976, and shows how few VHF channels now remain, compared with the substantial number of UHF channels still awaiting assignment to public broadcasting.

Major federal funding for educational and public stations was introduced during the 1960s (see Unit 360). Amounts were then increased at the end of that decade, after the creation of the Corporation for Public Broadcasting (CPB). The substantial growth of public television in the 1970s, evident in **Table 180-A**, was made possible by even greater federal government funding and by a national policy of encouraging public television alternatives to commercial television. Since about 1970, public television stations, operating under many different kinds of financial constraints, have outstripped the growth in the number of commercial television stations, though the differences in growth rate are small.

Table 180-D lists the expanding numbers of stations "receivable per community," which is another type of measure of the increasing numbers of television stations on the air. However, the spread of cable television (see Unit 190), with its multiple channels for subscribers, is also partly responsible for this upward trend in the number of stations receivable in a community. Nevertheless, according to the data presented here, most homes in the United States have access to the three main network signals, plus one or more educational/public independent stations.

Sources

FCC figures for **Table 180-A** are for January 1 of each year and refer only to stations on the air, regardless of license status. A.D. Little Co., which arranged the FCC figures contained in **Tables 180-B** and **180-C**, based the market rankings on number of prime-time television households as of December 1968. However, the reader should note that data for 1958 and 1965 is for February, while 1968 information is for December. Moreover, in **Table 180-B**, 1975 information is for July 1; and in **Table 180-C**, 1976 information is also for July 1. Thus, there are differences among the rankings up to 1968, and in the 1975-76 information as well. However, these differences should not be significant enough to make the basic comparisons invalid.

Statistics offered in **Table 180-D** are based on A.C. Nielsen's ratings research and are therefore estimates by sample, not actual counts for all markets.

Further Information

The reader will find useful historical information on television in the FCC Office of Network Study (1958), in Barnouw (1975), in Head (1976), and in the sources noted in Unit 170. Information on the industry is summarized each year in *Broadcasting Yearbook* and *Television Factbook*, the major trade directories. Those interested in the most current data should consult *Broadcasting* or *Variety*, or write to the National Association of Broadcasters (for information concerning commercial stations) or the Corporation for Public Broadcasting (for information concerning educational/public television).

Table 181–A.
Number of Network Affiliate Television Stations
in U. S., 1947–1977

	NBC Affiliates		CBS Affiliates		ABC Affiliates		Total Stations	Total Network Stations	
	Number	Percent	Number	Percent	Number	Percent		Number	Percent
1947	2	16.7 %	1	8.3 %	1	8.3 %	12	4	33 %
1948	9	56.3	3	18.8	6	37.5	16	16	100
1949	25	49.0	15	29.4	11	21.6	51	50	98
1950	56	57.1	27	27.6	13	13.3	98	96	98
1951	63	58.9	30	28.0	14	13.1	107	107	100
1952	64	59.3	31	28.7	15	13.9	108	108	100
1953	71	56.3	33	26.2	24	19.0	126	125	99
1954	164	46.3	113	31.9	40	11.3	354	317	90
1955	189	46.0	139	33.8	46	11.2	411	374	91
1956	200	45.4	168	38.1	53	12.0	441	421	95
1957	205	43.5	180	38.2	60	12.7	471	445	94
1958	209	42.2	191	38.8	69	13.9	495	469	95
1959	213	41.8	193	37.8	79	15.5	510	485	95
1960	214	41.6	195	37.9	87	16.9	515	496	96
1961	201	38.1	198	37.6	104	19.7	527	503	95
1962	201	37.2	194	35.9	113	20.9	541	508	94
1963	203	36.4	194	34.8	117	21.0	557	514	92
1964	212	37.6	191	33.9	123	21.8	564	526	93
1965	198	34.8	190	33.4	128	22.5	569	516	91
1966	202	34.5	193	33.0	137	23.4	585	532	91
1967	205	33.6	191	31.3	141	23.1	610	537	88
1968	207	32.6	192	30.2	148	23.3	635	547	86
1969	211	31.9	190	28.7	156	23.6	662	557	84
1970	215	31.8	193	28.5	160	23.6	677	568	84
1971	218	32.0	207	30.4	168	24.6	682	593	87
1972	218	31.5	209	30.2	172	24.8	693	599	86
1973	218	31.3	210	30.1	176	25.3	697	604	87
1974	218	31.3	212	30.4	181	26.0	697	611	88
1975	219	30.8	213	30.0	185	26.0	711	617	87
1976	218	30.7	213	30.0	182	25.6	710	613	86
1977	212	29.1	210	28.8	190	26.1	728	612	84

Source: FCC (for total number of stations) and the television networks (for number of their affiliates) as presented in Sterling and Kittross (1978), p. 515.

Interpretation of Tables

Whereas radio network systems developed over a period of two decades and then declined in the late 1950s (see Unit 171), television began as and remains a network-dominated medium. As **Table 181-A** reveals, the present network-affiliation levels in the television industry are only slightly lower than the saturation levels reached in the early 1950s.

From the beginning, NBC has been the largest television network, though CBS is also able to reach the entire country. ABC, because it began acquiring affiliates much later, and because it operated so long under severe financial constraints, was always the third network in both size and importance. However, ABC's ratings strength since 1976 appears to be improving its ability to gather more and better station affiliates.

Table 181-B.
Number of Network-Affiliate and Independent Television Stations in U. S., by Market Group, 1958–1975

Market Group	Network Affiliates				Non-Affiliated Independents				Total Commercial Stations			
	1958	1965	1968	1975	1958	1965	1968	1975	1958	1965	1968	1975
Markets 1-10:												
Number of Stations	29	30	30	31	12	17	34	36	41	47	64	67
Percent of All Commercial Stations	71%	64%	47%	46%	29%	36%	53%	54%	100%	100%	100%	100%
Markets 11-50:												
Number of Stations	113	118	119	126	12	17	38	37	125	135	157	163
Percent of All Commercial Stations	90%	87%	76%	77%	10%	13%	24%	23%	100%	100%	100%	100%
Subtotal (Markets 1-50):												
Percent of All Commercial Stations	86%	81%	67%	68%	14%	19%	33%	32%	100%	100%	100%	100%
Markets 51-100:												
Number of Stations	136	144	148	170	3	4	6	6	139	148	154	176
Percent of All Commercial Stations	98%	97%	96%	97%	2%	3%	4%	3%	100%	100%	100%	100%
Markets 101 and up:												
Number of Stations	169	196	214	216	5	6	27	7	174	202	241	222
Percent of All Commercial Stations	97%	97%	89%	97%	3%	3%	11%	3%	100%	100%	100%	100%
Total, All Market Groups:												
Number of Stations	447	488	511	608	32	44	105	86	479	532	616	694
Percent of All Commercial Stations	93%	92%	83%	88%	7%	8%	17%	12%	100%	100%	100%	100%

Sources: Data for 1958-1968: A. D. Little Co. (1969), pp. 142, 193, citing information from *Television Factbook* (February 1958, February 1965, December 1968). 1975 data for "top-100 markets": *Broadcasting Yearbook 1976.* 1975 data for "market groups 101 and up": provided to the editors by the Association of Independent Television Stations, Inc.

Not represented in **Table 181-A** are the two attempts to create a permanent fourth television network. The more recent and least successful was the United (formerly Overmyer) Network, which broadcast an evening program to 106 stations in early 1967. The system continued for a month before it ran out of funds. The earlier attempt, the Dumont Network, lasted for six years during the 1950s. Because there were only a few market areas at the time with four allocated channels, the Dumont Network was never able to attract a sufficient number of primary affiliates. *Broadcasting Yearbook* reports that Dumont had contracts—usually secondary or even tertiary affiliations—with 45 stations in 1949, 52 in 1950, 62 in 1951-52, and 133 in 1953. Its affiliation figures reached a peak of 195 stations in 1954, then dipped to 158 during the next year. The Dumont Network ceased operations in September 1955.

Table 181-A includes primary affiliates only. However, many of the nonaffiliated independent stations represented in the totals in Table 181-B have secondary network affiliations, which permit them to carry network programs that are not picked up by the local primary affiliate. In some smaller markets, these independent stations may even have contracts with two or three networks, giving them the freedom to choose programs from all of the companies. This phenomenon was especially common in the early days of television, when there were limited numbers of stations in a market area (see Unit 180). Today, such a situation is more unusual, since most markets have access to the three network signals.

Sources

The information in Table 181-A was reported by the television networks themselves. Part of this data has also been published in Lichty and Topping (1975), p. 193.

The A.D. Little Company supplied information for the years 1958, 1965, and 1968 in Table 181-B. The Little Company's source was the February 1958, February 1965, and December 1968 editions of *Television Factbook*. Little ranked the markets by "number of prime-time TV households in 1968," which is apparently a reference to the Arbitron Company's "Areas of Dominant Influence" (ADIs). The data for 1975 regarding the top-100 markets were figured by the editors from information supplied by *Broadcasting Yearbook 1976*. For markets 101 and up, the editors relied on research done by the Association of Independent Television Stations, Inc., which supplied information as of April 1, 1975.

The reader should note in Table 181-B that the total number of network affiliates for 1975 includes 65 satellite-affiliate stations not listed in the market-breakdown columns. The reader should also be aware that the editors defined a "network affiliate" as a station with contractual right of first refusal on network programs. Clearly, the data presented in this table is subject to wide variations in reliability, since it was drawn from several different sources. The editors believe, however, that the resulting overall percentage trends represent actual conditions.

Further Information

The sources listed in Units 170 and 180 are of value to the reader seeking further information on television network affiliates. The FCC's *Network Broadcasting* (1958) is especially useful. For discussion of the possibilities of a fourth regular network, see Park (1973). *Broadcasting Monthly* and *Broadcasting Industry* regularly report current network statistics on size, ratings, and finances. Unfortunately, the television networks themselves usually do not respond to letters of inquiry from the public.

Cable Television Systems and Services   190

Interpretation of Tables

Cable television originated in 1949, when communities in poor reception areas began erecting "community" antennas on nearby hills. Cables were run from these antennas to the homes of subscribers, who would underwrite costs by paying an installation charge and a monthly maintenance fee. By the mid-1960s, cable systems had expanded into areas already served by one or more TV signals, in order to pull in a diversity of distant signals. By the late 1960s, an increasing number of cable systems were originating their own programming as well (see Unit 560).

From 1965 to early 1972, the FCC limited expansion of cable systems into the top 100 markets, until a detailed and definitive set of rules could be issued for the regulation of cable systems. Throughout this period, a combination of economic uncertainty and ever-more-complicated layers of local, state, and federal regulations severely limited the potential ot cable tele-

Table 190–A.
Growth of Cable Television Systems in U. S., 1952–1977

Year	Number of Systems	Number of Subscribers (add 000)	Percent of TV Homes with Cable	Average Number of Subscribers per System
1952	70	14	0.1 %	200
1953	150	30	0.2	200
1954	300	65	0.3	217
1955	400	150	0.5	375
1956	450	300	0.9	667
1957	500	350	0.9	700
1958	525	450	1.1	857
1959	560	550	1.3	982
1960	640	650	1.4	1,016
1961	700	725	1.5	1,036
1962	800	850	1.7	1,063
1963	1,000	950	1.9	950
1964	1,200	1,085	2.1	904
1965	1,325	1,275	2.4	962
1966	1,570	1,575	2.9	1,003
1967	1,770	2,100	3.8	1,186
1968	2,000	2,800	4.4	1,400
1969	2,260	3,600	6.1	1,593
1970	2,490	4,500	7.6	1,807
1971	2,639	5,300	8.8	2,008
1972	2,841	6,000	9.6	2,112
1973	2,991	7,300	11.1	2,441
1974	3,158	8,700	13.0	2,755
1975	3,506	9,800	14.3	2,795
1976	3,651	10,800	15.5	2,958
1977	3,800	11,900	17.3	3,132

Sources: Data originated by *Television Digest*, reprinted in annual issues of *Television Factbook* and in *Statistical Trends in Broadcasting* annual.

Note: All figures are estimates and are as of January 1 each year.

vision to become a dominant new communications industry. By 1976-77, cable system expansion had begun again as a result of improving economic conditions and several court decisions in 1977 which struck down the FCC's restrictive pay-cable regulations.

Tables 190-A and 190-B illustrate the relatively slow growth of cable systems throughout the United States during the past two decades. Table 190-B reveals the more rapid expansion of cable in low-population suburban counties, where reception is sometimes less reliable and where the FCC regulatory policies have been less restrictive. Cable growth in major urban areas (the "A" counties in Table 190-B) has generally been limited by: (1) the high cost of building cable systems in cities, (2) the difficulty of supplying innovative programming to residents already well-served by broadcast television and other media; (3) the confusion over the complex cable regulations, especially prevalent in the major market areas, and (4) the difficulties of obtaining investment capital for the less affluent core-city areas.

Cable system expansion has also been limited in the rural areas (the "D" counties), where the costs involved in connecting widely dispersed populations are prohibitive. In view of these facts, it seems likely that most cable system growth will continue to be found in the suburban areas (the "B" and "C" counties). However, the lifting of the FCC's pay-cable restrictions in 1977 should

Table 190-B.
Percentage of U. S. TV Households with Cable Service, by County Size, 1968–1976

County Size[a]	1968	1969	1970	1971	1972	1973	1974	1975	1976
"A" counties	1.1%	1.6%	1.7%	2.4%	3.3%	3.8%	4.3%	4.9%	6.3%
"B" counties	3.9	4.8	5.1	6.1	7.5	8.7	9.5	11.4	14.1
"C" counties	15.2	16.8	17.4	20.1	22.5	24.9	25.7	27.3	29.5
"D" counties	9.4	10.2	10.6	12.3	13.7	14.7	15.4	16.6	17.9
All Counties[b]	4.4%	6.1%	7.6%	8.8%	9.6%	11.1%	13.0%	14.3%	15.5%

Sources: Data originated by *Television Digest*, based on Nielsen Television Index, A. C. Nielsen Company data. Reprinted in annual issues of *Television Factbook* and in *Statistical Trends in Broadcasting* annual.

Notes: All data are for May of each year, except 1970 (March) and 1969 (November). (a) County-size categories come from A. C. Nielsen Co. (1976), p. 53. "A"—All counties in the 25 largest metropolitan areas according to the 1970 census. "B"—All counties not in "A" with populations of over 150,000 or in metropolitan areas over 150,000. "C"—All counties not in "A" or "B" with populations over 35,000 or in metropolitan areas over 35,000. "D"—All other counties. (b) These figures are from Table 190-A, the fourth column: "Percent of TV Homes with Cable."

promote cable growth generally, since pay-cable operations offer a good potential for highly profitable returns on an investment.

Table 190-C, in combination with the data of Table 190-A, suggests that cable television did not begin to serve a significant proportion of the country's population (perhaps 5 percent) until after 1968. The service then tripled in another eight years. It is important to be aware, however, that statistics concerning cable growth can be misleading. Cable systems with fewer than 1,000 subscribers outnumber all other size categories. Yet the largest cable systems, with 10,000 or more subscribers, have grown substantially since 1970, while the smaller systems have remained essentially static in number. If data on the mean and median number of subscribers per system were available, the real effect of additional large systems (see Unit 290) would be more apparent than the simple growth trend indicated by the "average" column of Table 190-A.

Table 190–C.
Number of Cable Television Systems in U. S., by Size of System, 1970–1976

Size of Systems (Number of Homes)	1970	1971	1972	1973	1974	1975	1976
20,000+ Homes	8	12	22	31	42	53	68
10,000-19,999 Homes	50	60	83	119	142	171	181
5,000-9,999 Homes	144	176	215	252	289	328	345
2,000-4,999 Homes	402	458	566	593	644	685 }	1,407
1,000-1,999 Homes	423	462	500	545	605	639 }	
500-999 Homes	427	476	514	587	577	602 }	1,688
Below 500 Homes	776	765	843	852	851	862 }	
Systems of Unspecified Size	260	169	96	53	40	65	26
Total Number of Subscribers	2,490	2,578	2,839	3,032	3,190	3,405	3,715

Sources: Data originated by *Television Digest*, reprinted in annual issues of *Television Factbook* and in *Statistical Trends in Broadcasting* annual.

Note: Data is for various months: September (1974-1976), June (1973), and March (1970-1972).

Table 190–D.
Number of Pay-Cable Operations in U. S., 1973–1976

Year	Pay-Cable Operations	Pay-Cable Subscribers
1973	10	18,400
1974	45	66,900
1975	75	264,575
1976 (June)	253	766,100
1976 (December)	364	977,809

Source: Paul Kagan Associates, *The Pay-TV Newsletter*, April 1, 1973; May 15, 1974; June 30, 1975; June 30, 1976; December 31, 1976.

Pay-cable channels carry programming which is not available on "regular" broadcast television. The cable systems charge subscribers a special fee for this service, in addition to the usual monthly cable-maintenance fees. As **Table 190-D** shows, the number of cable systems carrying one or more pay-channels increased sharply between 1973 and 1977. Even so, present figures for pay-cable represent only a fraction of the total number of cable systems in the United States. And among the cable systems carrying pay-channels, only about 25 percent of their subscribers have been paying for regular reception of the additional pay-cable programming. There is also a high turnover or "churn" rate among these subscribers. The reversal of FCC pay-cable regulations should encourage a period of rapid expansion for the cable industry, paced by the increasing demand for pay-cable services.

Sources

Data for **Tables 190-A, 190-B,** and **190-C** were taken from the Blair Company's annual *Statistical Trends in Broadcasting*. The original source of these figures was *Television Factbook*, which features an annual survey of cable systems in the United States. **Table 190-A** figures are estimates for January 1 of each year. The A.C. Nielsen Company estimates contained in **Table 190-B** are for May of each year, with two exceptions: November of 1969 and March of 1970. **Table 190-C** information is for various months: March for 1970, 1971, and 1972; June for 1973; and September for 1974, 1975, and 1976.

Table 190-D data are drawn from Paul Kagan Associates surveys published in the *Pay TV Newsletter* census issues. This is the best available information on the number of pay-cable operations in the United States. However, the reader should be aware that, due to the nature of the industry and the absence of any FCC clearinghouse of cable data (there is no cable-licensing system comparable to that for broadcasting stations), all of these figures are necessarily estimates.

Further Information

For an introduction to what cable is and how it operates, the reader should refer to LeDuc (1973), Baer (1974), and Hollowell (1975). Standard directories on the subject include the *Cable Sourcebook*, *CATV and Station Coverage Atlas*, and *Television Factbook*. The major trade association is the National Cable Television Association. Another useful organization is the Cable Television Information Center, which is consumer-oriented and provides both publications and advice.

SECTION 2

Ownership and Control of the Media

Table 200–A.
Intra-Market Ownership Concentrations among the Daily
Media (Newspapers and Broadcast Stations) in U. S., 1922–1970

	1922	1930	1940	1950	1960	1970
Total Daily Media Concentration						
Top 10	.06	.12	.16	.30	.29	.28
Top 25	.08	.12	.18	.32	.29	.27
Top 50	.06	.10	.20	.32	.29	.27
Top 100	.06	.09	.21	.32	.30	.27
Broadcasting Concentration						
Top 10	- -	.02	.02	.34	.28	.28
Top 25	- -	.03	.04	.33	.29	.27
Top 50	- -	.02	.04	.32	.28	.27
Top 100	- -	.01	.06	.28	.27	.28
Concentration per 1000 Population						
Top 10						
Outlets	.018	.014	.011	.016	.018	.019
Voices	*.017*	*.012*	*.010*	*.011*	*.013*	*.013*
Top 25						
Outlets	.024	.016	.013	.018	.022	.027
Voices	*.022*	*.014*	*.011*	*.012*	*.015*	*.016*
Top 50						
Outlets	.026	.018	.016	.024	.028	.032
Voices	*.026*	*.013*	*.014*	*.016*	*.020*	*.021*
Top 100						
Outlets	.028	.021	.020	.031	.036	.046
Voices	*.027*	*.017*	*.017*	*.020*	*.025*	*.029*

Sources: For "Top 10" and "Top 100" figures in Total Daily Media and Broadcasting sections: Sterling (1975), table 2, p. 253. For "Top 25" and "Top 50" figures in Total Daily Media and Broadcasting sections: Sterling (1974), tables 4, 5, "Supplement." For Concentration and Population: Sterling (1975), table 6, p. 256. See text for definition of market groups, outlets, and voices and for secondary sources.

Interpretation of Table

Table 200-A illustrates the concentrations of ownership among daily newspapers and commercial radio and television stations located within a single market area in the United States. (Cross-market ownership trends are described in Units 221 and 260-280.) The focus in this unit is on ownership within the top 100 Standard Metropolitan Statistical Areas (SMSAs)—a marketing designation based on the size of a population potentially reached by a "media outlet" (in this case, a *daily* newspaper or broadcast station). The top 100 SMSAs include about 80 percent of the U.S. population.

The first section of **Table 200-A** shows the ratio of "media voices" to "media outlets" among the top 10, 25, 50, and 100 SMSAs, or market areas. As noted above, "media outlets" are individual daily newspapers or radio or television stations. "Media voices," in the context of this table, are owners who control one or more media outlets located within a *single* market area. Thus, the first section of the table indicates the proportion of individual owners among *all* daily newspapers and broadcast stations within each market in the top 100 market areas. The higher the figure, the greater the concentration of ownership among the media outlets in a single market.

The reader will note that concentrations of ownership increased steadily from 1922 to 1940 as the result of a decline in the number of daily papers and a rise in press-radio station combinations (see Unit 260). The figures then indicate a substantial jump in 1950, when AM radio station owners began to establish the new television and FM radio services. Since 1950, the expanding broadcast industry (see Units 170 and 180) and the increasing numbers of independently owned radio and television stations have kept the ownership-concentration levels notably stable.

The middle section of **Table 200-A** deals with ownership-concentration levels in broadcasting. As the figures indicate, there was a very low degree of "duopoly" (ownership of more than one media outlet of the *same type* in a single market) prior to 1940. After World War II, when AM radio station owners began to establish AM-FM and radio-television combinations, the ratio of voices (owners) to outlets (stations in a single market) increased markedly—an indication of greater levels of ownership concentration. These ratios can be expected to increase further in future years as fewer new stations are established and the high prices for existing stations restrict the market to well-financed corporations already in the business of station-ownership.

The bottom section of **Table 200-A** details the ratios of media outlets and media voices per 1,000 population. The figures indicate the changing number of daily broadcast stations and newspapers (outlets) and single-market owners (voices) per 1,000 people in the top 10, 25, 50, and 100 SMSAs. Note that from 1922 until 1940, both outlet and ownership concentrations declined in proportion to the population. This decline resulted mainly from a decrease in the number of daily newspapers during this period. Another factor was the decreasing number of new AM radio stations established during the Depression years.

After World War II, with the many newly established radio and television services, the number of media outlets increased faster than the population. By 1970, however, this curve had flattened enough to suggest that there will be a downward turn by 1980.

Sources

In gathering and calculating the ratios for **Table 200-A**, the editors used the top 100 market cities as they had been ranked by the U.S. Census Bureau in 1967. Of course, these rankings changed both before and after 1967, but the editors felt that the use of a constant (the 1967 ranking of the cities) would facilitate the comparison of the data for markets over the past half-century. The "cost" of this approach includes some notably false rankings, especially up to 1950.

The editors also found it necessary to treat all media outlets as equal in importance, despite the fact that there is a considerable difference in economic impact between a TV/radio/newspaper operation in a top 10 market area and a small daily newspaper at the bottom of the top 100 market rankings. Dealing only with the top 100 markets also leaves out many smaller cities, which are the main areas of single-market ownership concentrations.

The figures in **Table 200-A** were based on handcounted data from secondary sources. This procedure introduced an error ratio of roughly 3 percent. The secondary sources used by the editors are as follows: The newspaper data was taken from appropriate annual issues of *Editor and Publisher Yearbook*. Broadcast station data for 1922 was from the Department of Commerce (1922); for 1930, from the Federal Radio Commission (1930); and for 1940-1970, from appropriate issues of *Broadcasting Yearbook*. The top 100 market figures were drawn from Sterling (1975) and from Sterling, "Supplement" (1974).

Further Information

The best overview of research and policy on media ownership is found in Baer, Geller et al. (1974), which includes a useful critique of previous studies. Fuller details of these studies can be found in Sterling (1971) and Sterling (1975). A defense of the status quo in media ownership is delivered in Seiden (1975). For a dated but still strongly written and documented attack on concentration trends in the media, see Rucker (1968). The many other studies of media ownership tend to deal either with print or with broadcast media. See the other units in Section 2 for further references.

Table 201–A.
U. S. Companies with Holdings in Three or More Media Industries, by Number and Category of the Holdings, 1977

Companies with Holdings in Six or More Media Industries

Name of Company	Book Publishing Holdings	Newspaper Publishing Holdings	Magazine Publishing Holdings	Film Production and Movie Theater Holdings	Broadcasting Station Holdings	Cable System Holdings	Music Publishing and Recording Holdings	Other Media Holdings	*Fortune* Corporate Ranking, 1976[a]
American Broadcasting Companies, Inc.	1	- -	5	1 Film Production Company 277 Movie Theaters	14 Radio, 5 TV Stations	- -	10 Record Labels	A Radio/TV Network	170
CBS, Inc.	9	- -	20	Educational Film Production	14 Radio, 5 TV Stations	20% of Some Canadian Systems	3 Recording Companies	A Radio/TV Network	102
Cox Broadcasting Corporation	2	17	16	Film Distribution	10 Radio, 5 TV Stations	36 Operating Systems	- -	Television Production	846
Metromedia, Inc.	1	- -	- -	- -	12 Radio, 6 TV Stations	- -	Music Publishing	Outdoor Advertising Direct Mail Advertising Television Production	562
The New York Times Co.	3	15	8	Educational Film Production	2 Radio, 1 TV Stations	- -	Educational Recordings	1 News Service A Data Bank	394
R. C. A., Inc.	6	- -	- -	Documentary Film Production	8 Radio, 5 TV Stations	- -	1 Record Subsidiary	A Radio/TV Network Radio/TV/Audio Equipment Manufacturing A Common Carrier System Electronics Manufacturing Videodisc Manufacturing	31

Table 201–A. (Cont'd.)

Name of Company	Book Publishing Holdings	Newspaper Publishing Holdings	Magazine Publishing Holdings	Film Production and Movie Theater Holdings	Broadcasting Station Holdings	Cable System Holdings	Music Publishing and Recording Holdings	Other Media Holdings	Fortune Corporate Ranking, 1976[a]
Time, Inc.	5	17	5	Time-Life Films	1 TV Station	1 System	Record Production	Television Production, Pay-Cable Film Distribution	217
Times-Mirror Co.	10	5	4	--	2 TV Stations	17 Operating Systems	--	50% Ownership of a News Service	232
Warner Communications, Inc.	3	--	3 Magazine Distributors	Film Production	--	147 Operating Systems	7 Record Labels	Television Production, Video Computer Games (Atari, Inc.)	261
The Washington Post Co.	1	4	1	--	1 Radio, 4 TV Stations	--	--	Television Production, 50% Ownership of a News Service	452

Companies with Holdings in Five Media Industries

Name of Company	Book Publishing Holdings	Newspaper Publishing Holdings	Magazine Publishing Holdings	Film Production and Movie Theater Holdings	Broadcasting Station Holdings	Cable System Holdings	Music Publishing and Recording Holdings	Other Media Holdings	Fortune Corporate Ranking, 1976[a]
Doubleday & Co.	9	--	6	--	7 Radio Stations	1 System	--	A Specialized TV Network	--
Filmways, Inc.	3	--	11	Feature Film Production	--	--	1 Record Company	Television Production	998
MCA, Inc.	3	--	--	4 Feature Film Production/ Distribution Companies	--	--	3 Record Companies	Television Production, Videodisc Manufacturing	267
General Electric Co.	--	--	--	Film Production	8 Radio, 3 TV Stations	11 Operating Systems	--	Television Production, Radio/TV/ Audio Equipment Manufacturing	9
Media General, Inc.	--	7	1	--	2 Radio, 1 TV Stations	1 System	--	Newsprint Production	673
Meredith Corp.	1	24	22	--	5 Radio, 4 TV Stations	--	--	Book Club	691

Table 201–A. (Cont'd.)

Companies with Holdings in Four Media Industries

Name of Company	Book Publishing Holdings	Newspaper Publishing Holdings	Magazine Publishing Holdings	Film Production and Movie Theater Holdings	Broadcasting Station Holdings	Cable System Holdings	Music Publishing and Recording Holdings	Other Media Holdings	*Fortune* Corporate Ranking, 1976[a]
Playboy Enterprises, Inc.	1	--	2	Theaters Film Production	--	--	1 Record Company	Television Production Book Club	674
Starr Broadcasting Corp.	2	--	1	14 Theaters	10 Radio, 4 TV Stations	--	1 Record Distributor	--	--
Avco Corp.	--	--	1	Film Production	3 Radio Stations	--	1 Record Company	--	305
Capitol Cities Communications, Inc.	1	13	6	--	13 Radio, 6 TV Stations	--	--	--	641
Combined Communications Corp.	--	1	--	--	7 Radio, 7 TV Stations	--	--	Television Production Outdoor Advertising	702
Gulf & Western, Inc.	7	--	--	4 Feature Film Production/Distribution Companies	--	--	Music Publishing Company	Television Production	57
The Hearst Corp.	1	9	26	--	7 Radio, 3 TV Stations	--	--	--	--
Columbia Pictures Industries, Inc.	--	--	--	Film Production	5 Radio, 2 TV Stations	--	1 Record Company	Television Production	488
McGraw-Hill, Inc.	5	--	73	2 Educational Film Companies	4 TV Stations	--	--	--	323
Newhouse Newspapers	--	22	5	--	7 Radio, 6 TV Stations	14 Operating Systems	--	--	--
Teleprompter Corp.	--	--	--	Film Distribution	--	123 Operating Systems	1 Business Music Company (Musak)	Television Production	--
Twentieth Century-Fox Film Corp.	--	--	--	Feature Film Production	3 TV Stations	--	Music Publishing and Records	Television Production	472

Table 201–A. (Cont'd.)

Name of Company	Book Publishing Holdings	Newspaper Publishing Holdings	Magazine Publishing Holdings	Film Production and Movie Theater Holdings	Broadcasting Station Holdings	Cable System Holdings	Music Publishing and Recording Holdings	Other Media Holdings	Fortune Corporate Ranking, 1976[a]
Viacom International, Inc.	--	--	--	Film Distribution	--	32 Communities Served	2	Television Production	--
WGN Continental Broadcasting Co.	--	6	--	--	4 Radio, 4 TV Stations	13 Communities Served	--	Television Production	--
Westinghouse Electric Corp.	--	--	--	--	9 Radio, 5 TV Stations	7 Operating Systems	Recorded Educational Materials	Consumer Electronics, Phonographs, Etc.	22

Companies with Holdings in Three Media Industries

Name of Company	Book Publishing Holdings	Newspaper Publishing Holdings	Magazine Publishing Holdings	Film Production and Movie Theater Holdings	Broadcasting Station Holdings	Cable System Holdings	Music Publishing and Recording Holdings	Other Media Holdings	Fortune Corporate Ranking, 1976[a]
H & E Balaban Corp.	--	--	--	A Theater Chain	4 TV Stations	1 System	--	--	--
Bonneville International Corp.	--	1	--	--	11 Radio, 2 TV Stations	1 Operating System	--	--	--
Cadence Industries	1	--	2	A Theater Chain	--	--	--	A Common Carrier System	--
Chronicle Publishing Co.	--	1	--	--	2 TV Stations	6 Operating Systems	--	--	--
The Daily Press, Inc.	--	2	--	--	2 Radio Stations	2 Systems	--	--	--
Dakota-North Plains Corp.	1	--	1	--	2 Radio Stations	--	--	--	--
Dow Jones & Co., Inc.	2	23	1	--	--	--	--	Business Information Systems	555
Dun & Bradstreet Companies, Inc.	5	--	23	--	5 TV Stations	--	--	--	--
William R. Dunaway	--	2	2	--	2 Radio Stations	--	--	--	--
Esquire, Inc.	3	--	1	Education Films	--	--	--	--	--
Field Enterprises, Inc.	2	2	--	--	5 TV Stations	--	--	--	--

Table 201–A. (Cont'd.)

Name of Company	Book Publishing Holdings	Newspaper Publishing Holdings	Magazine Publishing Holdings	Film Production and Movie Theater Holdings	Broadcasting Station Holdings	Cable System Holdings	Music Publishing and Recording Holdings	Other Media Holdings	*Fortune* Corporate Ranking, 1976[a]
Gannett Co.	1	55	--	--	2 Radio, 1 TV Stations	--	--	Polling Company (Louis Harris, Inc.)	426
General Tire and Rubber Co.	--	--	--	A Theater Chain	13 Radio, 4 TV Stations	42 Operating Systems	--	--	768 (RKO General Only)
Greater Media, Inc.	--	1	--	--	14 Radio Stations	3 Systems	--	--	--
W. F. Hall Printing Corp.	Printing	--	Printing	Educational Films	--	--	--	Educational Television Production	903
Harcourt Brace Jovanovich	11	--	74	2 Educational Film Companies	--	--	--	--	560
Illini Publishing Co.	--	1	2	--	1 Radio Station	--	--	--	--
The Journal Co.	--	2	--	--	2 Radio, 1 TV Stations	2 Systems	--	--	--
Landmark Communications, Inc.	--	6	--	--	3 Radio, 2 TV Stations	41 Communities Served	--	--	--
Lee Enterprises, Inc.	--	19	--	2 Film Companies	6 Radio, 4 TV Stations	--	--	--	--
Macmillan, Inc.	12	--	Distribution	Film Distribution	--	--	--	--	376
McClatchy Newspapers	--	3	--	--	7 Radio, 2 TV Stations	12 Communities Served	--	--	--
McCracken Newspapers	--	6	--	--	2 Radio Stations	1 System	--	--	--
Mickelsen Media, Inc.	--	3	--	--	2 Radio Stations	3 Operating Systems	--	--	--
Minneapolis Star-Tribune Co.	--	2	--	--	2 Radio, 2 TV Stations	1 System	--	--	--

Table 201–A. (Cont'd.)

Name of Company	Book Publishing Holdings	Newspaper Publishing Holdings	Magazine Publishing Holdings	Film Production and Movie Theater Holdings	Broadcasting Station Holdings	Cable System Holdings	Music Publishing and Recording Holdings	Other Media Holdings	Fortune Corporate Ranking, 1976[a]
Providence Journal-Bulletin	--	1	--	--	2 Radio Stations	13 Operating Systems	--	--	--
E. W. Scripps Co.	--	17	--	--	3 Radio, 5 TV Stations	--	--	United Press International	--
Sonderling Broadcasting Corp.	--	--	--	56 Theaters	11 Radio, 1 TV Stations	--	--	TV Production Radio/TV Distribution	--
South Bend Tribune	--	1	--	--	2 Radio, 2 TV Stations	10 Communities Served	--	--	--
Southland Publishing Co.	--	1	--	--	3 Radio Stations	2 Systems	--	--	--
Stauffer Publishing Co.	--	18	--	--	8 Radio, 1 TV Stations	1 System	--	--	--
Steinman Stations, Inc.	--	1	1	--	2 Radio, 2 TV Stations	--	--	--	--
Transamerica Corp.	--	--	--	Film Distribution	1 Radio, 2 TV Stations	--	12 Labels	--	--
Triad Stations, Inc.	--	1	--	--	4 Radio Stations	3 Systems	--	--	--
Tribune Publishing Co.	--	1	--	--	2 Radio Stations	9 Operating Systems	--	--	--
Truth Publishing Corporation	--	1	--	--	2 Radio Stations	4 Communities Served	--	--	--
UA-Columbia Cablevision/UA Theatre Circuit	--	--	--	604 Theaters	--	34 Operating Systems	--	Television Production	--
WOMETCO Enterprises, Inc.	--	--	--	Film Processing 48 Theaters	1 Radio, 3 TV Stations	13 Operating Systems	--	--	667

Sources: Data compiled by editors from the following: Book publishing: Karian (1975); *The Bowker Annual* (1976); *Standard and Poor's Directory of Corporations, 1976, Vol. 3; Standard and Poor's Standard Corporation Descriptions* (June 1977, July 1977). Newspaper publishing: *1977 Editor and Publisher International Yearbook; Broadcasting Yearbook 1977; Standard and Poor's Standard Corporation Descriptions* (June 1977, July 1977). Magazine publishing: *Broadcasting Yearbook 1977; Standard Rate and Data Service; Consumer Magazine and Farm Publication Rates and Data* (1977); *Business Publication Rates and Data* (1977). Film production: *Standard and Poor's Directory of Corporations, 1976, Vol. 3; Standard and Poor's Standard Corporation Descriptions* (June 1977, July 1977). Broadcasting and cable: *Broadcasting Yearbook 1977; Broadcasting's Cable Sourcebook 1977; Standard and Poor's Standard Corporation Descriptions* (June 1977, July 1977); Pavlakis (1974); *Standard and Poor's Directory of Corporations, 1976, Vol. 3; Standard and Poor's Standard Corporation Descriptions* (June 1977, July 1977). Recording industry: Shemel (1977). *Fortune* magazine corporate ranking: *Fortune* (May 1977, June 1977).
Note: (a) *Fortune* magazine corporate rankings are available only if a company is among the top 1,000 U.S. corporations.

Table 201-B.
U. S. Companies with Three or More Holdings in Two Media Industries,
by Number and Category of the Holdings, 1977

Name of Company	Publishing Holdings	Broadcasting Station Holdings	Other Media Holdings
Donrey Media Group	33 Newspapers	5 Radio, 3 TV Stations	- -
Fuqua Industries	- -	2 Radio, 3 TV Stations	198 Movie Theaters Film Production/ Processing Company
General Cinema Corp.	- -	2 Radio, 1 TV Stations	663 Movie Theaters Film Production Company
Harte-Hanks Newspapers	26 Newspapers	4 TV Stations	- -
Jefferson-Pilot Corp.	9 Newspapers	9 Radio, 2 TV Stations	- -
Knight-Ridder Newspapers	53 Newspapers	8 Radio, 1 TV Stations	- -
Lindsay-Schaub Newspapers	10 Newspapers	4 Radio Stations	- -
McNaughton Stations	4 Newspapers	8 Radio Stations	- -
Morgan Murphy Stations	6 Newspapers	2 Radio, 5 TV Stations	- -
Multimedia, Inc.	7 Newspapers	12 Radio, 5 TV Stations	- -
Park Broadcasting, Inc.	9 Newspapers	13 Radio, 7 TV Stations	- -
Post Corporation	14 Newspapers	3 Radio, 4 TV Stations	- -
Sammons Communications, Inc.	- -	4 Radio Stations	50 Operating Cable Systems
Seaton Stations	8 Newspapers	4 Radio, 1 TV Stations	- -
State Telecasting Co.	6 Newspapers	3 TV Stations	- -
Storer Broadcasting Co.	- -	6 Radio, 7 TV Stations	Cable Systems Serving 61 Communities
Wehco Media, Inc.	9 Newspapers	4 Radio, 1 TV Stations	- -
Xerox Corp.	5 Book Publishers 4 Magazines	- -	- -

Source: Compiled by editors from sources listed for Table 201-A.

Interpretation of Tables

While much attention has been given to broadcast and newspaper chains and to cross-owner-ship of media outlets, there has been relatively little research on the recent phenomenon of multi-media firms in the communications industry. Unit 201 estimates the extent to which such com-panies have acquired holdings in several different media across all markets.

Table **201-A** names those companies which have holdings in *three or more* different media. Radio and television stations are considered here as one medium. This was done mainly because the large number of radio-television cross-ownerships would have greatly lengthened this list and included a disproportionate number of small companies.

Companies are listed alphabetically within sections which designate the number of different types of media they own. Additionally, Table **201-A** gives the ranking of each company in the "Fortune 500" (or "Second 500") list of the largest American corporations. This information will allow the reader to estimate the size of multi-media owners in comparison to other sectors of the economy. Since Table **201-A** is a measurement for only one point in time, it is not possible to discuss trends.

Two limitations on this data should be mentioned. First, company holdings change rapidly. Most of the figures in Table **201-A** are accurate to the end of 1976, with some mergers and purchases from 1977 included. However, some new additions or divestitures are likely to have occurred since the figures in this list were assembled.

Second, Table **201-A** probably underestimates the number of multi-media ownerships. The firms were located by comparing the names of owners in one medium with the names of owners in other media. But subsidiaries of a company will often be listed by a different name than that of the parent company. The editors attempted to compensate for this situation by consulting several sources which deal specifically with cross-ownership. Once a company seemed likely to be a multi-media owner, the editors checked its corporate description, including a list of its subsidiaries.

Unfortunately, in the case of privately owned companies, this was not possible. In addition, it is likely that some combinations simply eluded the editors. The reader may rest assured, however, that the data for any company on the list comes from at least one established and reliable industry source.

While preparing Table **201-A**, the editors realized that a number of companies did not own outlets in three or more media, but still controlled far more in the industry than would be indicated by their categorization as a cross-media chain owner. Thus, Table **201-B** lists companies that own chains of outlets (three or more holdings) in each of *two* different media. In order to eliminate the large number of newspaper-broadcasting cross-ownerships, as well as a number of very small cross-holdings in other media, the Table **201-B** list was restricted to companies with at least three holdings in each media.

Sources

Tables **201-A** and **201-B** were compiled by the editors especially for this volume. Initially, the editors consulted the listings of newspaper-broadcasting and broadcasting-cable cross-ownerships in *Broadcasting Yearbook* and *Broadcasting's Cable Sourcebook*. The names in these lists, as well as the list of group owners in broadcasting and cable, were then compared with the names of group owners in *Editor and Publisher International Yearbook* (for newspapers), in *Standard Rate and Data Service Consumer and Farm Publications* and *Business Publications* (for magazines), and in Karian (1975) (for books). The editors also examined Karian's (1975) listing of conglomerate ownerships of book publishers. The *Bowker Annual* list of book trade mergers was used to update Karian.

Next, the editors arranged their entries according to the Standard Industrial Classification (SIC) code for the mass-media industries in Standard and Poor's *Index of Corporations*. Each entry was then matched against every other entry on the evolving list. Finally, to provide a common basis for estimating holdings, the editors checked their list of companies with holdings in two or more media against the listings in Standard and Poor's *Standard Corporation Descriptions*.

Further Information

Phillips (1977) provides an interesting and current view of media conglomeration. Bunce (1976) discusses the situation with respect to broadcasting. See also Baer, Geller et al. (1974), Seiden (1975), and the dated but still useful Rucker (1968).

Table 202-A.
Number, Gross Receipts, and Employment of Minority-Owned Media Firms in U. S., 1969 and 1972

Category of Firms	1969 Minority-Owned Firms Number of Firms	1969 Minority-Owned Firms Gross Receipts	1969 Minority-Owned Firms with Paid Employees Number of Firms	1969 Number of Employees	1969 Gross Receipts	1972 Minority-Owned Firms Number of Firms	1972 Minority-Owned Firms Gross Receipts	1972 Minority-Owned Firms vs. All Firms in Category[a] % of Minority Firms	% of Minority-Firm Gross Receipts	1972 Minority-Owned Firms with Paid Employees Number of Firms	Number of Employees	Gross Receipts	All Firms in Category. Percent Changes 1969-72 Number of Firms	Gross Receipts
Printing and Publishing	1,099	$61,076	368	2,559	$56,655	1,496	$129,566	3.5%	0.4%	446	3,980	$114,441	36%	112%
Newspapers	69	22,274	55	944	22,084	89	18,938	1.1	0.2	71	927	18,417	29	-15
Periodicals	20	1,708	17	74	1,681	26	23,541	1.0	0.7	19	410	23,431	30	1,278
Books	35	2,231	11	118	2,125	18	8,352	0.9	0.2	14	N/A	N/A	-49	274
Miscellaneous Publishing	19	1,565	11	60	1,535	20	4,210	1.0	0.4	14	N/A	N/A	5	169
Commercial Printing	177	19,876	156	1,001	19,690	308	51,258	1.4	0.5	247	1,838	49,730	74	158
Blankbooks and Bookbinding	14	824	9	48	785	18	2,431	1.2	0.3	13	90	2,372	29	195
Printing Trade Services	22	2,432	19	144	2,404	37	4,355	1.4	0.6	27	187	4,209	68	79
Printing and Publishing, n.s.k.[c]	743	10,166	90	170	6,351	980	16,481	N/A	N/A	41	176	3,818	32	62
Bookstores	46	2,939	35	120	2,804	316	6,243	4.0	0.7	35	189	3,557	(b)	112
Radio and Television Broadcasting	39	6,090	28	344	6,059	37	11,338	N/A	N/A	35	N/A	N/A	-5	86
Motion Pictures	228	11,636	92	765	10,715	418	14,766	N/A	N/A	106	1,040	11,899	93	2.7
Production and Services	109	3,137	23	N/A	N/A	219	4,815	2.6	0.2	26	128	3,656	105	65
Distribution and Services						4	346			3	N/A	N/A		
Motion Picture Theaters	110	8,190	67	619	7,820	157	9,088	1.2	0.5	76	901	7,787	43	11
Motion Pictures, n.s.k.[c]	9	309	2	N/A	N/A	38	517	N/A	N/A	1	N/A	N/A	322	67

Sources: Minority-owned firms data: U. S. Bureau of the Census, *1972 Survey of Minority-Owned Business Enterprises* (1975). General industry data: *1972 Census of Manufactures.* Motion picture data: U. S. Bureau of the Census, *1972 Census of Selected Service Industries.*

Notes: (a) Comparisons with all establishments and receipts should be made with extreme caution. See comments in text. (b) The percent change was not calculated because the small 1969 base figure and the great spread between the 1969 and 1972 figures make any meaningful comparison impossible. (c) N.s.k. —"Not specified by kind."

Table 202–B.
Number of Minority-Owned Radio, Television, and Cable Outlets in U. S., 1977

Type of Outlet	Total Number of Outlets	Minority-Owned Outlets
Commercial VHF Television	514	1
Commercial UHF Television	208	7
Noncommercial Television	243	0
Commercial AM Radio	4469	32
Commercial FM Radio	2845	9
Noncommercial Radio	861	2
Cable Television Systems (Operating)	3450	6
Cable Television Franchises	N/A	30

Source: Communications Resource Center (1977).

Interpretation of Tables

In 1969, the federal government carried out the first comprehensive national survey of U.S. businesses owned by ethnic and racial minorities. This survey has now been made a continuing part of the economic censuses taken every five years by the U.S. Census Bureau. The most recent information available is for 1972.

Table 202-A presents the 1969 and 1972 Census Bureau data on minority-owned *media* firms. It is interesting to compare these statistics with the Census Bureau's data on all minority firms. In 1972, for example, minority-owned firms in all businesses, including the mass media, totalled 381,935—an increase of 59,977, or 19 percent, over 1969. Gross receipts for these firms were $16,556 million—an increase of $5,917 million, or 56 percent, from 1969. A comparison of these percent change figures with the percent change figures in the last two columns of Table 202-A reveals that, in most cases, minority-owned mass media firms made gains—both in number of firms and in total receipts—much in excess of those made by minority-owned businesses as a whole. Losses are apparent only in the number of book publishing companies and broadcasting businesses, and in the receipts of newspapers and motion picture theaters.

Table 202-A also includes a comparison of the number and gross receipts of minority-owned firms versus all U.S. firms. These data reveal that minorities own mass media firms in numbers disproportionately low to their presence in the population. Also, it is evident that minority-owned firms tend, on the whole, to have a lower-than-average share of U.S. gross business receipts.

These percentages should be taken as estimates, however, because the data-collection procedures for minority-owned businesses make any precise comparisons with other census figures very difficult. Specifically, the Census Bureau counted the number of minority-owned *firms* in its survey of minority businesses, whereas it counted the number of *establishments* for all of its other surveys. Since one firm can own any number of establishments, the number of firms in a particular field or business is likely to be smaller than the number of establishments. Thus, to the extent that minority chain-owners exist, the number of minority-owned media establishments is probably underestimated.

At the same time, the minority share of the media industries may be overestimated with regard to gross receipts. This is because the Census Bureau reports totals for *all* minority-owned firms filing a business tax return, whereas its several surveys of all U.S. firms are restricted to certain minimum income levels. Thus, establishments with incomes below these minimum levels are not included in the Census Bureau totals. However, the very small firms which are excluded make up only a tiny percentage of overall receipts, so the difference here is probably slight.

Table 202-B offers a comparison of the number of minority-owned outlets in television, radio, and cable television, with the number of outlets for those entire industries. Only in the category of UHF television does minority ownership exceed 1 percent of the total.

Sources

The source of **Table 202-A**, the U.S. Census Bureau's *Survey of Minority-Owned Business Enterprises*, is now a part of the quinquennial economic censuses by the federal government. The *Survey* is a systematic attempt to gauge the extent of minority ownership in the United States. Besides giving national totals for minority ownership, the survey breaks down its information by specific minority groups—including black, Spanish origin, American Indian, Asian-American, and other—and examines the data by regional division, state, Standard Metropolitan Statistical Area (SMSA), size of firm, and legal form of organization.

The Census Bureau has also developed sampling procedures which attempt to estimate the number of companies owned by persons of Spanish origin but not Spanish surname. This means that some sampling error may affect the total figures. Experts suggest that there is a 95 percent chance that the number of firms owned by those of Spanish origin is correct within a plus or minus range of 20 percent. The figures for gross receipts are believed to be accurate within a plus or minus range of 6 percent.

Since the Census Bureau's procedures are based on examination of both Internal Revenue Service and Social Security Administration reports, and supplemented by mail canvasses, they can be considered quite reliable. The reader with further questions about the survey's procedures should consult the introductory and supplementary material published along with the reports.

The Communications Resource Center—the editors' source for **Table 202-B**—gathered its information from the FCC and various industry sources, including its own records. Most of the figures for total outlets are comparable to data presented in sources cited in this volume's units on broadcasting.

Further Information

A review of works on minority participation in media ownership has been prepared by Ledding and Baer (1973).

Ownership Concentration: Book Publishers — 210

Interpretation of Tables

Table 210-A shows the number, dollars earned, and percent of total sales of U.S. book publishing establishments for 1958, 1963, 1967, and 1972. Over this 14-year period, establishments with 250 employees or more gained an increasing share of total industry sales. In 1958, for example, these large companies made up 3.4 percent of all establishments and received 44 percent of the industry's sales. In 1972, they made up 4.6 percent of all establishments and accounted for 64 percent of the industry's sales. Apparently, the current trend is toward increasing sales dominance by the large firms.

Table 210-B covers the same 14-year period and offers another view of sales concentrations and competition in the book publishing industry. In measuring the proportions of shipments/sales claimed by the leading four, eight, twenty, and fifty companies in different categories of book publishing, **Table 210-B** would seem to indicate a genuinely competitive industry structure. For example, although some increases occurred in the share of *overall* shipments made by the top fifty firms, the share accounted for by the four and eight leading companies have remained almost constant.

However, closer examination of the shipment/sales ratios for specific categories of book publishing reveals that certain segments of the industry are not so competitive after all. In the field of technical, scientific, and professional books, for instance, the share accounted for by the top four companies rose from 27 to 39 percent between 1958 and 1972.

This fact, in itself, does not indicate a concentrated industry structure. The reader should note that the top four firms in most industries control at least one-third of all sales. Moreover, recent figures for general reference book publishing (traditionally the most concentrated field) and general trade book publishing show a significant decline in sales concentrations. None of these figures take into account any mergers which have occurred since 1972, nor do they record cross-media conglomerates (see Unit 201).

Table 210–A.
Number, Dollars Earned, and Percentage Shares of Total Sales
of U. S. Book Publishing Establishments, by Number of Employees, 1958–1972

Number of Establishments

Number of Employees	1958	1963	1967	1972
1 to 4	411	471	496	604
5 to 9	155	152	135	160
10 to 19	104	114	104	134
20 to 49	93	117	116	125
50 to 99	58	48	63	67
100 to 249	51	53	62	59
250 to 499	15	19	27	29
500 to 999	9	10	10	17
1,000 to 2,499	7	8	8	9
2,500 and over	- -	1	1	1
TOTAL	903	993	1022	1205

Dollars Earned in Millions

Number of Employees	1958	1963	1967	1972
1 to 4	$ 24.1	$ 33.5	$ 32.3	$ 54.9
5 to 9	32.5	32.7	39.8	57.8
10 to 19	33.5	49.7	60.6	88.2
20 to 49	117.3	129.4	124.4	178.9
50 to 99	156.4	124.7	198.0	196.9
100 to 249	210.9	329.4	419.1	441.4
250 to 499	108.1	170.2	396.9	541.1
500 to 999	159.1	310.8	275.5	645.8
1,000 to 2,499	191.5	354.4	588.3	651.8
2,500 and over	- -	(a)	(a)	(a)
TOTAL	$1033.4	$1534.8	$2134.8[b]	$ 2856.8

Percent of Total Sales

Number of Employees	1958	1963	1967	1972
1 to 4	2.33 %	2.18 %	1.51 %	1.92 %
5 to 9	3.15	2.13	1.86	2.02
10 to 19	3.24	3.24	2.84	3.09
20 to 49	11.33	8.43	5.83	6.26
50 to 99	15.14	8.13	9.27	6.89
100 to 249	20.41	21.46	19.63	15.45
250 to 499	10.46	11.09	18.59	18.94
500 to 999	15.40	20.25	12.90	22.61
1,000 to 2,499	18.54	23.09	27.57	22.82
2,500 and over	- -	- -	- -	- -
TOTAL	100.00 %	100.00 %	100.00 %	100.00 %

Sources: 1958-1967 data: Vanier (1973), pp. 13-14, citing *Census of Manufactures* data. 1972 data: *1972 Census of Manufactures*, p. 27A-24.

Notes: (a) Information deleted by government to avoid disclosing data for individual companies. Data included in total for next small category. (b) Figures may not add because of rounding.

Table 210-B.
Ownership Concentrations among U. S. Book Publishing Firms,
by Percent of Shipments and Type of Books, 1958-1972

Type of Books	1958	1963	1967	1972	% Change 1958-1972
ALL BOOK PUBLISHING					
Total Shipments					
(millions of dollars)	$1010.7	$1547.8	$2255.3	$2915.4	
% of Total Shipments by:					
Four Largest Firms	16	18	16	16	0
Eight Largest Firms	26	29	27	27	1
Twenty Largest Firms	45	52	52	52	7
Fifty Largest Firms	65	73	75	75	10
TEXTBOOKS					
Total Shipments					
(millions of dollars)	$281.7	$471.1	$733.6	$809.6	
% of Total Shipments by:					
Four Largest Firms	33	32	29	33	0
Eight Largest Firms	50	54	50	54	4
Twenty Largest Firms	76	81	79	80	4
Fifty Largest Firms	93	94	94	95	2
TECHNICAL, SCIENTIFIC, PROFESSIONAL BOOKS					
Total Shipments					
(millions of dollars)	$116.0	$156.3	$240.2	$403.0	
% of Total Shipments by:					
Four Largest Firms	27	32	38	39	12
Eight Largest Firms	43	49	54	57	14
Twenty Largest Firms	71	68	74	76	5
Fifty Largest Firms	91	87	91	92	1
RELIGIOUS BOOKS					
Total Shipments					
(millions of dollars)	$58.6	$81.1	$110.4	$131.2	
% of Total Shipments by:					
Four Largest Firms	30	22	27	36	6
Eight Largest Firms	45	37	46	51	6
Twenty Largest Firms	70	65	74	76	6
Fifty Largest Firms	90	89	96	97	7
GENERAL TRADE BOOKS					
Total Shipments					
(millions of dollars)	$274.7	$458.2	$657.7	$1006.7	
% of Total Shipments by:					
Four Largest Firms	39	30	28	29	-10
Eight Largest Firms	53	46	46	47	-6
Twenty Largest Firms	72	59	70	74	2
Fifty Largest Firms	90	89	91	92	2

(Continued on p. 78.)

Sources

All of the material in this unit comes from the *Census of Manufactures*, which is carried out by the U.S. Census Bureau during those years ending in either "2" or "7." The data are generally reliable.

Further Information

The best single work on concentration in book publishing is Vanier (1973), while Lofquist (1976) provides a valuable statistical review. Mergers in the book trade are recorded each year in the *Bowker Annual*.

Table 210–B. (Cont'd.)

Type of Books	1958	1963	1967	1972	% Change 1958-1972
GENERAL REFERENCE BOOKS[a]					
Total Shipments					
(millions of dollars)	$163.6	$207.3	$216.3	$235.2	
% of Total Shipments by:					
Four Largest Firms	--[b]	87	81	71	-16[c]
Eight Largest Firms	--	96	91	82	-14[c]
Twenty Largest Firms	--	100	--[d]	94	-6[c]
Fifty Largest Firms	--	(e)	100	99+	--
OTHER BOOKS AND PAMPHLETS					
Total Shipments					
(millions of dollars)	$96.0	$154.8	$200.1	--[f]	
% of Total Shipments by:					
Four Largest Firms	--	37	48	--	--
Eight Largest Firms	--	48	61	--	--
Twenty Largest Firms	--	68	78	--	--
Fifty Largest Firms	--	85	92	--	--
BOOK PUBLISHING NOT SPECIFIED BY KIND OF BOOK					
Total Receipts					
(millions of dollars)	$20.2	$18.9	$97.0	$155.6	

Source: Lofquist (1976), pp. 12-27, citing *Census of Manufactures* data.

Notes: (a) Before 1972, the category "General Reference Books" was classified as "Subscription Reference Books, Hardbound" and did not include such reference books as dictionaries, thesauruses, and atlases. Therefore, the 1972 data are not completely comparable to earlier years. (b) The published totals for reference books included individual products primary to other industries. Thus, the percentage shares for these totals are not available. (The other products included in the reference book totals were added in order to avoid the disclosure of sales figures for individual companies.) (c) These percent-change figures are for the years 1963-1972. (d) This information was withheld to avoid disclosure of sales figures for an individual company. (e) The *total* figure for shipments of reference books was accounted for by the 20 largest firms. (f) This product category was omitted in 1972.

Bookstore Ownership

21

Interpretation of Table

Table 211-A shows the number and total sales of single- and multi-unit bookselling establishments in the United States. Traditionally, bookstores have been small, single-unit businesses. In 1958, 90 percent of all U.S. bookstores and 72 percent of all bookstore sales were made by stores which were not part of chains. By 1972, the percentage of stores operated by single-establishment firms had declined to 81 percent, and their percentage of sales had fallen to 58 percent. Such statistics indicate a definite trend toward multi-unit firms, even though nearly one-third of all stores remain small, one- or two-person operations with no paid employees. Four-fifths of all bookstores are still individually owned.

The greatest shift in the share of sales has been to the largest bookstore chains. In 1958, there were no chains with more than 50 stores. By 1972, multi-unit companies with more than 50 stores accounted for 11.5 percent of all bookstore sales. Moreover, the share of sales received by two-store firms declined during this same 15-year period, a fact that emphasizes the sales power of the larger groups. The two leading chain-owners of bookstores, Waldenbooks and B. Dalton Bookseller, exemplify this trend. Waldenbooks now has more than 400 stores nationwide, while B. Dalton has 290, with sales up by 30 percent or more in each of the last three years.

Table 211–A.
Number, Sales, and Percentage of Single- and Multi-Unit Bookstores in U.S.,
by Number of Stores Owned, 1958–1972

	Number of Stores			
	1958	1963	1967	1972
Total, All Bookstores	2,885	3,154	2,960[a]	7,830
Percentage of Total Which Are:[b]				
Single-Unit Stores	90.1%	86.2%	76.2%	81.2%
Operated by Single-Establishment Firms	88.2	84.2	74.2	79.8
Operated by Multi-Establishment Firms[c]	1.9	2.0	2.0	1.4
Multi-Unit Stores	9.9	13.8	23.8	18.8
2 Units	4.2	6.1	7.0	3.7
3 Units	.9	1.7	1.6	2.3
4 to 5 Units	1.6	2.0	2.9	2.1
6 to 10 Units	.6	1.6	1.9	2.1
11 to 25 Units	1.5	1.0	2.7	1.6
26 to 50 Units	1.1	1.0	1.6	1.7
51 to 100 Units	0	.4	5.3	2.6
101 or more Units	0	0	0	2.7
Total, 6 or more Units	3.2	4.0	11.5	10.7

	Sales (millions of dollars)			
	1958	1963	1967	1972
Total, All Bookstores	$196.3	$279.5	$427.6[a]	$877.6
Percentage of Total Sales by:				
Single-Unit Stores	72.2%	67.9%	67.7%	58.4%
Operated by Single-Establishment Firms	68.3	63.2	59.4	53.9
Operated by Multi-Establishment Firms[c]	3.9	4.7	8.3	4.5
Multi-Unit Stores	27.8	32.1	32.3	41.6
2 Units	10.2	11.7	9.2	8.3
3 Units	1.3	2.5	3.1	5.3
4 to 5 Units	3.7	7.3	3.5	4.5
6 to 10 Units	{ 12.6	2.7	3.6	3.1
11 to 25 Units		{ 8.0	5.9	5.1
26 to 50 Units			{ 7.0	3.7
51 to 100 Units	0			{ 11.5
101 or more Units	0	0	0	
Total, 6 or more Units	12.6	10.7	16.5	23.4

Sources: *Census of Business, 1958, 1963, 1967*; and *Census of Retail Trade, 1972.*

Notes: (a) Includes only those bookstores with payrolls. Other years include all bookstores. (b) Percentages are computed on the total number of bookstores in operation *for the entire year.* These totals are: 1958—2,733, 1963—2,845; 1967—2,886; 1972—6,695. (c) Data in this category are for single establishments of multi-unit firms which operate in unrelated kinds of retail business.

A recent report by the U.S. Department of Commerce (Lofquist, 1976-1977, p. 15) also stresses the trend toward corporate and cooperative ownership of bookselling establishments during these years. According to this report, individual proprietorships and partnerships represented 79 percent of all establishments in 1958. Corporations held 18 percent of all stores, while a category entitled "Other, including cooperatives" made up only 3 percent of the total. But, in 1972, the percentage of stores organized as corporations had increased to 35 percent, and the category of "Other, including cooperatives" had risen to 10 percent. Moreover, the entire number of U.S. bookstores increased from 2,885 in 1958 to 7,830 in 1972. Thus, the rise in the actual number of "other" stores (mainly cooperatives) was more than tenfold, from 75 to 780 establishments.

Table 211-A does not go beyond 1972. However, since 1972, the number and sales of book-stores have continued their dramatic growth. Department of Commerce estimates for 1976 placed the number of stores in the United States at approximately 12,000, with sales of about $1.3 billion (see Unit 111). Although such spectacular estimates of activity in the field since 1972 may tend to overshadow the census figures offered in **Table 211-A**, the patterns shown here are still valid.

Sources

Data in **Table 211-A** come from the U.S. Census Bureau's *Census of Retail Trade* (part of the *Census of Business* before 1972) and are generally considered reliable. The information is gathered approximately every five years through mail questionnaires sent to bookstores throughout the United States. Additional material is obtained from the Social Security Administration and the Internal Revenue Service. The Census Bureau's definition of a bookstore is a store which deals primarily in the sale of new books and periodicals, although other merchandise may also be sold. Stationery stores, book clubs, news dealers, and newsstands are not included.

Further Information

The *Census of Retail Trade* remains the best single source of national aggregated information about bookstores. It includes breakdowns by state, region, size of establishment, legal form of organization, and products sold. Analyses of its data can be found in occasional articles in *Printing and Publishing* (Lofquist, 1976-1977) and *Publishers Weekly* (Dessauer, 1976). Since the 1960s, the Census Bureau has also measured bookstore sales on a monthly basis, using a sample of 103 bookstores. Their net change in sales—in percent—is reported in *Monthly Retail Trade: Sales and Accounts Receivable*, a Department of Commerce publication.

Market Competition: Newspaper Publishers 220

Table 220–A.
U. S. Cities with Daily Newspapers, 1923–1973

Year	Total Cities with Newspapers	Cities Having Only One Paper	Cities Having Two or More Papers	
			Cities	% of Total
1923	1,297	795	502	38.7%
1933	1,426	1,183	243	17.0
1943	1,416	1,279	137	9.7
1948	1,392	1,283	109	7.8
1953	1,453	1,364	91	6.3
1958	1,447	1,377	70	4.8
1963	1,476	1,425	51	3.5
1968	1,493	1,450	43	2.9
1973	1,519	1,482	37	2.4

Source: Rosse, et al. (1975).

Table 220–B.
Number, Percentage, and Sales Ratios of Newspaper Firms
in Multi-Paper Cities, 1923–1973

Year	Total Number of Firms in U. S.	Total Number of Firms in Multi-Paper Cities	% of Firms in Multi-Paper Cities	% of All Daily Papers Sold by Firms in Multi-Paper Cities	% of U. S. Population in Multi-Paper Cities
1923	1,977	1,182	59.8 %	88.8 %	- -
1933	1,745	562	32.2	73.9	- -
1943	1,597	318	19.9	64.2	- -
1948	1,536	253	16.5	62.0	26 %
1953	1,582	218	13.7	54.2	- -
1958	1,545	168	10.9	51.7	21
1963	1,552	127	8.2	43.3	- -
1968	1,547	97	6.3	36.1	15
1973	1,566	84	5.4	32.2	13

Source: Rosse, et al. (1975).

Interpretation of Tables

In **Table 220-A**, "newspapers" are defined as independent newspaper *firms*. Two newspapers operating under a joint contract of some kind or owned by the same local company would be counted as one newspaper in this analysis. Thus, **Table 220-A** outlines the decline in the number of U.S. cities having access to more than one locally published, independently owned daily newspaper. In 1923, nearly 39 percent of U.S. cities had more than one independent daily newspaper. By 1973, this figure had dropped to less than 3 percent.

Table 220-B rearranges the same data to show the declining number of newspaper firms with competition in the same city. A "newspaper firm" is an independent local company in this analysis. Each local company owned by a chain is counted separately, but two local newspapers operating under a joint agreement or owned by the same local company are counted as one firm. In 1923, nearly 60 percent of all newspaper firms had local competition. By 1973, the percentage had fallen to just over 5 percent.

Table 220-B also shows the diminishing percentage of daily papers sold by firms in multi-paper cities—a decline from 89 to 32 percent during the same 50-year period. Even during the 25 years prior to 1973, that percentage of the population served by competing dailies dropped to half of what it had been in 1948.

Table 220-C offers another view of newspaper competition and points up the dangers of relying on only one form of measurement. In this table, the editors have employed the standard industrial measure of the percentage of sales made by the top four, eight, twenty, and fifty firms. The reader will note that, compared to other industries, the newspaper industry shows fairly low sales concentrations.

However, there is a problem with looking at the data in this way. With this kind of measurement, all sales data for the nation are aggregated. Consequently, it is not possible to examine the common occurence of one-newspaper cities and the effects of such local concentrations on the public's access to information. Moreover, this kind of measurement does not take into account the large number of newspaper companies in operation. Although the reader may note that the top 50 firms made 61 percent of all sales in 1972, he may not realize that these same 50 firms represent only two-thirds of 1 percent of the 7,461 daily and weekly newspaper firms counted that year.

Sources

The information in **Tables 220-A** and **220-B** was drawn from Rosse et al. (1975), who relied on the *Editor and Publisher International Yearbook*, the standard directory of the trade. It is worth

Table 220–C.

Percentage Share of Total Newspaper Receipts for the 4, 8, 20, and 50 Largest U. S. Newspaper Companies, by Type of Paper and Source of Income, 1958–1972

Type of Newspaper and Source of Income	Total Receipts[a] (millions of dollars)	Percent Share of Total			
		4 Largest Companies	8 Largest Companies	20 Largest Companies	50 Largest Companies
All Newspapers					
1958	$3458.3	18%	25%	36%	53%
1963	4254.7	15	22	36	53
1967	5549.8	16	25	40	56
1972	7901.1	17	29	44	61
% Change 1958-1972		-6	16	22	15
Daily and Sunday Newspapers: Receipts from Subscriptions and Sales					
1958	916.7	25	32	46	63
1963	1064.4	20	28	43	61
1967	1309.1	19	29	47	64
1972	1745.5	20	33	51	70
% Change 1958-1972		-20	3	11	11
Daily and Sunday Newspapers: Receipts from Advertising					
1958	2208.7	18	26	39	57
1963	2727.5	15	24	39	58
1967	3652.5	18	28	45	64
1972	5207.9	20	32	49	69
% Change 1958-1972		11	23	26	21
Weekly and Other Newspapers: Receipts from Subscriptions and Sales					
1958	62.6	11	14	20	28
1963	82.9	18	22	29	38
1967	78.2	26	33	41	54
1972	106.9	21	28	38	50
% Change 1958-1972		91	100	90	79
Weekly and Other Newspapers: Receipts from Advertising					
1958	235.2	3	5	9	16
1963	296.0	6	8	13	20
1967	243.2	5	10	18	30
1972	386.5	5	10	20	34
% Change 1958-1972		67	100	122	113

Source: Lofquist (1976), p. 17.

Note: (a) Total newspaper receipts for newspapers not specified by kind include the following amounts: 1972, $454.4 million; 1967, $266.8 million; 1963, $83.9 million; and 1958, $35.2 million.

noting the one major change which Rosse and his colleagues made in the way they arranged the *Yearbook* data. They used the newspaper firm, rather than the newspaper publication, as their basic unit of analysis. As a result, papers produced under joint operating agreements or sharing any major part of their operations were counted as one firm, while members of chains in different cities were counted as separate newspapers. This method was appropriate for an analysis of local monopoly, but it is not useful in studying chain ownerships (see Unit 221).

Table 220-C was based on a U.S. Commerce Department summary of the figures collected in the *Census of Manufactures* (Lofquist, 1976).

Further Information

Owen (1975) provides an interesting discussion of the phenomenon of geographic newspaper monopoly, the economic forces behind it, and its policy implications. Baer et al. (1974) discuss the concentration of mass media ownership and review other works on this topic. For related information on newspaper chain ownership, see Unit 221.

Table 221–A.
Number, Percentage, and Circulation Share of
Chain-Owned Daily Newspapers in U. S., 1900–1976

	Number of Chains	Number of Chain-Owned Dailies	Total Number of Dailies	% of Chain-Owned Dailies	% of Total Daily Circulation of Chain-Owned Dailies	Mean Number of Dailies per Chain
1900[a]	8	27	- -	- -	10%	3.4
1910	13	62	- -	- -	- -	4.7
1923	31	153	2036	7.8%	- -	4.9
1930	55	311	1942	16.0	43.4	5.6
1935	59	329	1950	16.8	41.6	5.6
1940	60	319	1878	17.0	- -	5.3
1945	76	368	1749	21.0	42.0	4.8
1953	95	485	1785	27.0	45.3	5.1
1960	109	552	1763	31.3	46.1	5.1
1966	156	794	1754	45.3	57.0	5.1
1971	157	879	1749	50.3	63.0	5.6
1976	168	1061	1765	60.1	71.0	6.3

Sources: All data for 1900: Estimated by Mott (1962), p. 648. Number of Chains, Chain-Owned Dailies, and Dailies per Chain, 1910-1971: Prepared by Raymond B. Nixon as quoted in *Editor and Publisher*, February 23, 1974. Percentage of Total Circulation, 1930-1966: Prepared by Raymond B. Nixon as quoted in Bottini (1967), p. 2. Percentage of Total Circulation, 1971: Emery (1972), p. 629. Total Number of Dailies, 1923-1971: *Editor and Publisher International Yearbooks.* Number of Dailies and Chain-Owned Dailies, 1976: *Advertising Age*, December 27, 1976, p. 6. Number of Chains and Percentage of Total Circulation, 1976: Bagdikian (1977), p. 19. Other 1976 data were calculated by the editors.

Note: (a) Estimate.

Interpretation of Tables

Table 221-A demonstrates the steady rise in the number of newspaper chains and chain-owned dailies in the United States since 1900. The proportion of newspaper circulation controlled by chains has risen from 10 to more than 70 percent. It is interesting to note that since the mid-1930s—the heyday of public concern about newspaper giants like Hearst—the percentage of chain-owned dailies has tripled and the percentage of chain-controlled circulation has almost doubled.

Table 221-B shows the 50 leading newspaper chains in 1972, as well as the percentage of national daily circulation accounted for by each chain. A more recent study by Bagdikian (1977) found that the top 25 daily-newspaper chains controlled 52 percent of all daily circulation in 1976, a significant increase from the 38 percent shown for 1960 in Table 221-B.

Bagdikian also lists the 1976 leaders in ownership of daily newspapers: Gannett (73 dailies), Thomson (57), Knight-Ridder (34), Walls (32), Newhouse (30), Freedom (25), Harte-Hanks (24), Scripps League (20), Worrell (19), Cox (18), and Stauffer (18). The top ten circulation leaders for 1976 were:

Knight-Ridder	3,725,000	Times-Mirror	1,750,000
Newhouse	3,530,000	Dow Jones	1,700,000
Chicago Tribune	2,995,000	Hearst	1,550,000
Gannett	2,940,000	Cox	1,200,000
Scripps-Howard	1,750,000	New York Times Co.	1,005,000

Table 221–B.
Total Circulation and Number of Daily Newspapers Owned
by the 50 Largest Newspaper Publishers in U. S., 1972

Rank	Name of Group	Number of Daily Newspapers Owned	Total Circulation	Percentage of Circulation Among All Papers	Percentage of Circulation Among Top 50 Groups
1	Tribune Co.	8	3,612,089	5.8%	9.8%
2	Newhouse Newspapers	23	3,307,043	5.3	9.0
3	E. W. Scripps Co.	49	2,419,007	3.9	6.6
4	Gannett Newspapers	50	2,284,964	3.7	6.3
5	Knight Newspapers	10	1,952,019	3.1	5.3
6	Hearst Newspapers	8	1,764,832	2.8	4.8
7	Times-Mirror Co.	4	1,731,977	2.8	4.7
8	Dow Jones and Co.	15	1,535,276	2.5	4.2
9	Ridder Publications	17	1,307,119	2.1	3.6
10	James M. Cox Newspapers	12	1,024,173	1.6	2.8
11	Cowles Newspapers	7	936,139	1.5	2.6
12	New York Times Co.	7	910,142	1.5	2.5
13	Thomson Newspapers	45	896,382	1.4	2.5
14	Central Newspapers	7	765,511	1.2	2.1
15	Copley Newspapers	14	688,335	1.1	1.9
16	Robt. McLean Newspapers	2	652,742	1.0	1.8
17	Kansas City Star	3	652,166	1.0	1.8
18	Harte-Hanks News	20	623,377	1.0	1.7
19	Media General, Inc.	6	573,545	0.9	1.6
20	Freedom Newspapers	19	527,416	0.8	1.4
21	Booth Newspapers, Inc.	8	524,678	0.8	1.4
22	Block Newspapers	5	508,034	0.8	1.4
23	Landmark Communications	6	464,902	0.7	1.3
24	Lee Newspapers	14	421,776	0.7	1.0
25	Pulitzer Publishing Co.	2	374,232	0.5	1.0
26	Bulletin Company of Norwich	2	341,713	0.5	0.9
27	McClatchy Newspapers	3	340,618	0.5	0.9
28	Capital Cities Broadcasting	3	339,519	0.5	0.9
29	Morris Communications	10	335,631	0.5	0.9
30	Ingersoll Newspapers	10	321,773	0.5	0.9
31	A. H. Belo Corp.	7	313,783	0.5	0.9
32	Donrey Media Group	26	305,163	0.5	0.8
33	Multimedia Newspapers	7	288,293	0.5	0.8
34	Speidel Newspapers	11	286,571	0.5	0.8
35	Howard Publications	11	283,286	0.5	0.8
36	Carmage Walls	20	281,816	0.5	0.8
37	Stauffer Publications	15	244,799	0.4	0.7
38	Seattle Times Co.	2	231,333	0.4	0.6
39	Florida Publishing	3	216,405	0.3	0.6
40	South Bend Newspapers	8	210,735	0.3	0.6
41	Worrell Newspapers	17	193,115	0.3	0.5
42	Ogden Newspapers	10	188,976	0.3	0.5
43	Fentress Newspapers	6	187,790	0.3	0.5
44	S. W. Calkins Newspapers	7	187,557	0.3	0.5
45	Lindsay-Schaub News	7	183,326	0.3	0.5
46	Horvitz Newspapers	6	183,214	0.3	0.5
47	State Record Co.	3	181,790	0.3	0.5
48	Worcester Telegraph and Gazette	4	161,897	0.3	0.4
49	John P. Harris News	9	145,134	0.2	0.4
50	Ewing Newspapers	3	140,890	0.2	0.4
	Total		36,547,003		

Source: Baer, et al.. (1974), p. 40, based on raw data from *Editor and Publisher International Yearbook, 1973.*

Sources

Table 221-A was compiled from a number of reports which had been calculated from either the information in *Editor and Publisher International Yearbook* or the data prepared by Raymond B. Nixon for his annual listings for *Editor and Publisher*. Nixon acquires information on the amount of group ownership each year by sending out questionnaires to newspapers.

Table 221-B was compiled by Baer et al. (1974) from data in the *Editor and Publisher International Yearbook*. *Editor and Publisher* is the first-ranking, standard newspaper industry directory; all coverage of English-language daily newspapers by *Editor and Publisher* is generally considered complete and historically comparable.

Further Information

Three interesting recent articles on this subject are by Bagdikian (1977), Phillips (1977), and deLesseps (1977). A major literature review, with annotated bibliography and summary assessment, was done by Baer et al. (1974) in the same volume from which Table 221-B was taken. The reader should also refer to the discussion of chain ownership and newspaper-broadcasting cross-ownership in Gormley (1976), and in Units 200, 201, 220, and 261 of this book.

Ownership Concentration: Magazine Publishers 230

Interpretation of Table

Table 230-A presents a breakdown, by type of magazine, of the receipts accounted for by the top four, eight, twenty, and fifty largest periodical publishing companies in the United States in 1958, 1963, 1967, and 1972. The reader will note that, in almost all categories, periodical publishing has generally become less concentrated. A few categories, such as specialized business and professional periodicals, represent a minor divergence from this trend.

It is important to understand the limitations of the figures presented in Table 230-A. First, only those companies whose primary activity is producing periodicals have been included in the tally. Consequently, such large magazine chains as those owned by the New York Times Company and the Times-Mirror Company (both newspaper publishers) or by McGraw-Hill (basically a book publisher) would not be included. Second, because nonprofit corporations are often excluded from these figures, the editors have no way of measuring the revenue generated by the considerable numbers of journals produced by these organizations.

Information on concentration of ownership in the magazine industry is far less available than similar data for the radio, television, and newspaper industries. This is unfortunate because certain categories of periodicals in Table 230-A still show a significant degree of concentration—despite the general trend away from ownership concentration in the industry. For example, 80 percent of all general periodical revenues for 1972 went to the top 20 companies.

Lists of chain owners in periodical publishing are equally difficult to obtain. The only listings available appear to be those published by the Standard Rate and Data Service in their directories of general, farm, and business periodicals. But the scope of coverage in these lists is not clear, and in some cases, subsidiary chains were indistinguishable from parent firms (Standard Rate and Data Service, 1976). Inquiries made to *Folio* (the magazine of magazine management), the U.S. Department of Commerce, and the Magazine Publishers Association failed to yield further information.

Sources

The information in Table 230-A comes from the *Census of Manufactures*, a survey carried out every five years by the U.S. Census Bureau. Despite its limits, the *Census of Manufactures* is considered one of the most valid and reliable sources of periodical industry information. See Appendix A for a detailed discussion of this source.

Further Information

See Unit 201 for a discussion of media conglomerates which include some magazine chains.

Table 230–A.
Revenue Accounted for by the 4, 8, 20, and 50 Largest Periodical Publishers in U. S., 1958–1972

Type of Periodical	Total Revenue (millions)	Percent of Total Revenue			
		4 Largest Companies	8 Largest Companies	20 Largest Companies	50 Largest Companies
All Periodicals					
1958	$1,578.4	31%	40%	54%	67%
1963	2,035.5	26	39	56	69
1967	2,668.2	23	36	53	68
1972	3,187.0	22	33	50	65
Farm Periodicals, Receipts from Subscriptions and Sales					
1958	11.3	44	59	78	97
1963	8.5	50	68	90	99+
1967	11.3	41	63	85	99+
1972	14.2	38	55	81	99+
Farm Periodicals, Receipts from Advertising					
1958	55.4	43	59	80	97
1963	45.6	48	65	87	99+
1967	45.7	43	59	81	99
1972	61.7	39	61	84	99+
Specialized Business and Professional Periodicals, Receipts from Subscriptions and Sales					
1958	86.3	N/A	N/A	N/A	N/A
1963	122.7	23	30	44	62
1967	149.6	31	41	58	77
1972	262.2	31	40	59	77
Specialized Business and Professional Periodicals, Receipts from Advertising					
1958	294.1	N/A	N/A	N/A	N/A
1963	412.7	28	37	49	65
1967	524.9	34	45	59	73
1972	648.0	26	36	52	71
General Periodicals, Receipts from Subscriptions and Sales					
1958	343.1	N/A	N/A	N/A	N/A
1963	456.7	38	56	80	93
1967	593.5	37	55	80	92
1972	828.8	36	56	79	90
General Periodicals, Receipts from Advertising					
1958	543.9	59	73	91	98
1963	710.6	53	72	92	97
1967	879.5	48	67	90	97
1972	889.0	40	60	84	94
Other Periodicals (except Shopping News, Directories, or Catalogs)					
1958	265.4	N/A	N/A	N/A	N/A
1963	230.2	35	46	64	81
1967	284.2	30	44	65	84
1972	282.1	28	45	65	84
Periodicals, n.s.k.[a]					
1958	39.6	N/A	N/A	N/A	N/A
1963	48.5	N/A	N/A	N/A	N/A
1967	179.5	N/A	N/A	N/A	N/A
1972	201.1	N/A	N/A	N/A	N/A

Source: Lofquist (1976).

Note: (a) n.s.k. – "not specified by kind."

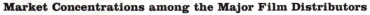

Table 240–A.
Market Concentrations among the Major Film Distributors in U. S., 1948–1967

Year	Estimated Total U. S. Film Rentals From Theaters	Estimated Share of Seven Film "Majors"	
		Amount	Percent of Total
1948	$378	$288	76%
1954	371	317	85
1958	415	272	66
1963	412	236	57
1967	503	354	74

Source: Crandall (1975), p. 60, using data from *Census of Business*.

Table 240–B.
Percentage Share of Sales by Top 4, 8, 20, and 50 U. S. Film Equipment Companies, 1958–1972

	Number of Companies Reporting	Percent of Sales Controlled by:			
		Top 4	Top 8	Top 20	Top 50
Equipment Companies					
1958	N/A	69%	81%	93%	99%
1963	N/A	57	71	86	98
1967	N/A	58	69	85	98
1972	N/A	59	72	89	99
Production-distribution-service Companies					
1972	8,555	29	44	56	64

Source: *1972 Census of Manufactures*.

Interpretation of Tables

During the late 1940s and early 1950s, a series of consent decrees between the U.S. Department of Justice and the motion picture industry successfully ended the government's longtime efforts to separate the production (the major studios) and the exhibition (the theaters) segments of the industry. It was the government's contention that the economic dominance of the movie industry by the eight Hollywood "majors" constituted restraint of competition. The major studios agreed to sell their theaters (see Unit 141), but as **Table 240-A** suggests, their financial dominance of the industry has lessened only marginally from the 80 percent levels of control they enjoyed in the pre-decree years.

This continued dominance seems particularly evident when one notes in **Table 240-A** that the figures represent film-rental revenues of only seven of the original eight major studios. The RKO

Studio was closed down in 1955; therefore, RKO earnings were subtracted from the totals for this table in order to make the figures comparable. If the RKO revenues are added to the 1948 and 1954 figures, the total post-decree film-rental income of the major studios becomes 86 percent in 1948 and 90 percent in 1954.

The figures in **Table 240-A** also illustrate the serious difficulties of the major film studios in adjusting both to the advent of television and to the economic handicaps of post-decree conditions. The large film production companies began to recover their strong role in the industry only during the late 1960s and early 1970s. (See Unit 140 for data on the film production of the major studios over four decades; see Unit 341 for financial data.)

Another indication that the oligopolistic conditions in the film industry may be lessening somewhat can be found in **Table 240-B**, which shows declining levels of sales dominance among the top four and top eight companies that manufacture motion picture equipment (both professional and home). The decline in revenues in 1958 and especially in 1963 is considerable. However, the source of this data (Crandall, 1975) explains that the 1963 decline represents an exceptionally bad year for Hollywood. The reader should also note that, despite the declines over the past two decades, equipment firms continue to control three quarters of this industry's sales.

For motion picture production, distribution, and service companies (financially detailed in Unit 340), ownership information is available only for 1972. As combined in **Table 240-B**, these 1972 figures really tell us little of value in assessing the industry.

Sources

The data for **Table 240-A** are drawn from Crandall (1975), who based his computations on *Census of Business* figures. His discussion of how he figured the major studios' share of total rentals covers three pages, so the interested reader is advised to refer to this source for a complete explanation. **Table 240-B** data comes from the 1972 *Census of Manufactures*.

Further Information

Conant (1960) is the standard source for the discussion of ownership concentrations and the effects of the consent decrees in the motion picture industry. The Conant material has been updated by Crandall (1975). For a discussion of theater ownership, see Unit 141. Film conglomerates are detailed in Unit 201.

Motion Picture Theater Ownership

24

Interpretation of Tables

Writing in 1946, Morris Ernst referred to the U.S. movie industry's "infantile skittishness in respect to statistics." Ernst's comment was echoed three decades later in the trade weekly *Variety*, which noted that many important statistics, "for reasons apparent only to the obscure working of the minds of exhibitors and their organizations, have been kept secret." This evasiveness within the motion picture industry is particularly evident in regard to the ownership of theaters and the number of theaters held by individual companies. As a consequence, the two tables in this unit provide only a portion of the theater ownership picture.

Table 241-A traces the rise and decline of the old studio-theater combinations, which were eventually broken up by the antitrust consent decrees of the late 1940s and early 1950s. The increasing concentrations of ownership until 1945, and the decline since that time, are clearly shown in the table. However, the figures are misleading in one important respect: Nearly all of the important first-run movie theaters in the major cities were controlled by the major studios, and thus the percentage of industry dominance by these theater chains was far greater than the figures suggest. The studio-owned chains probably controlled at least one-quarter of all theater seats in 1945 (since the studio chains owned the biggest theaters). Moreover, a higher percentage of these seats were in the most profitable first-run theaters in the major cities.

Table 241-B lists the six largest theater chains in the United States as of early 1975. In 1970, some 700 theater chains or circuits controlled four or more theaters each (53 percent of all movie

Table 241–A.
Number of Chain-Owned Movie Theaters in U. S. before and after
Government Decree of Divestiture, 1931–1959

Name of Chain (and Successor Company after Divestiture)	1931[a]	1940	1945	Year of Decree (Year)	Theaters	Year after Divestiture	1957	1959
Paramount Pictures (ABC-Paramount)	971	1,273	1,395	(1949)	1,424	650	534	496
20th-Century Fox (National Theatres, Inc.)	521	538	636	(1951)	549	356	321	250
Warner Bros. (Stanley Warner Corp.)	529	557	501	(1951)	436	334	297	240
Loew's, Inc. (Loew's Theatres, Inc.)	189	122	135	(1952)	129	112	100	111
RKO Corp. (RKO Theatres Corp.)	161	132	109	(1948)	124	89	82	89
Chains Under Joint Control	N/A	200+	361		N/A	N/A	N/A	N/A
Total Number of Chain Theaters	2,437	2,622	3,137		2,662	1,541	1,334	1,186
Percent of All Theaters	11.1%	13.8%	15.3%		14.3%	N/A	8.2%	7.3%

Sources: Data is from Conant (1960), pp. 26 and 108; except for 1940 data, which is from Huettig (1944), pp. 134-135; and for 1959, which is from Schnapper (1976). Percentage figures are based on total number of theaters listed on Table 140-A, except for the 1957 and 1959 data, which was based on Table 140-B.

Note: (a) 1931 total includes 66 theaters owned by Universal Theaters Corporation, not otherwise listed.

Table 241–B.
Largest Movie Theater Chains in U. S., 1975

Chain	Number of Theaters
General Cinema	500
United Artists	500
Mann Theaters	200
Commonwealth	200
ABC Theaters	185
Cinemette	150
Total	1,735[a]

Source: *Variety* (January 8, 1975).

Note: (a) This total represents approximately 12.5 percent of all theaters in the U. S.

theaters in the nation), while 6,800 companies or individuals controlled the remaining 47 percent. (Note that ABC Theaters is a continuation of the ABC-Paramount chain listed in **Table 241-A**.)

By the late 1970s, there were renewed pressures from several areas of government for a new investigation of the motion picture industry. The concern focused in particular on the role of large media conglomerates (see Unit 201) in the film and television industries and on a number of alleged financial improprieties and anticompetitive procedures in the production, distribution, and exhibition of feature films and television programming. In 1976, for example, Warner Bros. was ordered by the Justice Department to cease the occasional practice of "four-walling"—a strategy in which the distributor rented a theater for the run of one of its films, thereby collecting all revenue from the film rather than splitting the proceeds with an exhibitor. This practice was held in violation of the consent decrees of the 1940s and early 1950s.

Another controversial practice in the industry is "blind bidding," in which a producer/distributor requires theater operators to bid for films as yet unmade. The consequence of this practice is that the theaters are often stuck with a poorly received film at a far higher rental price than would otherwise have been the case. Finally, there has been considerable concern, both within and outside the film industry, about the concentrations of theaters, especially the newer, multi-screen suburban-based operations, in large national chains. There also seems to be a trend toward regional dominance of a given area's theaters by two or three owners.

Most of these concerns are directed once again at ownership concentrations in the motion picture industry—especially at the theater or exhibition levels. There was talk early in 1978 that Congress was considering extensive hearings into these questions. Clearly, if such an investigation does materialize, one beneficial result will be a greater availability of statistical information on the industry.

Sources

Except for the 1940 and 1959 figures, the data in **Table 241-A** are drawn from Conant (1960). Data for 1940 are from Huettig (1944), and the 1959 information comes from Schnapper (1976). The total shown for 1931 includes 66 theaters owned by Universal Theaters Corp., which is not represented on the table. The percentage figures at the bottom of the table were calculated by the editors on the basis of the total number of theaters listed in Unit 140, **Tables 140-A** and **140-B**. The information in **Table 241-B** is from *Variety* (January 8, 1975) and is rounded, representing what the source terms "simply approximations."

Further Information

For a historical overview of movie theater ownership in the United States, see Conant (1960). For current information, one must keep watch on the two major trade periodicals, *Variety* and *Boxoffice*.

Ownership Concentration: Recording Industry

250

Interpretation of Table

Statistics on the record and tape industry are difficult to compile because of the multiplicity of labels issued by each of hundreds of firms in the United States. **Table 250-A** illustrates the control of the industry by the top four, eight, twenty, and fifty record/tape-producing firms in the United States. Note that sales dominance by the top twenty firms has declined steadily and substantially since 1947. This is due mainly to an increasing number of new companies in the industry. To a lesser extent, the decline has resulted from growth in the number of imports (both recordings and matrices) from abroad.

Sources

These data are taken from the 1972 *Census of Manufactures*.

Table 250–A.
Percentage Share of Sales by Top 4, 8, 20, and 50 Record Manufacturers in U. S., 1947–1972

Year	Number of Companies Reporting	Percent of Sales Controlled by:			
		Top 4	Top 8	Top 20	Top 50
1947	96	79 %	87%	94 %	N/A
1954	135	70	80	88	N/A
1958	85	76	83	90	98%
1963	128	69	75	85	94
1967	306	58	67	81	92
1972	537	48	61	76	85

Source: *1972 Census of Manufactures.*

Further Information

There is no consistent source of ownership information on the recording industry. Denisoff (1975) provides the best background information on the popular recording industry, and *Billboard* is the most important trade periodical. See also the citations in the Further Information sections of Units 150 and 201. Several of the relatively new communications conglomerates include recording firms as a part of their holdings—see Unit 201.

Ownership Patterns: Broadcasting Industry   260

Interpretation of Tables

This is the first of several units which analyze the ownership of both commercial and public broadcast stations in the United States. **Table 260-A** provides summary information on the number and prices of commercial radio and television stations sold over the 40-year period from 1938 to 1976. The recent marked decline in the sales of combination radio-television operations is due to a 1971 FCC ruling which requires divestiture of such combinations by the new owner within a specified period of time after purchase.

As **Table 260-A** indicates, the prices of broadcast stations rose rather sharply in the late 1960s and early 1970s. Clearly, the inflation rate during those years was largely responsible for these increases. But another important factor in this trend has been the scarcity of new broadcast channels. The lack of opportunities to place new stations on the air makes existing stations all the more valuable and expensive. The result is a narrowing of the number of potential buyers with sufficient capital to purchase a station—which means that more and more stations are being absorbed by the larger and wealthier group owners (see Units 200, 201, and 280).

Table 260-B shows trends in group ownership of broadcast stations within each of the top 100 markets. The larger numbers on the table indicate higher proportions of intra-market group ownership. In the 1940s, there was a generally acknowledged de facto limitation on the total number of stations which could be controlled by a single owner, but group owners controlled about 40 percent of the AM radio stations in the top markets. In 1954, the FCC formally limited a single owner to any combination of seven AM radio stations, seven FM radio stations, and seven television stations (with no more than five of the television stations in the VHF category). Thus, an owner might have sets of one AM station, one FM station, and one television station in each of seven

Table 260–A.
Number of Radio and Television Stations Sold in U. S., with Average Price per Transaction, 1938–1976

Year	Number of Transactions				Average Price per Each FCC-Approved Transaction			Inflation Index (1972=100)
	Radio Only	TV Only	Radio/ TV	Total	Radio Only	TV Only	Radio/ TV	
1938	20	--	--	20	$ 46,039	--	--	28.3
1940	12	--	--	12	98,708	--	--	28.8
1942	21	--	--	21	92,404	--	--	32.5
1944	58	--	--	58	226,871	--	--	36.6
1946	52	--	--	52	441,589	--	--	43.9
1954	187	27	18	232	54,674	$ 885,435	$1,456,295	59.7
1956	316	21	24	361	103,049	849,066	2,717,169	62.9
1958	407	23	17	447	122,526	730,273	3,580,742	66.0
1960	345	21	10	376	150,039	1,091,915	2,464,840	68.7
1962	306	16	8	330	195,793	1,437,977	2,352,843	70.6
1964	430	36	20	486	121,620	2,396,513	3,359,288	72.7
1966	367	31	11	409	208,811	986,259	2,591,864	76.8
1968	316	20	9	345	225,667	1,679,403	5,284,070	82.6
1970	268	19	3	290	321,988	4,602,846	346,155	91.4
1972	239	37	--	276	478,764	4,240,699	--	100.0
1974	369	24	5	398	457,989	4,957,644	3,960,000	116.4
1976	413	32	1	446	437,442	3,389,364	1,800,000	133.9

Sources: 1938-1946 data: FCC (1947), p. 87. 1954-1976 data: *Broadcasting* (January 31, 1977), p. 23.

Note: Inflation index is the GNP.

cities, or 21 single stations in 21 different cities. In actual practice, however, group owners have concentrated in either radio or television and have focused their ownership in the largest markets.

Although the inception of FM radio and television—as well as many new AM radio stations—had decreased group ownership levels in broadcasting by the early 1950s, these levels have since increased nearly to pre-World War II figures. **Table 260-C** presents what scattered information is available on group ownership of radio stations only. As with broadcasting generally, the overall trend in radio is toward increasing ownership concentrations.

Table 260-D provides information on ownership concentrations among companies which manufacture broadcast-related equipment. From 1954 to 1972, the concentration of control in the manufacture of radio and television receivers decreased slightly. However, this decline is due more to massive imports (see Units 750 and 760) than to the increasing number of manufacturing

Table 260–B.
Proportion of Intra-Market Ownership of Broadcast Stations in U. S.,
by Market Group, 1922–1970

| Market Group | Percent of Intra-Market Control | | | | | |
	1922	1930	1940	1950	1960	1970
Top 10	.16	.17	.40	.25	.35	.38
Top 25	.10	.11	.40	.19	.32	.34
Top 50	.05	.10	.45	.17	.31	.34
Top 100	.02	.06	.39	.14	.29	.32

Source: Sterling (1975), p. 255, table 5.

Table 260–C.
Number and Percentage of AM Radio Stations Controlled
by Group Owners in U. S., 1929–1967

Year	Total Number of Stations	Number of Group Owners	Number of Group-Owned Stations	Percent of AM Stations under Group-Ownership
1929	600	12	20	3.3%
1939	764	39	109	14.3
1951	2,232	63	253	11.3
1960	3,398	185	765	22.5
1967	4,130	373	1,297	31.4

Sources: 1929 data: Agee (1949), p. 414, table 2. All other data: Rucker (1968), p. 189, table 14.

firms. (The 1954 data on radio/TV receivers is also not strictly comparable to later information.) Ownership concentrations in the production of cathode-ray picture tubes have also declined slightly, but it is noteworthy that more than half of the companies which were operating in 1963 no longer report any manufacturing activity. (Competition from imports and the increased complexity of color tubes are probably the major factors in the decreasing numbers of companies in this field.) The "radio-television equipment" category is a very broad one which includes all broadcast and studio equipment.

Sources

Table 260-A is based on FCC data and materials from *Broadcasting* (January 31, 1977). Both sources provide information for the odd-numbered years omitted on the table, but apparently there is no consistent information available for the years 1947-1953. The editors computed averages by dividing dollar totals by the number of stations sold in each category. Only those sales approved by the FCC are included. However, since any license transfer must be approved by the FCC, these figures are probably quite accurate. The averages for any one year may be skewed by unusually large or small sales.

Table 260-B was taken from Sterling (1975). The reader should refer to Unit 200 for an analysis of this study. Table 260-C is from Rucker (1968)—except for the 1929 figures, which come

Table 260–D.
Percentage of Broadcast-Equipment Sales Controlled
by Top 4, 8, 20, and 50 U. S. Manufacturers, 1954–1972

Company Type and Year	Number of Companies Reporting	Percent of Sales Controlled by:			
		Top 4	Top 8	Top 20	Top 50
Radio-TV Receiving Sets[a]					
1954[b]	N/A	42 %	62 %	87%	N/A %
1963	322	41	62	82	94
1967	303	49	69	85	95
1972	343	49	71	86	96
Cathode-Ray TV Picture Tubes					
1963	148	91	95	97	99
1967	95	84	98	99+	99+
1972	69	83	97	99+	99+
Radio-Television Equipment[c]					
1963	1,001	29	45	69	84
1967	1,111	22	37	61	81
1972	1,524	19	33	58	77

Source: *1972 Census of Manufactures.*

Notes: (a) Includes phonographs and P.A. systems. (b) 1954 information is not directly comparable with data for later years, as means of computing companies in the category changed. (c) Includes electronic communication equipment and parts (except telephone and telegraph), high energy particle accelerator systems and parts, and other related equipment.

from Agee (1949). Figures include all types of group owners, as well as those with newspaper interests. Because data were originally drawn from several different sources, each of which developed its own definitions and counting procedures, the figures in **Table 260-C** should be viewed as approximations. Finally, **Table 260-D** was taken from the 1972 edition of the ever-useful *Census of Manufactures*.

Further Information

The handiest annual summation of sales activity and prices for broadcast stations is found in *Broadcasting* in either late January or early February. Aggregate lists also appear in *Broadcasting Yearbook* and *Television Factbook*. The latter also contains detailed sales and ownership histories of all television stations in the United States.

Most current writing on group ownership in broadcasting focuses on television. Contemporary views of the issues and data appear in Bunce (1976) and Howard (1976). The reader seeking data favoring group ownership should check Cherington et al. (1971) and Seiden (1975), while Rucker (1968) offers a strong, statistics-studded argument against concentration. The best overview of studies and data on ownership concentration is Baer and Geller et al. (1974), and a useful legal analysis critical of the status quo is Branscomb (1975). Although there is no published continuing analysis of group ownership in the broadcast industry, statistics and comment do appear regularly in *Broadcasting, Television Digest*, and *Access*.

Table 261–A.
Newspaper Ownership of Broadcast Stations in U. S., 1922–1976

	AM Stations			FM Stations			Television Stations		
		Newspaper-Owned			Newspaper-Owned			Newspaper-Owned	
	Total Stations	Number	Percent of Total	Total Stations	Number	Percent of Total	Total Stations	Number	Percent of Total
1922	382	48	12.6 %	--	--	--	--	--	--
1923	556	60	10.7	--	--	--	--	--	--
1924	530	38	7.2	--	--	--	--	--	--
1925	571	33	5.8	--	--	--	--	--	--
1926	528	38	7.2	--	--	--	--	--	--
1927	681	38	5.6	--	--	--	--	--	--
1928	677	41	6.1	--	--	--	--	--	--
1929	606	34	5.6	--	--	--	--	--	--
1930	618	36	5.8	--	--	--	--	--	--
1931	612	68	11.1	--	--	--	--	--	--
1932	604	78	12.9	--	--	--	--	--	--
1933	599	80	13.4	--	--	--	--	--	--
1934	583	90	15.4	--	--	--	--	--	--
1935	585	122	20.9	--	--	--	--	--	--
1936	616	159	25.8	--	--	--	--	--	--
1937	646	180	27.9	--	--	--	--	--	--
1938	689	203	29.5	--	--	--	--	--	--
1939	722	226	31.3	--	--	--	--	--	--
1940	765	250	32.7	--	--	--	--	--	--
1941	831	249	29.9	--	--	--	--	--	--
1942-44				[No available data for this period.]					
1945	919	260	28.4	46	17	36.9 %	8	1	12.5 %
1946	948	271	28.6	48	N/A	N/A	6	N/A	N/A
1947	1,062	319	30.0	140	N/A	N/A	12	N/A	N/A
1948	1,621	444	27.3	458	331	72.3	16	N/A	N/A
1949	1,912	463	24.2	700	280	40.0	51	13	25.5
1950	2,086	472	22.6	733	273	37.2	98	41	41.8
1951	2,232	487	21.8	676	231	34.2	107	45	42.1
1952	2,331	485	20.8	637	212	33.3	108	49	45.4
1953	2,391	478	20.0	580	199	34.3	126	87	69.0
1954	2,521	469	18.6	560	183	32.7	354	130	36.7
1955	2,669	465	17.4	552	170	30.8	411	149	36.3
1956	2,824	463	16.4	540	156	28.9	441	160	36.3
1957	3,008	441	14.7	530	142	26.7	471	156	33.1
1958	3,196	440	13.8	537	145	27.0	495	168	33.9
1959	3,326	431	12.9	578	143	24.7	510	181	35.5
1960	3,456	429	12.4	688	145	21.1	515	175	33.9
1961	3,547	N/A	N/A	815	N/A	N/A	527	N/A	N/A
1962	3,618	412	11.4	960	147	15.3	541	161	29.8
1963	3,760	N/A	N/A	1,081	N/A	N/A	557	N/A	N/A
1964	3,854	381	9.9	1,146	147	12.8	564	174	30.9
1965	4,044	383	9.5	1,270	159	12.5	569	181	31.8
1966	4,065	391	9.6	1,446	170	11.8	585	174	29.7
1967	4,121	387	9.4	1,643	177	10.8	610	172	28.2
1968	4,190	383	9.1	1,753	181	10.3	635	177	27.9
1969	4,265	381	8.9	1,938	191	9.9	662	183	27.6

Table 261–A. (Cont'd.)

	AM Stations			FM Stations			Television Stations		
	Total Stations	Newspaper-Owned		Total Stations	Newspaper-Owned		Total Stations	Newspaper-Owned	
		Number	Percent of Total		Number	Percent of Total		Number	Percent of Total
1970	4,292	394	9.2 %	2,184	245	11.2 %	677	189	27.9 %
1971	4,343	402	9.3	2,196	248	11.3	682	191	28.0
1972	4,374	318	7.3	2,304	209	9.1	693	176	25.4
1973	4,395	325	7.4	2,411	171	7.1	697	178	25.5
1974	4,407	304	6.9	2,502	211	8.4	697	179	25.7
1975	4,432	321	7.2	2,636	236	9.0	711	193	27.1
1976	4,463	N/A	N/A	2,767	N/A	N/A	710	N/A	N/A

Sources: 1922-1960 data: Sterling (1969), pp. 227-236, 254, tables 1 and 2. Sterling drew his material from Willey and Rice (1933), p. 196 (for 1922-1930 data as of June 30); Wagner (1976), p. 189 (for 1931-1941 data as of January 1); and Levin (1960), p. 53 (for 1945-1960 data as of January 1). 1961-1976 data: *1976 Statistical Abstract*, p. 539, table 840, using material initially gathered and published by *Broadcasting Yearbook*.

Note: All data are for "on-air" stations as of January 1, except: 1962—September 1, 1961; 1964—September 30, 1963; 1965—October 31, 1964; 1966—October 31, 1965; 1967—November 10, 1966; 1968—November 1, 1967; 1969—December 4, 1968; 1970—December 1, 1969; 1971—February 1, 1971; 1972—December 1, 1971; 1973—December 1, 1972; 1974—December 1, 1973; 1975—December 1, 1974. "Total" column for AM radio includes educational operations, which after about 1940 maintained a fairly steady figure of 37-38 stations. For FM and television, however, "total" means commercial stations only.

Interpretation of Table

Table 261-A reveals national trends in cross-ownership of newspapers and broadcast stations, whether in a single Standard Metropolitan Statistical Area (SMSA) market or in different markets (see Unit 200 for a discussion of SMSA markets). Historically, most cross-ownership of media outlets has been within single markets. In 1955, for example, 82 percent of newspaper-owned television stations occupied the same market as their owners. But by 1974, only 46 percent of such stations occupied their owners' market areas (Bunce, 1976, p. 45). Apparently, a new pattern has developed.

To some extent, this shift may be due to increasing regulatory attempts to discourage common ownership of multiple means of advertising and news communication within a single market area. Critics first expressed this concern in the late 1930s, when newspaper owners began to buy up AM radio stations as a means of protecting themselves from radio's potential competition in news coverage and advertising. From 1941 to 1944, the FCC investigated this phenomenon and heard arguments from both sides regarding newspaper-broadcasting cross-ownership. However, no specific conclusions were reached.

In the years following World War II, the press became a prominent owner of both FM radio and television stations. At the same time, its control of AM radio began a slight and then an absolute decline. Newspaper control of both AM and FM radio continued to drop through the 1950s, as more stations controlled by non-newspaper owners went on the air. The press-owned portion of television stations also decreased, though very slowly and less dramatically, from initial levels of over one-third of all television operations on the air to approximately one-fourth of these outlets in the 1960s.

These declines relieved regulatory concern to such an extent that, when the FCC finally did issue new rules in 1975, media cross-owners escaped forced divestiture in all but eight small cities, where the *only* newspaper controlled the one radio or television station in town. However, the data accumulated by the FCC during its 1970-1975 investigation soon became the basis of new litigation. In the Spring of 1977, the Court of Appeals for the District of Columbia ordered the FCC to reconsider the issue; and this time, the end result was a complete prohibition of same-market cross-ownership combinations. As this volume went to press, the Supreme Court had not yet decided the case on appeal.

Unlike national trends in common ownership, regional patterns of concentration still have not been adequately documented. Many critics suggest that cross-ownership problems are most serious among the small, one-paper, one-station markets. Other critics are more concerned about the major, top-20 markets, where newspaper-television combinations are centered. And so the arguments continue—with the newspapers stating that they have as much right as anybody to control stations, while their opponents stress the dangers (not only for news and entertainment communication, but for advertising as well) that could result from such concentrations of ownership among different media in the same market.

Sources

The **Table 261**-A figures through 1960 are based on information in Sterling (1969), which in turn was drawn from Willey and Rice (1933), for 1922-1930 data as of June 30; from Wagner (1976), for 1931-1941 data as of January 1; and from Levin (1960), for 1945-1960 data as of January 1. Data after 1960 were initially gathered and published by *Broadcasting Yearbook*. The editors employed these data as they were aggregated in the 1976 *Statistical Abstract*.

Figures for total stations on the air (commercial only, except for AM, which includes about 25 educational stations) were taken from the sources listed in Units 170 and 180. All percentages were calculated by the editors. With so many different sources and means of data-gathering, the reader is cautioned to avoid a strict comparison of all the information in **Table 261**-A, and to focus instead on the overall trends.

Further Information

Newspaper-owned or -controlled radio and television stations are listed annually in *Broadcasting Yearbook*. *Television Factbook* also provides information on press-television station ties. The most important historical analysis of newspaper-broadcasting cross-ownership is Levin (1960), updated by Levin (1971). The reader will find the newspaper industry's views and studies in "Comments of American Newspaper Publishers Association in Opposition" (1971). Baer, Geller, and Grundfest (1974) present a useful policy option review. See also Unit 201 for information on cross-media ownership and cross-owned chains.

Network Ownership of Television Stations 262

Interpretation of Table

Table 262-A provides current (1978) information on network-owned and operated (O&O) television and radio stations in the United States, with an emphasis on television as the more important medium. Under each of the three networks—ABC, CBS, and NBC—the table lists all of the network's O&O television stations, in the order of their SMSA-market ranking (see Unit 200 for a discussion of SMSA markets). A station's call letters and channel number are identified on the first line; the second line notes the year the station was constructed (C) or purchased (P). The letter R is added if there is also a network radio O&O station in that city. Entries in italics indicate an O&O station which is no longer owned by the network. The *second* date in these italicized entries is the year when the network sold the station.

A fundamental goal of the networks has been to locate all of their O&O stations in the largest markets in the country. To a remarkable degree they have succeeded. In terms of the potential number of households reached, the networks hold the top three positions among group owners of television stations in this country (see Unit 280). ABC, the newest network, has always had the fewest affiliate stations. However, the network's phenomenal programming successes in recent years have considerably strengthened its financial position vis-a-vis the other two networks.

Both CBS and NBC have bought and sold several stations over the years; and in the late 1950s, both experimented briefly with two UHF stations before concluding that the financial prospects of UHF were dim (see **Table 380**-C). Regarding the previous CBS ownership of television stations in Los Angeles (KTTV), Washington, and Minneapolis-St. Paul, the reader should note that the network held only minority shares (45 to 49 percent in each case) of these stations.

NBC and the independent Group W (Westinghouse) stations were involved in a bizarre decade-long struggle involving affiliate stations in Cleveland (where NBC was based) and the larger market of Philadelphia (where Group W had a station which NBC coveted). In 1955, NBC forced a trade, providing Westinghouse with $3 million and the Cleveland station (WKYC) in exchange for Group

Table 262–A.

Founding Year and Other Characteristics of Network-Owned Television Stations in U. S., 1976

Market Ranking and Number of TV Households	% of All U. S. Households	ABC-Owned Stations	CBS-Owned Stations	NBC-Owned Stations
1. New York 6,326,300	8.8 %	WABC/7 (1948, C, R)	WCBS/2 (1941, C, R)	WNBC/4 (1941, C, R)
2. Los Angeles 3,814,500	5.3	KABC/7 (1949, C, R)	KNXT/2 (1951, P, R) *KTTV/11 (1948-51, P)*	KNBC/4 (1947, P)
3. Chicago 2,646,500	3.7	WLS/7 (1948, C, R)	WBBM/2 (1953, P, R)	WMAQ/5 (1948, C, R)
4. Philadelphia 2,247,700	3.1	- -	WCAU/10 (1958, P, R)	*WRCV/3 (1955-65, P)*
5. San Francisco 1,743,200	2.4	KGO/7 (1949, C, R)	(R only)	(R only)
6. Boston 1,713,200	2.4	- -	(R only)	- -
7. Detroit 1,554,200	2.2	WXYZ/7 (1948, C, R)	- -	- -
8. Washington 1,373,200	1.9	(R only)	*WTOP/9 (1950-54, P)*	WRC/4 (1947, C, R)
9. Cleveland 1,297,200	1.8	- -	- -	WKYC/3 *(1948-55, C)* (1965, P)
12. Houston 944,000	1.3	(R only)	- -	- -
13. Minneapolis-St. Paul 934,100	1.3	- -	*WCCO/4 (1952-54, P)*	- -
15. St. Louis 916,300	1.3	- -	KMOX/4 (1957, P, R)	- -
21. Milwaukee 668,100	.9	- -	*WXIX/18 (1954-59, P)*	- -
22. Hartford 651,400	.9	- -	*WHCT/18 (1956-58, P)*	*WNBC/30 (1956-58, P)*
28. Buffalo 617,600	.9	- -	- -	*WBUF/17 (1955-58, P)*

Sources: Dates and station characteristics: Sterling and Kittross (1978), p. 266, and Lichty and Topping (1975), p. 194, table 13. Markets and TV households: Arbitron Television's *ADI Book 1976-77*, pp. 8-10.

Note: Listings show the television station call letters and channel number on first line, and in parentheses below the year the station began operations for that network. The symbol C indicates the station was constructed by the network; P indicates purchased by the network from a previous owner; R indicates a combination AM-FM radio station owned by the network in that market. Those stations in italics are no longer network-owned. The end date indicates the year the network relinquished control of the station.

W's KYW in Philadelphia. Investigations by the Department of Justice, Congress, and the FCC eventually led to an undoing of this deal in 1965, when NBC agreed to return to its Cleveland base. The Cleveland station is thus the only O&O station which has been controlled by a network at two separate times.

Most network O&O station operations are radio-television combinations, but an FCC ruling in 1971 requires radio-television station combinations within the same market to be divested once they are sold (see Unit 260 for a more complete discussion of this ruling). Thus, this pattern of ownership will gradually change as the networks sell their stations (most likely their radio affiliates) in order to buy others.

Sources

Due to the public nature of station ownership, and the small number of stations involved, the information in Table 262-A is very accurate. Market rankings and the figures for number and percentage of television households are drawn from Arbitron Television's *ADI Book, 1976-77*. The other information in the table comes primarily from Sterling and Kittross (1978), with some input from Lichty and Topping (1975).

Further Information

For historical information on network radio stations, see the FCC's *Report on Chain Broadcasting* (1941). Background on the network television stations can be found in the FCC's *Network Broadcasting* (1958). Financial information on the television networks is found in Unit 380; programming information is in Unit 582. The reader will also find useful discussions of network O&O stations in Rucker (1968), in an ownership report by Baer et al. (1974), Owen (1975), and Bunce (1976). Lists of network-owned and operated television and radio stations appear annually in *Broadcasting Yearbook*. *Television Factbook* details all current information regarding television O&O stations.

Group Ownership of Television Stations

280

Interpretation of Tables

Group ownership has always been a way of life for commercial television in the United States, and the concentration of station ownership increases annually. **Table 280-A** provides an overall picture of this trend, showing a rise both in the number of group owners in this country and in the proportion of commercial television stations controlled by group owners (defined as a single owner holding at least two stations).

The peculiar percentage drop in group ownership in the 1950s was due to the large number of new stations going on the air at that time. As fewer new stations were established and more channels changed hands through sales, the proportion of group-owned television stations resumed its steady rise. Besides the FCC restrictions on same-market ownership (see Units 260 and 262), the only apparent limiting factor on further group-ownership in the industry is the number of UHF stations now operating. Note in **Table 280-B** the substantially lower group holdings among UHF stations.

Tables **280-B** and **280-C** illustrate the higher concentrations of group ownership in the largest SMSA markets, although this trend is also evident in nearly all other market categories over the past two decades. (See Unit 200 for a discussion of SMSA markets.) Among the top 15 group owners of television stations (ranked in **Table 280-C** according to their net weekly audience), the networks and RKO occupy four of the five top slots in each sample year. The network and RKO stations also occupy the largest markets in the nation. Likewise, Group W, WGN-Continental, Storer, and Triangle (sold to Capitol Cities in the early 1970s)—all companies controlling stations in the larger market areas—have maintained a steady position among the top 10 audience-ranked companies.

Thus, **Table 280-C** demonstrates that the *number* of stations controlled by an ownership group is not as important as the markets in which the group stations operate. For example, in 1959, WGN-Continental's *two* stations ranked sixth among all group owners, whereas owners with five and six stations appear much lower in the listings. The "percentage of households" columns in **Table 280-C** represent the proportion of national households included in the markets in which each group owner operates.

Table 280–A.
Number and Percentage of Group-Owned Television Stations in U. S., 1948–1976

Year	Number of Groups	Number of Group-Owned Stations	Total Commercial Stations	% of Group Control
1948	3	6	16	37.5%
1949	10	24	51	47.1
1950	17	52	98	53.1
1951	19	53	107	49.5
1952	19	53	108	49.1
1953	38	104	126	82.5
1954	48	126	354	35.6
1955	62	165	411	40.1
1956	60	173	441	39.2
1957	65	192	471	40.8
1958	82	241	495	48.7
1959	85	249	510	48.8
1960	84	252	515	48.9
1961	87	260	527	49.3
1962	89	268	541	49.5
1963	97	280	557	50.3
1964	106	299	564	53.0
1965	109	310	569	54.5
1966	111	324	585	55.4
(Data for 1967-1974 not available.)				
1975	115	405	711	57.0
1976	119	415	710	58.0

Sources: First two columns (through 1966) from Kroeger (1966), pp. 30-31; third column taken from figures in Table 180-A. Data for 1975-76 from Howard (1976).

Sources

In **Table 280-A**, the information through 1966 comes from Kroeger (1966). The 1975-76 data are from Howard (1976). The 1956 and 1966 information in **Table 280-B** is drawn from Cherington et al. (1971). The time period for these data is not specified, but they appear to be as of the early Spring for each year.

The 1976 information in **Table 280-B** covers only the top 100 markets and is therefore not strictly comparable with the other figures. The information is drawn from Howard (1976), and the time period for the figures is as of January 1, 1977. The reader should also note that for 1956 and 1966, the percentage columns refer to the ratio of group-owned versus independent stations in each market category. For 1976, the percentages refer to the proportion of group-owned stations to *all* commercial stations in the top 100 markets.

In **Table 280-C**, the 1959 and 1967 data come from Larson (1976). The 1975 data are from Howard (1976b), who cites *Television Factbook* as the primary source. The "percentage of households" columns are estimates, but the overall ownership rankings can be considered accurate.

Further Information

The trade journal *Broadcasting* includes an annual summary of broadcast station sales in its late January or early February issue. Similar, though usually less detailed lists, appear in *Broad-*

Table 280–B.
Number and Percentage of Group-Owned Television Stations in U. S.,
by Market Size, 1956–1976

	Markets 1-10	Markets 1-50	Markets 11-50	Markets 51-100	Markets 101 and up	Total Stations
1956[a]						
All TV Stations		163		134	159	456
Group-Owned Stations		92		48	65	205
% Group-Owned		56.4 %		35.8 %	40.8 %	- -
1966[a]						
All TV Stations		193		164	235	592
Group-Owned Stations		134		112	150	396
% Group-Owned		69.4 %		68.3 %	63.8 %	- -
1976[b] (Group-Owned Stations Only)						
VHF						
Number of Stations	38		97	71	N/A[c]	N/A
% of Stations	95 %		80 %	70 %	N/A	N/A
UHF						
Number of Stations	16		19	26	N/A	N/A
% of Stations	59%		46%	51%	N/A	N/A
All Stations						
Total Number of Stations	54		116	97	N/A	N/A
Total % of Stations	81%		73%	61%	N/A	N/A

Sources: 1956, 1966: Cherington, et al. (1971), p. 40, exhibit 2. 1976: Howard (1976), p. 9.

Notes: (a) Data reported as of early Spring; (b) Data reported as of January 1; (c) Data for 1976 is limited to top 100 markets only.

casting Yearbook and Television Factbook. The latter also features detailed sales and ownership histories of all television stations in the United States.

There are a number of current books on group ownership in the television industry. Recent summaries of the issues and data are found in Bunce (1976) and Howard (1976). Cherington et al. (1971) and Seiden (1975) provide data and arguments favoring group ownership in the industry, while Rucker (1968) offers a carefully argued study criticizing this trend. Branscomb (1975) also makes an interesting legal analysis which is critical of the status quo. The best overview of studies and data on ownership concentration is by Baer and Geller et al. (1974). Analysis and comment on the group ownership issue are also regular features of *Broadcasting*, *Television Digest*, and *Access*.

Table 280–C.

Number of Stations, Weekly Circulation, and Percentage of Households of the Top 15 Group Owners of Television Stations, 1959, 1967, 1975

1959

Ownership Unit	Number of Stations Owned	Net Weekly Circulation (millions)	Percent of Households
1. CBS	5	11.3	22%
2. RCA (NBC)	5	10.8	21
3. ABC	5	9.6	19
4. RKO General	4	5.4	11
5. Westinghouse	5	4.7	9
6. WGN-Continental	2	4.5	9
7. Metropolitan	4	3.9	8
8. Storer	5	3.3	6
9. Triangle	6	2.8	5
10. Avco	5	1.9	4
11. Scripps-Howard	3	1.9	4
12. Newhouse	6	1.8	4
13. Hearst	3	1.7	3
14. Times-Mirror	1	1.7	3
15. Time Inc.	4	1.6	3

1967

Ownership Unit	Number of Stations Owned	Net Weekly Circulation (millions)	Percent of Households
1. CBS	5	13.9	23%
2. ABC	5	13.3	22
3. RCA (NBC)	5	13.3	22
4. Metromedia	4	9.1	15
5. RKO	5	7.9	13
6. Group W	5	7.0	12
7. WGN-Continental	4	6.7	11
8. Storer	6	4.5	8
9. Cox	5	3.7	6
10. Triangle	6	3.5	6
11. Chris-Craft	3	3.1	5
12. Taft	6	3.0	5
13. Autry-Golden West	3	2.7	5
14. Scripps-Howard	4	2.6	4
15. Avco	5	2.6	4

1975

Ownership Unit	Number of Stations Owned	Net Weekly Circulation (millions)	Percent of Households
1. CBS	5	15.1	22%
2. RCA (NBC)	5	14.5	21
3. ABC	5	14.5	21
4. Metromedia	6	11.7	17
5. RKO	4	8.7	13
6. Westinghouse	5	8.6	12
7. WGN-Continental	4	7.3	11
8. Kaiser	7	6.2	9
9. Capitol Cities	6	5.1	7
10. Storer	7	5.0	7
11. Cox	5	4.5	6
12. Taft	6	4.3	6
13. WKY-System	6	3.4	5
14. Scripps-Howard	5	3.3	5
15. Post-Newsweek	4	3.3	5

Sources: 1959 and 1967 data: Larson (1977), pp. 32-33. 1975 data: Howard (1976b), p. 404, citing information from *Television Factbook*.

Note: "Net Weekly Circulation" figures indicate how many millions of households are served by each of the group owners. "Percent of Households" represents the proportion of households included in the market in which each group owner operates.

Table 281–A.
Number and Percentage of Public Television Stations in U. S.,
by Category of Ownership, 1959–1976

Ownership Category	1959	1962	1964	1966	1967	1968	1969	1970	1971	1972	1973	1974	1975	1976
Colleges and Universities														
Number	9	12	24	29	27	31	58	59	61	67	72	74	76	78
Percent	*.26*	*.19*	*.27*	*.26*	*.23*	*.21*	*.31*	*.30*	*.29*	*.30*	*.31*	*.30*	*.30*	*.29*
Public School Systems														
Number	3	19	19	19	21	22	22	24	23	21	20	20	19	19
Percent	*.09*	*.31*	*.22*	*.17*	*.18*	*.15*	*.12*	*.12*	*.11*	*.09*	*.08*	*.08*	*.08*	*.07*
State and/or Municipal Authorities														
Number	10	13	20	24	34	52	57	60	67	74	81	84	87	97
Percent	*.29*	*.21*	*.23*	*.21*	*.29*	*.36*	*.30*	*.31*	*.32*	*.33*	*.34*	*.35*	*.35*	*.36*
Community Organizations														
Number	13	18	25	41	37	41	52	52	56	61	63	65	69	73
Percent	*.37*	*.29*	*.28*	*.36*	*.31*	*.28*	*.28*	*.27*	*.27*	*.27*	*.27*	*.27*	*.27*	*.27*
Total Stations	35	62	88	113	119	146	189	195	207	223	236	243	251	267

Sources: 1959 data: Joint Council on Educational Television (1959). 1962-1970 data: *One Week of Educational Television* series. 1971-1976 data: Corporation for Public Broadcasting reports.

Interpretation of Table

Ownership of public television (PTV) stations is reported in **Table 281-A** in the four owner-ship categories commonly recognized in the industry: (1) colleges and universities, (2) public school systems, (3) state and/or municipal agencies, and (4) community organizations. The top line in the table shows the number of stations (not licensees) in each ownership category; the italicized lower line represents the percentage of all PTV stations within each category.

Colleges and universities, already experienced with educational radio, were the first in the field of educational television. Iowa State University put WOI-TV on the air in 1950, two years before the FCC's allocation of frequencies for educational stations had been established. Public school systems have always been the smallest ownership category, and their position has declined even further in recent years, due mainly to the serious budgetary problems in most school districts.

State/municipal agencies include not only several state-run networks and a few local operations (such as the City of New York's WNYC-TV), but also four nondomestic licensees in American Samoa, Guam, Puerto Rico, and the Virgin Islands. Since 1970, state/municipal authorities have operated the largest bloc of PTV stations. The state authorities, and the number of transmitters controlled by them, are Alabama (9), Connecticut (3), Georgia (9), Kentucky (14), Maine (3), Mississippi (8), Nebraska (8), New Jersey (4), and South Carolina (7). The Alabama system has earned the dubious distinction of being the first educational licensee to lose its license at renewal, due to charges of discrimination in employment and programming. The eventual status of the Alabama Educational Television Commission's nine stations remains unclear as this volume goes to press.

Community organizations are privately created nonprofit corporations and foundations, usually consisting of some combination of community cultural organizations. Some of the most important program-producing public stations in the country fall into this category, including WGBH in Boston, WNET in New York, KCET in Los Angeles, WETA in Washington, WQED in Pittsburgh, and KQED in San Francisco.

Sources

Table 281-A figures for 1959 come from the Joint Council on Educational Television (1959). The 1962-1970 information is from the *One Week of Educational Television* series. All remaining data were taken from Corporation for Public Broadcasting (CPB) reports. Although all of the information is for various dates in the Spring of each year, the variation in dates creates a few very slight numerical discrepancies among the different sources. However, due to the public nature of station ownership, the figures in **Table 281-A** can be considered generally accurate.

Further Information

The National Association of Educational Broadcasters (NAEB) publishes an annual directory of public television, the *NAEB Directory of Public Telecommunications*, with details on all of the ownership groups. The NAEB, along with the other two key agencies, the CPB and the Public Broadcasting Service (PBS), will also supply current and historical information on the PTV systems. Other useful statistical information on public television ownership appears in the CPB's annual *Public Television Licensees*. Background reading on the development, operation, and future of public broadcasting appears in Cater and Nyhan (1976) and Wood and Wylie (1977).

Ownership of Cable Systems   29

Interpretation of Tables

As with other media, the trend in cable system ownership in recent years has been toward greater concentration. **Table 290-A** shows the number and percentage of cable systems controlled by selected categories of owners during each year from 1969 to 1976. Although the data up to 1972 are sketchy, a pattern of control by broadcasters and publishers is clear.

Table 290–A.
Number of Cable (CATV) Systems in U. S., by Category of Ownership, 1969–1976

	1969 (February)		1970 (March)		1971 (March)		1972 (March)		1973 (June)		1974 (June)		1975 (September)		1976 (September)	
	Number of Systems	Percent of Systems Surveyed	Number of Systems	Percent of Systems Surveyed	Number of Systems	Percent of Systems Surveyed	Number of Systems	Percent of Systems Surveyed	Number of Systems	Percent of Systems Surveyed	Number of Systems	Percent of Systems Surveyed	Number of Systems	Percent of Systems Surveyed	Number of Systems	Percent of Systems Surveyed
Number of CATV Systems Surveyed	2300	--	2490	--	2578	--	2839	--	3032	--	3190	--	3405	--	3715	--
Category of Ownership:																
Broadcasters	741	32%	910	37%	766	30%	1077	38%	1048	35%	1178	37%	1090	32%	1183	32%
Newspapers	220	7	207	8	175	7	180	6	308	10	463	15	486	14	476	13
Publishers							75	3	221	7	230	7	247	7	492	13
TV Programming Producers/Distributors	N/A	N/A	N/A	N/A	N/A	N/A	217	8	604	20	744	23	772	23	729	20
Theater Owners	N/A	N/A	N/A	N/A	N/A	N/A	97	3	130	4	146	5	296	9	313	8
Telephone Companies	150	7	146	6	132	5	57	2	50	2	143	4	61	2	69	2
Community or Subscriber Ownership	N/A	N/A	N/A	N/A	N/A	N/A	81	3	75	3	83	3	88	3	96	3
TV Manufacturers	N/A	N/A	N/A	N/A	N/A	N/A	N/A	N/A	320	11	606	19	630	19	455	12

(Note: A brace in the original joins Newspapers and Publishers for 1969, 1970, and 1971, indicating combined figures of 220/7, 207/8, and 175/7 respectively.)

Source: *Television Factbook*, annual issues.

Table 290–B.
Number of Pay-Cable Subscribers Served by Top 8 Distributing Companies in U. S., 1970–1976

Note: All subscriber totals are in thousands.

Name of MSO	1970 Ranking	1970 Subscribers	1971 Ranking	1971 Subscribers	1972 Ranking	1972 Subscribers	1973 Ranking	1973 Subscribers	1974 Ranking	1974 Subscribers	1975 Ranking	1975 Subscribers	1976 Ranking	1976 Subscribers
American Television and Communications Corp.	7	112	3	180	3	264	4	275	4	375	4	490	3	550
Cablecom-General, Inc.	5	123	7	123	9	150	8	170	10	154	10	187	13	166
Communications Properties, Inc.	N/A	N/A	N/A	N/A	8	154	N/A	N/A	8	190	8	247	8	255
Cox Cable Communications Corp.	3	190	2	197	5	242	5	245	7	240	5	375	5	413
Cypress Communications Corp.	6	120	6	140	[sold to Warner, September 1972]									
H & B Communications Corp.	1	242			[merged with TelePrompter]									
Jerrold Corp.	N/A	N/A	9	100			[sold to Sammons]							
Sammons Communications, Inc.	N/A	N/A	N/A	N/A	6	200	6	200	6	245	7	271	7	286
Tele-Communications, Inc.	N/A	N/A	5	142	4	249	3	320	3	400	2	539	2	551
TelePrompter Corp.	2	243	1	535	1	658	1	680	1	831	1	1084	1	1070
Time-Life	8	106	8	106	10	118	N/A	N/A	N/A	N/A	9	188	10	189
Viacom International, Inc.	4	150	4	150	7	183	7	190	5	254	6	290	6	304
Warner Communications, Inc.	N/A	N/A	N/A	N/A	2	342	2	360	2	405	3	523	3	550
Total Subscribers for Top 8 MSOs		1286		1873		2292		2440		2940		3819		3979
Percent of All Cable Subscribers		28.6%		35.3%		38.2%		33.4%		33.8%		39.0%		36.8%

Sources: 1970-1973 data is from Perry (1974), pp. 5-7, using original data from *Moody's Industrial Manual* and *TV Factbook* and is as of January 1 of each year; 1974 data was provided to the editors by NCTA and is as of September 1973; 1975 and 1976 data is from *Television Digest's* "Special Western Cable Television Show Supplement" issues, p. 1 and is as of October 1 of each year.

Table 290–C.
Number and Percentage of Pay-Cable Subscribers Served
by Top 5 Distributing Companies in U. S., 1975–1976

Name of Company	31 March 1975		30 June 1976	
	Number of Subscribers	Percent of Total Subscribers	Number of Subscribers	Percent of Total Subscribers
Home Box Office (Time, Inc.)	90,000	48%	475,000	62%
Telemation Program Services	33,000	17	176,000	23
Optical Systems (Pioneer Systems, Inc.)	50,000	27	49,000	6
Warner Star Channel	8,000	4	34,000	5
Pay TV Services	6,000	3	13,000	2
Total Subscribers for Top 5 Companies	187,000	99%	747,000	98%

Source: Paul Kagan Associates, Inc., *The Pay TV Newsletter.*

Table 290-B shows the gradual increase in the number and proportion of cable subscribers served by the top eight Multiple System Operators (MSOs). The totals shown are for the top eight systems only, regardless of the other figures contained in some of the columns. Table 290-C provides what little information is available thus far on the distributors and producers of pay-cable programming. The data reveal that two or three firms dominate the pay-cable industry. By mid-1977, the Home Box Office system claimed over 700,000 subscribers.

Sources

Table 290-A is taken from annual listings published in *Television Factbook*, which gathers its data through annual surveys of the industry. Because some lesser ownership categories are omitted in this table, and because the figures include multiple listings of owners falling into more than one ownership category, the subtotals of cable systems do not always equal the total number of systems surveyed.

The 1970-73 data in Table 290-B are taken from Perry (1974), who cited a variety of sources, including *Moody's Industrial Manual* and *Television Factbook*. All of these data are as of January 1 for each year. The 1974 figures are actually for September 1973 and were provided to the editors by the National Cable Television Association (NCTA). The 1975-76 data (as of October 1 of those years) come from *Television Digest's* "Special Western Cable Television Show Supplement" issues. All of the information in Table 290-B is based on annual reports or survey responses by cable system operators.

Table 290-C is constructed from the census issues of *The Pay TV Newsletter* of Paul Kagan Associates. As the rounded numbers suggest, the table is made up of estimates of total subscribers.

Further Information

Television Digest contains regularly updated listings of the top 50 cable system operators, as well as listings of the largest individual systems, of the systems by state, and of other data. Some of this information is reprinted in *Television Factbook* or can be obtained from the National Cable Television Association (NCTA). *The Pay TV Newsletter* is the most commonly cited source for all information on pay-cable.

SECTION 3

Economics of the Media Industries

Table 300–A.
U. S. Gross National Product (GNP), 1900–1976

Year	GNP in Current Dollars (billions)	GNP in Constant Dollars (billions)	GNP Index (1972=100)	GNP Percent of Real Change	GNP Per Capita Dollars
1900	$ 18.7	N/A	N/A	N/A	N/A
1901	20.7	N/A	N/A	N/A	N/A
1902	21.6	N/A	N/A	N/A	N/A
1903	22.9	N/A	N/A	N/A	N/A
1904	22.9	N/A	N/A	N/A	N/A
1905	25.1	N/A	N/A	N/A	N/A
1906	28.7	N/A	N/A	N/A	N/A
1907	30.4	N/A	N/A	N/A	N/A
1908	27.7	N/A	N/A	N/A	N/A
1909	33.4	$ 180.8	18.5	N/A	$2.00
1910	35.4	186.0	19.0	2.9%	2.01
1911	35.8	191.8	18.7	3.1	2.04
1912	39.4	201.3	19.6	5.0	2.11
1913	39.6	203.3	19.5	1.0	2.09
1914	38.6	195.9	19.7	-3.6	1.98
1915	40.0	193.3	20.7	-1.3	1.92
1916	48.3	207.8	23.2	7.5	2.04
1917	60.4	212.1	28.5	2.1	2.05
1918	76.4	248.7	30.7	17.3	2.41
1919	84.2	230.4	36.6	-7.4	2.20
1920	91.5	214.2	42.7	-7.0	2.01
1921	69.6	199.8	34.9	-6.7	1.84
1922	74.2	229.3	32.4	14.8	2.08
1923	85.3	254.0	33.6	10.8	2.27
1924	84.9	256.1	33.1	0.8	2.24
1925	93.3	275.8	33.8	7.7	2.38
1926	97.2	291.6	33.3	5.7	2.48
1927	95.1	292.9	32.5	0.4	2.46
1928	97.1	295.8	32.8	1.0	2.45
1929	103.4	315.3	32.8	6.6	2.59
1930	90.7	286.1	31.7	-9.3	2.32
1931	76.1	264.7	28.7	-7.5	2.13
1932	58.3	229.0	25.5	-13.5	1.83
1933	55.8	224.2	24.9	-2.1	1.79
1934	65.3	241.6	27.0	7.8	1.91
1935	72.5	263.3	27.5	9.0	2.07
1936	82.7	299.4	27.6	13.7	2.34
1937	90.7	313.1	29.0	4.6	2.43
1938	84.6	300.1	28.3	-4.2	2.31
1939	90.8	322.1	28.2	7.3	2.46
1940	100.0	347.5	28.8	7.9	2.59
1941	124.9	411.5	30.4	18.4	2.96
1942	158.3	487.6	32.5	18.5	3.36
1943	192.0	545.2	35.2	11.8	3.84
1944	210.5	575.3	36.6	5.5	4.10
1945	212.3	564.1	37.6	11.2	3.98
1946	209.6	477.6	43.9	-15.3	3.36
1947	232.8	468.3	49.7	1.9	3.24
1948	259.1	487.7	53.1	4.1	3.31
1949	258.0	490.7	52.6	0.6	3.28

Table 300–A. (Cont'd.)

	GNP in Current Dollars (billions)	GNP in Constant Dollars (billions)	GNP Index (1972=100)	GNP Percent of Real Change	GNP Per Capita Dollars
1950	286.2	533.5	53.6	8.7	3.50
1951	330.2	576.5	57.3	8.1	3.72
1952	347.2	598.5	58.0	3.8	3.80
1953	366.1	621.8	58.9	3.9	3.88
1954	366.3	613.7	59.7	-1.3	3.76
1955	399.3	654.8	61.0	6.7	3.94
1956	420.7	668.8	62.9	2.1	3.96
1957	442.8	680.9	65.0	1.8	3.96
1958	448.9	679.5	66.0	-0.2	3.89
1959	486.5	720.4	67.5	6.0	4.05
1960	506.0	736.8	68.7	2.3	4.08
1961	523.3	755.3	69.3	2.5	4.11
1962	563.8	799.1	70.6	5.8	4.28
1963	594.7	830.7	71.6	4.0	4.39
1964	635.7	874.4	72.7	5.3	4.56
1965	688.1	925.9	74.3	5.9	4.77
1966	753.0	981.0	76.8	5.9	4.99
1967	796.3	1,007.7	79.0	2.7	5.07
1968	868.5	1,051.8	82.6	4.4	5.24
1969	935.5	1,078.8	86.7	2.6	5.32
1970	982.4	1,075.3	91.4	-0.3	5.25
1971	1,063.4	1,107.5	96.0	3.0	5.35
1972	1,171.1	1,171.1	100.0	5.7	5.61
1973	1,306.6	1,235.0	105.8	5.3	5.87
1974	1,418.2	1,214.0	116.4	-1.8	5.73
1975	1,516.3	1,191.7	127.3	-2.0	5.58
1976	N/A	1,264.7	133.9	6.1	5.88

Source: Bureau of Economic Analysis, U.S. Department of Commerce.

Interpretation of Tables

The three tables in this unit provide the basic national economic descriptors that underlie all financial information on the communications industries in the United States. The concern in this unit is with two closely related economic factors: (1) the actual growth in the U.S. economy in this century, and (2) a method of controlling for the effects of inflation in order to permit fair comparisons of economic data over the years.

Table 300-A provides data on the U.S. Gross National Product (GNP) from 1900 to 1976, both in the current dollars of each year and in *constant* dollars, which are calculated here, and throughout this book, with 1972 as the base index year (1972=100). As defined by the U.S. Department of Commerce, the Gross National Product is

the market value of the output of goods and services produced by the nation's economy, before deduction of depreciation charges and other allowances for business and institutional consumption of durable capital goods. Other business products used up by business in the accounting period are excluded. The nation's economy in this context refers to the labor and property supplied by residents of the nation. Gross National Product comprises the purchase of goods and services by consumers and government, gross private domestic investment (including the change in business inventories), and net exports.

Table 300–B.
U. S. Consumer Price Index (CPI), 1900–1977

Year	Index (1972=100)	Year	Index (1972=100)
1900	20.0	1940	33.5
1901	20.0	1941	35.2
1902	20.8	1942	38.9
1903	21.5	1943	41.3
1904	21.5	1944	42.1
1905	21.5	1945	43.0
1906	21.5	1946	46.7
1907	22.3	1947	53.4
1908	21.5	1948	57.5
1909	21.5	1949	57.0
1910	22.3	1950	57.5
1911	22.3	1951	62.1
1912	23.1	1952	63.4
1913	23.7	1953	63.9
1914	24.0	1954	64.2
1915	24.3	1955	64.0
1916	26.1	1956	65.0
1917	30.6	1957	67.3
1918	36.0	1958	69.1
1919	41.3	1959	69.7
1920	47.9	1960	70.8
1921	42.8	1961	71.5
1922	40.1	1962	72.3
1923	40.8	1963	73.2
1924	40.9	1964	74.1
1925	41.9	1965	74.4
1926	42.3	1966	77.6
1927	41.5	1967	79.8
1928	40.9	1968	83.2
1929	40.9	1969	87.6
1930	40.3	1970	92.8
1931	36.4	1971	96.8
1932	32.6	1972	100.0
1933	31.0	1973	106.2
1934	32.0	1974	117.9
1935	32.8	1975	128.7
1936	33.1	1976	136.1
1937	34.3	1977[a]	142.7
1938	33.7		
1939	33.2		

Sources: Bureau of Labor Statistics, as reprinted in *Historical Statistics* (1975) for 1912-1970 data, and in *Statistical Abstract* for 1971-1977 data.

Note: Figures converted to 1972 base by the editors. (a) This figure is for the first six months of 1977.

For the purposes of this book, the most important column in **Table 300-A** is the GNP Index, technically known as the "GNP Implicit Price Deflator." The GNP Index or Price Deflator is the ratio of the Gross National Product in current prices to the GNP in constant prices based (in this book) on the index year of 1972. Much of the economic data in this section will be compared to this 1972 dollar index to control for the effects of inflation. The editors have used 1972 as the standard economic base year for two reasons: (1) the federal government is already in the process of switching over its GNP data to that year; and (2) a price deflator should be based on a relatively recent year for more effective comparisons, and that base year or period should have been relatively

Table 300–C.
Basic U. S. Personal Income and Expenditure Statistics, 1946–1976

Year	Disposable Personal Income			Personal Consumption Expenditure		
	Total (billions)	Percentage of Change	Per Capita	Total (billions)	Percentage of Change	Per Capita
1946	$332.4	- -	$2,342	$301.4	- -	$2,124
1947	318.8	-4.1%	2,203	306.2	1.6%	2,116
1948	335.5	5.2	2,279	312.8	2.2	2,125
1949	336.1	-.2	2,244	320.0	2.3	2,137
1950	361.9	7.7	2,377	338.1	5.7	2,220
1951	371.6	2.7	2,399	342.3	1.2	2,210
1952	382.1	2.8	2,425	350.9	2.5	2,227
1953	397.5	4.0	2,482	364.2	3.8	2,274
1954	402.1	1.2	2,467	370.9	1.8	2,275
1955	425.9	5.9	2,567	395.1	6.5	2,381
1956	444.9	4.5	2,634	406.3	2.8	2,406
1957	453.9	2.0	2,639	414.7	2.1	2,411
1958	459.0	1.1	2,625	419.0	1.0	2,396
1959	477.4	4.0	2,685	441.5	5.4	2,483
1960	487.3	2.1	2,697	453.0	2.6	2,507
1961	500.6	2.7	2,725	462.2	2.0	2,516
1962	521.6	4.2	2,796	482.9	4.5	2,589
1963	539.2	3.4	2,849	501.4	3.8	2,650
1964	577.3	7.1	3,009	528.7	5.4	2,755
1965	612.4	6.1	3,152	558.1	5.6	2,872
1966	643.6	5.1	3,274	586.1	5.0	2,982
1967	669.8	4.1	3,371	603.2	2.9	3,036
1968	695.2	3.8	3,464	633.4	5.0	3,156
1969	702.3	2.5	3,515	655.4	3.5	3,234
1970	741.6	4.1	3,620	668.9	2.1	3,265
1971	769.0	3.7	3,714	691.9	3.4	3,342
1972	801.3	4.2	3,837	733.0	5.9	3,510
1973	854.7	6.7	4,062	767.7	4.7	3,649
1974	840.8	-1.6	3,468	759.1	-1.1	3,582
1975	855.5	1.7	4,006	770.3	1.5	3,607
1976	890.5	4.1	4,140	813.7	5.6	3,783

Sources: Data based on Bureau of Economic Analysis calculations appearing in *Historical Statistics* and *Statistical Abstract.*

Note: Index converted to 1972 base by Wharton Econometric Forecasting Associates, University of Pennsylvania.

quiet economically. The 1972 base fits these criteria in that it predates the 1973 inflationary swell which followed the Vietnam War and the dramatic oil-price increases.

The best known of the indexes used by the federal government to calculate the GNP Price Deflator figures is the Consumer Price Index (CPI), which is shown for the years 1900-1976 in **Table 300-B.** The Consumer Price Index measures changes in retail prices of goods and services bought by urban wage earners and clerical workers. Often referred to as the "Cost of Living Index," the Consumer Price Index will usually parallel GNP patterns to a degree. The CPI is also the best comparative inflationary control for such media data as cost of newspapers or magazines, book prices, and radio and television receiver prices. The figures in **Table 300-B** are national annual averages of the monthly CPI reports.

Table 300-C provides a measure of income and overall consumer expenditures in the post-World War II years. Nearly all of the data in this table are already converted to constant (1972) dollars, thereby allowing an easy comparison of true changes in "disposable personal income" and in "personal consumption expenditures." (The former is the personal income that remains after all tax and other obligatory payments to government. The latter includes the market value of purchases of goods and services by individuals and nonprofit institutions, plus the value of food, clothing, housing—rentals but not purchases—and financial services received by individuals and non-profit institutions as income in kind.)

The "median family income" category in **Table 300-C** is the average annual income received by families with a male head of household. These figures are expressed here in both current and constant (1972) dollars.

Sources

For a discussion of both the reliability and the development of the data in **Table 300-A**, the reader should refer to *Historical Statistics* (1975), pp. 183-184. Note, however, that the data here have been converted with 1972 as the base index year, rather than the 1958 base used in *Historical Statistics*.

Table 300-B is based primarily on U.S. Bureau of Labor Statistics data, as reprinted in *Historical Statistics* (1975) (the 1971-76 data are reprinted in the *Statistical Abstract*). The CPI figures prior to 1912 were estimated by the editors from other sources and then adapted for as much comparability as possible with later index figures. For a discussion of the CPI's development and reliability, see *Historical Statistics* (1975), pp. 191-192.

In **Table 300-C**, the median annual family income figures come from the U.S. Census Bureau, as reprinted in *Historical Statistics* (1975). The data since 1974 are not strictly comparable due to revised procedures by the Census Bureau. The statistics for disposable personal income and for personal consumption expenditures are based on U.S. Bureau of Economic Analysis calculations, with basic data found in *Historical Statistics* and *Statistical Abstract*. These are estimates rounded to represent national annual averages, but the base data are considered quite accurate by the U.S. Department of Commerce.

Further Information

Historical Statistics (1975), Part 1, chapters E, F, and G, provides a helpful background discussion on the development, uses, and validity of these government economic descriptors up to 1970. The annual *Statistical Abstract* provides similar information for the years after 1970. In early 1978, the Consumer Price Index was split into two parts each month—a new "All-Urban Index," which represents 80 percent of the nation's population, and the previously existing "Wage-earner Index," which covers about 40 percent of the population. See the *New York Times* (December 30, 1977), p. B4, for background on this change.

Consumer Expenditures for Media Products and Services 301

Interpretation of Tables

Table 301-A was developed by the editors as a special "Consumer Price Index" for various kinds of media-related expenditures by U.S. consumers since 1935. Using 1972 as the base year (1972=100) for this index, the reader can compare the variations in the costs to the public of the different media products and services. **Table 301-B** then translates these cost indicators into the constant (1972) dollar sums expended on the media by the American consumer per year per household.

Unfortunately, comparisons between the two tables are limited by the aggregations of media categories in **Table 301-B**. The combination of maps with books in **Table 301-B** remains fairly comparable, given the presumed dominance of book expenditures in that category. But the mixing of newspapers with periodicals and sheet music, or of broadcast receivers with recordings and musical instruments, makes it nearly impossible to get a clear image of the true dollar value of consumer spending in these areas.

Only the categories of "motion picture admissions" and "radio-TV repairs" are identical in both tables and therefore fully comparable. Indeed, the U.S. Commerce Department's special Consumer Price Index (CPI) series for the motion picture industry was used by the editors to establish the constant dollar figures for the other media categories. The reader should be aware, however, that because of the use of this special CPI series for motion pictures, the figures for motion pictures admissions are not directly comparable to the other media categories in **Table**

Table 301–A.
U. S. Consumer Price Index for Media Expenditures, 1935–1976

Note: Base index figure of 100 is for the year 1972.

	Overall Recreational Expenditures	Newspapers	Periodicals	Motion Picture Admissions	Stereo Disc Recordings	Portable Tape Recorders	Table Radios	Television Receivers	Radio-TV Repairs
1935	34.0	22.8	--	17.6	--	--	--	--	--
1936	34.6	23.1	--	18.0	--	--	--	--	--
1937	35.6	23.6	--	18.7	--	--	--	--	--
1938	36.8	24.9	--	19.0	--	--	--	--	--
1939	36.9	25.4	--	18.7	--	--	--	--	--
1940	37.5	25.6	--	19.2	--	--	--	--	--
1941	38.8	25.9	--	20.2	--	--	--	--	--
1942	40.7	27.0	--	21.3	--	--	--	--	--
1943	44.1	29.1	--	23.2	--	--	--	--	--
1944	48.9	30.2	--	26.8	--	--	--	--	--
1945	50.8	31.0	--	28.2	--	--	--	--	--
1946	52.5	32.1	--	29.0	--	--	--	--	--
1947	55.9	35.1	--	30.4	--	--	--	--	--
1948	58.9	38.6	--	30.7	--	--	--	--	--
1949	61.0	41.0	--	31.4	--	--	--	--	--
1950	60.6	41.3	--	31.3	--	--	133.5	--	--
1951	62.4	42.4	--	31.8	--	--	146.6	157.1	--
1952	62.6	44.5	--	32.1	--	--	148.0	138.6	--
1953	63.3	46.3	--	33.6	--	--	146.5	133.3	--
1954	62.6	46.3	--	35.8	--	--	140.7	124.5	--
1955	62.5	47.2	--	37.6	--	--	135.4	117.4	--
1956	63.4	47.4	--	38.4	--	--	130.9	117.9	--
1957	65.7	51.9	--	40.3	--	--	133.5	123.0	--
1958	68.3	55.3	--	41.8	--	--	130.4	126.2	--
1959	69.5	55.9	--	43.2	--	--	128.8	126.8	--
1960	71.1	57.0	--	45.9	--	--	126.5	127.7	--
1961	72.7	58.4	--	48.3	--	--	124.3	124.4	--
1962	74.3	59.6	--	50.4	--	--	120.3	118.3	--
1963	76.7	63.3	--	52.4	--	--	118.5	115.3	--
1964	77.4	68.3	70.2	56.6	94.8	111.0	115.9	112.7	--
1965	78.1	70.4	71.8	61.1	94.0	108.5	109.7	107.8	--
1966	79.4	72.8	74.0	65.7	93.6	106.8	102.9	102.6	--
1967	81.4	75.6	76.1	70.7	93.2	106.0	101.1	100.5	--
1968	85.3	80.3	79.9	77.4	92.0	102.4	100.7	100.3	--
1969	88.5	84.2	85.1	83.8	92.5	101.9	100.1	100.1	--
1970	92.3	90.2	89.7	91.9	93.1	100.6	99.9	100.3	--
1971	97.1	98.0	95.2	97.2	96.5	99.9	99.6	100.6	99.7
1972	100.0	100.0	100.0	100.0	100.0	100.0	100.0	100.0	100.0
1973	102.5	102.6	102.9	104.1	101.1	99.0	100.5	98.5	101.6
1974	109.0	117.5	105.0	111.1	105.5	101.0	103.0	99.4	103.6
1975	117.6	131.9	125.0	120.7	114.1	101.2	105.2	102.1	107.0
1976	123.1	137.6	140.9	125.4	115.3	101.7	106.4	103.4	109.0

Source: Consumer Price Index.

301-B. In 1935, for example, if we were to use the general CPI recreational expenditures figures, rather than those from the CPI film industry series, the motion picture admission figure would be only $50.44 instead of the more accurate $97.44. The editors used the separate CPI series for motion pictures in order to attain the most accurate film data, even at the cost of cross-media comparability.

Taken together, even with the limitations noted above, the two tables demonstrate the increasing costs of the print media as compared to the other media, and the declining index for broadcast receivers and recorders. The declines in the latter are due mainly to heavy competition from foreign manufacturers in recent years.

Sources

The data for **Table 301-A** are taken from the Consumer Price Index, which is issued on a monthly basis by the Bureau of Labor Statistics (BLS) of the U.S. Department of Labor. The figures prior to 1962—from the CPI (September 1962)—were originally expressed on a base index of 1957=100. Data since 1962 come from summary December issues of the CPI. The 1962-71

Table 301-B.
Annual Per-Household Media Expenditures by U. S. Consumers, 1935-1976

Note: All figures in constant 1972 dollars.

	Books, Maps	Newspapers, Magazines, Sheet Music	Motion Picture Admissions	Radio-TV Sets, Recordings, Musical Instruments	Radio-TV Repairs
1935	$16.59	$41.36	$ 97.44	$ 22.50	$ 1.91
1936	18.26	43.00	105.61	29.21	1.85
1937	20.41	43.18	108.13	32.33	1.94
1938	17.69	41.15	102.79	27.15	2.01
1939	17.78	43.59	102.30	33.04	2.20
1940	17.85	44.94	109.53	37.68	2.45
1941	18.33	45.72	111.73	43.63	2.58
1942	19.62	47.39	131.64	42.73	3.10
1943	22.51	51.53	149.04	24.78	3.70
1944	24.80	48.51	134.89	17.14	3.97
1945	27.30	50.66	137.13	18.05	4.63
1946	29.38	54.82	152.80	55.68	5.73
1947	24.29	56.86	134.08	63.95	6.40
1948	24.46	57.55	121.03	60.73	7.28
1949	24.37	56.51	109.55	65.10	8.34
1950	25.54	56.64	100.94	91.73	10.73
1951	27.84	56.43	92.21	80.21	12.66
1952	27.64	59.25	85.24	82.40	13.79
1953	28.27	60.49	76.16	88.14	14.77
1954	27.42	62.08	73.04	92.73	16.39
1955	28.98	62.46	73.67	95.89	17.25
1956	30.67	60.64	72.23	94.76	18.49
1957	30.12	60.46	56.25	86.56	19.24
1958	29.65	59.78	47.02	81.57	19.75
1959	30.44	59.22	42.93	84.51	19.97
1960	30.34	57.65	39.45	79.99	20.62
1961	31.13	52.03	36.92	81.16	21.19
1962	31.63	56.65	34.24	82.31	21.18
1963	33.33	58.22	32.52	86.38	21.32
1964	37.09	57.48	29.92	98.00	21.40
1965	36.74	59.34	30.41	112.38	20.80
1966	39.68	67.49	29.16	133.85	20.40
1967	38.31	66.49	26.93	144.18	20.72
1968	37.42	68.19	27.49	146.38	20.38
1969	37.80	64.51	26.85	148.29	19.65
1970	40.26	66.64	26.10	151.83	18.44
1971	39.13	67.41	25.82	151.58	18.08
1972	37.94	70.27	24.66	164.44	18.33
1973	39.58	83.55	27.66	175.65	19.07
1974	39.84	92.52	32.15	174.22	16.28
1975	40.61	89.70	29.57	174.28	16.92
1976	40.02	90.21	32.69	179.10	16.43

Sources: 1957-1958 data: *Historical Statistics* (1975), series H 878-893. 1958-1959 data: *National Income and Product Accounts of the United States, 1929-74* (1977), pp. 90-91. 1973-1976 data: *Survey of Current Business* (July 1977), table 2.6, p. 29. Although not specified on the table, the number of households each year was developed from McCombs (1972), pp. 74-75, for 1935-1954 figures; *Historical Statistics* (1975), series A 288-319, for 1955-1970 figures; and *Current Population Reports* (August 1977), series P-20, No. 311, table A, for 1971-1976 figures.

data were also originally calculated with the base index of 1957=100, while the data after 1971 were expressed on a new base index of 1967=100.

The editors converted all of these index figures to a base of 1972=100 (conversions were made from the 1957 to the 1967 index, then converted again to the 1972 index figures shown in the table). All of the relevant index figures available from the Bureau of Labor Statistics are included in this table. The few gaps in this material are due to the fact that many of the media-related indexes were not being figured by the BLS until the mid-1960s. The reader should refer to any issue of the Consumer Price Index for a detailed discussion of how the index is derived and how the data are limited.

As with **Table 301-A**, the information in **Table 301-B** was developed by the editors, using the several primary government sources listed below. The available data were converted by the editors to a per-household basis by dividing the number of U.S. households into the total aggregate consumer-expenditures figure. Then the figures were converted again to constant (1972) dollars in order to control for inflation.

The data for number of households each year, though not specified on the table, were developed from the following sources: McCombs (1972), for the 1935-54 figures; *Historical Statistics* (1975), for the 1955-70 figures; and *Current Population Reports* (August 1977), for the 1971-76 figures.

The media-expenditures data were obtained by dividing total recreational expenditures figures from the following three sources:

- *Historical Statistics* (1975), for data through 1957-58. (This source was used only through 1957 for the two "radio-TV" categories. All other columns used this source through 1958.)

- *National Income and Product Accounts of the United States, 1929-74* (1977), for data from 1958-59 through 1972. (See the comments below regarding this source.)

- *Survey of Current Business* (July 1977), for 1973-76 figures.

The accuracy of the information in **Table 301-B** is somewhat limited by the use of several different sources and by the federal government's substantial revision in the mid-1970s of much of the data for the 1958-72 period. Thus, the figures shown here will *not* agree with those derived from, say, *Historical Statistics*, since the post-1958 information was substantially revised and appears in its revised form only in the recently published *National Income and Product Accounts of the United States, 1929-74*. The differences per column range to $20 and more in some years.

Further Information

The most current source for information on media-related consumer expenditures is the monthly Consumer Price Index. The December issue of the CPI also provides annual figures and comparisons with the previous year. Information on actual dollar expenditures per household can be traced back to 1929 in *Historical Statistics* (1975), series H 878-893. The latest and most consistent single source on consumer expenditures is the reference book by the U.S. Commerce Department's Bureau of Economic Analysis, *National Income and Product Accounts of the United States, 1929-1974* (1977). An interesting earlier analysis of much of this information, and many other related statistical runs from 1929 to the late 1960s, is found in McCombs (1972).

Consumer vs. Advertiser Investments in the Media
30?

Interpretation of Tables

It is generally assumed that advertising is the primary source of support for most of the mass media in the United States. But as **Tables 302-A** and **302-B** demonstrate, this assumption is an exaggeration. Books and films, of course, are supported almost entirely by direct consumer investment, with only negligible levels of advertising revenue. And even in the newspaper, magazine, and broadcasting industries, the data indicate that the support role of advertising has been less important over the years than one would have expected.

Table 302–A.
Consumer vs. Advertiser Investment in Newspapers and Magazines
in U.S., 1947–1972

	Newspapers				Magazines			
	Advertising Receipts	Percent of Total Receipts	Consumer Expenditures	Percent of Total Receipts	Advertising Receipts	Percent of Total Receipts	Consumer Expenditures	Percent of Total Receipts
1947	$1,192.4	66.5%	$ 599.9	33.5%	$ 612.5	60.1%	$ 407.0	39.9%
1954	2,043.7	71.0	834.9	29.0	863.5	61.9	530.6	38.1
1958	2,443.9	71.4	979.3	28.6	982.9	63.9	555.9	36.1
1963	3,032.5	72.5	1,147.3	27.5	N/A	N/A	N/A	N/A
1967	3,895.7	73.7	1,387.3	26.3	1,499.4	61.7	930.1	38.3
1972	5,600.3	75.1	1,853.7	24.9	1,693.4	56.6	1,298.3	43.4

Source: *Census of Manufactures.*

Table 302–B.
Consumer vs. Advertiser Expenditures
for the U. S. Broadcasting Industry, 1930–1974

Five-Year Period	Average Annual Consumer Expenditures		Average Annual Advertiser Expenditures	
	Receiver Purchase/ Repair	Percent of Total Expenditures	Radio-Television Advertising	Percent of Total Expenditures
1930-34	$ 1,141,000	95%	$ 57,640	5%
1935-39	1,818,000	92	150,080	8
1940-44	1,113,000	80	285,980	20
1945-49	3,615,000	88	515,100	12
1950-54	8,106,000	88	1,075,600	12
1955-59	7,216,000	79	1,870,080	21
1960-64	7,887,000	75	2,649,260	25
1965-69	12,200,000	75	4,095,600	25
1970-74	21,074,000	79	5,691,600	21

Source: Calculated by the editors from data in Tables 660-A and 660-B, which utilized data from *Broadcasting Yearbook 1977*, pp. B-175 (television) and C-310-311 (radio).

Note: Add 000 to dollar figures, which represent averages of current dollar values for five-year periods.

Table 302-A compares, for several selected post-war years, the total advertising receipts of U.S. newspapers and magazines, with the total consumer expenditures (subscriptions and per-copy sales) for these print media. In the case of newspapers, the support role of advertising has become *more* important in recent years, despite the steadily increasing prices per copy for newspapers (see Unit 322). Whereas two-thirds of the income of newspapers came from advertising in 1947, the proportion had risen to three-quarters by the early 1970s. Earlier data, not reprinted here, indicate that during the 1920s, only about one-half of newspaper income derived from advertising. (See Unit 321 for a breakdown of advertising and circulation revenues in the newspaper industry.)

Magazines, in contrast, are moving in the opposite direction—back to their original position of being almost entirely reader-supported. The trend here is recent and very gradual, and there are considerable differences by type of magazine (see Unit 330). More specialized magazines, for example, generally require much greater reader support. However, the increases in the U.S. postal rates for magazines in the 1970s, along with a number of other economic factors (higher paper and printing costs, declining readership, competition from television), have resulted in a general trend toward more reader support of the publication costs of all types of magazines.

Table 302-B offers a comparison of advertiser and consumer expenditures in the broadcasting industry. We generally think of radio and television as strictly advertiser-supported media. But in doing so, we are overlooking the consumer's investment in receivers and in the repair of this equipment. Thus, Table 302-B directly compares the average consumer investment in the broadcasting industry (for receiver purchase and repair) over five-year periods, versus the average total advertiser expenditures in the industry. Clearly, the public's investment has been far greater than that of the advertiser.

The sharp increases in consumer expenditures in the 1950-54 and 1965-74 periods were due to the initial wave of purchases, first, of black-and-white television sets and then of the more expensive color receivers. The decline in consumer expenditures in the 1940-44 period are due to a ban on the manufacture of radios during most of the war years. (See Unit 660 for further data on consumer investments in receivers, and Units 370 and 380 for figures on the broadcast industry's advertising revenues.)

Sources

The information in Table 302-A comes from appropriate issues of the *Census of Manufactures*. Daily, Sunday, and weekly newspapers are included in the newspaper figures in this table. The magazine figures combine data from various subcategories of periodicals—usually farm publications, specialized business and professional magazines, general magazines (comics, women/home, general interest/entertainment, and general news), and a miscellaneous category of "other" periodicals (religious magazines, newspaper supplements, etc.).

Table 302-B data on consumer expenditures for radio/television receivers were calculated by the editors from the figures on sales of broadcast receivers in Tables 660-A and 660-B. These figures, in turn, were taken from *Broadcasting Yearbook 1977*. Because there was no available information on *radio* retail sales for the years 1950-57, the editors estimated an average sales figure of $2.1 billion for both the 1950-54 and 1955-59 periods. (The averaged total for radio sales for 1945-49 was $2.6 billion; for 1960-64, $1.9 billion.) The reader should refer to the "Sources" section in Unit 660 for a discussion of some other serious reliability problems with the figures in Tables 660-A and 660-B. However, the trend indicated by these data remains valid.

Radio-TV repair figures, which were added by the editors to the consumer-expenditures totals, were taken from *Historical Statistics* (1975), for the years 1930-1970, and from *Statistical Abstract* for 1970-1974. The editors averaged the totals for each five-year period.

The advertiser-expenditures totals were calculated by the editors from the revenue figures in Units 370 (radio) and 380 (television). See those units for the several government and industry sources of the base data.

Due to the averaging and the wide variety of sources for Table 302-B, the figures must be regarded as little more than approximate estimates, which are intended only to indicate trends.

Further Information

For a very interesting attempt to arrive, by a different route, at answers to the question of advertiser versus consumer support of the mass media, see McCombs (1972).

Table 303–A.
Estimated Annual Expenditures of Advertisers in U. S., 1890–1934

Year	Total in Current Dollars	Total in Constant (1972) Dollars	Percent Change in Constant Dollars
	Note: All dollar figures are in millions.		
1890	$ 300	N/A	N/A
1900	450	N/A	N/A
1904	750	N/A	N/A
1909	1,000	$5,405	N/A
1914	1,100	5,584	3.3%
1915	1,100	5,314	-4.8
1916	1,240	5,345	-0.6
1917	1,380	4,842	-9.4
1918	1,240	4,039	-16.6
1919	1,930	5,273	30.6
1920	2,480	5,808	10.1
1921	1,930	5,530	-4.8
1922	2,200	6,790	22.8
1923	2,400	7,143	5.2
1924	2,480	7,492	4.9
1925	2,600	7,692	2.7
1926	2,700	8,108	5.4
1927	2,720	8,369	3.2
1928	2,760	8,415	0.1
1929	2,850	8,689	3.3
1930	2,450	7,729	-11.0
1931	2,100	7,317	-5.3
1932	1,620	6,353	-13.2
1933	1,325	5,321	-16.2
1934	1,650	6,111	14.8

Sources: Current dollar figures from Robert J. Coen of McCann-Erickson, Inc. Editors added constant dollar figures based on GNP price deflator.

Interpretation of Tables

This unit provides some aggregate national data on trends in advertiser expenditures on the various media in the United States. **Table 303-A**, which estimates the total annual advertiser expenditures from 1890 through 1934, primarily illustrates the impact of World War I and the Great Depression on the advertising industry. **Table 303-B** continues this time series with both aggregate and individual-media figures for the 1935-1976 period.

In **Table 303-B**, the category of radio and television "spot" advertising refers to commercials which are placed by an advertiser or agency on a regional or national basis, without using the services of the radio or television networks. In other words, the commercials are "spotted" by advertisers among the specific stations or areas they wish to reach. Some network stations or affiliates may carry this advertising, but the networks themselves are not parties to the advertising contract. The "miscellaneous" category in **Table 303-B** includes such advertising vehicles as weekly newspapers, telephone directory yellow pages, point-of-purchase advertising, and handbills. These miscellaneous figures are estimates based on a standard 20 percent of the total figure.

Table 303–B.
Total Advertiser Expenditures on U. S. Media,
by Medium and Type of Advertising, 1935–1976

Type of Advertising	1935	1936	1937	1938	1939
	Note: All figures in millions of dollars.				
Newspapers					
Total Expenditures	$ 761	$ 842	$ 870	$ 782	$ 793
National	148	166	166	148	152
Local	613	676	704	634	641
Magazines					
Total Expenditures	130	154	181	158	169
In Weekly Magazines	54	67	83	75	88
In Women's Magazines	51	57	60	52	49
In Monthly Magazines	25	30	38	31	32
Farm Publications Expenditures	10	12	19	14	17
Television					
Total Expenditures	- -	- -	- -	- -	- -
Network	- -	- -	- -	- -	- -
Spot	- -	- -	- -	- -	- -
Local	- -	- -	- -	- -	- -
Radio					
Total Expenditures	113	122	165	167	184
Network	63	75	89	89	99
Spot	15	23	28	34	35
Local	35	24	48	44	50
Direct Mail Expenditures	282	319	333	324	333
Business Papers Expenditures	51	61	70	61	69
Outdoor					
Total Expenditures	31	38	44	43	44
National	23	28	33	32	33
Local	8	10	11	11	11
Miscellaneous					
Total Expenditures	342	382	418	381	401
National	168	192	211	200	213
Local	174	190	207	181	188
Total Expenditures					
National	890	1,030	1,130	1,060	1,120
Local	830	900	970	870	890
GRAND TOTAL	$1,720	$1,930	$2,100	$1,930	$2,010
Total in Constant (1972) Dollars	$6,255	$6,993	$7,241	$6,820	$7,128

Clearly, newspapers are the largest advertising medium, mainly because of their continued dominance of local advertising. Radio was given a boost during World War II, when paper-rationing limited the opportunities to advertise in the print media. However, after the war, the radio networks lost much of their national advertising business to television, which very quickly rose to the dominant position in broadcasting by using the structural and financial base already established by radio.

Table 303-C, based on the figures in **Table 303-B**, reveals each advertising medium's percentage share of the total advertiser expenditures. The table also shows the real growth (or decline) of advertiser expenditures according to the constant (1972) dollar totals at the bottom of **Table 303-B**.

Table 303-D provides a 13-year time series on changes in the advertising rates of the various media. The table is in the form of a cost-per-thousand (CPM) index, with the base figure of 100 for the year 1970. The CPM rate index is the common denominator that allows comparison be-

Table 303–B. (Cont'd.)

Type of Advertising	1940	1941	1942	1943	1944
Newspapers					
Total Expenditures	$ 815	$ 844	$ 797	$ 899	$ 886
National	161	162	141	180	191
Local	654	682	656	719	695
Magazines					
Total Expenditures	186	201	187	259	305
In Weekly Magazines	103	117	107	154	172
In Women's Magazines	49	52	52	66	82
In Monthly Magazines	34	32	28	39	51
Farm Publications Expenditures	19	19	18	25	29
Television					
Total Expenditures	- -	- -	- -	- -	- -
Network	- -	- -	- -	- -	- -
Spot	- -	- -	- -	- -	- -
Local	- -	- -	- -	- -	- -
Radio					
Total Expenditures	215	247	260	314	393
Network	113	125	129	157	192
Spot	42	52	59	71	87
Local	60	70	72	86	114
Direct Mail Expenditures	334	353	329	322	326
Business Papers Expenditures	76	89	98	142	177
Outdoor					
Total Expenditures	45	53	44	42	56
National	34	37	31	29	39
Local	11	16	13	13	17
Miscellaneous					
Total Expenditures	420	444	427	487	528
National	225	242	228	270	309
Local	195	202	199	217	219
Total Expenditures					
National	1,190	1,280	1,220	1,455	1,655
Local	920	970	940	1,035	1,045
GRAND TOTAL	$2,110	$2,250	$2,160	$2,490	$2,700
Total in Constant (1972) Dollars	$7,326	$7,401	$6,646	$7,074	$7,377

tween media advertising priced in different ways—that is, by lines or column inches in the print media or by airtime for broadcasting. The index enables the advertiser to determine which medium is the most economical means of reaching 1,000 households with a given advertising message. The figures in **Table 303-D** are aggregate national CPMs, but advertisers also develop specialized CPMs for particular characteristics of the audience, such as sex, location, age, and interests.

Actual CPM-advertising rates have generally climbed sharply since the mid-1960s, especially among newspapers and the television networks. As **Table 303-E** indicates, only the radio networks show a decline in advertising rates in 1975. Because the figures in **Table 303-E** are derived from a wide range of sources, it is unlikely that any two lists purporting to provide such national data will agree. Suffice it to say that increases in magazine and radio advertising rates have been small in comparison to the increases for the higher-demand local newspapers and national television advertising outlets.

Table 303–B. (Cont'd.)

Type of Advertising	1945	1946	1947	1948	1949
Newspapers					
Total Expenditures	$ 919	$1,155	$1,471	$1,745	$1,911
National	203	238	323	379	463
Local	716	917	1,148	1,366	1,448
Magazines					
Total Expenditures	344	405	464	477	458
In Weekly Magazines	188	202	246	258	245
In Women's Magazines	97	127	133	133	129
In Monthly Magazines	59	76	85	86	84
Farm Publications Expenditures	32	36	49	56	55
Television					
Total Expenditures	- -	- -	- -	- -	58
Network	- -	- -	- -	- -	30
Spot	- -	- -	- -	- -	9
Local	- -	- -	- -	- -	19
Radio					
Total Expenditures	424	455	506	562	571
Network	198	200	201	211	203
Spot	92	98	106	121	123
Local	134	157	199	230	245
Direct Mail Expenditures	290	334	579	689	756
Business Papers Expenditures	204	211	233	251	248
Outdoor					
Total Expenditures	72	86	121	132	131
National	50	60	79	89	88
Local	22	26	42	43	43
Miscellaneous					
Total Expenditures	555	658	837	958	1,022
National	327	368	466	522	557
Local	228	290	371	436	465
Total Expenditures					
National	1,740	1,950	2,500	2,795	2,990
Local	1,100	1,390	1,760	2,075	2,220
GRAND TOTAL	$2,840	$3,340	$4,260	$4,870	$5,210
Total in Constant (1972) Dollars	$7,553	$7,608	$8,571	$9,171	$9,905

Sources

The data in **Tables 303-A** and **303-B** were supplied directly by Robert J. Coen of McCann-Erickson, Inc., who has been developing these statistics since 1950. The base for Mr. Coen's work was established by his two predecessors in the Marketing Services Research Department of McCann-Erickson. All of the figures are estimates, and their validity varies greatly, depending on the medium in question. Most accurate are the broadcast figures, which are taken from FCC annual financial reports. Coen reports that the newspaper and magazine information has been verified by several different sources and may be also considered fairly accurate. The newspaper data are for daily and Sunday papers only.

The outdoor, direct mail, and miscellaneous categories are most subject to wide variations, but Coen estimates that the overall trends and total figures are within 10 percent of actual practice. The more recent information is generally the most reliable.

Table 303-C was calculated by the editors from the information in **Table 303-B**. The **Table 303-D** data for 1965-1970 are taken from *Encyclomedia: 1977 Newspaper Edition*, which collected the information from the following sources:

Table 303–B. (Cont'd.)

Type of Advertising	1950	1951	1952	1953	1954
Newspapers					
Total Expenditures	$2,070	$2,251	$2,464	$2,632	$2,685
National	518	529	537	606	607
Local	1,552	1,722	1,927	2,026	2,078
Magazines					
Total Expenditures	478	535	575	627	629
In Weekly Magazines	261	297	325	351	363
In Women's Magazines	129	143	149	158	152
In Monthly Magazines	88	95	101	118	114
Farm Publications Expenditures	58	64	70	71	71
Television					
Total Expenditures	171	332	454	606	809
Network	85	181	256	320	422
Spot	31	70	94	145	207
Local	55	81	104	141	180
Radio					
Total Expenditures	605	606	624	611	559
Network	196	180	162	141	114
Spot	136	138	141	146	135
Local	273	288	321	324	310
Direct Mail Expenditures	803	924	1,024	1,099	1,202
Business Papers Expenditures	251	292	365	395	408
Outdoor					
Total Expenditures	142	149	162	176	187
National	96	101	109	119	126
Local	46	48	53	57	61
Miscellaneous					
Total Expenditures	1,122	1,267	1,402	1,523	1,600
National	608	696	767	846	899
Local	514	571	635	677	701
Total Expenditures					
National	3,260	3,710	4,100	4,515	4,820
Local	2,440	2,710	3,040	3,225	3,330
GRAND TOTAL	$5,700	$6,420	$7,140	$7,740	$8,150
Total in Constant (1972) Dollars	$10,634	$11,204	$12,310	$13,141	$13,652

- For newspapers—Newspaper Advertising Bureau and J. Walter Thompson Co. (Estimates are based on the cost of 1,000 lines in black-and-white.)

- For consumer magazines—Magazine Advertising Bureau and J. Walter Thompson Co. (Estimates are based on the cost of a one-page, four-color advertisement.)

- For network radio—the radio networks, RADAR research, and J. Walter Thompson Co. (Estimates are based on the cost of 60-second announcements.)

- For radio spots—Pulse, Inc., and J. Walter Thompson Co. (Estimates are based on the cost of 60-second announcements.)

- For network television, prime-time, daytime, and spots—A. C. Nielsen Co. and J. Walter Thompson Co. (Estimates are based on the cost of 30-second announcements.)

Table 303–B. (Cont'd.)

Type of Advertising	1955	1956	1957	1958	1959
Newspapers					
Total Expenditures	$3,077	$3,223	$ 3,268	$ 3,176	$ 3,526
National	712	754	768	724	773
Local	2,365	2,469	2,500	2,452	2,753
Magazines					
Total Expenditures	691	758	777	734	832
In Weekly Magazines	397	440	451	425	479
In Women's Magazines	161	166	165	151	168
In Monthly Magazines	133	152	161	158	185
Farm Publications Expenditures	72	73	71	67	71
Television					
Total Expenditures	1,035	1,225	1,286	1,387	1,529
Network	550	643	690	742	776
Spot	260	329	352	397	486
Local	225	253	244	248	267
Radio					
Total Expenditures	545	567	618	620	656
Network	84	60	63	58	44
Spot	134	161	187	190	206
Local	327	346	368	372	406
Direct Mail Expenditures	1,299	1,419	1,471	1,589	1,688
Business Papers Expenditures	446	496	568	525	569
Outdoor					
Total Expenditures	192	201	199	192	193
National	130	136	134	130	130
Local	62	65	65	62	63
Miscellaneous					
Total Expenditures	1,793	1,948	2,012	2,020	2,206
National	1,002	1,111	1,169	1,184	1,280
Local	791	837	843	836	926
Total Expenditures					
National	5,380	5,940	6,250	6,340	6,855
Local	3,770	3,970	4,020	3,970	4,415
GRAND TOTAL	$9,150	$9,910	$10,270	$10,310	$11,270
Total in Constant (1972) Dollars	$15,000	$15,755	$15,800	$15,621	$16,696

The 1971-78 data in **Table 303**-D are estimates from Ted Bates & Co., as reprinted in *Broadcasting*. Based on the same unit-cost structures outlined above, the Ted Bates figures are, in general, closer to actual industry buying experience than the 1965-1970 data from *Encyclomedia*.

Because *Encyclomedia* also includes figures through 1975, the editors were able to compare the Ted Bates and the *Encyclomedia* findings for the 1971-1975 period. For newspapers, the two sets of figures are very close, with only 1-3 percentage points of variance. For magazines, the variance is about 5 points; for spot radio, about 1-3 points; and for prime-time network television, about 4 points. Larger differences are found in the two sets of figures for network radio (10 percentage points), for network daytime television (2-18 points—the latter in 1975), and for spot television (from 5 points in 1971 to 40 points by 1975). In every case except magazines, the Ted Bates figures are the lower of the two.

Table 303–B. (Cont'd.)

Type of Advertising	1960	1961	1962	1963	1964
Newspapers					
Total Expenditures	$ 3,681	$ 3,601	$ 3,659	$ 3,780	$ 4,120
National	778	744	722	702	773
Local	2,903	2,857	2,937	3,078	3,347
Magazines					
Total Expenditures	909	895	942	1,002	1,074
In Weekly Magazines	525	508	519	540	583
In Women's Magazines	184	187	200	218	231
In Monthly Magazines	200	200	223	244	260
Farm Publications Expenditures	66	62	65	66	66
Television					
Total Expenditures	1,627	1,691	1,897	2,032	2,289
Network	820	887	976	1,025	1,132
Spot	527	548	629	698	806
Local	280	256	292	309	351
Radio					
Total Expenditures	693	683	736	789	846
Network	43	43	46	56	59
Spot	222	220	233	243	256
Local	428	420	457	490	531
Direct Mail Expenditures	1,830	1,850	1,933	2,078	2,184
Business Papers Expenditures	609	578	597	615	623
Outdoor					
Total Expenditures	203	180	171	171	175
National	137	122	115	115	117
Local	66	58	56	56	58
Miscellaneous					
Total Expenditures	2,342	2,320	2,430	2,567	2,773
National	1,364	1,366	1,437	1,520	1,630
Local	978	954	993	1,047	1,143
Total Expenditures					
National	7,305	7,315	7,695	8,120	8,720
Local	4,655	4,545	4,735	4,980	5,430
GRAND TOTAL	$11,960	$11,860	$12,430	$13,100	$14,150
Total in Constant (1972) Dollars	$17,409	$17,114	$17,606	$18,296	$19,464

The closeness of the two sets of figures for most of the media categories suggests that the estimation process by the two sources is quite good. The marked variance for spot television is probably due to the greater difficulty—and, therefore, lesser reliability—of calculating a national index average for such a large and segmented field as spot television advertising.

The average advertising rates in **Table 303-E** were gathered from the following sources:

● Newspapers—supplied directly to the editors by the Newspaper Advertising Bureau. The Newspaper Advertising Bureau based its figures on a May 1977 study by the Marketing Services Research Department of McCann-Erickson, Inc., using various trade and government primary sources. The Research Department of McCann-Erickson can also supply 1975-1976 rates by size of circulation.

Table 303–B. (Cont'd.)

Type of Advertising	1965	1966	1967	1968	1969
Newspapers					
Total Expenditures	$ 4,426	$ 4,865	$ 4,910	$ 5,232	$ 5,714
National	784	887	846	889	943
Local	3,642	3,978	4,064	4,343	4,771
Magazines					
Total Expenditures	1,161	1,254	1,245	1,283	1,344
In Weekly Magazines	610	658	651	657	662
In Women's Magazines	269	280	282	284	308
In Monthly Magazines	282	316	312	342	374
Farm Publications Expenditures	71	70	68	68	64
Television					
Total Expenditures	2,515	2,823	2,909	3,231	3,585
Network	1,237	1,393	1,455	1,523	1,678
Spot	892	988	988	1,131	1,253
Local	386	442	466	577	654
Radio					
Total Expenditures	917	1,010	1,048	1,190	1,264
Network	60	63	64	63	59
Spot	275	308	314	360	368
Local	582	639	670	767	837
Direct Mail Expenditures	2,324	2,461	2,488	2,612	2,670
Business Papers Expenditures	671	712	707	714	752
Outdoor					
Total Expenditures	180	178	191	208	213
National	120	118	126	137	138
Local	60	60	65	71	75
Miscellaneous					
Total Expenditures	2,985	3,257	3,304	3,552	3,814
National	1,745	1,896	1,909	2,020	2,131
Local	1,240	1,361	1,395	1,532	1,683
Total Expenditures					
National	9,340	10,150	10,210	10,800	11,400
Local	5,910	6,480	6,660	7,290	8,020
GRAND TOTAL	$15,250	$16,630	$16,870	$18,090	$19,420
Total in Constant (1972) Dollars	$20,525	$21,654	$21,354	$21,900	$22,399

- Magazines—Chapin (1957), for the 1950 rates, and Magazine Publishers Association for the 1965 and 1975 figures.

- Radio—the 1965 figures were supplied to the editors by James Quinn of the J. Walter Thompson Research Department. The 1975 data were taken from "How Media Costs in Nine Media Changed in 6 Years, 1970-1975," in *Media Decisions* (August 1976).

- Television—A. C. Nielsen Co., as reprinted in *Broadcasting Basics II* (Fall 1976).

Table 303–B. (Cont'd.)

Type of Advertising	1970	1971	1972	1973	1974	1975	1976[a]
Newspapers							
Total Expenditures	$ 5,704	$ 6,198	$ 7,008	$ 7,595	$ 8,001	$ 8,442	$ 9,910
National	891	991	1,103	1,111	1,194	1,221	1,502
Local	4,813	5,207	5,905	6,484	6,807	7,221	8,408
Magazines							
Total Expenditures	1,292	1,370	1,440	1,448	1,504	1,465	1,789
In Weekly Magazines	617	626	610	583	630	612	748
In Women's Magazines	301	340	368	362	372	368	457
In Monthly Magazines	374	404	462	503	502	485	584
Farm Publications Expenditures	62	57	59	65	72	74	86
Television							
Total Expenditures	3,596	3,534	4,091	4,460	4,854	5,263	6,721
Network	1,658	1,593	1,804	1,968	2,145	2,306	2,857
Spot	1,234	1,145	1,318	1,377	1,497	1,623	2,154
Local	704	796	969	1,115	1,212	1,334	1,710
Radio							
Total Expenditures	1,308	1,445	1,612	1,723	1,837	1,980	2,277
Network	56	63	74	68	69	83	104
Spot	371	395	402	400	405	436	493
Local	881	987	1,136	1,255	1,363	1,461	1,680
Direct Mail Expenditures	2,766	3,067	3,420	3,698	3,986	4,181	4,813
Business Papers Expenditures	740	720	781	865	900	919	1,035
Outdoor							
Total Expenditures	234	261	292	308	309	335	383
National	154	172	192	200	203	220	252
Local	80	89	100	108	106	115	131
Miscellaneous							
Total Expenditures	3,848	4,088	4,597	4,958	5,277	5,571	6,636
National	2,126	2,202	2,437	2,575	2,755	2,882	3,465
Local	1,722	1,886	2,160	2,383	2,522	2,689	3,171
Total Expenditures							
National	11,350	11,775	13,030	13,775	14,730	15,410	18,550
Local	8,200	8,965	10,270	11,345	12,010	12,820	15,100
GRAND TOTAL	$19,550	$20,740	$23,300	$25,120	$26,740	$28,230	$33,650
Total In Constant (1972) Dollars	$21,389	$21,604	$23,300	$23,743	$22,972	$22,176	$24,989

Source: Robert J. Coen of McCann-Erickson, Inc.

Note: (a) 1976 figures are preliminary.

Further Information

Advertising textbooks will provide background in this field. The reader may also wish to consult Daniells (1976), chapter 18, for information on many marketing and advertising data sources. Important periodicals in the field include *Advertising Age*, *Media Decisions*, and *Marketing Communications*. However, the primary source for information on advertising expenditures in this country continues to be the Marketing Services Research Department of McCann-Erickson, Inc.

Table 303–C.
Percentage of Total Advertiser Expenditures Shared by Individual U. S. Media, 1935–1976

Year	Newspapers	Magazines	Farm Publications	Television	Radio	Direct Mail	Business Papers	Outdoor Signs	Miscellaneous Other Media	% Real Change (Constant Dollars)
1935	45	8	*	--	7	17	3	2	18	-4
1936	44	9	*	--	7	17	3	2	19	+12
1937	42	9	*	--	8	16	3	2	19	+4
1938	41	9	*	--	9	17	3	2	19	-6
1939	40	9	*	--	9	17	4	2	19	+5
1940	39	10	*	--	10	16	4	2	19	+3
1941	38	10	*	--	11	16	4	2	19	+10
1942	37	9	*	--	12	15	5	2	20	-0
1943	36	11	*	--	13	13	6	2	20	+6
1944	33	12	*	--	14	12	7	2	20	+4
1945	32	13	*	--	15	10	7	3	20	+2
1946	34	13	*	*	14	10	6	3	20	+1
1947	35	12	*	*	12	14	5	3	20	+13
1948	36	11	*	*	12	14	5	3	20	+7
1949	37	9	*	1	11	14	5	3	19	+8
1950	36	9	*	3	11	14	5	3	19	+7
1951	35	9	*	5	10	14	5	3	20	+5
1952	35	9	*	6	9	14	5	2	20	+10
1953	34	9	*	8	8	14	5	2	20	+7
1954	33	8	*	10	7	15	5	2	20	+4

Table 303-C. (Cont'd.)

Year	Newspapers	Magazines	Farm Publications	Television	Radio	Direct Mail	Business Papers	Outdoor Signs	Miscellaneous Other Media	% Real Change (Constant Dollars)
1955	34	8	*	11	6	14	5	2	20	+10
1956	33	8	*	12	6	14	5	2	20	+5
1957	32	8	*	12	6	14	6	2	20	- -
1958	31	7	*	13	6	15	5	2	20	-1
1959	32	8	*	13	6	15	5	2	20	+7
1960	31	8	*	13	6	15	5	2	20	+4
1961	31	8	*	14	6	16	5	2	19	-2
1962	30	8	*	15	6	16	5	1	19	+3
1963	29	8	*	16	6	16	5	1	19	+4
1964	29	8	*	16	6	15	4	1	20	+6
1965	29	8	*	17	6	15	4	1	20	+5
1966	29	8	*	17	6	15	4	1	20	+6
1967	29	7	*	17	6	15	4	1	20	-1
1968	29	7	*	18	7	14	4	1	20	+3
1969	29	7	*	19	7	14	4	1	20	+2
1970	29	7	*	18	7	14	4	1	20	-5
1971	30	7	*	17	7	15	3	1	20	+1
1972	30	6	*	18	7	15	3	1	20	+8
1973	30	6	*	18	7	14	3	1	20	+2
1974	30	6	*	18	7	15	3	1	20	-3
1975	30	5	*	19	7	15	3	1	20	-3
1976	30	5	*	20	7	14	3	1	20	- -

Source: Computed by authors from figures in Table B.

Notes: Asterisk (*) indicates a figure of less than 1 percent. Data prior to 1935 are not strictly comparable to later figures (see *Printer's Ink*, June 16, 1938).

Table 303–D.
Cost-per-Thousand (CPM) Advertising-Rate Index for
the U. S. Media, 1965–1978

| | Newspapers | General-Interest Magazines | Radio | | Television | | |
			Network	Spot	Network, Prime-Time	Network, Daytime	Spot
1965	82	94	107	92	91	80	96
1966	87	95	106	97	95	91	99
1967	87	95	104	98	95	91	102
1968	90	95	100	98	99	93	105
1969	94	98	100	100	102	98	107
1970	100	100	100	100	100	100	100
1971	103	97	99	102	93	87	98
1972	106	102	89	108	100	84	92
1973	112	104	89	108	112	95	91
1974	119	110	89	109	121	105	93
1975	141	118	90	115	123	110	93
1976	156	120	99	129	133	137	93
1977	170	122	108	140	168	176	122
1978	183	131	123	152	187	202	114

Sources: 1965-1970 data: *Encyclomedia: 1977 Newspaper Edition*, p. 32. (See Unit 303 text for list of primary sources of these data.) 1971-1978 data: *Broadcasting* (February 6, 1978), p. 53. (See text for derivation, which varies somewhat from 1965-1970 data.)

Table 303–E.
Average Cost-per-Thousand (CPM) Advertising Rates of
the Various U. S. Media, 1950–1975

	1950	1965	1975
Daily Newspapers	$3.50	$5.17	$9.26
Sunday Newspapers	2.65	3.76	7.02
Consumer Magazines (B&W ad)	2.86	4.05	4.85
Consumer Magazines (color ad)	4.04	5.62	6.62
Radio (network)	N/A	1.18	1.14
Radio (spot)	N/A	1.51	1.88
Television (primetime network)	N/A	3.93	4.81
Television (daytime network)	N/A	1.45	2.24

Source: Newspapers: Newspaper Advertising Bureau. Magazines: 1950 data from Chapin (1957), p. 73; 1965 and 1975 data from Magazine Publishers Association. Radio: 1965 data supplied to the editors by James Quinn of J. Walter Thompson; 1975 data from *Media Decisions* (August 1976), p. 58. Television: A.C. Nielsen Company data reprinted in *Broadcasting Basics II* (Fall 1976), p. 9.

Table 310–A.
Sales Totals and Consumer Expenditures
in the U. S. Book Publishing Industry, 1909–1976

Note: All figures are in millions of dollars.

Year	Sales Totals—Census Bureau		Sales Totals—Bowker/AAP[b]		Consumer Expenditures—Bureau of Economic Analysis	
	Current Dollars	Constant (1972) Dollars[a]	Current Dollars	Constant (1972) Dollars	Current Dollars	Constant (1972) Dollars
1909	$ 55.8	$ 301.6	- -	- -	- -	- -
1914	63.4	321.8	- -	- -	- -	- -
1919	116.3	317.8	- -	- -	- -	- -
1921	118.9	340.7	- -	- -	- -	- -
1923	127.6	379.8	- -	- -	- -	- -
1925	114.3	338.2	- -	- -	- -	- -
1927	167.9	516.6	- -	- -	- -	- -
1929	181.6	553.7	- -	- -	$ 309	$ 942
1931	140.8	490.6	- -	- -	253	882
1933	81.7	328.1	- -	- -	152	610
1935	113.0	410.9	- -	- -	183	665
1937	144.1	496.7	- -	- -	243	838
1939	149.1	528.7	- -	- -	226	801
1943	306.4	870.5	- -	- -	366	1,040
1945	293.4	776.2	- -	- -	520	1,383
1947	463.8	933.2	$ 435.1	$ 875.5	531	1,068
1954	708.9	1,187.4	575.7	964.3	806	1,350
1958	1,033.1	1,565.3	885.5	1,341.7	1,022	1,548
1959	1,148.7	1,701.8	998.9	1,479.9	1,088	1,612
1960	1,303.3	1,897.1	1,131.0	1,646.3	1,139	1,658
1961	1,382.3	1,994.7	1,240.1	1,789.5	1,212	1,749
1962	1,527.8	2,164.0	N/A	N/A	1,287	1,823
1963	1,534.6	2,143.3	1,685.7	2,354.3	1,413	1,973
1964	1,728.6	2,377.7	1,825.8	2,511.4	1,612	2,217
1965	1,767.1	2,378.3	2,022.3	2,721.8	1,648	2,218
1966	1,996.3	2,599.3	2,316.2	3,015.9	1,840	2,396
1967	2,134.8	2,702.3	2,320.0	2,936.7	1,847	2,338
1968	2,099.4	2,541.6	2,594.0	3,140.4	1,941	2,350
1969	2,417.2	2,788.0	2,763.2	3,187.1	2,082	2,401
1970	2,434.2	2,663.2	2,924.3	3,199.5	2,356	2,578
1971	2,739.3	2,853.4	2,917.8	3,039.4	2,461	2,564
1972	2,856.8	2,856.8	3,017.8	3,017.8	2,530	2,530
1973	3,142.9	2,970.6	3,213.6	3,037.4	2,769	2,617
1974	3,356.3	2,883.4	3,569.9	3,066.9	3,034	2,607
1975	3,590.0[c]	2,820.1	3,850.7	3,024.9	3,397	2,668
1976	N/A	N/A	4,185.2	N/A	3,590	N/A

Sources: U. S. Census Bureau figures, 1909-1974: *Census of Manufactures and Annual Survey of Manufactures,* annual issues; 1975 figures: *U. S. Industrial Outlook, 1977.* Bowker/AAP figures, 1947-1970: *The Bowker Annual,* annual issues; 1971-1976 figures: Association of American Publishers (AAP), *Industry Statistics, 1976.* Consumer expenditures figures, 1929-1972: U. S. Department of Commerce, Bureau of Economic Analysis (1977), pp. 90-91, 337. 1973-1976 figures: U. S. Department of Commerce, Bureau of Economic Analysis (July 1976), p. 34.

Notes: (a) The calculation of constant dollars is based on the GNP deflator. (b) AAP is the Association of American Publishers. (c) The 1975 figure is a Census Bureau estimate.

Table 310–B.
Book Sales of U. S. Publishers, by Type of Book, 1947–1972

Note: All figures are in thousands of dollars.

Type of Book	1947	1954	1958
Total Sales	$455,790	$665,419	$1,010,713
Textbooks	N/A	N/A	281,572
Elementary, hardbound		57,365	76,632
Elementary, paperbound		10,242	11,603
High School, hardbound	55,068	31,927	58,191
High School, paperbound		2,118	2,024
College, hardbound	52,513	50,241	81,377
College, paperbound		1,484	2,767
Work Books, paperbound	13,227	24,097	40,300
Standardized Tests	- -[a]	- -[a]	8,678
Textbooks, n.s.k.[b]	- -	- -	- -
Subscription Reference Books, hardbound	63,851	89,825	163,569
Technical/Scientific/Professional Books	45,837	63,635	116,021
Law Books	- -	- -	36,400
Medical Books	- -	- -	21,400
Business Books	- -	- -	9,400
Other Tech/Sci/Pro Books	- -	- -	48,821
Tech/Sci/Pro Books, n.s.k.	- -	- -	- -
Religious Books	N/A	N/A	58,643
Bibles/Testaments	9,285	19,125	23,064
Hymnals/Devotionals/Prayer Books			8,064
Other Religious Books, hardbound	19,608[c]	17,007[c]	15,999
Other Religious Books, paperbound			11,516
Religious Books, n.s.k.			- -
General Books	N/A	N/A	274,739
Book Club Books	65,423[d]	- -[d]	95,684
Wholesaled, paperbound		- -[e]	47,680
Adult Trade, hardbound	69,963	133,117	64,669
Adult Trade, paperbound		36,049	5,374
Juvenile, $1 and over	20,289	50,835	40,218
Juvenile, under $1			21,114
General Books, n.s.k.	- -	- -	- -
Other Books and Pamphlets	N/A	N/A	96,003
Other Books, hardbound		15,489	52,148
Other Books, paperbound, music	20,070[f]	23,316[g]	12,737
Other Books, paperbound, other			
Pamphlets, religious			11,668
Pamphlets, music	20,656	25,094	19,450
Pamphlets, other			
Other Books and Pamphlets, n.s.k.			- -
Books and Pamphlets, n.s.k. (firms with 10 or more employees)			
Books and Pamphlets, n.s.k. (firms with less than 10 employees)	- -	11,774	20,166

Interpretation of Tables

The trend of book sales in the United States for most of this century can be seen in **Table 310-A**, which offers total sales figures from the U.S. Bureau of the Census, *The Bowker Annual* and the Association of American Publishers (AAP), and the U.S. Bureau of Economic Analysis (BEA). Three series of data are provided in this table because each source has its own relative advantages in describing the development of the industry. The particular differences among the three series will be discussed below in the "Sources" section.

Basically, the growth of the book publishing industry has paralleled the nation's overall economic development, with a dip during the Great Depression and an expansion during World War II which continued until the mid-1960s. Book publishing experienced an especially notable spurt of growth during the mid-1950s, partly because of rising adult literacy, but mainly because of greater numbers of children and new government commitments to schools, universities, and libraries.

Table 310–B. (Cont'd.)

Type of Book	1963	1967	1972
Total Sales	$1,547,713	$2,255,300	$2,915,400
Textbooks	471,100	733,600	809,600
Elementary, hardbound	112,689	180,600	162,400
Elementary, paperbound	21,668	24,300	57,500
High School, hardbound	97,811	122,700	132,400
High School, paperbound	8,849	14,900	12,800
College, harbound	131,725	226,600	277,300
College, paperbound	14,867	32,700	45,100
Work Books, paperbound	61,050	88,600	88,700
Standardized Tests	19,328	28,500	14,200
Textbooks, n.s.k.[b]	3,113	14,700	19,200
Subscription Reference Books, hardbound	207,300	216,300	198,500
Technical/Scientific/Professional Books	156,342	240,200	403,000
Law Books	57,384	74,000	146,900
Medical Books	24,148	41,000	58,100
Business Books	5,592	20,100	42,000
Other Tech/Sci/Pro Books	63,015	93,500	135,100
Tech/Sci/Pro Books, n.s.k.	6,203	11,600	19,900
Religious Books	81,120	110,400	131,200
Bibles/Testaments	26,421	36,700	52,600
Hymnals/Devotionals/Prayer Books	8,201	15,400	9,000
Other Religious Books, hardbound	31,296	29,700	30,000
Other Religious Books, paperbound	12,599	15,700	28,300
Religious Books, n.s.k.	2,603	12,900	11,300
General Books	458,152	657,700	1,006,700
Book Club Books	143,418	201,500	131,300
Wholesaled, paperbound	60,543	67,700	90,300
Adult Trade, hardbound	108,515	148,900	232,100
Adult Trade, paperbound	34,485	82,700	220,500
Juvenile, $1 and over	72,678	107,500	88,200[h]
Juvenile, under $1	31,257	35,100	- -[h]
General Books, n.s.k.	7,256	14,300	
Other Books and Pamphlets	154,842	188,100	N/A
Other Books, hardbound	84,402	108,100	68,100
Other Books, paperbound, music	{25,900	N/A	10,300
Other Books, paperbound, other		14,900	18,900
Pamphlets, religious	{2,100	2,100	N/A
Pamphlets, music		N/A	6,200
Pamphlets, other	32,924	41,600	N/A
Other Books and Pamphlets, n.s.k.	6,605	21,400	25,200
Books and Pamphlets, n.s.k. (firsm with 10 or more employees)	{18,894	60,800	94,800
Books and Pamphlets, n.s.k. (firms with less than 10 employees)		36,200	60,700

Sources: 1947-1963 data: Lofquist (1970), p. 25. 1967 and 1972 data: *1972 Census of Manufactures*, pp. 27A-31 and 27A-32.

Notes: (a) Sales figures for standardized tests in 1947 and 1954 were included in the "Pamphlets, other" category. (b) n.s.k.: not specified by kind. (c) These sums did not include paperbound religious books. In 1947, the sales of paperbound prayer books amounted to $1,558,000. The value of hymnals in 1954 was $3,048,000. (d) Book-club sales for 1948 and 1954 were included in the figure for "Adult Trade, hardbound." (e) Wholesaled paperbound book sales in 1947 and 1954 were reported in the "Adult Trade, paperbound" category. (f) Mail-order book sales were included in this general category of "Other" in 1947. (g) Paperbound religious books were included in this category in 1947 and 1954. (h) Data were deleted to avoid revealing information about a single company.

Table 310–C.
AAP-Estimated Sales Totals and Percentage Growth for the U. S. Book Publishing Industry, by Type of Book, 1971–1976

Note: All dollar figures are in millions.

	1971	1972		1973			1974			1975			1976		
	Sales	Sales	% Changes from 1971	Sales	% Changes from 1972	% Changes from 1971	Sales	% Changes from 1973	% Changes from 1971	Sales	% Changes from 1974	% Changes from 1971	Sales	% Changes from 1975	% Changes from 1971
Trade Books (Total)	$ 422.7	$ 442.0	4.6%	$ 460.1	4.1%	8.8%	$ 522.7	13.6%	23.6%	$ 549.2	5.1%	29.9%	$ 573.3	4.4%	35.6%
Adult, Hardbound	242.0	251.5	3.9	264.8	5.3	9.4	308.2	16.4	27.3	313.4	1.7	29.5	331.0	5.6	36.8
Adult, Paperbound	69.6	79.6	14.3	86.7	8.9	24.5	97.3	12.2	39.8	111.2	14.3	59.1	117.8	5.9	69.3
Juvenile, Hardbound	108.9	106.5	-2.2	98.8	-7.2	-9.3	103.1	4.4	-5.3	109.6	6.3	0.6	109.1	-0.5	0.2
Juvenile, Paperbound	2.2	4.4	100.0	9.8	122.7	345.5	14.1	43.9	540.9	15.0	6.4	581.8	17.4	16.0	690.9
Religious Books (Total)	108.5	117.5	8.3	124.7	6.1	14.9	130.6	4.7	20.4	154.6	18.4	42.5	171.2	10.7	57.8
Bibles, Testaments, Hymnals, Prayerbooks	54.4	61.6	13.2	66.5	7.9	22.2	67.5	1.5	24.1	76.6	13.5	40.8	83.6	9.1	53.7
Other Religious	54.1	55.9	3.4	58.2	4.1	7.5	63.1	8.4	16.6	78.0	23.6	44.2	87.6	12.3	61.9
Professional Books (Total)	353.0	381.0	7.9	405.4	6.4	14.8	466.3	15.0	32.1	501.2	7.5	42.0	559.0	11.5	58.4
Technical, Scientific	122.3	131.8	7.8	138.4	5.0	13.2	158.3	14.4	29.4	175.5	10.9	43.5	195.2	11.2	59.6
Business, Other Professional	178.3	192.2	7.8	206.2	7.3	15.6	236.3	14.6	32.5	242.3	2.5	35.9	266.8	10.1	49.6
Medical	52.4	57.0	8.8	60.8	6.7	16.0	71.7	17.9	36.8	83.4	16.3	59.2	97.0	16.3	85.1
Book-Club Books	229.5	240.5	4.8	262.4	9.1	14.3	283.6	8.1	23.6	303.4	7.0	32.2	343.1	13.1	49.5
Mail-Order Publications	194.6	198.9	2.2	221.2	11.2	13.6	247.0	11.7	26.9	279.8	13.3	43.8	348.9	24.7	79.3
Mass-Market Paperbacks (Total)	228.8	252.8	10.5	297.1	17.5	29.9	308.9	4.0	35.0	356.2	15.3	55.7	415.4	16.6	81.6
Rack-Sized	226.7	250.0	10.3	292.2	16.9	28.9	298.7	2.2	31.8	336.6	12.7	48.5	394.0	17.1	73.8
Not Rack-Sized	2.1	2.8	33.3	4.9	75.0	133.3	10.2	108.2	385.7	19.6	92.2	833.3	21.4	9.2	919.0
University Press Books	39.3	41.4	5.3	42.6	2.9	8.4	46.1	8.2	17.3	48.8	5.8	24.2	53.5	9.6	36.1
Elementary/Secondary Textbooks	496.6	497.6	-0.2	547.9	10.1	10.3	598.8	9.3	20.1	643.1	7.4	29.5	640.1	-0.5	28.9
College Textbooks	371.5	375.3	-1.0	392.2	4.5	5.6	453.4	15.6	19.9	530.6	17.0	42.8	564.0	6.3	51.8
Standardized Tests	25.3	26.5	4.8	28.8	8.7	13.8	34.2	18.7	25.2	36.7	7.3	45.0	40.0	9.0	58.1
Subscription Reference Books	301.0	278.9	-7.3	262.2	-6.0	-12.9	280.2	6.8	-6.9	258.1	-7.9	-14.2	286.5	11.0	-4.8
Audiovisual/Other Educational Media (Total)	106.2	116.2	14.8	117.8	1.4	16.4	143.0	21.4	41.3	137.3	-4.0	35.7	142.0	3.4	40.3
El-Hi	87.5	101.2	15.7	102.8	1.6	17.5	125.4	22.0	43.3	119.6	-4.6	36.7	123.1	2.9	40.7
College	9.1	9.2	1.1	9.1	-1.1	0.0	10.8	18.7	18.7	10.4	-3.7	14.3	11.1	6.7	22.0
Other	4.6	5.8	26.1	5.9	1.7	28.3	6.8	15.3	47.8	7.3	7.4	58.7	7.8	6.8	47.8
Other Book Sales	45.8	49.2	7.4	51.2	4.1	11.8	55.1	7.6	20.3	51.7	-6.2	12.9	48.2	-6.8	5.2
Total Sales	$2,917.8	$3,017.8	3.4%	$3,213.6	6.5%	10.1%	$3,569.9	11.1%	22.3%	$3,850.7	7.9%	32.0%	$4,185.2	8.7%	43.4%

Source: Association of American Publishers (1977), pp. 18-19.

Table 310-D.
Receipts, Operating Expenses, and Capital Expenditures of the U. S. Book Publishing Industry, 1939-1975

Note: All dollar figures in millions.

Year	Value of Industry Receipts		Cost of Materials, Fuels, etc.		Payroll, All Employees		Wages, Production Workers Only		New Capital Expenditures	
	Current Dollars	Constant (1972) Dollars	Current Dollars	Percent of Receipts	Current Dollars	Percent of Receipts	Current Dollars	Percent of Receipts	Current Dollars	Percent of Receipts
1939	$ 154.6	$ 548.2	$ 50.9	33%	$ 37.7	24%	$ 8.5	5%	N/A	N/A
1947	463.9	933.4	200.9	43	104.3	22	20.1	4	N/A	N/A
1954	708.9	1,187.4	301.7	43	144.8	20	29.3	4	$ 7.5	1%
1958	1,033.1	1,565.3	413.3	40	191.9	19	44.5	4	13.1	1
1963	1,534.6	2,143.3	582.3	38	280.7	18	59.5	4	25.4	2
1967	2,134.8	2,702.3	762.8	36	389.9	18	76.6	4	55.1	3
1972	2,856.8	2,856.8	959.9	34	557.6	20	128.6	5	48.4	2
1975	3,486.3	2,738.6	1,162.8	33	666.5	19	139.3	4	75.9	2

Sources: 1939 Payroll, All Employees: *1939 Biennial Census of Manufactures*. All other data: 1939-1954: *1963 Census of Manufactures*; 1958-1972: *1972 Census of Manufactures*; 1975: *Annual Survey of Manufactures 1975*.

Note: The calculation of constant dollars was based on the Gross National Product deflator.

The extent of this growth is apparent when one calculates the average (arithmetic mean) annual growth rate of book industry sales in constant (1972) dollars—the "real" growth rate. In these terms, the growth rate of the industry rose from 4.8 percent between 1945 and 1954, to 7.2 percent between 1954 and 1964. By contrast, during the next ten years, from 1965 to 1974, the growth rate was only 2.2 percent. This decline in book publishing growth can be explained largely by the end of the "baby boom" and its effect on educational needs, and by a general tightening of the economy.

The book publishing industry's development can be seen more clearly in **Table 310-B**, which breaks down U.S. book sales according to the type of book. From 1958 to 1967, the average annual growth rate (in constant dollars) for all books sold was 7.2 percent. In the five-year period from 1967 to 1972, real growth was only .4 percent. The rates of growth for the larger sub-categories of books in these two periods were:

	1958-1967	1967-1972
All books	7.2%	0.4%
Textbooks	9.0	-2.7
Subscription reference books (mainly encyclopedias)	1.1	-6.2
Technical, scientific, and professional books	6.3	5.8
Religious books	5.2	-1.3
General books (trade, juvenile, and mass market paperbacks)	8.0	3.9

While all categories of books had smaller growth rates after 1967, the breakdown above shows that the greatest reduction occurred in sales of textbooks and subscription reference books. Of course, these are the two categories which would be expected to drop if the main influence on the market were a decline in spending by schools and libraries. On the other hand, all categories of books and buyers interpenetrate, and each segment of the book industry has its own cycles and competitive environment. Thus, the reader should not substitute this brief review for a more thorough analysis of the industry.

Table 310-C presents a categorical breakdown of annual book sales as compiled by the Association of American Publishers, which has been collecting these statistics on an annual basis since 1971. Comparison of the 1976 and 1971 data reveals a trend similar to that discussed in **Table 310-B**. The growth of the industry as a whole during this period was 43.4 percent (in current dollars). Subscription reference books, elementary and secondary texts, books from university presses, and trade books generally lagged behind the average, although some subcategories within these same classifications, such as adult trade paperbacks, did somewhat better. On the other hand, sales of professional, religious, mass-market paperback, and college textbooks were higher than the overall book trade; while juvenile paperbound books and other than rack-sized mass-market paperbacks showed extraordinary increases during this period.

Table 310-D compares receipts with operating expenses and capital expenditures in the book publishing industry. In constant (1972) dollars, industry receipts have exhibited little growth since 1967. However, the percentages of revenues accounted for by the major cost categories (materials, fuels, payroll, and capital expenditures) have either remained relatively constant or have declined, indicating no major squeeze on profits from these sources. Any general judgments about book industry trends are difficult to make from such aggregate statistics.

Sources

In **Table 310-A**, the Census Bureau's data for 1909 through 1939, and for the census years of 1947, 1954, 1958, 1963, and 1972, are found in the *Census of Manufactures*. Since no censuses were made between 1939 and 1947, the Census Bureau provides estimates for these years. The source of the data for the noncensus years since 1947 is another Census Bureau publication, the *Annual Survey of Manufactures*.

Before 1939, book publishing was not separated from commercial printing in published data of the Census Bureau. However, the Bureau has since reviewed these data and separated out the book industry figures. Regarding these pre-1939 figures, Lofquist (1970, p. 15) cautions that "care should be taken not to place too great emphasis on what appear to be abrupt year-to-year changes. These changes are probably the result of census changes in category definitions or industry coverage." Since 1947, the numbers are more reliable. The figures from the *Annual Survey* may be considered slightly less accurate, because this source estimates total industry activity from a yearly sample of publishers.

The information from the second source of **Table 310-A**, the AAP and *The Bowker Annual*, differs from the Census Bureau material in several important ways. In its *Industry Statistics* (1977, pp. 18-19), the AAP gives the following advice:

> Readers comparing the estimated data with Census reports should recall that the U.S. Census does not provide data on most university presses or on other institutionally sponsored and not-for-profit publishing activities, nor on the audiovisual and other media materials which are included in [the AAP table on book industry sales]. On the other hand, AAP estimates have traditionally excluded coloring books, Sunday School materials, and certain pamphlets which are incorporated in Census data. Furthermore, some substantial differences in classification will be encountered between the Census and AAP reports, even though total sales shown in the table have been reconciled with Census findings.

The AAP figures prior to 1971 (when the AAP began its work) were collected for *The Bowker Annual*, and it is difficult to ascertain their accuracy. The compiler of these statistics changed several times during the 1947-1970 period, projections were substituted for annual figures for some years, and revisions based on subsequently available census data were often made. For these reasons, it is best to regard these pre-1971 AAP/Bowker data as educated estimates by persons with a good knowledge of the trade but less than solid statistical methods.

The third set of figures in **Table 310-A**, from the Bureau of Economic Analysis of the U.S. Department of Commerce, are derived from the estimates of personal consumption expenditures prepared for the Commerce Department's National Income and Products Accounts, which is the basis for the total annual figure known as the Gross National Product. The advantages of these figures are that they represent *consumer* expenditures, rather than industry sales, and that they have been reconciled with the total statistics for national economic output.

The disadvantages of these figures are that they do not separate out expenditures for maps and that they undergo considerable revision from time to time without sufficient explanation by the BEA as to the purposes and procedures of the revisions. The editors also suspect that the BEA has a general tendency to adjust sales of goods downward and sales of services upward. Such revisions by the BEA make comparisons with other series difficult.

Table 310-B data also come from the *Census of Manufactures* and are subject to the same general evaluation offered above. However, the sales measured in **Table 310-B** are for *book* products only, whether or not the books are sold by companies defined as part of the book publishing industry; whereas the figures in **Table 310-A** include some sales of *non*book products, but only if these products were sold by book publishing companies. This explains why the totals in **Table 310-B** do not equal those in **Table 310-A**.

In 1972, for example, the book publishing industry was responsible for $2.5 billion in book sales, out of a total of $2.9 billion for all companies selling books. Other than book publishers, the companies that produced the largest volume of books were periodical publishing firms, which sold $333.9 million worth of books in 1972. Similarly, the $2.5 billion in *book* sales by *book* publishers represents only 88 percent of all receipts by the book publishing industry. The book industry also sold $136.5 million worth of periodicals and had miscellaneous receipts accounting for the rest of the total receipts of the industry.

Table 310-C is made up of AAP estimates which are based on a survey of industry firms. The survey responses are then extended to the total industry, using Census Bureau data as a guideline. In 1976, the companies responding to the AAP questionnaires accounted for about 60 percent of all estimated industry sales—an impressively high response rate. However, since the replies are voluntary, the reader must not discount the possibility of systematic bias resulting from the respondents' self-selection. It is also likely that the AAP samples overrepresent the large publishers who are association members, although questionnaires are sent to many nonmembers as well.

The estimates in **Table 310-C** include only domestic and export sales. The indigenous sales activities of foreign subsidiaries of American publishers are not covered in the figures. The "audio-visual and other media" figures in the table refer only to the sales of book publishers, not to the total of all audio-visual and other media sales. The "other sales" category refers only to sheet sales (except those to prebinders) and sales of miscellaneous merchandise.

Table 310-D was drawn from appropriate issues of the *Census of Manufactures* and the *Annual Survey of Manufactures*.

Further Information

The Census Bureau and the AAP are presently the two most widely accepted sources of book industry sales statistics. However, there are two other sources which present useful information on this industry: *Publishers Weekly*, which features several articles each year on book sales, and the Book Industry Study Group, which has recently begun a series of studies of book trade economics. The most recent effort of the Book Industry Study Group is *Book Industry Trends: 1977* (Dessauer, Doebler, and Nordberg, 1977), the first of a planned annual series of five-year forecasts of book publishing, wholesaling, and retailing. John Dessauer, currently the leading book industry statistician, is the statistical consultant for both the AAP and the Book Industry Study Group. His analyses frequently appear in *Publishers Weekly*.

The Department of Commerce presents quarterly analyses of book, periodical, newspaper, and other printing and publishing in its journal, *Printing and Publishing*, which is issued by the Domestic and International Business Administration. It is the best currently available source on information about government statistics on publishing. Some interesting recent articles in this quarterly, as well as in *Publishers Weekly*, include the following: Dessauer (1977, 1976, 1973); Grannis (1977a, 1977b, 1977c, 1976); Noble (1977, 1976); Nordberg (1976); and Lofquist (1970).

Book industry statistics are included in each issue of *The Bowker Annual*. Interesting discussions of the book publishing business that do not include many statistics but are nevertheless very useful include Dessauer (1974), *Publishers Weekly* (1976), and Smith (1966). Vanier's (1973) work on the book industry market structure is also helpful. A classic source of early data is *Cheney's Economic Survey of the Book Industry* (1960), which in many ways still provides insightful methods for analyzing the industry.

Book Distribution Finances 31

Table 311–A.
Number, Annual Sales, Employee/Proprietor Totals, and Payroll of U. S. Bookstore Establishments, 1929–1976

Note: All dollar figures in millions.

| Year | Number of Establishments | | Annual Sales | | Number of Employees | | Total Payroll |
	All Establishments	Establishments with a Payroll	All Establishments	Establishments with a Payroll	Paid Employees	Proprietors and Partners	
1929	2,809	N/A	$ 117.0	N/A	N/A	2,451	$ 18.3
1939	2,845	N/A	73.8	N/A	13,038	2,156	13.9
1948	2,905	N/A	267.7	N/A	23,836	2,359	47.5
1954	2,642	1,728	151.2	$138.7	8,301	2,260	19.0
1958	2,885	1,675	196.3	178.4	10,168	2,633	24.4
1963	3,154	2,164	279.5	264.6	12,439	2,608	36.3
1967	N/A	2,960	N/A	427.6	18,010	N/A	61.7
1972	7,830	4,991	907.0	853.9	28,703	4,973[a]	118.1
1976[b]	12,000	N/A	13,000.0	N/A	40,000	N/A	N/A

Sources: 1929-1967: Lofquist (1971), pp. 8-11. 1972: *1972 Census of Retail Trade.* 1976: Lofquist (1977).

Notes: (a) This is an estimate derived by multiplying the number of partnerships by two and then adding that figure to the number of proprietors. (b) The 1976 figures are estimates from Lofquist (1977).

Table 311–B.
Estimated Consumer Expenditures for Books in U. S., by Channel of Distribution, 1972 and 1976

| Channel of Distribution[a] | 1972 | | 1976 | | 1972-1976 | |
	Millions of Dollars	Millions of Units	Millions of Dollars	Millions of Units	Percent Change in Dollar Expenditures	Percent Change in Unit Expenditures
General Retailers	$ 813.0	404.0	$1,365.8	483.5	68.0 %	19.7 %
College Stores	566.1	198.4	849.7	181.4	50.1	-8.6
Libraries and Institutions	345.8	88.4	406.3	75.3	17.5	-14.8
Schools	646.0	343.2	760.3	284.5	17.7	-17.1
Direct-to-Consumer Sales	802.9	170.7	1,144.2	184.3	42.5	8.0
Others	53.3	55.0	64.0	34.7	20.1	-36.9
Totals	$3,226.8	1,259.6	$4,590.7	1,243.7	42.3 %	-1.3 %

Source: Dessauer, Doebler, and Nordberg (1977), pp. 267-270, 283-286, 307-310.

Note: (a) See the Unit 311 text for definitions of the various channels of distribution.

Table 311–C.
Estimated Book Sales by Wholesalers and Jobbers in U. S.,
by Channel of Distribution, 1972 and 1976

| | 1972 | | 1976 | | 1972-1976 | |
| | Millions of Dollars | Millions of Units | Millions of Dollars | Millions of Units | Percent Change in Dollar Sales | Percent Change in Unit Sales |
Channel of Distribution[a]						
General Retailers	$175.8	207.9	$331.4	256.0	88.5 %	23.1 %
College Stores	45.5	45.0	66.5	41.9	46.2	-6.9
Libraries and Institutions	218.1	63.3	274.1	53.1	25.7	-16.1
Schools	117.9	75.7	104.3	53.5	-11.5	-29.3
Export Sales	24.2	10.1	37.0	11.7	52.9	15.8
Totals	$581.3	401.3	$813.5	416.0	39.9 %	3.7 %

Source: Dessauer, Doebler, and Nordberg (1977), pp. 233-235, 245-247, 263-265.

Note: (a) See the Unit 311 text for definitions of the various channels of distribution.

Interpretation of Tables

Table 311-A outlines the growth of the bookselling business in the United States, from 1929 to 1976. It is apparent that the number of bookselling establishments remained remarkably constant for nearly 30 years. During this early period, sales growth was also extremely modest. In fact, in terms of constant (1972) dollars, 1963 was the first year to top the bookstore sales registered in 1929.

Since 1958, however, the growth of booksellers has accelerated greatly. Between 1958 and 1976, the number of bookselling establishments increased 415 percent, from 2,885 to approximately 12,000 stores. Meanwhile, estimates of sales rose from $196.3 million to $1.3 billion—an increase of more than 560 percent. Sales data for the first ten months of 1976 (Lofquist, 1976/77) indicated some leveling off, but it is not yet possible to determine whether the remarkable growth trend begun in the mid-1960s is now coming to an end.

While bookstores have been growing in number and sales, other channels of book sales have reduced their activity—at least in terms of the number and constant dollar value of consumer-purchased books. The figures in Table 311-B indicate that all channels of distribution have shown sales increases over the five-year period between 1972 and 1976. However, much of this increase is actually due to inflation. Relative purchasing trends can be seen more clearly in the purchase of "units"—that is, individual books or sets of books which are priced together. Only general retailers and direct-to-consumer sales programs increased their unit sales during these five years.

The category of "general retailers" includes all retail outlets except "college stores"; the "direct-to-consumer" category refers to sales by publishers and book clubs to individual consumers, as well as to industry and government. The "other" category includes special and remainder sales and other transactions outside the normal marketing pattern. All remainder-book sales, regardless of the category of the seller, are included in this category of "other." The decline in unit purchases by schools, college bookstores, libraries, and other institutions can be attributed to the decline in elementary school enrollment, the general tightening of the economy, and a new fiscal conservatism on the part of institutions supporting libraries. (See Unit 314 for a description of the finances and book acquisitions of libraries.)

In Table 311-C, the 1972 and 1976 sales activities of book wholesalers and jobbers are compared according to most of the same channels of distribution listed in Table 311-B (the "direct-to-consumer" and "other" categories have been eliminated, and an "export" category has been added). The general sales pattern is also the same. Again, general retailing is the area which shows an increase in unit sales, while the institutionally linked sectors have fallen behind. Exports have also increased for book wholesalers and jobbers.

Perhaps the most interesting way to judge the growth of book wholesaling and jobbing is to compare Tables 311-B and 311-C directly. In this way, it becomes clear that wholesalers have outperformed consumer expenditures in both the general retail and college store markets, while they have lagged behind consumer outlays in the areas of libraries and schools. This trend gains significance when the reader understands that, traditionally, distribution to bookstores has not been a major wholesale activity. On the other hand, wholesalers have long played a part in sales to libraries, and here the record parallels that of the market generally.

Sources

Table 311-A is based on data from the U.S. Census Bureau's *Census of Retail Trade*, which includes bookstores (its definition: "establishments primarily selling new books and periodicals") in its reports. Data from bookselling establishments in nonprofit institutions, such as church bookstores and college bookstores run by the schools, are omitted from the Bureau's listings. Also, paperback racks in discount houses, book clubs, department store sales, and news dealers and newsstands are not included in the analysis. Within these stated limits, the data collected by the *Census of Retail Trade* are considered valid and reliable. The estimates for 1976 come from William S. Lofquist, editor of the Department of Commerce's *Printing and Publishing* (Lofquist, 1976/77).

Tables 311-B and 311-C are taken from two publications of the Book Industry Study Group, a nonprofit corporation organized in February of 1976 to facilitate research and assist in the exchange of ideas among members of the book industry. All statistical compilations for these two tables were done by John P. Dessauer, who is also the statistician for the Association of American Publishers (AAP) and other book trade associations, a contributing editor for *Publishers Weekly*, and the leading private statistician for the book industry.

The sources used by Dessauer in compiling the estimates found in Tables 311-B and 311-C include the following: the *Census of Manufactures*; a series of library surveys conducted by the National Center for Education Statistics; and a variety of surveys by the AAP, the Association of American University Presses, the Evangelical Christian Publishers Association, and the National Association of College Bookstores. Data for wholesalers comes from AAP canvasses of wholesalers in 1972 and 1976, as well as from "direct communication with sources in the field" (Dessauer, Doebler, and Nordberg, 1977, p. 150). As with many other book trade sources, the exact method ology of these surveys and of Dessauer's work was not revealed to the editors. Consequently, only the statistician's fine reputation and credits can be mentioned here as a measure of the validity of his work.

A special note must be made concerning Table 311-B. When using this table, the reader should understand how its source distinguishes between estimated publishers' sales (such as those shown in Table 310-C) and estimated consumer expenditures on books. As Dessauer (1976, p. 39) explains:

> U.S. consumer expenditures are monies spent by individuals, institutions, or other ultimate customers for books (such as government and industry) in the United States and the District of Columbia. They differ from publishers' receipts reported in AAP surveys in two ways: they do not include export sales, and they incorporate applicable mark-ups of retailers and wholesalers. These could be single mark-ups, in cases where the publisher sells directly to a retailer or to a library jobber, or double mark-ups in cases where the publisher sells to a wholesaler who in turn supplies a retailer. Of course, no mark-ups are involved in instances where the publisher sells directly to individuals or institutions. . . .
>
> Remember that not all consumer purchases are made at list price. Institutions normally buy at a discount; and even in retail outlets, books are frequently sold at reductions from the full price. There are, moreover, special, premium, and remainder sales of both hardcover and softcover titles which have to be taken into account. As for units, multi-volume sets, even of encyclopedias, have been counted as single units.

Estimates of consumer expenditures are extrapolated from data on publishers' sales. But since publishers' net sales are computed by deducting "returns" (refunds for unsold books) from current gross sales, a lag of several months is created insofar as these figures reflect the actual experience of wholesalers and retailers. The reader must taken this delay factor into account when assessing the validity of these estimates for the exact period of time specified.

Further Information

The two Book Industry Study Group reports offer considerably more data than could be presented here, including both projections and historical data. In addition, Dessauer, Doebler, and Nordberg (1977) present essays on the current condition of the book industry, data on publishers' sales, and annual figures for both a five-year historical period (from 1972 to 1976) and a five-year projection period (from 1977 to 1981). The breakdowns throughout the 166 pages of tables in this source are quite detailed and cross-tabulate the year, the channel of distribution, and the category of book for estimates of publishers' sales, wholesalers' and jobbers' sales, and consumer expenditures.

Parts of the Study Group reports and related studies often appear in *Publishers Weekly*. However, the constant updating of estimates, as new sources of data become available, tends to produce discrepancies between estimates of the same figures in different articles.

Another source of information about bookstores is *Printing and Publishing* magazine, published by the Department of Commerce. The reader may wish to check two recent articles appearing in that publication: Lofquist (1976/77) and Lofquist (1977). The first deals generally with bookstore growth, while the second analyzes growth by geographic region.

Book Production Costs   312

Table 312–A.
Revenue, Expenses, and Earnings of U. S. Trade Book Publishers, 1976

	Amount	Average Percent of Net Sales	Range of Net Sales for Middle 50% of Firms		
Gross Sales	$460,157	117.4	106.6%	to	121.4%
Returns and Allowances	68,105	17.4	8.0	to	21.5
Net Sales	392,053	100.0	100.0	to	100.0
Net Sales of Imports, Exports, and Domestic Distributed Editions	22,947	5.9	4.3	to	32.2
All Other Net Sales	369,106	94.1	100.0	to	100.0
Total Cost of Sales	225,849	57.6	51.2	to	60.1
Manufacturing	158,732	41.8	35.9	to	46.0
Royalties	53,714	14.1	7.9	to	18.4
Imports, Exports, and Domestic Distributed Editions	6,390	1.7	1.2	to	14.6
Unspecified	7,013				
Gross Margin on Sales	166,205	42.4	39.9	to	48.8
Other Publishing Income	34,702	8.9	3.0	to	13.0
Total Operating Expenses	172,267	43.9	41.4	to	52.2
Editorial	18,964	5.0	3.2	to	7.1
Production	6,632	1.8	1.1	to	2.8
Marketing	60,042	16.0	13.6	to	19.5
Fulfillment	37,135	9.9	7.2	to	10.8
General/Administrative	42,423	11.3	10.0	to	15.0
Unspecified	7,072				
Net Income from Operation	28,638	7.3	1.4	to	11.8
Non-Publishing Income (or Expenses)	-583	-0.1	-1.5	to	1.5
Interest Income (or Expenses)	-1,840	-0.5	-2.5	to	-0.4
Misc. Other Income (or Expenses)	1,227	0.3	0.1	to	2.1
Unspecified Income (or Expenses)	31				
Net Income (or Loss) before Taxes	28,056	7.2	-0.6	to	11.3
Federal, State, and Local Income Taxes	15,354	3.9	1.7	to	5.8
Net Income (or Loss) after Taxes	12,702	3.2	-0.4	to	5.9

Source: Association of American Publishers (1977), p. 29.

Note: The figures in this table are drawn from the survey reports of 42 publishers.

Table 312–B.
Revenue, Expenses, and Earnings of U. S. Publishers of Professional Books, 1976

	Amount	Average Percent of Net Sales	Range of Net Sales for Middle 50% of Firms		
Gross Sales	$195,840	114.9%	109.9%	to	118.0%
Returns and Allowances	25,355	14.9	9.9	to	18.0
Net Sales	170,485	100.0	100.0	to	100.0
Net Sales of Imports, Exports, and Domestic Distributed Editions	10,385	6.1	6.8	to	35.4
All Other Net Sales	160,100	93.9	89.7	to	100.0
Total Cost of Sales	69,355	40.7	29.5	to	48.2
Manufacturing	48,173	28.5	18.9	to	34.9
Royalties	16,071	9.5	5.8	to	11.6
Imports, Exports and Domestic Distributed Editions	4,547	2.7	3.6	to	15.9
Unspecified	564				
Gross Margin on Sales	101,130	59.3	51.8	to	70.5
Other Publishing Income	2,025	1.2	0.7	to	2.2
Total Operating Expenses	78,428	46.0	40.1	to	57.4
Editorial	8,153	4.8	3.6	to	9.1
Production	3,101	1.8	1.0	to	2.2
Marketing	36,202	21.5	13.0	to	23.2
Fulfillment	9,648	5.7	5.3	to	9.5
General/Administrative	20,527	12.2	10.6	to	16.9
Unspecified	798				
Net Income from Operation	24,728	14.5	5.4	to	16.8
Non-Publishing Income (or Expenses)	147	0.1	-2.6	to	0.6
Interest Income (or Expenses)	-241	-0.1	-1.9	to	0.2
Misc. Other Income (or Expenses)	-178	-0.1	-0.8	to	0.3
Unspecified Income (or Expenses)	566				
Net Income (or Loss) before Taxes	24,875	14.6	5.9	to	17.6
Federal, State, and Local Income Taxes	12,273	7.2	2.6	to	8.2
Net Income (or Loss) after Taxes	12,602	7.4	3.5	to	12.0

Source: Association of American Publishers (1977), p. 58.

Note: The figures in this table are drawn from the survey reports of 23 publishers.

Interpretation of Tables

Tables 312-A through 312-E detail the 1976 operating finances of various sectors of the book industry, as reported in a survey by the Association of American Publishers (AAP). Two sectors of the industry, university presses and subscription reference book publishers, are not included here, since the AAP has not reported their operating data.

These presentations of revenue, expenses, and earnings provide a picture of the general state of the book publishing industry and the differences among the following sectors: trade books, professional books, mass-market paperbacks, and El-hi and college textbooks. The "average percent of net sales" in each table is the arithmetical average, while the "middle 50 percent" figures refer to those firms which fall between the 26th and the 75th percentiles in the rank order of the reporting group. This latter measure gives some idea of the variation from the average, while excluding the extreme cases. Since the percentage of sales for mass-market paperback publishers is based on gross sales, rather than net sales (as is the case with publishers in the other four sectors), the reader should take care in making comparisons.

Table 312–C.
Revenue, Expenses, and Earnings of U. S. Publishers
of Mass-Market Paperbacks (Rack-Sized Books Only), 1976

	Amount	Average Percent of Gross Sales	Range of Gross Sales for Middle 50% of Firms		
Gross Sales	$323,562	100.0%	100.0%	to	100.0%
Incentives	5,019	1.6	0.2	to	2.5
Returns and Allowances	99,014	30.6	24.8	to	43.7
Additional Credited Provisions	10,582	3.3	0.6	to	8.8
Total Returns and Credits	114,615	35.4	27.9	to	49.9
Net Sales	208,947	64.6	50.1	to	72.1
Total Cost of Sales	126,177	39.0	34.7	to	44.4
Manufacturing	56,632	17.5	16.3	to	19.5
Royalties	57,488	17.8	10.8	to	19.5
Freight and Duty	12,057	3.7	3.1	to	5.8
Gross Margin on Sales	82,770	25.6	13.9	to	32.9
Total Operating Expenses	62,927	19.4	12.6	to	22.7
Fulfillment Expenses	12,687	3.9	2.1	to	5.3
Order Entry and Customer Service	3,406	1.1	0.3	to	3.6
Shipping and Warehousing	9,281	2.9	1.0	to	5.1
EDP/Systems Expenses	2,861	0.9	0.3	to	1.5
Editorial	3,080	1.0	0.6	to	1.1
Production	2,055	0.6	0.4	to	1.2
Marketing	27,486	8.5	5.9	to	9.8
General/Administrative	15,402	4.8	2.5	to	5.6
Interest Expense (or Income)	617	0.2	0.1	to	0.5
Other Expenses (or Income)	-1,261	-0.4	-1.6	to	0.0
Net Income before Taxes and Management Fees	19,843	6.1	-3.2	to	13.1

Source: Association of American Publishers (1977), p. 82.

Note: The figures in this table are drawn from the survey reports of six publishers.

The AAP has been collecting similar information since 1971. However, comparisons with previous years are not presented here, because the number and identity of reporting publishers changes each year. The reader should consult Noble (1977) for some interpretations of trends, or contact the AAP for the full report, which is for sale to nonmembers and distributed free of charge to members.

Table 312-F covers 11 years—from 1965 through 1975—of sales, net income, and profit margin trends for six major, publicly held book publishing companies. Each of these corporations has been among the 10 largest book publishers at least once in the last decade. Their fortunes vary considerably. However, in general, the 1975 data reveal that these publishers are achieving profit margins which are slightly lower than 1965 levels, but somewhat better than the levels achieved in the early 1970s. Although the profit margins on the table range from a deficit to 26.2 percent, these large book publishing companies look fairly vital. Compared to the rest of American industry, their profits seem neither exorbitant nor anemic.

Sources

The information presented in the annual survey of the Association of American Publishers, some of which is available in **Tables 312-A** through **312-E**, is furnished by both association mem-

Table 312–D.
Revenue, Expenses, and Earnings of U. S. Publishers of El-Hi Textbooks, 1976

	Amount	Average Percent of Net Sales	Range of Net Sales for Middle 50% of Firms		
Gross Sales	$560,664	103.5%	103.0%	to	104.7%
Returns and Allowances	18,921	3.5	3.2	to	4.8
Net Sales	541,743	100.0	100.0	to	100.0
Total Cost of Sales	190,890	35.2	32.4	to	39.6
Paper, Printing, Binding, and Duplication	158,001	29.2	27.4	to	33.3
Royalties	32,889	6.1	5.2	to	7.7
Gross Margin on Sales	350,853	64.8	60.4	to	67.6
Other Publishing Income	5,673	1.0	0.2	to	1.9
General	4,387	0.8	0.1	to	1.3
From Foreign Subsidiaries	1,286	0.2	0.3	to	2.9
Unspecified	0				
Total Operating Expenses	285,091	52.6	46.3	to	66.1
Plant	30,992	5.7	3.9	to	7.9
Editorial	23,776	4.4	3.6	to	5.3
Production	8,103	1.5	0.9	to	2.2
Marketing	108,521	20.0	18.8	to	26.1
Fulfillment	44,969	8.3	6.6	to	10.7
General/Administrative	68,732	12.7	10.7	to	16.1
Net Income from Operation	71,436	13.2	-3.3	to	19.2
Non-Publishing Income (or Expenses)	-1,041	-0.2	-2.8	to	0.2
Interest Income (or Expenses)	-1,987	-0.4	-2.7	to	0.0
Misc. Other Income (or Expenses)	945	0.2	0.0	to	0.3
Net Income (or Loss) before Taxes	70,393	13.0	-3.8	to	19.4
Federal, State, and Local Income Taxes	37,198	6.9	2.9	to	10.5
Net Income (or Loss) after Taxes	33,195	6.1	-3.2	to	10.2

Source: Association of American Publishers (1977), p. 106.

Note: The figures in this table are drawn from the survey reports of 28 publishers.

bers and nonmembers, who voluntarily respond to the AAP questionnaires. The annual reports are prepared for publishers and others who are seeking detailed and reliable information about the industry. As a result, they do not suffer from the spirit of press agentry that sometimes infects the reports of other trade associations.

Of course, there are a number of limitations to the value of any survey data. There is no guarantee, for example, that the responding sample is representative of the total range of publishers within a particular sector of the industry. Nevertheless, a comparison of the estimated sales of the industry with the total sales of the reporting publishers should give the reader some idea of the relation of the sample to an entire sector's activity. The report always includes sufficient raw data to allow some intuitive estimate of how the respondents compare with the rest of the industry.

Another limitation of this data is that about 30 percent of the figures are merely estimations made by the publishers themselves. The AAP takes pains to specify definitions and instructions for these estimates, but the possibility for error still exists. On the other hand, this method of gathering data provides information on aspects of publishing that otherwise would simply not be available. A number of observers of the book industry, including Noble (1977) and Grannis (1977),

Table 312–E.

Revenue, Expenses, and Earnings of U. S. Publishers of College Textbooks, 1976

	Amount	Average Percent of Net Sales	Range of Net Sales for Middle 50% of Firms		
Gross Sales	$526,733	117.7%	115.7%	to	122.6%
Returns and Allowances	79,372	17.7	15.7	to	22.6
Net Sales	447,361	100.0	100.0	to	100.0
Net Sales of Imports, Exports, and Domestic Distributed Editions	36,477	8.2	5.2	to	100.0
All Other Net Sales	410,884	91.8	94.8	to	100.0
Total Cost of Sales	161,162	36.0	35.5	to	40.1
Paper, Printing, Binding, and Duplication	88,068	19.7	18.4	to	23.0
Royalties	67,702	15.1	13.6	to	17.1
Imports, Exports, and Domestic Distributed Editions	5,392	1.2	1.0	to	8.8
Gross Margin on Sales	286,199	64.0	59.9	to	64.5
Other Publishing Income	1,963	0.4	0.2	to	0.5
Total Operating Expenses	205,439	45.9	45.7	to	59.6
Plant	29,906	6.7	5.1	to	9.6
Editorial	26,490	5.9	4.9	to	9.2
Production	6,683	1.5	0.9	to	2.3
Marketing	63,230	14.1	12.9	to	18.2
Fulfillment	29,293	6.5	5.5	to	8.7
General/Administrative	49,837	11.1	10.3	to	13.8
Net Income from Operation	82,723	18.5	3.1	to	17.4
Non-Publishing Income (or Expenses)	-608	-0.1	-1.4	to	0.1
Interest Income (or Expenses)	-384	-0.1	-1.2	to	-0.2
Misc. Other Income (or Expenses)	-224	-0.1	-0.3	to	0.3
Unspecified Income (or Expenses)	0				
Net Income (or Loss) before Taxes	82,115	18.4	2.6	to	16.9
Federal, State, and Local Income Taxes	38,522	8.6	1.6	to	8.4
Net Income (or Loss) after Taxes	43,593	9.7	1.3	to	8.7

Source: Association of American Publishers (1977), p. 130.

Note: The figures in this table are drawn from the survey reports of 29 publishers.

have recently praised the usefulness of the AAP report. The reader should see Unit 310 for further discussion of AAP estimates and their relation to other sources of data.

The figures in **Table 312-F** are collected from the annual reports of firms listed by *Standard and Poor's Industry Surveys,* a noted supplier of business information. The editors consider the data to be valid and reliable.

Further Information

The AAP annual survey supplies detailed breakdowns for many of the line items listed in **Tables 312-A** through **312-E.** Articles commenting on this data appear periodically in *Publishers Weekly,* and some of the data is usually reprinted in *The Bowker Annual.* See Unit 310 for some overall sales figures to which these operating statements can be compared.

Table 312-F.
Index of Sales, Net Income, and Profit Margin of Six Major U. S. Publishers, 1965–1975

Note: Sales and income index figures are calculated on a base of 100 for the year 1967.

Year	Grolier			McGraw-Hill			Harcourt Brace Jovanovich			Macmillan			Scott, Foresman			Prentice-Hall		
	Sales	Net Income	% Profit Margin[a]	Sales	Net Income	% Profit Margin	Sales[b]	Net Income	% Profit Margin	Sales	Net Income	% Profit Margin	Sales	Net Income	% Profit Margin	Sales	Net Income	% Profit Margin
1965	78	106	14.5 %	72	78	16.7 %	57	80	24.9 %	68	85	15.6 %	70	83	24.1 %	78	70	22.5 %
1966	88	117	15.2	91	103	18.2	76	102	23.5	84	102	15.4	100	140	26.2	89	94	25.6
1967	100	100	13.1	100	100	16.5	100	100	18.0	100	100	12.5	100[c]	100	21.6	100	100	24.6
1968	104	96	12.6	114	100	15.4	134	100	15.4	160	143	13.4	105	107	22.7	115	108	24.8
1969	119	122	13.6	117	91	13.4	141	116	16.4	209	165	12.7	106	101	21.4	128	124	24.9
1970	133	136	14.5	116	73	11.0	147	110	14.7	214	71	7.6	112	100	19.7	136	126	23.5
1971	148	125	10.3	118	70	9.8	170	124	13.8	207	95	8.7	119	106	21.8	143	135	23.0
1972	168	110	11.7	126	82	12.1	177	131	14.4	211	136	11.5	123	109	21.6	153	139	24.1
1973	173	deficit	10.2	138	98	12.8	194	112	14.0	225	153	11.3	134	127	22.7	163	153	24.1
1974	145	deficit	deficit	149	108	13.2	225	166	13.7	250	144	10.4	183	141	19.2	187	153	21.4
1975	143	deficit	5.2	157	118	14.0	265	198	15.0	256	119	10.7	219	216[d]	23.8	206	159	20.9

Source: *Standard and Poor's Industry Surveys: Communication*, October 9, 1975; October 14, 1976.

Notes: (a) Profit margins are derived by dividing operating income by sales. Operating income is usually the balance left from sales after deduction of operating costs, promotional and administrative expenses, local and state taxes, and provisions for bad debts and pensions; but before other income and before deductions for depreciation, debt service charges, federal taxes, and any special reserves. (b) Figures for Harcourt Brace Jovanovich represent *net* sales and other revenues. (c) Index base for Scott, Foresman represents sales/net income as of April of the *following* calendar year. All other companies report these figures as of December of the same calendar year. (d) Figure reflects a LIFO accounting system.

Table 313–A.
Average Book Prices in U. S., 1947–1976

Year	Hardcover Trade/Technical		Trade and Higher Priced Paperback		Mass Market Paperback	
	Current Dollars	Constant (1972) Dollars[a]	Current Dollars	Constant (1972) Dollars[a]	Current Dollars	Constant (1972) Dollars[a]
1947/49	$ 3.59	$ 6.41	N/A	N/A	N/A	N/A
1953	4.13	6.46	N/A	N/A	N/A	N/A
1956	4.61	7.09	N/A	N/A	N/A	N/A
1958	5.12	7.41	N/A	N/A	N/A	N/A
1960	5.24	7.40	N/A	N/A	N/A	N/A
1961	5.81	8.13	N/A	N/A	N/A	N/A
1962	5.90	8.16	$2.12	$2.93	$ .53	$ .73
1963	6.55	8.95	2.27	3.10	.58	.79
1964	6.93	9.35	2.41	3.25	.59	.80
1965	7.65	10.28	2.50	3.36	.63	.85
1966	7.94	10.23	2.95	3.80	.64	.82
1967	7.99	10.01	3.09	3.87	.69	.86
1968	8.47	10.18	3.05	3.67	.78	.94
1969	9.37	10.70	3.58	4.09	.91	1.04
1970	11.66	12.56	4.81	5.18	.95	1.02
1971[b]	13.25	13.69	5.09	5.26	1.01	1.04
1972	12.99	12.99	4.24	4.24	1.12	1.12
1973	12.20	11.49	3.73	3.51	1.17	1.10
1974	14.09	11.95	4.38	3.72	1.28	1.09
1975	16.19	12.58	5.24	4.07	1.46	1.13
1976	16.32	11.99	5.53	4.06	1.60	1.18

Sources: 1947/49-1974: *Bowker Annual*, appropriate years; 1975, 1976: *Publisher's Weekly* (1977).

Notes: (a) Constant dollar conversion based on Consumer Price Index. (b) Figures for 1971 and later years are computed as "price per volume" rather than per title. Caution should be used in comparing 1971-76 figures with figures for previous years.

Interpretation of Tables

Table 313-A lists the average prices of hardcover trade/technical books, trade and higher priced paperback books, and mass-market paperbacks for the period 1947/49 through 1976. Over most of this 30-year period, there has been a generally steady rise in prices—both in current and constant (1972) dollars—for all three categories of books. However, except in the case of mass-market paperbacks, the constant dollar prices for books peaked in 1971 and have fluctuated somewhat below that peak since then. Unfortunately, 1971 is also the year in which the survey for these prices switched from a price-per-title to a price-per-*volume* basis. Consequently, it is difficult to assess the validity of the 1971-1976 figures in comparison to the earlier data.

Table 313-B offers a detailed breakdown, by book subject matter, of the 1976 figures in Table 313-A. The price indexes on the table, which are based on a value of 100 for the average 1967-69 price for each subject category, provide an indication of the relative price increases for the different subjects. The reader will note that there is a considerable variation both in book prices and in price increases by subject matter. Mass-market paperback prices show the greatest overall

Table 313–B.
Average Book Prices in U. S., by Book Subject Matter, 1976

Note: Index figures are calculated on a base of 100 for the years 1967-69.

Subject Category	Hardcover Trade/Technical		Trade and Higher Priced Paperback		Mass Market Paperback	
	Average Price	Price Index	Average Price	Price Index	Average Price	Price Index
Agriculture	$14.01	128.1	$ 5.19	150.9	$1.77	148.7
Art	19.91	133.3	5.66	138.0	1.46	108.1
Biography[a]	14.81	115.7	4.26	132.7	1.82	135.8
Business	16.22	130.3	7.44	114.3	1.95	178.9
Education	12.95	126.2	5.75	148.6	1.73	104.8
Fiction	9.87	152.6	3.42	152.7	1.52	150.5
General Works[b]	21.89	86.9	5.67	58.7	1.74	143.8
History	16.63	111.5	5.35	149.4	1.94	141.6
Home Economics[b]	10.23	129.8	4.32	153.2	1.80	151.3
Juveniles	5.87	134.3	2.56	193.9	1.22	148.8
Language[b]	16.25	114.8	6.61	132.7	1.73	100.0
Law	19.19	111.9	11.62	254.3	1.82	119.0
Literature	14.65	121.8	5.05	135.8	1.88	156.7
Medicine	23.43	144.7	7.97	149.0	1.86	151.2
Music	15.73	116.3	5.85	135.4	1.90	172.7
Philosophy, Psychology[b]	13.96	133.7	4.98	138.3	1.79	142.1
Poetry, Drama	12.41	116.9	3.55	122.8	1.92	119.3
Religion	12.47	127.2	3.32	132.3	1.71	127.6
Science	23.95	149.2	8.37	156.4	1.59	117.8
Sociology, Economics[b]	20.03	118.3	5.57	135.5	1.87	123.0
Sports, Recreation	11.40	107.0	4.23	148.4	1.75	148.3
Technology	20.47	127.1	7.21	75.1	2.00	155.0
Travel[b]	16.73	130.9	4.75	138.5	2.59	169.3
Total	**$16.32**	**125.6**	**$ 5.53**	**130.4**	**$1.60**	**142.9**

Sources: *Publishers Weekly* (February 13, 1977), pp. 52-56. Index figures are based on 1972 data in *The Bowker Annual* (1975), pp. 180-182.

Notes: (a) These figures include biographies placed in other categories by the Library of Congress. (b) New category. Index base is for 1967 and 1969 rather than 1967 through 1969.

increases, particularly in the areas of music, medicine, and law. For hardcover trade/technical books, the most significant increases have been in sociology and economics, religion, and education. The trade and higher priced paperback books have experienced their greatest price hikes in law, books for juveniles, literature, science, and fiction.

Table 313-C presents the average prices of novels, works of biography, and histories from 1929 through 1976. Although the figures shown here are likely to be less valid than those shown in Tables 313-A and 313-B (see "Sources" discussion below), this series has the advantage of offering continuous data for nearly 50 years. The table indicates that over the past 20 years, the percentage of price increases have been about the same for all three categories of books. Between 1956 and 1966, for example, prices in each category rose between 45 and 55 percent. Between 1966 and 1976, the increases were between 65 and 69 percent. During these same two periods, the Consumer Price Index for all commodities increased 19 percent (1956-1966) and 75 percent (1966-1976).

Table 313-D presents a series of average book prices, by type of book, for 1972 and 1976. These estimates were determined by balancing estimated consumer expenditures against estimates of publishers' sales. Between 1972 and 1976, the greatest price increases were among paperbound college texts, adult paperbound trade books, college texts generally, and juvenile paperback trade

Table 313–C.
Average Hardbound Trade Book Prices in U. S., 1929–1976

Year	Novels	Biography	History
1929	$2.25	$ 4.11	$ 4.35
1939	2.38	3.40	3.34
1941	2.58	3.30	3.89
1948	2.97	3.98	5.06
1950	3.02	4.47	5.21
1952	3.26	4.66	5.45
1954	3.50	4.40	5.56
1956	3.63	4.96	5.49
1958	3.90	4.92	6.52
1960	4.09	5.75	6.99
1962	4.52	6.43	7.08
1964	4.86	6.24	7.85
1966	5.28	7.69	8.25
1968	5.82	13.73	9.95
1970	6.27	9.95	10.55
1972	6.96	10.12	12.30
1974	7.68	12.31	12.91
1976	8.74	12.87	13.96

Sources: 1929-1941: *Bowker Annual* (1961). 1948-1976: *Publisher's Weekly*, annual statistical issues.

books. The smallest price increases since 1972 are found among mail-order publications and hardbound religious books.

Sources

The data in **Tables 313-A** and **313-B** were taken from annual averages of the new book prices recorded throughout the year in the "Weekly Record" section of *Publishers Weekly*. These weekly listings of new titles serve as the standard announcement of a book's existence to the trade.

The practice of calculating annual averages of these weekly listings began as a project of the Resources and Technical Services Division of the American Library Association, in cooperation with the U.S. Office of Education. The project was designed to develop a uniform standard by which price changes in library materials might be evaluated. The first series of prices using this method was published by Schick and Kurth (1961). Since then, annual averages of prices and price changes have been carried in the annual statistical issues of *Publishers Weekly* and in *The Bowker Annual* (which supplements this data with information from the Library of Congress).

For many years, this was the leading measure of price changes in the book trade. Recently, however, a number of shortcomings have been found with these averages. First of all, average prices are based upon the publisher's list price; they are not checked against sales figures. Consequently, if lower priced books sell many more copies than higher priced books, the average-price listings would be higher than the average prices actually paid. For this reason, Dessauer (1976, p. 43) points out that the *Publishers Weekly* series generally overestimates the average prices being paid.

Further, some categories of books, such as U.S. government publications and university theses, are excluded from the averages. Although such exclusions are not unreasonable, the reader should also note that some categories of books included in the tally are underreported. Grannis (1977, p. 33) states that these underreported categories include "undetermined numbers of textbooks" and "probably more than 1,000" paperback titles each year.

Finally, R. R. Bowker Company has recently decided to end its reliance on this annual statistical series and substitute another series based on an 18-month data-collection period. Bowker has found that many titles dated in a given year do not reach its computers, or those of the Library

Table 313–D.
Average Per-Book Consumer Expenditures in U. S., by Type of Book, 1972 and 1976

Type of Book	Average Price, 1972	Average Price, 1976	Index: Average Price Increase, 1976 (1972=100)
Trade Books	$ 3.07	$ 4.33	141.0
Adult, Hardbound	5.02	6.67	132.9
Adult, Paperbound	1.58	2.79	176.6
Juvenile, Hardbound	2.94	4.28	145.6
Juvenile, Paperbound	.75	1.24	165.3
Religious Books	2.76	3.66	132.6
Hardbound	7.14	9.11	127.6
Paperbound	1.27	2.05	161.4
Professional Books	4.86	7.26	149.4
Hardbound	9.78	15.40	157.5
Paperbound	2.39	3.64	152.3
Book Club Publications	2.12	3.15	148.6
Hardbound	2.88	4.48	155.6
Paperbound	1.24	1.82	146.8
Mail-Order Publications	9.43	11.61	123.1
Mass Market Paperbacks	.95	1.50	157.9
University Press Publications	4.86	7.20	148.1
Hardbound	8.39	11.92	142.1
Paperbound	1.96	3.05	155.6
El-Hi Textbooks	1.87	2.67	142.8
Hardbound	3.79	5.24	138.3
Paperbound	1.15	1.79	155.7
College Textbooks	4.44	7.46	168.0
Hardbound	8.15	11.63	142.7
Paperbound	2.56	4.73	184.8
Subscription Reference Books	186.29	266.40	143.0
Total, All Books	2.56	3.69	144.1
Hardbound	5.85	8.34	142.6
Paperbound	1.27	2.00	157.5

Source: Calculated by the editors from data in Dessauer, Doebler, and Nordberg (1977), pp. 270, 286.

Note: The editors calculated the estimated average prices by dividing the total dollar sales in each book category by the total unit sales. (Both totals were rounded to the nearest hundred thousands.) The index for price changes was calculated by dividing 1976 estimated average prices by 1972 estimated average prices (both rounded to nearest cent).

of Congress, until several months later. In 1976, the first year in which the new series was employed, Bowker found considerable price differences between the 18-month tally and the 12-month tally (Grannis, 1977, p. 33).

The data for **Table 313-C** are based on annual hand-counts by the *Publishers Weekly* staff of the prices for books advertised in the Fall announcement issues of *Publishers Weekly*. In 1976, the prices of 174 novels, 130 biographies, and 151 volumes of history were included in the averages under the following definitions: "Novels, except Mystery, Western, S-F, Gothic," "Biography, Memoirs, Letters," and "History, including Pictorial, but not Art books."

The major problem with this method is that it is difficult to estimate the extent to which a book's appearance in a paid advertisement qualified it as a representative of its subject matter and price range. There is obviously no scientific basis for validity in these averages. Still, they continue a series which was begun in less sophisticated days and has some historical value.

Table 313-D represents an ambitious attempt to overcome some of the shortcomings of the previous series in this unit. It estimates all consumer expenditures—including the expenditures of libraries, schools, and other institutional markets—by applying the factors of mark-ups, remainder sales, and similar trade practices to the data on publishers' sales.

The source of this material is John P. Dessauer, Inc.—a trade, rather than academic, source. Consequently, the editors are not able to describe the full methodology used to determine these estimates. Nevertheless, Dessauer's recent work is probably the best available estimate of what the average consumer is actually paying for a given kind of book, while the material from the "Weekly Record" in *Publishers Weekly* represents the best approximation of the prices at which books are being offered and the best indication of the extent to which publishers are responding to inflationary pressures by raising prices.

Further Information

The Bowker Annual regularly publishes many of series discussed above, as well as the prices of British and other foreign books and periodicals.

Library Finances and Personnel

314

Table 314–A.
Number, Annual Operating Expenditures, and Size of Collections and Professional Staffs of Public Libraries in U. S., 1962 and 1974

	1962	1974	Percent Change
Number of Public Libraries[a]	7,257	8,307	14.5%
Size of Collections			
Book Collections (millions of volumes)	N/A	387.6	N/A
Total, All Print Materials (millions)[b]	241.4	397.0	64.5
Total, Nonprint Materials (thousands)	N/A	45,577	N/A
Audiovisual Materials (thousands)	N/A	8,309	N/A
All Other Materials (thousands)	N/A	37,268	N/A
Size of Professional Staffs[c]	19,855	36,131	82.0
Population Served (millions)	155.7	198.6	27.6
Total Annual Operating Expenditures (millions)	$317	$1,018	221.0
Average per Capita Expenditures for Population Served	$2.04	$5.13	151.0
Expenditures in Constant (1972) Dollars (millions)	$449	$875	94.9
Average per Capita Expenditures in Constant (1972) Dollars	$2.88	$4.41	53.0

Source: Ladd (1977), pp. 69, 99.

Notes: (a) Of the 7,257 public libraries in the United States in 1962, 6,565 reported adequately on collections and 6,318 reported adequately on professional staffs. In 1974, a survey sample of 1,460 libraries was used to estimate the characteristics of the total number of 8,307. In Ladd's (1977) analysis, the percent increase figures were based on the number of libraries furnishing adequate data in 1962 and the total number of libraries in 1974. The editors of this volume have preferred to compare the size of the total numbers for both years. (b) This category includes volumes of bookstock and bound periodicals, plus titles of books and periodicals in all types of microforms. (c) Includes librarians, media audiovisual specialists, and other full-time professional staff members. Does not include technical, clerical, or other library staff (43,533 in 1974) or plant operation maintenance staff (6,335 in 1974). The total number of full-time professional and nonprofessional staff people in 1974 was 86,003.

Table 314–B.
Number, Annual Operating Expenditures, and Size of Collections and
Professional Staffs of College and University Libraries in U. S., 1963 and 1975

	1963	1975	Percent Change
Four-Year Colleges[a]			
Number of Libraries	1,339	1,745	30.3%
Collections (millions of volumes)	88.3	274	210.3
Size of Professional Staff	4,696	10,934	132.8
Annual Operating Expenditures (millions)	$201.4	$483	139.8
Two-Year Colleges			
Number of Libraries	591	1,121	89.7
Collections (millions of volumes)	8.0	43	437.5
Size of Professional Staff	969	3,869	299.3
Annual Operating Expenditures (millions)	$11.6	$160	1,279.3
All Institutions, Including Universities[a]			
Number of Libraries	2,075	3,026	45.8
Collections (millions of volumes)	215	612	184.7
Size of Professional Staff	11,200	22,880	104.3
Annual Operating Expenditures (millions)	$213	$1,071	402.8
Number of Students Served (millions)	4.3	10.2	137.2

Source: Ladd (1977), pp. 162, 181, 224. Percent change calculated by editors.

Note: (a) The method of classifying institutions changed between 1963 and 1975. In 1963, the category of "four-year colleges" included universities, but in the tabulations of collections and professional staff, larger academic libraries with significantly greater average sizes, were pulled out of the subcategory and included only in the "all institutions" data.

The collections of the 129 libraries treated this way in 1963 all exceeded 300,000 volumes, and their total holdings were 118.7 million volumes.

The professional staff in 145 academic libraries in 1963 exceeded 15 full-time-equivalent positions, and these libraries, with a total professional staff of 5,545, only had their figures added in the "all institutions" totals.

In 1975, the distinction is clear. "Four-year colleges" includes no universities. University data are in the "all institutions" category only.

Interpretation of Tables

Tables 314-A and 314-B present comparisons of library collections, staffs, and operating expenditures for two periods, 1962-1963 and 1974-1975. This information is available because of the efforts of the National Center for Education Statistics (NCES), which sponsored the first large-scale samplings of historically comparable information on a cross-section of U.S. libraries.

Table 314-A, from a report prepared for the National Commission on Libraries and Information Science, is based on data from the Office of Education and the NCES. The data show that the number of public libraries increased fairly slowly in the years between 1962 and 1974, but that library staffs, collections, and expenditures (even in constant dollars) have expanded more quickly. The 8,307 public libraries in this country now possess nearly 400 million books (or their equivalent in other print materials) and about 45,000 nonprint items.

Table 314-B shows similar trends for all college and university libraries. Two-year-college libraries have exhibited the greatest growth, both in numbers and in collections. As a whole, college and university libraries have outperformed public libraries in most aspects of growth.

In Table 314-C, the reader will find an overview of the major characteristics and annual expenditures of public school libraries and media centers in 1973-1974. Nearly 75,000 school libraries in the United States serve more than 43 million students, or about 39 out of every 40 public school enrollees. According to Ladd (1977, p. 107), these libraries and media centers are located in about 84 percent of the nation's approximately 89,000 public schools.

Table 314–C.
Annual Expenditures, Number of Staff, Size of Collection and Number of Pupils Served by Public School Libraries and Media Centers in U. S., 1973 and 1974

Number of Schools with Libraries/Media Centers	74,625
Expenditures[a]	
Salaries and Wages	$818,205,114
Supplies and Materials	
Books	$162,293,435
Periodicals	$24,237,062
Audiovisual	$71,379,882
Equipment	$66,720,088
Other Expenditures	$39,448,526
Total	$1,182,284,107
Pupils Served[b]	43,929,114
Certificated Staff[b]	
Women	55,281
Men	7,378
Total	62,659
Books[b]	
Added During the Year	37,486,930
Total at End of the Year	506,964,551
Total Audiovisual Materials at End of the Year[b]	68,023,961

Source: Eldridge (1976).

Notes: (a) Figures are for the 1973-74 school year. (b) Figures are for 1974.

Table 314-D provides estimates of the cost of books and other media acquisitions by libraries in the United States in 1973-1974. The main value of this table is that it suggests the range of expenditures for a variety of materials in several media, with the percentage of expenditures for books by four categories of libraries: (1) college and university libraries, (2) public libraries, (3) special libraries, and (4) school libraries. The purchasing power of these institutions is such that trends in one medium—for example, price increases in periodicals—may affect trends in another medium—such as the volume of book sales.

Sources

Table 314-A is based upon two different surveys of public libraries—one performed by the U.S. Office of Education in 1962, the other by the National Center for Education Statistics in 1974. The surveys are described in the "Sources" section of Unit 112. The data in Table 314-B were also derived from general surveys by the Office of Education and the NCES, and the Table 314-C data are based on a NCES sample survey of public school libraries and media centers in the 1973-1974 school year (see Unit 112 for details). Further information about the validity and reliability of all of these surveys and data can be found in the NCES reports on the surveys (National Center for Educational Statistics, 1977a, 1977b). Table 314-D is taken from two publications of the Book Industry Study Group (see "Sources" section of Unit 311 for a description of the Study Group and their reports).

Table 314–D.
Estimated Value of Books and Other Materials Purchased
by Libraries in U. S., 1973–1974

Note: All dollar figures are in millions.

	Dollars	Units
College and University Libraries		
Books (Total)	$ 179.1	21.60
Domestic	115.6	14.40
Imports	45.7	3.81
Government and Special	17.8	3.39
Periodicals	105.9	3.53
Audiovisuals	14.7	.74
Microform	14.6	- -
Binding	21.1	- -
Total College and University Libraries	**$ 335.4**	- -
Public Libraries		
Books (Total)	$ 138.1	31.90
Domestic	131.3	30.37
Imports	0.7	.01
Government and Special	6.1	1.52
Periodicals	13.4	.74
Audiovisuals	11.1	.56
Microform	2.2	- -
Binding	2.8	- -
Total Public Libraries	**$ 167.6**	- -
Special Libraries		
Books (Total)	$ 77.5	8.23
Domestic	51.2	4.97
Imports	18.3	1.52
Government and Special	8.0	1.74
Periodicals	68.1	1.62
Audiovisuals	7.8	.39
Microform	9.4	- -
Binding	11.4	- -
Total Special Libraries	**$ 174.2**	- -
School Libraries		
Books	$ 184.4	75.61
Periodicals	27.5	2.04
Audiovisuals	81.6	4.12
Microform	.7	- -
Binding	.6	- -
Total School Libraries	**$ 294.8**	- -
ALL LIBRARIES	**$ 972.0**	- -

Source: Dessauer (1976), p. 23.

Further Information

Reports of the NCES and reports and publications of the Association of Research Libraries, the Medical Library Association, the American Library Association, and other such associations are filled with detailed information about their member libraries. Considerable summary information about libraries, including bibliographic references, can also be found in *The Bowker Annual* and in such periodicals as Bowker's *Library Journal*.

Table 320–A.
Total Receipts of U. S. Newspaper Industry vs. Receipts
from Newspaper Products Only, 1914–1957

| | Total Industry Receipts | | Receipts from Newspaper Products Only | |
| | Current Dollars | Constant (1972) Dollars | Total Income (Sale of Advertising and Newspapers) | Percent of Total from Advertising |
Year				
	Note: All dollar figures are in millions.			
1914	N/A	N/A	$ 283.6	65
1919	N/A	N/A	566.3	70
1921	N/A	N/A	734.3	71
1923	N/A	N/A	803.5	72
1925	$ 971.2	$2,873.4	892.1	74
1927	1,049.3	3,228.6	977.6	74
1929	1,149.9	3,505.8	1,073.1	74
1931	947.6	3,301.7	886.5	71
1933	701.4	2,816.9	667.8	64
1935	813.1	2,956.7	762.2	66
1937	922.3	3,180.3	861.7	67
1939	904.9	3,208.9	845.7	64
1947	1,917.3	3,857.7	1,792.3	67
1949	2,325.3	4,420.7	2,232.3	67
1950	2,435.1	4,543.1	2,338.3	68
1951	2,573.2	4,490.8	2,499.9	70
1952	2,763.1	4,764.0	2,672.4	70
1953	2,955.0	5,017.0	2,832.6	71
1954	3,091.0	5,247.9	2,926.5	71
1955	3,395.7	5,566.7	3,210.2	73
1956	3,612.4	5,743.1	3,396.4	73
1957	3,703.9	5,698.3	3,477.3	73

Sources: 1914-1937 data: *Biennial Survey of Manufactures.* 1947 and 1954 data: *Census of Manufactures*, appropriate issues. Data for all other years: *Annual Survey of Manufactures*, appropriate issues.

Note: The calculation of constant dollars is based on the Gross National Product deflator.

Interpretation of Tables

Tables 320-A and 320-B illustrate the growth trends in the receipts of the American newspaper industry from 1914 to 1975. The tables distinguish between receipts from newspaper products only and from the newspaper industry as a whole in order to account for companies which are primarily in the business of producing other products, but also publish newspapers. In addition, some newspaper companies have other sources of revenue exclusive of their newspaper operations. Finally, the U.S. Census Bureau uses one or the other of these series as the total for various categorical breakdowns of newspaper industry data.

The basic message of both series of figures in Table 320-A and 320-B is that the newspaper industry has experienced growth, both in current and constant (1972) dollars, for most of the 60-year period. The fortunes of the industry tend to parallel the general direction of the economy as a whole. For example, the effects of the Great Depression on newspaper revenues are apparent. But since the industry itself has prospered while the actual number of newspapers has declined (see Unit 120), it appears that the growth of the survivors has counterbalanced the demise of some newspapers.

Table 320-B.
Total Receipts of U. S. Newspaper Industry vs. Receipts from Newspaper Products Only, by Type of Newspaper, 1958–1975

Note: All dollar figures are in millions.

	All Newspapers	All Newspapers		Daily/Sunday Newspapers	Daily/Sunday Newspapers	Weekly/Other Newspapers	Weekly/Other Newspapers
	Total Receipts, All Newspaper Products	Total Receipts, Newspaper Industry	Total Industry Receipts, Constant (1972) Dollars	Total Receipts	Percent of Receipts from Advertising	Total Receipts	Percent of Receipts from Advertising
1958	$ 3,458.3	3,628.0	$5,581.5	$3,125.4	71	$297.8	79
1959	3,767.3	3,946.6	5,846.8	3,396.7	72	320.1	78
1960	3,920.2	4,136.6	6,021.3	3,531.7	72	337.1	78
1961	3,954.6	4,182.0	6,034.6	3,588.4	71	329.6	78
1962	4,089.2	4,319.5	6,233.0	3,716.6	71	340.2	77
1963	4,254.7	4,483.6	6,262.0	3,791.9	72	378.9	78
1964	4,620.4	4,820.4	6,630.5	4,123.2	72	401.1	78
1965	4,886.1	5,156.1	6,939.6	4,343.3	73	425.6	78
1966	5,256.0	5,520.2	7,187.8	4,688.2	74	489.0	78
1967	5,549.8	5,757.1	7,287.5	4,961.6	74	321.4	76
1968	5,938.2	6,191.2	7,495.4	5,323.4	73	371.6	76
1969	6,538.2	6,822.8	7,869.4	5,848.9	74	439.5	75
1970	6,636.1	6,966.6	7,622.1	5,870.9	72	560.6	76
1971	7,036.6	7,354.5	7,660.9	6,272.3	71	548.1	76
1972	7,908.4	8,270.1	8,270.1	6,960.6	75	493.4	78
1973	8,495.7	8,868.4	8,382.2	7,488.4	76	624.8	79
1974	9,186.6	9,567.9	8,219.8	8,118.7	75	840.0	79
1975	10,042.8	10,468.4	8,223.4	8,825.7	74	976.8	81

Sources: 1963, 1967, and 1972 data: *Census of Manufactures*, appropriate issues. Data for all other years: *Annual Survey of Manufactures*, appropriate issues.

Note: The calculation of constant dollars is based on the Gross National Product deflator.

In **Table 320-B**, the Census Bureau tallies the total receipts and the newspaper-product receipts of daily and Sunday newspapers and weekly/other newspapers. From this breakdown, which the Census Bureau initiated in 1958, one can see that the daily and Sunday share of total receipts has been holding firm at about 89 or 90 percent. These figures provide some justification for Bagdikian's (1976/77, p. 19) comment that concern over the mortality of daily newspapers has

Table 320-C.

Table 320-C.
Average Advertising Rates of Daily and Sunday Newspapers in U. S., 1921–1976

Note: All index figures are calculated on a base of 100 for the year 1972.

	Morning Dailies			Evening Dailies			Sunday Newspapers			Consumer Price Index
	Agate Line Rate	Milline Rate	Index of Milline Rate	Agate Line Rate	Milline Rate	Index of Milline Rate	Agate Line Rate	Milline Rate	Index of Milline Rate	
1921	$ 26.00	$2.59	50.8	$ 60.01	$ 3.29	47.5	$ 44.25	$2.32	46.6	42.8
1925	33.20	2.66	52.2	72.37	3.39	49.0	54.24	2.32	46.6	41.9
1930	35.51	2.52	49.4	87.02	3.45	49.9	62.34	2.36	47.4	40.3
1935	37.30	2.58	50.6	88.10	3.71	53.6	59.66	2.12	42.6	32.8
1940	38.17	2.37	46.5	89.95	3.59	51.9	68.57	2.11	42.4	33.5
1945	57.12	2.24	43.9	114.33	3.24	46.8	81.59	2.02	40.6	43.0
1950	77.99	2.65	52.0	156.55	3.83	55.3	123.54	2.41	48.4	57.5
1955	95.01	3.12	61.2	190.92	4.46	64.5	147.72	2.91	58.4	64.0
1960	121.02	3.63	71.2	229.56	5.09	73.6	170.18	3.55	71.3	70.8
1965	136.61	3.96	77.6	260.51	5.44	78.6	182.56	3.73	74.9	74.4
1970	171.76	4.79	93.9	313.49	6.50	93.9	230.25	4.66	93.6	92.8
1975	258.47	7.19	141.0	461.51	9.56	138.2	358.74	7.10	142.6	128.7
1976	285.83	7.95	155.9	481.43	10.02	144.8	388.10	7.50	150.6	136.1

Source: *Editor and Publisher International Yearbook*, appropriate annual issues.

been a "report of an exaggerated death." (The reader should note that the sums of the columns for "daily/Sunday" and "weekly/other" newspaper receipts do not equal the total figures for the newspaper industry because of the presence in the latter category of receipts for newspapers "not specified by kind.")

Through **Table 320-B**, the reader may also trace the relative financial importance of advertising revenues, as opposed to subscriptions and sales. Overall industry receipts from advertising have fluctuated between about 70 and 75 percent. Weeklies appear to be slightly more dependent

Table 320-D.
Receipts, Selected Operating Costs, and Capital Expenditures of U. S. Newspaper Industry, 1925–1975

Note: All dollar figures are in millions.

	Total Industry Receipts		Cost of Materials, Fuels, etc.		Payroll, All Employees		Wages, Production Workers Only		New Capital Expenditures	
	Current Dollars	Constant (1972) Dollars	Current Dollars	Percent of Total Receipts	Current Dollars	Percent of Total Receipts	Current Dollars	Percent of Total Receipts	Current Dollars	Percent of Total Receipts
1925	$ 971.2	$2,873.4	$ 296.8	31%	N/A	N/A	$ 180.1	19%	N/A	N/A
1927	1,049.3	3,228.6	306.0	29	N/A	N/A	194.7	19	N/A	N/A
1929	1,149.9	3,505.8	305.0	27	N/A	N/A	211.4	18	N/A	N/A
1931	947.6	3,301.7	235.3	25	N/A	N/A	189.7	20	N/A	N/A
1933	701.4	2,816.9	151.1	22	N/A	N/A	138.9	20	N/A	N/A
1935	813.1	2,956.7	180.5	22	N/A	N/A	164.5	20	N/A	N/A
1937	922.3	3,180.3	221.1	24	N/A	N/A	185.8	20	N/A	N/A
1939	904.9	3,208.9	231.1	26	N/A	N/A	164.0	18	N/A	N/A
1947	1,917.3	3,857.7	518.6	27	$ 743.9	39%	372.8	19	N/A	N/A
1954	3,019.0	5,247.9	946.8	31	1,262.8	41	667.1	22	$ 75.5	2%
1958	3,628.0	5,581.5	1,112.4	31	1,499.9	41	779.0	21	148.2	4
1963	4,483.6	6,262.0	1,281.2	29	1,784.6	40	935.2	21	135.2	3
1967	5,757.1	7,287.5	1,573.6	27	2,223.7	39	1,121.5	19	246.7	4
1972	8,270.1	8,270.1	2,045.2	25	3,170.8	38	1,537.8	19	359.6	4
1974	9,567.9	8,219.8	2,528.0	26	3,598.5	38	1,669.3	17	408.2	4
1975	10,468.4	8,223.4	2,879.1	28	3,784.7	36	1,715.7	16	366.7	4

Sources: 1925-1954 data: *1963 Census of Manufactures.* 1958-1972 data: *1972 Census of Manufactures.* 1974-1975 data: *Annual Survey of Manufactures, 1975.*

Note: Calculation of constant dollars is based on the Gross National Product deflator.

upon ad revenue than dailies. From 1958 to 1975, the percentage of income from advertising in the weekly/other newspapers has also remained quite stable, at around 78 percent. On the other hand, the proportion of income from advertising in daily/Sunday newspapers has recently crept up a few points.

Table 320-C charts the growth of one segment of newspaper advertising income—the advertising rates of morning daily, evening daily, and Sunday newspapers (see also Tables 303-D and 303-E). The "agate line rate" in each newspaper category represents the average charge of all daily or Sunday newspapers for one agate line (one line of 5½ point type) of advertising. The "milline rate" is the cost of one agate line per million circulation. The increase in milline rates would seem to indicate a more rapid growth in the price of advertising than in circulation. However, since prices in general tend to rise, the editors have computed indexes for the milline rates and compared these indexes to the Consumer Price Index (CPI) in order to more accurately depict the trend in newspaper advertising rates. The comparison shows that, for most of the 55-year period, the growth in circulation was such that advertising rates roughly paralleled the Consumer Price Index. In recent years, though, there has been a tendency for the milline rate to rise faster than the CPI.

Table 320–E.
Number, Payroll, Revenue, and Major Expenses of
Weekly Newspaper Establishments in U. S., by Number of Employees, 1972

| | Number of Establishments | All Employees | | Production Workers Only | | | Value Added by Manufacture | Cost of Materials | Value of Receipts | Capital Expenditures | End-of-Year Inventories |
		Number of Employees (thousands)	Total Payroll	Number of Employees (thousands)	Total Man-hours (millions)	Total Wages					
All Weekly Establishments[a]	6,659	65.1	$404.5	36.6	59.9	$188.3	$831.6	$274.0	$1.105.2	$48.8	$24.5
Establishments with an Average of:											
1 to 4 Employees	3,572	6.6	38.7	4.9	7.0	18.3	105.0	35.1	140.1	12.6	3.4
5 to 9 Employees	1,428	9.5	55.8	5.8	10.0	27.9	124.0	41.2	165.2	N/A	4.1
10 to 19 Employees	883	11.8	72.1	6.9	11.8	35.4	147.3	45.0	192.4	9.4	5.8
20 to 49 Employees	597	17.6	103.6	9.5	15.5	47.8	206.9	65.7	272.2	13.0	5.8
50 to 99 Employees	122	8.1	53.0	4.1	6.6	21.9	99.3	36.4	135.7	4.6	2.6
100 to 249 Employees	43	6.3	43.4	3.1	5.1	20.5	75.7	27.7	103.4	6.3	2.5
250 to 499 Employees	11	3.4	26.8	1.5	2.4	11.0	48.7	15.1	63.8	2.3	1.0
500 to 999 Employees	3	1.6	11.2	.8	1.3	5.6	24.8	7.7	32.4	.7	.5
Weekly Establishments Covered Only by Government Records [b]	4,388	14.2	83.7	9.5	15.1	40.7	203.9	68.6	272.4	10.8	7.0

Source: *1972 Census of Manufactures*, p. 27A-23.

Notes: (a) Includes all newspapers not classified as "daily." (b) Census Bureau report forms were not mailed to companies that operated only small establishments—generally single-unit companies with less than 10 employees. Payroll and sales data for these companies were obtained from administrative records supplied to other agencies of the Federal Government. These payroll and sales data were then used in conjunction with industry averages to estimate the balances of the items shown in the table. Data are also included in the respective size classes shown for this industry.

Table 320-D compares U.S. newspaper industry receipts with some of the major operating expenses for newspapers from 1925 through 1974. It is clear that the percentage of expenditures for materials and payroll has declined, especially over the past 20 years. However, the share of income invested in new capital equipment has increased somewhat. Overall, this trend indicates that the newspaper industry is dealing adequately with its costs. As Bratland (1977, p. 11) states:

> Climbing ad revenues together with circulation gains, newsprint conservation programs, labor-management cooperation, and further technical developments in newspaper production have improved the outlook for daily newspapers; a growth rate of 7 to 8 percent per year is expected into the 1980s.

While we may debate some of the assumptions in this analysis, these tables do seem to indicate the vitality of the newspaper industry as a whole.

Table 320-E provides Census Bureau figures on the number, employment levels, sales figures, and other general statistics regarding all nondaily (weekly and other) newspapers in the United States in 1972. The totals in this table are probably low, because the Census Bureau currently counts only those newspapers employing one or more persons during the census year. Many small weeklies are run by individuals or families, often with unpaid contributors or other help. In addition, the Bureau does not count weekly/other newspapers published by nonprofit organizations or by businesses (such as printers) whose primary activity is something other than newspaper publishing.

However, taking these limitations into consideration, we can draw some interesting conclusions regarding the structure of the nondaily newspaper industry. For example, the field is largely made up of newspapers employing less than five persons—a total of 3,572 such establishments in 1972. Although this segment of the industry represents more than half (54 percent) of the establishments listed in Table 320-E, it accounts for only 13 percent of the total receipts. On the other hand, the 57 largest nondaily newspapers—representing only .86 of 1 percent of the industry—account for 18 percent of all income. This size distribution contrasts sharply with daily newspapers, where 92 percent of all establishments employ 20 employees.

Sources

The information in Tables 320-A, 320-B, 320-D, and 320-E comes from the U.S. Census Bureau's *Census of Manufactures* and *Annual Survey of Manufactures*. The data for the census years—those years up to 1947, plus 1954, 1958, 1963, 1967, and 1972—are somewhat more reliable than the other figures, which were based upon sample surveys carried out in the noncensus years. Thus, the census years represent the best bases for the measurement of industry growth.

The advertising rate information in Table 320-C was collected by *Editor and Publisher*, which has been publishing this information since 1921 in its *International Yearbook*. *Editor and Publisher* is the standard source of trade information to the newspaper industry, and its data are considered valid and reliable.

Further Information

Encyclomedia is a most useful reference periodical on the newspaper industry. The reader should refer especially to volume I, no. 1 of *Encyclomedia*, the *1977 Newspaper Edition*, which offers a 274-page collection of data on newspapers, including general dimensions of the medium (advertising and readership statistics); newspaper costs, circulation, and coverage on a market-by-market basis, the cost-per-thousand for eight important population segments; the reach and frequency of newspaper supplements and comics; and much more. The book is available from the publishers of *Media Decisions*, 342 Madison Ave., New York, N.Y. 10017.

Owen (1975) provides an important discussion of newspaper finances in the context of the overall media structure in this country. The American Newspaper Publishers Association (ANPA) also publishes a number of financial reports on the industry, as does Knowledge Industry Publications—see, for example, Compaine (1973). Finally, a regular reading of *Editor and Publisher* is strongly recommended for anyone wanting to keep up in this field.

Table 321-A.
Revenues, Net Income, Operating Expenses, and Physical Characteristics of a 34,000-Circulation, 7-Day U. S. Newspaper, 1972–1976

Revenues and Net Income

	1972		1973		1974		1975		1976	
	Revenues	% of Total	Revenues	% of Total	Revenues	% of Total	Revenues	% of Total	Revenues	% of Total
Advertising:										
Local	$1,359,500	41.6%	$1,496,000	42.5%	$1,548,900	42.0%	$1,680,700	40.9%	$1,795,771	40.0%
National	141,900	4.3	126,100	3.6	172,700	4.7	168,500	4.1	205,398	4.6
Classified	456,700	14.0	501,900	14.2	531,800	14.4	606,000	14.8	710,243	15.8
Legal	38,600	1.2	40,800	1.2	46,000	1.2	44,000	1.1	53,612	1.2
Preprints	132,100	4.0	185,600	5.3	204,500	5.5	243,500	5.9	262,614	5.8
All Advertising Revenues	$2,128,800	65.1%	$2,350,400	66.7%	$2,503,900	67.9%	$2,742,700	66.8%	$3,027,638	67.4%
Circulation	1,085,200	33.2	1,126,400	32.0	1,130,400	30.7	1,304,100	31.8	1,392,153	31.0
Other Revenue	55,900	1.7	45,400	1.3	53,500	1.5	58,700	1.4	70,794	1.6
Total Revenues	**$3,269,900**	**100.0%**	**$3,522,200**	**100.0%**	**$3,687,800**	**100.0%**	**$4,105,500**	**100.0%**	**$4,490,585**	**100.0%**
Net Income before Taxes	653,800	20.0	899,500	25.5	910,700	24.7	1,048,400	25.5	1,198,376	26.7
Provision for Income Taxes	340,000	10.4	476,700	13.5	482,700	13.1	471,800	11.5	575,200	12.8
Net Income	**$ 313,800**	**9.6%**	**$ 422,800**	**12.0%**	**$ 428,000**	**11.6%**	**$ 576,600**	**14.0%**	**$ 623,176**	**13.9%**

Table 321-A. (Cont'd.)

Operating Expenses and Payroll

	1972 Expenses	1972 % of Total	1973 Expenses	1973 % of Total	1974 Expenses	1974 % of Total	1975 Expenses	1975 % of Total	1976 Expenses	1976 % of Total
Newsprint, Ink	$ 386,900	14.8%	$ 406,900	15.5%	$ 421,500	15.2%	$ 528,900	17.3%	$ 612,930	18.6%
Press Room	199,200	7.6	179,500	6.8	138,900	5.0	147,500	4.8	144,777	4.4
Composing Room	399,400	15.3	363,100	13.8	353,400	12.7	312,200	10.2	288,595	8.8
Advertising Department	238,500	9.1	255,000	9.7	267,200	9.6	289,800	9.5	342,223	10.4
Circulation	256,200	9.8	265,300	10.1	265,600	9.6	278,200	9.1	302,490	9.2
Editorial	414,300	15.8	422,000	16.1	467,000	16.8	567,900	18.6	592,758	18.0
General, Administrative	438,600	16.8	400,400	15.3	434,000	15.6	370,600	12.1	403,228	12.2
Building	45,800	1.7	60,400	2.3	85,500	3.1	95,400	3.1	90,094	2.7
Employee Benefits	166,400	6.4	165,100	6.3	178,900	6.4	253,600	8.3	292,378	8.9
Depreciation	68,000	2.6	103,600	4.0	160,400	5.8	205,000	6.7	217,975	6.6
Bad Debts	2,800	.1	1,400	.1	4,700	.2	8,000	.3	4,761	.2
Total Operating Expenses	**$2,616,100**	**100.0%**	**$2,622,700**	**100.0%**	**$2,777,100**	**100.0%**	**$3,057,100**	**100.0%**	**$3,292,209**	**100.0%**
Payroll	$1,202,100	46.1	$1,276,000	48.7	$1,272,900	45.8	$1,350,800	44.2	$1,399,231	42.5

Interpretation of Tables

Table 321-A displays the financial profile (revenues, operating expenses, payroll, and net income) of a single 34,000-circulation, seven-day American newspaper. *Editor and Publisher*, the source of the table, regards this profile as "typical," but the actual identity of the paper has been

Table 321–A. (Cont'd.)

	Physical Characteristics			
	1973	1974	1975	1976
Number of Issues	365	360	360	360
Number of Pages	10,170	9,042	9,462	9,578
Number of Columns (final edition)	81,360	72,336	75,696	76,624
Division of Space (inches):				
Paid Advertising	711,900	1,082,500	906,955	926,023
% of Total	41.7%	68.8%	55.0%	55.6%
Reading, Promotion	996,700	490,800	739,433	740,549
% of Total	58.3%	31.2%	45.0%	44.4%
Total	1,708,600	1,573,300	1,646,388	1,666,572
Average Daily Circulation	35,130	34,304	34,020	34,470

Sources: *Editor and Publisher*, June 1, 1974, pp. 9, 25; April 26, 1975, p. 15; May 1, 1976, p. 24; March 26, 1977, p. 9.

kept secret. The breakdown of figures here allows the reader to see, in the short range, how various revenues and costs have influenced the newspaper's format and operation, and what the overall profit picture has been for the years 1972 through 1976.

During this five-year period, the relative influence of various sources of income remained relatively constant for this newspaper, with a slight increase in the emphasis on advertising. Newsprint and ink claimed an increasing share of expenses, while payroll costs declined. The reader may also note an increasing amount of depreciation, indicating some capital investment. The percentage of net income for this paper has been good and, on the average, shows a steady rise.

Table 321-B provides a similar balance sheet for another larger (250,000 circulation) seven-day newspaper. The general picture is one of stability, with a slight curvilinear trend in some categories of circulation, income, and expense. Circulation and profits have generally risen between 1950 and 1976, although the most recent figures show a decline. The proportion of income from advertising rose to a peak toward the end of the 1960s, but has declined since. Both newsprint and ink costs declined, but now are rising somewhat. The general profit picture of this "typical" large-city newspaper—at least, before taxes—is good.

Table 321-C provides some basic information on the revenues, income, and profits of the major *publicly owned* newspaper publishing companies. (The vast majority of newspaper firms are privately owned, and their operating data are impossible to come by.) As a group, the publicly owned companies tend to be large, part of a chain, and involved in other activities besides newspaper publishing. (See Unit 201 for a listing of many of these same companies as multi-media conglomerates.)

Table 321-C will help the reader gain some idea of the variety of financial circumstances among such firms. For example, in 1976, the total return on revenues ranged from 4.5 to 18.8 percent in this group, with newspaper pretax income varying as a percent of revenues from 5.4 to 38.3 percent.

Sources

Tables 321-A and 321-B are presentations of the actual balance sheets of two newspapers, for selected years. Both tables were published originally by *Editor and Publisher*, and **Table 321-B** was compiled under the auspices of the Newspaper Analysis Service. The editors accept these data as valid and reliable. However, they question the general applicability of these specific statistics to the rest of the newspaper industry. Although comparison of these data with the aggregate figures in Unit 320 yields similar percentages, it is impossible to judge the accuracy of any general industry-wide conclusions which the reader may draw from **Tables 321-A** and **321-B**.

Table 321-C reproduces information collected by *Editor and Publisher* from the annual reports filed by the companies involved. The editors assume the accuracy of these data.

Table 321–B.
Revenues, Operating Expenses, and Net Income of a 250,000-Circulation, 7-Day U. S. Newspaper, 1950–1976

Revenues	1950	1956	1962	1968	1974	1976
Advertising:						
Retail	$2,961,514	$ 4,455,735	$ 5,984,896	$ 7,789,247	$13,643,424	$14,468,242
National	1,217,573	2,017,829	1,778,824	1,705,926	1,612,038	2,041,846
Classified	995,198	1,707,458	2,075,479	3,622,071	6,136,531	6,637,902
Circulars/Inserts	- -	- -	- -	224,510	531,827	692,234
Total Advertising Revenue	**$5,174,285**	**$ 8,181,022**	**$ 9,839,199**	**$13,341,754**	**$21,923,820**	**$23,840,224**
% of Total Revenues	70.8%	76.4%	77.8%	80.9%	81.1%	76.6%
Circulation:						
City	1,210,407	1,429,932	1,750,788	2,009,116	3,401,590	5,022,518
Country	909,177	1,078,737	1,008,265	1,080,392	1,566,298	2,234,168
Total Circulation Revenue	**$2,119,584**	**$ 2,508,669**	**$ 2,759,053**	**$ 3,089,508**	**$ 4,967,888**	**$ 7,256,686**
% of Total Revenues	29.0%	23.5%	21.8%	18.7%	18.4%	23.3%
Other Revenue	16,141	13,059	45,215	65,636	149,404	33,917
% of Total Revenues	0.2%	0.1%	0.4%	0.4%	0.5%	0.1%
Total Revenues	**$7,310,010**	**$10,702,751**[a]	**$12,643,467**	**$16,496,898**	**$27,041,112**	**$31,130,827**

Expenses	1950	1956	1962	1968	1974	1976
Direct Expenses:						
Editorial	$ 844,386	$1,035,519	$ 1,229,470	$ 1,578,976	$ 2,339,433	$ 2,773,465
% of Total Revenues	11.6%	9.7%	9.7%	9.6%	8.7%	8.9%
Advertising	317,193	519,945	603,934	767,669	1,206,174	1,584,137
% of Total Revenues	4.3%	4.9%	4.8%	4.6%	4.4%	5.1%
Mechanical	975,943	1,482,545	1,830,209	2,269,919	4,001,338	4,423,796
% of Total Revenues	13.4%	13.9%	14.5%	13.8%	14.8%	14.2%
Newsprint, Ink	2,261,351	3,476,278	3,732,711	4,747,319	8,029,952	9,391,241
% of Total Revenues	30.9%	32.4%	29.5%	28.8%	29.7%	30.2%
Total Direct Expenses	**$4,398,873**[b]	**$6,514,288**[a]	**$ 7,396,324**	**$ 9,363,883**	**$15,576,897**	**$18,172,639**
% of Total Expenses	60.2%	60.9%	58.5%	56.8%	57.6%	58.4%
Indirect Expenses:						
Building	145,489	175,269	192,526	284,600	511,312	740,279
% of Total Expenses	2.0%	1.6%	1.5%	1.7%	1.9%	2.4%
Circulation	660,841	1,036,613	1,086,318	1,304,456	2,037,088	2,560,300
% of Total Expenses	9.0%	9.7%	8.6%	7.9%	7.6%	8.2%
Administrative	555,023	745,549	970,429	1,301,235	2,300,940	3,165,871
% of Total Expenses	7.6%	7.0%	7.7%	7.9%	8.5%	10.2%
Total Indirect Expenses	**$1,361,353**	**$1,957,431**	**$ 2,249,273**	**$ 2,890,291**	**$ 4,849,340**	**$ 6,466,450**
% of Total Expenses	18.6%	18.3%	17.8%	17.5%	18.0%	20.8%
Deductions:						
Supplements	98,205	106,733	110,461	103,246	49,034	57,610
Bad Debts	18,721	28,073	48,559	36,945	33,715	73,396
Depreciation	67,119	116,596	224,767	309,906	543,265	573,339
Misc. Adjustments	16,650	5,000	- -	100,000	275,487	257,260
Total Deductions	**$ 200,695**	**$ 256,402**	**$ 383,787**	**$ 550,098**[a]	**$ 901,501**	**$ 961,605**
% of Total Expenses	2.7%	2.4%	3.0%	3.3%	3.3%	3.1%[b]
Total Expenses	**$5,960,921**[b]	**$8,728,121**[a]	**$10,029,385**[a]	**$12,804,273**[a]	**$21,327,738**	**$25,600,694**
% of Total Revenues	81.5%	81.6%	79.3%	77.6%	78.9%	82.2%
Net Income before Taxes	**$1,349,089**[b]	**$1,974,630**	**$ 2,614,081**[a]	**$ 3,692,626**[b]	**$ 5,713,374**	**$ 5,530,133**
% of Total Revenues	18.5%	18.4%	20.7%	22.4%	21.1%	17.8%
Average Net Paid Circulation	225,876	246,880	242,860	253,604	260,350	254,665

Source: Newspaper Analysis Service, as reprinted in various issues of *Editor and Publisher.*

Notes: (a) Totals do not add due to rounding. (b) Mathematical errors in original source corrected by editors.

Table 321–C.
Revenues and Net Income of Selected U. S. Newspaper Firms, 1976

Note: All dollar figures are in millions.

	Affiliated Publications	Capital Cities Communications	Dow Jones Co.	Gannett Company	Harte-Hanks Newspapers	Knight-Ridder	Lee Enterprises	Media General	Multimedia	New York Times Co.	Post Corporation	Speidel Newspapers, Inc.	Thompson Newspapers	Times-Mirror Co.	Washington Post Co.
Total Revenues of Firm	$121.9	$212.2	$274.9	$413.3	$116.7	$677.5	$69.8	$199.0	$79.0	$445.7	$25.5	$57.0	$217.6	$975.6	$375.7
Total Net Income of Firm	$5.5	$35.6	$30.3	$48.0	$10.5	$47.4[a]	$9.4	$16.1	$10.0	$22.3	$2.1	$10.2	$40.8	$69.5	$24.5
Percent Return on Total Revenues	4.5%	16.8%	11.0%	11.6%	9.0%	7.0%	13.5%	8.1%	12.6%	5.0%	8.2%	17.8%	18.8%	7.1%	6.5%
Revenues, Income—Newspaper Operations Only:															
Total Newspaper Revenues	$119.6	$47.2[b]	$212.3[c]	--	$103.5	--	$53.0[c]	$94.0	$40.0	$318.5	--	$57.0	$217.6	$426.1	$168.7[d]
Pretax Income	--	--	--	--	--	--	--	--	--	$17.3[c]	--	$20.3	$83.7	$48.5	$11.8[d]
Pretax Income as Percent of Newspaper Revenues	--	--	--	--	--	--	--	--	--	5.4%[c]	--	35.6%	38.5%	11.4%	7.0%
Circulation Revenues	$41.1	$7.2[b]	--	--	$22.8[c]	--	--	$18.2	--	--	--	$12.0	--	--	$34.0
Advertising Revenues	$78.4	$40.1[b]	--	--	$91.1[c]	--	--	$74.7	--	--	--	$41.2	--	--	$131.6
Newspaper Revenues as Percent of Total Revenues	98.1%	22.3%	77.2%	--	88.7%	--	76.0%[e]	47.2%	50.6%	71.5%	--	100.0%	100.0%	43.7%	44.9%

Source: *Editor and Publisher*, May 14, 1977, pp. 17-20.

Notes: (a) Estimate based on percentage reports. (b) Includes both trade and consumer newspaper revenues. (c) Includes the sale of equities; real 1976 net income was $52.3 million. (d) Newspaper-division income includes newsprint manufacture, feature syndication, and one-third interest in the *International Herald Tribune*. The total "newspaper only" income can be estimated at $165.6 million. (e) *Editor and Publisher* percentage.

Further Information

Editor and Publisher often prints articles which deal with the financial state of the newspaper industry. These articles are written from a number of vantage points, and anyone who wishes to gain a cumulative impression of the newspaper trade should read *Editor and Publisher* regularly. Along with each of the annual articles which accompany the statistics given in **Tables 321**-A and **321**-B, the reader will find a description of the major events that occurred in the newspaper's operations during that year. This description is so helpful in drawing an interpretation that the reader who is seriously interested in studying these tables should refer to this original source.

Standard and Poor's Industry Surveys presents data from annual company reports and other major sources, as well as an overall industry analysis. The basic analysis is published each fall. At other times during the year, short supplements update some of the information and commentary regarding particular industry characteristics and stock prospects. The new *Encyclomedia: 1977 Newspaper Edition*, to be revised annually, also contains a wealth of data on newspaper industry economics for both national and individual local markets.

Newspaper Prices   322

Interpretation of Tables

The most useful available information on the rise of daily newspaper prices—including both subscription and single-copy sales—is the editors' special Consumer Price Index (CPI) for newspapers, which is listed (along with indexes for the other media) in **Table 301**-B. A look at this table reveals that, until 1955 or so, the rise in newspaper prices generally followed rising prices for other commodities. For the next 15 years, however, the actual growth rate of newspaper prices was somewhat more rapid than that of the U.S. Commerce Department's general Consumer Price Index for recreational expenditures. Since 1971, the price index for newspapers has fluctuated around the CPI for all commodities—a couple of points higher in some years, a couple of points below in other years.

Table 322-A outlines the increases in single-copy prices for daily and Sunday newspapers from 1966 to 1975. The major trend for dailies is a nearly universal increase in price from 10 cents to 15 cents. In this same 10-year period, Sunday newspapers rose from 15 or 20 cents in 1966 to 25 or 35 cents by 1975. A comparison of these price increases with the index of prices in **Table 301**-B reveals that during the same 10-year period, copy prices for dailies rose 59 percent and Sunday newspaper prices rose 73 percent, while the price index for all newspapers rose 81 percent.

The difference in the percentage-increase figures for the two series is at least partly explained by the fact that they are not precisely comparable. In **Table 301**-B, daily, Sunday, and weekly newspapers are combined, as are subscription and single-copy prices. In **Table 322**-A, the figures cover single-copy prices only and include newspapers in Canada and the U.S. Territories as well as the United States. However, the editors suspect that the main reason for the difference is the fact that subscription prices (represented only in **Table 301**-B) have tended to rise faster than single-copy sales.

Sources

Table 322-A comes from a survey which the American Newspaper Publishers Association (ANPA) conducts annually, using information from the Audit Bureau of Circulations' *Daily Newspaper Circulation Rate Book*. The Audit Bureau of Circulations is the major source of independent information on the accuracy of the circulation claims of publishers. Both advertisers and the trade rely upon this source, and the editors consider its information reliable.

Further Information

The ANPA is continuing its survey and usually releases the results in its *General Bulletin*. For information concerning the editors' Consumer Price Index for newspapers, see Unit 301.

Table 322–A.
Single-Copy Price of Daily and Sunday Newspapers in U. S.,
U. S. Territories, and Canada, 1966–1975

	Daily Newspapers									
	1966	1967	1968	1969	1970	1971	1972	1973	1974	1975
Number of Daily Newspapers Selling at:										
3-9 Cents	636	449	251	151	88	54	43	31	31	13
10 Cents	1,212	1,392	1,589	1,680	1,606	1,481	1,407	1,316	832	433
11-14 Cents	1	2	2	9	8	23	36	29	12	6
15 Cents	4	5	9	19	146	290	350	476	938	1,237
16-19 Cents	0	0	0	0	0	0	0	0	2	1
20 Cents	2	2	3	3	5	5	4	4	42	157
21-24 Cents	0	0	0	0	0	0	0	0	2	0
25 Cents	0	0	0	0	1	1	1	1	4	13
30 Cents	0	0	0	0	0	1	1	2	0	1
Average (Mean) Price (Cents)	8.6	9.0	9.5	9.7	10.2	10.7	10.9	11.3	12.7	14.3

	Sunday Newspapers									
Number of Sunday Newspapers Selling at:										
1-9 Cents	23	17	9	6	2	1	1	0	2	0
10 Cents	140	120	104	91	90	79	79	74	64	37
11-14 Cents	1	0	0	0	0	0	0	0	0	0
15 Cents	171	173	160	145	116	94	90	89	68	61
16-19 Cents	0	0	0	0	0	0	0	0	0	0
20 Cents	166	161	161	160	140	126	127	97	66	49
21-24 Cents	0	0	1	0	0	0	0	0	0	0
25 Cents	58	81	101	128	163	183	194	222	203	173
30 Cents	5	5	17	16	30	47	46	56	49	62
35 Cents	1	3	11	26	35	43	42	51	112	157
40 Cents	0	1	0	0	3	6	8	10	27	37
45 Cents	0	0	0	0	0	0	0	0	3	3
50 Cents	0	0	1	1	4	6	5	7	23	51
55 Cents	0	0	0	0	0	0	0	0	0	1
60 Cents	0	0	0	0	0	0	0	0	1	4
75 Cents	0	0	0	0	0	0	0	0	1	1
Average (Mean) Price (Cents)	16.0	16.8	18.1	19.1	20.5	21.8	21.8	22.7	25.8	29.1

Source: American Newspaper Publishers Association General Bulletin No. 3, January 21, 1976, pp. 12-15.

Table 330–A.
Total Receipts of U. S. Periodicals Industry vs. Receipts
from Periodical Products Only, 1914–1975

Note: All dollar figures are in millions.

Year	Total Receipts from Periodical Products Only		Total Industry Receipts	
	Current Dollars	Percent of Receipts from Advertising	Current Dollars	Constant (1972) Dollars
1914	$ 135.6	52.8%	N/A	N/A
1919	240.0	64.5	N/A	N/A
1921	270.9	57.3	N/A	N/A
1923	351.3	60.6	N/A	N/A
1925	429.5	60.9	N/A	N/A
1927	482.0	63.4	N/A	N/A
1929	507.4	63.6	N/A	N/A
1931	407.3	59.8	N/A	N/A
1933	269.3	52.4	N/A	N/A
1935	329.6	56.5	N/A	N/A
1937	407.8	57.8	N/A	N/A
1939	409.0	54.9	$ 420.0	$1,489.4
1947	1,019.5	60.1	1,059.4	2,131.6
1954	1,413.1	61.1	1,469.8	2,462.0
1958	1,639.1	62.3	1,729.5	2,620.5
1963	2,035.5	61.0	2,295.7	3,206.3
1967	2,668.2	62.5	3,095.9	3,918.9
1972	3,197.7	56.6	3,521.3	3,521.3
1975	3,817.0	53.8	4,379.7	3,440.5

Sources: 1914-1972 data: *Census of Manufactures*, appropriate annual issues. 1975 data: *Annual Survey of Manufactures, 1975*, table 9.

Note: The calculations of constant dollars were based on the Gross National Product deflator.

Interpretation of Tables

Table 330-A shows the overall financial growth of the U.S. magazine industry, which currently draws annual receipts of more than four billion dollars. Prior to 1939, the U.S. Census Bureau did not classify periodicals separately from newspapers. Consequently, the editors based the figures for earlier census years on revenues for periodical *products*, rather than for the periodicals industry as a whole. This procedure eliminates revenues received by magazine publishers from other businesses, such as newspapers, but it includes revenues resulting from periodicals published by companies engaged in some other business.

From 1939 on, both sets of figures—receipts from the sale of periodicals and receipts of the periodicals industry—are available. The reader will note that the two series are roughly parallel, although industry receipts show a slight tendency to grow faster than product receipts. This pattern

Table 330–B.
Total Advertising Revenues of Magazines in U. S., 1915–1976

Year	Revenue[a]	Number of Magazines	Average Revenue per Magazine[b]
1915	$ 28,132,691	35	$ 3,883,049
1916	36,860,499	35	4,539,470
1917	45,223,924	35	4,533,727
1918	58,432,486	61	3,120,227
1919	94,379,404	63	4,093,131
1920	129,466,442	62	4,890,324
1921	93,935,750	63	4,272,331
1922	97,766,190	63	4,789,643
1923	117,636,976	65	5,386,308
1924	131,769,520	64	6,220,238
1925	151,168,716	68	6,577,128
1926	165,041,971	68	7,288,552
1927	181,100,282	68	8,194,583
1928	180,999,963	67	8,236,256
1929	196,266,975	66	9,066,287
1930	192,118,660	67	9,045,561
1931	157,250,602	71	7,717,063
1932	110,574,191	71	6,107,384
1933	97,357,882	113	3,460,137
1934	117,658,996	110	3,961,582
1935	122,907,779	124	3,604,334
1936	141,648,135	110	4,665,617
1937	160,026,658	114	4,840,492
1938	141,164,557	105	4,750,616
1939	150,838,687	119	4,494,865
1940	165,643,598	111	5,181,544
1941	178,507,634	105	5,592,344
1942	173,592,683	106	5,038,975
1943	227,265,849	111	5,816,591
1944	268,944,087	102	7,204,117
1945	302,816,776	104	7,743,882
1946	379,436,624	111	7,786,670
1947	440,071,463	108	8,198,664
1948	458,677,139	98	8,814,273
1949	440,881,448	94	8,916,784
1950	458,451,328	91	9,399,117
1951	513,850,604	93	9,642,714
1952	553,815,162	93	10,267,244
1953	603,113,826	102	10,038,847
1954	597,141,926	86	11,630,671
1955	657,332,732	93	11,587,039
1956	691,728,403	89	12,356,485
1957	738,639,661	85	13,369,044
1958	693,092,038	83	12,652,283
1959	783,767,628	83	13,989,605
1960	853,165,143	83	14,962,297
1961	831,257,680	82	14,628,122
1962	875,236,035	84	14,758,465
1963	931,565,582	88	14,784,878
1964	996,593,319	89	15,402,583
1965	1,083,347,797	94	15,511,409
1966	1,170,517,360	96	15,876,158
1967	1,161,033,926	95	15,470,139
1968	1,196,055,761	95	15,242,204
1969	1,243,371,660	93	15,420,516
1970	1,180,717,188	94	13,742,693
1971	1,190,130,415	83	14,936,376
1972	1,210,529,086	86	14,075,920
1973	1,316,015,996	92	13,520,342
1974	1,372,261,464	94	12,541,689
1975	1,328,730,467	93	11,223,428
1976	1,621,992,896	93	N/A

Source: Publishers Information Bureau.

Notes: (a) Figures include both general magazines and national farm magazines through 1970; general magazines only after 1970. Sunday newspaper supplements are excluded. (b) These figures are in constant (1972) dollars as computed by the editors.

Table 330–C.
Total Receipts of U. S. Periodicals Industry,
by Type of Periodical, 1958–1975

Note: All dollar figures are in millions.

1958

Type of Periodical	Total Industry Receipts	Percent of Total from Sales/Subscriptions	Percent of Total from Advertising
Total, All Periodicals	$1,639.1	N/A	N/A
Total, Farm Periodicals	66.7	16.9%	83.1%
General	47.6	17.0	83.0
Specialized	19.1	16.8	83.2
Total, Business/Professional Periodicals	380.4	22.7	77.3
Industrial/Technical/Engineering	212.0	14.3	85.7
Merchandising	72.2	9.3	90.7
Professional/Institutional/Services	96.4	51.2	48.8
Unspecified Business/Professional	N/A	N/A	N/A
Total, General Periodicals	887.0	38.7	61.3
Comics	21.8	96.3	3.7
Women/Home Services	207.2	35.7	64.3
General Interest/Entertainment	530.2	39.9	60.1
General News	101.4	28.4	71.6
Business News	26.3	29.7	70.3
Unspecified General Periodicals	N/A	N/A	N/A
Total, Other Periodicals	265.4	53.5	46.5
Religious	N/A	N/A	N/A
Sunday Supplements[a]	N/A	N/A	N/A
Unspecified Other Periodicals	N/A	N/A	N/A
Periodicals (not elsewhere classified)	N/A	N/A	N/A
Total, Unspecified Periodicals	39.6	N/A	N/A

indicates that periodical publishers are diversifying and taking on other activities. In 1972, the main other business of periodical publishers was book publishing, an activity which accounted for about $334 million of the periodicals industry revenues for that year.

Up to the Great Depression, the industry maintained steady growth. The Depression created a dip, and as **Table 330**-A reveals, recovery was slow until 1939. After World War II, the industry gained momentum, experiencing its most rapid growth between the mid-1950s and mid-1960s. Since then, the industry's receipts—measured in real dollars—have started to decline. As explained in Unit 130, however, the number of periodicals has continued to grow. Evidently, the average revenue per periodical is less now, and some claim that the percent trend is away from large, general-circulation periodicals and toward smaller, more specialized magazines.

The reader will also note, in **Table 330**-A, the annual percentage of industry receipts from advertising. This series appears to parallel the growth of the industry as a whole, increasing as overall revenues grow and declining in periods of retrenchment. At present, periodicals are becoming more financially dependent on circulation, while their overall revenues are declining in real terms.

Table 330-B presents figures on the advertising revenues of those general and farm magazines listed in the records of the Publishers Information Bureau. The magazines surveyed here are generally the larger, general-circulation magazines which are members of the Magazine Publishers Association (MPA). Although they represent only a tiny fraction of the total number of periodicals, they claim a healthy portion of the total advertising receipts.

The data in **Table 330**-B are not precise. A certain number of periodicals may leave or join the MPA each year, and this creates year-by-year fluctuations which are difficult to trace, especially without knowledge of the periodicals involved. It is therefore difficult for the reader to know whether to attribute these changes to an overall industry trend or merely to changes in the MPA sample. However, even when this source of error is taken into consideration, it is apparent that the average real growth in advertising revenues roughly follows the same course as the overall financial

Table 330–C. (Cont'd.)

Type of Periodical	1963		
	Total Industry Receipts	Percent of Total from Sales/Subscriptions	Percent of Total from Advertising
Total, All Periodicals	$2,035.5	N/A	N/A
Total, Farm Periodicals	54.1	15.7%	84.3%
General	43.1	15.3	84.7
Specialized	10.8	16.7	83.3
Total, Business/Professional Periodicals	535.4	22.9	77.1
Industrial/Technical/Engineering	247.4	12.5	87.5
Merchandising	126.7	16.0	84.0
Professional/Institutional/Services	121.3	46.2	53.8
Unspecified Business/Professional	39.8	38.4	61.6
Total, General Periodicals	1,167.3	39.1	60.9
Comics	11.4	95.6	4.4
Women/Home Services	316.0	35.5	64.5
General Interest/Entertainment	659.3	42.3	57.7
General News	140.5	24.7	75.3
Business News	28.0	45.7	54.3
Unspecified General Periodicals	11.8	55.9	44.1
Total, Other Periodicals	230.2	N/A	N/A
Religious	71.9	91.4	8.6
Sunday Supplements[a]	67.3	38.6	61.4
Unspecified Other Periodicals	4.3	N/A	N/A
Periodicals (not elsewhere classified)	86.6	71.0	29.0
Total, Unspecified Periodicals	48.5	N/A	N/A

Type of Periodical	1967		
	Total Industry Receipts	Percent of Total from Sales/Subscriptions	Percent of Total from Advertising
Total, All Periodicals	$2,668.2	N/A	N/A
Total, Farm Periodicals	57.0	19.8%	80.2%
General	41.1	22.4	77.6
Specialized	15.9	13.2	86.8
Total, Business/Professional Periodicals	674.5	22.2	77.8
Industrial/Technical/Engineering	352.7	12.7	87.3
Merchandising	145.0	16.8	83.2
Professional/Institutional/Services	159.4	45.3	54.7
Unspecified Business/Professional	17.4	47.7	52.3
Total, General Periodicals	1,473.0	40.3	59.7
Comics	8.9	95.5	4.5
Women/Home Services	362.2	32.4	67.6
General Interest/Entertainment	847.3	46.0	54.0
General News	204.2	28.6	71.4
Business News	39.9	37.6	62.4
Unspecified General Periodicals	10.5	41.9	58.1
Total, Other Periodicals	284.2	N/A	N/A
Religious	81.9	84.2	15.8
Sunday Supplements[a]	68.5	30.7	69.3
Unspecified Other Periodicals	11.7	N/A	N/A
Periodicals (not elsewhere classified)	122.1	70.2	29.8
Total, Unspecified Periodicals	179.5	N/A	N/A

Table 330–C. (Cont'd.)

| | 1972 | | |
Type of Periodical	Total Industry Receipts	Percent of Total from Sales/Subscriptions	Percent of Total from Advertising
Total, All Periodicals	$3,197.7	N/A	N/A
Total, Farm Periodicals	75.9[b]	18.7%	81.3%
General	48.7	21.1	78.9
Specialized	26.7	14.6	85.4
Total, Business/Professional Periodicals	910.1	28.8	71.2
Industrial/Technical/Engineering	359.0	22.1	77.9
Merchandising	296.6	27.6	72.4
Professional/Institutional/Services	249.6	39.2	60.8
Unspecified Business/Professional	4.9	63.3	36.7
Total, General Periodicals	1,728.5	48.2	51.8
Comics	N/A	N/A	N/A
Women/Home Services	487.9	39.6	60.4
General Interest/Entertainment	855.2	56.3	43.7
General News	322.9	34.3	65.7
Business News	33.1	62.5	37.5
Unspecified General Periodicals	N/A	N/A	N/A
Total, Other Periodicals	282.1	N/A	N/A
Religious	102.4	89.2	10.8
Sunday Supplements[a]	46.4	20.0	80.0
Unspecified Other Periodicals	4.9	N/A	N/A
Periodicals (not elsewhere classified)	128.4	68.9	31.1
Total, Unspecified Periodicals	201.1	N/A	N/A

trend profiled in **Table 330-A**. According to **Table 330-B**, real advertising revenues reached their height in 1966 and have been declining ever since.

Table 330-C offers the Census Bureau's figures for periodical revenues, broken down by type of periodical during selected years from 1958 through 1975. The editors have omitted similar data for earlier years because the categories of the breakdown were different prior to 1958, and the two series therefore lack historical comparability.

When the 1958 figures in **Table 330-C** are measured against those for 1972—the most current year for which a full range of figures is available—it is clear that the greatest rates of growth among periodicals have been in the areas of trade magazines (classified as "marketing"); general news magazines; professional, institutional, and service periodicals; and women's magazines. Farm magazines and magazines that provide business news to the general public showed declines in real income during this 15-year period, while technical periodicals and general interest and entertainment magazines showed positive rates of growth—although the growth rates were below the industry's average for the period.

In **Table 330-D**, the periodicals industry receipts are compared with selected operating expenses of the industry. Except for a very recent rise in the percentage of costs of materials, the general trend in the balancing of receipts and expenses has been favorable for the industry. In 1958, materials, fuels and payroll made up 66 percent of periodicals industry revenues. By 1975, this figure had dropped to 60 percent.

With the possible exceptions of the recording and cable industries, periodical finances are probably the most opaque of all the mass media. No widespread trade organization has been established—although the Magazine Publishers Association is active in its section of the market. The one trade publication, *Folio: The Magazine of Magazine Management*, is of recent origin. *Folio* has indicated an interest in magazine publishing statistics, but it has yet to present any comprehensive historical series.

The reader must understand, then, that these aggregate data, by themselves, present only a superficial picture of a complicated and diverse industry. For each generalization, the industry offers a number of specific exceptions. The reader may find it helpful to compare information given here with that provided in Units 303 and 630.

Table 330–C. (Cont'd.)

Type of Periodical	1975 Total Industry Receipts	Percent of Total from Sales/Subscriptions	Percent of Total from Advertising
Total, All Periodicals	$3,817.0	N/A	N/A
Total, Farm Periodicals	(92.1)[c]	22.0%	78.0%
General	N/A	N/A	N/A
Specialized	N/A	N/A	N/A
Total, Business/Professional Periodicals	1,114.8	30.6	69.4
Industrial/Technical/Engineering	N/A	N/A	N/A
Merchandising	N/A	N/A	N/A
Professional/Institutional/Services	N/A	N/A	N/A
Unspecified Business/Professional	N/A	N/A	N/A
Total, General Periodicals	2,128.0	55.4	44.6
Comics	N/A	N/A	N/A
Women/Home Services	N/A	N/A	N/A
General Interest/Entertainment	N/A	N/A	N/A
General News	N/A	N/A	N/A
Business News	N/A	N/A	N/A
Unspecified General Periodicals	N/A	N/A	N/A
Total, Other Periodicals	302.2	N/A	N/A
Religious	N/A	N/A	N/A
Sunday Supplements[a]	N/A	N/A	N/A
Unspecified Other Periodicals	N/A	N/A	N/A
Periodicals (not elsewhere classified)	N/A	N/A	N/A
Total, Unspecified Periodicals	(179.9)[c]	N/A	N/A

Sources: 1958-1963 data: *Census of Manufactures*, as quoted in Hokkanen (1971). 1967-1972 data: *1972 Census of Manufactures*. 1975 data: *Annual Survey of Manufactures*.

Notes: Totals for 1958-1963 may not add because of rounding. (a) Category includes Sunday comics and magazines. (b) Figure includes $.5 million in receipts from unspecified farm periodicals. (c) The figures shown in parentheses have associated standard errors exceeding 15 percent. Thus, at the product class level, these estimates may be of limited reliability (see text).

Sources

Tables **330**-A, **330**-C, and **330**-D were constructed from data gathered either for the *Census of Manufactures* or the *Annual Survey of Manufactures*, which are published by the U.S. Census Bureau. These sources are generally regarded as authoritative within the limits of their definitions. As noted on **Table 330**-C, the 1975 figures in parentheses have associated standard errors exceeding 15 percent. Thus, at the product-class level, these estimates may be of limited reliability. However, the figures may be combined with other product-class totals and summed to the four-digit level in order to achieve acceptable reliability.

Table **330**-B comes from the Publishers Information Bureau, a trade organization which has close ties and some personnel in common with the MPA. On occasion, the MPA is very selective about what it will or will not release for analysis, and the editors suspect that promotion of the association's data may form a part of the group's statistical strategy. Moreover, assessment of Table **330**-B is likely to be flawed by the difficulty of identifying the scope of the figures from year to year. Still, this table does provide another view of magazine finances from an industry source, and the editors find that it tends to confirm as many negative as positive trends.

Table 330–D.
Receipts, Selected Operating Expenses, and Capital Expenditures of U. S. Periodicals Industry, 1939–1975

Note: All dollar figures are in millions.

	Total Industry Receipts		Cost of Materials, Fuels, etc.		Payroll, All Employees		Wages, Production Workers Only		New Capital Expenditures	
	Current Dollars	Constant (1972) Dollars	Current Dollars	Percent of Total Receipts	Current Dollars	Percent of Total Receipts	Current Dollars	Percent of Total Receipts	Current Dollars	Percent of Total Receipts
1939	$ 420.0	$1,489.4	$ 157.0	37%	N/A	N/A	$ 25.0	6%	N/A	N/A
1947	1,059.4	2,131.6	421.0	40	$235.7	22%	64.5	6	N/A	N/A
1954	1,469.8	2,462.0	664.0	45	312.7	21	68.2	5	$14.5	1%
1958	1,729.5	2,620.5	764.7	44	386.7	22	56.8	3	35.1	2
1963	2,295.7	3,206.3	958.1	42	461.1	20	65.6	3	33.8	1
1967	3,095.9	3,918.9	1,234.1	40	633.7	20	80.5	3	58.0	2
1972	3,521.3	3,521.3	1,410.0	40	709.7	20	84.6	2	56.8	2
1974	4,059.4	3,487.5	1,656.9	41	808.2	20	104.3	3	56.1	1
1975	4,379.7	3,440.5	1,746.9	40	876.9	20	118.9	3	66.7	2

Sources: 1939-1954 data: *1963 Census of Manufactures.* 1958-1972 data: *1972 Census of Manufactures.* 1974-1975 data: *Annual Survey of Manufactures, 1975.*

Note: Calculation of constant dollars was based on the Gross National Product deflator.

Further Information

Perhaps the best single book on the magazine industry is Peterson's *Magazines in the Twentieth Century* (1964). Although dated, this work still offers the best comprehensive history of magazines currently available. Compaine (1974) provides an interesting and more current analysis of the industry. Other works to consult include Wolseley (1969, 1973), Wood (1971), Ford (1969), and Tebbel (1969). A bibliography for the study of magazines has also been prepared by Schacht (1972).

Table 331–A.

Table 331–A.
Average Annual Library Subscription Price for Periodicals in U. S.,
with Library-Subscription and Consumer Price Indexes, 1947–1976

Note: Price index figures are calculated on a base of 100 for the year 1972.

	Average Annual Library Subscription Price (Current Dollars)	Average Annual Library Subscription Price Index	Consumer Price Index: Periodicals Only	Consumer Price Index: All Measured Commodities
1947			N/A	53.4
1948	$3.62	27.4	N/A	57.5
1949			N/A	57.0
1950	3.91	29.6	N/A	57.5
1951	4.02	30.4	N/A	62.1
1952	4.12	31.1	N/A	63.4
1953	4.24	32.0	N/A	63.9
1954	4.34	32.8	N/A	64.2
1955	4.44	33.6	N/A	64.0
1956	4.56	34.5	N/A	65.0
1957	4.70	35.5	N/A	67.3
1958	4.92	37.2	N/A	69.1
1959	5.13	38.8	N/A	69.7
1960	5.32	40.2	N/A	70.8
1961	5.63	42.6	N/A	71.5
1962	5.92	44.7	N/A	72.3
1963	6.31	47.7	N/A	73.2
1964	6.64	50.2	70.2	74.1
1965	6.95	52.5	71.8	74.4
1966	7.44	56.2	74.0	77.6
1967	8.02	60.6	76.1	79.8
1968	8.65	65.4	79.9	83.2
1969	9.31	70.4	85.1	87.6
1970	10.41	78.7	89.7	92.8
1971	11.66	88.1	95.2	96.8
1972	13.23	100.0	100.0	100.0
1973	16.20	122.4	102.9	106.2
1974	17.71	133.9	105.0	117.9
1975	19.94	150.7	125.0	128.7
1976	22.52	170.2	140.9	136.1

Sources: Library Subscription Prices: *The Bowker Annual*, appropriate editions, utilizing data from the American Library Association. Consumer Price Indexes: Bureau of Labor Statistics (1975, 1963).

Note: All figures are as of December 31 of the year given. Figures may not add due to rounding.

Interpretation of Tables

Prices for periodicals have been rising, as have prices for most other commodities. **Table 331-A** shows, however, that periodical price increases during the past 30 years have not been uniform across all classes of publications. The data here offer a comparison of the average library subscription price for periodicals with the Consumer Price Index (CPI) for periodicals and for all measured commodities. The data indicate that the average price of publications purchased by libraries has risen at a very rapid rate since 1947, much ahead of the general rise in prices. This is undoubtedly explained by the fact that the library price survey includes a large number of scholarly publications,

Table 331–B.
Average Single-Copy Price of 50 Major Magazines in U. S., 1960–1976

Year	Average Single Copy Price		Average Yearly Subscription Price	
	Current Dollars	Constant (1972) Dollars	Current Dollars	Constant (1972) Dollars
1960	$.39	$.55	$ 4.58	$6.47
1961	.41	.57	4.68	6.55
1962	.41	.57	4.79	6.63
1963	.42	.57	4.89	6.68
1964	.46	.62	5.25	7.09
1965	.46	.62	5.32	7.15
1966	.49	.63	5.51	7.10
1967	.51	.64	5.60	7.02
1968	.55	.66	6.05	7.27
1969	.58	.66	6.52	7.44
1970	.63	.68	7.16	7.72
1971	.63	.65	7.38	7.62
1972	.64	.64	7.57	7.57
1973	.68	.64	7.72	7.27
1974	.81	.69	8.86	7.51
1975	.88	.68	9.66	7.51
1976	.99	.73	10.88	7.99

Source: Magazine Publishers Association. Data was based on reports to the Audit Bureau of Circulations, effective December 31st of each year.

whereas the Consumer Price Index for periodicals is limited to 13 general-interest, large-circulation magazines. The price of the popular magazines listed with the CPI has lagged behind the price trends for all commodities.

Table 331-B presents average single-copy and subscription prices, from 1960 through 1976, for the 50 leading popular magazines. (The top 100 magazines in 1976 are listed in **Table 630-D.**) Over this 17-year period, the deflated price of magazines has risen both for single copies and sub-scriptions—although the constant (1972) dollar prices from 1970 to 1975 remained at or below their 1970 level.

Table 331-C presents additional information drawn from the same library price survey em-ployed in **Table 331-A.** Listed here are the average prices of periodicals in a variety of different subject areas. The reader will note considerable variation among subject areas, not only in price levels but also in rates of increase. Journals in the category of "Chemistry and Physics" lead the chart on both counts. In 1977, their average annual library-subscription price was $93.76, which represents an increase of 283 percent since the 1967-1969 base period. On the other hand, the least expensive periodicals on the list are those published for children. Their 1977 subscription prices averaged only $5.82. The subject area with the smallest overall price increase is "Law," in which prices have merely doubled since 1967-1969.

Sources

The information on average periodical prices listed in **Tables 331-A** and **331-C** was taken from work which is done annually by the Library Materials Price Index Committee of the Resources Section of the American Library Association's Resources and Technical Services Division. In the Spring of each year, this group checks current issues of a large sample of periodicals for their latest subscription rates for libraries. Results of this survey are published annually—usually in July or August—in *Library Journal*, and then reprinted during the following year in *The Bowker Annual*.

To be included in the survey, a periodical must conform to the following definition: "a pub-lication which constitutes one issue in a continuous series under the same title, published more than

Table 331-C.
Average Annual Subscription Price of U. S. Periodicals, by Subject Area, 1967–1977

Note: Base index figure of 100 is equivalent to the average price for the years 1967-1969.

Subject Area	1967-69 Average Price	1972 Average Price	1972 Index	1973 Average Price	1973 Index	1974 Average Price	1974 Index	1975 Average Price	1975 Index	1976 Average Price	1976 Index	1977 Average Price	1977 Index
All U. S. Periodicals	$ 8.66	$13.23	152.8	$16.20	187.1	$17.71	204.5	$19.94	230.3	$22.52	260.0	$24.59	283.9
Agriculture	4.68	6.35	135.7	7.21	154.1	8.12	173.5	9.70	207.3	10.75	229.7	11.58	247.4
Business and Economics	7.54	9.95	132.0	12.25	162.5	13.90	184.4	15.26	202.4	16.98	225.2	18.62	246.9
Chemistry and Physics	24.48	45.46	185.7	56.61	231.5	65.47	267.4	76.84	313.9	86.72	354.2	93.76	383.0
Children's Periodicals	2.60	3.24	124.6	3.27	125.8	3.72	143.1	4.69	180.4	5.32	204.6	5.82	223.0
Education	6.34	9.51	150.0	11.34	178.9	12.64	199.4	14.72	232.2	16.00	252.4	17.54	276.7
Engineering	10.03	16.04	160.0	23.37	233.0	24.38	243.1	26.64	265.6	31.87	317.7	35.77	356.6
Fine and Applied Arts	6.71	8.42	125.5	9.16	136.5	9.84	146.7	11.09	165.3	12.42	185.1	13.72	204.5
General Interest Periodicals	7.28	9.62	132.1	10.05	138.5	11.43	157.0	14.36	197.3	15.24	209.3	16.19	222.4
History	6.04	8.25	136.6	8.95	148.2	9.57	158.4	11.14	184.4	11.94	197.7	12.64	209.3
Home Economics	6.45	10.25	158.9	12.21	189.3	12.31	190.9	14.24	220.8	17.86	276.9	18.73	290.4
Industrial Arts	6.87	8.98	130.7	9.57	139.3	9.63	140.2	10.59	154.2	12.51	182.1	14.37	209.2
Journalism and Communications	5.72	8.68	151.7	13.05	228.2	13.13	229.6	14.70	257.0	15.90	278.0	16.97	296.7
Labor and Industrial Relations	3.01	3.92	130.2	6.02	200.0	6.71	222.9	7.40	245.9	10.33	343.2	11.24	373.4
Law	8.71	11.15	128.0	13.19	151.4	14.56	167.2	15.00	172.2	16.21	186.1	17.36	199.3
Library Science	6.27	9.40	150.0	10.48	167.2	12.53	199.8	14.18	226.2	15.96	254.5	16.97	270.7
Literature and Language	5.38	7.45	138.5	8.14	151.3	9.16	170.3	10.41	193.5	11.60	215.6	11.82	219.7
Math, Botany, Geology, and General Science	15.30	22.63	148.0	26.99	176.4	30.27	197.8	35.95	235.0	42.51	277.8	47.13	308.0
Medicine	19.38	29.59	152.7	33.60	173.4	36.31	187.3	42.38	218.7	47.47	244.9	51.31	264.8
Philosophy and Religion	5.27	7.16	135.9	8.12	154.1	8.84	167.7	9.05	171.7	9.94	188.6	10.89	206.6
Physical Education and Recreation	4.89	6.39	130.7	6.83	139.7	7.17	146.6	7.80	159.5	9.27	189.6	10.00	204.5
Political Science	6.18	8.47	137.1	9.69	156.8	10.79	174.6	12.79	207.0	13.09	211.8	14.83	240.0
Psychology	14.55	20.98	144.2	23.17	159.2	25.79	177.3	27.51	189.1	29.39	202.0	31.74	218.1
Sociology and Anthropology	6.11	9.12	149.3	11.28	184.6	13.03	213.3	14.85	243.0	17.11	280.0	19.68	322.1
Zoology	13.39	22.39	167.2	24.07	179.8	24.78	185.1	27.37	204.1	31.34	234.1	33.69	251.6
Total Number of Periodicals	6,944	2,537		2,861		2,955		3,075		3,151		3,218	

Source: *The Bowker Annual* (1977), p. 333, utilizing data from the American Library Association.

twice a year over an indefinite period, individual issues in the series being numbered consecutively or each issue being dated." In addition, the periodical must be published in the United States. If it is also published in another country, the place of publication in the United States must be listed first, and the first currency listed for subscription payments must be U.S. dollars. The periodical must be priced, and its subject matter must be of interest to libraries. Newspapers are excluded.

The survey sample includes nearly all eligible American periodicals listed in the following H. W. Wilson Company periodical indexes: *Reader's Guide to Periodical Literature, Business Periodicals Index, Index to Legal Periodicals, Applied Science & Technology Index, Art Index, Biological & Agricultural Index, Education Index, Humanities Index, Social Sciences Index,* and *Library Literature.* Titles are selected also from the National Library of Medicine's *Index Medicus* and from the *Subject Index to Children's Magazines.*

When the latest issue of a periodical cannot be checked for prices, its subscription rate is taken from library records, from publishers' price lists, or from subscription agents' catalogs. In a few cases, current prices cannot be determined and the previous year's prices are used instead—though this practice is never continued for more than one year.

Subject categories for publications are based on Dewey and Universal Decimal Classifications, modified somewhat to better fit the actual distribution of periodicals. The number of periodicals in each subject area is kept relatively constant, and titles which have transferred to foreign publishers, changed to nonperiodical frequency, or ceased publication are replaced by other established titles in the field. Subject areas in which very few magazines or journals are published—fiction and biography, for example—are excluded.

While these data are gathered and published to help librarians prepare their budgets, many librarians have found that their actual costs for periodicals average more than these figures. One possible explanation for this is that librarians may be more selective in their purchasing than the survey group is in its choice of sample publications (Atkinson, 1975, p. 176).

The CPI for periodical prices, which appears in **Table 331-A**, is not collected by the same city-by-city survey method as most of the other prices in the overall index of commodities. Rather, the U.S. Bureau of Labor Statistics (BLS) gathers information from semiannual reports of the Audit Bureau of Circulations on the average prices of 13 popular periodicals: *Reader's Digest, Sports Illustrated, Good Housekeeping, Ladies' Home Journal, Seventeen, Glamour, Time, National Geographic, Popular Mechanics, Photoplay, McCalls, Scholastic Magazine,* and *Better Homes and Gardens.* At the time this "market basket" of magazines was chosen—sometime before 1967—*Life* and *Look* were also included. When they ceased publication, they were not replaced.

The editors accept the accuracy of the Audit Bureau's price quotations, since this group is the major monitor of circulation activity in the magazine publishing field. However, the CPI for periodicals remains a limited measure of the price increases of periodicals, in that the 13 magazines listed above have several characteristics which tend to make them unrepresentative, including circulation size, general orientation, and number of years in business. The periodicals index is in the process of being revised, and this new index should be based on a much larger sample of magazines. (For a discussion of the CPI for periodicals and for all commodities, see Units 300 and 301.)

Table 331-B was prepared from annual figures collected by the Magazine Publishers Association (MPA). Collecting the price information for this top 50 group is a simple matter, and the editors are confident that the MPA is performing the task competently. However, to the extent that publications move in and out of this top 50 group from year to year, a source of error is introduced into any analysis of year-to-year trends. Sorting out year-to-year price changes from changes in the composition of the MPA sample is next to impossible. The 1977 figures in **Table 331-C** were taken from the *Library Journal* (July 1977), pp. 1462-1467.

Further Information

Two important studies of scholarly journals have recently appeared: King et al. (1976) deal with scientific and technical journals, while Fry and White (1976) treat scholarly and research journals in general.

Table 340–A.
Total Production and Services Expenditures
of U. S. Motion Picture Industry, 1921–1947

Note: All dollar figures are in thousands.

| | Number of Establishments | Salaries and Wages | | Total Other Expenditures | Total Expenditures |
		Total	Percent of Expenditures		
1921	127	$ 37,693	48.7	N/A	$ 77,397
1923	97	38,425	44.5	N/A	86,418
1925	132	49,017	52.3	$ 44,619	93,636
1927	142	74,936	55.8	59,407	134,343
1929	142	85,028	46.2	99,074	184,102
1931	140	N/A	N/A	N/A	154,436
1933	92	71,344	59.8	47,999	119,343
1935	129	104,430	64.5	57,435	161,865
1937	83	139,551	70.6	58,190	197,741
1939	178	142,543	66.1	73,157	215,700
1947	277	293,046	63.7	167,097	460,143

Source: *Census of Manufactures 1947*, Volume II, p. 837, table 1.

Interpretation of Tables

Table 340-A provides summary information on the production and services expenditures of the U.S. motion picture industry during the 1921-1947 period. The category of industry "establishments" includes studios producing theatrical films, producers of nontheatrical films, and the various service companies for the industry. Of the 277 establishments listed for 1947, 100 were theatrical producers, 127 produced nontheatrical films, and 50 supplied laboratory and other services. The "total other expenditures" column (titled "total cost of work done" in the source) represents production costs for the films, rental fees for the use of studio facilities, laboratory charges, and miscellaneous other costs. Both the distribution and exhibition aspects of the motion picture industry are excluded from the figures in the table.

Readers will note, in Table 340-A, the generally increasing proportion of industry expenditures for salaries. These increases are due both to the rising salaries paid to top stars and to the increasing unionization of the industry. It would be useful to compare industry receipts during this period, but unfortunately, there appear to be no reliable and consistent figures available.

Table 340-B continues the time series data of Table 340-A for the period from 1954 to 1972. Industry receipts are available for these years and are included in the table. Table 340-B also provides a breakdown of production and distribution expenditures for "regular" (theatrical) motion pictures and for films shot for television. Note the higher proportion of salary expenditures in the production segments of the industry, as compared to either distribution (film exchanges) or services. Again, these high salary percentages are due to the large fees demanded by film stars and craft-union members. The reader should also note the great fluctuations in the number of motion-picture producing establishments from year to year, and the increasing proportion of the industry which is devoted to made-for-television filming.

Sources

The data in Table 340-A were taken from the *Census of Manufactures*. The total expenditures figures for the years 1921 and 1923 are not completely comparable to the totals for later

Table 340–B.
Total Receipts and Expenditures of U. S. Motion Picture Industry, with Breakdown for Production/Distribution of Theatrical and Television Films, 1954–1972

Note: All dollar figures are in thousands.

| | Number of Establishments | Total Receipts[a] | Salaries and Wages | | Total Expenditures |
			Total	Percent of Expenditures	
1954					
Production:					
Theatrical	417	$ 74,209	$201,517	61.5	$327,743
TV	206	60,968	28,748	N/A	N/A
Distribution:					
Theatrical	700	624,978	73,150	12.5	587,153
TV	80	23,994	3,786	20.3	18,625
Services	503	156,181	60,301	N/A	N/A
1958					
Production:					
Theatrical	668	154,040	208,258	57.1	364,957
TV	312	95,596	89,189	60.4	147,658
Distribution:					
Theatrical	721	710,512	62,554	12.1	517,209
TV	111	90,980	12,431	17.6	70,629
Services	609	191,655	70,816	48.5	146,151
1963					
Production:					
Theatrical	720	134,460	194,131	39.6	490,189
TV	527	270,602	120,363	51.7	232,914
Distribution:					
Theatrical	730	824,686	72,702	12.1	601,447
TV	131	228,704	17,766	15.5	114,393
Services	663	208,092	83,998	53.6	156,638
1967					
Production:					
Theatrical	909	176,251	319,611	N/A	N/A
TV	686	447,038	148,042	N/A	N/A
Distribution:					
Theatrical	710	855,114	57,722	N/A	N/A
TV	147	367,848	37,881	N/A	N/A
Services	843	344,911	126,750	N/A	N/A
1972					
Production:					
Theatrical	1,392	238,517	217,911	N/A	N/A
TV	1,138	464,471	241,094	N/A	N/A
Distribution:					
Theatrical	877	1,381,491	135,023	26.5	509,045
TV	151	319,648	33,301	17.5	190,136
Services	855	389,419	168,161	52.7	318,957

Sources: 1954-1967 data: *Census of Business, Selected Services* for 1954 (Vol. V, part 8), 1958 (Vol. V, part 8), 1963 (Vol. VI, part 8), and 1967 (Vol. 5, part 1). 1972 data: *1972 Census of Selected Service Industries* (Vol. I, part 3).

Note: (a) For production companies only, "total receipts" includes income from film rentals received directly from exhibitors, from outright sales of films, and from miscellaneous sources other than film rentals (see text).

years, because the "other expenditures" data were not recorded in those early years of the industry. Thus, the totals for 1921 and 1923 include only salaries and wages plus the *value* of film productions at the various studios. In 1931, the *Census of Manufactures* recorded the salaries of production-department employees only. These salaries totaled $70,637,000.

The figures in **Table 340**-B are from appropriate issues of the *Census of Business, Selected Services* and, after 1970, the *Census of Selected Service Industries*. All of the data are for establishments with a payroll—a category that encompasses 95-98 percent of all of the revenues and expenditures in the industry. The figures in the "total receipts" column include film rentals received by the production companies directly from exhibitors, earnings from outright sales of films by the producers, and miscellaneous nonrental receipts to the producers. Receipts from independent distributors and those from distribution offices owned by a production company are *not* included here. As a consequence of this unusual breakdown of income of the film production companies, it is impossible to arrive at legitimate gross profit figures for the industry.

Further Information

Information on the motion picture industry is generally quite limited and found mainly in the various trade periodicals (see Unit 342). The Census Bureau references cited above are the single most consistent sources of information on the motion picture industry, but they suffer from an aggregation of data. Readers are also directed to the annual reports of the film production companies, which can be found in many libraries (see Unit 341). For general background information, see Conant (1960), Jarvie (1970), Bluem and Squire (1972), and Jowett (1976).

Finances of the Major Film Production Companies · 341

Interpretation of Tables

Most media industries in the United States are widely diversified both in location and ownership. However, the motion picture industry from its earliest years has been centered in a few major firms—traditionally eight of them—located in the Los Angeles area. **Table 341**-A provides a record of the after-tax net profits of these firms for the past four decades, from the midst of the Depression to the present. The figures demonstrate the dramatic variations possible in this business, which weathered the Depression and flourished during the war years only to be devastated in the 1950s by the consent decrees (see Unit 240), the increasing pressures of unemployment and resultant unionism, and the ever-stronger competition from television.

Note in **Table 341**-A that the profit peaks of the major studios in the 1942-1947 period were all but gone just five years later, so that by the post-decree year of 1952, profits were either very low or had declined into substantial losses. (The figures in parentheses indicate a loss.) In 1966-1969, three of the weaker companies (Paramount, Warner Bros, and United Artists) fell prey to large conglomerates and now operate as subsidiaries. However, in two of these cases (Paramount and United Artists), the mergers did not prevent further declines and even losses in subsequent years.

Table 341-B covers the same firms for a shorter space of years—the five-year period from 1972 to 1976. In listing the percentage of sales and profits from film (both theatrical and made-for-television) among the eight major producing companies, the table shows declining film income for many of the companies. For three of the firms (Columbia, MGM, and Warner Bros.), film output has also made up a lesser percentage of company sales in the five-year period, suggesting that the businesses have diversified in the face of declining film income.

On the other hand, in about half the cases where comparable data are available for the same year, the proportion of profit from film has been higher than the proportion of film sales. Not specifically shown in **Table 341**-B, but strongly operative in the figures, is the fact that television, not theatrical film is increasingly the primary motion picture product of these companies. Both theatrical and television films are included in the sales and profit figures in the table.

A table showing average feature-film production costs would be a logical addition to this unit, but the editors found it virtually impossible to collect any consistent time-series data on this subject. (See Crandall, 1975, p. 86 ff., for a discussion of this problem.) Conant (1960, p. 77) suggests that a typical "A" film of the early 1930s cost about $200,000 and that there was a tenfold increase in production costs by 1956. But according to Conant, there has been little fluctuation in the *average* costs of production since the mid-1950s.

Table 341–A.
Net Profits or Losses of the Eight Major Motion Picture Production Companies in U. S., 1932–1976

Note: All figures in millions. Losses in parentheses, representing figures after taxes and write-offs, before special credits.

	Columbia	Loew's, Inc./ MGM	Paramount[a]	20th Century-Fox	United Artists[b]	Universal	Warner Bros.	Walt Disney
1932	$ 0.6	$ 8.0	- -	N/A[c]	N/A[c]	N/A[c]	$ (14.1)	N/A[c]
1933	0.7	4.3	- -	$ 1.7	N/A	$ (1.0)	(6.3)	N/A
1934	1.0	8.6	- -	1.3	N/A	(0.2)	(2.5)	N/A
1935	1.8	7.5	- -	3.1	N/A	(0.7)	0.7	N/A
1936	1.6	10.6	$ 4.0	7.7	N/A	(1.8)	3.2	N/A
1937	1.3	14.3	6.0	8.6	N/A	(1.1)	5.9	N/A
1938	0.2	9.9	2.8	7.2	N/A	(0.5)	1.9	N/A
1939	0.0	9.5	2.8	4.2	N/A	1.2	1.7	N/A
1940	0.5	8.7	6.4	(0.5)	N/A	2.4	2.7	N/A
1941	0.6	11.0	9.2	4.9	N/A	2.7	5.5	$ (0.8)
1942	1.6	11.8	13.1	10.6	N/A	3.0	8.6	(0.2)
1943	1.8	13.4	14.6	10.9	N/A	3.8	8.3	0.4
1944	2.0	14.5	14.7	12.5	N/A	3.4	6.9	0.5
1945	1.9	12.9	15.4	12.7	N/A	4.0	9.9	0.4
1946	3.5	17.9	39.2	22.6	N/A	4.6	19.4	0.2
1947	3.7	10.5	28.2	14.0	N/A	3.2	22.0	0.3
1948	0.5	4.2[d]	22.6	12.5	N/A	(3.2)	11.8	(0.1)
1949	1.0	6.0	20.8[e]	12.4	N/A	(1.1)	10.5	(0.1)
1950	1.9	7.6	6.6	9.5[f]	N/A	1.4	10.3	0.7
1951	1.5	7.8	5.5	4.3	0.3	2.3	9.4	0.4
1952	0.8	4.6	5.9	4.7	0.4	2.3	7.2	0.5
1953	0.9	4.5	6.7	4.8	0.6	2.6	2.9[g]	0.5
1954	3.6	6.3	8.1	8.0	0.9	3.8	3.9	0.7
1955	4.9	5.0	9.4	6.0	2.7	4.0	4.0	1.4
1956	2.6	4.6	4.3	6.2	3.1	4.0	2.1	2.6
1957	2.3	(0.5)	5.4	6.5	3.3	2.8	3.4	3.6
1958	(5.0)	0.8	4.6	7.6	3.7	(2.0)	(1.0)	3.9
1959	(2.4)	7.7	4.4	2.3	4.1	4.7	9.4	3.4
1960	1.9	9.6	7.0	(2.9)	4.3	6.3	7.1	(1.3)
1961	(1.4)	12.7	5.9	(22.5)	4.0	7.5	7.2	4.5
1962	2.3	2.6	3.4	(39.8)	3.8	12.7	7.6	6.6
1963	2.6	(17.5)	5.9	9.1	(0.8)	13.6	5.7	7.0
1964	3.2	7.4	6.6	10.6	9.3	14.8	(3.9)	7.0
1965	2.0	7.8	6.3	11.7	12.8	16.2	4.7	11.0
1966	2.0	10.2	N/A[h]	12.5	13.6	13.6	6.5	12.4
1967	6.0	14.0	N/A	15.4	15.5	16.5	3.0	11.3
1968	10.0	8.5	N/A	13.7	19.5[i]	13.5	10.0	13.1
1969	6.0	(35.0)	N/A	(36.8)	16.2	2.5	(52.0)[j]	15.8
1970	6.0	(8.2)	(2.0)[k]	(77.4)	(45.0)	13.3	33.5	22.0
1971	(29.0)	7.8	(22.0)[k]	6.5	1.0	16.7	41.6	26.7
1972	(4.0)	9.2	31.2[k]	6.7	10.8	20.8	50.1[l]	40.3
1973	(50.0)	2.1	38.7	10.7	14.0	25.6	47.4	N/A
1974	(2.3)	26.8	18.7	10.9	9.9	59.2	48.5[m]	48.5
1975	10.5[n]	31.8	29.9	22.7	11.5	95.5	9.1[o]	61.7
1976	11.5	31.9	49.6	10.7	16.0	90.2	61.2	74.6

Sources: 1932-1972 data: Jowett (1976), pp. 483-484, using data from company annual reports and *Moody's Industrial Manual*. 1973-1976 data: *Moody's Industrial Manual* and (for United Artists) *Moody's Bank and Finance Manual*.

Notes: (a) In reorganization until 1936. (b) Not a listed corporation until 1950. (c) Editorial insertion; does not appear in original table. (d) Divorcement: Loew's Theatres hived off. (e) Divorcement: United Paramount Theatres hived off, with profits of $16.7 million in 1948 and $17.6 million in 1949. (f) Divorcement: National Theatres hived off. (g) Divorcement: Stanley Warner hived off. (h) Bought by Gulf & Western; financial figures burned. (i) Bought by Transamerica Corporation. (j) Warner Bros. bought by Kinney Services, which changed its name to Warner Communications in 1971. (k) Operating-loss profits. (l) Breakdown of profits: records and music—$23.8 million; films—$15.8 million; publishing—$2 million; cable television—$1.8 million. (m) Percentage breakdown of profits: 38% from theatrical films; 6% from TV films. (n) $5.2 million gain on exchange of debentures; total is net with deferred income taxes. (o) Includes reduction in carrying value of investment in National Kinney Corp.

Table 341–B.
**Film Income as a Percentage of Sales and Net Operating Profit of the
Eight Major Motion Picture Production Companies in U. S., 1972–1976**

Company	1972 Sales	1972 Profit	1973 Sales	1973 Profit	1974 Sales	1974 Profit	1975 Sales	1975 Profit	1976 Sales	1976 Profit
Columbia	75%	N/A	68%	N/A	61%	N/A	52%	N/A	52%	N/A
Disney	24	60%	22	37%	21	41%	22	40%	20	36%
MCA	59	64	54	48	60	57	63	68	63	67
MGM	94	80	95	80	61	43	46	34	46	30
Paramount	64	N/A	66	N/A	56	N/A	89	N/A	87	N/A
20th Century-Fox	70	35	60	N/A	66	50	71	73	72	64
United Artists	64	94	65	98	N/A	N/A	N/A	N/A	N/A	N/A
Warner Bros.	38	32	38	43	44	62	38	46	34	33

Source: Standard and Poor's *Industry Survey: Leisure Time, Basic Analysis*, issues for years following those listed on table. Data were originally collected from company annual reports.

The *International Motion Picture Almanac* (1975) reports the following proportional breakdown of production costs for feature films in the mid-1970s: story costs (5 percent), production and direction costs (5 percent), sets and other physical properties (35 percent), stars and cast (20 percent), studio overhead (20 percent), income taxes (5 percent), leaving a net percent average profit after taxes of 10 percent.

Sources

The data in both **Tables 341**-A and **341**-B are from secondary sources and therefore involve some simplification and summarization of the often-complicated annual financial reports of the major film production companies. For a more comprehensive picture of the finances of these firms, the reader should refer directly to the annual reports of each company. However, as **Table 341**-B indicates, the specific role of film production in the sales and profit of these companies is often not made available in their public documents.

The three companies which are now a part of large conglomerates (Warner, Paramount, and United Artists) present special difficulties to the researcher, since their annual statements are often combined with other leisure-related businesses controlled by the parent company. In addition, the financial figures for Paramount for 1966 (and perhaps for subsequent years as well) were burned when the studio was taken over by Gulf and Western (see **Table 341**-A, note h).

Further Information

For broad background information on the motion picture industry, see Conant (1960), Crandall (1975), and Jowett (1976). Each of these sources includes many summarized statistics. Back volumes of the annual *Moody's Industrial Manual* also include summarized financial reports of the important film production companies. Scattered current financial information appears in the various trade periodicals, especially *Variety*.

Table 342–A.
**Total Receipts and Percentage of Income from Admissions
among Indoor and Drive-In Motion Picture Theaters in U. S., 1939–1972**

	Four-Wall Theaters		Drive-In Theaters	
	Receipts	Percent from Admissions[a]	Receipts	Percent from Admissions[a]
1939	$ 673,045	N/A	N/A	N/A
1948	1,566,890	79.4	N/A	N/A
1954	1,170,401	80.5	$225,910	72.3
1958	928,128	85.8	230,417	76.6
1963	803,458	87.4	253,766	77.4
1967	969,991	89.7	313,012	79.5
1972	1,402,758	88.6	413,158	79.3

Note: All dollar figures are in thousands.

Sources: The 1939 and 1948 total figures (which include both conventional and drive-in theaters) are from Chapin (1957), p. 133. 1948 percent from admissions is from *1948 Census of Business*, Vol. VI, p. 9.05. 1954-1972 data: *1972 Census of Selected Service Industries* (1975), pp. 3-4.

Note: (a) Receipts other than admissions include concessions.

Interpretation of Tables

Consistent information on motion picture exhibition is as hard to come by as data on motion picture production and distribution. The tables in this unit provide what little trend data is publically available. **Table 342-A** lists the receipts and the percentage of receipts from admissions for both "four-wall" (indoor) and drive-in theaters in the census years since 1939. The rising percentages of receipts from admissions suggest that concession income is decreasing in importance for theater owners. To some extent, of course, these percentages also reflect the increasing prices of admission, one of the trends illustrated in **Table 342-B**.

The constant (1972) dollar column in **Table 342-B** clearly indicates 1945-1946 as the peak admissions years for the film industry—though 1946-1948 are often cited as peak years for actual numbers of people going to theaters (see Unit 640). The table also demonstrates that, even with today's higher-priced theater tickets, levels of admissions income still have not reached the peak levels attained over two decades ago. The other columns in **Table 342-B** are self-explanatory, though the reader should pay particular attention to consumer expenditure patterns and the far more important place held by films prior to World War II, as well as their fairly static position over the past decade.

Table 342-C provides a very rough historical profile of aggregate motion picture theater corporation income. The most outstanding trend here is the great year-to-year fluctuations which have occurred—the profit peaks of the late 1940s, the mid-1950s (reflecting the new wide-screen and the short-lived 3-D innovations), and the mid-1960s (due mainly to road-show films).

Table 342-D offers four summary views of how the typical dollar of theater income was spent in 1931, 1948, 1956, and 1970. Film rental, house expenses, and taxes claim a steady percentage of income over the decades. Salaries have gone up, especially since 1970, and so have advertising costs, with the result that the profit ratio continues to decline.

Sources

This information has been pieced together from a wide variety of sources, representing many different research methods and aims. Only **Tables 342-A** and **342-B** may be said to have some

Table 342–B.
Total Admissions Income and Average Single-Admission Price
of U. S. Motion Picture Theaters, with Admissions Expenditures
as a Percentage of Selected Consumer Expenditures, 1921–1975

	Admissions to Film Theaters (millions)	Constant (1972) Dollars (millions)	Admissions as a Percentage of:			Estimated Average Admission Price
			Personal Consumption Expenditure	Recreational Expenditure	Spectator Amusement Expenditure	
1921	$ 301	$ 703	- -	- -	- -	- -
1923	336	824	- -	- -	- -	- -
1925	367	876	- -	- -	- -	- -
1927	526	1,267	- -	- -	- -	- -
1929	720	1,760	.9%	16.6%	78.9%	- -
1930	732	1,816	1.1	18.4	82.1	- -
1931	719	1,975	1.2	21.8	84.2	- -
1932	527	1,617	1.1	21.6	83.5	- -
1933	482	1,555	1.1	21.9	84.1	- -
1934	518	1,619	1.0	21.2	82.9	- -
1935	556	1,695	1.0	21.1	82.7	$ .25
1936	626	1,891	1.0	20.7	82.5	- -
1937	676	1,971	1.0	20.0	82.6	- -
1938	663	1,967	1.0	20.5	81.3	- -
1939	659	1,985	1.0	19.1	80.3	.27
1940	735	2,194	1.0	19.5	81.3	- -
1941	809	2,298	1.0	19.1	81.3	.29
1942	1,022	2,627	1.2	21.6	84.9	- -
1943	1,275	3,087	1.3	25.7	87.6	- -
1944	1,341	3,185	1.2	24.7	85.8	- -
1945	1,450	3,372	1.2	23.6	84.6	.40
1946	1,692	3,623	1.2	19.8	81.9	.41
1947	1,594	2,985	1.0	17.2	79.6	.43
1948	1,506	2,619	.9	15.5	78.5	.43
1949	1,451	2,546	.8	14.5	77.5	.45
1950	1,376	2,393	.7	12.3	77.3	.44
1951	1,310	2,110	.6	11.3	76.3	.45
1952	1,246	1,965	.6	10.3	75.3	.45
1953	1,187	1,858	.5	9.3	73.9	.48
1954	1,228	1,913	.5	9.4	73.4	.51
1955	1,326	2,072	.5	9.4	73.6	.53
1956	1,394	2,145	.5	9.3	73.4	.54
1957	1,126	1,673	.4	7.3	68.0	.57
1958	992	1,436	.3	6.3	64.5	.65
1959	954	1,369	.3	5.6	60.7	- -
1960	956	1,350	.3	5.4	57.9	- -
1961	955	1,336	.3	5.1	56.7	- -
1962	945	1,307	.3	4.7	53.8	- -
1963	942	1,287	.3	4.4	51.8	.85
1964	951	1,283	.2	4.0	49.5	.93
1965	1,067	1,434	.3	4.1	50.3	1.01
1966	1,119	1,442	.2	4.0	48.4	1.09
1967	1,128	1,414	.2	3.5	46.9	1.20
1968	1,294	1,555	.2	3.7	48.8	1.31
1969	1,400	1,598	.2	3.7	48.2	1.42

internal consistency in that regard. **Table 342-C** is impossible to evaluate empirically given the lack of data on its derivation. The **Table 342-D** figures are all estimates (see the table notes). All of the data presented in Unit 342 should be used carefully and thought of as merely supporting trends, rather than definitively proving them.

Table 342–B. (Cont'd.)

	Admissions to Film Theaters (millions)	Constant (1972) Dollars (millions)	Admissions as a Percentage of:			Estimated Average Admission Price
			Personal Consumption Expenditure	Recreational Expenditure	Spectator Amusement Expenditure	
1970	$1,521	$1,639	.3%	3.7%	48.4%	$1.55
1971	1,626	1,680	.2	3.7	48.4	1.65
1972	1,644	1,644	.2	3.4	47.2	1.70
1973	1,965	1,850	.2	3.6	50.8	1.77
1974	2,264	1,920	.3	3.7	52.2	1.87
1975	2,274	1,767	.2	3.5	49.5	2.05

Sources: Admissions data: 1921-1929 from *Historical Statistics* (1975), series H-884 (p. 401); 1930-1975 from "U. S. Boxoffice Receipts in Relation to Personal Consumption Expenditures," Bureau of Economic Analysis, Social and Economic Statistics Administration, U. S. Department of Commerce, supplied to editors by Motion Picture Association of America. Constant dollar figures derived from Consumer Price Index, and figured by editors (see Unit 300 for CPI deflators). All data on admissions as a percentage of personal consumption, recreational expenditure, and spectator amusement expenditure from the same source. Estimated average admission prices through 1957 from Conant (1960), p. 4, taken in turn from U. S. Bureau of Labor Statistics, *Admission Price Index*. Data from 1958 through 1974 from Jowett (1976), p. 482, as supplied by MPAA Research Department. 1975 admission price figure from *Statistical Abstract* (1976), p. 219, table 360, which also parallels 1970's MPAA data.

Table 342–C.
Pre-Tax Profits of U. S. Motion Picture Theater Corporations, 1948–1972

Note: All figures are in millions.

Year	Profits before Taxes	Year	Profits before Taxes
1948	$142	1961	$ 23
1949	128	1962	6
1950	112	1963	19
1951	101	1964	86
1952	84	1965	104
1953	80	1966	131
1954	136	1967	94
1955	124	1968	138
1956	89	1969	13
1957	55	1970	93
1958	15	1971	15
1959	44	1972	1
1960	49		

Source: U. S. Department of Commerce, Bureau of Economic Analysis, as reprinted in National Association of Theater Owners (1976), p. 45.

Further Information

No single source provides regularly updated theater statistics. However, readers are directed to the statistical section of the *International Motion Picture Almanac*, and to *Cash Box*, *Boxoffice*, and *Variety* among the trade periodicals.

Table 342–D.
Percentage Breakdown of Typical Operating Expenditures
for Motion Picture Theaters in U. S., 1931–1970

Operating Expenses	Percentage of Theater Income Expended			
	1931	1947	1956	1970
Film Rental and Handling	33.3%	32.0%	35.0%	34.4%
Advertising and Publicity	3.3	N/A	8.0	9.0
Salaries	18.3	16.0	16.0	26.6
Heat, Light, Power	2.5	N/A	8.0	N/A
Rent	15.0	15.0	20.0	N/A
Taxes	6.9	6.0	4.0	N/A
Insurance	.9	N/A	N/A	N/A
Depreciation and Repairs	3.2	N/A	N/A	N/A
Misc. Expenses	2.0	20.0	3.0	24.5
Total	85.4%	89.0%	94.0%	94.5%
Profit	14.6%	11.0%	6.0%	5.5%

Sources: 1931 data: Lewis (1933), p. 315. 1947 data: Watkins (1947), p. 19. 1956 data: *Standard and Poor's Industry Surveys: Amusements* (May 3, 1956), p. A-62. 1970 data: *International Motion Picture Almanac* (1975), p. 35A.

Recording Industry Finances

350

Interpretation of Tables

Cycles of prosperity and depression in the recording industry are evident in **Table 350-A.** Between 1921 and 1976, the industry experienced four major dips. The first of these, in the early 1920s, was created by radio competition and complicated by the limitations of the phonographs then in use. The second dip took place in the early 1930s—the result of the Depression. Then, during the war years, shortages of shellac (the base material of records at that time) limited the industry's growth, as did the near-ban on recording which was imposed by the American Federation of Musicians because of a labor dispute. Finally, in the late 1940s and early 1950s, public confusion and concern over the "battle of the speeds"—RCA's 45 rpm records and CBS's 33 rpm records—had a short-term deleterious effect on the industry as a whole.

Table 350-B provides a breakdown, by the various disc and tape products, of the industry's sales for the past decade. These figures do not agree with the totals given in **Table 350-A**, but such variance in data is a common occurrence in this industry. Even so, it is clear that LPs, with their higher sale prices, dominate the industry financially. In the area of tapes, **Table 350-B** shows the decline of the 4-track and reel-to-reel formats—along with quad tapes of all kinds—and the great popularity of 8-track cartridges. An examination of constant (1972) dollar totals, presented at the bottom of **Table 350-B**, reveals that inflationary price increases are responsible for much of the industry's growth in the past decade.

Table 360-C provides two different recent views of how the typical recording-industry income dollar is expended. The two sections of the table include essentially the same data, and taken together, they provide a fairly clear breakdown of industry expenses for typical popular music recordings. Flexibility for retail record/tape discounting is evident in the price to retailers ("distributor's price") shown on the table. (There will often be considerable variance between classical, popular and talk recordings on some of the expenses incurred.)

Table 350-D presents the total receipts and operating expenses of record manufacturers since 1939. The pattern in expenditures is quite static over the 35-year period.

Table 350–A.
Total Annual Sales of U. S. Recording Industry, 1921–1975

Note: All dollar figures are in millions.

Year	Sales in Current Dollars	Sales in Constant (1972) Dollars	Percent of Real Change
1921	$ 105.6	$ 246.7	N/A
1922	92.4	230.4	-7%
1923	79.2	194.1	-16
1924	68.2	166.7	-14
1925	59.4	141.8	-15
1926	70.4	166.4	+17
1927	70.4	169.6	+2
1928	72.6	177.5	+5
1929	74.8	182.9	+3
1930	46.2	114.6	-37
1931	17.6	48.4	-58
1932	11.0	33.7	-30
1933	5.5	17.7	-47
1934	6.6	20.6	+16
1935	8.8	26.8	+30
1936	11.0	33.2	+24
1937	13.2	38.5	+16
1938	26.4	78.3	+103
1939	44.0	132.5	+69
1940	48.4	144.5	+9
1941	50.6	143.8	- -
1942	55.0	141.4	-2
1943	66.0	159.8	+13
1944	66.0	156.8	-2
1945	109.0	253.5	+62
1946	218.0	466.8	+84
1947	224.0	419.5	-10
1948	189.0	328.7	-22
1949	173.0	303.5	-8
1950	189.0	328.7	+8
1951	199.0	320.5	-2
1952	214.0	337.5	+5
1953	219.0	342.7	+2
1954	213.0	331.8	-3
1955	277.0	432.8	+30
1956	377.0	580.0	+34
1957	460.0	683.5	+18
1958	511.0	739.5	+8
1959	603.0	865.1	+17
1960	600.0	847.5	-2
1961	640.0	895.1	+6
1962	687.0	950.2	+6
1963	698.0	953.6	- -
1964	758.0	1,022.9	+7
1965	862.0	1,158.6	+13
1966	959.0	1,235.8	+7
1967	1,051.0	1,317.0	+7
1968	1,124.0	1,351.0	+3
1969	1,170.0	1,335.6	-1
1970	1,182.0	1,273.7	-5
1971	1,251.0	1,292.4	+1
1972	1,383.0	1,383.0	+7
1973	1,436.0	1,352.2	-2
1974	2,200.0	1,866.0	+38
1975	2,360.0	1,833.7	-2

Source: Recording Industry Association of America.

Table 350–B.
Total Annual Sales of U. S. Recording Industry,
by Types of Disc and Tape Recordings, 1966–1976

Type of Recording	1966 Total Receipts	1967 Total Receipts	1967 Percent Change	1968 Total Receipts	1968 Percent Change	1969 Total Receipts	1969 Percent Change	1970 Total Receipts	1970 Percent Change	1971 Total Receipts	1971 Percent Change	1972 Total Receipts	1972 Percent Change	1973 Total Receipts	1973 Percent Change	1974 Total Receipts	1974 Percent Change	1975 Total Receipts	1975 Percent Change	1976 Total Receipts	1976 Percent Change
Discs																					
LPs	$ 783	$ 874	12%	$ 949	9%	$ 995	5%	$1,017	2%	$1,132	11%	$1,203	6%	$1,246	4%	$1,356	9%	$1,485	10%	$1,663	12%
Singles	176	177	--	175	-1	175	--	165	-6	165	--	180	9	190	6	194	2	212	9	245	16
Total Disc Sales	$ 959	$1,051	10%	$1,124	7%	$1,170	4%	$1,182	1%	$1,297	10%	$1,383	7	$1,436	4%	$1,550	8%	$1,697	9%	$1,908	12%
Pre-Recorded Tapes																					
8-Track Cartridges	N/A	$ 60	--	$ 155	158%	$ 300	94%	$ 378	26%	$ 385	2%	$ 425	10%	$ 489	15%	$ 549	12%	$ 583	6%	$ 678	16%
4-Track Cartridges	N/A	36	--	40	10	21	-48	5	-76	--	--	--	--	--	--	--	--	--	--	--	--
Cassettes	N/A	6	--	17	183	75	341	77	3	96	25	102	6	76	-26	87	15	99	13	146	47
Reel-to-Reel	N/A	20	--	22	10	20	-10	18	10	12	-33	8	-33	4	-50	3	-25	2	-34	--	--
Quadraphonic (all formats)	N/A	--	--	--	--	--	--	--	--	--	--	6	--	12	100	11	-6	8	-27	5	-38
Total Tape Sales	50	$ 122	144%	$ 234	92%	$ 416	78%	$ 478	15%	$ 493	3%	$ 541	10%	$ 581	7%	$ 650	12%	$ 692	6%	$ 829	20%
Total Sales, All Recordings	**$1,009**	**$1,173**	--	**$1,358**	--	**$1,586**	--	**$1,660**	--	**$1,790**	--	**$1,924**	--	**$2,017**	--	**$2,200**	--	**$2,389**	--	**$2,737**	--
Total in Constant (1972) Dollars	$1,300	$1,470	--	$1,632	--	$1,811	--	$1,789	--	$1,849	--	$1,924	--	$1,899	--	$1,866	--	$1,878	--	$2,011	--
Percent of Real Change	--	--	13%	--	11%	--	11%	--	-1%	--	3%	--	4%	--	-1%	--	-2%	--	1%	--	7%

Source: *Standard and Poor's Industry Surveys: Leisure Time, Basic Analysis* (November 11, 1976), p. L 23.

Table 350–C.
Representative Production Cost, Profit, and Retail Price
of the Typical Recording in U. S., 1975 and 1976

Standard and Poor Figures (1975)

Manufacturer's Costs (per album):	
Recording Expense and Artists' Advances	$ .30
Payments to Publisher ($.02 per song)	.24
Musicians' Trust Fund Fee	.08
Manufacturing Cost	.50
Jacket and Inner Sleeve	.15
Artists' Royalty	1.00
Freight to Distributor	.03
Advertising, Selling, Administration	.50
Manufacturer's Profit:	**$1.00**
Manufacturer's Price to Distributor	$3.80
Expenses and Profit of Distributor and Retail Outlet	3.18
Retail Album Sale Price	**$6.98**

Warner Communications Figures (1976)

	Album	Tape	Single
Retail List Price	$6.98	$7.97	$1.29
Distributor's Price	3.36	4.01	.58
Manufacturer's Price (estimated)	2.90	3.60	.48
Manufacturer's Variable Costs:			
Mechanicals ($.02 per song)	$.20	$.20	$.04
American Federation of Musicians	.07	.06	.015
Manufacturing and Packaging	.52	.65	.19
Artist's Royalty	From 5% to 15% of retail price.		
Manufacturer's Fixed Costs:			
Recording Expense[a]	From $15,000 to $150,000 per album. Single is taken from album.		
Artist's Advances[a]	From nothing to substantial amounts for major artists.		
Advertising, Promotion, Tour Support	Broad range.		
Cover Preparation and Art	$3,000.		
Indirect Costs to Manufacturers:			
Distribution organization; sales, promotion, and marketing operations; and general and administrative expenses.	These vary in a wide range, depending upon the size of the total operation.		

Sources: *Standard and Poor's Industry Surveys: Leisure Time, Basic Analysis*. 1975 data: November 20, 1975, p. L 22. 1976 data: November 20, 1976, p. L 23-24. 1976 data were attributed to Warner Communications.

Note: (a) These costs are typically recoupable against artists' royalties, if any are earned.

Sources

The Recording Industry Association of America (RIAA) is the source for current information on record industry economics, and its data often appear in *Billboard* and *Variety*. Both **Tables 350-A** and **350-B** are RIAA estimates, but the RIAA has not released information to the public on how these estimates are reached. The early figures in **Table 350-A** are revisions made after 1945 from earlier published listings. The RIAA explains that this was made possible by better and more complete reporting by its members.

Table 350-D.
Total Receipts, Operating Costs, and Capital Expenditures of U. S. Recording Industry, 1939–1974

Note: All dollar figures are in millions.

	Total Industry Receipts		Cost of Materials		Payroll, All Employees		Wages, Production Workers Only		New Capital Expenditures	
	Current Dollars	Constant (1972) Dollars	Current Dollars	Percent of Total Receipts	Current Dollars	Percent of Total Receipts	Current Dollars	Percent of Total Receipts	Current Dollars	Percent of Total Receipts
1939	$ 9.4	$ 33.3	$ 3.0	32%	N/A	N/A	$ 1.1	12%	N/A	N/A
1947	110.2	221.7	38.9	35	$ 29.2	26%	22.8	21	N/A	N/A
1954	92.5	154.9	33.9	37	23.3	25	15.7	17	$ 2.9	3%
1958	148.7	225.3	58.7	39	33.4	22	23.7	16	4.0	3
1963	180.2	251.7	54.1	30	47.0	26	33.0	18	8.7	5
1967	276.4	349.9	95.2	34	85.1	31	54.0	20	7.1	3
1972	567.7	567.7	191.5	34	145.5	26	100.0	18	16.9	3
1974	586.9	504.2	242.0	41	151.7	26	99.4	17	20.5	3

Sources: *Census of Manufactures*, except for 1974 figures, which are from *Annual Survey of Manufactures, 1974.*

Table 350-C information was originally published in *Standard and Poor's Industry Survey: Leisure Time* (1975, 1976). No other source was credited for the 1975 data, but the 1976 data were attributed by Standard and Poor to Warner Communications. **Table 350-D** figures are taken from the U.S. Census Bureau's *Census of Manufactures* and *Annual Survey of Manufactures.*

The reader should note that **Tables 350-A, 350-B,** and **350-C** are based on retail price listings. This is a consistent means of showing changes in the industry; but it is also a very misleading one, since records and tapes are frequently sold at substantial discounts. Factory (wholesale) price listings would be a better basis for judging real growth.

Further Information

Aside from some individual company annual reports and occasional articles in investment publications, there is no consistent public reporting of data on the economics of the record industry. Moreover, some companies, such as Columbia and RCA Victor, do not issue reports which are separate from their controlling firms. Consequently, the reader seeking further information in this area is advised to consult *Billboard* and *Variety*.

Public Broadcasting Station Finances

36

Table 360–A.
Total Income and Operating Expenditures of Public Television Stations in U. S., 1970–1975

Note: National totals are in millions of dollars.
Per-Station averages are in thousands of dollars.

	1970	1971	1972	1973	1974	1975
National Totals						
Income	$105.5	$149.2	$168.3	$190.4	$220.7	$277.1
Direct Operating Expenditure	$83.7	$113.4	$122.9	$137.2	$161.7	$200.1
Number of PTV Stations[a]	195	207	223	236	243	252
Per-Station Averages						
Income	$541.0	$720.8	$754.7	$806.8	$908.2	$1,099.6
Direct Operating Expenditure	$429.2	$547.8	$551.1	$581.4	$665.4	$794.0

Source: Data supplied directly to the editors by CPB.

Note: (a) The number of stations supplied by CPB does not match the total number of educational stations in Table 180-A. This is likely due to slight variance of dates between the sources—dates for data here not supplied by CPB.

Interpretation of Tables

The four tables in this unit illustrate recent trends in public television station income and expenses, as well as a limited view of public radio economics. **Table 360-A** provides both national and average per-station figures for fiscal-year income and direct operating expenditures (the latter does *not* include capital expenses and in-kind expenditures). These figures indicate that average per-station income has increased just over 100 percent during the six-year period from 1970 to 1975. Direct operating expenditures have increased about 83 percent in the same period.

Table 360-B lists the sources of public television station income in terms of the proportional contribution of each source. The percentages are calculated on the basis of aggregate national data. These figures indicate that federal government support for public television stations has nearly doubled, from 12 percent in 1966 to 27 percent in 1976. In contrast, support from local governments and school boards has declined by half (see Unit 281 for the ownership ramifications of this decline). There has been a like decline for foundation support, due at least partially to the Ford Foundation's withdrawal from a portion of its major role in supporting public television over the years (see Unit 361). Somewhat as a result of these declines, the support of individuals (by direct payment, subscriptions, or auctions) has tripled.

Table 360-B.
Percentage Breakdown of Income Sources for Public Television Stations
in U. S., 1966–1976

Income Source	1966	1967	1968	1969	1970	1971	1972	1973	1974	1975	1976
Public Broadcast Agencies[a]	--	5%	7%	5%	8%	11%	11%	10%	12%	14%	} 27%
Federal Government	12%	10	6	7	5	6	9	7	7	8	
State Governments and Boards of Education	27	16	24	29	28	33	24	30	31	29	25
Local Governments and School Boards	19	23	23	24	21	14	13	13	12	9	8
Universities and Colleges	11	10	11	6	9	7	12	8	8	7	9
Foundations	14	15	9	8	9	11	12	10	7	7	6
Subscribers and Auctions	6	8	10	9	10	9	10	14	15	16	14
Business/Industry, Other	11	13	9	11	10	9	9	8	8	10	11

Source: Data supplied directly to the editors by CPB.

Note: (a) Primarily CPB, but also includes such agencies as CTW, PBS and National Educational Radio, etc.

Table 360-C provides an aggregate percentage breakdown of the direct operating costs of public television stations. The figures illustrate a predictable trend—the increase in the funds that are expended directly by the stations for development and fund-raising. This trend is, of course, parallel to the increases in direct public support noted in Table 360-B.

The financial information on public radio in Table 360-D is subject to some significant limitations which are discussed below. Still, the table provides a very rough approximation of the overall and per-station finances of public radio.

Sources

The data for all of the tables in this unit come from the Office of Communication Research of the Corporation for Public Broadcasting (CPB). Some of the data are published in the CPB's *Public Television Licensees* and *CPB-Qualified Public Radio Stations*. These CPB annuals, issued

Table 360–C.
Percentage Breakdown of Direct Operating Costs
of Public Television Stations in U. S., 1970–1975

Expense Item	1970	1971	1972	1973	1974	1975
Technical	26%	23%	22%	24%	24%	22%
Programming	16	15	14	14	11	14
Production	22	29	27	26	29	29
Instructional and School Services	8	8	7	6	6	5
Development and Fund Raising	4	4	4	6	6	7
Promotion	3	3	3	3	3	3
Training and Personnel Development	- -	- -	1	1	1	2
General and Administrative	15	14	17	16	16	14
Other	6	5	6	5	5	4

Source: Data supplied directly to the editors by CPB.

Table 360–D.
Total Income and Operating Costs of CPB-Qualified Public Radio Stations
in U. S., 1970–1975

	Note: National totals are in millions of dollars. Per-station averages are in thousands of dollars.					
	1970	1971	1972	1973	1974	1975
National Totals						
Income	$11.2	$14.1	$17.7	$21.8	$26.0	$31.3
Direct Operating Costs	$8.6	$10.6	$12.9	$15.9	$19.2	$24.7
Number of Stations						
All Educational Radio	443	502	541	603	682	747
CPB-Qualified Public Radio	91	103	121	144	155	165
Per-Station Averages						
Income	$123.1	$136.9	$146.3	$151.4	$167.7	$189.7
Direct Operating Expenditure	$94.3	$101.9	$106.7	$110.5	$123.6	$149.5

Source: Data supplied directly to the editors by CPB.

under various titles since 1970, provide accurate fiscal-year information based on surveys of all public television stations and the limited number of "qualified" public radio stations. The 1966-1968 data in **Table 360-C** precede the establishment of the CPB and are therefore found in annual publications of the National Association of Educational Broadcasters (NAEB).

The information on public radio in **Table 360-D** is severely limited in its completeness and accuracy, mainly because the CPB-qualified stations analyzed in the CPB annual are but a small fraction (20 percent) of all public radio stations on the air. In an attempt to compensate for these omissions, the editors combined the number of CPB-qualified educational FM radio stations with the roughly 30 public AM stations which are not listed in CPB publications. These stations are omitted by the CPB because they do not meet the minimal staff and budget levels which qualify a station for CPB support and survey inclusion. Thus, the CPB-qualified stations are nearly always the bigger and better-financed operations—another reason why the figures in **Table 360-D** must be considered rough and even misleading.

Further Information

The Office of Communication Research of the CPB is the current repository and analysis center for information about public broadcasting stations back to about 1970, and sometimes before. For detailed information on the earlier years, see the National Association of Educational Broadcasters publications, the *Carnegie Commission Report* (1967), and Schramm and Nelson (1972).

The reader should also keep in mind that despite the care of the CPB's survey procedures and analysis, all of the data in these four tables are gathered and reported for a purpose: to back up the CPB's annual requests for funding from Congress. Thus, there is likely to be a touch of advocacy in the development and arrangement of these figures.

National Public Broadcasting Finances

361

Table 361–A.
Total Federal Government Appropriations for Public Broadcasting in U. S., 1967–1978

	Educational Broadcasting Facilities Program	Children's Television Workshop	Corporation for Public Broadcasting	Total Federal Government Support	Federal Support in Constant (1972) Dollars
		Note: All figures in millions of dollars.			
1967	$32.0[a]	- -	- -	$ 32.0	$40.5
1968	0.0	$1.4	- -	1.4	1.7
1969	4.4	1.6	$ 5.0	11.0	12.7
1970	5.1	1.0	15.0	21.1	23.1
1971	11.0	2.9	23.0	36.9	38.4
1972	13.0	7.0	35.0	55.0	55.0
1973	13.0	6.0	35.0	54.0	51.0
1974	15.7	4.0	47.5	67.2	57.7
1975	12.0	5.5	62.0	79.5	62.5
1976	12.9	5.4	96.0[b]	114.3	85.4
1977	15.0	5.0	103.0	123.0	N/A
1978	N/A	N/A	107.2	N/A	N/A

Source: United States Office of Education, for columns 1 and 2; CPB for column 3; the editors for column 5.

Notes: (a) Single authorization. Covers 1963-1967 inclusive. (b) Includes $17.5 million for the transition quarter to allow for the change in the federal fiscal year.

Interpretation of Tables

The four tables in this unit provide detailed information on the important role played by the federal government in public broadcasting over the past decade. The tables also present a retrospective look at the even longer involvement of the Ford Foundation in subsidizing public broadcasting activities.

Most federal money for public broadcasting enters the system along one of the three main routes shown in **Table 361-A**: (1) through the Educational Broadcasting Facilities Program, which was approved in 1962 but not actually funded until 1967; (2) through grants to the Children's Television Workshop (CTW); and (3), most recent and sizable, through grants to the Corporation

Table 361-B.
Budgetary Breakdown of Revenues and Expenses of Corporation for Public Broadcasting, 1969–1976

Note: All figures in thousands of dollars.

Budget Item	1969[a]	1970[a]	1971	1972	1973	1974	1975	1976
			Revenues					
Federal Appropriations	$5,000	$15,000	$23,000	$35,000	$35,000	$47,750	$62,000	$78,500
Federal Grants and Contracts	- -	12	711	225	36	113	90	106
Nonfederal Contributions[b]	2,753	1,173	5,113	5,601	4,025	5,597	9,334	5,577
Earned Interest	206	251	235	694	353	853	1,330	952
Carry-over of Year-end Net Assets from Previous Year	- -	1,045	1,128	2,210	3,634	1,647	3,771	4,538
Unliquidated Budget Commitments from Previous Year	- -	940	1,368	1,296	597	966	1,411	5,017
TOTAL	$7,959	$18,421	$31,555	$45,026	$43,645	$56,925	$77,936	$94,690

for Public Broadcasting (CPB). Naturally, CPB grants go to CTW as well, and these grants are also federal money (see **Table 361-C** for details). In addition, the CPB issues grants to broadcasting facilities (see **Table 361-B**). The categories in **Table 361-A** represent the basic levels of support, ignoring subsequent "cross-fertilization" between programs.

Not shown in **Table 361-A** are grants from the National Endowment for the Arts and the National Endowment for the Humanities, both of which provide program funding. Additional funding will also dribble down through other sources, such as research grants from the National Science Foundation; but the channels listed in **Table 361-A** represent the lion's share of the support for public broadcasting.

Table 361-B provides a detailed look at the fiscal-year budgets of the CPB since 1969. Among the eight expenses categories listed in the budget, the following might be clarified with some additional commentary:

1. Expenditures for "PTV Program Production" primarily involve the major annual grants to PBS, CTW, and the producing PTV stations for programming. CPB has

Table 361-B. (Cont'd.)

Budget Item	Expenses							
	1969[a]	1970[a]	1971	1972	1973	1974	1975	1976
Grants and Awards[c]	$3,986	$10,252	$24,587	$37,165	$37,273	$48,056	$63,883	$74,948
PTV Program Production	--	4,897	9,902	15,308	16,131	17,124	17,444	14,849
Program Distribution	--	957	6,775	9,818	9,100	8,146	9,948	11,459
Public Radio Programs	--	151	1,085	2,291	3,501	3,931	5,383	5,541
Communication Research	--	--	--	--	92	75	239	439
Engineering and Development	--	--	--	53	151	109	372	1,290
Development of Program Quality	--	498	222	767	367	105	133	326
Support for Station Operations	--	4,244	4,374	7,002	6,960	18,211	30,012	40,666
Program Promotion and Advertising	--	--	2,054	1,142	1,062	355	352	378
Programs Administered by CPB	1,197	3,857	1,224	987	693	787	1,002	792
Administrative Support	791	1,816	2,237	2,643	3,065	2,900	3,496	4,393
Current Unliquidated Budget Commitments	940	1,368	1,296	597	966	1,411	5,017	9,305
Carry-over of Year-end Net Assets to Next Year	1,045	1,128	2,210	3,634	1,647	3,771	4,538	5,252
TOTAL	$7,959	$18,421	$31,555	$45,026	$43,645	$56,925	$77,936	$94,690

Source: Corporation for Public Broadcasting, *Annual Report*. Some figures do not add due to rounding.

Notes: (a) 1969-1970 figures are unchecked and unverifiable. (b) Nonfederal contributions are almost entirely from businesses and foundations. (c) For definitions of "Grants and Awards" subcategories, see text.

been increasingly criticized in recent years for spending relatively little of its funds directly for programming—about 15 percent in 1976.

2. "Program Distribution" is nearly always a single grant to PBS for running the interconnected network.

3. "Public Radio Programs" refers to both production and distribution expenditures, with most of these funds going to National Public Radio.

4. "Engineering and Development" expenditures are generally research-oriented and do not include grants to stations for technical improvements.

5. "Development of Program Quality" refers to special support for experimentation and for the support of talent outside of public broadcasting.

6. Expenditures for "Support of Station Operations" are mainly grants to stations for general operating expenses.

Table 361-C.
Income Sources of the Children's Television Workshop, 1968–1977

Note: All figures in thousands of dollars

	1968	1969	1970	1971	1972	1973	1974	1975	1976	1977
Federal Funding										
Office of Education	$1,340	$1,330	$655	$2,600	$7,000	$6,000	$4,000	$5,500	$5,231	$5,000
Office of Economic Opportunity and Office of Child Development	50	300	300	300	--	--	--	--	--	--
National Institute for Alcohol Abuse and Alcoholism	--	--	--	--	--	--	--	250	--	--
National Endowment for the Humanities	--	--	--	--	--	--	--	48	1,000	--
National Cancer Institute	--	--	--	--	--	--	--	197	--	--
Others	25	--	--	--	--	--	--	--	--	--
Corporation for Public Broadcasting	--	--	750	500	2,000	5,000	5,000	2,200	25	--
Public Broadcasting Service	--	--	--	--	--	--	--	4,255	4,165	3,601
Commercial Stations	--	--	--	115	241	303	188	178	123	136
Foundations										
Carnegie Corporation of New York	--	100	1,400	600	1,000	500	--	--	--	--
The Ford Foundation	--	250	1,288	1,000	1,000	2,000	--	2,025	500	525
The John & Mary Markle Foundation	--	--	250	--	--	--	--	--	--	--
The Robert Wood Johnson Foundation	--	--	--	--	--	38	292	1,396	--	--
The Commonwealth Fund	--	--	--	--	--	50	--	100	--	--
Edna McConnell Clark Foundation	--	--	--	--	--	100	250	25	--	--
The Surdna Foundation	--	--	--	--	--	--	--	100	--	--
Others	--	--	160	10	119	88	--	66	--	54
Commercial Firms										
Mobil Oil Corporation	--	--	--	250	250	--	100	25	--	--
General Telephone & Electronics Corporation	--	--	--	--	--	--	50	--	--	--
Xerox Corporation	--	--	--	--	260	740	--	--	--	--
Exxon Corporation	--	--	--	--	--	38	--	--	--	--
Aetna Life Insurance Company	--	--	--	--	--	--	450	1,154	--	--
Others	--	11	26	--	48	--	--	650	--	--
Non-Broadcasting Activities										
Magazine Sales	--	--	104	639	1,439	1,051	1,330	2,093	2,793	4,013
Royalties on Products	--	--	--	642	897	944	2,050	1,702	4,217	6,238
International Programming	--	--	15	363	851	2,936	1,510	2,946	2,462	1,568
Other	--	1	16	176	113	242	263	314	9	41
Total	$1,415	$1,992	$4,964	$7,195	$15,218	$20,030	$15,483	$25,194	$20,525	$21,176

Source: Children's Television Workshop

Note: All figures are for fiscal years ending in June.

That "Sesame Street" and its offshoots have been successful (as well as expensive) is demonstrated by the increasing levels of CTW fundings shown in **Table 361-C**. Most of this funding has come from direct federal government grants, but the reader might also note that CTW-program "spin-offs" (magazine sales and product royalties) have also been providing revenues to CTW since 1972. In 1977, this spin-off income represented the biggest single source of support for CTW.

Table 361-D details the support of public broadcasting (especially television) by the Ford Foundation. Beginning in the early 1950s, Ford money has been crucial to the establishment of national public broadcasting, as well as of many of the earliest educational television stations.

Sources

Though much of the information in this unit is self-reported, it can be considered accurate because it is part of the public record and annually audited. **Table 361-A** was compiled by the U.S. Office of Education, the CPB, and the editors. **Table 361-B** was done by the CPB.

Table 361-C information was supplied to the editors by the CTW. **Table 361-D** is adapted from Ford Foundation data which were based, in turn, on the foundation's own audited annual reports.

Table 361–D.
Ford Foundation Grants/Expenditures for Public Broadcasting, 1951–1977

Fiscal Year	TV and Radio	Radio Only[a]
1951	$ 1,439,091	$ 492,800
1952	2,646,106	0
1953	4,490,021	150,905
1954	4,776,068	0
1955	3,139,195	0
1956	9,979,675	0
1957	4,749,720	74,750
1958	3,965,932	200,000
1959	11,126,112	12,600
1960	7,708,701	1,500
1961	8,140,359	15,000
1962	19,580,006	0
1963	7,423,652	0
1964	7,560,522	0
1965	7,171,903	0
1966	16,288,700	0
1967	23,000,544	38,000
1968	10,998,411	36,500
1969	25,301,843	185,572
1970	17,098,172	75,000
1971	18,155,198	0
1972	19,103,000	0
1973	10,683,699	0
1974	28,974,773	0
1975	3,680,000	0
1976	15,063,034	0
1977[b]	1,242,552	0
Totals	$293,486,989	$1,282,627

Sources: "Ford Foundation Activities in Noncommercial Broadcasting, 1951-76" (New York: Ford Foundation, 1976), p. 23. 1977 data from CPB *Status Report* (1977), p. 5.

Notes: (a) Radio only figures refer only to monies specifically for radio. These figures are included in first column. Combined radio-TV grants are listed only in first column. (b) To April 30 only.

Further Information

For more information on government funding of public broadcasting, see the annual congressional hearings and committee reports regarding CPB and other related appropriations. The Office of Education, in the Department of Health, Education and Welfare, keeps track of and can supply information about the Educational Broadcasting Facilities Program and the CTW grants. For information on CPB, CTW and the Ford Foundation, the reader might consult the published annual reports of each, as well as the material cited in Unit 360 of this book. For further information on the role of various foundations in public broadcasting, see Lashner (1976 and 1977) and *Role of Private Foundations in Public Broadcasting* (1974).

Table 370-A.
Total Revenues and Expenses of the Average Commercial Radio Station in U. S., 1960–1975

Note: All dollar figures are in thousands.

	1960		1970		1975 Full-Time AM		1975 Full-Time FM	
	Amount	Percent	Amount	Percent	Amount	Percent	Amount	Percent
Revenue								
Total Time Sales	$110.3	100%	$162.3	100%	$269.4	100%	$139.9	100%
Networks	0	0	0	0	0	0	0	0
Spot	15.9	14	20.2	13	31.0	12	11.2	8
Local	94.4	86	142.0	88	238.4	88	128.7	92
Expenses	101.8	100	151.7	100	251.1	100	138.4	100
(Total Salaries)	(65.8)	--	(84.0)	--	(131.5)	--	(66.8)	--
Technical	10.9	11	12.6	8	18.3	7	11.5	8
Program	33.5	33	46.7	31	72.8	29	41.7	31
Selling	18.7	18	28.1	19	48.7	19	29.6	20
General and Administrative	38.7	38	64.3	42	111.3	44	55.6	40
Outside News Service	N/A	--	N/A	--	5.2	--	2.6	--
Music License Fee	N/A	--	4.6	--	6.9	--	3.1	--
Depreciation/Amortization	5.6	--	7.4	--	11.9	--	9.9	--
Interest	N/A	--	N/A	--	1.8	--	.9	--
Profit (before taxes)	8.4	8	10.5	7	14.9	6	-.7	-.5

Source: National Association of Broadcasters, *Radio Financial Report* (annual), 1961, 1971, and 1976.

Note: Number of stations surveyed: 1960—1,118, 1970—1,374, 1975—1,058 full-time AM and 321 FM stations. Percentages may vary slightly due to rounding.

Interpretation of Tables

As the tables in this unit illustrate, there are a number of different ways to approach the economics of commercial radio stations. Table 370-A offers a breakdown of national data into the "average" revenues and expenses of the "typical" local radio station. In addition, the 1975 figures on this table provide a further breakdown for the comparison of full-time AM station and FM station finances. Since less than half of all AM stations in existence today are full-time (see Unit 170), the financial variance between the two types of services (full-time and part-time) is worth noting.

Of course, like all statistical averages, the data in Table 370-A can be misleading. In 1975, for example, the National Association of Broadcasters (NAB) reported a number of large-market

Source: FCC, annual financial reports on the radio industry, partially reprinted in the *Annual Report*.

Note: (a) Independent FM stations are not included in the totals after 1968.

Table 370–B.
Revenues, Expenses, and Pre-Tax Earnings of Commercial Radio Networks and Stations in U. S., 1937–1976

Note: All dollar figures are in millions. Figures in parentheses indicate losses.

Year	Total Number of Stations	Networks and Network O & O Stations					Other Stations[a]				Total, All Stations		
		Number of Networks	Number of Stations	Total Revenues	Total Expenses	Pre-Tax Earnings	Number of Stations Reporting	Total Revenues	Total Expenses	Pre-Tax Earnings	Total Revenues	Total Expenses	Pre-Tax Earnings
1937	629	3	N/A	N/A	N/A	N/A	N/A	N/A	N/A	N/A	$ 114.2	$ 91.6	$ 22.6
1938	660	3	23	$ 54.8	$ 35.5	$ 9.2	637	$ 65.5	$ 56.9	$ 9.5	111.4	92.5	18.9
1939	705	3	23	48.4	37.6	11.0	682	75.3	62.6	12.8	123.9	100.1	23.8
1940	765	3	31	56.4	42.2	14.1	734	90.6	71.5	19.1	147.1	118.8	33.3
1941	817	3	33	62.0	44.2	18.0	784	106.6	79.6	27.1	168.8	124.0	44.8
1942	851	4	32	63.7	46.8	16.9	819	115.1	87.4	27.7	178.8	134.2	44.6
1943	841	4	31	76.6	53.0	23.6	810	138.6	95.8	42.8	215.3	148.8	66.5
1944	875	4	32	94.6	68.4	26.2	843	180.7	116.6	64.1	275.3	185.0	90.3
1945	911	4	28	100.9	77.9	23.1	873	198.3	137.8	60.5	299.3	215.7	83.6
1946	1025	4	29	102.0	82.6	19.4	996	220.6	168.5	57.1	322.6	246.1	76.5
1947	1464	4	27	104.4	84.8	19.6	1437	259.3	207.1	52.2	368.7	291.9	71.8
1948	1824	4	27	109.1	91.0	18.1	1797	298.0	252.0	46.1	407.0	342.9	64.1
1949	2021	4	27	108.1	90.6	17.5	1994	305.7	266.9	38.8	413.8	357.5	56.3
1950	2229	4	26	110.5	91.5	19.0	2208	334.0	284.8	49.2	444.5	376.3	68.2
1951	2266	4	25	104.0	93.9	10.1	2241	346.4	299.0	47.4	450.4	392.9	57.5
1952	2380	4	25	100.6	89.4	11.2	2355	369.1	320.2	48.9	469.7	409.6	60.1
1953	2479	4	22	97.3	86.9	10.4	2457	378.0	333.4	44.6	475.3	420.3	55.0
1954	2598	4	21	88.6	80.4	8.2	2577	361.0	327.3	33.7	410.5	407.7	41.8
1955	2742	4	19	78.3	72.4	5.9	2724	375.0	335.0	40.0	453.4	407.4	46.0
1956	2966	4	19	70.2	69.8	0.4	2947	410.4	361.6	48.8	480.6	431.4	49.2
1957	3164	4	21	73.5	73.5	0.0	3143	444.4	389.8	54.6	517.9	463.3	54.6
1958	3290	4	23	69.4	73.0	(3.7)	3267	453.7	412.8	40.9	523.1	485.8	37.3
1959	3528	4	19	60.4	64.9	(4.5)	3529	499.6	452.7	46.9	560.0	517.6	42.4
1960	3688	4	19	63.0	66.0	(3.0)	3669	534.7	485.8	48.9	597.7	551.8	45.9
1961	3610	4	19	61.5	61.3	0.2	3591	522.1	490.2	31.8	583.6	511.6	32.0
1962	3698	4	19	64.1	61.9	2.2	3679	562.7	518.2	44.5	626.8	580.1	46.7
1963	3832	4	19	68.9	63.0	5.0	3813	600.7	548.6	52.1	669.7	611.6	53.1
1964	3896	4	19	71.1	66.8	4.3	3877	648.0	578.5	69.3	719.2	645.4	73.8
1965	3941	4	19	74.4	71.3	3.0	3922	702.4	624.4	78.0	776.8	695.8	81.1
1966	4019	4	19	79.4	75.8	3.6	4000	773.2	676.2	97.0	852.7	752.1	100.6
1967	4068	4	19	77.1	79.1	(2.0)	4057	807.6	720.5	87.0	884.7	799.6	85.0
1968	4161	4	20	81.3	86.5	(5.2)	4141	913.4	790.9	122.5	994.7	877.4	117.3
1969	4194	4	20	84.5	85.0	(0.5)	4174	955.8	844.1	111.7	1040.3	929.2	111.2
1970	4209	4	20	86.1	84.4	1.7	4189	991.2	888.9	102.2	1077.4	973.4	104.0
1971	4252	4	20	97.0	89.4	7.5	4232	1079.4	969.2	110.2	1176.3	1058.6	117.8
1972	4271	4	20	106.3	93.4	12.9	4251	1185.7	1051.7	134.1	1292.1	1145.0	147.0
1973	4267	4	18	102.3	96.3	6.0	4269	1254.5	1137.3	117.3	1356.9	1233.6	123.3
1974	4267	4	18	104.4	102.1	2.3	4343	1305.3	1212.8	92.5	1409.7	1314.9	94.8
1975	4355	7	17	118.4	109.5	9.0	4338	1361.3	1274.7	86.5	1479.7	1384.3	95.4
1976	4363	7	17	143.8	133.4	10.2	4346	1543.1	1396.0	147.2	1686.9	1529.4	157.5

stations with profit ratios of 13.5 percent—that is, more than $322,400. Yet in the same year, a small station in a small town of under 10,000 population might profit only 2.6 percent or about $2,600.

Table 370-B provides nearly 40 years of data comparing the economics of the networks and their stations with the economics of all other radio stations. Although radio networks are once again approaching the high income levels they first attained in the 1940s, this apparent prosperity is actually the result of the inflation in this decade.

Table 370-C, based on the raw financial figures in Table 370-B, lists the profit ratios for the radio networks, their owned-and-operated (O&O) stations, and all other AM and AM-FM stations. The ratios were derived by the editors by dividing earnings by revenues in each category. The results are profit ratios before taxes. The proportion of total radio industry profits (last two columns) was derived by dividing network and O&O station earnings by total earnings (these figures were then checked by dividing other station earnings by total earnings).

The table illustrates the decline in network radio as a strong financial element in the industry after the rise of television. Note that nearly all of the profit after about 1955 comes from the stations. Compare these results with those for the television industry (Tables 380-B and 382-C), in which network domination is the rule, following the old radio pattern.

Table 370–C.
Pre-Tax Profit Ratios of Network and Other Commercial Radio Stations in U. S., 1937–1976

Note: Figures in parentheses indicate loss. Dashes indicate less than 1% either way.

	Profit Ratios			Proportion of Total Profits	
	Networks and O & O Stations	Other Stations	Total Radio	Networks and O & O Stations	Other Stations
1937	N/A	N/A	20%	N/A	N/A
1938	17%	15%	17	49%	51%
1939	23	17	19	46	54
1940	25	21	23	42	58
1941	29	25	27	40	60
1942	27	24	25	38	62
1943	31	31	31	35	65
1944	28	35	33	29	71
1945	23	31	28	28	78
1946	19	26	24	25	75
1947	19	20	20	27	73
1948	17	15	16	28	78
1949	16	13	14	31	69
1950	17	15	15	28	72
1951	10	14	13	18	82
1952	11	13	13	19	81
1953	11	12	12	19	81
1954	9	9	9	20	80
1955	8	11	10	13	87
1956	--	12	10	--	100
1957	--	12	11	--	100
1958	--	9	7	(1)	100
1959	(1)	9	8	(11)	100
1960	(1)	9	8	(7)	100
1961	--	6	5	--	100
1962	3	8	7	5	95
1963	9	9	9	10	90
1964	6	11	10	6	94
1965	4	11	10	4	96
1966	5	13	12	4	96
1967	--	11	10	(2)	100
1968	(1)	13	12	(4)	100
1969	--	12	11	--	100
1970	1	10	10	2	98
1971	8	10	10	6	94
1972	12	11	11	9	91
1973	6	9	9	5	95
1974	2	7	7	2	98
1975	8	6	6	9	91
1976	7	10	9	7	93

Source: Calculated by the editors from the figures in Table 370-B.

Table 370-D provides what little aggregate data is available on commercial FM radio after 1948. While most of these statistics concern independent stations (stations not owned by an AM-station company), fuller information on AM-owned FM stations has been made available since 1969. These figures indicate that only just recently has the FM radio industry become profitable—first among the AM-owned FM stations, and then, in 1976, among the independent FM stations as well. But these data are limited severely by the fact that some 1,500 other FM stations (nearly all AM-owned), do not report their FM finances separately. (The figures in Tables 370-A, 370-B, and 370-C all include FM-station revenues which are not reported separately.)

Table 370-D.
Total Revenues, Expenses, and Pre-Tax Earnings of Commercial FM Radio Stations in U. S., 1948–1976

Note: All dollar figures are in millions. Figures in parentheses indicate losses.

Year	Number of Stations	Independent FM Stations				FM Stations Owned by AM Stations				Total, All Stations		
		Number of Stations	Total Revenues	Total Expenses	Pre-Tax Earnings	Number of Stations	Total Revenues	Total Expenses	Pre-Tax Earnings	Total Revenues	Total Expenses	Pre-Tax Earnings
1948	682	87	$ 1.1	$ 4.2	$ (3.1)	--	--	--	--	$ 1.7	--	--
1949	723	104	1.6	5.1	(3.5)	--	--	--	--	3.6	--	--
1950	699	86	1.4	4.0	(2.6)	--	--	--	--	2.8	--	--
1951	626	66	1.2	3.0	(1.8)	--	--	--	--	3.0	--	--
1952	611	56	1.1	2.1	(1.0)	--	--	--	--	2.6	--	--
1953	594	45	.8	1.6	(.8)	--	--	--	--	2.1	--	--
1954	528	43	.8	1.4	(.6)	--	--	--	--	1.9	--	--
1955	493	38	1.0	1.4	(.4)	--	--	--	--	1.9	--	--
1956	472	51	1.4	1.8	(.4)	--	--	--	--	2.4	--	--
1957	499	67	2.0	2.5	(.5)	--	--	--	--	3.1	--	--
1958	533	93	2.5	3.2	(.7)	--	--	--	--	4.0	--	--
1959	662	148	4.3	5.9	(1.6)	--	--	--	--	5.7	--	--
1960	789	218	5.8	8.2	(2.4)	--	--	--	--	9.4	--	--
1961	938	249	7.1	9.7	(2.6)	--	--	--	--	10.0	--	--
1962	993	279	9.3	12.5	(3.2)	--	--	--	--	13.9	--	--
1963	1071	294	11.4	14.6	(3.2)	--	--	--	--	16.3	--	--
1964	1175	306	12.8	15.8	(3.0)	--	--	--	--	19.7	--	--
1965	1381	338	15.7	19.0	(3.3)	--	--	--	--	24.7	--	--
1966	1575	381	19.4	22.7	(3.3)	--	--	--	--	32.3	--	--
1967	1706	405	22.6	26.8	(4.2)	--	--	--	--	39.8	--	--
1968	1888	433	28.3	32.2	(3.9)	--	--	--	--	53.2	--	--
1969	1961	442	33.4	38.9	(5.5)	179	$ 12.1	$16.9	$(4.8)	67.4	$ 55.8	$(10.3)
1970	2105	464	40.6	46.8	(6.2)	225	18.9	23.8	(4.9)	84.9	70.6	(11.1)
1971	2235	527	55.3	64.4	(9.0)	241	26.3	32.3	(6.0)	115.0	96.7	(15.0)
1972	2328	590	77.4	86.2	(8.8)	275	37.5	41.4	(3.9)	151.9	127.6	(12.7)
1973	2390	616	96.1	106.1	(10.0)	361	57.5	58.3	(.8)	198.3	164.4	(10.8)
1974	2552	678	128.0	141.1	(13.1)	397	65.4	63.0	2.9	248.2	204.1	(10.2)
1975	2669	703	142.9	152.4	(9.4)	477	102.4	97.7	4.7	245.3	250.1	(4.7)
1976	N/A	744	N/A	N/A	4.3	563	N/A	N/A	16.9	332.5	311.4	21.2

Source: FCC, annual financial reports on the broadcasting industry, partially reprinted in the *Annual Report*.

Notes: This table is misleading in that it refers only to the FM stations reporting financial data—often a minority of the total FM stations on the air. In addition, until 1969, the financial information from FM stations *owned by AM stations* was included in the FCC reports for all radio stations (see Table 370-B).

As with other advertising media, including newspapers and television, the income of the radio industry is somewhat cyclical, depending on both the overall state of the economy and the state of the advertising business. In "good" years, radio industry income has increased by 50-60 percent over the previous year, but lack of growth, or even decline (when inflation is taken into effect), is also an expected occurence in the industry.

Overall, the radio industry is very profitable, though a relatively few large stations take the lion's share of the profits. Moreover, two large groups of stations—daytime AM stations and independent FM stations—continue to face a "soft" income situation. In 1976, for example, of 4,275 reporting AM or AM-FM stations, some 1,400 reported losing money, while 329 of 672 independent FM stations also lost money. Thus, as in television (see Unit 380), there are distinct groups of "haves" and "have nots" in radio broadcasting.

Sources

Data for **Table 370-A**, drawn from the NAB's annual *Radio Financial Report* (1961, 1971, 1976), were gathered by a survey of all stations. Although not all stations responded to this survey, the NAB research department reports that its results generally parallel those of the FCC's more definitive research. **Tables 370-B** and **370-D** were taken from the FCC's *AM and FM Broadcast Financial Data*, which includes independent FM stations until 1961 and AM-owned FM stations to 1969. Again, not all stations were included in these tallies. Only the column of "Total Revenues" under "Total, All Stations" includes all income to all FM stations, regardless of control. The total columns for expenses and earnings include only the combined totals of the independent FM and AM-owned FM stations. The figures in the table may not add due to rounding.

Despite the above limitations, all of the information collected here is likely to be accurate, since it is the result of a legally required, detailed financial report of all licensees with income. As noted above, **Table 370-C** is based on the figures given in **Table 370-B**.

Further Information

Financial information on radio is more difficult to obtain than financial information on television. The two standard sources are the NAB and the FCC, and the data issued by these sources are often reprinted at length in *Broadcasting. Statistical Trends in Broadcasting* (annual), *Broadcasting Yearbook* (annual), and *Television Factbook* (annual) all contain summary market breakdowns for radio, and the Radio Advertising Bureau can supply more specific data. For projections of radio's place in the near future, see *Radio in 1985* (1977).

Commercial Television Station Finances

38

Interpretation of Tables

The three tables presented in this unit provide an overview of the revenues, expenses, earnings, and profit ratios of commercial television stations in the United States. The reader will note in **Tables 380-A** and **380-B** that television profit ratios are a good deal higher than those of *radio* stations (see **Tables 370-A** and **370-B**, and Unit 382). However, averages of television statistics, such as the figures in **Tables 380-A** and **380-B**, can be misleading. For example, a major-market, VHF, network-affiliate station may have a profit of over $5 million (and a profit ratio of 33 percent or better), while a small-market, VHF, independent station might realize only $100,000 before taxes (about a 7 percent profit ratio). Moreover, UHF stations, almost without exception, do not do nearly as well as their VHF competitors.

Another key factor in the financial performance of both VHF and UHF stations is the matter of network affiliation. According to the FCC, in 1975, 87 percent of VHF network-affiliate stations, but only 73 percent of VHF independents, made a profit. In that same year, only 52 percent of UHF stations—affiliated and independent—drew a profit (see **Table 380-C**). Similar annual performance statistics over the past two decades form a fairly consistent pattern.

Table 380-B presents the official FCC data on television station economics for the years 1948 through 1976 (the information on profit ratios is supplied by the editors). The "commercial stations" columns include all VHF and UHF, network-affiliate and independent stations, but exclude the 15 network owned-and-operated (O&O) stations. The "industry total" columns include data on the O&O stations, to give the reader a broader view of television economics. However, for the full picture, the reader should use this table in conjunction with the tables in Unit 382 to compare the television networks and their O&O stations with all other commercial stations.

Table 380-C compares VHF and UHF commercial stations from the end of the FCC freeze on channel capacity in 1953 (see Unit 180) through 1975. The differences between UHF and VHF profitability are evident. A decline in UHF station profits after 1967 was undoubtedly due to the many new stations going on the air at that time (nearly all stations tend to lose money in the start-up process). By the mid-1970s, however, UHF stations appeared to be breaking into the black once again.

Table 380–A.
Budgetary Breakdown of Revenues and Expenses
of Commercial Television Stations in U. S., 1960–1975

Note: All dollar figures are in thousands.

Budget Item	1960 All TV Stations[a]		1970 All TV Stations		1970 UHF Stations Only		1975 Network Affiliates		1975 UHF Stations Only	
	Amount	Percent of Total	Amount	Percent of Total	Amount	Percent of Total	Amount	Percent of Total	Amount	Percent of Total
Revenue:										
Total Time Sales	$962.8	100%	$1792.7	100%	$978.0	100%	$2430.0	100%	$1787.2	100%
Network sales	251.3	26	342.4	19	75.3	8	364.5	15	132.3	7
Spot sales	413.0	43	735.0	41	340.3	35	957.4	39	704.2	39
Local sales	298.5	31	715.3	40	562.4	58	1108.1	46	950.7	53
Expenses:										
Total Salaries[b]	$318.7	- -	$573.0	- -	$360.5	- -	$681.2	- -	$528.6	- -
Technical costs	124.0	16	206.4	15	155.4	16	229.7	14	223.0	15
Programming costs	280.9	37	475.8	36	357.3	36	599.1	35	523.7	36
Promotional costs	97.9	13	171.6	13	122.7	12	238.2	14	199.5	14
General and Administrative costs	262.5	34	486.5	36	354.4	36	634.7	37	520.8	36
Outside News Service fees	N/A	- -	N/A	- -	N/A	- -	17.1	- -	9.0	- -
Music License fees	N/A	- -	N/A	- -	N/A	- -	43.4	- -	27.9	- -
Depreciation/Amortization	78.9	- -	142.5	- -	110.4	- -	151.0	- -	116.4	- -
Film/Tape costs	85.4	- -	110.9	- -	74.0	- -	132.0	- -	115.2	- -
Interest	N/A	- -	N/A	- -	N/A	- -	4.9	- -	25.6	- -
Income (before taxes)	$139.2	15%	284.9	18%	$-54.8	-6%	$420.7	20%	$95.1	6%

Source: National Association of Broadcasters, *Television Financial Report* (1961, 1971, 1976).

Notes: (a) The number of TV stations reporting each year are as follows: 1960–277 stations. 1970–"All Stations," 677; "UHF Stations Only," not available. 1975–"Network Affiliates," 346; "UHF Stations Only," 84. (b) "Total Salaries" figures overlap the other budgetary-expense items, in that salary expenses are sometimes included in these other items.

Table 380–B.
Total Revenues, Expenses, Pre-Tax Earnings and Profit Ratios of Commercial Television Stations in U. S., 1948–1976

Note: All dollar figures are in millions. Figures in parentheses indicate losses.

Year	All Non-O&O Stations[a]					% of Total TV Industry Profits	All Commercial Stations[b]				
	Number of Stations	Revenue	Expenses	Earnings before Taxes	Profit Ratio		Number of Stations	Revenue	Expenses	Earnings before Taxes	Profit Ratio
1948	40	$ 3.9	$ 12.4	$ (8.5)	(218)%	--	50	$ 8.7	$ 23.6	$ (14.9)	(171)%
1949	84	15.0	29.0	(13.5)	(90)	--	98	34.3	59.6	(25.3)	(74)
1950	93	50.4	49.6	.8	2	--	107	105.9	115.1	(9.2)	(9)
1951	98	107.3	76.7	30.6	29	74%	108	235.7	194.1	41.6	18
1952	107	144.0	98.4	45.6	32	82	122	324.2	268.7	55.5	17
1953	318	201.0	151.0	50.0	25	74	334	432.7	364.7	68.0	16
1954	394	286.3	232.5	53.8	19	60	410	593.0	502.7	90.3	15
1955	421	370.0	288.5	81.5	22	55	437	744.7	594.5	150.2	20
1956	459	454.6	350.4	104.2	23	55	475	896.9	707.3	189.6	21
1957	485	475.3	386.0	89.3	19	56	501	943.2	783.2	160.0	17
1958	495	513.3	418.4	94.8	18	55	514	1,030.0	858.1	171.9	17
1959	504	587.8	453.4	134.4	23	60	521	1,163.9	941.6	222.3	19
1960	515	627.9	479.0	148.9	24	61	530	1,268.6	1,024.5	244.1	19
1961	525	643.0	493.0	150.0	23	63	540	1,318.3	1,081.3	237.0	18
1962	539	732.0	531.8	200.2	27	64	554	1,486.2	1,174.6	311.6	21
1963	550	776.9	569.9	207.0	27	60	565	1,597.2	1,254.0	343.2	21
1964	560	864.6	605.5	259.1	30	62	575	1,793.3	1,377.7	415.6	23
1965	573	941.0	654.7	286.3	30	64	588	1,964.8	1,516.9	447.9	23
1966	593	1,036.7	730.6	306.1	30	62	608	2,203.0	1,710.1	492.9	22
1967	604	1,058.8	804.3	254.5	24	61	619	2,275.4	1,860.8	414.6	18
1968	627	1,212.9	897.0	316.0	26	64	642	2,520.9	2,026.1	494.8	20
1969	658	1,328.9	1,001.3	327.5	25	59	673	2,796.2	2,242.6	553.6	20
1970	671	1,351.1	1,064.6	286.4	21	63	686	2,808.2	2,354.4	453.8	16
1971	673	1,371.4	1,127.2	244.3	18	63	688	2,750.3	2,361.2	389.2	14
1972	648	1,581.1	1,242.3	338.8	21	61	663	3,179.4	2,627.3	552.2	17
1973	651	1,706.8	1,341.4	365.4	21	56	666	3,464.8	2,811.7	653.1	19
1974	659	1,855.2	1,448.9	406.3	22	55	669	3,776.3	3,039.2	737.1	20
1975	654	2,024.7	1,558.8	465.9	23	60	669	4,094.1	3,314.1	780.0	19
1976	666	2,594.1	1,798.5	795.6	31	64	680	5,198.5	3,948.3	1,250.2	24

Source: FCC, annual financial reports on the television industry, partially reprinted in the FCC's *Annual Report*.

Notes: Figures may not total due to rounding. (a) Includes all commercial stations (VHF and UHF, independent and affiliate) except the 15 network-owned and operated stations. (b) Includes network-owned and operated stations.

Table 380–C.
Total Revenues, Expenses, and Pre-Tax Earnings
of Commercial VHF and UHF Television Stations in U. S., 1953–1976

Note: All dollar figures are in millions. Figures in parentheses indicate losses.

Year	Number of Stations Reporting	Revenue	Expenses	Earnings before Taxes	% of Stations Reporting Profits
1953					
VHF	206	$ 190.6	$ 134.3	$ 56.3	N/A
UHF	112	10.4	16.7	(6.3)	N/A
1954					
VHF	269	260.9	197.1	63.8	N/A
UHF	125	25.4	35.4	(10.0)	N/A
1955					
VHF	318	342.2	255.5	86.7	63
UHF	103	28.5	33.0	(4.5)	27
1956					
VHF	364	422.1	316.0	106.1	73
UHF	95	32.5	34.4	(1.9)	39
1957					
VHF	397	448.6	355.8	92.8	81
UHF	88	26.7	30.2	(3.5)	32
1958					
VHF	416	487.2	390.1	97.1	71
UHF	76	26.1	28.3	(2.2)	37
1959					
VHF	427	559.8	424.9	134.9	78
UHF	77	28.0	28.5	(.5)	51
1960					
VHF	439	597.1	448.5	148.6	81
UHF	76	30.8	30.5	.3	50
1961					
VHF	444	611.6	461.0	150.6	79
UHF	81	31.4	32.0	(.6)	39
1962					
VHF	456	697.6	498.3	199.3	81
UHF	83	34.4	33.5	.9	57
1963					
VHF	464	737.8	531.0	206.8	83
UHF	86	39.1	38.9	.2	58
1964					
VHF	468	820.3	563.9	256.4	85
UHF	92	44.3	41.6	2.7	68
1965					
VHF	473	891.3	604.8	286.5	87
UHF	100	49.7	49.9	(.2)	66
1966					
VHF	479	976.9	663.5	313.5	87
UHF	114	59.8	67.1	(7.4)	59
1967					
VHF	471	989.9	717.7	272.2	83
UHF	133	68.9	86.6	(17.7)	42
1968					
VHF	473	1,122.1	776.5	345.6	86
UHF	154	90.9	120.4	(29.5)	45
1969					
VHF	489	1,214.9	844.2	370.7	83
UHF	169	114.0	157.2	(43.2)	35
1970					
VHF	491	1,226.6	894.7	331.9	82
UHF	180	124.5	170.0	(45.5)	32
1971					
VHF	491	1,223.3	946.3	277.0	81
UHF	182	148.2	180.8	(32.7)	32
1972					
VHF	490	1,395.6	1,040.9	354.7	86
UHF	173	185.4	201.4	(15.9)	44
1973					
VHF	489	1,497.4	1,124.3	373.1	86
UHF	177	209.4	217.0	(7.7)	47
1974					
VHF	494	1,626.9	1,215.9	411.1	86
UHF	175	228.2	233.1	(4.9)	47
1975					
VHF	477	1,762.2	1,305.8	456.2	86
UHF	177	262.6	252.7	9.9	52
1976					
VHF	460	2,231.1	1,500.4	730.7	91
UHF	178	363.0	298.2	64.8	67

Source: National Association of Broadcasters, *Television Financial Report* (1961, 1971, 1976).

Sources

For a discussion of source validity for the tables in this unit, the reader should refer to the "Sources" section in Unit 370; for the tables in this unit were constructed from parallel sources and are subject to the same general limitations. While **Table 380-B** does not include all stations on the air (see Unit 180), it is the most complete listing available. The accuracy of the data through 1957 in **Tables 380-B** and **380-C** is somewhat limited, because many of the television stations listed for those early years were actually on the air during only part of a year, and many UHF stations went dark each year. Also, there is an apparent lack of consistency in the FCC's reporting of profitable stations in those years.

Further Information

Official television station financial information is found in the FCC's *TV Broadcast Financial Data* (annual), which is substantially reprinted in the FCC's *Annual Report* and in *Broadcasting*. The National Association of Broadcasters produces annual volumes on both radio and television. Its *Television Financial Report* is an especially useful survey containing many market and revenue breakdowns. All of these sources provide some market-by-market information.

Summaries of financial information appear in *Television Factbook* and *Broadcasting Yearbook*, as well as in reports and publications of the John Blair Company. *Broadcasting Monthly*, a special analysis for investors, is a fine source for practical, up-to-date financial statistics on the networks and major group owners. However, for deeper analysis, the reader should consult Bunce (1976), Owen, et al. (1974), and Owen (1975).

Network Television Finances 38

Interpretation of Tables

Television network earnings come from two sources: the networks themselves and their owned-and-operated (O&O) stations (five in each network, for a total of 15). Because the network stations are in the largest broadcast markets (see Unit 262), these stations typically achieve annual profits of three to five million dollars (a 30 percent or more margin of profit). Thus, the network O&O stations contribute substantially to overall network earnings.

The networks themselves were money-losers in the early years of television, due to the costs of interconnection and programming. In the mid-1950s, they began to achieve limited profits, but the O&O stations remained the major sources of overall network earnings. By 1971, however, the demand for network time exceeded supply and drove up the network charges for advertising time. As a result, the networks surged ahead of their O&O stations in total earnings.

The dramatic changes in 1971 also resulted partially from outside regulations: Cigarette advertising was banned on January 1, 1971, and the FCC's prime-time access rule was invoked in September of that year. **Table 381-A** shows that network profit margins more than doubled in the 1970s, while the O&O station margins, although still substantial, had slipped from the high levels of a decade before. The old argument that the networks could not survive without O&O station income is clearly no longer applicable.

Table 381-B documents several important changes in network television advertising patterns between 1965 and 1975. During this period, for example, the total number of minutes for television advertising increased about 10 percent, while the number of television commercials grew by more than 100 percent. The latter development occurred as the 30-second commercial unit became the industry norm—a change forced in large part by the sharply rising charges for network time.

Those cost increases also led to substantial changes in the ways that programming was supported. Most television programs in the early 1950s were entirely supported by a single advertiser which had a strong identity with a given show. This had been the pattern for radio network programming. By the mid-1950s, however, sponsored television shows had declined to 39 percent of all prime-time programs, while "participating-advertiser" programs were clearly on the rise. The participating-advertiser program is produced by the network, which then sells advertising time at a set rate to any advertiser willing to pay the charges. The advertiser has no influence over the

Table 381–A.
Total Revenues, Expenses, Pre-Tax Earnings, and Profit Margins
of Television Networks and Network-Owned Stations in U. S., 1948–1976

Note: All dollar figures are in millions. Figures in parentheses indicate losses.

	Number of Networks	Number of Network-Owned Stations	Combined Network/Station Revenues and Earnings					Networks Only			Network-Owned Stations		
			Revenues	Expenses	Pre-Tax Earnings	Profit Margin	% of Total TV Industry Profits	Pre-Tax Earnings	Percent Change	Profit Margin	Pre-Tax Earnings	Percent Change	Profit Margin
1948	4	10	$ 4.8	$ 11.2	$ (6.4)	(133)%	--	N/A	N/A	N/A	N/A	N/A	N/A
1949	4	14	19.3	31.4	(12.1)	(63)	--	N/A	N/A	N/A	N/A	N/A	N/A
1950	4	14	55.5	65.5	(10.0)	(18)	--	N/A	N/A	N/A	N/A	N/A	N/A
1951	4	15	128.4	117.4	11.0	9	26%	N/A	N/A	N/A	N/A	N/A	N/A
1952	4	15	180.2	170.3	9.9	5	18	N/A	N/A	N/A	N/A	N/A	N/A
1953	4	16	231.7	213.7	18.0	8	26	N/A	N/A	N/A	N/A	N/A	N/A
1954	4	16	306.7	270.2	36.5	12	40	N/A	N/A	N/A	N/A	N/A	N/A
1955	4	16	374.0	306.0	68.0	18	45	N/A	N/A	N/A	N/A	N/A	N/A
1956	3	16	442.3	356.9	85.4	19	45	N/A	N/A	N/A	N/A	N/A	N/A
1957	3	16	467.9	397.2	70.7	15	44	N/A	N/A	N/A	N/A	N/A	N/A
1958	3	19	516.7	439.7	77.0	15	45	N/A	N/A	N/A	N/A	N/A	N/A
1959	3	17	576.1	488.2	87.9	15	40	$ 32.0	--	7.3%	$ 55.9	--	40.6%
1960	3	15	640.7	545.5	95.2	15	39	33.6	5.0%	6.8	61.6	10.2%	42.2
1961	3	15	675.3	588.3	87.0	13	37	24.7	(26.5)	4.7	62.3	1.1	41.9
1962	3	15	754.2	642.8	111.4	15	36	36.7	48.6	6.3	74.7	19.9	44.1
1963	3	15	820.3	684.1	136.2	17	40	56.4	53.7	8.9	79.8	6.8	43.3
1964	3	15	928.7	772.2	156.5	17	38	60.2	6.7	8.4	96.3	20.7	44.5
1965	3	15	1,023.8	862.2	161.6	16	36	59.4	(1.3)	7.5	102.2	6.1	43.5
1966	3	15	1,166.3	979.5	186.8	16	38	78.7	32.5	8.7	108.1	5.8	41.2
1967	3	15	1,216.6	1,056.5	160.1	13	39	55.8	(29.1)	5.9	104.3	(8.5)	39.6
1968	3	15	1,307.9	1,129.2	178.8	14	36	56.4	1.1	5.5	122.4	17.4	42.0
1969	3	15	1,467.3	1,241.3	226.1	15	41	92.7	64.4	8.1	133.4	9.0	41.3
1970	3	15	1,457.1	1,289.6	167.5	11	37	50.1	(46.0)	4.4	117.3	(12.1)	37.5
1971	3	15	1,378.9	1,234.0	144.9	11	37	53.7	7.2	4.9	91.2	(22.3)	32.0
1972	3	15	1,598.4	1,385.0	213.4	13	39	110.9	106.5	8.7	102.5	12.4	31.3
1973	3	15	1,758.0	1,470.3	287.7	16	44	184.9	66.7	13.2	102.8	0.3	29.1
1974	3	15	1,921.1	1,590.3	330.8	17	45	225.1	21.7	14.6	105.7	2.8	28.2
1975	3	15	2,069.4	1,755.3	314.2	15	40	208.5	(7.4)	12.5	105.7	0.0	26.7
1976	3	15	2,604.4	2,149.8	454.6	17	36	295.6	41.8	14.0	159.0	50.4	34.9

Sources: FCC figures as released annually (see Unit 380), with profit margins and percentage change figures added by editors (some from *Broadcasting Monthly* [May-June 1977], p. 25).

Table 381-B.
Number and Type of Commercials and Total Commercial Minutes on U. S. Network Television, 1965–1975

Year	Total Number of Commercial Minutes (3 Networks)	Percent of Commercials by Length		Number of Commercials		Number of Prime-Time Programs by Type of Advertising	
		30 Seconds	60 Seconds	Number	Index	Sponsored	Participating
1965	N/A	N/A	N/A	N/A	N/A	32	51
1967	100,000	6%	94%	103,000	100	20	60
1969	100,424	15	85	108,600	105	6	67
1971	99,867	49	51	132,300	128	3	63
1973	101,955	71	29	158,000	153	0	70
1975	109,135	92	7	208,447	202	N/A	N/A

Sources: Total number of Commercial Minutes, Percent of Commercials by Length, and Number of Commercials, 1965-73, from Group W (1976), as reported in *Broadcasting* (September 6, 1976), p. 25. 1975 data from *Broadcasting Monthly*. Number of Prime-Time Programs by Type of Advertising from unpublished research by L. W. Lichty.

Note: Data in first five columns are for the indicated calendar year, while the last two columns represent *seasons* (the "season" in 1965, for example, extended from September 1964 to August 1965).

program other than selecting the time at which the commercial will appear. The advertiser merely "participates" in covering the production and broadcast costs of the show.

By the early 1970s, the regularly sponsored weekly show had disappeared from prime-time television, and few such sponsors were left in the daytime hours. The participating-sponsor format, combined with the predominance of 30-second commercials, has greatly contributed to viewer (and advertiser) complaints of "clutter" on the air.

Table 381-C traces prime-time cost trends for 30- and 60-minute television series between 1949 and 1973. The costs represent seasonal *averages* for all types of programs, since quiz and audience participation shows, as well as variety and "talk-show" formats, are generally far less expensive than dramatic series. By the 1976-77 season, program costs per prime-time hour had exceeded $300,000 in most cases.

Table 381–C.
Program Costs of Prime-Time Network Television, 1949–1973

Year	Number of Prime-Time Programs	Average Episode Cost: 60-Minute Programs			Average Episode Cost: 30-Minute Programs		
		Number of Programs	Current Dollars	Constant (1972) Dollars	Number of Programs	Current Dollars	Constant (1972) Dollars
1949	33	6	$ 7,000	$ 13,233	27	$ 3,100	$ 5,860
1950	52	12	13,500	25,187	40	7,200	13,433
1951	102	24	23,600	41,187	78	10,500	18,325
1952	94	19	30,100	51,897	75	13,100	22,586
1953	87	13	36,000	61,121	76	16,200	27,504
1954	100	13	39,800	66,667	87	17,100	28,643
1955	105	17	48,000	78,689	88	22,300	36,557
1956	98	17	62,200	98,887	81	30,600	48,649
1957	97	23	57,200	88,000	74	33,100	50,923
1958	111	20	75,200	113,939	91	36,100	54,697
1959	99	23	75,000	111,111	76	36,300	53,778
1960	103	29	90,000	131,004	74	37,500	54,585
1961	98	33	91,200	131,601	65	41,300	59,596
1962	92	44	94,000	133,144	48	45,000	63,739
1963	82	44	111,600	155,866	38	55,000	76,816
1964	76	45	119,300	164,099	31	56,500	77,717
1965	83	40	131,200	176,581	43	59,400	79,946
1966	88	35	145,000	188,802	53	65,400	85,156
1967	80	39	159,000	201,266	41	76,900	97,342
1968	72	39	179,000	216,707	32	87,500	105,932
1969	73	39	185,000	213,379	34	88,000	101,499
1970	74	39	198,400	217,068	33	N/A	N/A
1971	68	35	200,000	208,333	31	98,700	102,813
1972	68	25	N/A	N/A	30	N/A	N/A
1973	64	21	208,461	197,033	31	104,194	98,482

Source: Copyrighted and unpublished data from L. W. Lichty.

Table 381-D provides a breakdown of production costs for sample television shows over the 1950-1974 period. "Above-the-line" costs (salaries and fees for the creative staff, writers, and actors) have increased steadily as actors' unions and directors' and writers' guilds have been able to demand higher-paying contracts earlier in the life of a television series. "Below-the-line" costs (wages of production personnel and costs of materials, facilities, and services) have also increased steadily and markedly over the years, partly because of the greater sophistication—and, therefore, higher costs—of both television programming and television and film equipment. However, the primary sources of these cost increases are union-contract wages for production personnel and the general effects of inflation on materials and services.

By the 1960s, program-production costs were typically met by an independent packaging agency, which capitalized the project and hired the creative personnel, then sold the completed program to the network for a lump-sum payment. Very often, this payment does not cover program costs, which are fully recouped only when the program or series is sold to stations in syndication for rebroadcast.

Sources

The data in Table 381-A are derived from FCC figures, which are first printed in mimeo releases and then reprinted in the FCC's *Annual Report* and in *Television Factbook* (see Unit 380). The profit margin and percentage-change figures were calculated by the editors (some of these figures were also found in *Broadcasting Monthly* [May-June 1977]). Because all financial figures are rounded to the nearest hundred-thousand, totals may not add exactly. Specific network and O&O station data are not broken out in FCC reports prior to 1959.

The figures in Table 381-B, which are aggregates for all three networks, come mainly from Group W (1976), as reported in *Broadcasting* (September 6, 1959). The last two columns are from unpublished research by L. W. Lichty of the University of Wisconsin. Unlike the rest of the table, these figures refer to prime-time programs only. Since Group W provided no figures for 1975, information from *Broadcasting Monthly* is included for that year.

Table 381–D.
Breakdown of Production Costs for Selected Categories
of Network Television Programming, 1950–1974

Cost Item	Typical Live Drama—1950 (Half Hour)	Typical Film Mystery—1952 (Half Hour)	"Defenders" 1961 (Hour)	"Bonanza" 1969 (Hour)	Typical Film Drama—1974 (Half Hour)
Above the Line Costs					
Script	$ 500	$ 1,000	$ 8,000	$ 7,750	$ 7,500
Producer, Director	450	750	15,706	22,990	18,000
Miscellaneous	- -	- -	2,400	11,380	5,000
Cast	1,100	2,750	17,500	55,885	27,000
Total, Above the Line Costs	$2,050	$ 4,500	$ 43,606	$ 98,005	$ 57,500
Percent of Total Costs	*29%*	*35%*	*40%*	*46%*	*49%*
Below the Line Costs					
Production Staff	- -	$ 540	$ 2,152	$ 3,053	$ 2,000
Cameraman, Camera	- -	800	3,704	5,379	2,500
Grips, Set Operations	- -	250	3,300	6,869	2,000
Electrical	- -	889	3,360	6,276	2,500
Scenery	- -	- -	6,000	4,479	3,500
Sound Recording	- -	654	2,023	6,310	3,000
Makeup, Hair Dressing	- -	238	815	4,199	500
Set Dressing, Props	750	550	3,537	5,722	2,500
Location	- -	50	1,805	6,463	- -
Transportation	- -	200	925	1,511	1,000
Stage, Studio	- -	850	4,525	13,550	15,000
Film Editing	- -	875	2,590	8,704	4,000
All Other Costs: rerecord, stock, titles, royalties, wardrobe, misc.	4,120	2,421	30,009	41,015	21,000
Total, Below the Line Costs	$4,870	$ 8,317	$ 64,745	$113,530	$ 59,500
Total Costs for One Episode	$6,920	$12,817	$108,351	$211,535	$117,000
Total in Constant (1972) Dollars	*$12,910*	*$22,098*	*$156,351*	*$243,985*	*$100,515*

Source: Lichty and Topping (1975), p. 444, table 40.

All the data in **Table 381-C** are from copyrighted and soon-to-be published data of L. W. Lichty (in progress), based on averages of published information for different types of prime-time programs. A. D. Little Co. (1969) is the source of the information on costs of pilot programs (television shows produced as a sample of a proposed series). These figures on pilot programs costs are aggregates of all three national networks. All cost data in **Table 381-C** are for programs on the air in the third week in January of each season.

The production cost figures in **Table 381-D** were gathered by Lichty and Topping (1975), who used several trade periodical articles as sources. Two of the sample programs—"Defenders" and "Bonanza"—were above average in cost for those years. A script for "Defenders" cost about twice the 1961 norm. The 1974 drama sample, which is based on a real production budget rounded to the nearest $500 for each cost item, did not involve superstars or special settings. Since information of this type is not commonly published, these random examples of series costs provide the most accurate picture the editors were able to obtain.

Further Information

More analysis and statistics showing relationships of information in both **Tables 381-A** and **381-B** are available in *Broadcasting Monthly*, *Broadcasting Industry*, and *Broadcasting Basics II* (1976). See also *Broadcast Advertising Research* (BAR) for regular analyses of television network advertising information. For financial information on the separate networks (with the exception of NBC, whose financial information is not broken out separately from owner RCA), see the networks' annual reports and *Broadcasting Monthly*.

Table 390–A.
Total Assets, Revenues, Expenses, and Net Income
of U. S. Cable Television Systems, 1976

	Reporting Cable Systems (80%)	FCC Estimate for All Systems (100%)
Number of Cable Systems	1,954	2,443
Average Monthly Subscriber Rate	$6.21	$6.21
Total Annual Revenues	$715,934,481	$894,918,101
Total Annual Operating Expenses	$453,888,149	$567,360,186
Total Annual Net Income (after taxes)	$21,507,450	$26,884,313
Percent of Profit Margin (before depreciation, interest)	3%	3%
FCC Estimates for "Average" Cable System:		
Annual Revenue	- -	$376,000
Annual Income	- -	$15,000
Profit Margin	- -	4%
Total Assets	$1,705,221,351	$2,131,526,689

Source: Federal Communications Commission, "CATV Industry Financial Data for the Period November 1975-October 1976" (June 10, 1977).

Interpretation of Table

Until recently, there was no consistent source which provided national information on the revenues, expenses, and income of cable television (CATV) systems in the United States. In June of 1977, however, the FCC issued the first of an annual series of financial reports on cable, similar to those for the radio and television industries (see Units 370 and 380). For various reasons (late returns, incomplete answers, etc.), about 20 percent of the CATV systems operating in this country were not included in this first FCC report; so the Commission based its report on the 80 percent actual data and estimated figures for the missing 20 percent. Table 390-A presents the results of that first survey, which covers the operating period from November 1975 through October 1976.

Regarding pay-cable systems, Paul Kagan Associates, in correspondence with the editors, estimated the 1976 income for pay-cable operations at $92.4 million, with an additional $5.2 million for apartment-building services, bringing the total income up to $97.6 million. Average monthly per-subscriber income was $7.97 for home pay-cable systems and $10.01 for apartment systems.

Sources

Table 390-A was constructed from FCC figures in "CATV Industry Financial Data for the Period November 1975-October 1976." All of the figures are estimates.

Further Information

Along with the sources listed in Unit 190, two recent publications of some value are Ross (1974) and Scott (1976). Also, two organizations which the reader may wish to contact are the Cable Television Information Center of the Urban Institute, and the National Cable Television Association, a trade association. For pay-cable, the most important source is Paul Kagan Associates, *The Pay TV Newsletter*. The FCC's second annual financial report on cable systems, covering 1976-1977 data, is due for release in mid-1978.

SECTION 4

Employment and Training in the Media Industries

Table 400–A.
Number of Employees in the Mass Media Industries in U. S.,
by Industry, 1947–1976

Note: All figures are in thousands.

	Book Industry	Newspaper Industry	Periodicals Industry	Motion Picture Industry	Radio and Television Broadcasting Industry	Total Non-Farm Employment
1947	50.7	248.5	65.7	252.0	N/A	43,881
1948	49.2	265.3	64.4	249.0	N/A	44,891
1949	48.4	275.8	63.5	250.0	N/A	43,778
1950	48.9	280.1	62.7	248.0	N/A	45,222
1951	50.8	282.2	65.3	245.4	N/A	47,849
1952	52.6	284.9	66.5	240.1	N/A	48,825
1953	55.7	289.1	67.3	234.0	N/A	50,232
1954	55.4	293.5	68.1	230.7	N/A	49,022
1955	57.3	302.1	69.0	231.6	N/A	50,675
1956	61.5	311.9	69.8	225.8	N/A	52,408
1957	65.2	314.9	68.4	211.1	N/A	52,894
1958	65.3	314.1	68.8	199.1	86.9	51,363
1959	66.8	318.5	69.7	195.1	88.9	53,313
1960	69.9	325.2	70.3	189.6	92.4	54,234
1961	70.9	325.9	70.7	186.5	93.9	54,042
1962	71.8	327.6	69.7	178.3	95.3	55,596
1963	72.7	328.9	68.2	176.5	99.1	56,702
1964	77.0	335.7	68.6	177.4	102.9	58,331
1965	81.3	345.4	69.7	185.1	106.9	60,815
1966	88.4	351.2	71.7	187.5	113.6	63,955
1967	93.3	355.1	75.0	194.3	119.6	65,857
1968	95.3	358.1	75.9	196.0	123.0	67,951
1969	98.5	368.1	75.3	206.7	128.8	70,442
1970	100.5	372.2	75.5	203.9	132.5	70,920
1971	97.2	376.5	69.4	197.4	134.8	71,222
1972	95.3	376.5	68.1	191.1	133.7	73,714
1973	92.8	382.3	68.7	189.3	135.2	76,896
1974	94.2	383.5	69.2	204.5	150.5	78,413
1975	92.2	378.5	69.3	202.0	152.4	77,051
1976	87.8	382.8	69.9	202.5	157.4	79,443

Sources: 1947-1973: Bureau of Labor Statistics, *Employment and Earnings, United States, 1909-1975.* 1974-1976: Bureau of Labor Statistics, *Employment and Earnings* (March 1977).

Interpretation of Tables

Table 400-A presents the total number of employees in the book, newspaper, magazine, motion picture, and broadcast industries in the United States. The total U.S. nonfarm employment statistics are also given as a point of comparison. Every industry, except motion pictures, shows an absolute increase in numbers of employees over the 30-year period shown in the table. However, there are considerable variations in the patterns of growth of the different media industries.

Book publishing employment rose steadily from 1947 to 1970—with an especially high rate of growth during the 1960s—and then declined after 1970. Since the industry's employment trend roughly follows its production record (see Unit 310), the editors conclude that the recent decline

Table 400–B.
Index of Employment in the Mass Media Industries in U. S.,
by Industry, 1958–1976

Note: Index figures are calculated on a base of 100 for the year 1958.

Year	Book Industry	Newspaper Industry	Periodicals Industry	Motion Picture Industry	Radio and Television Broadcasting Industry	Non-Farm Employment
1958	100	100	100	100	100	100
1959	102	101	101	98	102	104
1960	107	104	102	95	106	106
1961	109	104	103	94	108	105
1962	110	104	101	90	110	108
1963	111	105	99	89	114	110
1964	118	107	100	89	118	114
1965	125	110	101	93	123	118
1966	135	112	104	94	131	125
1967	143	113	109	98	138	128
1968	146	114	110	98	142	132
1969	151	117	109	104	148	137
1970	154	118	110	102	152	138
1971	149	118	101	99	155	139
1972	146	120	99	96	154	144
1973	142	122	100	95	156	150
1974	144	122	101	103	173	153
1975	141	121	101	101	175	150
1976	134	122	102	102	181	155

Source: The indexes were calculated by the editors from the figures in Table 400-A.

in employment is mainly due to a parallel slump in production resulting from a decreasing demand for school and library books.

Newspaper publishing employment peaked in 1974 and has remained fairly constant since then. The editors suspect that the present leveling off is due to technological innovations in production facilities; for the payroll for production workers has declined faster than the payroll of all other newspaper employees (see **Table 320-C**).

Employment in the periodicals industry has remained fairly constant since 1955, except for a prominent bulge in employment during the three years from 1968 to 1970. This bulge at the end of the 1960s may represent the appearance of a number of new, specialized magazines which overlapped the last years of existence of several large-circulation general publications, such as *Life*, *Look*, and *Saturday Evening Post*.

The employment curve of the motion picture industry shows a decline until 1963, and then a steady growth in the years that follow. Like the employment figures, the production and distribution data for the film industry also represent a much greater rate of growth since 1963 (see **Table 440-B** for disaggregated employment totals in the production/distribution and exhibition/services segments of the industry). This pattern reflects a stabilization of the movie-theater business and an increase in production for television.

Of all the employment trends shown here, the broadcasting industry has the most positive record. Since the U.S. Bureau of Labor Statistics (BLS) began collecting these data in 1958, the number of people working in broadcasting has risen in every year but 1972. The pace has slowed somewhat in recent years: Between 1971 and 1976, the average growth rate was 3.1 percent, compared with 3.5 percent between 1966 and 1971 and 3.9 percent between 1961 and 1966. Still, broadcasting is the only medium listed here which continues to outpace the growth of overall nonfarm employment.

Table 400-B converts the raw data in **Table 400-A** into index figures, making comparisons among the media and total nonfarm employment an easier task. The editors have chosen 1958 as the base year for this comparison because it is the first year for which broadcasting data are available.

Sources

Tables **400-A** and **400-B** do not include statistics for cable television or for the recording industry, because the BLS, which collected the data in this section, does not provide figures for either of those two industries. The BLS also does not separate radio from television broadcasting. Consequently, rather than juxtaposing employment statistics from different sources—and thereby introducing the possibilities of misleading or inaccurate comparisons—the editors have included employment information from other sources in the specific units of Section 4 which deal with each medium.

One series of employment statistics used extensively in later units of this section is the U.S. Census Bureau's *Census of Manufactures* and *Annual Survey of Manufactures*. The Bureau of Labor Statistics (1976a) offers this explanation of the differences between its figures and those of the Census Bureau:

> The major reasons for noncomparability are different treatment of business units considered parts of an establishment, such as central administrative offices and auxiliary units; the industrial classification of establishments; and different reporting patterns by multi-unit companies. There are also differences in the scope of industries covered; e.g., the *Census of Business* excludes professional services, public utilities, and financial establishments, whereas these are included in BLS statistics.

The best description of the data and collection procedures of the BLS is found in the *BLS Handbook of Methods for Surveys and Studies*. The latest edition (Bureau of Labor Statistics, 1976b) is *Bulletin 1910*. This work provides excellent and clear descriptions of the sources of data, sampling procedures, concepts employed in defining the survey, estimating procedures, seasonal adjustments, limitations of the data, and other facets of the process used to gather and present this information. The researcher wishing to analyze or manipulate these data would do well to begin with this source.

Briefly, the employment statistics in **Tables 400-A** and **400-B** are collected by state employment agencies, in accordance with specific guidelines provided by the BLS. The information comes from a sample of establishments throughout the 50 states and in the District of Columbia. In 1975, for example, more than 160,000 reporting units were surveyed for data on nonagricultural employment. Although only annual figures are provided here, information is collected each month and presented in the monthly BLS production, *Employment and Earnings*.

The BLS survey's definition of "employee" is of interest. It includes permanent and temporary employees, full- and part-time employees, and employees on paid sick leave, paid holiday, or vacation. A person working in two separate establishments is counted twice, while proprietors, self-employed persons, and unpaid family workers are not counted at all. In some industry sectors which include a significant number of "mom-and-pop" concerns (such as weekly newspapers), the omission of unpaid family workers could make a difference. The editors assume that the figures for newspapers probably exclude some weekly newspaper workers, although the data are not broken down by period of publication.

Further Information

Annual averages of the BLS data appear in each March issue of *Employment and Earnings*. The BLS also publishes a summary volume of this information every few years. The latest of these summaries is *Employment and Earnings, 1909-1975* (Bureau of Labor Statistics, 1976a).

The reader may also wish to consult *The Information Economy* (Porat et al., 1977) a series of nine volumes released by the Office of Telecommunications of the U.S. Department of Commerce. These reports represent the first attempt to rigorously define the extent of information activity in our economy. These reports include analyses not only of industries dealing primarily with information, but also of those sectors of all industries which are information-related. Major findings contained in this series are presented in the first two volumes.

These reports are based primarily upon Dr. Marc Uri Porat's Ph.D. dissertation (Porat, 1976), which extends and organizes the investigation begun by Machlup (1962) in *The Production and Distribution of Knowledge in the United States*. These two works are worth consulting for perspectives on the role of the information or knowledge industries in the American economy.

Table 401–A.
Number of Employees in Selected Media Occupations in U. S., 1900–1970

Note: All figures are in thousands of persons, 14 years and older.

Occupation	1900	1910	1920	1930	1940	1950[a]	1960[a]	1970[a]
Authors	3	4	7	12	14	17	29	26
Bookbinders	26	17	19	19	19	33	28	36
Librarians	3	7	15	30	39	57	85	124
Library Attendants/Assistants	1	3	2	2	24	13	33	129
Laborers, Printing and Publishing	4	5	8	11	10	12	13	5
Operatives, Printing and Publishing	16	42	48	51	59	80	97	N/A
Apprentices, Printing Trades	4	12	12	11	10	16	12	N/A
Printing Pressmen and Plate Printers		20	19	31	36	51	75	160
Engravers, except Photoengravers					9	10	12	9
	136	22	23	28				
Photoengravers and Lithographers					23	29	25	33
Compositors and Typesetters		128	140	184	181	182	183	163
Editors and Reporters	32	36	39	61	66	93	103	151
Newsboys	7	30	28	39	58	101	197	188
Advertising Agents/Salesmen	12	11	25	40	41	35	35	65
Radio Operators	N/A	4	5	5	7	17	29	29
Radio/TV Repairmen	N/A	N/A	N/A	N/A	N/A	79[b]	106	141
Actors/Actresses	N/A	N/A	N/A	N/A	21	20	13	15
Ushers	N/A	N/A	N/A	N/A	22	26	16	16
Motion Picture Projectionists	N/A	4	10	20	24	27	18	16

Source: *Historical Statistics of the U. S.* (1975), Series D 233-682, pp. 140-145.

Notes: (a) The classifications of occupations were revised in 1950 and again in 1960 and 1970. Therefore, the figures from these three decennial censuses are not strictly comparable either to the pre-1950 figures or to one another. However, *Historical Statistics* lists 1950 data in 1960 categories and 1960 data in 1970 categories so that more precise comparisons can be made. (b) The 1960 occupational classification was used for this 1950 figure.

Interpretation of Table

Table 401-A lists the number of persons employed in each of several media-related occupations. Because the figures were gathered during the decennial U.S. census, these statistics reflect individuals' reports of their occupations, rather than the employers' records used for similar tables in the *Census of Manufactures* and the Bureau of Labor Statistics' industry series. As such, the figures in Table 401-A do not represent overall employment for an industry.

Indeed, to the extent that people are likely to inflate their occupational titles for the census reports, these figures are misleading. We might expect, for example, that the ratio of "librarians" to "library assistants" is not a particularly accurate depiction of the actual job situation. Another limiting factor in the interpretation of these data is that some of the occupations listed here could be found in many different industries.

As a general rule, however, the fortunes of various occupations do tend to parallel the fortunes of the industries that provide most of the employment for these occupations. For example, motion picture-related occupations have been declining—although, in the case of actors and actresses, there has been a slight up-swing from a 1960 low. Library and broadcasting occupations increased significantly during the 1960s, while the fortunes of the listed printing and newspaper trades were mixed.

Sources

The decennial U.S. census, based on extensive questioning of individual households, is the nation's most exhaustive measure of its population. At the same time, the difficulty of gaining cooperation for so extensive an effort tends to result in population figures which, in fact, underestimate the actual population count of the country. This same limitation affects the accuracy of data on employment levels and occupations. The reader seeking a detailed analysis of this problem should consult Johnston and Wetzel (1969).

Since **Table 401**-A deals with trends, rather than absolute numbers, the Census Bureau's underestimation of employment levels probably presents less of a problem here than the Bureau's revisions of figures for each of the last three censuses. Data for most of the occupations listed have been affected to some extent by this revision process. For example, the data presented for actors and actresses, editors and reporters, and operatives in printing, publishing, and allied trades have been changed by an amount equal to more than 10 percent of their numbers.

Further Information

Each month, the Census Bureau collects data based on household interviews from a sample survey of the population. This process provides comprehensive information on the total number of persons in the United States who are 16 years of age or older, and who are either employed or unemployed. These interviews also involve such personal and economic data as sex, race, marital status, specific occupation, hours of work, and duration of unemployment. The information is collected by trained interviewers from a sample of about 47,000 households throughout the country. The data are then published in the U.S. Bureau of Labor Statistics' *Employment and Earnings*. This monthly publication also provides employment and earnings information collected from employers' records (see Units 400 and 402).

Minority and Female Employment in the Media　402

Interpretation of Tables

The best available data comparing female employment levels in the media with female employment in the entire U.S. nonfarm labor force are collected by the U.S. Bureau of Labor Statistics (BLS). The results of several such BLS surveys for the book, newspaper, periodical, motion picture, and broadcasting industries appear in **Table 402**-A. Unfortunately, the BLS does not separate radio and television broadcasting, nor does it provide information on the recording or cable television industries (see Units 450, 460, and 490).

Table 402-A shows that the number and percentage of women employed in the media industries have increased since 1960 (the first year in which data on female employment were collected). However, the percentage of female to male employees differs significantly among the media. For example, the book and periodical publishing industries now employ a substantially larger proportion of women than the average for all nonagricultural employment in this country, while broadcasting and newspaper publishing still lag considerably behind the national average. Except for a slight decline in recent years, women's employment in motion picture production and exhibition has just about kept pace with the national average.

When attention is shifted from the overall proportion of women's employment to the rate of growth of that proportion, the comparison changes. The periodical industry, which is the only one of these media with an absolute majority of women in its labor force, shows the slowest rate of growth in the proportion of female employees since 1964 (the year when comparisons with the labor force as a whole first became possible). The book publishing industry, which hires the second greatest proportion of women, has the second slowest rate of growth. At the other extreme, the newspaper and broadcasting industries, which employ the lowest percentages of women among the media listed here, have been catching up at a rate which exceeds that of the labor force as a whole.

The meaning of these trends in terms of social equity is more difficult to determine. The overall percentage of women in the periodical industry labor force appears equal to their presence

Table 402–A.
Number and Percentage of Women Employed in the Mass Media Industries and in the Total Non-Agricultural Labor Force in U. S., 1960–1976

Note: All employee figures are in thousands.

	Book Industry		Newspaper Industry		Periodicals Industry		Motion Picture Industry		Broadcasting Industry		Total Non-Agricultural Labor Force	
	Number of Women Employees	Percent of Total Employees in Industry	Number of Women Employees	Percent of Total Employees in Industry	Number of Women Employees	Percent of Total Employees in Industry	Number of Women Employees	Percent of Total Employees in Industry	Number of Women Employees	Percent of Total Employees in Industry	Number of Women Employees	Percent of Total Non-Agricultural Labor Force
1960	30.7	43.9%	65.2	20.0%	31.3	44.5%	66.3	35.0%	20.9	22.6%	N/A	N/A
1961	30.8	43.4	66.1	20.3	31.4	44.4	64.1	34.4	21.4	22.8	N/A	N/A
1962	30.8	42.9	67.8	20.7	31.6	45.3	60.7	34.0	21.4	22.5	N/A	N/A
1963	31.0	42.6	69.9	21.3	31.9	46.8	59.8	33.9	22.2	22.4	N/A	N/A
1964	32.7	42.5	72.6	21.6	32.5	47.4	58.8	33.1	23.0	22.4	19,672	33.7%
1965	34.7	42.7	75.9	22.0	33.1	47.5	59.1	33.3	23.6	22.1	20,671	34.0
1966	39.2	44.3	80.3	22.9	34.3	47.8	60.8	32.4	24.8	21.8	22,180	34.7
1967	42.8	45.9	84.0	23.7	35.5	47.3	64.4	33.1	26.9	22.5	23,284	35.4
1968	44.7	46.9	88.0	24.6	35.7	47.0	66.4	33.9	28.2	22.9	24,395	35.9
1969	46.5	47.2	93.9	25.5	35.8	47.5	69.5	33.6	30.5	23.7	25,568	36.3
1970	47.9	47.7	97.5	26.2	36.1	47.8	71.3	35.0	31.1	23.5	26,060	36.7
1971	46.3	47.6	98.9	26.7	33.5	48.3	73.5	36.7	32.2	23.9	26,301	36.9
1972	46.1	48.4	104.2	27.7	32.9	48.3	75.4	39.5	34.7	26.0	27,404	37.2
1973	46.3	49.9	111.6	29.2	32.9	47.9	79.0	41.7	36.9	27.3	28,924	37.6
1974	48.0	51.0	117.7	30.7	33.9	49.0	77.3	37.8	40.2	26.7	30,026	38.3
1975	46.6	50.5	120.2	31.8	35.1	50.6	75.6	37.4	44.4	29.1	30,157	39.1
1976	43.0	49.0	124.6	32.5	35.7	51.1	77.1	38.1	46.6	29.6	31,498	39.6

Source: U. S. Bureau of Labor Statistics, *Employment and Earnings, United States, 1909-1975* (1976).

Note: The percentage-of-total figures were calculated by dividing the number of women employees by the appropriate figure for total employment in each industry (see Table 400-B).

Table 402–B.
Percentage of Minority Group and Male-Female Employees
in the Printing/Publishing, Newspaper, and Motion Picture Industries
in U. S., 1966 and 1973

	Printing/ Publishing Industry		Newspaper Industry		Motion Picture Industry		All U.S. Industries	
	1966	1973	1971[a]	1973	1966	1973	1966	1973
All Employees	100.0%	100.0%	100.0%	100.0%	100.0%	100.0%	100.0%	100.0%
Male	69.1	65.5	77.6	74.7	70.2	60.6	68.5	63.2
Female	30.9	34.5	22.4	25.3	29.8	39.4	31.5	36.8
White Employees	N/A	90.0	93.2	92.4	N/A	83.6	88.6	84.2
Male	N/A	59.4	72.2	69.0	N/A	50.9	59.6	53.7
Female	N/A	30.6	21.0	23.4	N/A	32.7	29.0	30.5
All Minority Employees	N/A	10.0	6.8	7.6	N/A	16.4	11.4	15.8
Male	N/A	6.1	5.4	5.8	N/A	9.7	7.9	9.5
Female	N/A	3.9	1.4	1.9	N/A	6.7	3.5	6.3
Black Employees	4.8	6.6	4.7	5.1	5.1	7.9	8.2	10.6
Male	3.1	3.9	3.8	3.8	3.7	4.8	5.7	6.3
Female	1.7	2.7	.9	1.3	1.4	3.1	2.5	4.3
Spanish-Surname Employees	1.7	2.7	1.7	1.9	4.5	6.4	2.5	4.1
Male	1.2	1.8	1.4	1.5	3.3	3.7	1.7	2.6
Female	.6	.9	.3	.4	1.2	2.6	.8	1.5
Asian Employees	N/A	.5	.2	.4	N/A	1.6	.5	.8
Male	N/A	.3	.2	.2	N/A	.9	.3	.4
Female	N/A	.2	.1	.1	N/A	.7	.2	.3
American Indian Employees	N/A	.2	.2	.2	N/A	.5	.2	.4
Male	N/A	.1	.1	.1	N/A	.3	.1	.2
Female	N/A	.1	.0	.0	N/A	.2	.1	.1

Source: Equal Employment Opportunity Commission (1968, 1975).

Note: (a) 1971 is the first year for which data on the newspaper industry was separated from the other printing and publishing industries.

in the population—and substantially above their participation in the U.S. labor force as a whole. Thus, from a policy perspective, one might say that no further increases are "necessary" in this industry. One might also say that no policy problem is posed by the slower rates of increase among industries (such as book publishing) which have had unusually high levels of female employees for many years. Of course, these overall statistics do not measure other equally significant aspects of the problem, such as promotion, salaries, and the decision-making authority of women employees.

Another interesting comparison which can be made on **Table 402**-A involves the newspaper and broadcasting industries. Broadcasting is the only medium which is regulated in terms of its employment practices—in theory, at least. Yet the overall increase in the percentage of female employees in the *unregulated* newspaper industry has been significantly greater than that for broadcasting. Clearly, there are forces other than regulation which can change the composition of an industry's labor force.

It is possible, for example, that the increases in female employment in the newspaper industry have less to do with any end to discrimination by management than with changes in technology. Many production jobs previously performed by members of the white male-dominated crafts unions have been replaced recently by computer-related positions which emphasize clerical skills. Thus, if more women are being hired for these types of clerical jobs, their representation in the newspaper labor force may be increasing without any upgrading in their job status.

Table 402–C.
Occupational Distribution of Minority Group and Male-Female Employees in the Printing/Publishing, Newspaper, and Motion Picture Industries and in the Total Non-Agricultural Labor Force in U. S., 1973

Printing/Publishing Industry

	White Collar Occupations						Blue Collar Occupations				Other
	Total White Collar Employment	Officials and Managers	Professionals	Technicians	Sales Workers	Office and Clerical	Total Blue Collar Employment	Skilled Craft	Operatives	Laborers	Service Workers
All Employees	48.3%	8.8%	8.3%	2.7%	7.8%	20.5%	49.3%	23.9%	17.0%	8.3%	2.5%
Male	40.4	11.8	9.0	3.3	9.5	6.8	56.7	32.5	16.7	7.6	2.8
Female	63.1	3.1	7.0	1.6	4.7	46.6	35.1	7.7	17.7	9.8	1.7
White Employees	49.9	9.5	8.9	2.8	8.3	20.4	48.3	25.0	15.9	7.3	1.8
Male	42.1	12.7	9.5	3.3	10.1	6.5	55.9	34.0	15.5	6.4	1.9
Female	65.0	3.4	7.5	1.7	5.0	47.4	33.5	7.7	16.7	9.1	1.5
All Minority Employees	33.8	2.6	3.6	2.4	3.3	21.9	57.9	13.9	26.9	17.2	8.2
Male	24.0	3.5	4.1	3.1	3.6	9.8	64.6	18.0	27.9	18.7	11.4
Female	48.9	1.3	2.7	1.4	2.8	40.7	47.7	7.6	25.3	14.8	3.3
Black Employees	32.9	2.3	2.9	2.0	3.3	22.4	56.5	10.9	28.1	17.5	10.6
Male	22.1	3.1	3.2	2.5	3.5	9.9	62.6	13.5	29.8	19.3	15.3
Female	48.2	1.2	2.4	1.2	3.1	40.2	47.8	7.2	25.7	14.9	4.0
Spanish-Surname Employees	30.6	2.6	3.1	2.5	3.1	19.4	65.3	19.8	27.0	18.5	4.1
Male	22.6	3.4	3.7	3.0	3.5	9.0	72.2	26.0	26.9	19.3	5.3
Female	45.7	1.2	2.0	1.4	2.2	38.9	52.3	8.3	27.0	17.0	1.9
Asian Employees	60.4	4.5	14.5	7.7	3.5	30.3	38.0	14.0	14.3	9.7	1.6
Male	53.4	6.4	18.2	10.7	4.6	13.5	44.6	17.4	14.9	12.3	2.0
Female	70.2	2.0	9.4	3.5	2.0	53.3	28.8	9.3	13.4	6.1	1.0
American Indian Employees	39.6	8.6	5.1	2.9	4.1	18.9	58.0	32.3	17.6	8.0	2.4
Male	31.9	11.3	5.6	3.8	3.8	7.4	65.2	41.7	16.0	7.5	2.8
Female	57.5	2.3	4.1	.8	4.6	45.8	41.2	10.5	21.5	9.2	1.3

Table 402–C. (Cont'd.)

Newspaper Industry

| | White Collar Occupations | | | | | | Blue Collar Occupations | | | | Other |
	Total White Collar Employment	Officials and Managers	Professionals	Technicians	Sales Workers	Office and Clerical	Total Blue Collar Employment	Skilled Craft	Operatives	Laborers	Service Workers
All Employees	51.7%	8.0%	11.9%	2.2%	10.8%	18.8%	45.6%	28.1%	11.8%	5.6%	2.7%
Male	42.2	9.7	12.1	2.4	10.1	7.8	54.7	34.7	14.0	6.1	3.1
Female	79.9	2.8	11.5	1.5	12.7	51.4	18.4	8.8	5.5	4.1	1.7
White Employees	52.7	8.4	12.5	2.2	11.0	18.6	45.5	29.2	11.3	5.0	1.8
Male	43.4	10.3	12.6	2.4	10.5	7.6	54.6	36.1	13.2	5.3	2.0
Female	80.2	2.9	12.0	1.5	12.7	51.0	18.5	8.9	5.5	4.1	1.3
All Minority Employees	39.6	2.8	5.4	1.7	7.9	21.8	46.6	15.1	18.8	12.8	13.7
Male	27.5	3.3	5.4	1.7	6.3	10.7	56.3	17.6	22.9	15.8	16.2
Female	76.8	1.5	5.4	1.5	12.7	55.7	16.9	7.4	6.1	3.4	6.2
Black Employees	38.9	2.5	5.0	1.5	8.3	21.6	43.2	9.8	20.1	13.3	17.9
Male	26.2	2.9	4.6	1.5	6.3	10.9	52.5	11.1	24.8	16.6	21.3
Female	76.8	1.3	6.1	1.5	14.2	53.6	15.3	5.7	6.3	3.3	7.9
Spanish-Surname Employees	38.2	3.3	5.0	1.6	7.2	21.1	55.7	27.1	16.9	11.7	6.1
Male	27.5	3.7	5.7	1.7	6.3	10.0	65.7	32.1	19.8	13.8	6.9
Female	77.9	1.9	2.5	1.3	10.5	61.8	19.0	8.9	5.9	4.2	3.1
Asian Employees	55.0	2.9	12.5	3.9	5.4	30.3	43.6	16.9	13.1	13.5	1.4
Male	44.2	3.8	15.3	5.0	5.2	14.9	54.1	17.3	17.0	19.8	1.7
Female	75.2	1.2	7.4	1.8	5.9	59.0	23.9	16.2	5.9	1.8	.9
American Indian Employees	42.2	7.6	8.0	1.5	6.9	18.3	54.4	33.6	12.8	8.0	3.4
Male	32.3	8.3	8.0	1.9	5.8	8.3	63.8	38.7	15.7	9.4	3.9
Female	73.7	5.3	7.9	.0	10.5	50.0	24.6	17.5	3.5	1.8	1.8

Table 402–C. (Cont'd.)

Motion Picture Industry

	White Collar Occupations						Blue Collar Occupations				Other
	Total White Collar Employment	Officials and Managers	Professionals	Technicians	Sales Workers	Office and Clerical	Total Blue Collar Employment	Skilled Craft	Operatives	Laborers	Service Workers
All Employees	47.6%	11.0%	5.7%	4.4%	5.2%	21.4%	26.0%	10.9%	9.2%	5.9%	26.4%
Male	41.4	15.7	6.8	6.6	3.6	8.8	33.3	16.3	11.1	5.9	25.2
Female	57.2	3.7	4.1	1.1	7.5	40.7	14.7	2.6	6.2	5.8	28.1
White Employees	50.1	12.4	6.0	4.7	5.5	21.5	25.6	11.5	8.8	5.3	24.3
Male	44.1	17.7	7.2	6.9	4.0	8.2	33.6	17.4	11.1	5.2	22.3
Female	59.4	4.2	4.1	1.3	7.7	42.1	13.1	2.3	5.2	5.6	27.5
All Minority Employees	35.2	3.4	4.5	2.9	3.6	20.8	27.9	8.2	11.1	8.6	36.9
Male	27.5	5.0	4.7	4.6	1.2	12.0	31.7	10.9	11.1	9.6	40.8
Female	46.2	1.1	4.2	.4	6.9	33.6	22.5	4.3	11.1	7.1	31.3
Black Employees	39.9	2.7	5.4	2.4	5.4	23.9	16.9	4.5	7.6	4.8	43.3
Male	28.1	3.8	4.9	3.7	1.3	14.4	21.1	6.3	8.5	6.4	50.8
Female	57.8	1.1	6.2	.4	11.7	38.5	10.4	1.8	6.2	2.4	31.8
Spanish-Surname Employees	28.2	3.8	3.7	3.0	1.5	16.2	45.1	13.6	16.8	14.8	26.6
Male	25.1	5.8	4.5	4.7	1.3	8.7	48.1	17.3	15.2	15.6	26.9
Female	32.7	.8	2.5	.6	1.8	26.9	41.0	8.3	19.0	13.7	26.3
Asian Employees	39.7	4.5	4.3	5.0	1.8	24.0	14.1	5.2	6.8	2.0	46.3
Male	34.5	7.2	5.6	8.4	.4	12.9	19.3	8.4	8.0	2.8	46.2
Female	46.4	1.0	2.6	.5	3.6	38.5	7.3	1.0	5.2	1.0	46.4
American Indian Employees	34.1	4.9	.8	4.1	5.7	18.7	29.3	8.9	8.9	11.4	36.6
Male	28.2	5.6	1.4	7.0	1.4	12.7	35.2	14.1	12.7	8.5	36.6
Female	42.3	3.8	.0	.0	11.5	26.9	21.2	1.9	3.8	15.4	36.5

Table 402–C. (Cont'd.)

	Total U.S. Labor Force										
	White Collar Occupations						Blue Collar Occupations				Other
	Total White Collar Employment	Officials and Managers	Professionals	Technicians	Sales Workers	Office and Clerical	Total Blue Collar Employment	Skilled Craft	Operatives	Laborers	Service Workers
All Employees	48.4%	9.9%	8.4%	4.5%	9.4%	16.3%	43.7%	12.8%	22.1%	8.8%	7.9%
Male	41.3	13.6	9.4	4.9	8.1	5.3	52.7	18.7	24.2	9.8	6.0
Female	60.6	3.4	6.6	3.9	11.6	35.1	28.2	2.6	18.4	7.2	11.2
White Employees	52.2	11.1	9.2	4.7	10.2	16.9	41.3	13.5	20.6	7.2	6.5
Male	45.2	15.3	10.4	5.2	8.9	5.4	50.0	19.8	22.5	7.8	4.7
Female	64.5	3.8	7.1	3.9	12.6	37.1	26.0	2.5	17.2	6.3	9.5
All Minority Employees	28.1	3.0	3.8	3.3	5.0	13.0	56.2	8.8	30.0	17.4	15.7
Male	19.2	3.9	3.7	2.8	4.1	4.8	67.4	12.6	33.7	21.0	13.4
Female	41.7	1.6	3.9	4.1	6.5	25.7	39.0	2.8	24.2	12.0	19.2
Black Employees	25.3	2.5	2.5	3.1	4.5	12.7	56.8	7.8	31.8	17.2	17.9
Male	15.3	3.1	2.1	2.2	3.5	4.3	69.9	11.5	37.0	21.5	14.8
Female	39.8	1.5	3.1	4.4	5.9	24.9	37.8	2.6	24.3	10.9	22.4
Spanish-Surname Employees	27.5	3.4	2.8	2.9	5.9	12.5	60.7	11.2	28.9	20.5	11.8
Male	20.4	4.5	3.1	3.0	4.8	5.1	68.4	15.4	30.3	22.6	11.3
Female	40.4	1.5	2.4	2.7	7.9	26.0	46.8	3.7	26.4	16.8	12.8
Asian Employees	67.4	5.4	25.9	7.9	6.8	21.2	22.4	5.8	11.0	5.5	10.3
Male	64.9	8.0	30.7	9.4	6.8	10.0	24.5	8.7	9.9	5.9	10.6
Female	70.4	2.3	20.2	6.1	6.9	35.0	19.7	2.4	12.4	5.0	9.8
American Indian Employees	34.8	7.3	4.4	3.6	8.1	11.4	56.6	14.3	26.7	15.6	8.6
Male	28.5	10.0	5.0	3.9	6.0	3.7	65.2	20.5	27.3	17.5	6.3
Female	45.6	2.9	3.4	3.1	11.7	24.6	41.9	3.8	25.9	12.2	12.9

Source: Equal Employment Opportunity Commission (1975).

On the other hand, tentative evidence supporting the impact of government regulation can also be found in **Table 402-A**. If one calculates the least-squares estimate of the average annual growth rate of that proportion of women employed in broadcasting before and after 1971 (the first year in which the FCC required stations to file employment statistics), it becomes apparent that, from 1960 to 1971, the percentage of female employees increased by only one-quarter of one percent per year. But, from 1971 to 1976, that average annual percentage increase jumped to a full 2 percent. That is, the percentage of women employed in broadcasting has been growing eight times faster since the FCC began collecting statistics which might affect regulatory decisions.

Even with the impetus of regulation, however, the broadcasting industry is still not increasing its percentage of female employees as quickly as the newspaper industry. Between 1971 and 1976, newspapers increased their percentage of female employees by 2.1 percent each year, although this figure represents only a 50 percent increase over the 1.4 percent average annual rate between 1960 and 1971. Since 1966, broadcasting has fallen to the lowest position among the media industries for their overall percentage of women employed.

Some of the limitations of overall employment percentages are mentioned above (see also the United States Commission on Civil Rights, 1977). Most significantly, these figures do not reveal the level of those jobs for which women or minorities have been hired, nor do they say anything about the relative salaries and other conditions attached to those jobs in the various demographic categories. Since 1966, the United States Equal Employment Opportunity Commission (EEOC) has been attempting to remedy these gaps by collecting statistics on the job levels at which women or minorities are employed. The BLS has also included disaggregation by sex on its questionnaires to employers, though it has not yet required that information be broken down by ethnic group. Therefore, the EEOC data and similar information required by the FCC represent the best figures currently available on the employment of minorities in the media.

Tables 402-B and **402-C** present some of that data. **Table 402-B** shows the overall employment percentages for printing and publishing, newspaper publishing, and motion picture production and exhibition, as well as for all U.S. nonfarm industries. These are the only mass media areas for which EEOC information is available. (See Unit 460 for the FCC data on minority and female employment in television.)

According to EEOC data, all of the listed media industries lag behind the national nonfarm average for minority employment. Moreover, it is again apparent that printing and publishing, as well as newspaper publishing, employ fewer women than the national average. The reader should note, however, that the size of the newspaper industry tends to overwhelm book and periodical publishing when their statistics are aggregated. Thus, an average of all publishing figures in **Table 402-A** results in a figure which is still less than the average for total nonfarm female employment, despite the above-average percentage of women in book and periodical publishing. It is also notable that, when one compares the data in **Tables 402-A** and **402-B** for the newspaper and motion picture industries, the EEOC figures for total female employment are much lower.

Table 402-C presents a 1973 breakdown by job category for each of the industries on which EEOC data are available. All figures represent percentages, and the following example, drawn from the data concerning the newspaper industry, may assist the reader in interpreting the table:

> Of all white male employees in newspaper publishing, 10.3 percent were officials and managers, while 12.6 percent were classed as "professionals." Of all minority females, only 1.5 percent were classified as officials and managers, and 5.4 percent were listed as professionals. The job areas showing the highest concentration of minority females were office and clerical (55.7 percent), sales work (12.7), and skilled crafts (7.4 percent). By way of comparison, only 7.6 percent of all white males in the newspaper industry held office and clerical jobs during that year, while 10.5 percent were employed as sales workers and 36.1 percent worked at skilled crafts.

Sources

Data in **Table 402-A** were taken from BLS surveys done by state employment agencies each month. Briefly, these surveys involve sampling 160,000 business establishments in all industries. Survey results are compared quarterly with baseline information provided by the legally required unemployment insurance records. Survey procedures have been fairly consistent over the past 20 years, and generally, the process seems to provide reasonably valid and reliable data. A more complete description of these surveys can be found in the discussion of sources for Unit 400. The reader seeking a detailed discussion of the methods involved in the collection and analysis of this information should consult the Bureau of Labor Statistics report (1976b).

The information in **Tables 402-B** and **402-C** comes from the EEOC's annual *Equal Employment Opportunity Report*. One important limitation on these data is the considerable length of time required for their compilation. For example, as of the summer of 1977, the most current figures available were those for 1973.

Another limitation is created by the fact that only employers with 100 or more employees are required to file reports. This restriction could definitely affect reports for the newspaper industry, since, according to the *Census of Manufactures*, more than 92 percent of all newspapers and more than 63 percent of all *daily* newspapers employed less than 100 employees in 1972.

Additional limitations might be summarized as follows: (1) some temporary employees are excluded from the survey; (2) religious corporations, associations, societies, and educational institutions are exempted from coverage; (3) the reporting program is a self-assessment system and only statements proven to be "willfully false" are punishable by law; (4) some employers—about 11 percent in 1973—fail to respond to the survey; and (5) employers are discouraged from directly asking for employees' racial or ethnic identifications, so that they generally use "the visual survey or 'headcount' method" instead. Moreover, no figures are collected for Hawaii because of that state's unique racial composition. Clearly, data collection in this sensitive area is still in a rather primitive state, and it is difficult to establish a basis for comparing this information with figures from other sources.

Further Information

The BLS data are published monthly in *Employment and Earnings*, and each March issue of that publication lists annual averages for the preceding year. EEOC data is available not only as national aggregate figures, but also in breakdowns by state and Standard Metropolitan Statistical Areas (SMSAs). For sources of employment information on television broadcasting, see Unit 460.

Another source of employment data, by sex and job category, is the decennial population census. These censuses provide the basis for the Census Bureau's subject report entitled *Occupation by Industry*. An example of the recent report for 1970, with some analysis, can be found in Cook (1973).

Educational Programs for Media Professionals   403

Interpretation of Tables

One indication of the growth of media industries and their increasing need for qualified personnel is the expansion of media education in American colleges and universities. Although separate professional schools also exist—especially in the fields of broadcasting and film—this unit concentrates on institutions of higher education, which are, more than ever, the focus for well-rounded professional/academic training.

Table 403-A provides limited information on library education—the oldest of the academic-training programs for media occupations. Expansion of the book industry and enhanced federal support for libraries are reflected in the increasing numbers of library degrees granted during the 1960s and 1970s. Library-science programs have also undergone important changes over the past three decades, changing in the 1950s from a fifth-year undergraduate orientation to a concentrated one- or two-year Master's degree requirement. These changes have involved significant curricular modifications as well.

Table 403-B surveys the development of educational programs for journalism. The programs began early in this century, with 30 colleges offering journalism courses by 1912, and more than 450 schools establishing such programs by the 1930s. Journalism education is still a growth industry, as is evident from the 1970-1977 figures in **Table 403-B**. Increases in enrollments during the 1970s were undoubtedly sparked, in part, by the conspicuous successes of such investigative reporters as Seymour Hersh and Woodward and Bernstein. But, with a limited number of job openings available in newspaper and broadcast journalism, many journalism graduates have found it necessary to enter public relations and other fields—see the **Table 403-C** data from The Newspaper Fund surveys.

Table 403-D presents figures for broadcasting education, a field which is closely related to journalism on many campuses. Courses in radio appeared as early as the 1920s, but structured undergraduate and graduate radio programs were established mainly in the land-grant colleges of the Middle West during the 1930s (in most cases, the programs grew out of departments of

Table 403-A.
Educational Programs, Student Enrollments, and Number of Degrees Granted in Library Science in U.S., 1940–1974

	1940	1945	1950	1955	1960	1963-64	1967-68	1970-71	1973-74
Number of Colleges/Universities with Library Programs									
Undergraduate Schools	N/A	N/A	N/A	N/A	N/A	N/A	182	176	137
Graduate Schools	N/A	N/A	N/A	N/A	N/A	86	117	125	115
Total Schools	N/A	N/A	70	84	98	N/A	299	301	252
Number of Schools Accredited by ALA[a]	30	34	36	35	32	31	39	49	53
Number of Students in Library Programs									
Undergraduate	1,687	1,798	2,760	2,698	4,333	N/A	11,187	7,597	6,320
Graduate	240	140	99	91	79	N/A	10,973	14,204	15,913
Total	1,927	1,938	2,859	2,789	4,412	N/A	22,160	21,801	22,233
Number of Library Degrees Granted (all levels)	1,049	982	1,611	1,780	2,262	3,375	6,106	6,932	8,005

Sources: Schools, enrollment figures, 1940-1960: Carroll (1970), pp. 62-63; 1963-1971: American Library Association data, cited in *Bowker Annual*; 1973-1974: ALA data cited in Weintraub and Reed (1974), pp. 3, 8, 12, 16, 18. Degrees granted: ALA data, cited in *Bowker Annual*.

Note: (a) American Library Association.

Speech). Development in this field over the past 20 years has been steady and has included such related areas as telecommunications, communication arts, and educational media.

Film education, treated in **Table 403-E**, is the most recent area of media education to be developed. This field grew rapidly after the inception of regular film programs during the 1950s, and the increased fascination with the medium among college students since the mid-1960s has accelerated the demand for such programs in schools. An interesting parallel statistic to this table,

Table 403-B.
Educational Programs, Student Enrollments, and Number of Degrees Granted in Journalism in U. S., 1941–1977

	1941	1950	1955	1960	1965	1970	1975	1977
Number of Colleges/Universities with Journalism Programs	34	70	96	101	119	162	196	183
Number of Students in Journalism Programs								
Undergraduate	6,855	9,458	9,462	10,349	17,313	29,414	57,840	60,515
Graduate	340	749	696	1,041	1,916	3,692	5,593	5,027
Total	7,195	10,207	10,158	11,390	19,229	33,106	63,433	65,962
Number of Journalism Degrees Granted								
Undergraduate	N/A	N/A	N/A	2,614	2,897	6,524	11,619	12,872
Graduate	N/A	N/A	N/A	310	519	1,077	1,553	1,715
Total	N/A	N/A	N/A	2,924	3,416	7,601	13,172	14,587

Sources: 1941 data: Rogers (1945). 1950-1955 data: Dr. Paul Peterson, Ohio State University. 1955-1965 data verified in Katzen (1975), p. 21. 1960-1970 data: Peterson in *Journalism Quarterly*, first yearly issues. 1977 data: *Journalism Educator* (January 1978).

and to **Tables 403-A, 403-B,** and **403-C** as well, is the number of books published on media subjects each year. In fact, the number of film and other media books—both scholarly and popular—has increased dramatically over the past decade.

Sources

In **Table 403-A,** the data for schools and enrollments from 1940-1960 were supplied by Carroll (1970). Data after 1960 and degrees-granted figures were taken from the regular surveys by the American Library Association (ALA), which are reported in separate publications and through shorter articles in *The Bowker Annual*. All surveys on which **Table 403-A** was based were sent to both accredited and non-accredited schools, and brought substantial rates of return, especially from the ALA-accredited institutions. Yet, until recently, there has been little consistency in what data were reported from year to year, making assessment of trends prior to the mid-1960s a difficult task.

Table 403–C.

Occupational Distribution of Journalism Graduates in U. S., 1965–1975

	1965	1970	1975
Percentage Employed in Media Industries			
Total, All Media	50.0%	42.3%	58.2%[a]
Daily Newspapers	17.2	16.8	16.8
Weekly Newspapers	3.6	2.7	6.4
Wire Services	1.2	1.0	.9
Public Relations	8.6	9.7	10.9
Advertising	8.5	6.1	3.7
Magazines	4.9	1.7	3.3
Television	3.2	2.9	4.7
Radio	2.8	1.4	6.0
Percentage Employed in Other Fields			
Total, All Other Fields	50.0%	57.7%	41.8%
Graduate Schools	12.0	7.7	6.4
Military	8.0	6.2	- -
Teaching (including journalism)	3.0	5.3	3.7
Other Fields	6.0	6.3	24.0
Traveling, unreported, unemployed, etc.	21.0	32.3	7.7

Source: Annual surveys of *The Newspaper Fund.*

Notes: Size of sample, 1965: N=2,677 of 3,416 journalism graduates; 1970: N=5,258 of 7,601 journalism graduates; 1975: N=548 of 900 persons specified only as "those surveyed." (a) Includes 5.5 percent "other media jobs" not otherwise specified or listed.

Table 403-B figures were gathered from Katzen (1975), Rogers (1945), and various issues of *Journalism Educator* since 1960. Data in *Journalism Educator* are collected through mail surveys sent to the heads of journalism programs throughout the country. Since 1967, this effort has been conducted by Dr. Paul Peterson of Ohio State University, who supplied some of the 1950s enrollment figures for **Table 403-B.** Apparently, no information regarding the number and characteristics of journalism faculty members has been gathered.

The **Table 403-C** information on the post-graduate employment of journalism students in media and other fields was drawn from annual surveys by The Newspaper Fund. These surveys involve approximately 75 percent of all journalism graduates in a given year.

Table 403-D, taken from Sterling (1977), was originally based on biennial reports by Niven (1956, 1961, 1970, and 1975). Undergraduate information applies to juniors and seniors only, although 1970 and 1975 data include 2,400 and 3,600 students attending programs in two-year colleges. No information on the number of degrees granted each year was available. Niven's data were gathered by mail surveys of departments known to offer courses or a degree program in broadcasting or broadcast-related education. Faculty statistics include instructors and, for some schools, graduate assistants. Consequently, the totals are somewhat inflated—perhaps by 3 to 5 percent.

Table 403-E data for 1970 and 1975 are based on a mail survey by the American Film Institute (AFI) (1970, 1975). The 1977 data were supplied directly to the editors by Dennis Bohnenkamp of the AFI. The former sources include both television and film data, but the information presented in **Table 403-D** primarily concerns film. The 1975-1977 faculty statistics include faculty for both film and television programs, so the faculty increases from 1970 are misleading.

Further Information

Background regarding library education may be obtained through Davis (1976) and Carroll (1970). Both sources cite many other studies, and Carroll includes a good deal of statistical material from 1930 on. In addition, the Library Education Division of the ALA conducts regular surveys of the field and can supply reports dating back to 1963.

Table 403–D.
Educational Programs, Student Enrollments, and Number of Faculty in Broadcasting in U. S., 1956–1975

	1956	1960	1965	1970	1975
Number of Colleges/Universities with Broadcasting Programs					
Undergraduate Degree Programs	86	96	127	173	205
Graduate Degree Programs	58	62	77	110	126
Total Degree Programs	144	158	204	283	331
Number of Students in Broadcasting Programs					
Undergraduate[a]	3,149	3,009	3,527	9,017	17,251
Graduate	566	543	953	1,815	2,115
Total	3,715	3,552	4,480	10,832	19,366
Number of Faculty in Broadcasting Programs					
Full-Time Instructors	N/A	272	345	631	983
Part-Time Instructors	N/A	245	392	572	707
Total	N/A	517	737	1,203	1,690

Source: Sterling (1977); based on Niven (1956, 1961, 1966, 1970, 1975).

Note: (a) Juniors and seniors only, except for 1970 and 1975 figures, which include 2,400 (1970) and 3,600 (1975) students attending two-year colleges.

Table 403–E.
Educational Programs, Student Enrollments, and Number of Faculty in Film in U. S., 1970, 1975 and 1977

	1970	1975	1977
Number of Colleges/Universities with Film Programs			
Schools with Film Degrees/Programs/Majors	96[a]	240	473
Schools Offering Some Courses	331[a]	551	601
Total Schools	427	791	1,074
Total Film Courses Offered	1,669	3,873	4,153
Number of Students in Film Programs			
Undergraduate Majors	3,015	8,345	N/A
Graduate Majors	1,216	1,170	N/A
Total Majors	4,231	9,515	8,335
Number of Faculty in Film Programs			
Full-Time Instructors	304	1,179	2,828
Part-Time Instructors	565	1,443	1,390
Total	869	2,622	4,218

Sources: American Film Institute (1970, 1975), and AFI data supplied directly to the editors (1977).

Note: (a) These figures are for 1971.

Journalism education is dealt with primarily in the publications noted above in the "Sources" section. The January issue of *Journalism Educator* each year is traditionally the standard directory to the field of journalism education. For data on where journalism graduates are employed, as well as other post-graduate information, the reader should contact The Newspaper Fund.

Background on broadcast education appears in Sterling (1977), which cites many other review articles on the subject. However, the best statistics in this area are those prepared by John M. Kittross for the *Journal of Broadcasting*, based on material in Niven (see "Sources" section above). The prime source for film education information is the American Film Institute's regular *Guide to College Courses in Film and Television*.

In general, the best overview of higher education for the media in both the United States and selected foreign countries is Katzen (1975). Not considered separately in this unit are programs on media education, for which no consistent statistical information could be found. Most of these programs operate from Schools of Education. The *Hope Reports* are the standard information source for the entire educational media and audio-visual field.

Characteristics and Job Functions of Journalists

40

Table 404–A.
Number and Characteristics (Sex, Education, and Experience) of News Media Employees in U. S., by Medium, 1971

News Media	Full-Time Editorial Employees	Percent of Total Editorial Employees	Percent Who Are Female	Percent Who Are College Graduates	Percent Who Have a Journalism Degree	Percent Employed on First Media Job
Total Editorial Employees	69,500	- -	- -	- -	- -	- -
Newspapers						
Daily	38,000	56%	22%	63%	33%	58%
Weekly	11,500	17	27	44	20	14
News Magazines	1,900	3	30	88	13	2
Total Print Media	52,200	- -	- -	- -	- -	- -
Broadcasting						
Radio-TV	7,000	10	11	59	15	5
Radio Only	7,000	10	5	37	9	16
Total Broadcasting Media	14,000	- -	- -	- -	- -	- -
Wire Services	3,300	5	13	80	39	5

Source: Johnstone, Slawski, and Bowman (1976), appendix tables 2.1, 2.7, 3.2, 3.10, 4.4.

Note: "Radio-TV" indicates television only, and Radio-TV combination operations; while radio only includes only individual radio operations (or AM-FM combinations). Under percentage of college graduates, a further break-down is provided: network broadcasting: 66%; non-network broadcasting: 45%.

Interpretation of Tables

The News People, a detailed sociological portrait of American broadcast and press journalists by Johnstone, Slawski, and Bowman (1976), provided the first in-depth survey of the backgrounds, residences, and job functions of the men and women in this profession. Some of the more valuable data from this study are summarized on the three tables in this unit.

Table 404–B.
Region, City Size, Age, Sex, and Ethnic Origin of Journalists,
Compared with U. S. Labor Force and Total Population, 1971

Characteristics	Journalists	Civilian Labor Force over 18	Total Population
Regional Location			
Northeast	36%	24%	24%
North Central	23	29	28
South	25	30	31
West	16	17	17
City Size			
1,000,000 and over	41	— —	35
500,000-1,000,000	14	— —	7
250,000-500,000	15	— —	6
50,000-250,000	18	— —	10
10,000-50,000	8	— —	8
Under 10,000	4	— —	34[a]
Median Age	36.5	39.2	— —
Sex			
Male	80 %	66 %	49 %
Female	20	34	51
Ethnic Origin[b]			
Anglo-Saxon	39	— —	24
German	18	— —	17
Irish	14	— —	10
Scandinavian	5	— —	4
French	4	— —	2
Black	4	— —	15
Other	17	— —	28

Source: See previous table. Data here from appendix tables 2.2, 2.3, 2.5, 2.6, and 2.9.

Notes: (a) Includes rural population (27%). (b) For "Ethnic Origin" category, total population column refers only to *adult* population.

Table 404-A estimates the total number of full-time editorial employees in the various news media, along with figures on how many of these employees are female, college graduates, and holders of a journalism degree. The final column of the table identifies the media which most frequently provide "entry jobs" for journalists.

Table 404-B compares selected characteristics of journalists, the civilian labor force over age 18, and the total U.S. population. Among the interesting findings: Compared to both the labor force and the general population, journalists tend to be more urbanized and more densely located in the Northeast. American journalists are also marginally younger, predominantly male, and heavily Anglo-Saxon in ethnic background.

Table 404-C indicates that the job patterns of print and broadcast journalists are quite similar. Newspaper journalists appear to have more opportunities for specialized reporting and features, and broadcasters are markedly younger than press journalists.

Table 404–C.
Distribution of Job Functions and Median Age of Journalists in U. S., 1971

Functions	Print Sector (N=4,353)		Broadcast Sector (N=937)		Total Sample (N=5,292)
	Percent	Median Age	Percent	Median Age	Percent
News Gathering/Reporting/Writing					
Total who do reporting	78%	––	81%	––	79%
Cover specialized newsbeat	37	35	24	31	35
Write editorials	28	45	21	34	27
Write a column	29	41	––	––	24
Write features	12	37	4	––	10
Write commentary	6	38	13	29	8
Write reviews	5	42	––	––	4
Produce news documentaries or specials	––	––	12	33	3
Produce or host a discussion program	––	––	8	30	2
News Editing/Processing					
Total who edit or process	72	42	70	30	72
Total who do rewrites	57	––	52	––	56
News Management/Supervision					
Total with such duties	42	––	43	––	42
Influence hiring and firing	28	45	31	33	28
Supervise one or more reporters	27	––	32	––	28
In charge of a department	16	42	18	––	17
Manage a budget	12	––	17	––	13
Manage entire news operation	11	47-49	10	36	11
Overall median age	––	38	––	31	––

Source: See table A. This data from appendix tables 5.1 and 5.2, with some excisions and figure rounding. Bases were weighted to arrive at last column.

Sources

The Johnstone, Slawski, and Bowman study (1976) was based on a national sample of nearly 5,300 journalists during April of 1971. The findings of the researchers are therefore estimates based on this sample. The Johnstone et al. volume is recommended to the reader for its interesting conclusions and detailed description of the sociological methods used by the researchers in developing their data.

Further Information

In addition to *The News People*, and the literature cited in its bibliography, the reader is referred to Units 420, 460, and 700 of this book.

Table 410–A.

Total Employees and Payroll in the Book Publishing Industry and in All Manufacturing Industries in U. S., 1947–1975

	Book Publishing Employees (thousands)	Index (1972=100)	All Manufacturing Employees (thousands)	Index (1972=100)	Book Publishing Payroll (millions)	Index (1972=100)	All Manufacturing Payroll (millions)	Index (1972=100)
1947	39.9	70	14,294.0	79	$104.3	19	$ 39,695.6	25
1948	N/A	N/A	N/A	N/A	N/A	N/A	N/A	N/A
1949	33.0	58	13,566.9	75	105.6	19	41,482.0	26
1950	39.9	70	14,467.1	80	127.6	23	46,642.8	29
1951	N/A	N/A	15,309.6	85	N/A	N/A	54,741.5	34
1952	42.6	75	15,732.7	87	155.5	28	59,598.2	37
1953	N/A	N/A	16,693.1	93	N/A	N/A	66,492.9	41
1954	34.7	61	15,645.5	87	144.8	26	62,962.7	39
1955	35.7	63	16,335.5	91	161.1	29	69,096.6	43
1956	40.0	70	16,694.4	93	184.9	33	74,015.1	46
1957	38.0	67	16,621.1	92	189.8	34	76,314.6	48
1958	38.5	67	15,423.1	86	191.9	34	73,875.2	46
1959	39.9	70	16,062.9	89	211.2	38	81,203.6	51
1960	42.4	74	16,149.9	90	233.3	42	83,672.5	52
1961	43.9	77	15,729.6	87	249.0	45	83,677.4	52
1962	47.0	82	16,154.7	90	277.4	50	89,819.2	56
1963	46.8	82	16,231.9	90	280.7	50	93,283.3	58
1964	53.1	93	16,485.7	91	330.9	59	98,685.3	62
1965	50.4	88	17,250.5	96	322.5	58	106,643.2	66
1966	54.0	95	18,200.3	101	359.8	65	117,157.4	73
1967	52.0	91	18,492.0	103	389.9	70	123,480.6	77
1968	51.9	91	18,681.0	104	398.1	71	132,568.4	83
1969	56.4	99	19,155.6	106	457.0	82	142,645.1	89
1970	55.7	98	18,289.5	101	480.1	86	141,886.4	88
1971	59.9	105	17,426.3	97	535.7	96	144,246.3	90
1972	57.1	100	18,034.4	100	557.6	100	160,433.2	100
1973	59.2	104	18,870.4	105	610.4	109	178,316.5	111
1974	54.4	95	18,712.8	104	621.5	111	190,574.3	119
1975	54.0	95	17,216.3	95	666.5	120	190,943.4	119

Sources: Book publishing employees and payroll, 1947-1972 data: *U. S. Census of Manufactures*, 1954, 1958, 1963 and 1972; 1973-1976 data: *U. S. Industrial Outlook 1977*. All manufacturing employees and payroll, 1947-1972 data: *U. S. Census of Manufactures*, General Summary, 1972; 1973 data: *Annual Survey of Manufactures 1972*; 1974-1975 data: *Annual Survey of Manufactures 1975*.

Interpretation of Tables

Table 410-A compares total employment and payroll in the book publishing industry with that of all manufacturing industries in the United States, from 1947 to 1975. These figures from the U.S. Census Bureau differ significantly from the book industry employment figures collected by the U.S. Bureau of Labor Statistics (BLS), in that the Census Bureau totals are broken down into book publishing and book *printing*. In order to focus more closely on publishing, the editors have decided to exclude the book-printing employment figures (estimated at 44.6 million persons in 1975) from Table 410-A. However, it is worth noting that, according to the Census Bureau, the book industry employment *total* (printing and publishing) for 1975 was 98.6 thousand persons, a figure which is fairly close to the 92.2 thousand reported by the BLS. For discussion of the reasons why the two figures are not closer, the reader should see Unit 400.

Table 410-A shows that book publishing employment remained fairly constant from 1947 until 1959, then entered a period of growth which continued until 1971. Since that time, the publishing industry's fortunes have followed roughly the same course as U.S. manufacturing industries in general. It is interesting to note that throughout the 1960s the employment picture for the pub-

Table 410–B.
Average Weekly Earnings, Hours, and Overtime Hours of Book Production Workers and of All Manufacturing Workers in U. S., 1947–1976

	Weekly Earnings, Book Workers	Index: Book Industry Earnings	Weekly Earnings, All Manufacturing Workers	Index: All Manufacturing Earnings	Weekly Hours, Book Workers	Weekly Hours, All Manufacturing Workers	Weekly Overtime Hours, Book Workers	Weekly Overtime Hours, All Manufacturing Workers
1947	$ 52.57	34	$ 49.17	32	40.8	40.4	N/A	N/A
1948	55.99	36	53.12	34	39.1	40.0	N/A	N/A
1949	58.14	37	53.88	35	39.0	39.1	N/A	N/A
1950	63.83	41	58.32	38	39.5	40.5	N/A	N/A
1951	67.20	43	63.34	41	40.0	40.6	N/A	N/A
1952	71.15	46	67.16	43	40.2	40.7	N/A	N/A
1953	73.38	47	70.47	46	40.1	40.5	N/A	N/A
1954	76.02	49	70.49	46	39.8	39.6	N/A	N/A
1955	76.99	49	75.70	49	40.4	40.7	N/A	N/A
1956	83.44	54	78.78	51	40.9	40.4	N/A	2.8
1957	84.00	54	81.59	53	40.0	39.8	N/A	2.3
1958	86.55	56	82.71	53	39.7	39.2	2.8	2.0
1959	92.34	59	88.26	57	40.5	40.3	3.4	2.7
1960	95.82	62	89.72	58	40.6	39.7	3.8	2.4
1961	99.06	64	92.34	60	40.6	39.8	3.7	2.4
1962	99.85	64	96.56	62	40.1	40.4	3.4	2.8
1963	104.49	67	99.63	64	40.5	40.5	3.5	2.8
1964	106.90	69	102.97	67	40.8	40.7	3.8	3.1
1965	110.68	71	107.53	70	41.3	41.2	4.2	3.6
1966	114.53	74	112.34	73	41.8	41.3	4.9	3.9
1967	113.93	73	114.90	74	40.4	40.6	3.5	3.4
1968	120.90	78	122.51	79	40.3	40.7	3.3	3.6
1969	130.33	84	129.51	84	40.1	40.6	3.5	3.6
1970	135.84	87	133.73	86	38.7	39.8	2.6	3.0
1971	147.02	94	142.44	92	39.1	39.9	2.9	2.9
1972	155.63	100	154.69	100	39.4	40.6	3.3	3.5
1973	161.43	104	166.06	107	39.4	40.7	3.5	3.8
1974	166.45	107	176.40	114	38.8	40.0	3.0	3.2
1975	172.13	111	189.51	123	37.5	39.4	2.2	2.6
1976	192.06	123	207.60	134	38.8	40.0	2.7	3.1

Sources: 1947-1973 figures: Bureau of Labor Statistics, *Employment and Earnings, United States, 1909-75*. 1974-1976 figures: Bureau of Labor Statistics, *Employment and Earnings* (March 1977).

Table 410–C.
Average Hourly Union Wage Rates in Book- and Job-Printing Trades in U. S.,
by Type of Trade, Region, and City Size, 1974

	Average Hourly Wage
Trade	
All Book- and Job-Printing Trades	$6.34
Bindery Workers (Journeymen II)	4.17
Bookbinders (Journeymen I)	6.63
Compositors (Hand)	7.11
Electrotypers	6.22
Machine Operators	6.97
Machine Tenders (Machinists)	7.35
Mailers	5.69
Photoengravers	7.74
Press Assistants and Feeders	6.09
Pressmen, Cylinder	6.73
Pressmen, Platen	5.86
Stereotypers	6.78
Cameramen	6.82
Platemakers	6.23
Strippers	6.69
Region	
Total United States	6.34
New England	5.89
Middle Atlantic	6.92
Border States	6.36
Southeast	5.62
Southwest	4.97
Great Lakes	6.17
Middle West	5.59
Mountain	5.09
Pacific	6.35
City Size	
1,000,000 or more	7.51
500,000 to 1,000,000	6.72
250,000 to 500,000	6.47
100,000 to 250,000	5.96
All Cities	6.34

Source: Bureau of Labor Statistics, *Union Wages and Hours: Printing Industry, July 1, 1974* (Bulletin 1881).

Notes: Average hourly wage rates exclude holiday, vacation or other benefit payments made regularly or credited to the worker each pay period. The rate for each trade was weighted by the number of union members at each hourly wage rate. Regions used in this study include: New England: Connecticut, Maine, Massachusetts, New Hampshire, Rhode Island, and Vermont; Middle Atlantic: New Jersey, New York and Pennsylvania; Border States: Delaware, District of Columbia, Kentucky, Maryland, Virginia and West Virginia; Southeast: Alabama, Florida, Georgia, Mississippi, North Carolina, South Carolina and Tennessee; Great Lakes: Illinois, Indiana, Michigan, Minnesota, Ohio, and Wisconsin; Middle West: Iowa, Kansas, Missouri, Nebraska, North Dakota and South Dakota; Southwest: Arkansas, Louisiana, Oklahoma and Texas; Mountain: Arizona, Idaho, Colorado, Montana, New Mexico, Utah and Wyoming; and Pacific: Alaska, California, Nevada, Oregon and Washington. Hawaii was excluded from the survey.

Table 410-D.
Occupational Distribution of Book Publishing Employees in U. S., by Type of Books Published, 1976

	Trade and Religious Books		Professional Books		Mass Market Paperbacks[a]		Book Clubs/Mail-Order Publishers		El/Hi Textbooks	
	Average Percentage of Employees	Mid-Range Percentage of Employees[b]	Average Percentage of Employees	Mid-Range Percentage of Employees[b]	Average Percentage of Employees	Mid-Range Percentage of Employees[b]	Average Percentage of Employees	Mid-Range Percentage of Employees[b]	Average Percentage of Employees	Mid-Range Percentage of Employees[b]
Editorial	17.9%	15.8 to 25.3%	28.4%	18.5 to 28.9%	7.0%	6.1 to 7.5%	1.3%	1.3 to 8.4%	18.0%	14.6 to 21.2%
Production	7.5	5.7 to 9.2	11.6	6.1 to 10.6	3.7	2.7 to 6.5	3.1	3.8 to 31.7	5.8	3.7 to 9.2
Art	N/A	N/A	N/A	N/A	1.7	1.5 to 2.3	N/A	N/A	N/A	N/A
Marketing										
Salesmen	9.2	6.1 to 15.7	2.9	3.4 to 10.1	22.3	12.6 to 32.9	N/A	N/A	18.3	15.2 to 28.5
Consultants	N/A	N/A	N/A	N/A	N/A	N/A	N/A	N/A	3.2	2.4 to 4.6
Sales Department	6.5	5.0 to 10.0	4.9	3.2 to 10.7	6.9	0.8 to 10.6	N/A	N/A	10.7[c]	N/A
Promotion	6.2	5.0 to 8.4	10.9	10.0 to 26.3	5.1[d]	3.0 to 9.8	N/A	N/A	2.9	1.1 to 4.0
Unspecified	0.2	N/A	0.3	N/A	N/A	N/A	N/A	N/A	N/A	N/A
Total Marketing	22.1	16.4 to 27.7	19.1	10.0 to 31.3	34.4	26.4 to 48.5	3.8	4.4 to 25.3	35.0	30.4 to 45.3
Fulfillment										
Order Processing	17.1	11.7 to 24.5	17.5	17.9 to 31.0	14.4	5.8 to 24.6	42.3	28.9 to 44.0	13.3	8.7 to 18.8
Credit/Accounts Receivable	N/A	N/A	N/A	N/A	5.8	4.2 to 10.5	N/A	N/A	N/A	N/A
Shipping/Warehousing	14.1	5.4 to 22.6	7.2	10.0 to 26.3	18.7	0.8 to 38.8	34.7	25.3 to 45.3	14.7	8.6 to 17.0
Unspecified	N/A	N/A	1.7	N/A	N/A	N/A	N/A	N/A	N/A	N/A
Total Fulfillment	31.2	19.0 to 38.0	26.4	30.6 to 45.7	38.9	28.6 to 48.8	77.0	40.4 to 76.0	28.0	17.7 to 39.2
Administrative Management	8.1	3.2 to 8.0	4.4	3.6 to 6.4	14.4	6.1 to 24.2	3.0	2.8 to 17.0	1.8	1.2 to 3.2
General Office	10.7	6.8 to 21.1	8.1	6.9 to 20.0	N/A	N/A	11.7	7.8 to 22.3	10.1	5.1 to 15.2
Other	2.6	1.7 to 6.7	2.1	1.6 to 13.9	N/A	N/A	N/A	N/A	1.3	1.1 to 2.5
Unspecified	N/A	N/A	0.3	N/A	N/A	N/A	N/A	N/A	N/A	N/A

Source: Association of American Publishers (1977), pp. 51, 75, 84, 92, 121.

Notes: (a) Publishers of rack-sized paperback books only. (b) The ''mid-range'' figures represent numbers at the 25th and 75th percentiles of the AAP-survey responses. These percentile figures permit the reader to assess the accuracy, or typicalness, of the arithmetical averages in the previous columns. See the text for a more complete discussion. (c) This figure is the sum of 3.5% employees in ''sales management'' and 7.2% employees in ''sales clerical.'' (d) Includes employees in publicity and advertising as well as promotion.

lishing industry seemed to be determined more by conditions within that particular industry than by the Vietnam War boom experienced by American industries as a whole. A look at the size of book industry payroll reveals that it, too, has generally increased more slowly than that for all manufacturers, except for a sizable upswing at the end of the 1960s, and again in the mid-1970s.

Table 410-B shows the average weekly earnings, hours, and overtime hours for book industry production workers. These figures are from the BLS and include both book publishing and book printing. For many years, book publishing employees received higher wages than the average manufacturing production worker. The two averages became approximately equal in 1972; and since then, the average weekly wage of the book industry production worker has lagged behind that received by workers throughout the rest of manufacturing in this country.

Table 410-C data, also from the BLS, show how the average hourly union wage rate in the U.S. book and job printing industries differs by trade, geographic region, and size of city. Generally, larger cities have higher paying printing operations, and the best paying regions of the nation for the printing trades are the Middle Atlantic, Pacific, and Border States. It is also apparent that the wages for some of the trades associated with the newer printing technologies, such as cameramen, platemakers, and strippers, are slightly less than that for some of the older trades, such as hand compositors and photoengravers.

Table 410-D shows the percentages of persons employed in the various occupational functions of the book publishing industry. These data illustrate the great diversity of the book publishing business and the importance of considering that diversity in any evaluation of the industry as a whole.

Among the several types of book publishers, there are major differences in the employment levels for editing, production, marketing, and fulfillment (shipping, order processing, etc.). For example, professional and elementary and secondary (El-hi) textbook publishers average the highest employment for editorial work, which is to be expected since texts and professional books require a good deal of editorial and graphic design work. In addition, El-hi textbook publishers employ more persons for marketing purposes than any other branch of publishing, although marketing employment among mass-market paperback publishers is also very high. Mass-market publishers rely heavily on salespeople who not only sell the books, but also take responsibility for stocking the shelves in the retail outlets they serve. The textbook publishers' need for an even larger sales force is probably due to their having to deal with a very complex bureaucracy of textbook buyers in a contracting and increasingly competitive market.

The reader will note that book clubs employ very large numbers of employees in the fulfillment aspects of their operations. This is to be expected, since the essential nature of a book club is its special methods of marketing and distribution.

The "mid-range" statistics in Table 410-D are those figures which fall between the 26th and 75th percentiles among the responses to the survey on which this table is based. This mid-range breakdown allows the reader to determine whether the arithmetical averages are "typical" of each segment of the book industry, or whether a few companies with extreme practices have skewed the mean.

Sources

The information in Table 410-A was collected by the U.S. Census Bureau in its *Census of Manufactures* and *Annual Survey of Manufactures*. The Census Bureau sends questionnaires to each manufacturing establishment for the censuses, while its annual surveys poll only a stratified probability sample of manufacturers. In 1975, for example, about 70,000 of the total 312,000 manufacturing establishments in the United States were samples for the *Annual Survey*. Larger establishments receive more complete coverage in these surveys. As a consequence, the standard errors of estimate for book publishing industry figures as a whole were as high as 33 percent in 1975. These data should therefore be treated with considerable caution.

Table 410-B comes from monthly surveys carried out by state employment agencies under standardized procedures developed by the Bureau of Labor Statistics. The BLS procedures are described in Units 400 and 420. Generally, the survey is considered valid and reliable. The best detailed discussion of this source is in the *BLS Handbook of Methods for Surveys and Studies* (Bureau of Labor Statistics, 1976b).

The BLS also collects the information presented in Table 410-C, but through a different annual survey. Each year, the BLS sends questionnaires to all the local unions in a sample of cities with populations of 100,000 or more. All cities with more than 500,000 population are also covered. Since cities in the 100,000-250,000 range are widely distributed throughout the United States, the data for that group are weighted in the regional and national aggregations to compensate for the cities not surveyed.

The information is up-to-date as of the first workday in July for the year concerned—in this case 1974—since most new wage agreements for the year have usually been negotiated by that time. Copies of actual agreements are also requested by the BLS, for comparison with the questionnaire responses. Personal visits are made to unions that do not respond to the mail questionnaires. The 1974 survey covered 70 cities and 104,000 printing workers, including commercial lithography and newspaper production workers, as well as book and job shop employees.

The average union wage rates provide comparisons among industries, trades, and cities for a given time. They do not accurately measure year-to-year changes, so only one year's figures are included here, although a longer series is available. Membership figures for the various trades or classifications do not remain constant, and these fluctuations may have a marked effect on average rates. Thus, in comparing these statistics, the reader should keep the following considerations in mind:

1.   The averages are influenced by the differences in union wage rates for individual cities, as well as by differences in the occupational composition of the printing trades in each city. Certain types of work are more prevalent in some cities than in others.

2.   A particular craft may not be covered by a collective bargaining agreement in some cities and therefore would be excluded from the survey, although all or part of the workers in that craft may be covered in other cities.

Table 410-D comes from data published in the *1976 Industry Statistics* of the Association of American Publishers (AAP). While the entire annual survey covers publishers representing about 60 percent of all book publishing sales, responses in certain subcategories and answers to certain questions are more limited. The number of publishers responding to the AAP questionnaire are listed below:

Trade and religious books: 29 publishers with 4,556 employees.
Professional books: 14 publishers with 1,088 employees.
Mass-market paperbacks: 4 publishers with 1,324 employees.
Book clubs/Mail-order books: 22 publishers with 2,518 employees.
El-hi textbooks: 14 publishers with 4,578 employees.

The editors cannot be sure of how representative these figures are of the entire industry. In the trade and religious book category, for example, 43 publishers responded to some questions, but *not* to the employment question on the survey; and this group of 43 publishers is responsible for 58 percent of the estimated total sales for the industry. Similarly, the mass-market paperback publishers responding only to parts of the AAP survey accounted for more than 90 percent of the estimated industry totals. The editors do not know the standing of the 29 trade and religious book publishers or the four mass-market paperback publishers who *did* respond to the employment questions. The same general situation prevails for the other categories of publishers.

Overall, then, the reader should regard **Table 410**-D as an informed but not definitive indication of possible differences among publishers. The AAP also publishes employee data for college text publishers, although this information was not included here because of its very different format.

Further Information

Monthly employment figures are presented in each issue of the BLS publication, *Employment and Earnings*, with annual averages for the preceding year appearing each March. Analyses of government statistics on employment and other subjects appear regularly in *Printing and Publishing*, a quarterly magazine of the Construction and Forest Products Division of the U.S. Department of Commerce.

Estimates of the book industry employment figures usually appear in the annual editions of *U.S. Industrial Outlook*, also published by the Department of Commerce. Comparisons of book industry employment with other media can be found in Unit 400, while information on the employment of women and minorities in the book industry appears in Unit 402.

Table 420–A.
Total Employment and Payroll in the Newspaper Industry and in All Manufacturing Industries in U.S., 1925–1975

	Employment					Payroll				
	Production Workers Only	All Newspaper Employees	All Newspaper Employees Index	All Manufacturing Employees	All Manufacturing Employees Index	Production Workers Only	All Newspaper Employees	All Newspaper Employees Index	All Manufacturing Employees	All Manufacturing Employees Index
	(thousands)	(thousands)	(1967=100)	(thousands)	(1967=100)	(millions)	(millions)	(1967=100)	(millions)	(1967=100)
1925	94.3	N/A	N/A	9,142.4	49	$ 180.0	N/A	N/A	$ 12,957.7	10
1927	98.1	N/A	N/A	9,072.1	49	195.0	N/A	N/A	13,123.1	11
1929	105.7	N/A	N/A	9,659.7	52	211.0	N/A	N/A	14,284.3	12
1931	97.9	N/A	N/A	N/A	N/A	190.0	N/A	N/A	N/A	N/A
1933	90.4	N/A	N/A	6,557.9	35	139.0	N/A	N/A	6,237.8	5
1935	99.0	N/A	N/A	8,262.3	45	164.0	N/A	N/A	9,564.8	8
1937	109.9	N/A	N/A	9,786.4	53	186.0	N/A	N/A	12,829.7	10
1939	96.7	N/A	N/A	9,527.3	52	164.0	N/A	N/A	12,706.1	10
1947	118.1	234.4	70	14,294.0	77	372.8	$ 743.9	33	39,695.6	32
1949	137.1	262.1	78	13,566.9	73	489.8	949.7	43	41,482.0	34
1950	146.0	267.3	80	14,467.1	78	549.0	1,000.9	45	46,642.8	38
1951	149.9	273.8	82	15,309.6	83	578.0	1,057.0	48	54,741.5	44
1952	149.2	275.5	82	15,732.7	85	612.0	1,123.8	51	59,598.2	48
1953	145.3	276.0	82	16,693.1	90	653.5	1,200.6	54	66,492.9	54
1954	148.5	280.9	84	15,645.5	85	667.1	1,257.1	57	62,962.9	51
1955	151.8	289.4	86	16,335.5	88	711.4	1,350.5	61	69,096.6	56
1956	154.8	299.3	89	16,694.4	90	756.8	1,448.4	65	74,015.1	60
1957	158.4	308.7	92	16,621.1	90	784.7	1,519.9	68	76,314.6	62
1958	154.7	295.6	88	15,423.1	83	779.0	1,499.9	67	73,875.2	60
1959	158.1	300.9	90	16,062.9	87	841.1	1,601.3	72	81,203.6	66
1960	159.9	307.4	92	16,159.9	87	882.9	1,673.9	75	83,672.5	68
1961	160.7	308.5	92	15,729.6	85	900.0	1,712.1	77	83,677.4	68
1962	163.2	310.7	92	16,154.7	87	929.5	1,761.0	79	89,819.2	73
1963	160.1	306.4	91	16,231.9	88	935.2	1,784.6	80	93,283.3	76
1964	166.3	317.9	95	16,485.7	89	997.8	1,901.1	85	98,685.3	80
1965	167.6	327.7	98	17,250.5	93	1,043.6	2,066.4	93	106,643.2	86
1966	167.6	333.5	99	18,200.3	98	1,091.4	2,121.2	95	117,157.4	95
1967	169.2	335.9	100	18,492.0	100	1,121.5	2,223.7	100	123,480.6	100
1968	169.7	338.5	101	18,681.0	101	1,187.7	2,368.7	106	132,568.4	107
1969	181.5	360.5	107	19,155.6	104	1,316.5	2,614.2	118	142,645.1	116

Table 420–A. (Cont'd.)

	Employment					Payroll				
	Production Workers Only	All Newspaper Employees	All Newspaper Employees Index	All Manufacturing Employees	All Manufacturing Employees Index	Production Workers Only	All Newspaper Employees	All Newspaper Employees Index	All Manufacturing Employees	All Manufacturing Employees Index
	(thousands)	(thousands)	(1967=100)	(thousands)	(1967=100)	(millions)	(millions)	(1967=100)	(millions)	(1967=100)
1970	168.2	349.1	104	18,289.5	99	$1,344.1	$2,715.5	122	$141,886.4	115
1971	164.4	346.4	103	17,426.3	94	1,408.6	2,868.7	129	144,246.3	117
1972	169.8	348.9	104	18,034.4	98	1,537.8	3,170.8	143	160,433.2	130
1973	167.3	353.2	105	18,870.4	102	1,613.9	3,385.3	152	178,317.2	144
1974	166.9	358.1	107	18,712.5	101	1,669.3	3,598.5	162	190,574.3	154
1975	166.5	361.7	108	17,216.3	93	1,715.7	3,784.7	170	190,943.4	155

Sources: Newspaper industry data, 1925-1939: *Biennial Census of Manufactures*, appropriate years; 1947-1954: *Census of Manufactures*, appropriate years; 1958-1972: *1972 Census of Manufactures*; all other years: *Annual Survey of Manufactures*, appropriate years. All manufacturing industries data: 1925-1972: *1972 Census of Manufactures*; 1973: *Annual Survey of Manufactures, 1973*; 1974-1975: *Annual Survey of Manufactures, 1975.*

Table 420-B.
Average Weekly Earnings, Hours, and Overtime Hours of Newspaper Production Workers and of All Manufacturing Workers in U. S., 1947–1976

	Newspaper Industry Average Weekly Earnings	Index (1972=100)	All Manufacturing Average Weekly Earnings	Index (1972=100)	Newspaper Industry Average Weekly Hours	All Manufacturing Average Weekly Hours	Newspaper Industry Average Weekly Overtime Hours	All Manufacturing Average Weekly Overtime Hours
1947	$ 61.96	35	$ 49.17	32	38.7	40.4	N/A	N/A
1948	69.68	40	53.12	34	38.8	40.0	N/A	N/A
1949	73.80	42	53.88	35	38.5	39.1	N/A	N/A
1950	75.36	43	58.32	38	38.1	40.5	N/A	N/A
1951	78.42	45	63.34	41	37.7	40.6	N/A	N/A
1952	81.91	47	67.16	43	37.4	40.7	N/A	N/A
1953	86.02	49	70.47	46	37.4	40.5	N/A	N/A
1954	87.32	50	70.49	46	37.0	39.6	N/A	N/A
1955	90.64	52	75.70	49	37.3	40.7	N/A	N/A
1956	93.74	53	78.78	51	37.2	40.4	N/A	2.8
1957	95.68	55	81.59	53	36.8	39.8	N/A	2.3
1958	97.82	56	82.71	53	36.5	39.2	2.6	2.0
1959	101.84	58	88.26	57	36.5	40.3	2.6	2.7
1960	105.70	60	89.72	58	36.7	39.7	2.6	2.4
1961	107.45	61	92.34	60	36.3	37.8	2.4	2.4
1962	110.35	63	96.56	62	36.3	40.4	2.5	2.8
1963	112.58	64	99.63	64	36.2	40.5	2.3	2.8
1964	116.84	67	102.97	67	36.4	40.7	2.4	3.1
1965	119.85	68	107.53	70	36.1	41.2	2.4	3.6
1966	125.24	71	112.34	73	36.3	41.3	2.7	3.9
1967	129.60	74	114.90	74	36.2	40.6	2.7	3.4
1968	136.08	78	122.51	79	36.0	40.7	2.7	3.6
1969	145.08	83	129.51	84	36.0	40.6	2.8	3.6
1970	150.59	86	133.73	86	35.6	39.8	2.5	3.0
1971	162.38	93	142.44	92	35.3	39.9	2.4	2.9
1972	175.35	100	154.69	100	35.5	40.6	2.5	3.5
1973	182.31	104	166.06	107	35.4	40.7	2.5	3.8
1974	190.70	109	176.40	114	34.8	40.0	2.2	3.2
1975	202.27	115	189.51	123	34.4	39.4	1.7	2.6
1976	216.09	123	207.60	134	34.3	40.0	1.6	3.1

Sources: 1947-1973 data: Bureau of Labor Statistics, *Employment and Earnings, United States, 1909-1975.* 1974-1976 data: Bureau of Labor Statistics, *Employment and Earnings* (March 1977).

Table 420–C.
Average Hourly Union Wage Rates in Newspaper Trades in U. S., 1949–1974, and by Type of Trade, Region, and City Size, 1971 and 1974

Average Hourly Wage Rate,[a] 1949-1974

Year	Hourly Rate
1949	$2.49
1955	3.01
1960	3.48
1961	3.56[b]
1962	3.65[b]
1963	3.75[b]
1964	3.84[b]
1965	3.94
1966	4.06[b]
1967	4.26[b]
1968	4.47[b]
1969	4.77[b]
1970	5.13
1971	5.65
1972	6.12[b]
1973	6.46[b]
1974	7.01

Interpretation of Tables

Table 420-A provides U.S. Census Bureau statistics on employment and payroll in the newspaper industry, and in all U.S. manufacturing industries, since 1925. Despite the decline in the number of newspapers in this century (see Units 120 and 121), newspaper employment has generally continued to rise in a gradual, stair-step fashion. However, a comparison of the Table 420-A data with the Bureau of Labor Statistics (BLS) figures in Tables 400-A and 400-B will show that the number of new newspaper jobs has lagged considerably behind employment in the general category of all "nonfarm enterprises," and behind both the book and broadcasting industries as well. Nevertheless, the newspaper industry remains by far the largest employer among the mass media, with more than 380,000 employees in 1976 (see Table 400-A).

Table 420-A also indicates that overall newspaper industry payrolls have grown at about the same pace as those for all U.S. manufacturing industries. However, Table 420-B, using figures from the Bureau of Labor Statistics, shows a slightly different trend in comparing the average weekly earnings, hours, and overtime hours of newspaper *production* workers with the earnings and hours of workers in all manufacturing production jobs. These figures indicate that while the average weekly earnings of newspaper industry production workers have been consistently above average among all manufacturing workers, the gap has been narrowing in the 1970s.

In 1947, for example, the average newspaper production worker's weekly wage was 26 percent higher than that of the average production worker in all manufacturing industries. By 1976, this figure had dropped to 4 percent. Between 1972 and 1976, the wages of newspaper production workers had increased only 23 percent, while wages in all manufacturing production jobs went up 34 percent. One factor in this relative decline in the average weekly wage for newspaper employees has been the decreasing number of hours and overtime hours that these employees work. However, the average hourly wage of newspaper production workers has also increased less rapidly than the hourly wage rate of manufacturing workers in general.

Table 420-C provides a listing of the average wage rates for selected newspaper trade occupations covered by union agreements. The wage rates are also compared by region in the United States and by city size. As one would expect, the large city newspapers and the more urbanized Middle Atlantic and Pacific Coast regions pay higher wages. However, one must consider the cost of living in these areas in order to adequately measure real differences in the wage rates.

Table 420–C. (Cont'd.)

Average Hourly Wage Rate,[a] by
Type of Trade, 1971 and 1974

	Hourly Rate, 1971	Hourly Rate, 1974
All Newspaper Trades	$5.65	$7.01
Daywork	5.46	6.82
Nightwork	5.83	7.19
Compositors, Hand	5.62	6.97
Daywork	5.50	6.86
Nightwork	5.74	7.07
Machine Operators	5.76	7.15
Daywork	5.59	6.97
Nightwork	5.90	7.30
Machine Tenders (Machinists)	5.61	7.01
Daywork	5.52	6.88
Nightwork	5.70	7.15
Mailers	5.41	6.70
Daywork	5.17	6.50
Nightwork	5.64	6.91
Photoengravers	6.12	7.42
Daywork	5.94	7.27
Nightwork	6.33	7.58
Pressmen (Journeymen)	5.63	7.01
Daywork	5.41	6.74
Nightwork	5.88	7.30
Pressmen-in-Charge	5.93	7.61
Daywork	5.69	7.33
Nightwork	6.18	7.89
Stereotypers	5.58	6.98
Daywork	5.28	6.69
Nightwork	5.90	7.27

Table 420-D is a compilation of the minimum weekly salaries guaranteed to reporters and photographers by Newspaper Guild agreements with the 100 newspapers listed. Contrary to the traditional view of the reporter as a notoriously underpaid worker, this survey includes some sizable salaries. After one year at the *New York Times*, for example, a reporter is guaranteed more than $24,000 a year. Of course, there is considerable variation in the chart. The newspaper with the lowest salary, the *Evening Telegram* in Superior, Wisconsin, pays its reporters only $10,400 per year after five years' service.

Sources

The information in **Table 420**-A is taken from the U.S. Census Bureau's *Census of Manufactures* and the *Annual Survey of Manufactures*. The figures prior to 1947 represent a retabulation of earlier Census Bureau data, since newspapers and periodicals were reported as a single category until 1939. The figures in the *Annual Surveys* are estimates made by inferences to the entire industry from a selected sample of respondents. Therefore, readers interested in using these data for analysis should consult the appropriate volumes of the *Annual Survey* to determine the Census Bureau's estimate of error for the statistics. Generally, these estimates are less than 10 percent.

The information in **Table 420**-B comes from the U.S. Bureau of Labor Statistics, which collects work-hour and wage data in the course of its monthly surveys on employment in the United States. The procedures of the BLS are described in detail in the "Sources" discussion in Unit 400. These data are generally valid and reliable. However, there are some particular features about them which are worth noting in the technical discussion in the Bureau's *Employment and Earnings 1909-1975* (1976a).

Table 420–C. (Cont'd.)

Average Hourly Wage Rate,[a] by Region of U.S.[c]		
	Hourly Rate, 1971	Hourly Rate, 1974
Total United States	$5.65	$7.01
New England	5.73	7.00
Middle Atlantic	6.13	7.71
Border States	5.60	7.45
Southeast	4.66	5.84
Southwest	4.69	5.66
Great Lakes	5.74	7.13
Middle West	5.36	6.47
Mountain	5.31	6.73
Pacific	5.86	7.22

Average Hourly Wate Rate,[a] by Size of City		
	Hourly Rate, 1971	Hourly Rate, 1974
1,000,000 or More	$5.93	$7.74
500,000 to 1,000,000	5.59	7.23
250,000 to 500,000	5.32	6.74
100,000 to 250,000	4.96	6.29
All Cities	5.65	7.01

Sources: 1949-1960, 1965 data: U. S. Bureau of Labor Statistics, quoted in Compaine (1974). 1961-1974 data: Bureau of Labor Statistics, *Union Wages and Hours: Printing Industry July 1, 1971* and *July 1, 1974* (Bulletins 1744 and 1881).

Notes: (a) Basic (minimum) wage rates, excluding holidy, vacation, or other benefit payments made regularly or credited to the worker each pay period. Average rates based on all union rates in effect on July 1 of each year. Each union rate was weighted by the number of union members at each reported hourly rate; (b) Figures based on products of known dollar figures and data of year-to-year percentage increases. Error due to this process is approximately 1 percent; (c) Regional breakdown in this study: *New England*: Connecticut, Maine, Massachusetts, New Hampshire, Rhode Island, and Vermont; *Middle Atlantic*: New Jersey, New York and Pennsylvania; *Border States*: Delaware, District of Columbia, Kentucky, Maryland, Virginia and West Virginia; *Southeast*: Alabama, Florida, Georgia, Mississippi, North Carolina, South Carolina, and Tennessee; *Great Lakes*: Illinois, Indiana, Michigan, Minnesota, Ohio, and Wisconsin; *Middle West*: Iowa, Kansas, Missouri, Nebraska, North Dakota, and South Dakota; *Southwest*: Arkansas, Louisiana, Oklahoma, and Texas; *Mountain*: Arizona, Idaho, Colorado, Montana, New Mexico, Utah, and Wyoming; and *Pacific*: Alaska, California, Nevada, Oregon, and Washington. Hawaii was excluded from the survey.

The Bureau of Labor Statistics collects the wage information presented in **Table 420-C** in an annual survey (as of the first workday in July) of all the local unions in a sample of cities with populations of 100,000 or more. All cities with more than 500,000 people are included in the survey, as are most cities in the 250,000 to 500,000 category. Because the cities in the 100,000 to 250,000 category are widely distributed throughout the United States, the data for that group are weighted in the regional and national aggregations in order to compensate for the cities which are not surveyed. (See the **Table 410-C** "Sources" discussion of the serious limitations of this BLS series.)

Table 420–D.
Top Minimum Weekly Salaries of Reporters for Selected U. S. Newspapers, 1977

Newspaper	Reporters' Top Minimum Salary[a]	Tenure Required for Top Minimum Salary
Washington (D.C.) Post and Star	$504.24	4 years
New York (N.Y.) Times[b]	463.13	1 year
New York (N.Y.) News	432.88	5 years
Garden City (N.Y.) Newsday (AFL-CIO)	428.00	4 years
Chicago (Ill.) Sun-Times	406.13	4 years
St. Paul (Minn.) Dispatch and Pioneer Press	393.50	5 years
Fresno (Calif.) Bee	392.25	5 years
Modesto (Calif.) Bee	392.25	5 years
Sacramento (Calif.) Bee	392.25	6 years
Minneapolis (Minn.) Tribune-Star	390.50	5 years
Buffalo (N.Y.) Evening News	390.17	5 years
St. Louis (Mo.) Post Dispatch	390.05	5 years
Oakland (Calif.) Tribune	380.75	6 years
Detroit (Mich.) News	385.80	4 years
Detroit (Mich.) Free Press	383.80	4 years
St. Louis (Mo.) Globe Democrat	375.15	5 years
Toronto (Ont.) Star	375.00	5 years
Philadelphia (Penn.) News and Inquirer	373.94	5 years
Highstown (N.J.) Daily Racing Form	372.15	5 years
Baltimore (Md.) Sun	372.00	2 years
Seattle (Wash.) Post-Intelligencer	371.50	5 years
Seattle (Wash.) Times	371.50	5 years
Sacramento (Calif.) Union	370.87	6 years
Denver (Colo.) Rocky Mountain News	367.00	4 years
Buffalo (N.Y.) Courier Express	365.15	4 years
Honolulu (Hawaii) Star Bulletin	364.00	4 years
Cleveland (Ohio) Plain Dealer	362.40	4 years
Mount Clemens (Mich.) Macomb Daily	358.00	4 years
Cincinnati (Ohio) Enquirer	348.00	5 years
Providence (R.I.) Journal Bulletin	346.00	4 years
Gary (Ind.) Post Tribune	345.08	4 years
Akron (Ohio) Beacon Journal (AFL-CIO)	345.00	4 years
Pittsburgh (Penn.) Post Gazette	345.00	4 years
Madison (Wisc.) Wisconsin State Journal	344.00	4 years
Madison (Wisc.) Capital Times	343.79	4 years
Denver (Colo.) Post	341.00	5 years
Baltimore (Md.) News American	336.00	5 years
Wilkes-Barre (Penn.) Times Leader	331.75	4 years
Memphis (Tenn.) Commercial Appeal and Press Scimitar	330.25	5 years
Pawtucket (R.I.) Times	325.25	4 years
Boston (Mass.) Globe	321.50	4 years
Columbus (Ohio) Citizen-Journal	321.00	5 years
Kenosha (Wisc.) News	320.00	5 years
Waukegan (Ill.) News-Sun	318.00	5 years
Harrisburg (Penn.) Patriot News	317.00	4 years
Scranton (Penn.) Times	315.26	3 years

In its annual surveys, the BLS requests copies of the actual union contracts in order to compare them with the questionnaire responses. Bureau representatives also make personal visits to unions which have not responded to the mail questionnaires. The survey of unions in 1974 included a sample of 104,000 workers in 70 cities.

Table 420-D is reprinted from *Editor and Publisher*, which obtained the information from the National Newspaper Guild. Of course, this listing is only a small fraction of the total number of daily newspapers in the country, but the editors were unable to procure data which would compare these newspaper pay scales to the union salaries paid at the papers not included in the table.

Table 420–D. (Cont'd.)

Newspaper	Reporters' Top Minimum Salary[a]	Tenure Required for Top Minimum Salary
Scranton (Penn.) Tribune and Scrantonian	$315.22	3 years
Monterey (Calif.) Peninsula Herald	315.00	5 years
Dayton (Ohio) Daily News	314.50	4 years
Youngstown (Ohio) Vindicator	313.50	5 years
Toledo (Ohio) Blade	313.23	4 years
Indianapolis (Ind.) Star	311.95	6 years
Hammond (Ind.) Times	310.25	4 years
Toronto (Ont.) Globe and Mail	308.00	5 years
Pottstown (Penn.) Daily News	303.86	5 years
Lansing (Mich.) State Journal	302.00	4 years
Ottawa (Ont.) Citizen	301.12	4 years
Winnipeg (Man.) Tribune	301.00	4 years
Sheboygan (Wisc.) Press	300.65	3 years
Rockford (Ill.) Star and Register Republic	300.50	5 years
Santa Barbara (Calif.) News and Press	300.00	6 years
Bay City (Mich.) Times	299.70	4 years
Kingston (N.Y.) Freeman	296.85	4 years
Peoria (Ill.) Journal Star	296.00	4 years
Malden and Medford (Mass.) News and Mercury	295.75	4 years
Erie (Penn.) Times and News	290.00	5 years
Lynn (Mass.) Item and Telegram	289.50	4 years
Joliet (Ill.) Herald News	289.00	3 years
Eugene (Oregon) Register Guard[b]	288.75	4 years
Jersey City (N.J.) Journal	288.30	3 years
Norfolk (Va.) Virginian Pilot	285.00	4 years
Brantford (Ont.) Expositor	283.10	4 years
Battle Creek (Mich.) Inquirer and News	282.00	4 years
Portland (Maine) Press Herald, Express and Telegram	281.00	4 years
Elgin (Ill.) Courier News (ITU)	276.50	4 years
Chicago (Ill.) Lerner Newspapers	275.61	flat
San Juan (Puerto Rico) El Mundo	274.00	5 years
Chattanooga (Tenn.) Times	273.52	4 years
Woonsocket (R.I.) Call	272.00	5 years
Yakima (Wash.) Herald and Republic	271.50	4 years
Richmond (Va.) Times Dispatch and News Leader	270.00	4 years
Waterbury (Conn.) American Republican	268.72	4 years
Pomona (Calif.) Progress-Bulletin	266.60	6 years
Canton (Ohio) Repository	260.00	4 years
Pueblo (Colo.) Star, Journal and Chieftain	259.00	5 years
Hilo (Hawaii) Tribune Herald	257.63	4 years
Springfield (Ohio) News and Sun (Unaf.)	255.75	5 years
San Antonio (Texas) Light	252.01	5 years
Ventura (Calif.) Free Press (Unaf.)	252.00	5 years
Watertown (N.Y.) Daily Times	252.00	6 years
Lowell (Mass.) Sun	251.20	4 years
Terre Haute (Ind.) Tribune-Star	239.00	5 years
Albany (N.Y.) Knickerbocker News	235.50	3 years
Newport News (R.I.) Daily Press and Times Herald (Unaf.)	235.00	6 years
Hazelton (Penn.) Standard Speaker	234.71	5 years
Stratford (Ont.) Beacon Journal (ITU)	228.75	5 years
Massillon (Ohio) Independent	224.00	5 years
Morgantown (W. Va.) Dominion Post	216.83	3 years
Superior (Wisc.) Evening Telegram (ITU)	200.00	5 years

Source: *1977 Editor and Publisher International Year Book*, p. V-32.

Notes: (a) These pay rates were established mainly through American Newspaper Guild contracts as of December 1, 1976. Other union contracts—the AFL-CIO and the ITU (International Telecommunications Union)—are indicated in parentheses, as are the unaffiliated (Unaf.) newspapers. (b) Wage contract includes a cost-of-living adjustment.

The Bureau of Labor Statistics compiles data on average hourly earnings in its monthly publication, *Employment and Earnings*. Annual averages appear in the March issue of this publication. The Bureau's annual survey of union wage rates includes data on stipulated union hours, as well as an index of year-to-year wage trends.

Commentaries on these BLS reports can be found in Lofquist (1972) and Cook (1976). The best description of the methodology involved in the BLS survey is the *BLS Handbook of Methods for Surveys and Studies* (1976b).

The summary of Newspaper Guild rates has recently been appearing annually in the *Editor and Publisher International Yearbook*.

Employment in the Magazine Industry

430

Interpretation of Tables

Table 430-A reviews total employment and payroll figures for the periodicals industry from 1939 to 1975. Generally, employment has followed the industry's sales pattern, with a peak during the boom years of the late-1960s. The average payroll for this industry has tended to grow more slowly than the payroll for all U.S. manufacturing industries over the past 30 years.

The relatively small number of periodical production workers—compared, for example, with newspaper employment (see Unit 420)—is due to the fact that most periodical publishers do not do their own printing, but instead contract with printers not classified in the same industry category. In addition, recent declines in the number of periodical production workers, compared to all periodicals industry employees, have been ascribed to the technological advances within the industry (Hokkanen, 1971).

Table 430-B presents data on the average weekly earnings, hours, and overtime hours of production workers in the periodicals industry, compared with production workers in all manufacturing industries. Here the situation is quite similar to that for newspaper production workers. Although weekly wages have remained higher than the overall U.S. manufacturing average, the gap is narrowing. The length of the work week in the periodicals industry tends to fluctuate according to the industry's economic fortunes, and lately the work week has been growing shorter.

Sources

The information in **Table 430-A** comes from the U.S. Census Bureau's *Census of Manufactures* and *Annual Survey of Manufactures*. The reader should refer to Unit 420 for comments on the validity of this information, since it was collected in the same way as that found in **Table 420-A**. Census Bureau data are generally regarded as valid and reliable—within the specific definitions given. The reader should note, however, that figures for the *Annual Survey* years (on this table, all years except 1939, 1947, 1954, 1958, 1963, 1967, and 1972) are based on a representative sample rather than a complete census of the entire industry. Consequently, these data are subject to a certain margin of error, usually less than 10 percent.

Table 430-B was constructed from monthly surveys of employment, earnings, and hours by state employment departments under the direction of the Bureau of Labor Statistics (BLS) of the U.S. Department of Labor. The reader should see the "Sources" discussion in Unit 400, as well as the comments on **Table 420-B**, which offers parallel information for the newspaper industry.

Further Information

Hokkanen (1971) has analyzed general trends in the periodicals industry, including employment, from 1947 to 1967. Although the industry's fortunes have declined from the aggregate peak achieved in the late-1960s, most of Hokkanen's analysis is still pertinent.

Each month, the Bureau of Labor Statistics publishes figures on total employment, the employment of women, employment of production workers, and production workers' earnings (both weekly and hourly), hours, and overtime hours in *Employment and Earnings*. Overall averages for each year are published by the BLS during March of the following year.

The reader is referred to Units 400 and 420 for additional sources.

Table 430–A.
Total Employment and Payroll of Production Workers and of All Employees in the U. S. Periodicals Industry, 1939–1974

	Employment					Payroll				
	Periodicals Industry			All Manufacturing		Periodicals Industry			All Manufacturing	
	Production Workers	All Employees	Index: All Employees	Employees	Index	Production Workers	All Employees	Index: All Employees	Employees	Index
1939	15.4	N/A	N/A	9,527.3	53	$ 25.0	N/A	N/A	$ 12,706.1	8
1947	19.5	69.0	104	14,294.0	79	64.5	$235.7	33	39,695.6	25
1949	21.4	73.9	111	13,566.9	75	75.1	288.8	41	41,482.0	26
1950	22.4	71.7	108	14,467.1	80	82.1	305.6	43	46,642.8	29
1951	16.3	59.4	89	15,309.6	85	63.2	275.1	39	54,741.5	34
1952	--	--	--	15,732.7	87	--	--	--	59,598.2	37
1953	13.4	58.3	88	16,693.1	93	60.9	290.0	41	66,492.9	41
1954	16.3	62.4	94	15,645.5	87	68.2	312.7	44	62,962.9	39
1955	16.3	65.1	98	16,335.5	91	70.3	336.9	47	69,096.6	43
1956	16.5	65.5	98	16,694.4	93	72.1	343.5	48	74,015.1	46
1957	14.6	63.7	96	16,621.1	92	62.6	345.4	49	73,614.6	46
1958	11.7	66.7	100	15,423.1	86	56.8	386.7	54	73,875.2	46
1959	12.4	67.4	101	16,062.9	89	62.0	419.3	59	81,203.6	51
1960	12.2	67.7	102	16,149.9	90	63.3	447.6	63	83,672.5	52
1961	11.8	68.2	102	15,729.6	87	62.7	467.2	66	83,677.4	52
1962	12.1	69.6	105	16,154.7	90	64.8	485.9	68	89,819.2	56
1963	12.3	67.7	102	16,231.9	90	65.6	461.1	65	93,283.3	58
1964	12.2	67.3	101	16,485.7	91	65.7	487.5	69	98,685.3	62
1965	14.0	70.0	105	17,250.5	96	79.1	510.0	72	106,643.2	66
1966	14.0	71.6	108	18,200.3	101	78.3	547.9	77	117,157.4	73
1967	14.5	74.1	111	18,492.0	103	80.5	633.7	89	123,480.6	77
1968	16.9	83.5	125	18,681.0	104	94.9	692.7	98	132,568.4	83
1969	16.0	85.1	128	19,155.6	106	105.6	727.7	103	142,645.1	89

Table 430–A. (Cont'd.)

	Employment					Payroll				
	Periodicals Industry			All Manufacturing		Periodicals Industry			All Manufacturing	
	Production Workers	All Employees	Index: All Employees	Employees	Index	Production Workers	All Employees	Index: All Employees	Employees	Index
1970	14.8	77.1	116	18,289.5	101	$112.6	$699.5	99	$141,886.4	88
1971	13.6	71.5	107	17,426.3	97	101.7	684.8	96	144,246.3	90
1972	11.2	66.6	100	18,034.4	100	84.6	709.7	100	160,433.2	100
1973	12.6	70.1	105	18,870.4	105	95.9	760.4	107	178,317.2	111
1974	13.0	71.7	108	18,712.8	104	104.3	808.2	114	190,574.3	119
1975	13.9	72.9	109	17,216.3	95	118.9	876.9	124	190,943.4	119

Sources: Periodicals industry data: 1939-1951, 1953-1963: *1963 Census of Manufactures*; 1964-1972: *1972 Census of Manufactures*; 1952, 1973, 1974: *Annual Survey of Manufactures* (1952, 1974). Manufacturing industry data: 1939-1972: *1972 Census of Manufactures*; 1973: *Annual Survey of Manufactures, 1974*. 1974-1975: *Annual Survey of Manufactures, 1975*.

Table 430–B.
Average Weekly Earnings, Hours, and Overtime Hours of Production Workers in the U. S. Periodicals Industry and in All Manufacturing Industries, 1947–1975

	Weekly Earnings in Periodicals Industry	Index: Periodicals Industry Earnings	Weekly Earnings in All Manufacturing	Index: All Manufacturing Earnings	Weekly Hours in Periodicals Industry	Weekly Hours in All Manufacturing	Weekly Overtime Hours in Periodicals Industry	Weekly Overtime Hours in All Manufacturing
1947	$ 63.71	34	$ 49.17	32	42.9	40.4	N/A	N/A
1948	65.85	35	53.12	34	40.5	40.0	N/A	N/A
1949	66.46	35	53.88	35	38.8	39.1	N/A	N/A
1950	70.21	37	58.32	38	39.4	40.5	N/A	N/A
1951	75.03	40	63.34	41	39.7	40.6	N/A	N/A
1952	79.00	42	67.16	43	39.9	40.7	N/A	N/A
1953	82.39	43	70.47	46	39.8	40.5	N/A	N/A
1954	83.74	44	70.49	46	39.5	39.6	N/A	N/A
1955	87.96	46	75.70	49	39.8	40.7	N/A	N/A
1956	91.37	48	78.71	51	39.9	40.4	N/A	2.8
1957	95.36	50	81.59	53	39.9	37.8	N/A	2.3
1958	97.50	51	82.71	53	39.0	39.2	2.6	2.0
1959	105.60	56	88.26	57	39.7	40.3	3.4	2.7
1960	109.18	58	89.72	58	39.7	39.7	3.5	2.4
1961	109.81	58	92.34	60	39.5	39.8	3.1	2.4
1962	111.67	59	96.56	62	39.6	40.4	3.1	2.8
1963	115.02	61	99.63	64	39.8	40.5	3.2	2.8
1964	122.01	64	102.97	67	40.4	40.7	4.0	3.1
1965	126.23	67	107.53	70	40.2	41.2	3.8	3.6
1966	130.65	69	112.34	73	40.2	41.3	4.2	3.9
1967	134.98	71	114.90	74	39.7	40.6	3.9	3.4
1968	151.20	80	122.51	79	41.2	40.7	4.1	3.6
1969	160.68	85	129.51	84	41.2	40.6	4.9	3.6

Table 430–B. (Cont'd.)

	Weekly Earnings in Periodicals Industry	Index: Periodicals Industry Earnings	Weekly Earnings in All Manufacturing	Index: All Manufacturing Earnings	Weekly Hours in Periodicals Industry	Weekly Hours in All Manufacturing	Weekly Overtime Hours in Periodicals Industry	Weekly Overtime Hours in All Manufacturing
1970	$169.29	89	$133.73	86	40.5	39.8	4.1	3.0
1971	177.68	94	142.44	92	40.2	39.9	3.8	2.9
1972	189.81	100	154.69	100	40.3	40.6	4.0	3.5
1973	203.41	107	166.06	107	40.2	40.7	4.0	3.8
1974	205.14	108	176.40	114	39.0	40.0	3.0	3.2
1975	206.05	109	189.51	123	38.3	39.4	2.4	2.6
1976	220.20	116	207.60	134	37.9	40.0	2.3	3.1

Sources: 1947-1973 data: Bureau of Labor Statistics, *Employment and Earnings, United States, 1909-1975.* 1974-1976 data: Bureau of Labor Statistics, *Employment and Earnings* (March 1977).

Table 440–A.
Number of Full-Time Employees, Total Annual Employee Earnings, and Average Annual Earnings per Employee in the U. S. Motion Picture Industry, 1929–1975

	Number of Employees (thousands)	Total Wages and Salaries (millions)	Average Annual Earnings per Employee	
			Current Dollars	Constant (1972) Dollars
1929	142	$ 308	$ 2,169	$5,303
1930	143	311	2,175	5,397
1931	140	305	2,179	5,986
1932	122	239	1,959	6,009
1933	119	225	1,891	6,100
1934	135	249	1,844	5,763
1935	148	280	1,892	5,768
1936	164	311	1,896	5,728
1937	177	349	1,972	5,749
1938	171	332	1,942	5,763
1939	172	339	1,971	5,937
1940	174	339	1,948	5,815
1941	184	371	2,016	5,727
1942	193	410	2,124	5,460
1943	204	459	2,250	5,448
1944	214	509	2,379	5,651
1945	215	552	2,567	5,970
1946	228	679	2,978	6,377
1947	229	694	3,031	5,676
1948	225	655	2,911	5,063
1949	225	660	2,933	5,146
1950	224	658	2,938	5,110
1951	223	680	3,049	4,910
1952	218	697	3,197	5,043
1953	211	689	3,265	5,110
1954	208	723	3,476	5,414
1955	206	774	3,757	5,870
1956	202	788	3,901	6,002
1957	192	782	4,073	6,052
1958	176	745	4,233	6,126
1959	172	775	4,506	6,465
1960	166	772	4,651	6,569
1961	164	815	4,970	6,951
1962	157	791	5,038	6,968
1963	155	806	5,200	7,104
1964	156	864	5,538	7,474
1965	160	967	6,044	8,124
1966	166	1,040	6,265	8,073
1967	171	1,100	6,433	8,061
1968	172	1,172	6,814	8,190
1969	180	1,278	7,100	8,105
1970	178	1,274	7,157	7,712
1971	177	1,277	7,215	7,454
1972	150	1,343	8,954	8,954
1973	154	1,429	9,279	8,737
1974	154	1,575	10,227	8,674
1975	154	1,674	10,870	8,446

Source: Bureau of Economic Analysis, U. S. Department of Commerce.

Table 440–B.
Number of All Employees and of Female Employees Only
in the Production/Distribution and the Theaters/Services Segments
of the U. S. Motion Picture Industry, 1958–1974

	Total Number of Industry Employees	Production/Distribution Employees		Theaters/Services Employees	
		All Employees	Female Employees	All Employees	Female Employees
1958	199,100	43,600	N/A	155,500	N/A
1959	195,100	44,900	N/A	150,200	N/A
1960	189,600	44,100	14,500	145,600	51,800
1961	186,500	46,800	14,400	139,700	49,700
1962	178,300	41,500	12,300	136,900	48,400
1963	176,500	41,100	11,900	135,500	48,000
1964	177,400	42,800	11,600	134,700	47,200
1965	185,100	48,500	12,300	136,600	46,800
1966	187,500	49,700	13,300	137,900	47,500
1967	194,300	53,300	14,700	141,000	49,800
1968	196,000	54,700	15,500	141,300	50,900
1969	206,700	61,000	17,800	145,700	51,700
1970	207,900	58,200	18,100	145,700	53,200
1971	200,500	54,800	18,500	145,700	54,900
1972	203,700	60,200	20,300	143,500	55,100
1973	209,100	63,900	22,700	145,200	56,300
1974	206,800	65,000	23,800	141,800	53,500

Source: Bureau of Labor Statistics (1976).

Note: Figures may not add due to rounding.

Interpretation of Tables

Table 440-A presents an overview of nearly 50 years of full-time equivalent (FTE) employment in all segments of the U.S. motion picture industry—production, distribution, and exhibition. Included in this table are total wage and salary figures, as well as average annual earnings per employee, for the years 1929 through 1975.

Table 440-B offers data on the number of female employees in the two major sectors of the motion picture industry—production and distribution, and exhibition and services. The total employment figures given here represent the average number of full- and part-time employees in the industry and are the base from which the FTE figures in Table 440-A were constructed. The reader will note that most employees in the motion picture industry—whether male or female—are in exhibition and services.

Table 440-C provides information on Hollywood union membership and employment in the film industry during November of 1972. This table shows a high degree of unemployment among these unions, even though November is normally a busy month for the industry personnel engaged in television production. (Typically, the unemployment rate is higher in the Spring, between television production cycles.)

Table 440-D lists the changing minimum daily, hourly, or weekly wage rates of union actors, writers, and one category of film technicians in Hollywood. Although this table does not show the proportion of these individuals employed in television series or in films for television (see Unit 460), such work is the prime reason for the slight upswing in Hollywood employment and wages since the mid-1960s.

Table 440-E is a summary listing of the average weekly wage rates of all production and distribution employees in the motion picture industry. As in the previous table, the reader will note the more rapid growth of wage rates after the mid-1960s, when television began to make greater use of film industry employees.

Table 440–C.

Number of Active and of Employed Hollywood Union Members, and Percentage of Unemployed Members, in the U. S. Motion Picture Industry–by Occupation, 1972

Occupation	Active Union Members in Hollywood	Employed Union Members	Percent Unemployed Members
Electricians (IBEW)[a]	358	297	17%
Electricians (MPEU)[b]	721	353	51
Makeup Artists	339	231	32
Property Workers	1,884	1,451	23
Grips	700[c]	210	30
Projectionists	240	216	10
Studio Teamsters	1,087	663	39
Costumers	822	739	10
Craft Workers	202	182	10
Ornamental Plasterers	200	60	70
Script Supervisors	106	73	31
Actors	13,000	1,950	85
Extras	2,645	661	75
Film Editors	1,739	1,617	7
Writers	3,000	N/A	N/A
Composers	412	N/A	N/A
Musicians	16,000	N/A	N/A
Cameramen	950	760	20
Sound Technicians	901	811	10
Directors	1,101	N/A	N/A
Art Directors	138	98	29
Set Directors	130[c]	N/A	N/A
Totals	46,675	10,372	- -

Sources: Office of Telecommunications Policy (1973), table 33, citing material from the Screen Actors Guild.

Notes: (a) International Brotherhood of Electrical Workers. (b) Motion Picture Electricians Union. (c) These figures are estimates.

Sources

Table 440-A was taken from mimeographed material provided by the Bureau of Economic Analysis (BEA) of the U.S. Department of Commerce. Tables 440-B and 440-E data were supplied by the U.S. Bureau of Labor Statistics (BLS) (1976).

Tables 440-C and 440-D were drawn from a report of the White House Office of Telecommunications Policy (OTP) (1973). The Table 440-C data came originally from the Screen Actors Guild (SAG), while the figures for Table 440-D came from both SAG and the Writers Guild. In each case, this information was reported by the unions to the OTP in an attempt to obtain aid for the unemployed among the Hollywood film industry unions. The single 1928 figure in Table 440-D was taken from Land (1968). The editors obtained the 1977 data and some revisions of earlier figures from the unions.

Further Information

The U.S. Equal Employment Opportunity Commission (EEOC) is beginning to report selected information on minority employment in the motion picture industry. However, that information has not been included here because it represents such a small percentage of total industry employment (see Unit 402). See Unit 460 for a comparison of film union earnings from television production and theatrical films.

Table 440–D.
Average Weekly Wate Rates of Hollywood Actors, Propmakers,
and Writers in the U.S. Motion Picture Industry, 1928–1977

	Daily Minimum Wage for Actors	Weekly Minimum Wage for Actors	Hourly Wage for Journeyman Propmakers	Weekly Minimum Wage for Writers
1928	N/A	N/A	$1.00	N/A
1935	$ 15	$ 65	1.28	N/A
1937	25	65	1.41	N/A
1941	25	100	1.71	N/A
1945	35	115	1.80	$125
1947	55	175	2.50	N/A
1952	70	250	2.75	250
1956	80	285	3.14	350
1960	100	350	3.37	385
1967	112	392	4.35	450
1971	138	483	5.11	525
1977	225	785	7.89	821

Sources: 1928 figure: Land (1968), p. 107; other years: Office of Telecommunications Policy (1973), table 21, citing material from the Screen Actors Guild (first three columns) and the Writers Guild.

Table 440–E.
Average Weekly Wage Rate of Production/Distribution Employees
in the U. S. Motion Picture Industry, 1951–1974

	Current Dollars	Constant (1972) Dollars
1951	$ 76.14	$122.60
1952	81.09	127.90
1953	80.99	126.74
1954	88.41	137.71
1955	93.17	145.58
1956	91.06	140.09
1957	98.83	146.85
1958	100.53	145.48
1959	112.05	160.76
1960	115.02	162.46
1961	120.50	168.53
1962	123.50	170.81
1963	131.55	179.71
1964	136.17	183.77
1965	148.08	199.03
1966	152.97	197.13
1967	155.93	195.40
1968	159.19	191.33
1969	178.04	203.24
1970	183.68	197.93
1971	187.62	193.82
1972	204.33	204.33
1973	220.42	207.55
1974	247.83	210.20

Source: Bureau of Labor Statistics (1976).

Table 450–A.
Number of Record Manufacturing, Music Store, and Record Store Employees in U. S., 1947–1975

	Manufacturing Employees	Music Store Employees	Record Store Employees
1947	10,045	19,360[a]	N/A
1950	6,600	N/A	N/A
1951	5,900	N/A	N/A
1952	5,500	N/A	N/A
1953	6,600	N/A	N/A
1954	6,200	17,535	N/A
1955	6,000	N/A	N/A
1956	6,400	N/A	N/A
1957	7,100	N/A	N/A
1958	7,400	24,241	5,539
1959	7,600	N/A	N/A
1960	8,200	N/A	N/A
1961	8,400	N/A	N/A
1962	9,200	N/A	N/A
1963	9,600	24,251	4,638
1964	9,900	N/A	N/A
1965	10,100	N/A	N/A
1966	11,000	N/A	N/A
1967	13,600	28,712	6,010
1968	14,500	N/A	N/A
1969	17,500	N/A	N/A
1970	18,700	N/A	N/A
1971	18,700	N/A	N/A
1972	20,300	37,363	10,752
1973	20,100	N/A	N/A
1974	19,700	N/A	N/A
1975	17,800	N/A	N/A

Sources: Record store employment: *Census of Retail Trade*, appropriate years. All other data: *Census of Manufactures* and *Annual Survey of Manufactures*, appropriate years.

Notes: All figures are approximate, and the store employment figures include only those music and record stores with payrolls. (a) This figure is for 1948.

Interpretation of Table

Information on employment in the U.S. recording industry is sparse. However, **Table 450-A** does present one dramatic industry employment trend which occurred during the mid-1960s and early 1970s, when the number of employees engaged in the manufacture of recorded discs and tapes rose from 9,900 in 1964 to 20,300 by 1972.

Several developments were responsible for the increased demand for prerecorded products and the corresponding increase in the number of industry employees: (1) the advent of stereo records in 1958 and the growing popular interest in high fidelity sound; (2) the availability of the new tape formats in the mid-1960s (see Unit 150); and (3) the revolution in popular music in the mid-1960s (the Beatles, Rolling Stones, Bob Dylan, etc.), which significantly enhanced and broadened the market for recordings. Unfortunately, comparable data on the number of persons employed in phonograph and tape equipment manufacture are not available separately. Instead, this information is aggregated with radio and television data in Unit 460.

As **Table 450-A** indicates, industry growth has also affected the number of persons employed in the distribution of recordings through music stores and record shops. The few figures presented here show steady increases in employment, although the reader should bear in mind that employment statistics available for music stores naturally include personnel who have nothing at all to do with recordings. Consequently, the best that can be gained from these particular figures is an "estimated impression."

Sources

Most of the figures for **Table 450-A** were taken from the U.S. Census Bureau's *Census of Manufactures* and the *Annual Survey of Manufactures*. Record store employment figures were gathered from the Census Bureau's *Census of Retail Trade* and are subject to several limitations. First, the *Census of Retail Trade* provides data for census years only and does not offer annually updated publications. Also, record shop employment was not separately reported prior to 1958. Finally, statistics collected from record shop proprietors could not be included in the record shop totals in **Table 450-A**, because this information was irregularly provided by the Census Bureau. For the years when such statistics are available, the overall data suggest that record shop employment is actually about one-third higher than shown on **Table 450-A**.

Further Information

Denisoff (1975) and Chapple and Garafalo (1977) provide useful background information and statistics on the recording industry. Both *Variety* and *Billboard* present current reports and analyses of the industry; and *Billboard's* annual *Directory and Buyer's Guide*, published in August or September, includes a series of summary statistics for the year. The *Census of Retail Trade* and *Census of Selected Service Industries* provide data on employment in the manufacture of phonographs, tape recorders and players, and other home music/entertainment equipment.

Employment in the Broadcasting Industry

460

Interpretation of Tables

Tables **460-A** through **460-E** provide most of what is known of national employment patterns in the broadcasting industry, and in broadcast-related manufacturing and retail and service industries. **Table 460-A** presents a count of employed personnel in radio and television stations and networks in the United States. Even though television networks and stations are far larger financial operations than their radio counterparts, there are many more radio stations in this country (see Units 170 and 180) and, therefore, far greater numbers of radio employees.

The reader will note the relatively slow growth of total broadcasting employment until the post-World War II years, when the burgeoning numbers of radio and television stations doubled industry employment by 1954. At that point, the industry's growth rate slowed down to evolutionary rather than revolutionary expansion, and it was 20 more years before the total doubled again. The reader should also note that the television network employment figures in **Table 460-A** do not include film industry personnel working on television series in Hollywood (see Unit 440 and **Table 460-C**). In addition, the total television-employment data for the 1970s include public television station employees, who represent about 15 percent of the totals.

Table 460-B provides average weekly salary figures for nonsupervisory personnel in the broadcasting industry, while **Table 460-C** lists the number of members and total annual member earnings for the major unions involved in network television production. In **Table 460-C**, the American Federation of Television and Radio Artists (AFTRA) includes most on-air personnel of the networks and large radio and TV stations. The sharp increases in AFTRA membership in 1969 and 1976 are not explained. The growth in those years may simply reflect differing methods or dates in counting membership.

The Screen Actor's Guild (SAG) is comprised of actors and actresses working in theatrical films, television films and series, and radio and television commercials. While detailed data are unavailable for the earlier years, the figures for 1965 through 1976 reveal that member earnings

Table 460–A.
Number of Radio and Television Network and Station Employees, 1930–1976

	Radio				Television			Total Number of Broadcast Employees
	Networks	AM/AM-FM Stations	FM Stations Only	Total Radio Employees	Networks	All Stations	Total Television Employees	
1930	N/A	N/A	--	6,000	--	--	--	6,000
1935	N/A	N/A	--	14,600	--	--	--	14,600
1938	N/A	N/A	--	22,500	--	--	--	22,500
1939	N/A	N/A	--	23,900	--	--	--	23,900
1940	N/A	N/A	--	25,700	--	--	--	25,700
1941	N/A	N/A	N/A	27,600	--	--	(a)	27,600
1942	N/A	N/A	N/A	29,600	--	--	(a)	29,600
1943	N/A	N/A	N/A	31,800	--	--	(a)	31,800
1944	N/A	N/A	N/A	34,300	--	--	(a)	34,300
1945	N/A	N/A	N/A	37,800	--	--	(a)	37,800
1946	N/A	N/A	N/A	40,000	--	--	(a)	40,000
1947	N/A	N/A	N/A	N/A	--	--	(a)	N/A
1948	N/A	N/A	N/A	48,300	--	--	(a)	48,300
1949	N/A	N/A	N/A	52,000	N/A	N/A	3,800	55,800
1950	N/A	N/A	N/A	N/A	N/A	N/A	9,000	N/A
1951	N/A	N/A	N/A	N/A	N/A	N/A	N/A	N/A
1952	N/A	N/A	N/A	51,000	N/A	N/A	14,000	65,000
1953	N/A	N/A	N/A	51,800	N/A	N/A	18,200	70,000
1954	N/A	N/A	N/A	42,600	N/A	N/A	29,400	72,000
1955	N/A	N/A	N/A	45,300	N/A	N/A	32,300	77,600
1956	N/A	N/A	N/A	47,600	N/A	N/A	35,700	83,300
1957	N/A	N/A	N/A	48,900	N/A	N/A	37,800	86,700
1958	N/A	N/A	N/A	48,900	N/A	N/A	39,400	88,200
1959	N/A	N/A	N/A	50,400	N/A	N/A	40,300	90,700
1960	1,200	50,500	1,300	53,000	9,600	31,000	40,600	93,600
1961	1,000	51,500	1,700	54,200	8,800	31,300	40,100	95,300
1962	1,100	53,000	2,000	56,100	9,100	32,800	41,900	98,000
1963	1,100	54,500	2,300	57,900	9,700	34,000	43,700	101,600
1964	1,200	56,600	2,400	60,200	10,700	35,000	45,700	105,900

from television commercial work outpaced both film and television series income. Here again, some figures cannot be readily explained. The near-doubling of television production income in 1971-1972, for example, is more likely due to differing ways of counting income than to an actual income increase of that magnitude. On the other hand, it is clear that television series production income among SAG members has increased rapidly in the inflationary 1970s, while theatrical film income has remained constant or, taking inflation into account, has dropped considerably.

Table 460-A. (Cont'd.)

	Radio				Television			Total Number of Broadcast Employees
	Networks	AM/AM-FM Stations	FM Stations Only	Total Radio Employees	Networks	All Stations	Total Television Employees	
1965	1,200	58,300	2,700	60,200	11,000	36,700	47,700	109,900
1966	1,100	60,500	3,200	64,800	11,200	39,100	50,300	115,100
1967	1,100	62,400	3,700	67,200	11,500	40,200	51,700	118,900
1968	1,100	65,600	4,000	70,700	12,200	43,100	55,300	126,000
1969	1,100	63,500	5,400	70,000	12,900	44,900	57,800	127,800
1970	1,100	63,800	6,100	71,000	13,200	45,200	58,400	129,400
1971	900	65,000	7,500	73,400	12,000	46,100	58,100	131,500
1972	900	66,600	8,700	76,200	12,400	46,900	59,300	135,500
1973	900	66,500	10,100	77,500	12,400	47,800	60,200	137,700
1974	900	67,900	11,300	80,100	13,200	48,800	61,900	142,000
1975	1,000	67,900	12,900	81,800	13,300	49,000	62,300	144,100
1976	900	70,800	14,600	86,300	13,800	51,000	64,800	151,100

Sources: 1930 figure: U. S. Department of Commerce estimate; 1935-1965 data: FCC, as printed in annual mimeographed financial reports for the radio and television industries; 1965-1975 data: FCC, as reprinted in the FCC's *Annual Report*; 1976 radio figures: FCC, as reprinted in *Broadcasting* (December 12, 1977), p. 45, table 6; 1976 television figures: *Broadcasting* (August 29, 1977), p. 37.

Note: (a) Television data for 1941-48 are included in the radio totals.

The figures from the Writer's Guild of America West are difficult to assess, since each year's total represents a combination of all television, film, and commercials income. If these figures were broken down into income sources, the greatest percentage would undoubtedly be for television production work. The Hollywood craft unions represent the aggregate earnings of several unions, and the method of data gathering is not known.

Table 460-D traces the gradual change in the employment of minorities and women by both commercial and noncommercial television stations. The reader will note that the "best" employ-

Table 460–B.
Average Weekly Salary of Non-Supervisory Employees
in the U. S. Broadcasting Industry, 1940–1974

| | Average Weekly Salary | |
	Current Dollars	Constant (1972) Dollars
1940	$ 43.51	$129.88
1941	45.15	128.27
1942	49.79	127.99
1943	52.26	126.54
1944	57.18	135.82
1945	60.05	139.65
1946	65.40	140.04
1947	69.14	129.48
1948	71.77	124.82
1949	77.41	135.81
1958	100.70	145.73
1959	104.88	150.47
1960	110.40	155.93
1961	109.06	152.53
1962	113.84	157.45
1963	118.84	161.99
1964	122.29	165.03
1965	125.84	169.14
1966	126.49	163.00
1967	130.72	163.81
1968	135.74	163.15
1969	142.11	162.23
1970	147.45	158.89
1971	159.22	164.48
1972	173.44	173.44
1973	184.39	173.63
1974	203.84	172.89

Sources: 1940-1941 data: *Broadcasting* (May 11, 1942); 1942-1949 data: UNESCO (1950), p. 487; 1958-1974 data: U. S. Department of Labor (1976).

ment record is for women at public television stations. It is also worth noting that much of the employment of women and minorities in all categories is part-time work. Not shown here is a breakdown of job levels for these groups (see "Sources" section below).

Table 460-E provides limited information on employment levels in selected broadcast-related industries—three categories of manufacturing firms and two retail and service categories. Clearly, these data do not present a complete picture of broadcast-related employment, since they do not include advertising, public relations, or miscellaneous other manufacturing and retail or service industries. This table is simply an indication of the size of the broadcasting industry's "support" groups.

The manufacturing figures in Table 460-E provide stark evidence of the increasing importation of broadcast equipment into the United States (see Units 750 and 760), and the resultant decrease of employment opportunities within the American economy. The steady declines in the electronic receiving-tubes industry are evidence of technological changes in the industry. Transistors and solid-state devices are increasingly used in place of tubes for most radio and television receivers. The retail radio-television store data in Table 460-E are incomplete, in that today's buyers can find this equipment in many other kinds of stores—for example, most department stores and general discount stores. The repair-shop employment figures suggest the growing complexity of servicing color television and transistor products.

Table 460–C.
AFTRA, SAG, Writers Guild West, and the Hollywood Craft Unions: Number of Members and/or Total Member Earnings from U. S. Network Television, 1961–1976

Note: All dollar figures are in millions.

| | AFTRA[a] | | Screen Actors Guild (SAG) | | | | | | Writers Guild of America West Total Member Earnings[b] | Hollywood Craft Unions Total Member Earnings[b] |
| | Number of Members | Total Member Earnings | Member Earnings from: | | | | Total Member Earnings | Number of Members | | |
			Television Production	Television Residuals	Television Commercials	Theatrical Films				
1961	--	$ 36.0	--	--	--	--	--	--	$26.0	--
1962	15,506	37.9	$21.6	$ 6.4	--	--	$ 73.7	14,365	27.0	$127.0
1963	16,351	41.4	19.7	7.7	--	--	76.9	14,650	27.0	135.0
1964	16,780	41.9	23.2	7.7	--	--	83.9	15,290	32.0	141.0
1965	17,073	47.9	26.6	7.3	$ 38.6	$25.7	97.8	16,117	32.0	175.0
1966	17,565	48.4	32.2	8.3	40.6	23.7	104.7	16,791	34.0	185.0
1967	18,184	50.3	24.8	11.1	46.3	26.6	108.9	18,471	37.0	186.0
1968	18,897	57.2	23.9	12.1	51.6	25.0	112.8	21,571	42.0	185.0
1969	21,076	62.4	25.4	10.5	57.1	27.6	121.2	21,600	45.0	203.0
1970	21,756	72.0	23.4	11.0	61.4	17.9	114.3	22,446	39.0	169.0
1971	22,752	69.3	20.5	13.5	59.2	20.6	114.4	24,996	37.0	163.0
1972	23,750	75.0	38.6	13.1	62.3	22.2	136.2	26,610	39.2	N/A
1973	24,576	75.0	37.4	11.0	73.5	25.3	147.2	27,904	42.6	N/A
1974	26,250	90.0	47.9	12.8	78.7	24.8	164.3	29,797	56.1	N/A
1975	26,973	93.0	53.0	18.9	86.3	24.4	182.8	31,522	72.6	N/A
1976	29,672	118.0	63.6	--	110.7[c]	33.7	208.0	32,434	76.0	N/A

Sources: 1961-1971 data: Office of Telecommunications Policy (1973) tables 16, 17, 22, 36. 1972-1976 data were obtained directly from the unions by the editors.

Notes: Figures may not add due to rounding. (a) American Federation of Television and Radio Artists. (b) Includes earnings from television commercials and theatrical films. (c) Includes television residuals.

Table 460–D.
Percentage of Minority and Female Employees
in U. S. Television Stations, 1971–1976

	1971	1972	1973	1974	1975	1976
Commercial Television Stations						
Minority Employees						
Full-Time Employees	8%	10%	11%	12%	13%	14%
Part-Time Employees	15	18	20	20	21	22
Total, All Minority Employees	9	11	12	13	13	15
Female Employees						
Full-Time Employees	22	22	23	24	25	26
Part-Time Employees	24	26	27	30	31	33
Total, All Female Employees	22	23	23	25	26	27
Public Television Stations						
Minority Employees						
Full-Time Employees	8	10	11	11	12	13
Part-Time Employees	10	9	9	10	11	11
Total, All Minority Employees	9	10	10	11	12	12
Female Employees						
Full-Time Employees	28	29	30	31	32	33
Part-Time Employees	25	25	31	32	34	38
Total, All Female Employees	27	28	30	31	32	34

Source: United Church of Christ Office of Communication, *Television Station Employment Practices*, appropriate annual issues.

Sources

Except for the 1930 figure, which is a U.S. Department of Commerce estimate, **Table 460-A** data were provided by the FCC. The figures are current as of the last day of each year and were rounded to the nearest 100 by the editors. Both full- and part-time employment are included in the totals. The FM radio data are for independent FM stations only; data on AM-FM combination stations appear in the AM/AM-FM column. The total broadcast-employees figures are provided by the editors and probably overstate the actual employment situation, since many radio or television station employees work in both media and would therefore be counted twice in the total figures. The editors had to recalculate the totals for radio, which were incorrectly reported in *Broadcasting*.

The salary data in **Table 460-B** are from *Broadcasting* for 1940-1941; UNESCO's *Press Film Radio, Volume IV* (1950) for 1942-1949; and the U.S. Department of Labor (1976) for 1958-1974. All constant dollar conversions (1972=100, using the Consumer Price Index) were done by the editors. **Table 460-C** data to 1971 were reported by the Office of Telecommunications Policy (OTP) (1973). The 1972-1976 figures were obtained directly from unions by the editors. These figures are thus unverified by any official or separate agency.

Table 460-D is based on FCC-gathered statistics which are reanalyzed each year by the Office of Communication of the United Church of Christ in its annual publication, *Television Station Employment Practices*. The category of "minorities" includes blacks, orientals, American Indians, and Hispanic Americans. The United Church of Christ warns that station-reported data may overestimate minority employment, especially in higher-ranking jobs (one reason that such information has not been included here). Part of the problem is also due to the fact that the categories used in FCC forms are standard government categories which do not particularly fit the broadcasting industry.

In **Table 460-E**, the manufacturing data through 1972 were taken from the *Census of Manufactures*, and the more recent data came from the *Annual Survey of Manufactures*. The employment figures for radio and television receivers also include the manufacture of phonographs, tape recorders, and other home music/entertainment equipment. The *Census of Retail Trade* provided figures for retail radio-television stores, and the *Census of Selected Service Industries* is the source of data on radio-television repair shops. Employment figures for stores and repair shops do not include proprietors of these establishments, since these data were not consistently reported in the sources.

Table 460–E.
Number of Employees in Broadcast-Related Manufacturing Firms and in Radio-TV Retail Stores and Repair Shops, 1933–1975

	Manufacturing Firms			Retail Radio-TV Stores	Radio-TV Repair Shops
	Radio and TV Receivers[a]	Cathode-ray TV Picture Tubes	Electronic Receiving Tubes		
1933	N/A	N/A	N/A	N/A	6,123
1948	N/A	N/A	N/A	14,676	10,262
1954	N/A	N/A	N/A	19,941	18,281
1958	66,500	8,600	37,000	35,804	23,532
1959	74,900	7,600	37,400	N/A	N/A
1960	71,700	8,000	36,200	N/A	N/A
1961	76,800	7,500	27,200	N/A	N/A
1962	83,000	6,800	26,600	N/A	N/A
1963	81,300	10,900	25,800	30,611	25,012
1964	86,500	11,300	21,900	N/A	N/A
1965	100,100	14,300	22,300	N/A	N/A
1966	130,200	24,700	24,300	N/A	N/A
1967	116,700	27,600	21,000	46,376	29,415
1968	112,500	27,200	18,700	N/A	N/A
1969	105,500	23,400	17,100	N/A	N/A
1970	89,700	19,200	14,300	N/A	N/A
1971	89,900	17,200	12,200	N/A	N/A
1972	86,500	15,800	11,400	99,673	38,015
1973	92,100	16,900	9,300	N/A	N/A
1974	87,700	15,500	8,100	N/A	N/A
1975	69,000	13,300	5,700	N/A	N/A

Sources: Manufacturing data 1933-1972: *Census of Manufactures 1972*; 1973-1975: *Survey of Manufactures*, appropriate years. Radio-TV stores: *Census of Retail Trade*, appropriate years. Radio-TV repair shops: *Census of Selected Service Industries*, appropriate years.

Note: (a) Includes auto radios and tape players, public address systems, and music distribution apparatus.

Further Information

For more details on broadcast employment patterns, see the FCC's annual *Employment in the Broadcasting Industry* and the United Church of Christ's annual series cited above. A recent report criticizing the manner in which FCC statistics for television are collected and presented is *Window Dressing on the Set: Women and Minorities in Television* (United States Commission on Civil Rights, 1977). This report deals with employment statistics, as well as with the portrayal of women and minorities on television, both in drama and news, and the regulation and enforcement efforts of the federal government in this area. In its critique of the employment statistics, the Commission on Civil Rights presents an alternative survey analysis to illustrate the failure of the FCC's statistical effort.

The only detailed analysis of broadcast employment and unionization is Koenig (1970). For more specific information regarding individual unions, the reader should contact each union directly. Regular reports of employment patterns and union developments—including strikes—are found in *Broadcasting*. For data on broadcast journalism, see Units 404 and 700.

Table 490–A.

Number of Employees and Proportion of Minority and Female Employees in Cable Television Systems in U. S., 1973 and 1974

	1973	1974
Total Number of Cable Systems (estimate)	N/A	3,200
Total Number of Cable Employees (estimate)	N/A	24,300
Reporting Cable Systems[a]	650	1,040
Number of Employees	10,890	17,300
Proportion of Minority Employees	10%	9%
Proportion of Minorities in High-Paying Jobs	N/A	38
Proportion of Minorities in Lower-Paying Jobs	N/A	62
Proportion of Female Employees	27	26
Proportion of Females in High-Paying Jobs	N/A	15
Proportion of Females in Lower-Paying Jobs	N/A	85

Source: Federal Communications Commission, "Cable Industry EEO Study, 1975."

Note: (a) Includes only cable systems with five or more employees.

Interpretation of Tables

The reader who wishes to investigate the business aspects of cable television may feel frustrated by the lack of specific information available (see Unit 390). Certainly this is true in the area of employment by the nation's cable systems. The FCC has been collecting basic employment statistics on the industry, but only for cable systems having more than five employees—a minority among all of the operating systems in this country.

Table 490-A summarizes the data gathered during a single detailed survey conducted by the FCC in 1974. This survey also includes some data for the previous year. The figures indicate that, in terms of number of employees, the cable television industry represents about 17 percent of the total broadcasting industry.

Sources

Table 490-A was constructed from data in the FCC's *Cable Industry EEO Study, 1975.* Survey results were based on Form 395 filings by cable systems with more than five employees. The full report consists of a page of text and three pages of tables, including both raw statistics and percentage information. These figures must be considered estimates, since they are based on only about one-third of the nation's cable systems.

Further Information

While the FCC continues to collect information on cable system employment, no further reports have been issued since 1974. Presumably, specific statistics may be obtained from the Commission, although these data may not have been fully assembled and analyzed. The only other source for estimates regarding cable system employment is the National Cable Television Association (NCTA).

SECTION 5

**Content Trends
in the Media**

Table 500–A.
Results of Surveys Measuring the Most Frequent Source
of News for the U.S. Public, 1959–1976

	Radio	Television	Magazines	Newspapers	Other People	All Sources Mentioned	Don't Know/ No Answer
				"The most frequent source of news"			
1959	34%	51%	8%	57%	4%	154%	1%
1961	34	52	9	57	5	157	3
1963	29	55	6	53	4	147	3
1964	26	58	8	56	5	153	3
1967	28	64	7	55	4	158	2
1968	25	59	7	49	5	145	3
1971	23	60	5	48	4	140	1
1972	21	64	6	50	4	145	1
1974	21	65	4	47	4	141	--a
1976	19	64	7	49	5	144	--a

Source: Television Information Office (1977), p. 3, using data developed by The Roper Organization.

Note: (a) Less than 1 percent.

Interpretation of Tables

For a number of years, national opinion polls have been used to measure the American public's attitudes about and uses of the different mass media. This method of measurement has a number of limitations, the most important being the fact that the wording of questions and the categories for responses have an effect on the answers of the survey respondents. Consequently, a time-series of poll responses can be misleading or simply unuseable if the wording of the questions or the categories for responses differ significantly among the surveys being compiled.

During the late 1950s, the Television Information Office (TIO) began employing the Roper Organization to regularly measure public attitudes about the media and about television in particular. For this reason, some comparable annual survey information is available. Yet the figures collected for this survey must be somewhat suspect, in that they were sponsored by an organization dedicated to promoting the interests of television. The Gallup organization has conducted similar studies for the American Newspaper Publishers Association (ANPA), using different questions and coming up with different results. A third survey, performed by the National Opinion Research Center, also produced different, though related, results with a completely different set of questions. The tables in this unit present the results of these three public opinion polls.

Table 500-A features the results of several of the Roper polls, from 1959 through 1976, measuring the most frequently used news source for the American public. The wording of the question was: "I'd like to ask you where you usually get most of your news about what's going on in the world today—from the newspapers or television or magazines or talking to people or where?" The percentages in this table reveal an increasing reliance on television and a decreasing tendency to mention newspapers or radio as the most frequently consulted news source.

Table 500-B, also from a Roper Organization survey, addresses the subject of media credibility for the years 1939 through 1976. The question in 1939 was worded: "If you heard conflicting versions of the same story from these sources (radio, magazines, newspapers, an authority), which would you be most likely to believe?" For the other years, the question was very similar: "If you got conflicting or different reports of the same news story from radio, television, the maga-

Table 500–B.
Results of Surveys Measuring Public Trust in the Credibility of the U.S. News Media, 1939–1976

	"The most believable news medium"				Don't Know/ No Answer
	Radio	Television	Magazines	Newspapers	
1939[a]	40%	N/A	N/A	27%	20%
1959	12	29%	10%	32	17
1961	12	39	10	24	17
1963	12	36	10	24	18
1964	8	41	10	23	18
1967	7	41	8	24	20
1968	8	44	11	21	16
1971	10	49	9	20	12
1972	8	48	10	21	13
1974	8	51	8	20	13
1976	7	51	9	22	11

Sources: 1939 data: Peter (1941). All other years: Television Information Office (1975), using data developed by The Roper Organization.

Note: (a) The 1939 survey included a fifth "medium"—"an authority you heard speak"—which received 13 percent of the responses as the most believable news source.

zines, and the newspapers, which of the four versions would you be most inclined to believe—the one on radio or television or magazines or newspapers?"

The trend shown here is similar to that in **Table 500-A.** Television was judged the most credible news medium in 1961, and the percentage of people who agree with this judgment has grown considerably over the past 15 years. Meanwhile, the relative credibility of newspapers and radio has declined slightly.

Table 500-C, the results of the Gallup survey sponsored by the ANPA, asks a different question about the public's exposure to the news media and finds that more people mention newspapers, rather than television, as their news source. However, it should be noted that the percentage of people mentioning television rose from 1957 to 1973, while the percentage naming newspapers remained relatively constant. The wording of the Gallup Poll question was: "Did you read a newspaper yesterday, look at television news yesterday, or listen to radio news yesterday?"

A survey taken in March of 1977 by another polling organization, and quoted in a publication of the American Newspaper Publishers Association (Bogart, 1977, p. 3), presents similar figures concerning people's "daily exposure to the news" that year: 69 percent for newspapers, 62 percent for television news, and 49 percent for radio news.

Taking a different approach, **Table 500-D** measures the American public's confidence in the people who run television and the people who run "the press." The question for this survey: "I am going to name some institutions in this country. As far as the people running these institutions are concerned, would you say you have a great deal of confidence, only some confidence, or hardly any confidence at all in them?"

Apparently, there is some growth in the percentage of survey respondents who have "hardly any" confidence in the people running television, while there is a slight increase in the percentage of respondents who say they have "a great deal" of confidence in the people running the press. However, these trends are for a very short period of time (1973-1976), and the shifts of opinion are not large, especially if the possibility of sampling error is considered. Moreover, the wording of the question does not make it clear whether the respondents are being asked to distinguish between newspapers and television news, or between newspapers and television in general (that is, as both an entertainment and a news medium), or between television in general and "the press," which could include both print and broadcast journalism.

In reviewing all of these survey results, one is reminded of an *I Ching* metaphor: "The footprints run criss-cross." All of the survey research organizations involved have good reputations.

Table 500–C.
Results of Surveys Measuring the Public's Daily Use
of the U.S. News Media, 1957–1973

| | "The news source used yesterday" | | |
	Newspaper	Television Newscast	Radio Newscast
1957	71%	38%	54%
1965	71	55	58
1970	73	60	65
1973	70	62	59

Source: Based on a Gallup Poll reported in American Newspaper Publishers Association (1974), p. 41.

The choice of which results one accepts will usually depend on one's purposes. The most reasonable and objective approach to survey data of this kind is to supplement the material with other relevant information, such as audience characteristics, circulation, and news content.

The type of question asked by the Roper Organization in **Table 500-A** has come under particular criticism in recent years. The critics maintain that human behavior cannot be accurately measured by asking people what they "usually" do with their time. Instead, more specific questions, such as what the respondents actually did *yesterday*, are far more reliable measures of behavior (Welles, 1978). Greenberg and Roloff (1974) point out that individual respondent characteristics should be measured as well, since these characteristics (sex, age, socioeconomic status) inevitably affect the patterns of media use. Welles (1978, p. 14) also mentions that people "probably get different kinds of news from different media"—a factor that should be measured in this type of survey. In most cases, the survey organizations have attempted to respond to such criticisms by wording their questions more specifically and by broadening their surveys to include breakdowns by individual characteristics of the respondents.

Sources

The Roper Organization, the source of **Tables 500-A** and **500-B**, described its sample and sampling procedure as follows:

> A multi-staged, stratified, area probability sample is used for *Roper Reports* . . . It is a nationwide cross-section of the noninstitutionalized population, 18 years and older, living in the continental United States. It is representative of all ages 18 and over, all sizes of community, geographic areas, and economic levels. In each study—November and December—2,000 personal interviews were conducted by experienced, trained interviewers.

> The samples since 1971 have included 18 to 20 year olds because of the lowering of age limits for voting. It was determined, through weighting procedures and retabulating, that inclusion of this younger group did not affect results in total. This means that trend differences found in the studies are meaningful and *are* due to changes in attitude of the population as a whole. (Television Information Office, 1977, p. 24)

The reader should note that a national probability sample of 2,000 usually has a sampling error of not more than plus or minus 2 percent.

Table 500-C was taken from a report by the American Newspaper Publishers Association of a survey done by the Gallup Poll organization. While that ANPA report did not discuss the particular sampling methods used by the Gallup Poll, Gallup's procedures are generally quite similar to those of the Roper Organization. However, the Gallup sample in the earlier years included only those persons 21 years and older. The Gallup Poll now measures 18-20 year olds as well, but the responses of this age group were deleted from the later years of this series in order to make the figures historically comparable. It may be, then, that the differences in the responses to these surveys and those of the Roper Organization are due in part to the media preferences of 18 to 20 year olds. However, the differences in the wording of the questions by the two organizations

Table 500–D.
**Results of Surveys Measuring Public Confidence
in the Leadership of the Television and Newspaper Industries in U.S., 1973–1976**

"Confidence in the people running television"

	1973		1974		1975		1976	
	Number	Percent	Number	Percent	Number	Percent	Number	Percent
Total Sample Size	1,504	- -	1,484	- -	1,490	- -	1,499	- -
Total Number Responding	1,480	100.0%	1,464	100.0%	1,451	100.0%	1,464	100.0%
"A great deal"	278	18.8	347	23.7	265	18.3	279	19.1
"Only some"	875	59.1	861	58.8	853	58.7	779	53.2
"Hardly any"	327	22.1	256	17.5	333	23.0	406	27.7

"Confidence in the people running the press"

	1973		1974		1975		1976	
Total Sample Size	1,504	- -	1,484	- -	1,490	- -	1,499	- -
Total Number Responding	1,477	100.0%	1,463	100.0%	1,442	100.0%	1,463	100.0%
"A great deal"	346	23.4	383	26.2	354	24.6	424	29.0
"Only some"	911	61.7	821	56.1	823	57.0	776	53.0
"Hardly any"	220	14.9	259	17.7	265	18.4	263	18.0

Source: National Opinion Research Center (1973, 1974, 1975, 1976).

may well be the most significant factor in the responses.

The source of the information in **Table 500-D** is the National Opinion Research Center (NORC), an independent nonprofit research organization affiliated with the University of Chicago. In addition to conducting research, the NORC provides graduate training in survey research techniques. The data reproduced in **Table 500-D** are from the NORC's national data program for the social sciences, which it began in 1972 under the sponsorship of the National Science Foundation.

A total of 1,499 respondents were interviewed in March and April for the NORC survey. They were "a representative cross-section of the total population of the continental United States, 18 years of age or older, and living in noninstitutional arrangements." The sample design used a multi-stage probability sample, with quotas at the block level, and a full probability model with predesignated respondents. The use of the quota sample means that a mean squared sampling error cannot be directly estimated. However, the NORC estimates the sampling error for this design at about what it would be for a random sample of 1,000 respondents—around plus or minus 2 to 4 percent. The work of the National Opinion Research Center is considered of high quality and reliability.

Further Information

The organizations cited in this unit are the main sources of information regarding media uses and credibility. Numerous surveys have been done with similar questions and issues. The best way to track them down is to contact the person in charge of machine-readable data bases at a large, research-oriented, university library. In addition, the reader may wish to know that the data presented in **Table 500-D** were also reprinted in *Social Indicators 1976* (U.S. Bureau of the Census, 1977). Updated versions of this compendium may contain similar information.

Table 501–A.
Results of Surveys Measuring Media Sources of Information to the Public on Local, State, and National Elections in U.S., 1952–1976

	All Elections	Local Elections				State Elections				National Elections			
	1952	1964	1968	1972	1976	1964	1968	1972	1976	1964	1968	1972	1976
Newspapers	22%	42%	40%	41%	44%	41%	37%	39%	35%	36%	24%	26%	20%
Television	31	27	26	31	34	43	42	49	53	64	65	66	75
Radio	27	10	6	7	7	10	6	7	5	9	4	6	4
People	- -	18	23	23	12	8	9	9	6	4	4	5	3
Magazines	5	1	1	2	1	1	1	1	1	6	5	5	5
Other	- -[a]	7	4	5	6	4	4	3	3	3	2	2	1
Total Responses	- -[a]	105%	100%	109%	104%	107%	99%	108%	103%	122%	104%	110%	108%

Sources: 1952 data: Kraus and Davis (1976), p. 82, citing Campbell et al., *Scientific American* (May 1953). 1964-1976 data: Television Information Office, using data developed by The Roper Organization.

Notes: The 1952 survey was based on a sample of 1,700 voting-age citizens. The surveys for other years used a sample of about 2,000. (a) The 1952 survey included the four *media* categories only, plus two additional response categories: "More than one of the above"–9%, and "None of the four above"–6%.

Table 501–B.
Analysis of Daily Newspaper Editorial Support
for U.S. Presidential Candidates, 1932–1976

| | Support for Republican Candidate | | Support for Democratic Candidate | | Uncommitted Newspapers | |
	Percent of All Dailies	Percent of Total Circulation	Percent of All Dailies	Percent of Total Circulation	Percent of All Dailies	Percent of Total Circulation
1932	52.0%	N/A	40.5%	N/A	7.5%	N/A
1936	57.1	N/A	36.1	N/A	6.8	N/A
1940	63.9	69.2%	22.7	25.2%	13.4	5.6%
1944	60.1	68.5	22.0	17.7	17.9	13.8
1948	65.1	78.5	15.3	10.0	15.6	10.0
1952	67.3	80.2	14.5	10.8	18.2	9.0
1956	62.3	72.3	15.1	12.8	22.6	14.9
1960	57.7	70.9	16.4	15.8	25.9	13.3
1964	35.1	21.5	42.3	61.5	22.6	17.0
1968	60.8	69.9	14.0	19.3	24.0	10.5
1972	71.4	77.4	5.3	7.7	23.3	14.9
1976	62.4	62.3	12.1	22.6	25.5	15.1

Source: *Editor and Publisher*. 1932, 1936 data: (October 26, 1940), p. 7; 1940-1964 data: cited in Emery (1964), p. 486; 1968 data: (November 2, 1968), p. 9; 1972 data: (November 4, 1972), p. 9; 1976 data: (October 20, 1976), p. 5.

Note: Figures may not add to 100 percent due to rounding.

Interpretation of Tables

Table 501-A lists those media which various adult samples identified as their primary sources of information about local, state, and national election campaigns in the United States. The figures clearly demonstrate the increasing importance of television as an information source at all political campaign levels. Newspapers are the only other medium to show an increase, but only in the case of local election coverage. Even in 1952, when television was barely established nationwide, it had already become the highest ranking medium for political information.

Table 501-B summarizes what is known of daily newspaper editorial support for presidential candidates from 1932 to 1976. The reader will note that on only three occasions have Democratic party candidates received the support of more than one-third of all daily papers—during Roosevelt's first two campaigns and during Johnson's 1964 campaign. McGovern in 1972 and Carter in 1976 received the smallest levels of newspaper support since records have been kept. Analysis of editorial support by each newspapers' percentage of total daily newspaper circulation makes the trend of Republican party support even more extreme.

Table 501-C details the costs of political party advertising on radio and television during U.S. general elections. This information covers general elections at all levels—local, state, and national. Some interesting trends are evident here: the slowly increasing uses of radio and television by third parties; the greater use of both media by Republicans (although the two major parties spent equal amounts in 1972); and the fluctuating proportions of total campaign expenditures for airtime, with steady increases until 1964, then a leveling off, and, finally, a decline in overall spending levels in 1972.

Table 501-D lists the broadcast advertising and other media advertising costs of the presidential and vice-presidential campaigns of the two major parties in 1968, 1972, and 1976. With the exception of the lavishly financed 1972 Nixon campaign, media advertising has accounted for 35 to 60 percent of the total expenditures for each campaign. The 1976 general election was the first to include a federal ceiling on presidential campaign expenditures, accompanied by federal matching funds to help finance the campaigns.

Table 501–C.
Costs of Political Party Advertising on Radio and Television during the U.S. General Elections, 1952–1972

Note: All advertising costs are in thousands of dollars.

	1952	1956	1960	1964	1968	1972
Television Advertising Costs						
Network Time	N/A	$2,931	$ 2,927	$ 3,807	$ 7,362	$ 4,911
Local Station Time	N/A	3,755	7,125	13,689	19,725	19,655
Total Costs	$3,000	$6,686	$10,052	$17,496	$27,807	$24,566
Percentage of Costs Paid by:						
Republican Party	N/A	56%	54%	54%	56%	47%
Democratic Party	N/A	42	44	44	38	47
Third Parties	N/A	2	1	1	5	6
Radio Advertising Costs						
Network Time	N/A	$ 321	$ 79	$ 119	$ 663	$ 489
Local Station Time	N/A	2,900	4,064	6,988	12,654	13,021
Total Costs	$3,100	$3,221	$4,143	$7,107	$13,317	$13,510
Percentage of Costs Paid by:						
Republican Party	N/A	52%	51%	51%	55%	44%
Democratic Party	N/A	43	43	46	38	45
Third Parties	N/A	5	6	3	7	11
Total Advertising Costs	$6,100	$9,907	$14,195	$24,604	$40,403	$38,127
Percentage Change from Previous Election	- -	62%	45%	73%	64%	-6%
Total Costs of Election (millions)	$140	$155	$175	$200	$300	$425
Percent Spent on Broadcasting	4%	6%	8%	13%	13%	9%

Sources: Advertising costs: Alexander (1972), p. 324, citing Heard (1960) for 1952 data and the Federal Communications Commission's *Annual Report* (1973), p. 207, for 1956-1972 data. Total costs of election: Alexander (1972), p. 78.

Table 501-E compares the total minutes of political advertising on network television during general election years versus the average per-household viewing time for this advertising. These figures reveal the small percentage of political advertising which is seen in the average household —typically about 10 percent of the total amount of advertising airtime.

Table 501-F demonstrates that the average U.S. household views between 20 and 30 percent of the total hours of network television airtime devoted to the party conventions and to election night coverage. Levels of viewing are higher on election nights, but this apparently has no correlation with voting patterns. Note that the viewing levels for the closely contested 1968 and 1976 elections are not much different from those for the 1964 and 1972 landslide elections.

Finally, Table 501-G provides what limited information is available on the hours of free broadcast time provided by the radio and television networks to presidential and vice-presidential candidates (and/or their supporters) from 1956 through 1972. Fairly substantial amounts of free radio time were still made available to candidates in both the primary and general election periods in 1972. But the amount of free network television time in general elections had dwindled from 39 hours in 1960 to a mere 1 hour in 1972.

This dramatic drop is mainly due to the politically turbulent 1960s, when strong third-party candidates and vocal political dissenters of all stripes demanded rigid enforcement of the equal-time provisions and the Fairness Doctrine (Section 315) of the Communication Act, as amended in 1959. Network television management insisted that television airtime had become far too costly to give it away to all of the candidates who would seek equal exposure; hence, the networks simply stopped providing such time. In 1975, the FCC determined that live debates between candidates are news events and, therefore, exempt from equal-time obligations to minor candidates, so long as the debates are produced and controlled by an independent, nonpartisan organization. Broadcasters are barred from involvement in the event other than covering the debate live with cameras and microphones. This FCC ruling opened the way for the Ford-Carter debates in 1976.

Table 501–D.
Advertising and Other Media Costs
of the U.S. Presidential/Vice Presidential Election Campaigns, 1968–1976

Note: All dollar figures are in millions.

	1968		1972		1976	
	Nixon	Humphrey	Nixon	McGovern	Ford	Carter
Broadcast Media Advertising Costs	$ 8.1	$4.0	$3.9	$4.9	$ 7.9	$8.6
Television Advertising						
Network Time	6.3	2.2	2.2	2.3	2.5	3.3
Spot Time		1.4	3.9	1.8	3.9	4.2
Radio Advertising	1.8	.4	.6	.8	1.5	1.1
Print Media Advertising Costs	.9	.4	.7	1.0	1.3	.6
Broadcast/Print Media						
Production Costs	2.0	1.1	1.5	.8	1.7	.5
Costs of Campaign Materials	1.3	N/A	1.3	.4	.7	N/A
Total Media Costs	**$12.3**	**$6.3[a]**	**$8.2[a]**	**$7.2[a]**	**$11.6**	**$9.7**
Total Campaign Expenditures	$24.9	$10.3	$61.4	$21.2	$23.1	$23.4
Percent of Expenditures for Media	49.4%	61.2%	13.4%	34.0%	50.2%	41.5%

Sources: 1968 data: Alexander (1970), pp. 81, 84, 92. 1972 data: Alexander (1976), pp. 272, 290, 339. 1976 data: Provided directly to the editors by Herbert Alexander, who cited information from the Carter campaign and the GOP National Committee.

Note: (a) Includes other unspecified expenditures.

Sources

In **Table 501-A**, the 1952 information was taken from Kraus and Davis (1976), citing Campbell et al., in *Scientific American* (May 1953). The data were gathered by means of a survey questionnaire which was sent to over 1,700 voting-age citizens throughout the continental United States. Data for 1964 through 1976 were provided by the Roper Organization for the Television Information Office (TIO).

The TIO is the NAB's television public relations group, and the Roper surveys were clearly carried out with a persuasive purpose in mind—that is, in showing television as improving its already high position among the other media. During the two most recent election years, however, Roper asked a parallel question about which medium was most useful in learning about *issues*, and television did not do quite so well in that area.

Table 501-B data were gathered from issues of *Editor and Publisher*. Data for 1940 through 1964 are also cited in Emery (1964). During a few presidential campaigns, third parties played a role which is not shown separately in this table. In 1948, for example, Henry Wallace received support from 4 percent of the U.S. dailies (1.5 percent of the total U.S. circulation); and two decades later, George Wallace received the support of 1.2 percent of dailies (.3 percent of circulation). The librarian at *Editor and Publisher* reported to the editors that information in this area prior to 1932 cannot be obtained from any source.

Table 501-C data for 1952 are from Alexander (1972), citing Heard's *The Costs of Democracy*. Data for 1956-1972 are from the FCC's *Annual Report* (1973) and are based on all reporting stations for all election-year political campaign broadcasting. Alexander and others note that although the FCC surveys are the only consistent information available for the elections covered, they still did not include *all* stations and elections. Consequently, these data are best viewed as close estimates. (The reader should know that these FCC surveys were discontinued on creation of the Federal Election Committee, which gathers somewhat similar information, but does not attempt to collate or publish it.) The estimated total campaign costs which appear at the bottom of **Table 501-C** are from Alexander (1972).

Table 501–E.
Total Air Time and Average Per-Household Viewing Time
of Paid Political Party Advertising on U.S. Network Television, 1960–1972

Election Year and Political Party	Total Minutes of Aired Advertising	Average Minutes Viewed per Household	Viewed Minutes as Percent of Aired Minutes
1960			
Republican (Nixon)	830	71	8.5%
Democratic (Kennedy)	510	52	10.2
Total	1,340	123	9.2%
1964			
Republican (Goldwater)	760	56	7.4%
Democratic (Johnson)	375	35	9.3
Total	1,135	91	8.0%
1968			
Republican (Nixon)	710	74	10.4%
Democratic (Humphrey)	830	89	10.7
Independent (Wallace)	250	29	11.6
Total	1,790	192	10.7%
1972			
Republican (Nixon)	615	60	9.8%
Democratic (McGovern)	540	59	10.9
Others	95	6	6.3
Total	1,250	125	10.0%

Sources: 1960, 1964 data: Lichty et al. (1965), pp. 219, 223, tables 1, 2. 1968, 1972 data: A. C. Nielsen, *Network Television Audiences to Primaries, Conventions, Elections* (1976), p. 20.

Table 501-D data for 1968 are from Alexander (1970); the 1972 data are from Alexander (1976). Information for 1976 for the Democrats was reported by the Carter campaign directly to Herbert Alexander, who made it available to the editors. Republican information for 1976 was supplied to the editors by both Alexander and the GOP National Committee. While 1968 and 1972 data can be compared to official FCC reports, the 1976 information given here must be considered preliminary.

The reader should also keep in mind that the figures shown in **Table 501-D** were originally supplied by the respective campaigns. The details vary from year to year, and losing campaigns are often ended with limited details released. In view of the laxity of campaign reporting, the data for 1968 and 1972 should be considered approximations.

Two sources contributed to **Table 501-E**: the 1960 and 1964 campaign data were gathered from Lichty et al. (1965); the 1968 and 1972 campaign figures were taken from A. C. Nielsen's *Network Television Audiences to Primaries, Conventions, Elections* (1976). **Table 501-F** information through 1972 comes from the same A. C. Nielsen publication. The information for 1976 was gathered from the *Nielsen Newscast* No. 2 (1976), on the Democratic Convention; *Nielsen Newscast* No. 3 (1976), on the GOP Convention, and *Nielsen Newscast* No. 4 (1976), on the election night coverage.

Table 501-G was constructed from the information issued after each general election, from 1956 through 1972, by the FCC. General election and 1968 primary data come from Alexander (1976); the 1972 primary data are taken from *Broadcasting*. The 1960 television figures for the general election period include the airtime for the Kennedy-Nixon debates.

Further Information

The reader seeking an overview of the media's role in political campaigns should consult Chester (1969) for the historical context, Kraus and Davis (1976) for research findings and a

Table 501–F.
Average Television Viewing Hours Per-Household
during U.S. National Convention and Election Night Coverage, 1952–1976

	Network Hours Telecast	Average Hours Viewed per Household	Viewed Hours as Percent of Aired Hours
1952			
Republican Convention	57:30	10:30	18%
Democratic Convention	61:06	13:06	21
Election Night	N/A	N/A	N/A
1956			
Republican Convention	22:48	6:24	28
Democratic Convention	37:36	8:24	22
Election Night	N/A	2:42	N/A
1960			
Republican Convention	25:30	6:12	24
Democratic Convention	29:20	8:20	28
Election Night	N/A	4:30	N/A
1964			
Republican Convention	36:30	7:00	19
Democratic Convention	23:30	6:24	27
Election Night	7:36	2:35	34
1968			
Republican Convention	34:00	6:30	19
Democratic Convention	39:06	8:30	22
Election Night	13:18	3:38	27
1972			
Republican Convention	19:48	3:30	18
Democratic Convention	36:42	5:48	16
Election Night	6:20	2:10	30
1976			
Republican Convention	27:21	N/A	N/A
Democratic Convention	30:48	N/A	N/A
Election Night	9:00	3:02	34

Sources: 1952-1972 data: Nielsen Television Index, A. C. Nielsen, *Network Television Audiences to Primaries, Conventions, Elections* (1976), pp. 8, 9, 21. 1976 data: Democratic convention: Nielsen Television Index, A. C. Nielsen, *Nielsen Newscast* No. 2 (1976), pp. 10-11; Republican convention: *Nielsen Newscast* No. 3 (1976), pp. 8-9; election night: *Nielsen Newscast* No. 4 (1976), pp. 2-3.

Table 501–G.
Hours of Free Network Broadcast Time Given to U.S. Presidential/Vice Presidential
Candidates and Their Supporters during Election Years, 1956–1972

	Primaries Election Period		General Election Period	
	Television Networks	Radio Networks	Television Networks	Radio Networks
1956	N/A	N/A	29:38	32:23
1960	N/A	N/A	39:22	43:14
1964	N/A	N/A	4:28	21:14
1968	13:16	31:29	3:01	24:17
1972	20:00	31:00	1:00	19:00

Sources: All general election and 1968 primaries data: FCC figures cited in Alexander (1976), p. 329. 1972 primaries data: FCC figures cited in *Broadcasting* (May 14, 1973), p. 25.

bibliography, and Chaffee (1975) for research directions and methods. Although the FCC has issued reports on political broadcasting, covering the 1956-1972 elections, opinions differ on just how accurate and complete its data are.

The best sources for statistics and analyses of media advertising expenditures for election campaigns after 1960 are Alexander's quadrennial reviews (1962, 1966, 1971, and 1976). These reviews are based on both journalistic reports and data obtained directly from the major and independent party campaigns. The Citizen's Research Foundation, which Alexander directs (245 Nassau Street, Princeton, New Jersey 08540), is the collection point and the repository for much of the data reported here.

Subject Matter of Published Books 510

Interpretation of Tables

The R. R. Bowker Company has been collecting data on book title output in the United States since 1880. **Table 510-A** offers a breakdown by subject, and at 10-year intervals, of the total number of new book titles published in the United States from 1880 to 1960. If one compares two widely separated years, such as 1910 and 1960, the most striking characteristic of the distribution of titles among subjects is the absence of any major changes. When expressed as percentages of overall title output, the figures for 11 of the 23 subject categories in 1960 came within 1 percent of the figures for these same categories in 1910. The greatest decline took place in the number of titles classified as general literature, whereas the most significant increases were in fiction and books for juveniles.

Table 510-B also focuses on new book title output by subject, but covers the shorter and more current period from 1961 to 1975. This second table was made necessary because of the Bowker Company's change in its category definitions in 1961. However, the table is also of special interest because it seems to offer some evidence that book title output might be considered an indicator of short-term social trends.

To illustrate this possibility, we have divided **Table 510-B** into seven-year periods, from 1961 to 1968 and from 1968 to 1975. During this first period, total book title output in the United States increased 68 percent. The subject categories with the greatest growth were general works (172 percent), sociology/economics (152 percent), literature (137 percent), law (127 percent), business (121 percent), and education (111 percent). The categories showing the least growth were fiction (7 percent), agriculture (8 percent), religion (39 percent), biography (42 percent), sports and recreation (45 percent), and history (46 percent).

During the second seven-year period, this pattern changed. Overall title output increased only 30 percent, and the leading subject areas had become home economics (133 percent), sports and recreation (90 percent), agriculture (83 percent), medicine (79 percent), biography (75 percent), and sociology/economics (62 percent). Finally, six categories showed absolute decreases in title output between 1968 and 1975: travel (-33 percent), language (-13 percent), literature (-10 percent), education (-8 percent), juveniles (-8 percent), and religion (-1 percent).

While good subject breakdowns of overall title output have been available for some time, they are less available within particular categories of books. **Tables 510-C** and **510-D** come as close as possible to providing such information in regard to textbooks. However, these figures are not for new title output, or even for number of copies sold, but rather for dollar sales. Therefore, the relative expenditures for each textbook subject area must be seen not only in terms of the demand for titles in a given subject area, but also in terms of the *cost* of volumes on that subject.

Such figures can be misleading. One can assume, for example, that certain heavily illustrated textbooks in a given subject area would cost more, and that these additional costs might possibly inflate the relative importance of these textbooks as a popular subject area. Nevertheless, it could be quite interesting to use these data in making a historical run comparable to those for overall title output. Fortunately, the Association of American Publishers (AAP) has been collecting these dollar sales figures since 1971, and in time it may be possible to isolate some interesting trends.

Sources

The data in **Tables 510-A** and **510-B** were collected by the R. R. Bowker Company from annual summaries of the information sent to the "Weekly Record" section of *Publishers Weekly*,

Table 510–A.
Total Number of New Book Titles Published in U.S., by Subject Matter, 1880–1960

	1880	1890	1900	1910	1920	1930	1940	1950	1960
Agriculture, gardening	43	29	76	200	67	74	139	152	156
Biography	151	213	274	644	285	792	647	603	879
Business	- -	- -	- -	150	168	210	402	250	305
Education	131	399	641	423	111	240	349	256	348
Fiction	292	1,118	1,278	1,539	1,123	2,103	1,736	1,907	2,440
Fine Arts	44	135	167	245	100	230	222	357	470
Games, sports	32	82	51	145	60	142	182	188	286
General literature, essays and criticism	106	183	543	2,042	301	539	536	591	736
Geography, travel	115	162	192	599	166	385	308	288	466
History	72	153	257	565	539	431	853	516	865
Home economics	(a)	(a)	(a)	132	28	55	94	193	197
Juvenile	270	408	527	1,010	477	935	984	1,059	1,725
Law	62	458	543	678	109	75	202	298	394
Medicine, hygiene	114	117	218	544	207	318	472	443	520
Music	24	- -	- -	100	49	62	124	113	98
Philology	(b)	(b)	(b)	200	195	215	319	148	228
Philosophy, ethics	22	11	101	265	242	295	110	340	480
Poetry, drama	111	168	400	752	453	696	738	531	492
Religion	239	467	448	943	504	834	843	727	1,104
Science	56	93	184	711	231	462	493	705	1,089
Sociology, economics	99	183	269	784	396	523	876	515	754
Technical, military	63	133	153	707	352	351	611	497	698
Miscellaneous	30	42	34	42	24	60	88	345	282
Total	2,076	4,554	6,356	13,420	6,187	10,027	11,328	11,022	15,012

Source: Hokkanen (1970), p. 28, citing R. R. Bowker Co. data.

Notes: These data include pamphlets before 1920. (a) Grouped with "Agriculture and Gardening" before 1910. (b) Grouped with "Education" before 1910.

the book publishing industry's primary trade magazine. Government documents and university theses are not included in these summaries. In addition, certain classes of books are under-reported, including some textbooks, mass-market paperbacks, and small-press publications.

There have also been some problems in defining a "book" for the purposes of this count; and as a result, the accuracy of the figures before 1940 are somewhat clouded. For example, up until 1913, pamphlets were included with books in the title output figures; and until 1940, *Publishers Weekly* never made a distinction between books and pamphlets, leaving the definitions to individual publishers. In succeeding decades, the *Publishers Weekly* definition of what constitutes a "book" has been changed twice.

These changes probably have more impact on the total figures for each year (see Unit 110) than on the relative production in individual subject areas. However, the significant decrease in general works between 1910 and 1920 may have been the result of *Publishers Weekly's* elimination of pamphlets from the title figures between those dates.

There have also been some variations in the subject categories since 1880, but these changes are not a serious limitation. The category now called "sociology/economics" was once defined as "political and social" and has gone through a number of other redefinitions. Similarly, what is now listed in **Table 510-A** as "technical/military," was called "useful arts" in 1880; and "agriculture" in **Table 510-B** covers the same category of books as "agriculture/gardening" in **Table 510-A**.

Table 510-B.
Total Number of New Book Titles Published in U.S., by Subject Matter, 1961–1975

	1961	1964	1968	% Change 1961-1968	1972	1975	% Change 1968-1975
Agriculture	231	285	249	8	380	456	83
Art	620	906	1,117	80	1,470	1,561	40
Biography	790	948	1,123	42	1,986	1,968	75
Business	350	575	772	121	684	820	6
Education	534	1,232	1,125	111	1,292	1,038	-8
Fiction	2,630	3,271	2,811	7	3,260	3,805	35
General works	275	532	749	172	1,048	1,113	49
History	1,049	1,358	1,528	46	1,629	1,823	19
Home economics	191	237	312	63	596	728	133
Juveniles	1,626	2,808	2,482	53	2,526	2,292	-8
Language	307	801	502	64	479	438	-13
Law	256	346	581	127	716	915	57
Literature	888	1,454	2,106	137	2,525	1,904	-10
Medicine	776	1,211	1,277	65	1,839	2,282	79
Music	155	214	290	87	402	305	5
Philosophy, psychology	565	766	946	67	1,164	1,374	45
Poetry, drama	615	936	1,062	73	1,484	1,501	41
Religion	1,290	1,830	1,791	39	1,705	1,778	-1
Science	1,494	2,738	2,407	61	2,586	2,942	22
Sociology, economics	1,613	3,272	4,070	152	6,415	6,590	62
Sports, recreation	444	582	644	45	941	1,225	90
Technology	781	1,125	1,262	62	1,425	1,720	36
Travel	580	1,024	1,181	104	1,491	794	-33
Total	18,060	28,451	30,387	68	38,043	39,372	30

Source: R. R. Bowker Co., *The Bowker Annual*, appropriate issues, citing data from *Publishers Weekly*.

The sales data in **Tables 510-C** and **510-D** come from an annual survey by the Association of American Publishers of U.S. book publishers both within and outside the membership of the AAP. Because participation in the survey is voluntary, the possibility of bias in the sample does exist. However, the respondents furnishing data for these tables represent a fairly high proportion of total industry sales—89 percent for elementary textbooks, 69 percent for high school textbooks, and 70 percent for college textbooks—so the reader may assume the breakdown to be fairly representative of all publishers.

Further Information

Data on American book title output are printed in both *The Bowker Annual* and the yearly statistical issue of *Publishers Weekly*. It should be noted, however, that in 1977, Bowker changed to a new 18-month schedule for collecting information about the titles published in each calendar year. As a result, there will be a delay in the publication of these figures in *Publishers Weekly* until late summer; and, presumably, this delay will cause a corresponding lag in *The Bowker Annual* figures.

The best available historical analysis of title output statistics is Hokkanen (1970). Another interesting compilation of subject matter trends in books is Alice Payne Hackett's tally of best-sellers. Her year-by-year list of fiction best-sellers from 1900 to 1974, and of nonfiction from 1912 to 1974, is available in Anderson (1975).

Table 510–C.
Value and Percentage of Total Sales of Elementary and High School Textbooks in U.S., by Subject Matter, 1975 and 1976

Note: All sales figures in thousands of dollars.

Elementary Textbooks and Materials

Subject Matter	1975 Sales	1975 Percent of Total Sales	1976 Sales	1976 Percent of Total Sales
Language Arts				
Reading and Literature	$132,365	38.3%	$131,400	37.9%
English	29,723	8.6	24,921	7.2
Spelling	19,620	5.7	24,343	7.0
Handwriting	4,215	1.2	5,814	1.7
Unspecified	13,562	- -	10,112	- -
Total Language Arts	199,485	53.8	196,591	53.8
Science	36,248	9.8	28,069	7.7
Health	6,805	1.8	6,094	1.7
Social Studies	21,601	5.8	24,627	6.7
Mathematics	82,175	22.2	86,469	23.7
Music	9,994	2.7	9,022	2.5
Art	16	0.0	14	0.0
Foreign Languages	90	0.0	68	0.0
Other	14,171	3.8	14,414	3.9
Total Sales	**$370,585**	**100.0%**	**$365,367**	**100.0%**

High School Textbooks and Materials

Subject Matter	1975 Sales	1975 Percent of Total Sales	1976 Sales	1976 Percent of Total Sales
Literature	$ 12,453	8.1%	$ 13,167	8.2%
English	9,883	6.5	11,608	7.2
Science	28,596	18.7	29,699	18.5
Social Studies	17,476	11.4	18,250	11.4
Mathematics	22,405	14.6	22,865	14.2
Music	332	0.2	478	0.3
Art	249	0.2	128	0.1
Foreign Languages	8,438	5.5	8,457	5.3
Vocational				
Business Education	34,676	22.6	38,237	23.8
Industrial Arts	3,016	2.0	3,409	2.1
Other	10,762	7.0	9,997	6.2
Total Vocational Arts	48,454	31.6	51,643	32.1
Other				
Dictionaries	2,173	1.4	1,870	1.2
Unspecified	2,687	1.8	2,469	1.5
Total Other	4,860	3.2	4,339	2.7
Total Sales	**$153,146**	**100.0%**	**$160,634**	**100.0%**

Source: Association of American Publishers (1977), pp. 99-100.

Note: Figures may not add due to rounding.

Table 510–D.
Value and Percentage of Total Sales of College Textbooks in U.S.,
by Subject Matter, 1974–1976

	1974		1975		1976	
	Sales	Percent of Total Reported	Sales	Percent of Total Reported	Sales	Percent of Total Reported
English Language and Literature	$ 25,401	8.3%	$ 30,650	8.3%	$ 32,382	8.2%
Speech, Drama and Mass Media	8,178	2.7	9,174	2.5	9,649	2.5
French	2,342	0.8	2,597	0.7	3,109	0.8
German	1,725	0.6	1,544	0.4	1,654	0.4
Spanish	4,049	1.3	4,852	1.3	5,193	1.3
Other Foreign Languages	784	0.3	844	0.2	1,030	0.3
Music	3,740	1.2	4,155	1.1	4,796	1.2
Art and Architecture	5,094	1.7	5,531	1.5	5,831	1.5
Religion and Philosophy	3,982	1.3	4,665	1.3	5,102	1.3
Electrical Engineering	3,555	1.2	4,204	1.1	4,589	1.2
Other Engineering	14,023	4.6	11,400	3.1	13,731	3.5
Career and Occupational Education	10,496	3.4	11,431	3.1	13,168	3.3
Accounting	14,828	4.9	17,090	4.6	18,849	4.8
Business Education	5,488	1.8	12,540	3.4	16,099	4.1
Business Administration	21,746	7.1	31,196	8.5	33,532	8.5
Economics	9,791	3.2	12,725	3.5	14,265	3.6
Mathematics	22,274	7.3	27,794	7.6	29,599	7.5
Chemistry (Incl. Biochemistry)	11,492	3.8	13,627	3.7	15,255	3.9
Physics and Physical Science	8,138	2.7	8,768	2.4	8,583	2.2
Astronomy	1,452	0.5	1,115	0.3	1,582	0.4
Biology	11,173	3.7	13,442	3.7	14,622	3.7
Geology and Earth Science	5,134	1.7	6,354	1.7	6,069	1.5
Home Economics	1,851	0.6	2,048	0.6	2,398	0.6
Health and Physical Education	3,747	1.2	4,287	1.2	4,954	1.3
Sociology	12,885	4.2	14,424	3.9	14,558	3.7
Anthropology	4,337	1.4	4,618	1.3	4,314	1.1
Political Science, Public Service and Administration	10,216	3.3	12,505	3.4	12,484	3.2
History	12,097	4.0	14,529	4.0	14,375	3.7
Psychology	25,985	8.5	27,809	7.6	30,955	7.9
Education	18,843	6.2	20,765	5.6	21,628	5.5
Nursing and Allied Health	6,640	2.2	6,167	1.7	6,693	1.7
Geography	2,829	0.9	3,036	0.8	3,344	0.9
Computers	5,920	1.9	9,954	2.7	11,461	2.9
General Reference Dictionaries	1	0.0	1	0.0	6	0.0
Miscellaneous	5,041	1.7	11,793	3.2	7,220	1.8
Unspecified	0	- -	81	- -	120	- -
TOTAL	$305,267	100.0%	$367,715	100.0%	$393,199	100.0%

Source: Association of American Publishers (1977), p. 126.

Note: The figures are drawn from sales figures of 23 textbook publishers.

Table 520-A.
Analysis of Front-Page Content of the "New York Times," 1900–1970

	1900-05	1910-15	1920-25	1930-35	1940-45	1950-55	1960-65	1970
Average Number of Stories	24	17	13	13	10	12	13	12
Average Number of Pictures	.00	.14	.07	.07	.67	1.86	2.86	1.86
Average Number of Jumps	1	3	6	8	9	11	13	12
Type of Story:								
News	91%	88%	95%	92%	96%	96%	94%	90%
Feature	9	12	5	8	3	3	5	10
Time Orientation of Story:								
Immediate	87	86	72	67	61	64	59	57
Long-Range	13	14	27	33	39	36	40	43
Source of Story:								
Wire Services	1	0	4	16	9	7	8	4
Times (By-lined)	0	0	6	16	47	69	77	85
Times (Not By-lined)	99	100	90	68	44	24	15	11
Location of News Event in Story:								
City	23	23	30	25	12	29	28	21
State or Region	19	14	9	11	5	8	9	7
Nation	33	17	10	13	8	8	11	10
Washington, D.C.	5	9	19	23	24	23	25	38
World	19	37	32	29	52	32	27	23
Number of Stories in Two-Week Period	342	235	178	177	145	174	180	81

Source: Ogan (1975), pp. 340-344.

Interpretation of Tables

Measuring national trends in newspaper content is not an easy task. The studies that exist were usually created to fit the particular needs of the researchers at a specific time. Thus, there are no long-term national data on newspaper content trends, and the editors are able to offer only some interesting examples of the kinds of newspaper content analyses which have been done.

Table 520-A summarizes one small study which covers, at 10-year intervals, the changes in the content of the front page of the *New York Times*. Some characteristics of the *Times* have changed considerably since 1900. The number of completed stories on Page One has declined, for example, and the number of pictures and "jumps" (stories continued on the inside page) has increased. The overall ratio of news stories to features on the front page has remained roughly the

Table 520–B.
Analysis of News and Editorial Content in U.S. Daily Newspapers,
by Subject Matter and Circulation, 1971

	All Daily Newspapers	Dailies with Circulation of:		
		50,000 or less	50,001- 250,000	250,001 or more
All General Interest Items	66.8%	67.0%	66.6%	67.2%
State and Local News	12.7	15.2	12.0	9.5
General local news	7.3	9.6	6.8	4.1
State and local government	5.4	5.6	5.2	5.4
International News	10.2	9.5	10.2	11.5
Vietnam (not U. S. govt.) and other wars, rebellions	4.4	4.4	4.2	4.9
U. S. government (Vietnam), armaments, defense	2.8	2.6	2.7	3.4
Diplomatic news (U. S. and foreign)	3.0	2.5	3.3	3.2
U. S. Government, Domestic	6.9	6.6	6.9	7.7
Other General Interest	37.0	35.7	37.5	38.5
Crime	3.9	3.3	4.3	4.6
Education, school news	3.3	3.5	3.6	2.6
Comics	2.6	2.7	2.5	2.6
Cultural events, reviews	2.6	2.6	2.3	3.0
Public health, welfare	2.4	2.3	2.4	2.6
Puzzles, horoscopes	2.4	2.8	2.3	1.8
Accident, disaster, natural phenomena	2.4	2.5	2.3	2.2
Social problems, protest	2.1	2.1	1.9	2.3
Obituaries	2.1	2.2	2.1	1.8
Labor, wages	1.8	1.3	1.9	2.7
Environment	1.6	1.5	1.5	1.7
General nonlocal human interest	1.2	1.3	1.3	1.1
Racial, minorities	1.2	1.0	1.5	1.2
TV/radio logs	1.2	1.0	1.1	1.5
Weather	1.1	1.1	1.1	1.1
Science, invention	1.0	1.0	1.1	0.9
Travel	1.0	0.9	1.0	1.1
Tax	1.0	0.8	1.1	0.9
Entertainers, Hollywood	0.9	0.6	0.8	1.7
Letters to the editor	0.6	0.5	0.7	0.8
Religion	0.6	0.7	0.7	0.4
Men's Interest	21.1	19.6	21.7	22.9
Sports	14.2	14.0	15.2	12.9
Business, finance	6.9	5.6	6.5	10.0
Women's Interest	5.4	6.9	5.0	3.2
Fashion, society	3.9	5.3	3.6	1.9
Food, home, garden	1.5	1.6	1.4	1.3
Columns	5.3	5.4	5.4	4.8
Advice columns	3.1	3.2	3.2	2.5
Political columns	1.1	1.2	1.0	1.0
Humor columns	0.8	0.8	0.8	0.7
Gossip columns	0.3	0.2	0.4	0.6
Other items not classified elsewhere	1.4	1.1	1.3	2.0

Source: American Newspaper Publishers Association, *News and Editorial Content and Readership of the Daily Newspaper* (1973).

Note: All figures represent news or editorial items which are 5.5 column-inches or longer.

same, but there is a trend to more long-range and analytical stories and fewer stories about immediate news events.

Another change has been the focus on Washington, D.C., as the major source of front-page news. Coverage of events throughout the state of New York and in other parts of the country has diminished. Coverage of world news has generally increased during wartime, but, overall, such coverage has been declining steadily since 1945. Finally, it is noteworthy that since 1920, the *Times* has steadily increased the number of by-lines given to its reporters.

Table 520-B represents the results of a content analysis of a sample of daily newspapers in the United States. This analysis was part of a national content and readership study carried out by the News Research Center of the American Newspaper Publishers Association (ANPA) in 1971. The study was based on interviews in 200 "geographic areas representative of the 48 contiguous U.S. states," and any daily newspaper was included if it drew 5 percent or more of its readership from any of the 200 areas.

The authors of the study found that daily papers with more than 250,000 circulation tended to carry relatively more international items and fewer state and local news stories. Also, the ratio of "men's interest" to "women's interest" news was greater in the larger newspapers. Simple percentages can be misleading, however, and there are other factors which the reader must consider. For example, newspapers with larger circulations generally have more pages. Consequently, the same percentage of coverage for a content category actually represents a larger amount of space in the larger newspapers. (In this study, the average number of pages for a daily with a circulation of less than 50,000 was 23.7; dailies with a circulation of 50,000 to 250,000 averaged 40.2 pages; and dailies with more than 250,000 circulation averaged 65.4 pages.)

Sources

The information in **Table 520-A** was collected by Ogan and her associates (1975). They reported this description of their method:

> Coders divided into "news" or "feature" the stories appearing on each front page of a "constructed" week of 1900 and every five years thereafter through 1970. . . . Coders also divided stories according to whether they seemed to be of "immediate" value or "long-range" value from the point of view of the reader. . . . Coders first divided stories into "news" or "feature," then into "immediate" versus "long-range" categories. These two coding judgments required considerable training, but coder reliability reached acceptable levels . . . Coders also recorded whether the story came to the paper by means of a *Times* reporter or other source and where the event covered actually happened. These proved easy coding judgments.

Table 520-B comes from an ANPA News Research Center study done by Leo Bogart, Frank E. Orenstein, Stuart Tolley, and Charles Lehman (ANPA, 1973). All news and editorial items of 75 agate lines (about 5½ column inches) were included. The authors of this study estimated that approximately 69 percent of all stories in the newspapers they sampled were large enough to be included in their tally.

Further Information

One interesting content analysis for several large American dailies is Rivers and Rubin (1971). *Journalism Quarterly* includes Ogan (1975) as well as most of the numerous other content analyses of newspapers that have been done in recent years. The ANPA News Research Bureau has recently been collecting studies of readership and circulation, many of which include a variety of content variables. The reader can obtain additional information by writing to: Dr. Maxwell McCombs, ANPA News Research Center, School of Public Communications, Syracuse University, Syracuse, New York 13210.

Table 530–A.
Proportion of Advertising-to-Editorial Linage
in Content of U.S. Magazines, 1947–1976

Year	Number of Magazines in Sample	Percent Advertising Linage	Percent Editorial Linage
1947	33	53.1 %	46.9 %
1957	33	49.6	50.4
1961	33	44.6	55.4
1964	33	46.4	53.6
1966	49	46.6	53.4
1967	50	46.7	53.3
1969	49	47.3	52.7
1970	48	46.0	54.0
1971	48	46.8	53.2
1973	45	49.3	50.7
1975	45	46.5	53.5
1976	N/A	49.3	50.7

Source: Magazine Publishers Association, citing data from R. Russell Hall Company, *Magazine Editorial Reports*, appropriate issues.

Interpretation of Tables

Table 530-A compares the percentages of space devoted to advertising and editorial content in a relatively small sample (50 or less) of general circulation magazines in the United States. During the period covered on this table (1947-1976), the percentage of advertising content has fluctuated between 44.6 and 53.1 percent. Current data reveal an approximate 50-50 balance of advertising with editorial content.

Table 530-B focuses on the subject matter of the editorial content in 14 general circulation magazines: *Newsweek, Time, Good Housekeeping, Ladies' Home Journal, McCall's, Parents' Magazine, True Story, American Home, Better Homes and Gardens, House and Garden, House Beautiful, Redbook, Harper's Bazaar,* and *Vogue.* All of these magazines have been published since before 1938, and over this nearly 40-year period, they have been among the leading U.S. general circulation periodicals. Although some of the magazines have experienced relative declines in circulation in recent years, eight were still in the top 20 on the magazine list of the Audit Bureau of Circulations in 1976—and all 14 appeared in the top 100 list (see **Table 630-D**).

The most striking trend apparent in **Table 530-B** is the decline of popular magazine fiction. In 1938 and 1946, approximately 20 percent of the editorial space in these magazines was devoted to fiction. By 1976, this figure had declined to 7.4 percent. No other trend is so pronounced, but interesting increases over the period have occurred in the subject areas of national affairs, beauty and grooming information, food and nutrition, health and medical science, home furnishings and management, and cultural interests. Major percentage declines, in addition to those in fiction, occurred in farming and gardening and in features on wearing apparel and accessories.

Table 530–B.
Analysis of Content of 14 National Magazines in U.S.,
by Subject Matter and Proportion of Advertising, 1938–1976

	1938		1946		1956		1966		1976	
	Total Coverage (pages)	Percent of Total Pages	Total Coverage (pages)	Percent of Total Pages	Total Coverage (pages)	Percent of Total Pages	Total Coverage (pages)	Percent of Total Pages	Total Coverage (pages)	Percent of Total Pages
National Affairs	928.5	5.9%	1,196.9	7.1%	1,213.8	6.3%	1,662.0	8.4%	1,885.6	10.9%
Foreign/International	666.7	4.2	1,103.6	6.5	947.6	4.9	977.9	5.0	942.3	5.4
Amusement	504.7	3.2	501.6	3.0	634.3	3.3	731.6	3.7	710.2	4.1
Beauty, Grooming	227.9	1.4	271.0	1.6	341.7	1.8	573.0	2.9	778.5	4.5
Building	885.2	5.6	970.8	5.7	1,031.4	5.4	883.1	4.5	545.2	3.1
Business and Industry	435.1	2.8	414.4	2.4	688.3	3.6	640.2	3.2	555.7	3.2
Children	501.3	3.2	585.2	3.5	630.2	3.3	665.5	3.4	338.6	2.0
Farming and Gardening	630.5	4.0	504.4	3.0	526.7	2.7	333.7	1.7	237.8	1.4
Food and Nutrition	495.8	3.2	787.8	4.6	1,251.4	6.5	1,609.5	8.2	1,671.8	9.6
Health/Medical Science	159.6	1.0	247.3	1.5	317.9	1.7	362.0	1.8	529.2	3.0
Home Furnishings and Management	1,193.2	7.6	1,496.8	8.8	2,146.5	11.2	2,273.6	11.5	2,164.2	12.5
Sports, Recreation, Hobbies	248.0	1.6	235.5	1.4	301.5	1.6	268.4	1.4	273.5	1.6
Travel and Transportation	376.7	2.4	193.8	1.1	523.4	2.7	550.7	2.8	355.1	2.0
Wearing Apparel and Accessories	1,965.3	12.5	1,934.1	11.4	2,335.4	12.2	2,616.8	13.3	1,546.8	8.9
Cultural Interests	912.6	5.8	1,510.0	8.9	1,843.0	9.6	2,038.7	10.3	1,856.6	10.7
General Interest	1,433.3	9.1	1,131.5	6.7	1,314.7	6.9	1,050.4	5.3	1,040.0	6.0
Miscellaneous	912.6	5.8	580.4	3.4	774.5	4.0	643.8	3.3	650.8	3.7
Fiction	3,256.3	20.7	3,292.5	19.4	2,363.6	12.3	1,829.3	9.3	1,284.0	7.4
Total Editorial Content	**15,733.3**	**100.0%**	**16,957.6**	**100.0%**	**19,185.9**	**100.0%**	**19,710.2**	**100.0%**	**17,365.9**	**100.0%**
Total Editorial Content	15,733.3	57.2%	16,957.6	41.4%	19,185.9	48.2%	19,710.2	49.6%	17,365.9	49.0%
Total Advertising Content	11,753.1	42.8	23,988.4	58.6	20,631.1	51.8	20,052.3	50.4	18,074.8	51.0
Total Magazine Pages	**27,486.4**	**100.0%**	**40,946.0**	**100.0%**	**39,817.0**	**100.0%**	**39,762.5**	**100.0%**	**35,440.7**	**100.0%**

Source: Prepared especially for this volume by the R. Russell Hall Company (1977).

Sources

The data for both **Tables 530-A** and **530-B** come from the R. Russell Hall Company's *Magazine Editorial Reports*, although the summary information in **Table 530-A** was originally based on a tabulation by the Magazine Publishers Association (MPA).

The *Magazine Editorial Reports* is a monthly publication which classifies the editorial content of leading national magazines by subject matter. Magazine publishers use this information, in conjunction with circulation and readership information, for advertising, sales, and planning purposes. A sample will usually include between 40 and 60 leading general circulation magazines.

In **Table 530-A**, the percentages are based on the contents of different groups of magazines, depending on the samples for the years cited. In terms of measuring trends, this shifting of magazines in and out of the sample group probably introduces some error. **Table 530-B** does not share this limitation, since it is based on a content analysis of the same 14 magazines for the entire period.

The R. Russell Hall Company (formerly the Lloyd H. Hall Company) prepared **Table 530-B** especially for this volume. The company notes that the 18 content categories listed on the table have remained essentially the same over the years since 1938, when the service began. The data, then, may be considered historically comparable. The only apparent limitation to these data is that there is no way to separate content figures for the relatively large number of women's and home magazines from the figures for such publications as *Time* and *Newsweek*. Moreover, some publications are sensitive about the release of information about their individual magazines, and the Hall Company reports always honor this concern.

Further Information

A number of organizations collect editorial content information and distribute it to the magazine publishing trade. A list of these organizations is available from the Magazine Publishers Association in their publication, *Sources of Information About Magazines* (1973). Most of the groups do not prepare any reports for the general public.

At various intervals, MPA also releases statistics based on some of the services provided by these data-gathering organizations. Clients other than magazines can contract with these firms for various content analyses, as the editors did for **Table 530-B**.

Advertising content in national periodicals is monitored by Media Records, Inc. Summaries of their tabulations of national advertising revenues, by type of product, are published each year in the *U.S. Statistical Abstract*.

Subject Matter of Motion Pictures 540

Interpretation of Tables

The major sources of data on the subject matter in U.S. motion pictures vary widely in their approaches and in their definitions of subject-matter categories. In order to provide a reasonably comprehensive analysis of feature film content, the editors have had to assemble widely disparate information from several different sources for periods ranging from 1920 to 1976.

Table 540-A compares the subject matter of Hollywood over more than 30 years, as analyzed by three different sources. The Dale survey (1935) was an effort to delineate the "moral values" (and presumably any taints of "immorality") in the content of Hollywood features. The survey was based on an annual analysis of a randomly selected sample of 500 films. The actual films were not screened; the information was based, instead, on reviews written by a New York service catering to film exhibitors. Although the sample of films was selected at random, some attempt was made to keep selections in rough proportion to the number of films produced in a given year by each major motion picture firm. Interestingly, the Dale classification did not provide a separate category for Westerns, which have been a Hollywood staple since the beginnings of the industry.

The Cogley-MPAA classification system was based on the code ratings of the Motion Picture Association of America (MPAA). The analysis was further refined by Cogley (1956) into a workable and mutually exclusive set of categories. Because of differing classifications and approaches, the data from Dale and Cogley-MPAA are not as comparable as **Table 540-A** may lead readers to suppose.

Table 540-B is another MPAA analysis, this time of the source materials from which screenplays were written; and **Table 540-C** presents the MPAA's historically consistent content analysis of the newsreels produced in this country between 1931 and 1955. The figures in the latter are based on samples of *Movietone News, News of the Day, Paramount News, Pathé News,* and *Uni-*

Table 540–A.
Two Measures (Dale and Cogley/MPAA) of the Subject Matter of U.S. Feature Films, 1920–1930 and 1940–1953

Subject Matter	Dale Classification[a] 1920	1925	1930
Crime	24%	30%	27%
Mystery	3	2	5
War	2	2	4
Sex	13	17	15
Social Propaganda	1	- -	- -
Love	45	33	30
Children	- -	1	- -
History	- -	1	1
Comedy	12	13	16
Travel	- -	1	2

Subject Matter	Cogley/MPAA Classification[b] 1940	1944	1947	1950	1953
Crime/Detective	14%	10%	13%	20%	13%
Mystery/Spy	N/A	3	4	3	4
War/Military	N/A	2	2	4	7
Social Problems	15	11	28	12	9
Romance	2	3	10	11	16
Juvenile	4	3	1	1	2
History/Biography	3	2	2	4	5
Comedy	21	24	N/A	N/A	N/A
Action/Adventure	10	8	5	4	8
Westerns	18	18	25	27	18
Musicals	9	16	5	4	4
Other	4	- -	5	10	14

Sources: Dale classification data from Dale (1935), p. 17. Cogley/MPAA classification data: 1940, 1944: Motion Picture Association of America annual reports (1943, 1945); 1947-1953 data: MPAA reports summarized by Cogley (1956), pp. 282-283.

Notes: Due to differences in approach and classifications, the Dale data are not directly comparable to the Cogley/MPAA figures except in the broadest sense (see text for explanation). (a) Percentage figures are based on an analysis of 500 films released each year. The aim of the survey was to seek out "moral values" in the content of films. (b) Percentage figures are based on the Motion Picture Association of America (MPAA) categorization of all of the films submitted to the association for code ratings during the years indicated.

versal Newsreel. The "National Defense" category includes "home-front" news during World War II, while the "Foreign News" category does not entail coverage of the war.

Table 540-D, a detailed report from *Variety* on the current MPAA code-rating system, compares the record of the major and minor film production companies (Allied Artists, Universal, Columbia, MGM, and their affiliates) with the independent producers. Percentage figures after the number of films under each rating symbol denote the percentage of all films from that source (i.e., Majors-Minors, Independents or Total) in the yearly period indicated. The data suggest a trend by both camps away from films rated General (G) to those rated Parental Guidance (PG) and Restricted (R).

Table 540–B.
Analysis of Source Materials for U.S. Feature Film Screenplays, 1935–1954

	Original Screen Stories	Stage Plays	Novels	Biographies	Short Stories	Source Unknown	Miscellaneous
1935	47%	8%	27%	1%	7%	5%	5%
1936	68	7	17	- -	7	- -	1
1937	64	6	17	2	8	2	1
1938	58	6	26	- -	10	- -	1
1939	56	6	22	3	10	2	1
1940	62	10	21	2	4	- -	2
1941	63	10	10	1	15	1	1
1942	73	6	10	1	5	2	2
1943	75	6	10	1	1	4	4
1944	73	6	11	1	2	2	5
1945	65	7	15	- -	3	1	11
1946	61	5	15	- -	2	1	15
1947	58	4	22	- -	1	3	13
1948	56	6	18	- -	5	2	12
1949	68	4	18	1	4	- -	5
1950	73	4	16	1	2	- -	4
1951	67	6	16	1	6	- -	4
1952	67	5	17	- -	6	- -	5
1953	64	5	20	1	5	- -	5
1954	58	4	20	- -	4	- -	14
1955	52	8	24	1	9	- -	6
1956	51	6	21	2	12	- -	8
1966	48	4	37[a]		6	- -	5
1967	55	8	32[a]		- -	- -	5

Sources: Motion Picture Association of America data: 1935-1948: reprinted in Handel (1950), p. 22; 1949-1954: Cogley (1956), p. 281; 1955-1967: Motion Picture Association of America annual reports.

Notes: Figures may not add to 100 percent due to rounding. (a) The category given is "Books."

Sources

For a detailed discussion of the Dale survey and classification system in **Table 540-A**, see Dale (1935). The Cogley-MPAA data are taken from MPAA annual reports (1943, 1945) for the 1940-1944 figures, and from Cogley (1956) for the more recent years' figures. In order to match the later Cogley classifications as closely as possible, the editors recategorized some of the data for 1940 and 1944.

The information in **Table 540-B**, also from the MPAA, is reprinted in Handel (1950), for the years 1935 to 1948, and in Cogley (1956) for 1949-1954. As with **Table 540-A**, there is no way to judge the accuracy or the comparability of the categories or the figures.

The data in **Table 540-C** are taken from Dale (1935), for 1931-1932 figures, from the MPAA's annual report (1946), for 1936-1938, from Handel (1950), for 1939-1948, and from the MPAA annual report (1955) for the 1955 figures.

Table 540-D reports *Variety's* compilation of film ratings from the inception of the MPAA code system in November 1968.

Table 540–C.
Analysis of Subject Matter of Newsreels Produced in U.S., 1931–1955

Subject Matter	1931-32	1936	1937	1938	1939	1940	1941	1942	1943	1944	1945	1946	1947	1948	1955
National News:															
Aviation	6.3%	3.5%	3.6%	4.2%	3.1%	.8%	.9%	.1%	.2%	.4%	1.4%	3.2%	1.8%	1.7%	--
Disasters, Fires, etc.	4.4	4.3	5.0	3.8	3.4	3.1	2.6	2.3	1.4	1.7	1.9	3.0	4.0	2.1	--
Farm	--	.7	.6	.6	.2	.4	.2	.6	.7	1.7	.2	.5	.4	.4	--
Fashions, Styles	2.1	2.5	2.3	2.4	1.8	1.6	1.5	.9	.5	1.0	.9	1.5	1.2	2.3	--
Government	3.8	2.4	4.4	4.6	5.1	4.5	5.8	8.6	7.8	2.7	11.7	8.4	8.2	6.2	18.4%
Health	--	.4	.6	.6	.4	.4	.2	.1	.6	.9	.1	.6	.4	--[a]	--
Industrial Progress	2.1	.7	.6	2.9	.7	.9	.6	.1	1.0	.3	.3	.5	.1	.3	--
Labor	--	1.0	3.4	.7	.8	.1	1.5	.3	.7	.3	.8	2.4	1.3	1.0	--
National Defense[b]	10.0	2.2	2.5	2.6	4.1	13.7	24.7	23.3	22.2	13.3	3.4	7.1	4.3	4.5	8.7
Politics	7.2	4.8	.5	3.7	.8	7.3	.1	.1	.3	5.0	.1	.6	.3	6.1	--
Religion	2.7	.8	1.2	1.6	1.0	.6	.7	.4	1.0	1.5	.8	2.3	.8	1.0	--
Science	4.2	1.5	.5	.4	1.1	.2	.3	.1	.2	.2	.9	.7	.5	.7	--
Sports	21.2	23.8	27.2	27.4	26.1	25.0	26.2	15.3	8.6	9.1	9.4	18.3	26.2	23.1	25.5
Weather	--	2.5	1.1	1.4	.8	1.1	.4	.4	.2	.6	.3	.5	.9	.5	--
Miscellaneous	34.9	27.1	23.7	21.3	21.8	15.9	12.9	15.1	8.9	9.2	20.3	17.2	18.1	18.2	--
Foreign News[c]	1.0	21.8	22.8	21.8	18.3	5.8	4.2	2.9	2.1	1.4	23.7	29.7	29.3	30.3	32.7
War in Europe	--	--	--	--	10.5	18.6	15.8	15.0	28.9	37.7	9.7	--	--	--	--
War in Pacific	--	--	--	--	--	--	1.4	14.4	14.7	14.5	14.1	--	--	--	--
United Nations	--	--	--	--	--	--	--	--	--	--	--	3.5	2.2	1.6	--
Total Number of Newsreels Analyzed	1,724	4,755	4,956	5,250	4,940	4,947	4,948	4,454	3,810	3,491	3,133	3,559	3,484	3,541	3,673

Sources: 1931-1932 data: Dale (1935), p. 201. 1936-1938 data: Motion Picture Association of America annual report (1946), p. 41. 1936-1948 data: Handel (1950), p. 170. 1955 data: figured by the editors from data in Motion Picture Association of America annual report (1955), p. 14.

Notes: 1936-1939 data was compiled from Movietone News, News of the Day, Paramount News, Pathé News (Warner Pathé News after August 15, 1947), and Universal Newsreel. (a) Less than .1%. (b) Including domestic war activities after U. S. entry into World War II. (c) Excluding World War II coverage.

Table 540–D.
Distribution of MPAA-Code Ratings among Films Produced by the Major/Minor Studios and the Independent Motion Picture Companies in U.S., 1967–1976

| | MPAA-Code Ratings | | | | | | | | Total Distribution of Ratings | |
| | G | | PG | | R | | X | | | |
	Number of Films	Percent of All Releases[a]	Number of Films	Percent of All Releases[a]	Number of Films	Percent of All Releases[a]	Number of Films	Percent of All Releases[a]	Number of Films	Percent of All Releases[a]
1968-69										
Major/Minor Studios[b]	120	32%	154	42%	81	22%	16	4%	371	84%
Independents	21	30	18	26	22	31	9	13	70	16
Total	141	32%	172	39%	103	23%	25	6%	441	100%
1969-70										
Major/Minor Studios	59	22%	109	40%	91	34%	12	4%	271	61%
Independents	31	18	46	27	73	42	22	13	172	39
Total	90	20%	155	35%	164	37%	34	8%	443	100%
1970-71										
Major/Minor Studios	60	25%	105	44%	70	30%	3	1%	238	46%
Independents	41	15	91	33	100	36	45	16	277	54
Total	101	20%	196	38%	170	33%	48	9%	515	100%
1971-72										
Major/Minor Studios	74	29%	127	50%	51	20%	1	1%	253	50%
Independents	20	8	104	40	127	50	5	2	256	50
Total	94	19%	231	45%	178	35%	6	1%	509	100%
1972-73										
Major/Minor Studios	43	18%	112	47%	79	33%	3	1%	237	43%
Independents	42	13	72	23	182	58	17	5	313	57
Total	85	16%	184	33%	261	47%	20	4%	550	100%
1973-74										
Major/Minor Studios	36	20%	88	50%	55	31%	2	1%	177[c]	35%
Independents	36	11	97	30	177	54	17	5	327	65
Total	72	14%	185	37%	232	46%	15[c]	3%	504[c]	100%
1974-75										
Major/Minor Studios	28	18%	68	45%	54	35%	3	2%	153	36%
Independents	28	11	82	30	148	54	14	5	272	64
Total	56	13%	150	35%	202	48%	17	4%	425	100%

Note: Key to MPAA ratings: G—general audience; PG—parental guidance suggested; R—restricted to those 17 years or older unless accompanied by a parent or guardian; X—prohibited to those under 17 years.

Table 540–D. (Cont'd.)

| | MPAA-Code Ratings | | | | | | | | | Total Distribution of Ratings | |
| | G | | PG | | R | | X | | | | |
	Number of Films	Percent of All Releases[a]	Number of Films	Percent of All Releases[a]	Number of Films	Percent of All Releases[a]	Number of Films	Percent of All Releases[a]	Number of Films	Percent of All Releases[a]
1975-76										
Major/Minor Studios	24	16%	75	51%	45	30%	4	3%	148	30%
Independents	40	12	85	24	179	51	45	13	349	70
Total	64	13%	160	32%	224	45%	49	10%	497	100%
Totals, 1968-1976										
Major/Minor Studios	444	24%	838	45%	526	29%	40	2%	1,848	48%
Independents	259	13	595	29	1,008	49	174	9	2,036	52
Total	703	18%	1,433	37%	1,534	39%	214	6%	3,884	100%

Source: Motion Picture Association of America code ratings as reported in *Variety* (January 5, 1977).

Notes: (a) Percentage figures denote the proportion of all films released by each production category (Majors/Minors or Independents) during the year indicated. (b) The Major/Minor Studios category includes the following companies: Allied Artists, American International, Avco-Embassy, Buena Vista, Columbia, MGM, Paramount, 20th Century-Fox, United Artists, Universal, and Warner Bros., as well as all affiliated trademarks. (c) Errors in original. 177 should be 181, 15 should be 19, 504 should be 508.

Further Information

Dale (1935) is the most useful historic source for information on content trends in the early years of Hollywood motion pictures. Good statistics for the 1947-1954 period are available in Cogley (1956). Although literature on film content is voluminous, much of it is based on nostalgia and offers little quantitative data. For a valuable overview (with a bibliographical guide to further sources), see Manvell et al. (1972).

The standard source of data on newsreels is Fielding (1972). The editors have been unable to locate quantitative information on documentary films—but Barnouw (1974) provides a brief survey. For nontheatrical films, see Unit 140, and *Hope Reports* (various dates).

Table 550–A.
Analysis of the Content of Disc and Tape Recordings Produced in U.S.,
by Percentage of Retail Sales, 1961–1975

Type of Recording	Percent of Unit Sales— Disc Albums Only			Percent of Dollar Volume—Tapes and Discs	
	1961	1963	1965	1973	1975
Contemporary (popular, rock, soul)	51%	57%	57%	64%	61%
Country/Western	14	21	20	11	12
Middle of the Road	13	7	10	11	11
Classical	3	2	2	5	5
Comedy	8	6	3	2	2
Jazz	5	3	3	3	5
Children's	4	5	5	4	3
Other (spoken, ethnic, etc.)	3	1	1	1	2

Source: National Association of Record Merchandisers (NARM).

Interpretation of Tables

A visit to any local record outlet will show that popular rock and soul music dominate the recordings industry. But more specific, scientifically valid information on content trends for recordings does not seem to be available. Part of the problem is that the terminology in the recordings business changes as rapidly as popular music fads. How to define "progressive rock," and how to categorize the many kinds of nonclassical instrumental music, are but two examples of the problem. In addition, most information on types of recordings is based on dollar volume, which is not as reliable as unit volume figures, since the pricing of recordings varies considerably. For example, more classical records than top-selling popular albums are available on inexpensive labels. Finally, there are probably differences in content trends for disc and tape recordings (and even among the different tape formats), but there are no consistent data on such differences.

Table 550-A provides at least an outline of style trends for recordings over a 15-year period, with an emphasis on disc recordings (tapes make up less than 30 percent of the 1973 and 1975 data shown). Some tentative observations can be made on the basis of these figures: (1) country music has declined in popularity; (2) classics are selling better, (3) comedy record sales have dropped sharply, and (4) other categories of recordings have remained relatively stable over the period. It is difficult to draw any conclusions from the broad "contemporary" music category, since it incorporates changing trends in folk music, in all kinds of vocal and instrumental music, and in many styles of rock music.

Sources

The data in Table 550-A are taken from the annual statistical reports of the National Association of Recording Merchandisers, Inc. (NARM). In 1961, NARM members accounted for about 57 percent of the total industry's sales volume—a figure that rose to about 90 percent by the mid-1970s. The data for 1961-1965 represent the percentage of album unit sales; the figures for 1973 and 1975 combine tapes and discs and are based on the percentage of dollar volume.

Since the editors recategorized some of the data to allow more comparability, all of the figures should be considered approximations. The "contemporary" category combines popular, rock, folk, and soul music for the 1961-1965 figures. The middle-of-the-road (MOR) music data for the 1960s include "sound and percussion" recordings and movie soundtrack albums.

Further Information

General articles on style trends in the recordings industry appear regularly in *Billboard* and other trade periodicals, but statistical content analyses are rarely included in those publications. NARM is apparently the only other source of specific information on content trends in the industry.

Content and Airtime of Broadcast News Programming 56

Table 560–A.
Total Hours per Week of Regularly Scheduled Network Radio and Television News Programs in U.S., by Type of Program, 1930–1974

Programming Content	Number of Hours per Week									
	1930	1935	1940	1945	1950	1955	1960	1965	1969/70[a]	1973/4[b]
News Reporting										
Radio	2	7	18	34	30	39	N/A	N/A	133[c]	129[d]
Television	--	--	--	--	4	6	6	14	16	16
Forum-Interview and News Analysis/Commentary										
Radio	1	4	5	5	7	8	N/A	N/A	N/A	N/A
Television	--	--	--	--	5	6	4	2	2	2
Documentary and Information										
Radio	1	5	7	9	4	4	N/A	N/A	N/A	N/A
Television	--	--	--	--	1	4	3	8	3	6
Total										
Radio	4	16	30	48	41	51	N/A	N/A	133[e]	129[e]
Television	--	--	--	--	10	16	13	24	21	24
Radio and Television Combined	4	16	30	48	51	67	N/A	N/A	154[e]	153[e]

Sources: Radio data through 1955 based on Summers (1958) and calculated by C. H. Sterling and L. W. Lichty. Radio data for 1969 provided directly to editors by L. W. Lichty. Radio data for 1974 from Lichty and Topping (1975), p. 434, table 31. All television data from Unit 582, except for weekend daytime data, which is from L. W. Lichty.

Notes: The figures in the original sources were all expressed in quarter hours. The editors converted these figures to the nearest full hour. (a) Radio data are for 1969, television for 1970. (b) Radio data are for 1974, television for 1973. (c) Includes daytime and evening news programs on all national networks (including the four separate ABC-operated networks—hence, a few programs were duplicated, and those duplications are included in the total figure). (d) Includes all regularly scheduled day and night news analysis/commentary programming, but does not include forum-interview programs. (e) These totals exclude the very limited amount of radio programming in the forum-interview and documentary and information categories.

Table 560–B.
Total Averaged Hours of News Programming
by the Three U.S. Television Networks, 1970–1976

	Regularly Scheduled News Programs	Sponsored News Specials	Network-Sponsored News Specials	Total News Hours
1970-71[a]	289	72	25	386
1971-72	310	62	13	385
1972-73	326	72	25	423
1973-74	318	62	33	413
1974-75	313	43	44	400
1975-76	318	73	20	411

Source: Nielsen Television Index, A. C. Nielsen Company, *Television Audience* (1976), pp. 56, 62.

Note: (a) Seasons run from September thru April of years given.

Interpretation of Tables

The tables in this section provide a quantitative measure of the growth of broadcast journalism. Table 560-A lists the total weekly hours of *regularly scheduled* network radio and television news programs, with a breakdown by type of news program. While the data indicate a definite and steady growth in the number of radio newscasts, the trend in network television news is less consistent.

Table 560-B focuses on network television news programming from 1970 to 1976, showing the total averaged hours of regularly scheduled news for all three networks. About 80 percent of these figures are the standard evening news programs; the remaining 20 percent are sponsored news specials and network-sustained news specials which are usually scheduled on short notice in response to news events. A news-programming peak in the 1972-1973 season is probably due to the end of U.S. involvement in Vietnam and to coverage of the presidential election year.

Table 560-C provides averaged national figures for a sample week of nonentertainment programming by commercial television stations. The figures indicate the essentially static proportions of news, public affairs, and other nonentertainment programming between 1973 and 1976. Note that about half the news content comes from other than local sources—in most cases, from the networks.

Table 560-D offers comparative figures on the uses of television by recent Presidents—an issue of interest to the networks (for financial reasons) and to observers and scholars of national politics. One striking trend in this table is the increasing concentrations of *prime-time* presidential appearances early in a new administration. Another interesting revelation, for which there is no clear explanation, is the substantially higher amounts of television appearances by President Kennedy during the daytime hours.

Table 560-E lists the percentage of radio and television stations which broadcast editorials on a daily, weekly, or "only occasional" basis. The information in this table is not particularly reliable (see "Sources" section below), but it seems to indicate a trend of increasing station uses of the editorial after the mid-1960s. The pattern is erratic, but this is due more to survey limitations than to documented changes in the field.

Sources

The information in Table 560-A on radio news programming up to 1955 is from Summers (1958), as interpreted and arranged by L. W. Lichty and C. H. Sterling. The 1969 radio figures were provided to the editors by Lichty. The 1974 *total* radio data, from Lichty and Topping (1975), includes 55 hours per week of public affairs and documentary-information programming. Not included on this table are such programs as NBC's *Monitor*, which ran on weekends for many

Table 560-C.
Percentage of Prime-Time and Total Airtime Hours of Non-Entertainment Programming by Commercial Television Stations in U.S., by Source and Type of Programming, 1973–1976

Programming Content	1973 Percent of Prime-Time	1973 Percent of Total Time	1974 Percent of Prime-Time	1974 Percent of Total Time	1975 Percent of Prime-Time	1975 Percent of Total Time	1976 Percent of Prime-Time	1976 Percent of Total Time
All Local, Syndicated, Network Programs								
News	12%	9%	12%	9%	12%	10%	12%	9%
Public Affairs	5	4	3	4	5	5	3	4
Other Nonentertainment Programs	2	9	2	9	5	10	5	11
Total Nonentertainment Programs	19	22	17	22	22	25	20	24
Locally Produced Programs Only								
News	6	5	6	5	5	6	6	5
Public Affairs	1	2	1	2	1	2	1	2
Other Nonentertainment Programs	1	2	1	2	1	2	1	2
Total Nonentertainment Programs	8	9	8	9	7	10	8	9

Source: Federal Communications Commission, *Television Broadcast Programming Data*, appropriate annual issues.

Notes: This survey encompassed 694 stations in 1973, 699 in 1974, 686 in 1975, and 702 in 1976. Prime-time hours are 6-11 P.M. in the Eastern and Pacific time zones, 5-10 P.M. in the Central and Mountain zones. Total broadcast time is 6 A.M. to midnight.

Table 560–D.
Number and Total Hours of Presidential Appearances
on U.S. Network Television, 1960–1975

	Kennedy[a]	Johnson[a]	Nixon[a]	Ford[b]	Carter[c]
Number of Appearances, Prime-Time Only	4	7	14	12	4
Hours of Air Time, Prime-Time Only	1:54	3:20	7:03	7:00	2:15
Total Number of Appearances	50	33	37	19	25
Total Hours of Air Time	30:15	12:30	13:30	12:55	14:05

Sources: Kennedy, Johnson, and Nixon data: Minow et al. (1975), p. 171, table 1, which is based on figures reported to the *New York Times* by the White House Press Office. Ford data: Nielsen Television Index, A. C. Nielsen Company, *Nielsen Newscast* No. 3 (1975), pp. 6-7. Carter data provided to the editors by the Congressional Research Service, Library of Congress.

Notes: (a) First 19 months in office. (b) First 15 months in office. (c) First 8 months in office.

years, and the weekend interview program *Face the Nation*, which is also carried on television. The cumulative totals for 1969-1970 and 1973-1974 are therefore not directly comparable to the radio-TV figures shown for 1950 and 1955. Directly comparable figures would be higher.

The television data for **Table 560-A** were taken from the tables in Unit 582, with the addition of weekend daytime figures which were supplied by Lichty. The 1969-1970 and 1973-1974 columns on the table represent a combination of materials: the radio data are for 1969 and 1974; the television data for 1970 and 1973. The Mutual and DuMont networks are included in these figures where applicable.

The **Table 560-B** data are all from A. C. Nielsen Company's *Television Audience* (1976). Since the information for sponsored news programs was multiplied from monthly averages, the "total news hours" column is a close estimate.

The figures in **Table 560-C** are from the FCC's annual *Television Broadcast Programming Data*. These data are based on station reports of their schedules on random days throughout the year. The material is then collected into a composite sample week for all stations. Nearly all U.S. commercial television stations are included in the survey (compare the numbers of stations reporting for this table with the station totals listed in Unit 180).

Table 560-D, from Minow, Martin, and Mitchell (1975), is based on figures reported to the *New York Times* by the White House Press Office. Information on the Ford Administration comes from the A. C. Nielsen Company, *Nielsen Newscast* No. 3 (1975). The Nielsen material was converted by the editors into information comparable with the rest of the table. The Carter data were provided to the editors by the Congressional Research Service, Library of Congress.

Table 560-E is from issues of *Broadcasting Yearbook*, usually for the year after the date shown on the table. The data were gathered by mail survey and they are based in some cases on less than half of the broadcasting stations in the United States (compare the totals in Units 170 and 180). The proportion of stations which do *not* broadcast editorials is not listed separately, because that information was not supplied in most cases. Thus, these figures in **Table 560-E** are at best only very approximate and must be used with caution.

Further Information

The best regular review of broadcast journalism is Barrett (1968 to date). Serious studies of journalism abound, but the most useful of those with quantitative information are Wolf (1972), Epstein (1973), and Batscha (1975). Braestrup (1977) gives a wealth of information on television reporting of the Vietnam war, and Routt (1974) is useful for data on broadcast editorializing.

Table 560–E.
Percentage of U.S. Radio and Television Stations Which Broadcast Editorials, by Frequency of Such Broadcasts, 1959–1975

	1959	1961	1963[a]	1965	1967	1969	1971	1973	1975
AM Radio Stations									
Number of Stations Reporting	N/A	N/A	N/A	3,225	3,155	3,465	2,241	2,018	2,612
Percent Which Broadcast Editorials									
On a daily basis	3%	7%	7%	10%	11%	7%	10%	17%	17%
On a weekly basis	4	4	4	6	19	5	9	15	13
Only occasionally	23	25	22	45	33	37	45	68	70
Percent of Total Editorializing	30	37	33	61	63	49	64	N/A	N/A
FM Radio Stations									
Number of Stations Reporting	N/A	N/A	N/A	309	388	1,986	554	601	1,792
Percent Which Broadcast Editorials									
On a daily basis	3%	3%	7%	2%	9%	3%	8%	15%	15%
On a weekly basis	2	3	4	4	9	4	7	14	13
Only occasionally	15	13	22	26	28	29	32	72	72
Percent of Total Editorializing	19	20	33	31	46	36	46	N/A	N/A
Television Stations									
Number of Stations Reporting	N/A	N/A	N/A	383	444	449	390	410	463
Percent Which Broadcast Editorials									
On a daily basis	4%	7%	10%	13%	11%	12%	15%	26%	23%
On a weekly basis	3	6	5	10	8	10	9	20	20
Only occasionally	25	20	18	31	29	27	30	54	58
Percent of Total Editorializing	32	37	33	54	48	49	53	N/A	N/A

Source: *Broadcasting Yearbook*, appropriate issues.

Note: (a) AM and FM stations were combined in the 1963 survey.

Table 570–A.
Programming Content of AM and FM Radio Stations in U.S., by Size of Market, 1964–1976

Year and Size of Market	Number of Stations	Middle of the Road	Top 40/ Contemporary	Beautiful and Background	Country/ Western	Black/ Soul	Progressive Rock	News and Talk	Classical	Other
1964 (AM and FM)[a]										
Large, Multiple Station Markets	1,400	12%	10%	22%	6%	5%	-[b]	--	--	45%
Single Station Markets		22	9	21	12	1	--	--	--	35
1966 (FM only)										
Top 50 Markets	244	49	15	30	--	--	--	--	--	6
Other Markets	564	64	4	23	5	--	--	--	--	4
1968 (AM and FM)										
Top 50 Markets	1,076	40	15	13	11	7	--	--	--	14
1970 (FM only)										
All Markets	1,365	35	17	22	11	1	4%	1%	--	9
1971 (AM and FM) Top 100 Markets										
AM Stations	955	21	27	17	18	--	--	--	--	17
FM Stations	643	18	25	39	10	--	--	--	--	8
1973 (AM and FM)										
All Markets	4,193	22	26	8	21	14	3	3	3%	--
1975 (AM and FM) Top 40 Markets										
AM Stations	600	26	17	5	16	10	2	9	2	13
FM Stations	475	13	21	24	9	5	10	2	6	10
1976 (AM and FM)										
Top 50 Markets[c]	500	14	27	18	6	5	--	8	1	22

Sources: 1964–1973 data: Lichty and Topping (1975), p. 435, table 32. 1975 data: Cox Broadcasting Corp. (1976), p. 55, exhibit 16. 1976 data: *Broadcasting* (September 27, 1976), "The Many Worlds of Radio, 1976," p. 46.

Notes: (a) The percentages here refer only to musical content and therefore, are not strictly applicable to later figures. (b) Blank spaces generally indicate that the programming category has been included under "other." In some cases, however, the particular programming format was not broadcast that year. (c) This listing is based on the top 10 stations in the top 50 markets. Thus, while it encompasses the top 50 markets, the listing also excludes many stations in these markets which feature minority-taste programming.

Interpretation of Table

From its beginning, radio was primarily a medium providing music to the home. Even in the heyday of network radio, local program hours were dominated by "musical clock" programs. With the decline of the radio networks in the 1950s, "formula" or format radio dominated the airways, with either MOR (middle-of-the-road) musical programming, or a combination of music and talk geared to the average listener, or a repetitive and tightly structured format of "top 40" records and frequent commercials aimed at youthful listeners. Most FM stations either broadcast the same programs as their AM owners, or provided classical or background music.

About 1965, radio programming began to change. In a ruling that called for separation of AM-FM station programming, the FCC provided the impetus for the diversification of FM programming into popular and even "talk" formats previously limited to AM stations. At first, the FCC ruling affected only markets of 100,000 or more and about half of the total broadcasting time of each station, but a decade later, the ruling was extended to more airtime and smaller markets.

Table 570-A provides limited documentation of the trend to greater diversification in both AM and FM radio between 1964 and 1976. The numbers are not strictly comparable, since many different surveys, with varied definitions of programming content, are summarized here. Nonetheless, the trend to more diversification is evident by the mid-1970s.

The rise in use of a Country/Western musical format, which became increasingly popular in the Northeast in the 1960s, is of special interest. In the larger cities, black "soul" music and other types of minority programming gained popularity in the early 1970s. Thus far, only the largest markets are able to economically support "all-news" stations and "talk" formats. With increasing diversification, however, there is also duplication—one can now drive across the country and hear the same three or four basic radio formats with very few regional differences.

Sources

The data in Table 570-A for 1964 to 1973 were compiled and recategorized by Lichty and Topping (1975) from several different surveys. The 1964 figures are for musical formats only. The data for 1975 come from Cox (1976). The information for 1976 comes from "The Many Worlds of Radio, 1976" in *Broadcasting* (September 27, 1976). This article covered only the top 10 stations (in ratings) in the top 50 markets; thus, some data on minority-interest programming are excluded. Because of the many different sources and approaches, this table must be taken as only a rough approximation of actual trends.

Further Information

Most trade reports and research results on radio programming appear in *Broadcasting*. Information on programming formats can be found in *Broadcasting Yearbook* and in Standard Rate and Data Service's radio rate monthly. Contact the major radio trade associations for other information.

For historical tables covering selected stations in the period up to 1939, see Albig (1956). Radio network programs from 1927 to 1956 are detailed, with some statistical information, in Lichty and Topping (1975).

Commercial Television Station Programming

Interpretation of Tables

While information on network television programming trends is extensive and readily available (see Unit 582), data showing the "typical" weekly schedule of individual television stations are nowhere near so common or so easy to come by. Most such data tend to be limited by serious discontinuities.

Table 580-A reveals some of the trends developed over two decades of commercial television programming, from 1951 until 1970. Among the trends indicated by the figures: the limited amount of musical programming on television; the decline of variety shows; the expansion and then limited decline of drama, including comedy drama; the sharp drop in televised sports; the relatively low and fairly steady amounts of news, public affairs, and religious programming; and the fluctuating

Table 580–A.
Typical Weekly Programming Content of Commercial Television Stations
in Four Major U.S. Cities, by Percentage of Total Airtime, 1951–1970

| Programming Content | 1951 | | | 1952 | 1954 | 1958 | 1960 | 1970 |
	New York	Los Angeles	Chicago	New York	New York	Washington, D. C.	Los Angeles	Washington, D. C.
Variety	24%	26%	16%	17%	11%	5%	5%	14%
Music	4	6	3	3	7	7	3	3
Drama	25	25	26	36	46	46	54	38
Quiz/Personality	11	8	14	9	10	9	6	8
News	6	13	6	6	6	4	5	9
Information/Talk	7	5	5	8	8	8	9	6
Religious	1	1	- -	1	2	2	2	3
Children's	12	10	8	11	3	13	7	13
Sports	10	5	21	8	3	5	4	4
Miscellaneous	- -	- -	- -	- -	4	1	5	2

Sources: Lichty and Topping (1975), p. 442, table 38, utilizing (for 1951-1954) data from National Association of Educational Broadcasters, and (for 1958-1970) data from student term papers.

schedules of children's programming. The percentages shown here include both network and local programs, since they are based on *complete* station schedules for approximately one week.

Table 580-B compares the programming formats and sources of network-affiliate and independent television stations from 1954 to 1972. For affiliates, the reader will note two trends: (1) the increase in network programming (from one-half to two-thirds of total program time), and (2) the decline of local-live and syndicated-film programs, and the rise of syndicated and local videotaped programming after 1960. Among independent stations, both "made-for-TV," syndicated films and theatrical films have declined somewhat; but as of 1972, they still dominated nearly half of the programming hours. Syndicated and local videotaped programming moved into second place with 28 percent of all programming. The table also indicates that local-live programming is far more common on independent than on network-affiliate stations. The small percentage of network programming on the independent stations in 1972 usually occurred when a local affiliate refused the network offering.

Table 580-C provides a 25-year survey of the number of syndicated programs or program series (*not* individual episodes) available in a given month each year. All syndicated material up to 1960, and much of it after that date, was on film. However, by the 1970s, videotape was more commonly used for certain types of programming—especially news, quiz, sports, and some variety shows. The reader should take special note of the high percentage of available syndicated material which was "*first run*"—that is, it had not previously been aired on one of the national television networks. (The "off-network" programs are those that were first broadcast by a network and then released into syndication, for sale to stations as "re-runs.")

Table 580-D traces content trends in syndicated programs over a shorter period, from 1965 through 1974. Certain types of programming (variety, situation comedy, documentary, quiz shows, religion, and sports) have increased sharply over this period, while other genres, such as drama and cartoons, have either remained consistent or have declined somewhat. Taken together, **Tables 580-A** through **580-D** reflect the growing demand for syndicated material as the number of independent stations (chiefly UHF) have increased (see Units 180 and 181).

Table 580–B.

A Comparison of Programming Formats of Network-Affiliate and Independent Television Stations in U.S., by Percentage of Total Airtime, 1954–1972

	Programming Format and Source					
	Made-for-TV Films	Theatrical Films	Syndicated Videotaped Programs	Local Live Programs	Local Videotaped Programs	Network Programs
Network-Affiliate Stations						
1954	12%	17%	- -	21%	- -	50%
1956	14	15	- -	14	- -	56
1958	13	16	- -	13	- -	58
1960	13	13	.3%	11	1	63
1962	12	11	1	12	2	63
1964	11	10	2	11	3	64
1966	9	11	3	10	3	64
1968	7	8	7	10	2	63
1970	7	9	2	10	3	66
1972	7	8	7	10	2	63
Independent Stations						
1954	21	31	- -	47	- -	- -
1956	20	48	- -	23	- -	- -
1958	24	47	- -	29	- -	- -
1960	36	28	4	31	2	- -
1962	36	26	5	28	9	- -
1964	43	26	5	23	4	- -
1966	25	33	8	28	9	- -
1968	27	29	11	20	8	- -
1970	31	35	15	14	5	- -
1972	23	24	20	18	8	4

Source: *Broadcasting Yearbook*, annual surveys.

Note: Discrepancies in percentage totals ranging from 95% to 104% due to rounding errors in source.

Sources

Table 580-A is reprinted from Lichty and Topping (1975). The data through 1954 were gathered from surveys by the National Association of Educational Broadcasters (NAEB), which was attempting to persuade the FCC of the need for public (then educational) television allocations to offset the lack of public affairs and news programs on commercial stations. Data for 1958 through 1970 were taken by Lichty and Topping from student term papers. In all cases, these data represent a full week of programming on all stations in each of the cities. The selected week and the time of the year differ for each survey. Because of the differing survey methods, the variations in content categorization, and the varied numbers of stations in the surveyed cities, the reliability of this table is limited.

Table 580-B reprints figures for the even-numbered years from 20 years of surveys conducted by *Broadcasting Yearbook*. The data for these surveys were self-reported by the stations, and the number of respondent stations was never noted. These surveys were discontinued after 1973.

Table 580-C was derived by Hatcher (1976) from several different sources, and thus the data are not strictly comparable. The figures up to 1958 came from *Telefilm* (February 1959);

Table 580–C.
Number of Available Syndicated Television Program Series in U.S., 1951–1975

	Total Number of Syndicated Series	Number of "Off-Network" Series	Number of "First-Run" Series	Percentage of First-Run Series
1951	20	14	6	30%
1952	26	12	14	54
1953	26	7	19	73
1954	37	0	37	100
1955	52	10	42	81
1956	36	17	19	53
1957	29	9	20	69
1958	47	17	30	64
1959	43	N/A	N/A	N/A
1960	58	N/A	N/A	N/A
1965	137	60	77	56
1967	196	63	133	68
1968	244	98	146	60
1970	213	94	169	64[a]
1971	262	110	152	58
1972	181	80	111	58[b]
1973	198	65	133	67
1974	313	110	203	65
1975	312	102	210	67

Sources: Hatcher (1976), utilizing data from *Telefilm* (February 1959), p. 14, for the 1951-1958 figures, and *Films for Television* for the 1959-1960 figures. 1965-1971 data figured by Hatcher from Arbitron's *Syndicated Programming Analysis* (November 1965, February-March 1967, November 1968, 1970, 1971). 1972-1975 data from Nielsen Television Index, A. C. Nielsen Company, *Report on Syndicated Programs* (November of each year).

Notes: "Off-network" syndicated programs are those that were first broadcast by a network and then released into syndication for sale to television stations as "re-runs." "First-run" syndications are original programming which has never appeared on a network. (a) Figure should be 79 percent, given the data here, but the source reports it as 64 percent. (b) Figure should be 61 percent, but source reports it as 58 percent.

the 1959-1960 figures came from *Films for Television*, which did not break down the total figures. (Although not shown here, Hatcher also presents totals reported in *Films for Television* for 1951-1958. These figures differ only slightly from the totals given in **Table 580-C.**)

The **Table 580-C** data for 1965-1971 data were calculated by Hatcher from Arbitron's *Syndicated Programming Analysis*, and the figures for 1972-1975 came from A. C. Nielsen Company's *Report on Syndicated Programs*. Because this table does not take program length into account, it is difficult to estimate the amount of syndicated material which is actually available. Most syndicated material runs 30 minutes, although some 15-minute material appeared prior to 1960, and some longer material has been available since that date.

Table 580-D was based on the same sources noted above for **Table 580-C**, with the categorization done by Hatcher (1976).

Further Information

Data on syndicated television programs are currently reported by the A. C. Nielsen Company in its *Report on Syndicated Programs*. David's *TV Season* (annual) also includes some data on nationally syndicated material. The history of syndication is best summarized by Hatcher (1976) and the earlier sources he cites. In addition, *Variety* and *Broadcasting* often contain television programming information.

Table 580–D.
Table 580–D.
Number and Content of Syndicated Television Programs and Series Available in a Given Month Each Year in U.S., 1965–1974

	1965	1968	1970	1972	1974
Total Number of Syndicated Programs	146	267	263	191	313
Number of Programs Which are:					
Variety	22	31	36	20	39
Music	5	4	3	13	13
Drama	56	84	79	51	68
Situation Comedy	10	26	33	28	47
Cartoons	18	18	19	9	17
Documentary	8	20	14	3	16
Human Interest/Quiz/Panel	4	10	12	14	16
News/Public Affairs/Talk	3	14	12	19	11
Religion	18	34	33	25	60
Sports Play-by-Play	1	15	11	6	18
Other/Miscellaneous	1	11	11	3	8

Sources: Hatcher (1976), pp. 71-72, 109-110, citing 1965-1970 data from Arbitron, *Syndicated Programming Analysis*, appropriate issues; and 1972-1974 data from A. C. Nielsen Company, *Report on Syndicated Programs*, appropriate issues.

Public Television Station Programming 58

Interpretation of Tables

Over the two decades covered in **Table 581-A**, the figures illustrate the transformation of public television—referred to as *educational* television prior to 1967—from a strictly local-station medium, with some exchanged ("bicycled") film materials among the stations, to a national network with a full schedule of weekly programming. Program format information does not include network interconnection programming until after 1970, although some interconnected feeds began in 1967 through the Ford Foundation-supported Public Broadcasting Laboratory.

The program sources data show how much less self-reliant public stations have become since the early 1960s. They now get the majority of their programming from national sources (mainly the Public Broadcasting Service interconnection), and even state and regional exchanges and networks have given way to the national and syndicated materials. The format and sources structure of public television now bears a growing resemblance to that of the network-affiliated commercial stations.

Table 581-B reviews the content of public television's general programming and the age levels to which the PBS instructional programs are directed. (Most instructional programming is broadcast during school hours.) Note the increases in instructional programming during the mid-1960s—increases which, to some extent, paralleled the massive school and other educational funding available from the "Great Society" programs of that era. Decreased funding, combined with inflation and disillusionment with television instruction as the panacea for education's ills, brought levels of instructional programming down by a significant amount in the mid-1970s. After 1970, most of the children's programming shown on public television came from the Children's Television Workshop (CTW), which created such programs as *Sesame Street*.

In distinct contrast, the PBS programming for the general public has steadily increased in the 1970s, after a moderate decline in the mid-1960s. In specific categories of programming, a decline in art and culture and in public affairs is matched by a small but rising percentage of entertainment

Table 581-A.
Hours, Format, and Sources of Public Television Programming in U.S., 1954-1976

	Hours per Week		Program Format (percent of total hours)			Program Sources (percent of total hours)			
	Total, All Stations	Average per Station	Live	Film or Tape	Network Interconnect	Local	National	State/ Regional	Syndication
1954	197	N/A	58%	42%	--	N/A	N/A	N/A	N/A
1956	468	N/A	60	40	--	N/A	25%	N/A	N/A
1958	1,027	38	52	48	--	N/A	28	N/A	N/A
1962	2,596	42	N/A	N/A	--	52%	29	N/A	19%
1964	3,715	42	13	87	--	37	31	15%	18
1966	5,688	50	8	92	--	15	50	14	21
1968	8,534	56	9	91	--	13	51	21	15
1970	12,217	65	N/A	N/A	N/A	11	62	11	16
1972	15,600	71	3	63	34%	16	54	10	20
1974	25,642	74	3	52	46	11	62	10	17
1976	29,881	87	2	52	46	10	70	6	14

Sources: 1954-1958 data: Educational Television and Radio Center (1958). All other years: Corporation for Public Broadcasting; 1962-1972 data: *One Week of Educational Television* (series); 1974 data: *Public Television Program Content: 1974*, pp. 24, 28, and inside front cover; 1976 data: *Public Television Programming by Category: 1976* (1977), pp. 19, 22, and inside front cover.

programs—often motion pictures—as public stations have worked to broaden their appeal.

Table 581-C provides a trend study of the content of television programs distributed by the Public Broadcasting Service, the major national programming agency for the industry. Beginning with the second season listed here (1974), PBS programming was largely determined by the Station Program Cooperative (SPC), a complicated system of bidding and voting by individual public television stations for the selection of the PBS offerings each season. It is not yet possible to discern

Table 581-B.
Content of General and Instructional Programming by Public Television Stations in U.S., 1956–1976

	1956	1958	1962	1964	1966	1968	1970	1972	1974	1976
General Programming Categories:										
Public Affairs	11%	13%	N/A	13%	13%	14%	18%	19%	13%	13%
Children's	10	10	N/A	10	10	10	20	21	32	25
Cultural and Arts	17	16	N/A	10	14	9	11	7	9	10
Entertainment	N/A	N/A	N/A	2	3	8	7	5	9	10
Other	47	24	N/A	19	18	10	8	20	20	21
Total	85%	63%	54%	54%	58%	51%	63%	72%	83%	79%
Instructional Programming Categories:										
Primary (Grades K-3)	N/A	11%	N/A	23%	6%	8%	9%	7%	N/A	N/A
Intermediate (Grades 4-6)	N/A	}	N/A	}	13	14	11	10	N/A	N/A
Junior High (Grades 7-9)	N/A	16	N/A	7	7	8	6	4	N/A	N/A
Senior High (Grades 10-12)	N/A	}	N/A	11	8	10	6	4	N/A	N/A
College	N/A	N/A	N/A	5	9	8	5	1	N/A	N/A
Adult	N/A	N/A	N/A	}			}	3	N/A	N/A
Total	15%	27%	46%	46%	42%	49%	37%	28%	17%	21%

Sources: 1956-1958 data: Educational Television and Radio Center (1958). All other data: Corporation for Public Broadcasting: 1962-1972 data: *One Week of Educational Television* (series); 1974 data: *Public Television Program Content: 1974*, pp. 24, 28 and inside front cover; 1976 data: *Public Television Programming by Category: 1976* (1977), pp. 19, 22 and inside front cover.

any content trends resulting from the operation of the SPC. The total hours figures in the table do not include repeat feeds of programs by PBS.

Sources

The 1954-1958 data in **Table 581-A** and the 1956-1958 data in **Table 581-B** were taken from the Educational Television and Radio Center (1958). All other figures in both tables come from various reports and publications of the Corporation for Public Broadcasting (CPB). The source of **Table 581-C** is the *Status Report* (1977) of the CPB.

A major drawback in describing public television programming trends is the lack of consistent information on which to base conclusions. Each of the tables in this unit is somewhat misleading,

Table 581–C.
Content of Television Programming Distributed
by the U.S. Public Broadcasting Service (PBS), 1973–1976

	1973	1974	1975	1976
Total Hours of Programming	1,102	1,219	1,367	1,854
Content of Programming (as percentage of total hours):				
Cultural	34.3%	32.8%	26.3%	33.9%
Educational/Children's	26.0	25.9	32.3	26.5
Public Affairs	39.7	41.3	41.4	39.6

Source: Corporation for Public Broadcasting, *Status Report* (1977), p. 19.

in that the editors have had to combine different surveys, with different data-gathering approaches, in order to assemble figures which provide some comparability over time. Even since 1970, when the CPB took over the data-gathering and reporting process for the public television industry, there have been frequent and strange information discontinuities.

Another problem, which especially affects the **Table 581-A** figures, is that the data (particularly data reported up to the mid-1960s) have often included both general and instructional programs, and these two categories now tend to be reported separately. The editors have taken the general figures whenever they were available; but the reader is advised to keep this discontinuity in mind, since it unavoidably reduces the direct comparability of these figures.

Further Information

The only available, continuing statistical reports on public television programming are those issued by the CPB at two-year intervals. They contain extensively detailed information on both general and instructional programming. The CPB's annual statistical surveys also contain limited information on programming.

For background and related information on public television, see Katzman (1976), Cater and Nyhan (1976), and Blakely (1971). The operation of the Station Program Cooperative is described and criticized in Reeves and Hoffer (1976). In addition, the reader may wish to check the bimonthly issues of *Public Telecommunications Review* for background and occasional statistical reports.

Network Television Programming 582

Interpretation of Tables

Table 582-A traces the first 25 years—from 1949 through 1973—of prime-time network television programming. The table lists the number of quarter-hours per week devoted by the networks to each program category. All of the networks are included—even DuMont up to 1955—and programs are listed whether or not they were sponsored. The reader will note interesting cycles of invention, imitation, and decline in such subject areas as westerns, sports, quiz shows, and documentaries. The network westerns, for example, emerged between 1958 and 1962, then experienced a lasting plateau until 1969. But just five years later, there were no prime-time westerns at all. Situation comedy programs have maintained their popularity throughout this period.

Table 582-B traces daytime programming trends for the same 25-year period. The reader should note that not until 1958 did the networks collectively offer approximately as many daytime programmed hours as they do today.

Table 582–A.
Content of Prime-Time Network Television Programming in U.S., by Number of Quarter-Hours of Airtime per Week, 1949–1973

	1949	1950	1951	1952	1953	1954	1955	1956	1957	1958	1959	1960	1961	1962	1963	1964	1965	1966	1967	1968	1969	1970	1971	1972	1973
Variety																									
Special/Varied	--	--	--	2	--	--	22	32	22	10	10	22	4	8	8	4	4	4	4	4	4	4	4	8	19
Comedy	42	40	86	65	50	43	44	42	39	20	14	22	14	14	28	40	40	24	28	33	34	35	34	20	20
Amateur/Talent	8	10	18	14	10	10	6	8	10	6	4	4	--	--	--	--	4	4	4	4	--	--	8	--	--
Country and Western	6	--	--	--	--	--	4	8	4	4	4	4	--	--	--	4	4	4	--	--	--	8	8	--	--
General/Talk	--	--	34	--	--	--	30	30	20	35	45	35	35	39	40	39	81	42	42	66	66	96	96	96	51
Music																									
Musical Variety	15	22	27	26	8	12	8	15	26	40	36	22	18	20	30	28	28	26	16	22	28	24	20	8	12
Light Music	15	12	25	13	12	12	14	6	4	--	--	--	--	--	--	--	--	--	--	--	--	--	--	--	--
Drama																									
General	24	42	64	54	44	58	80	70	76	30	35	32	28	34	54	60	34	32	8	3	10	34	34	20	24
Motion Pictures	34	8	12	2	--	--	--	12	10	--	--	--	--	8	16	16	24	32	48	52	56	72	64	72	101
Women's Serials	3	--	2	2	--	--	--	--	--	--	--	--	--	--	--	--	4	6	4	4	4	--	--	--	--
Action/Adventure	--	8	6	11	10	4	6	16	22	16	16	24	32	22	26	18	32	54	70	65	28	18	6	8	16
Crime/Detective	2	12	16	28	22	18	12	8	6	18	32	48	40	48	20	18	8	12	10	24	40	24	46	48	44
Suspense	--	8	16	18	8	10	4	2	6	6	4	6	--	8	8	14	12	--	4	4	4	--	--	4	4
Westerns	--	2	10	6	7	6	6	16	16	40	64	70	54	46	36	34	24	34	38	34	38	22	22	16	4
Comedy/Situation	4	15	16	24	36	50	60	38	36	40	26	32	52	50	48	38	62	72	52	38	42	56	50	40	12
Animated Cartoons	--	2	--	--	--	--	--	--	--	--	--	--	6	12	6	2	6	2	--	--	2	2	--	--	42
Quiz and Panel																									
Audience Participation	10	18	22	18	18	24	18	24	26	22	8	6	4	8	4	6	2	--	4	6	6	6	4	--	--
Human Interest	10	14	13	16	12	15	10	8	6	10	8	6	6	2	2	4	2	2	2	--	--	--	--	--	--
Panel Shows	13	10	20	26	24	22	16	10	6	6	10	12	8	6	8	6	6	6	6	--	--	--	--	--	--
News Information																									
Newscasts	27	14	13	13	19	18	22	16	16	21	21	16	16	23	23	32	29	30	40	35	27	39	41	39	39
Forums/Interviews	14	12	8	14	19	11	5	2	2	--	2	--	10	--	2	2	2	--	--	--	--	--	--	--	--
Documentary/Information	4	4	4	2	4	8	10	10	12	12	10	8	28	26	22	16	20	12	12	12	16	8	8	6	8
Other Types																									
Religion	--	2	4	4	7	3	2	2	2	--	--	--	--	--	--	--	--	--	--	--	--	--	--	--	--
Talk	30	6	3	10	11	10	5	5	1	--	--	--	--	--	--	--	--	--	--	--	--	--	--	--	--
Children's Shows	29	63	40	21	10	5	10	5	5	4	4	--	--	--	--	--	--	--	--	--	--	--	--	--	--
Sports	62	52	82	33	31	34	29	13	6	6	7	8	6	4	4	6	--	--	--	--	--	--	--	--	--
Miscellaneous	10	8	5	7	11	--	--	--	--	--	--	--	--	--	--	--	--	--	--	--	--	--	--	--	--
Total Quarter Hours	362	386	546	427	373	373	423	398	379	346	360	375	361	380	385	387	428	384	388	402	405	446	437	385	392

Sources: Sterling and Kittross (1978), citing copyrighted data from L. W. Lichty.

Table 582-B.
Content of Daytime Network Television Programming in U.S., by Number of Quarter-Hours of Airtime per Week, 1949–1973

	1949	1950	1951	1952	1953	1954	1955	1956	1957	1958	1959	1960	1961	1962	1963	1964	1965	1966	1967	1968	1969	1970	1971	1972	1973
Variety																									
Special/Varied	—	—	—	—	—	—	—	—	—	—	—	—	—	—	—	—	—	—	—	—	—	—	—	—	—
Comedy	—	—	—	35	—	—	—	—	—	—	—	—	—	—	—	—	—	—	—	—	—	—	—	—	—
Amateur/Talent	—	—	—	—	—	—	—	—	—	—	—	—	—	—	—	—	—	—	—	—	—	—	—	—	—
Country and Western	—	—	—	—	—	—	—	—	—	—	—	—	—	—	—	—	—	—	—	—	—	—	—	—	—
General/Talk	10	10	13	129	79	86	166	166	114	76	70	60	40	50	70	45	40	40	40	40	40	50	50	50	60
Music																									
Musical Variety	5	—	20	20	40	50	30	10	10	55	50	30	30	20	20	10	10	10	20	—	—	—	—	—	—
Light Music	10	5	5	5	—	—	—	—	—	—	—	—	—	—	—	—	—	—	—	—	—	—	—	—	—
Drama																									
General	—	—	—	—	—	—	—	20	20	30	20	50	50	50	40	20	—	20	20	20	—	—	—	—	—
Motion Pictures	—	—	—	—	—	—	—	40	30	—	—	—	—	—	—	—	—	—	—	—	—	—	—	—	—
Women's Serials	—	—	5	30	20	45	84	40	55	65	70	80	100	70	60	70	120	150	110	108	138	158	180	160	160
Action/Adventure	20	—	—	—	—	—	—	—	—	—	—	20	20	—	—	—	—	—	—	—	—	—	—	—	—
Crime/Detective	—	—	—	—	—	—	—	—	—	—	—	50	—	—	—	—	—	—	—	—	—	—	—	—	—
Suspense	—	—	—	—	—	—	—	—	—	—	—	—	—	—	—	—	—	—	—	—	—	—	—	—	—
Westerns	—	—	15	—	—	10	—	—	—	10	—	50	10	10	—	20	20	—	—	—	—	—	—	—	—
Comedy/Situation	—	—	—	—	—	—	—	—	30	10	10	40	50	20	40	50	60	60	50	50	50	60	60	70	20
Animated Cartoons	—	—	—	—	—	—	—	—	—	—	—	10	—	—	—	—	—	—	—	—	—	—	—	—	—
Quiz and Panel																									
Audience Participation	20	30	24	28	42	44	40	40	50	80	140	80	100	140	110	120	100	100	128	128	117	68	70	90	130
Human Interest	15	5	8	1	25	25	20	30	35	45	40	40	50	30	20	20	10	10	20	20	8	—	—	—	—
Panel Shows	—	—	10	—	—	—	—	—	5	—	—	—	—	10	20	20	10	10	10	18	10	28	20	10	10
News Information																									
Newscasts	—	—	—	10	5	5	—	—	5	5	5	5	9	22	16	24	24	24	22	18	18	26	24	25	25
Forums/Interviews	—	—	—	—	—	20	—	—	—	—	—	—	—	—	—	—	—	—	—	—	—	—	—	—	—
Documentary/Information	—	—	—	—	—	—	—	—	—	—	—	—	—	—	—	—	—	—	—	—	—	—	—	—	—
Other Types																									
Religion	—	5	—	—	—	—	—	—	—	—	—	—	—	—	—	—	—	—	—	—	—	—	—	—	—
Talk	15	90	28	11	21	—	27	—	—	—	50	20	20	30	40	10	10	10	10	12	12	10	10	10	10
Children's Shows	10	40	30	15	—	35	32	70	40	25	25	15	15	40	20	20	20	20	20	20	20	20	20	20	20
Sports	—	—	—	—	—	—	—	—	—	—	—	—	—	—	—	—	—	—	—	—	—	—	—	—	—
Miscellaneous	—	—	—	—	—	—	—	—	—	—	—	—	—	—	—	—	—	—	—	—	—	—	—	—	—
Total Quarter Hours	105	185	158	284	232	320	399	416	394	401	480	550	494	492	456	429	424	454	450	434	413	420	434	435	435

Sources: Sterling and Kittross (1978), citing copyrighted data from L. W. Lichty.

Table 582–C.
Content of Prime-Time and Daytime Network Television Programming in U.S., by Number of Quarter-Hours of Airtime per Week, 1973–1977

	Number of Quarter Hours per Week				
	1973	1974	1975	1976	1977[a]
Prime-Time Programs (7-11 P.M.)					
Type of Program:					
Variety	20	8	16	28	16
Drama	40	68	68	52	72
Feature Film	64	58	40	46	40
Suspense/Mystery	68	76	84	66	44
Situation Comedy	48	30	44	50	68
Other	12	12	12	22	24
Total	252	252	264	264	264
Daytime Programs (10 A.M.-4:30 P.M.)					
Type of Program:					
Daytime Drama	148	138	158	175	175
Situation Comedy	20	10	10	30	50
Quiz/Audience Participation	158	188	168	120	120
News/Other	13	3	3	N/A	N/A
Total[b]	340	340	340	N/A	N/A

Sources: 1973-1975 prime-time data: Nielsen Television Index, A. C. Nielsen Company, *Television Audience 1976*, p. 36. 1973-1975 daytime data: *Television Audience 1975*, p. 79. 1976-1977 data: *Television Audience 1977*, pp. 36 and 39.

Notes: Hours are averages for the Fall season of each year. (a) 1977 figures are estimates. (b) Daytime totals do not add, due to rounding.

Table 582-C provides prime-time and daytime programming data for 1973 through 1977. However, the information here was drawn from a different source and should not be considered simply a continuation of Tables 582-A and 582-B.

Table 582-D categorizes the number of prime-time network specials in the even-numbered years since 1950. Two peaks—the first in 1960 and the second in the mid-1970s—indicate renewed popularity for this "one-shot" form of programming. The national elections of 1960, 1968, and 1972 are reflected by the increases in news/political/documentary specials for those years.

Table 582-E reveals some of the changes which have taken place (1) in programming formats (the decline of live programming and its replacement by film and tape), (2) in the sources of network-broadcast programs (the decline of network- and advertiser-produced programs in favor of programs produced by a "packaging" agency), and (3) in the length of programs (in general, they are getting longer). Most of the figures on this table are percentages of prime-time hours. The only exceptions are the format data, which cover *all* hours of network broadcasting.

Sources

Tables 582-A and 582-B were constructed from copyrighted data of L. W. Lichty of the University of Wisconsin-Madison. These data are reprinted in Sterling and Kittross (1978). Lichty gathered this information from various printed sources, then categorized and analyzed it with the assistance of Sterling. The data may be considered accurate for the third week of January of each year. However, with the advent of network "second seasons" in the early 1970s, these annual listings become less representative of the overall network programming for the year.

Table 582-C is an attempt by the editors to update Lichty's information, using different sources: A. C. Nielsen Company's *Television Audience 1976*, for prime-time data, and *Television Audience 1975* for daytime programming. Unlike Tables 582-A and 582-B, Table 582-C lists only sponsored shows. Moreover, whereas Table 582-C defines "prime-time" as 7-11 p.m., Table 582-A begins the prime-time category at 6 p.m. Similarly, the daytime hours covered in Table 582-C run from 10 a.m. to 4:30 p.m., whereas Table 582-B covers all network daytime hours up to 6 p.m. Table 582-C data were converted to quarter hours to increase their comparability with the other tables.

Table 582–D.

Number, Content, and Total Hours of Prime-Time Network Television "Specials" Broadcast in U.S., 1950–1974

Type of Special	1950	1952	1954	1956	1958	1960	1962	1964	1966	1968	1970	1972	1974
Variety	2	3	7	10	26	43	55	33	47	48	35	51	60
Drama	--	--	1	3	28	50	29	11	21	54	39	41	83
Documentary	3	2	3	11	14	19	58	30	37	43		59	79
Political	1	2	--	4	5	--	1	8	1	8	72	27	12
News	1	2	--	1	5	69	18	10	15	22	18	36	34
Sports	3	1	1	2	5	9	4	10	2	19	34	10	17
Other	19	20	28	12	24	15	20	28	25	34	34	44	62
Total Number of Specials	**29**	**30**	**40**	**43**	**107**	**205**	**185**	**130**	**148**	**228**	**198**	**268**	**347**
Total Number of Hours	*18*	*19*	*24*	*32*	*101*	*185*	*163*	*160*	*157*	*256*	*N/A*	*330*	*449*

Sources: 1950-1968: Bailey, *Journal of Broadcasting* (Summer 1970). 1970: Nielsen Television Index, A. C. Nielsen Co., *Television Audience* (1971), p. 131. 1972-1974: A. C. Nielsen, *Nielsen Newscast* No. 3, 1974, pp. 12-13.

In constructing **Table 582-D**, the editors consulted Bailey (1970) for information through 1968; A. C. Nielsen Company's *Television Audience 1971*, for the 1970 figures; and "Evening Network TV Specials," *Nielsen Newscast* No. 3 (1974) for the 1972 and 1974 figures. Information through 1968 is for mid-September through mid-June of each season; the 1970 data are for September through April; and the 1972 and 1974 figures represent the entire network programming season (October-September). Because of the multiplicity of sources and the variety of categori-

Table 582-E.

Format, Source, and Length of the Average Network Television Program in U.S., 1956–1972

	Program Format[a]			Program Source[b]				Program Length[b]					
	Film	Videotape	Live	Network	Sponsor	Packager	Combination	15 Minutes	30 Minutes	60 Minutes	90 Minutes	120 Minutes
1956	27%	– –	73%	N/A	N/A	N/A	N/A	N/A	N/A	N/A	N/A	N/A
1958	24	6%	70	30%	28%	42%	1%	.4%	63%	33%	2%	0%
1960	32	32	36	20	14	63	3	.7	47	51	N/A	N/A
1962	35	37	28	18	9	70	3	.3	30	62	2	6
1964	37	37	26	19	7	74	1	0	33	54	4	8
1966	39	38	23	15	4	79	2	0	29	55	2	14
1968	37	48	16	16	3	81	1	0	23	53	4	19
1970	36	49	14	N/A	N/A	N/A	N/A	0	23	52	6	19
1972	44	40	16	N/A	N/A	N/A	N/A	0	17	52	12	19

Sources: Format data: *Broadcasting Yearbook*, appropriate issues. Source data: A. D. Little Company (1969), p. 1, based on survey returns from the networks. Length data: 1958-1968: A. D. Little Company (1969), p. 10; 1970-1972: Columbia Broadcasting System, as printed in Office of Telecommunications Policy (1973), appendix table 4.

Notes: All figures are rounded percentages. (a) As percentage of total network broadcast hours. (b) As percentage of total prime-time hours.

zations involved in this table, the data should be considered more of a refined estimate than an actual census.

In **Table 582-E**, the format data were taken from *Broadcasting Yearbook*; the source information came from the A. D. Little Co. (1969) (based on survey returns from the networks); and the information on program length came from the A. D. Little Co. (1969) (for data through 1968) and from the Columbia Broadcasting Service (CBS), as printed in a report of the Office of Telecommunications Policy (1973). All figures on **Table 582-E** are rounded percentages. Excluded from the data on programming length was a 45-minute category that never accounted for more than 1 percent of network hours.

Further Information

Detailed information on programming content and costs regularly appears in *Broadcasting* and *Variety*. Terrace (1976) and David (annual, since 1975) are handy directories of program information for network and nationally syndicated shows. Additional information concerning network television programming also appears in A. C. Nielsen Company's *Television Audience* (annual) and in reports from Batten, Barton, Dunstine, and Osborn, Inc. (1976 to date).

Historical statistics for 1958 through 1968 can be found in A. D. Little Co. (1964 and 1969). Comparisons of network programming, especially by ratings, are available in *Broadcasting Monthly*, *Broadcasting Industry*, and *Broadcasting Basics*. The reader may also wish to check Units 382 (network economics) and 682 (network audiences). Further data regarding television journalism can be found in Unit 502.

Violence in Network Television Programming   583

Interpretation of Table

Table 583-A summarizes the major findings of 10 years of analysis of network television content. A research team, working under the direction of Dean George Gerbner of the University of Pennsylvania, has been attempting to quantify violence in network television programming, according to the type of program and the hour it is presented. Each year, this group issues the *Violence Profile* (the *Violence Index* until 1973), a report which analyzes and summarizes a number of measures of television programming by the Gerbner team:

1. The percentage of programs containing any violence.

2. The rate of violent episodes per program.

3. The rate of violent episodes per hour.

4. The percentage of major characters involved in any violence.

5. The percentage of major characters involved in any killing.

The results in categories 2 and 3 are doubled by the researchers in order to raise their relatively low numerical value (because they are not percentages) to the significance that the factors of frequency and saturation deserve. Higher numbers on the table therefore indicate "more" violence in that category of programming or on that network.

The reader will note a general decline in levels of televised violence until 1976, when a sharp upward turn occurred in most categories. "Family hour" programming (6 to 9 p.m.) has usually contained less violence than programming later in the evening. Comic-tone programs (other than cartoons) appear to have contained the least violence of all of the categories, while crime and action-adventure programs, along with cartoons, had high incidences of measured violence.

Sources

The data for **Table 583-A** come from Gerbner et al. (1976, 1977). The reader should be aware that there is considerable controversy among researchers about the validity of this information. This controversy concerns both the methods of the study and Gerbner's definition of violence in any program context (which, for example, gives comedy equal consideration with serious drama). Gerbner's methods are too involved to describe here, but they are fully explained in each annual *Violence Profile*.

The seventh annual *Violence Profile*, which appeared in 1976, was the last edition to contain specific annual data for the series; the eighth edition resorted to aggregating data from earlier years because of space limitations. This practice will be repeated in future editions.

Table 583–A.
Gerbner Violence Profile of the Content of Network Television Programming in U.S., 1967-1976

Note: Higher numbers in table indicate a higher level of violence within each programming category. See text for explanation of the derivation of figures.

	All Network Programs	Family-Hour Programs[a]	Later-Evening Programs[b]	All Weekend Daytime Programs	Televised Feature Films[c]	Cartoon Programs	Crime/Western/ Action-Adventure Programs[c]	Comic Tone Programs[c]	All ABC Programs	All CBS Programs	All NBC Programs
1967	199	212	148	251	182	251	248	110	222	151	220
1968	181	161	179	232	236	239	224	110	193	167	187
1969	183	137	156	259	169	262	220	96	164	183	205
1970	173	113	165	250	250	250	226	89	161	162	203
1971	175	152	170	208	228	232	211	109	142	194	189
1972	173	149	165	207	225	217	231	57	175	150	203
1973	161	127	137	212	186	218	213	67	138	174	172
1974	182	146	210	192	273	196	234	64	197	174	177
1975	180	101	208	221	263	233	219	88	187	155	201
1976	204	145	209	247	220	273	230	168	207	182	224
Average Violence Profile	*180*	*141*	*181*	*222*	*225*	*232*	*224*	*89*	*178*	*168*	*197*

Source: Gerbner et al., *Violence Profiles Nos. 7 and 8: Trends in Network Television Drama and Viewer Conceptions of Social Reality, 1967-1976* (1976, 1977), appendix tables.

Notes: (a) Family Hour is 6-9 P.M. (b) Later-evening hours are 9-11 P.M. (c) Excludes cartoons.

Further Information

The reader should consult the complete series of the *Violence Profile* for details of the research. Gerbner and Gross (1976) also provide a layman's summary of the research, its findings, and some of the data not reported here. For analysis of the data limitations, the reader should see the debate between the Gerbner staff and two NBC researchers in "Violence Ratings: A Dialogue" (1972-1973), and a later debate between CBS researchers and Gerbner's team in "The Violence Profile: An Exchange of Views" (1977).

Cable Television Programming   590

Interpretation of Tables

Two useful ways of measuring the increasing significance of cable television as a mass medium in the United States are: (1) to trace the growing channel capacities of cable systems, and (2) to identify the greater amounts of program origination from some of these systems. (See Unit 190 for other measures.)

Typical cable system capacity ranges between 6 and 12 channels, and as **Table 590-A** reveals, this statistic has remained virtually unchanged from 1966 through 1976. However, systems with five or fewer channels have constantly declined in number during this period, while systems with 12 or more channels have increased—from 30 systems in 1969 to nearly 900 by 1976. This trend toward increased capacity is due both to 1972 FCC regulations, which called for enhanced capacity under a complicated and often delayed procedure, and to greater demands for service.

Cable system program origination is often considerably less than "programming." The most common form of "programming" has been time and weather dials which are continuously scanned by an automatic camera, thereby providing "content" for one cable channel at the least possible expense. Another type of automated origination is a news ticker which runs across the television screen.

As in the case of channel capacity, part of the impetus to originate both automated and studio programming came from FCC regulations. For several years, cable systems with more than 3,500 subscribers were required to provide some local origination in addition to simply feeding local and imported television channels into the homes. The expansion of cable into major cities also contributed to origination, as cable operators discovered that such services were often of as much interest to audiences—or to advertisers—as the "regular" television signals. The high costs of operation have discouraged any rapid growth of nonautomatic originations. However, 1972 FCC regulations requiring local public-access cable channels have led to an increase in local-live (studio) capacity for cable systems.

Sources

The data presented in **Table 590-A**, based on a survey of the cable television industry, were taken from the annual *Television Factbook*. In the survey, systems were listed under as many self-reported categories as necessary. The categories varied from year to year, and the information was collected for various months. The figures should therefore be viewed as estimates of actual trends.

Further Information

The National Cable Television Association (NCTA) has issued annual *Origination Directories* which provide detailed regional and local information.

Table 590-A.
Number of Cable Television Systems in U.S.–by Channel Capacities of Systems, by Systems with Program Origination, and by Format and Content of Programming, 1966–1976

	1966	1969	1970	1971	1972	1973	1974	1975	1976
Number of Reporting CATV Systems	1,440	2,300	2,490	2,578	2,839	3,032	3,190	3,405	3,715
Systems with Program Origination	N/A	883	1,089	1,190	1,514	1,764	1,982	2,159	2,404
Systems with No Program Origination	N/A	1,417	1,401	1,388	1,325	1,114	1,208	1,246	1,311
Systems Planning to Originate Programming	N/A	156	416	430	418	154	245	232	216
Number of CATV Systems, by Channel Capacities									
Over 20 channels	N/A	N/A	N/A	N/A	N/A	N/A	N/A	382	444
13 to 20 channels	N/A	29	86	157	361	469	590	354	424
6 to 12 channels	N/A	1,559	1,720	1,882	2,026	2,181	2,302	2,415	2,647
5 channels	N/A	511	459	371	332	287	328	195	170
Under 5 channels	N/A	61	61	50	55	49	39	32	10
Unspecified	N/A	140	164	118	65	46	31	27	11
Number of CATV Systems, by Content:									
Automated Origination:	N/A	825	1,019	1,477	1,514	1,664	1,887	2,074	2,311
Time and Weather	430	797	984	1,206	1,309	1,597	1,812	1,989	2,224
News Ticker	52	88	116	159	211	288	337	410	513
Stock Ticker	1	15	18	35	63	124	163	191	237
Sports Ticker	N/A	N/A	N/A	N/A	N/A	42	76	103	162
Message Wheel	N/A	N/A	N/A	N/A	87	189	271	321	390
Music	40	61	74	77	70	62	49	46	N/A
Emergency Alert	N/A	13	10	N/A	20	20	38	74	N/A
Advertising	N/A	N/A	N/A	N/A	59	322	444	454	475
Other	N/A	N/A	5	N/A	39	58	79	103	248
Studio Originations:	N/A	282	399	524	594	768	912	949	1,030
Local Live	97	197	293	467	570	587	652	645	682
Film	28	35	54	N/A	N/A	181	224	224	228
Videotape	3	39	66	N/A	N/A	288	401	403	421
CATV Network	N/A	N/A	N/A	N/A	N/A	40	52	59	63
School Channel	N/A	N/A	15	N/A	N/A	N/A	81	103	181
Public Access	N/A	N/A	N/A	N/A	N/A	N/A	11	29	117
Advertising	N/A	N/A	4	57	151	233	295	298	306
Pay Cable	N/A	N/A	N/A	N/A	N/A	N/A	48	96	303
Other	103	N/A	89	N/A	24	130	80	97	125

Source: *Television Factbook*, appropriate issues.

SECTION 6

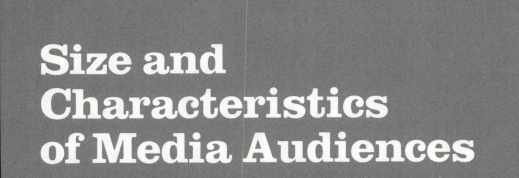

Size and Characteristics of Media Audiences

Table 600–A.
Number of Media Units per 100 Population in U.S., 1909–1972

Note: Population estimates are in thousands.

| | Estimated U. S. Population | Number of Copies | | | Number of Theater Seats | Number of Receivers | |
		Books	Daily Newspapers	Magazines		Radio	Television
1909	90,492	N/A	26.7	112.5	N/A	- -	- -
1914	99,118	N/A	29.0	130.7	N/A	- -	- -
1919	104,512	N/A	31.6	138.0	N/A	- -	- -
1923	111,950	N/A	31.9	134.7	6.8	.4	- -
1927	119,038	94.6	35.6	157.1	N/A	6.1	- -
1931	124,040	53.2	34.0	148.0	9.8	14.7	- -
1935	127,250	38.0	32.7	140.4	8.7	20.4	- -
1939	130,880	N/A	32.8	183.1	N/A	31.2	- -
1948	147,208	203.4	36.8	265.8	7.9	50.5	.1
1954	163,026	229.8	34.6	275.6	5.5	72.4	16.8
1958	174,882	271.7	33.6	224.1	4.8	80.1	27.0
1963	189,242	286.8	33.5	226.1	4.2	105.9	32.4
1967	198,712	363.9	33.5	200.3	3.1	132.2	37.6
1972	208,846	445.9	31.1	N/A	3.8	176.7	52.3

Sources: Population data: *Statistical Abstract*, appropriate years. Media data: *Census of Manufactures*, appropriate years.

Interpretation of Table

In the late 1940s, UNESCO developed a standard measure to assess the communications development of nations and to compare media development with population growth. The UNESCO standard called for a minimum of ten newspapers, five radio receivers, two movie-theater seats, and two television sets per 100 people. **Table 600**-A uses this standard, supplemented with information on books and magazines, to assess American media development in relation to population growth.

The table indicates that the number of books purchased per capita in the United States has sharply increased during the past 40 years. In contrast, newspaper circulation has been slipping since 1948, and the number of magazines per capita has also steadily declined over the past two decades. The number of movie-theater seats (here including car spaces at drive-in theaters) reached a peak just before the Depression and then declined until the last few years, when a turnaround occurred. The number of radio and television sets per 100 people has risen steadily. At present, the United States has far more books and radio sets than people.

In reviewing this material, the reader should keep in mind that a multiplicity of media units does not indicate diversity of content or degree of public access to those units, but merely reflects the numerical expansion of the media as compared to population. In addition, the UNESCO measure, which is very approximate, has several limitations as it is applied in this table (see the "Sources" section). Overall, however, the table is useful for tracing general trends.

Sources

With a few exceptions, the information in **Table 600**-A comes from U.S. Census Bureau publications—chiefly the estimated population figures listed in the *Statistical Abstract* and the unit-output data found in the *Census of Manufactures*. With regard to individual media, the editors offer the following comments on sources:

1. *Books*. The measure here is extremely conservative, in that it counts only those books actually published and sold in a given year. Because there is no adequate available information on the number of books in libraries or the aggregate number of books in print, it is not possible to make a comprehensive measure of all the books in circulation in the United States at any given time. This is most unfortunate since books have a longer life than any other medium.

The basic number of books for **Table 600-A** was figured from the *Census of Manufactures*, excluding two large categories—textbooks of all kinds and children's books—which were not as comparable to the other media as general adult-level books. The pre-1935 data did not cover the category "education," under the assumption that it mainly comprised textbooks. Comparable figures prior to 1927 are not available, because pamphlets and books were combined in earlier censuses and easily twice as many pamphlets as books appeared in most of those years.

2. *Daily newspapers*. The measure selected here was the national aggregate circulation of daily newspapers (thus excluding Sunday editions and other types of papers). This information is available in comparable form back into the late 1800s. As with books, the measure shows the number of copies per 100 people—*not* the number of separate titles.

3. *Magazines*. These figures reflect the national aggregate circulation for weekly, biweekly, monthly, and quarterly publications. Initially, magazines were listed in the *Census of Manufactures* by periodicity. After 1939, they were categorized by type, and this change may create some comparability problems.

4. *Theater seats*. The figures from 1948 on, from the *Census of Manufactures*, measure the total number of seats for indoor theaters and car spaces for drive-ins. Since most cars at outdoor theaters have two to four occupants, the capacity measure used in this table (one person per car) is understated. The base-capacity figures used here are found in Unit 141, which details the unofficial estimates used for the 1923, 1931, and 1935 data.

5. *Radio receivers*. The base data appear in Unit 660, and the reader should turn to that unit for an explanation of the limitations of the commercial information used to make these estimates. Figures for AM and FM radios are combined.

6. *Television receivers*. These figures are limited in the same way as the data on radio receivers. Totals for color and black-and-white television receivers are combined.

Further Information

See the various editions of UNESCO's *World Communications* for comparative per-capita data on other countries and specific regions of the world.

Characteristics of Book Readers

61

Interpretation of Tables

Studies of book readership and book-buying are generally conducted either privately for a specific publisher or trade association or for a public institution, such as a library, with limited resources and a primarily local interest. Therefore, the abundance of national data about television viewers or book industry finances is not matched with information on book readers and book buyers.

Table 610-A presents the results of the only known national survey of book readers in the last 10 years. This 1967 survey, sponsored by the National Advisory Commission on Libraries, asked the following question of its 1,500 respondents: "Now, thinking back over the past three months, would you tell me just how many books, paperbacks or hardcover, you have had occasion to read during this period?" The figures indicate that, at least in 1967, women read more books than men, young adults read more than their older counterparts, single people read more than people of any other marital status, and people with a higher educational level read more than less-educated people.

Tables 610-B and **610-C** were taken from two studies of the book-buying behavior of Americans: a 1966 study by the National Industrial Conference Board (now called The Conference Board) and a 1976 study by W. R. Simmons and Associates Research, one of the leading survey

Table 610–A.
Results of a Survey Measuring Book Readership in U.S.,
by Sex, Age, Marital Status, and Educational Level, 1967

Respondent Characteristics	Number of Responses	"Number of books read in past three months"							Total Responses
		1	2	3	4	5-8	9 or more	Can't Recall/ None	
Sex									
Male	779	5%	5%	9%	4%	9%	18%	50%	100%
Female	770	5	6	9	6	12	20	42	100
Age									
21-34 years	363	7	8	10	5	15	25	30	100
35-49 years	495	4	6	10	5	12	20	43	100
50 years and over	658	4	5	8	4	7	15	57	100
Marital Status									
Single	84	5	7	7	6	10	31	34	100
Married	1,283	5	6	9	5	11	19	45	100
Other	175	4	6	11	4	6	16	53	100
Education Level									
College	388	4	4	10	4	19	38	21	100
High school	816	6	8	11	5	11	18	41	100
Grade school	344	3	4	5	4	3	5	76	100
National Total	**1,549**	**5%**	**6%**	**9%**	**5%**	**11%**	**19%**	**45%**	**100%**

Sources: Knight and Nourse (1969), p. 83, citing data from a survey by the Academy for Educational Development for the National Advisory Commission on Libraries.

researchers in the country. The information in **Table 610-B** is based on the behavior of households, while the **Table 610-C** data are based on the responses of individuals. In addition, the two tables differ in the wording of the survey questions, in the methodologies of the two surveys, and in the categories by which the data are aggregated (see the "Sources" section below). Yet, given these differences, it is striking to note the similarities in the results of these two tables.

For example, both indicate that whites tend to buy more books than blacks. Both indicate that suburbanites buy the most books, while people living in rural areas purchase the least. And both indicate that book-buying increases steadily with education and income and that it tends to decrease for people over the age of 45. The only major point of difference between the two surveys lies in the relationship of family size to book-buying behavior. The 1966 study showed that the persons buying the most books tended to be in families of three or more, while the Simmons study showed single adults of both sexes as the biggest book buyers.

This possible discrepancy in family size might be explained by the inclusion of comic books as a subcategory of books in the 1966 survey. Parents are obviously the people who would be making most of the comic book purchases for their children. Comic books and parenthood are probably a factor as well in the high level of book purchasers among the 35-44 age group in **Table 610-B**. **Table 610-C** shows that the youngest adults (18 to 24 years) generally hold a slim lead over the 25 to 34 year old book-buyers and a considerable lead over the 35 to 44 year olds.

The major message of these surveys is that the book-buying market is what advertising people call "upscale." Book buyers are predominantly more affluent, more educated, and more urban than the population as a whole.

Sources

Table 610-A comes from a 1967 survey performed by the Academy for Educational Development, Inc., for the National Advisory Commission on Libraries. The following description of the survey is given in Knight and Nourse (1969):

Personal interviews were conducted with 1,549 adults during the period June 21-27, 1967 . . . The design of the sample was that of a replicated probability sample, down to

Table 610–B.
Distribution of Consumer Expenditures for Books in U.S.,
by Selected Family Characteristics and Type of Book, 1966

Family Characteristic	Distribution of All Families	All Books[a]	Type of Book		
			Pocket Editions	Comic Books	Hardbound Books
Geographical Region:					
Northeast	26.5%	25.5%	31.5%	28.0%	23.5%
North Central	27.0	23.5	22.0	22.0	24.0
South	29.0	27.0	23.0	29.5	28.0
West	17.5	24.0	23.5	20.5	24.5
White	88.5	93.5	93.5	83.5	94.5
Nonwhite	11.5	6.5	6.5	16.5	5.5
Market Location:					
In Metropolitan Areas:					
Central Cities	33.0	35.5	37.0	32.5	35.5
Urban Fringe	29.0	37.0	37.0	27.0	37.5
Other Areas	6.5	7.0	6.5	7.0	7.0
Outside Metropolitan Areas:					
Urban	15.5	10.0	11.5	17.5	9.0
Rural	16.0	10.5	8.0	16.0	11.0
Education of Head of Household:					
Grade School or less	29.5	11.0	12.0	21.5	9.5
Some High School	18.0	11.5	14.5	23.0	10.0
High School Graduate	29.0	29.0	28.5	30.0	29.0
Some College	10.0	16.0	15.5	12.5	16.5
College Graduate or higher	13.5	32.5	29.5	13.0	35.0
Family Income (before taxes):					
Under $3,000	16.0	2.0	2.5	4.5	1.5
$3,000-$5,000	15.0	7.5	7.5	11.0	7.0
$5,000-$7,500	21.0	14.5	15.0	21.5	14.0
$7,500-$10,000	19.0	19.5	21.0	23.0	19.0
$10,000 and over	29.0	56.5	54.0	40.0	58.5
Occupation of Head of Household:					
Professional/Technical	12.0	27.5	24.0	10.0	30.0
Managers/Officials	12.0	17.5	16.5	15.5	18.0
Clerical, Sales	11.5	14.0	14.0	13.5	14.0
Foremen, Craftsmen	16.0	16.0	18.0	21.5	15.0
Operatives	16.5	12.0	14.5	19.5	10.5
All other	32.0	13.0	13.0	20.0	12.5
Age of Head of Household:					
Under 25	6.5	5.5	6.5	2.5	5.5
25-34	18.0	26.0	24.0	20.0	27.0
35-44	20.5	30.5	30.0	41.5	29.5
45-54	19.5	21.0	21.5	25.5	21.0
55-64	15.5	10.0	11.0	8.0	10.0
65 and over	20.0	7.0	7.0	2.5	7.0
Family Size:					
One	19.5	12.5	12.5	3.0	13.5
Two	28.5	19.0	22.5	6.0	19.0
Three	16.5	21.5	19.5	17.0	22.0
Four	15.0	20.0	20.0	24.0	19.5
Five or more	20.5	27.0	25.5	50.0	26.0

Source: National Industrial Conference Board (1967).

Note: (a) Excludes "school" and "technical" books.

Table 610–C.
Results of a Survey Measuring Book Purchases in U.S.,
by Type of Book and Selected Characteristics of the Buyer, 1976/77

	"Purchased a book in the past six months"					
	Any Book		Paperback		Hardcover	
Type of Book Buyer	Women	Men	Women	Men	Women	Men
Race:						
White	40.0%	33.5%	34.7%	29.2%	17.7%	16.0%
Black	23.9	21.9	21.3	20.0	7.1	8.6
Marital Status:						
Married	38.4	29.0	32.8	25.0	16.5	12.9
Single	52.7	46.8	47.8	42.5	23.3	24.7
Other	27.8	25.7	24.8	21.1	12.1	11.7
Children in Household:						
Under 6 years	38.7	31.3	33.2	26.6	15.0	14.7
6-17 years	42.1	31.2	36.9	27.0	18.1	13.9
No child under 18	34.7	32.3	30.3	28.4	15.5	15.8
Locality:						
Metropolitan—Central City	39.2	35.1	34.4	30.4	17.4	16.0
Metropolitan—Suburban	41.6	36.6	36.8	32.3	17.9	18.1
Non-Metropolitan	31.2	22.6	25.9	19.5	13.3	9.9
Region:						
Northeast	40.0	37.9	36.3	34.5	15.9	17.9
Central	39.4	28.5	33.9	24.6	15.7	12.1
South	31.4	27.1	26.9	24.0	13.3	12.6
West	45.7	40.4	39.1	33.2	24.4	21.1
County Size:[a]						
"A" counties	43.2	36.7	37.9	32.0	18.7	17.6
"B" counties	38.0	35.1	33.4	30.3	16.3	18.2
"C" counties	36.2	31.0	30.3	28.0	16.1	12.3
"D" counties	26.3	16.5	22.7	14.0	11.2	6.5
Age:						
18-24 years	50.2	42.3	45.1	38.6	20.4	20.9
25-34 years	50.5	40.2	43.3	34.1	21.8	20.6
35-44 years	43.1	33.1	37.7	29.4	19.2	13.6
45-54 years	36.6	30.2	31.3	25.7	17.9	15.1
55-64 years	26.8	20.5	23.3	18.2	11.7	7.5
35-49 years	42.4	34.1	37.3	29.5	19.1	15.9
Occupation:						
Women:						
White collar	53.9		47.1		25.4	
Other employed	31.8		28.6		11.8	
Not employed	31.9		27.4		13.4	
Men:						
Professional/managerial		49.2		42.4		25.9
Clerical/sales		42.0		36.4		23.5
Other employed		26.1		23.2		10.7
Education:						
Attended college	61.1	53.6	52.9	46.3	31.6	30.5
High school graduate	40.3	30.1	35.0	26.6	16.3	11.4
Did not graduate high school	19.6	14.8	17.3	13.0	6.3	4.8

the block level in the case of urban areas, and to segments of townships in the case of rural areas. After stratifying the nation geographically and by size of community in order to insure conformity of the sample with the latest available estimate of the Census Bureau of the distribution of the adult population, sampling locations or areas were selected on a strictly random basis . . .

Since this sampling procedure is designed to produce a sample that approximates the adult civilian population (21 and older) living in private households in the United

Table 610–C. (Cont'd.)

Type of Book Buyer	Any Book		Paperback		Hardcover	
	Women	Men	Women	Men	Women	Men
Household Income:						
$20,000 and over	56.2%	42.6%	48.8%	36.7%	26.3%	22.6%
$15,000-$19,999	45.9	36.6	39.7	32.2	20.8	17.2
$10,000-$14,999	38.5	28.8	32.3	25.5	18.8	12.6
$8,000-$9,999	33.2	25.7	29.4	22.7	10.6	11.7
$5,000-$7,999	30.2	24.8	27.8	21.2	10.2	9.7
Less than $5,000	18.8	19.9	16.6	17.7	6.7	7.0
All Interviewees	38.1	32.3	33.1	28.2	16.5	15.2

Source: W. R. Simmons and Associates (1977).

Note: (a) "A" counties: All counties in the 25 largest metropolitan areas. "B" counties: All counties not in "A" category with populations of over 150,000 or in metropolitan areas over 150,000. "C" counties: All counties not in "A" category with population of over 35,000 or in metropolitan areas over 35,000. "D" counties: All other counties.

States (that is, excluding those in prisons and hospitals, hotels, religious and educational institutions, and on military reservations), the survey results can be applied to this population for the purpose of projecting percentages into number of people.

The editors generally regard the procedures reported for this survey as likely to produce valid and reliable results.

The data in **Table 610-B** are actually from surveys taken in 1961 and 1962, which were updated by manipulating the information to apply to 1966. The original study, in which 12,000 nonfarm households were interviewed, was conducted by the U.S. Bureau of Labor Statistics (BLS) to provide benchmark data for the Consumer Price Index. In that study, BLS interviewers asked detailed questions requiring members of the respondent family to reconstruct the previous year's receipts and disbursements. A detailed supplemental questionnaire, covering one week's expenditures for food and other frequently purchased items, was also completed. The reported receipts and disbursements were reviewed in the field for completeness, consistency, and balance of the family accounts. When the responses were unclear, families were re-interviewed.

The survey sample was constructed from a three-stage stratification design, with separate samples drawn for urban areas, rural areas in metropolitan counties, and rural areas in non-metropolitan counties. Details of the sampling procedure can be found in the National Industrial Conference Board reports (1965, 1967).

The rate of response to the survey was approximately 78 percent. The data were then adjusted by weighting the responses to conform to the *1960 Census of Population*, once the census figures had been matched with the definition of the survey sample. The 95 percent confidence interval for any survey response can be calculated from data in the report (National Industrial Conference Board, 1965).

The BLS survey suffers from a dependence on respondents' recall of income and expenditures over a year-long period. It is also subject to errors due to inaccurate sampling, reporting, and processing, and to the inability or refusal of some surveyed households to respond. However, the main limitations are the reliance on respondents' recall (the BLS changed this procedure in a similar 1972-1973 survey) and the probable errors introduced by the manipulation of the data for presentation in 1966.

Concerning this manipulation, the National Industrial Conference Board (1967) made this statement:

> Briefly described, the procedure used in updating the original survey findings to 1966 consisted of applying current demographic data to the 1960-1961 expenditure

figures. Although more sophisticated methodological approaches were explored, few appeared to provide more efficient results than the procedure finally elected. Quite evidently, this approach assumes that any change which may have occurred in total consumer expenditures for a particular product or service between the original survey and 1966 was experienced in about the same magnitude by all social and economic segments of the nation's household population. No pretention is made that this promise is without imperfections. Certainly there were cases where a particular segment of the market increased or decreased its outlays for a given item by more, or less, than other segments.

However, it can also be assumed with reasonable confidence that such differences are for the most part modest and not of meaningful account, given the uses intended with the data reported here. It is estimated that in some extreme cases, the figures shown in the volume over- or understate the importance of a particular market segment for a specific product by a percentage point or two.

The editors' impression of the data in **Table 610**-B is that they are much better than an estimate, but not to be used in any secondary data analysis without further study of the sources.

Table 610-C comes from the *Study of Selective Markets and the Media Reaching Them* (1976-1977), carried out by W. R. Simmons and Associates Research. The study was based on a national probability sample of 15,034 people who were 18 years of age or older and residing in the the continental 48 states. The interviewing was conducted from November 16, 1975, through September 1976.

The sample for the study was based on a multi-stage area probability design, disproportionately allocated to upper-income areas. Census tracts or minor civil divisions in which 25 percent or more of the families reported incomes of $25,000 or higher, or in which 50 percent or more reported incomes over $15,000 in the *1970 Census of Population*, were oversampled by a factor of 4.17 to 1. Census tracts or minor civil divisions in which fewer than 10 percent of the families reported incomes of $15,000 or more were undersampled by a ratio of 1 to 2.73.

Two other income categories between these extremes were used to stratify the sample, with the moderately high-income category oversampled (although less than the highest category), and the moderately low-income category slightly undersampled. To calculate the totals after the data were reported, however, the strata were reweighted to conform to their presence in the population. This means that the information given for the upper-income categories is more precise than that given for the lower-income categories, although coverage for all categories is good.

The Simmons survey was basically a panel study, in which respondents were personally interviewed twice. Between interviews, the respondents filled out a "product information booklet" containing a question on book-buying. The response rate to the first interview was 76.5 percent for all adults (80 percent for women and 73.5 percent for men). The response rate for the product information booklets was "more than 75 percent" of those who responded to the first interview, or somewhat more than 57.5 percent of the original sample.

W. R. Simmons has prepared a technical guide (*Simmons Media Studies*, 1977) describing the procedures of this survey in detail. Judging from this information, the results of the survey are valid and reliable. The Advertising Research Foundation audited Simmons' 1974-1975 study, which employed methods much like the current study, and found "nothing to cause serious concern" (*Simmons Media Studies*, 1976).

Further Information

W. R. Simmons and Associates Research has been carrying out studies of this kind for several years, although the specific product categories about which information is gathered may vary from year to year. Some useful reviews of the book readership literature have been written by Ennis (1972) and Mathews (1973). Considerable library-use information is available in Knight and Nourse (1969), and important historical data are available in Berelson (1949). The need for more research in this area is stressed by Heidbreder (1973) and Slanker (1977).

Table 620–A.
Total Circulation of Daily, Sunday, Weekly, and Other Newspapers in U.S., 1900–1976

Note: All figures are in thousands.

	All Daily Newspapers: Census of Manufactures	All Daily Newspapers: Editor and Publisher	Morning Dailies Only: Editor and Publisher	Evening Dailies Only: Editor and Publisher	All Sunday Newspapers: Editor and Publisher	All Sunday Newspapers: Census of Manufactures	All Weekly Newspapers: Census of Manufactures	All Other Newspapers: Census of Manufactures	Total, All U. S. Newspapers: Census of Manufactures
1900	15,102[a]	--	--	--	--	N/A	N/A	N/A	N/A
1904	19,633	--	--	--	--	12,022	18,809	N/A	50,464[b]
1909	24,212	--	--	--	--	13,347	20,946	N/A	58,505[b]
1914	28,777	--	--	--	--	16,480	21,851	N/A	67,108[b]
1919	33,029	--	--	--	--	19,369	20,741	N/A	73,139[b]
1920	--	27,791	N/A	N/A	17,084	--	--	--	--
1921	33,742	28,424	10,144	18,279	19,041	20,853	20,816	N/A	75,411[b]
1922	--	29,780	10,810	18,898	19,713	--	--	--	--
1923	35,471	31,454	11,475	19,979	21,463	24,512	16,425	N/A	76,408[b]
1924	--	32,999	12,365	20,634	22,220	--	--	--	--
1925	37,407	33,739	12,440	21,299	23,355	25,630	15,990	1,678	80,705
1926	--	36,002	13,336	22,666	24,435	--	--	--	--
1927	41,368	37,967	14,146	23,827	25,469	27,696	16,879	1,674	87,617
1928	--	37,973	13,995	23,977	25,772	--	--	--	--
1929	42,015	39,426	14,449	24,477	26,880	29,012	18,884	1,867	91,778
1930	--	39,589	14,434	25,155	26,413	--	--	--	--
1931	41,294	38,761	14,343	24,418	25,702	27,453	16,173	1,537	86,457
1932	--	36,408	13,700	22,700	24,860	--	--	--	--
1933	37,630	35,175	13,200	22,000	24,041	25,454	12,048	1,166	76,298
1934	--	36,709	14,000	22,700	26,545	--	--	--	--
1935	40,871	38,156	14,400	23,700	28,147	29,196	15,185	1,844	87,096
1936	--	40,292	15,300	25,000	29,962	--	--	--	--
1937	43,345	41,419	15,900	25,500	30,957	32,713	17,287	1,951	95,296
1938	--	39,572	15,100	24,500	30,481	--	--	--	--
1939	42,966	39,671	15,500	24,200	31,519	33,007	18,295	2,209	96,477

Table 620-A. (Cont'd.)

	All Daily Newspapers: Census of Manufactures	All Daily Newspapers: Editor and Publisher	Morning Dailies Only: Editor and Publisher	Evening Dailies Only: Editor and Publisher	All Sunday Newspapers: Editor and Publisher	All Sunday Newspapers: Census of Manufactures	All Weekly Newspapers: Census of Manufactures	All Other Newspapers: Census of Manufactures	Total, All U.S. Newspapers: Census of Manufactures
1940	--	41,132	16,114	25,018	32,371	--	--	--	--
1941	--	42,080	16,519	25,561	33,436	--	--	--	--
1942	--	43,375	17,111	26,264	35,294	--	--	--	--
1943	--	44,393	17,078	27,315	37,292	--	--	--	--
1944	--	45,955	18,059	27,896	37,946	--	--	--	--
1945	--	48,384	19,240	29,144	39,680	--	--	--	--
1946	--	50,928	20,546	30,382	43,665	--	--	--	--
1947	53,287	51,673	20,762	30,911	45,151	42,736	21,408	2,137	119,568
1948	--	52,285	21,082	31,203	46,308	--	--	--	--
1949	--	52,846	21,005	31,841	46,399	--	--	--	--
1950	--	53,829	21,266	32,563	46,582	--	--	--	--
1951	--	54,018	21,223	32,795	46,279	--	--	--	--
1952	--	53,951	21,160	32,791	46,210	--	--	--	--
1953	--	54,472	21,412	33,060	45,949	--	--	--	--
1954	56,410	55,072	21,705	33,367	46,176	46,350	30,336	3,257	136,353
1955	--	56,147	22,183	33,964	46,448	--	--	--	--
1956	--	57,102	22,492	34,610	47,172	--	--	--	--
1957	--	57,805	23,171	34,635	47,044	--	--	--	--
1958	58,713	57,418	23,161	34,258	46,955	48,262	26,177	3,651	136,803
1959	--	58,300	23,547	34,753	47,848	--	--	--	--
1960	--	58,882	24,029	34,853	47,699	--	--	--	--
1961	--	59,261	24,094	35,167	48,216	--	--	--	--
1962	--	59,849	24,563	35,286	48,888	--	--	--	--
1963	63,831	58,905	23,459	35,446	46,830	51,669	17,500c	3,600c	136,600
1964	--	60,412	24,365	36,048	48,383	--	--	--	--
1965	--	60,358	24,107	36,251	48,600	--	--	--	--
1966	--	61,397	24,806	36,592	49,282	--	--	--	--
1967	66,527	61,561	25,282	36,279	49,224	52,129	N/A	N/A	N/A
1968	--	62,535	25,838	36,697	49,693	--	--	--	--
1969	--	62,060	25,812	36,248	49,675	--	--	--	--
1970	--	62,108	25,934	36,174	49,217	--	--	--	--
1971	--	62,231	26,116	36,115	49,665	--	--	--	--
1972	64,996	62,510	26,078	36,432	49,339	51,945	N/A	N/A	N/A
1973	--	63,147	26,524	36,623	51,717	--	--	--	--
1974	--	61,877	26,145	35,732	51,679	--	--	--	--
1975	--	60,655	25,490	35,165	51,096	--	--	--	--
1976	--	60,977	25,858	35,119	51,565	--	--	--	--

Sources: All *Census of Manufactures* data: 1900-1967: *Historical Statistics of the United States: Colonial Times to 1970* (1975), p. 810; 1972: *1972 Census of Manufactures*. All *Editor and Publisher* data as follows: Total daily and Sunday newspapers, 1920-1970, and morning and evening newspapers, 1940-1970: *Historical Statistics of the United States, Colonial Times to 1970* (1975), p. 809. Morning and evening newspapers, 1921-1931: Willey and Rice (1933), p. 160. Morning and evening newspapers, 1932-1939: Chapin (1957), p. 9. Total, morning, evening, and Sunday newspapers, 1971-1975: *Statistical Abstract of the United States, 1974* and *1976*. All 1976 data: *1977 Editor and Publisher International Yearbook* (1976), p. 21.

Notes: (a) Includes a small number of periodicals. (b) Does not include "other" newspapers, which were not available prior to 1925. (c) Data are estimates based on the yearly subscription rate of reporting newspapers, as many small newspapers did not report circulation.

Interpretation of Tables

Table 620-A lists the average total circulation per issue for a number of different categories of newspapers between 1900 and 1976. Although there was a steady drop in the *number* of daily newspapers throughout this period (see Units 120 and 121), the figures in **Table 620-A** indicate that daily (and Sunday) newspaper circulation has generally risen since 1900. The only exceptions

Table 620–B.
Total Circulation of Daily Newspapers in U.S., by Size of City, 1948–1973

Note: All circulation figures are in thousands.

Size of City	1948	1958	1968	1973	Percent Change 1948-1973
Up to 10,000	1,676	1,753	1,741	1,758	4.9%
10,000 to 99,000	13,280	15,594	18,113	19,728	48.6
100,000 to 500,000	13,908	16,594	17,957	17,460	25.5
500,000 to 1 million	8,533	10,255	11,052	10,950	28.3
Over 1 million	13,947	13,013	11,955	11,389	-18.3
Total Circulation	51,344	57,209	60,818	61,285	19.4%

Source: Rosse et al. (1975), p. 40, citing data from *Editor and Publisher International Yearbook*.

are a dip during the Depression and another slight decline in the early 1970s. It is not clear whether the more recent circulation plateau is due to the recession years of 1974-1975, or whether more basic market forces are in operation. The *Editor and Publisher* figures for 1976 show a very slight increase, so it is possible that daily newspaper circulation figures will begin to rise again. On the other hand, when one combines the information in **Table 620-A** with the data on the number of U.S. households in Unit 100, it is apparent that daily newspaper circulation per household has been declining for some time.

Table 620-B breaks down the *Editor and Publisher* daily newspaper circulation figures by city size. The reader will note much greater increases in newspaper circulation in the middle-sized cities, as opposed to cities of less than 10,000 or more than 1 million. The very largest cities experienced a drop in daily newspaper circulation, while cities at the other end of the scale saw only slight increases in circulation.

Table 620-C ranks the 25 largest daily and Sunday newspapers in 1975. The circulation figures in the "All Daily Newspapers" segment of the table are for both morning and evening newspapers owned by a single company or operating under a joint operating agreement. The top 18 dailies on this list, constituting about 1 percent of all U.S. daily newspapers, accounted for about 21.5 percent of total circulation of dailies in 1975.

It would be useful to have a long-term source of information on the total circulation of the top newspaper chains, so that the reader could estimate what percentage of total annual newspaper circulation is controlled by what percentage of all newspaper companies (treating a chain as one company). Unit 220 lists the total circulation accounted for by all newspaper chains for some years, but this is as close as it is possible to get. However, one recent article by Bagdikian (1977) points out a trend in this area: In 1960, the 25 largest newspaper chains controlled 38 percent of all daily newspaper circulation, and this ownership rose to 52 percent by 1976. As Bagdikian commented, "Never before had so much been under the control of so few."

Table 620-D traces weekly newspaper circulation since 1956. According to the *Census of Manufactures* data in **Table 620-A**, weekly newspaper circulation had begun to decline after reaching a peak in 1954, but the more recent data in **Table 620-D** show that this trend of decline did not continue. Although the number of weekly newspapers has decreased since the mid-1950s, the circulation figures have risen quite steadily and, in the mid-1970s, quite markedly. Udell (1978) has also found data supporting an upward circulation trend among weekly newspapers.

Table 620–C.
The 25 Largest Circulation Daily and Sunday Newspapers in U.S., 1975

All Daily Newspapers

		Circulation
1.	New York Times	2,083,257
2.	Chicago Tribune	1,111,004
3.	Los Angeles Times	1,023,033
4.	New York Times	874,749
5.	Philadelphia Inquirer and News*	708,721
6.	Detroit News	684,852
7.	San Francisco Chronicle and Examiner†	650,607
8.	Kansas City Star and Times*	643,408
9.	New York Post	623,127
10.	Detroit Free Press	621,068
11.	Philadelphia Bulletin	599,917
12.	Chicago Sun-Times	570,509
13.	Washington Post	532,641
14.	Milwaukee Sentinel and Journal*	532,419
15.	Pittsburgh Press and Post-Gazette†	505,432
16.	Minneapolis Star and Tribune*	489,345
17.	Miami Herald and News†	478,553
18.	Boston Globe	472,104
19.	Altanta Constitution and Journal*	462,888
20.	Long Island Newsday	455,163
21.	Los Angeles Herald-Examiner	442,549
22.	Chicago News	439,846
23.	Cleveland Plain Dealer	407,892
24.	Louisville Courier-Journal and Times	400,628
25.	Indianapolis Star and News*	393,533

Morning Newspapers Only

		Circulation
1.	New York News	2,073,257
2.	Los Angeles Times	1,023,033
3.	New York Times	875,749
4.	Chicago Tribune	690,678
5.	Detroit Free Press	621,068
6.	Chicago Sun-Times	570,509
7.	Washington Post	532,641
8.	San Francisco Chronicle and Examiner†	474,521
9.	Philadelphia Inquirer and News*	452,524
10.	Cleveland Plain Dealer	407,892
11.	Miami Herald and News†	405,464
12.	Newark Star-Ledger	361,268
13.	Boston Herald American and Herald Advertiser*	359,281
14.	Kansas City Star and Times*	332,629
15.	Houston Post	297,195
16.	Boston Globe	286,640
17.	Saint Louis Globe-Democrat	277,284
18.	Dallas News	264,920
19.	Des Moines Register and Tribune*	245,802
20.	Portland Oregonian and Oregon Journal*	240,682
21.	Minneapolis Star and Tribune*	233,381
22.	Louisville Courier-Journal and Times	227,463
23.	Indianapolis Star and News*	224,051
24.	Denver Rocky Mountain News	219,544
25.	Memphis Commercial Appeal and Press-Scimitar*	218,721

Table 620–C. (Cont'd.)

	Evening Newspapers Only	Circulation
1.	Detroit News	684,852
2.	New York Post	623,127
3.	Philadelphia Bulletin	599,917
4.	Long Island Newsday	455,163
5.	Los Angeles Herald-Examiner	442,549
6.	Chicago News	439,846
7.	Chicago Tribune	420,326
8.	Washington Star-News	391,633
9.	Cleveland Press	375,258
10.	Milwaukee Sentinel and Journal*	353,124
11.	Long Island Press	326,818
12.	Kansas City Star and Times*	310,779
13.	Houston Chronicle	301,589
14.	Saint Louis Post-Dispatch	297,634
15.	Pittsburgh Press and Post-Gazette†	290,186
16.	Buffalo News	279,372
17.	Philadelphia Inquirer and News*	256,197
18.	Minneapolis Star and Tribune*	255,964
19.	Atlanta Constitution and Journal*	249,265
20.	Denver Post	245,175
21.	Dallas Times Herald	242,646
22.	Seattle Times	239,237
23.	Columbus Dispatch and Citizen-Journal†	223,489
24.	Baltimore News American	212,712
25.	Cincinnati Post	211,974

Sources

The information in **Table 620-A** comes from the U.S. Census Bureau's *Census of Manufactures*, and from *Editor and Publisher*, the leading trade magazine in the newspaper publishing industry. The differences in figures from the two sources are due to slightly different definitions of a "daily newspaper": *Editor and Publisher* includes only English-language dailies, whereas the Census Bureau includes a few foreign-language dailies. Both series exclude trade dailies and other daily publications not of interest to the general public.

The Census Bureau collects its data from a combination of mail questionnaires and examinations of social security and income tax records. The information is therefore generally considered reliable and valid, within the limits of its definitions. The circulation figures in the *Editor and Publisher International Yearbook* are considered the standard by the newspaper industry and are used by the industry in determining advertising rates and policies. The data can be regarded as reliable.

Table 620-B is from Rosse et al. (1975), who tabulated their data from the information for individual newspaper firms listed in the *Editor and Publisher International Yearbook*. The ultimate source of data, then, is reliable. The differences in the totals presented here and those given in the *Editor and Publisher International Yearbook* are probably due to different aggregation schemes. Rosse included as a single newspaper firm all "separate newspapers with joint editorship, advertising departments, publishing representatives, or press facilities." Double-counting under this definition could explain the discrepancies.

Table 620-C comes from the Standard Rate and Data Service (SRDS), another widely used trade source, which bases its figures on information from the Audit Bureau of Circulations or

Table 620–C. (Cont'd.)

Sunday or Weekend Newspapers

		Circulation
1.	New York News	2,866,959
2.	New York Times	1,467,059
3.	Los Angeles Times	1,207,482
4.	Chicago Tribune	1,165,026
5.	Detroit News	847,045
6.	Philadelphia Inquirer and News*	826,302
7.	Chicago Sun-Times	728,779
8.	Detroit Free Press	722,430
9.	Washington Post	712,625
10.	Pittsburgh Press and Post Gazette†	702,920
11.	Philadelphia Bulletin	674,825
12.	San Francisco Chronicle and Examiner†	667,121
13.	Minneapolis Star and Tribune*	640,756
14.	Boston Globe	623,648
15.	Atlanta Constitution and Journal*	558,603
16.	Newark Star Ledger	553,266
17.	Milwaukee Sentinel and Journal*	544,907
18.	Cleveland Plain Dealer	508,832
19.	Miami Herald and News†	505,008
20.	Boston Herald American and Herald Advertiser*	491,704
21.	Saint Louis Post-Dispatch	491,407
22.	Des Moines Register and Tribune*	480,884
23.	Los Angeles Herald-Examiner	460,027
24.	Kansas City Star and Times*	404,051
25.	Portland Oregonian and Oregon Journal*	401,472

Sources: Standard Rate and Data Service, *Daily Newspapers* (1975-1976), which based its figures on Audit Bureau of Circulation data and on publishers' statements.

Note: In this listing, newspapers are identified by the name and location of their advertising facilities. Thus, if two independently owned newspapers in a city share a joint advertising office (as in the case of the morning *San Francisco Chronicle* and the afternoon *San Francisco Examiner*), both papers are named in the individual rankings for each. The circulation figures, however, represent the sales of the *individual* papers (i.e., the *Chronicle* in the morning-paper listings and the *Examiner* in the evening-paper listings).

Other newspapers are listed jointly because of common ownership not only of the advertising facilities but of the two newspapers as well (e.g., the Minneapolis *Star* and *Tribune*). The jointly owned newspapers are marked with an asterisk (*); the independent newspapers which share advertising facilities are marked with a dagger (†).

from publishers' sworn statements. This table appears every two years in the SRDS publication, *Daily Newspapers*.

Table 620-D was drawn from two sources: Rucker (1968), citing information from the American Newspaper Representatives, Inc., and the American Newspaper Publishers Association (1977). The latter provided the 1970-1976 data.

Further Information

Valuable discussions of the forces affecting newspaper circulation appear in Owen (1975), Bagdikian (1971), Compaine (1973), and a just-published work by Udell (1978), who is an economic consultant to the American Newspaper Publishers Association.

Table 620–D.
Number and Total Circulation of Weekly Newspapers in U.S., 1956–1976

	Weekly Newspapers	Total Circulation
1956	8,478	18,529,199
1957	8,408	19,272,826
1958	8,368	19,725,952
1959	8,287	20,186,414
1960	8,274	20,974,388
1961	8,183	21,327,782
1962	8,178	22,797,449
1963	8,158	23,433,718
1964	8,151	23,975,549
1965	8,061	25,036,031
1966	8,003	26,088,230
1967	N/A	N/A
1968	N/A	N/A
1969	N/A	N/A
1970	7,610	29,422,487
1971	7,567	30,495,921
1972	7,553	31,997,341
1973	7,641	34,938,800
1974	7,612	35,792,409
1975	7,486	35,176,130
1976	7,579	38,006,868

Sources: 1956-1966 data: Rucker (1968), p. 30, citing American Newspaper Representatives, Inc. 1970-1976 data: American Newspaper Publishers Association (1977).

Characteristics of Newspaper Readers

621

Interpretation of Tables

Table 621-A describes newspaper readership in the United States according to a number of different demographic measures. According to the figures, slightly more men than women report newspaper readership (although the percentages in this table are very close in the breakdown by sex, other similar polls have confirmed this difference). The table also indicates that newspaper reading increases with education, urbanization, and affluence, and with age up to 60 years. A larger percentage of whites read newspapers, and newspapers are apparently read more often in the northeastern and central United States.

The main difference between Tables 621-A and 621-B is that the former is based on newspaper readership as reported by individuals, whereas Table 621-B presents expenditures for newspapers by household. Despite these differences, and the seven-year span between the surveys, the results in both tables are quite similar. In comparing the percentage of each demographic group's expenditures on newspapers with that group's presence in the population, Table 621-B reveals greater concentrations of expenditures for newspapers among residents of the Northeast, among whites, among suburban and central-city residents, and among the educated and affluent.

Sources

Table 621-A comes from a market research survey conducted by W. R. Simmons and Associates and published by the Newspaper Advertising Bureau. The methods of the survey are similar

Table 621–A.
Percentage of Newspaper Readers in U.S.,
by Sex, Age, Educational Level, and Other Characteristics, 1973

Characteristics of Readers	Percent Who Read Newspapers		
	All Adults	Male Adults	Female Adults
Total Adult Population	73%	74%	73%
Age			
18 to 24 years	64	68	61
25 to 34 years	70	70	71
35 to 49 years	77	77	78
50 to 64 years	79	80	79
65 and older	73	73	73
Education Level			
Some College or more	81	82	80
High School Graduate	77	77	77
1 to 3 Years of High School	68	70	67
Grade School or less	62	62	62
Annual Income			
$15,000 or more	82	84	81
$10,000 to $14,999	79	78	79
$5,000 to $9,999	69	68	70
Less than $5,000	61	59	62
Occupation			
Total Employed	74	75	73
Professional/Managerial	82	82	82
Clerical/Sales	76	79	75
Other	69	70	66
Total Unemployed	72	71	73
Race			
White	75	75	75
Nonwhite	60	63	57
Marital Status			
Married	76	76	76
Single	69	70	67
Divorced	64	58	67
Widowed	68	63	69
Presence of Children in Household			
One or more Children/Teenagers	72	74	71
One or more Children under 6 Years	69	71	67
No Children under 6 Years	75	76	75
No Children	75	74	75
Type of Locality			
Metropolitan:			
Central City	74	75	73
More than 500,000	74	78	70
50,000 to 499,999	74	72	75
Metropolitan Suburban	75	76	74
Nonmetropolitan	72	71	73

Characteristics of Readers	Percent Who Read Newspapers		
	All Adults	Male Adults	Female Adults
Region			
Northeast	77%	78%	76%
Central	78	79	77
South	67	67	68
West	71	72	70

Source: Data developed for the Newspaper Advertising Bureau by W. R. Simmons and Associates (1973).

Table 621–B.
Distribution of Consumer Expenditures for Newspapers in U.S.,
by Selected Family Characteristics, 1966

Family Characteristics	Distribution of All Families	Distribution of Expenditures on Newspapers
Region		
Northeast	26.5%	35.0%
North Central	27.0	28.5
South	29.0	21.5
West	17.5	15.0
Race		
White	88.5	91.5
Nonwhite	11.5	8.5
Market Location		
Metropolitan Areas		
Central Cities	33.0	35.0
Urban Fringe	29.0	35.0
Other Areas	6.5	6.5
Nonmetropolitan Areas		
Urban	15.5	13.5
Rural	16.0	10.0
Education Level of Head of Household		
Grade School or less	29.5	22.0
Some High School	18.0	18.0
High School Graduate	29.0	31.5
Some College	10.0	11.5
College Graduate or higher	13.5	17.0
Family Income (before taxes)		
Under $3,000	16.0	7.0
$3,000 to $5,000	15.0	10.5
$5,000 to $7,000	21.0	19.0
$7,500 to $10,000	19.0	22.0
$10,000 and over	29.0	41.5
Occupation of Head of Household		
Professional/Technical	12.0	15.5
Managerial/Official	12.0	15.5
Clerical/Sales	11.5	12.5
Foreman/Craftsman	16.0	17.5
Operative	16.5	15.0
All Other	32.0	24.0
Age of Head of Household		
Under 25 years	6.5	3.5
25 to 34 years	18.0	16.0
35 to 44 years	20.5	23.5
45 to 54 years	19.5	22.5
55 to 64 years	15.5	17.0
65 years and over	20.0	17.5
Family Size		
One Member	19.5	13.0
Two Members	28.5	30.5
Three Members	16.5	18.5
Four Members	15.0	16.5
Five Members or more	20.5	21.5

Source: National Industrial Conference Board (1967).

to those for Simmons and Associates' *1976-77 Study of Selective Markets and the Media Reaching Them*, which is described in the "Sources" section of Unit 610. The editors view the results of this survey as generally reliable, although it is subject to some sampling error (see Welles, 1978).

An interesting feature of the Simmons and Associates survey is the use of the "progressive step" method to determine if any newspapers were read "yesterday." Respondents were first asked, "What weekday newspaper have you read or looked into in the last few days?" After their response was recorded, they were asked, "When was the last time you read or looked into a copy of (the newspaper)?" If the answer to that question was "today," the interviewer then asked, "When was the last time before today?" If the answer to either of the previous two questions was "yesterday," the respondent was judged to have read a newspaper "yesterday." This method, which does not suggest "yesterday" in the question wording, has been used for a number of years and is considered by Simmons and Associates to be the best way to accurately measure newspaper readership.

Table 621-B comes from an analysis of the benchmark data of the federal government's Consumer Price Index. The survey was conducted by consultants of the National Industrial Conference Board. This is the same work from which the figures in **Table 610-B** were drawn, and the methods of the survey, with its limitations, are discussed in the "Sources" section of that unit. The principal flaw is that the data presented here have been updated to 1966 by mathematically adjusting results collected in 1961. The editors consider the numbers to be more reliable than gross estimates, but less accurate than survey data such as that in **Table 621-A**.

Further Information

Recently, W. R. Simmons and Associates has carried out similar studies of newspaper readership every two years. The American Newspaper Publishers Association (ANPA) also measures newspaper readership, on a less regular basis, in its *News Research Reports*. In addition, the ANPA News Research Center at the Syracuse University School of Public Communications has collected and indexed a number of newspaper readership and circulation studies of differing size and scope. The center provides bibliographies or relevant abstracts on request.

Audits and Surveys, Inc., has also conducted surveys on newspaper readership, including some which have been released by the Newspaper Advertising Bureau.

Magazine Circulation 630

Interpretation of Tables

There are no overall comprehensive estimates of the total circulation of periodicals in the United States. The problem is related to differences in definitions of periodicals, and to the difficulty of locating and recording data for the numerous obscure periodicals in this country (see Unit 130). Even among those periodicals which are well-known and regularly counted, the estimates of their total penetration among the U.S. population are inadequate (see the "Sources" section below).

Table 630-A presents the Magazine Publishers Association figures for the total per-issue circulation of general and farm magazines audited by the Audit Bureau of Circulations (ABC). These figures include the larger magazines of general appeal, as well as some smaller periodicals that specialize in the farm market. Most of these magazines are named in the list of top-ranking U.S. magazines (see **Table 630-D**).

Table 630-A reveals some interesting trends. Magazine circulation grew quite rapidly in the first half of this century, both absolutely and relative to the U.S. adult population. Circulation per 100 adults rose 101 percent between 1914 and 1919; and in the 1920s, this figure increased again by 49 percent. Sales dropped during the Depression, but even in the mid-1930s, magazine circulation grew 6 percent faster than the American population.

In the 1940s, growth resumed with a 37 percent rise in circulation, which slowed thereafter to 15 percent in the 1950s and 10 percent in the 1960s. Circulation per 100 adults reached its peak in 1969—since 1970, the figure has declined by 6.3 percent. However, the latest available count—157.5 copies per 100 adults in 1976—is slightly above the 157.3 posted in 1975. Also, although circulation of general and farm magazines has declined relative to the population, it has continued to increase both on an absolute basis (255,420,819 copies were distributed in 1976)

Table 630–A.
Number and Total Circulation of General and Farm Magazines,
and Number of Single Copies Purchased per 100 Adults in U.S., 1914–1975

| | Number of Magazines | Total Circulation per Issue | | Total Copies Sold | U. S. Adult Population[a] (thousands) | Single Copies Purchased per 100 Adults |
		Number of Single Copies Sold	Single Copies Sold as Percent of Total			
1914	54	N/A	N/A	17,912,922	67,556	26.5
1915	91	N/A	N/A	19,241,873	68,543	28.1
1916	96	N/A	N/A	32,638,114	69,514	47.0
1917	109	N/A	N/A	31,159,029	70,369	44.3
1918	123	N/A	N/A	35,177,156	69,865	50.4
1919	133	N/A	N/A	37,989,651	71,126	53.4
1920	146	N/A	N/A	44,094,717	72,675	60.7
1921	158	N/A	N/A	46,548,746	74,145	62.8
1922	164	N/A	N/A	47,160,809	75,233	62.7
1923	170	N/A	N/A	54,281,784	76,743	70.7
1924	173	N/A	N/A	54,175,705	78,487	69.0
1925	200	19,770,855	32.3%	61,276,667	79,905	76.7
1926	210	20,638,772	31.3	65,864,284	81,301	81.0
1927	215	21,844,921	31.1	70,236,215	82,775	84.9
1928	215	24,041,515	32.3	74,513,520	84,207	88.5
1929	231	27,953,966	36.2	77,173,748	85,565	90.2
1930	232	27,366,763	34.7	78,844,448	87,074	90.5
1931	195	26,090,582	34.8	75,051,854	88,232	85.1
1932	180	24,167,515	34.4	70,326,182	89,323	78.7
1933	187	23,564,124	34.0	69,347,429	90,436	76.7
1934	198	25,931,993	34.8	74,521,406	91,641	81.3
1935	204	26,668,266	35.1	75,973,645	92,867	81.8
1936	206	31,690,147	38.1	83,235,120	94,067	88.5
1937	213	34,793,579	39.0	89,287,722	95,252	93.7
1938	224	34,406,959	37.3	92,181,494	96,503	95.5
1939	229	36,368,268	38.8	93,774,577	97,761	95.9
1940	224	39,005,215	41.1	94,817,238	99,012	95.8
1941	213	44,575,854	44.2	100,934,784	100,182	100.8
1942	203	48,347,222	45.7	105,704,994	100,796	104.9
1943	209	54,933,809	49.3	111,344,026	100,530	110.8
1944	217	60,846,910	52.5	115,966,726	98,788	117.4
1945	219	65,707,419	54.2	121,240,485	97,903	123.8
1946	239	64,628,075	49.4	130,897,607	104,966	124.7
1947	243	61,926,080	45.7	135,567,060	106,783	127.0
1948	239	62,076,922	44.0	140,998,562	108,085	130.5
1949	246	60,495,940	42.1	143,712,572	109,288	131.5
1950	250	61,998,611	42.1	147,259,540	110,471	133.3
1951	247	64,157,748	42.3	151,503,536	111,111	136.4
1952	252	68,716,845	43.1	159,368,541	111,889	142.4
1953	258	68,109,367	41.8	163,034,506	112,870	144.4
1954	259	67,456,118	40.9	164,966,886	114,112	144.6

Table 630–A. (Cont'd.)

| | Number of Magazines | Total Circulation per Issue | | Total Copies Sold | U. S. Adult Population[a] | Single Copies Purchased per 100 Adults |
		Number of Single Copies Sold	Single Copies Sold as Percent of Total			
					(thousands)	
1955[b]	272	71,073,877	39.5%	179,965,231	115,505	155.8
1956	282	73,874,770	39.8	185,730,889	116,743	159.1
1957	278	68,305,833	37.7	181,410,348	118,208	153.5
1958	270	63,384,915	34.6	183,324,790	119,854	153.0
1959	274	62,609,711	33.7	185,589,166	121,438	152.8
1960	273	62,295,487	32.7	190,431,836	123,890	153.7
1961	273	60,696,623	31.0	195,663,452	125,303	156.2
1962	278	61,977,422	30.9	200,657,742	127,692	157.1
1963	274	62,578,172	30.8	203,223,239	129,797	156.6
1964	282	64,953,619	31.2	207,871,456	132,005	157.5
1965	275	66,538,850	30.9	215,486,748	133,909	160.9
1966	276	68,554,898	30.4	225,661,797	135,798	166.2
1967	279	71,275,957	30.7	232,124,659	137,877	168.4
1968	287	71,183,468	30.0	237,101,335	140,191	169.1
1969	302	71,587,283	29.6	241,793,220	142,616	169.5
1970	300	70,701,105	29.0	244,164,089	145,256	168.1
1971	293	73,296,562	30.2	242,453,893	148,646	163.1
1972	302	80,739,026	33.3	242,418,188	151,484	160.0
1973	306	83,947,248	34.1	245,901,842	154,154	161.0
1974	316	85,055,173	34.2	248,822,947	156,771	158.7
1975	327	85,580,704	34.1	250,831,209	159,490	157.3

Sources: Magazine Publishers Association. Population figures cited by MPA from the U. S. Bureau of the Census.

Notes: Includes magazines audited by the Audit Bureau of Circulation only. Circulation per issue figures are based on records of the second six months of each year. (a) U. S. residents aged 15 years or older. (b) For the first time, the *Reader's Digest* is included, with its circulation of 10,316,531.

and in single-copy sales (the percentage has risen from 29 percent in 1970 to 35.1 percent by 1976).

Another measure of overall periodical circulation growth is provided in **Table 630-B**, which is based on Census Bureau data collected in the *Census of Manufactures*, together with estimates and corrections by Theodore Peterson, a leading scholar of the magazine industry for many years. These figures suffer from a number of limitations which are discussed in the "Sources" section below. Indeed, according to one specialist in the U.S. Department of Commerce, the figures "carry little meaning." Certainly, it is very difficult to point out any trends in these data. Increases in the number of periodicals appear to be unrelated to the increases in circulation.

The breakdown of these figures by the type of magazine yields a little more information, however. **Table 630-C** shows that farm periodicals have experienced a decline in circulation, while general news, industrial, engineering, and technical periodicals have increased. Although **Table 630-C** also shows a sharp decrease in the circulations of professional, institutional, and service periodicals, the editors have reason to doubt this trend. A large number of these periodicals come from nonprofit publishers, who have a tax incentive for *not* listing their magazines as separately identifiable nonprofit operations.

Table 630–B.
Number and Total Circulation of All Periodicals in U.S., 1900–1963

Note: "Total Circulation" figures are in thousands.

	Number of Periodicals		Total Circulation	
	Peterson Data	Historical Statistics Data	Peterson Data	Historical Statistics Data
1900	3,500	N/A	65,000	N/A
1919	N/A	4,796	N/A	N/A
1921	N/A	3,747	N/A	N/A
1923	3,085	3,829	128,621	N/A
1925	3,635	4,496	153,375	179,281
1927	3,860	4,659	165,702	191,000
1929	4,500[a]	5,157	202,022	202,022
1931	4,887	4,887	183,527	183,527
1933	3,459	3,459	174,759	174,759
1935	4,019	4,019	178,621	178,621
1937	4,202	4,202	224,275	224,275
1939	4,985	4,985	239,693	239,693
1947	4,610	4,610	384,628	384,628
1954	N/A	3,427	N/A	449,285
1958	4,455	4,455	391,936	408,364
1963	N/A	N/A	N/A	427,915

Sources: Peterson (1964), pp. 57-59; *Historical Statistics of the United States* (1975), Series R 254-255.

Notes: Peterson figures are estimates based on Census Bureau data. The 1900 figures are rough estimates. (a) Reported by Peterson as "considerably more than 4,500."

The incentive arises from the fact that advertising profits of a nonprofit organization are taxable as "unrelated business income," but losses in subscription revenue can offset this ad income. Thus, if the magazine is offered as part of the membership in a nonprofit group, the amount of membership dues budgeted to the magazine directly affects the organization's tax write-off. The smaller the portion of dues allocated to the magazine, the greater the tax write-off and, hence, the incentive to merge the figures in reports to the *Census of Manufactures* (see Stevenson, 1976).

Table 630-D presents the 1976 rankings of the 100 leading magazines for which the Audit Bureau of Circulations collects circulation figures. Seven of the top 10 magazines in 1976 were in the top 10 in 1963, as were 13 of the top 20. Newcomers appeared at all levels, however, and 33 of the top 100 were not on the list in 1963.

Sources

The circulation figures in **Tables 630-A** and **630-D** come from the Audit Bureau of Circulations. A magazine publisher joins the ABC, or a similar organization, like the BPA (Business Publications Audit of Circulation, Inc.), so that its circulation and other statistics will be standardized and verified. The ABC examines the periodical's records, advising changes in record-keeping to allow adequate auditing. At least twice a year, the publisher files circulation statements of various kinds, depending on the relationship of paid circulation to nonpaid distribution. (The circulation figures listed in **Table 630-A** are for paid circulation.) Once a year, the publisher's records are audited to authenticate and verify the circulation statements. A detailed explanation of these operations is available in Green (1976).

The ABC figures are considered reliable for *individual* magazines because of the detailed methods used to develop these figures for advertisers and advertising agencies. However, the ABC figures have several limitations, due in large part to the voluntary nature of the Bureau's member-

Table 630–C.
Average Total Per-Issue Circulation of U.S. Periodicals,
by Type of Periodical, 1958–1972

Note: All figures are in thousands.

	1958	1963	1967	1972
Total, Farm Periodicals	18,850	14,305	12,115	13,103
General	14,872	12,087	10,219	11,092
Specialized	3,978	2,218	1,896	2,011
Total, Specialized Business/ Professional Periodicals	51,577	32,712	N/A	N/A
Industrial/Engineering/Technical	11,399	12,113	12,952	17,609
Merchandising	4,686	N/A	N/A	N/A
Professional/Institutional/Service	35,492	N/A	8,303	11,924
Total, General Periodicals	241,741	238,955	N/A	N/A
Comics	63,035	27,594	15,178	N/A
Women/Home Services	70,729	93,401	74,541	N/A
General Interest/Entertainment	98,378	102,501	136,567	N/A
General News	7,780	13,913	9,652	19,605
Business News	1,819	N/A	1,409	1,489
Total, Other Periodicals	96,196	141,943	N/A	N/A
Religious	N/A	58,595	57,358	N/A
Sunday Supplements[a]	N/A	34,325	24,912	16,828
Other, Unclassified Elsewhere	N/A	N/A	44,945	N/A

Source: *Census of Manufactures*, appropriate years.

Note: (a) Includes Sunday comics.

ship. Since the number of magazines included in the circulation totals varies from year to year, the reader cannot know whether annual fluctuations in circulation are due to changes in the audience's general buying behavior or to changes in the number of periodicals audited by the ABC. Further, the boundaries of the "general" and "farm" categories of periodicals are indistinct. It would be difficult to compare this count with any other.

The principal limitations on the *Census of Manufactures* data in **Tables 630-B** and **630-C** are the definition of "periodical" and "periodical publishing company" and the data-collection method of the Census Bureau. It is difficult to ascertain the relationship between the definition of the periodicals industry and the inclusion of product information. Technically, product information comes from all industries producing periodicals, but some limitations in reporting undoubtedly occur as the result of differences in classification. Also, for the fairly large number of periodicals with less than 10 employees, none of these figures are available—although other data, such as payroll information, are collected from administrative records.

The editors regard the figures in **Tables 630-B** and **630-C** as less reliable than other Census Bureau data, which are generally very good. Since 1958, the *Census of Manufactures* has not printed the total number of periodicals in the U.S.; and after 1963, no figures for total periodical circulation are available. In addition, starting with the 1977 economic censuses, the Census Bureau will discontinue the series on periodicals circulation figures.

Further Information

Information on the circulations of individual publications is fairly easy to come by. Standard Rate and Data Service and several other sources provide such information. The problem is to find meaningful aggregations of the numbers. Little has been written on the subject: Machlup (1962) provides some analysis, but his sources are limited to those we list above. Compaine (1974) is also of some use, although it is an expensive publication for commercial users.

Table 630–D.
Ranking and Circulation of the Top 100 Magazines in U.S., 1963 and 1976

1976 Rank	1963 Rank		1976 Circulation	1963 Circulation
1	2	TV Guide	20,249,384	9,315,367
2	1	Reader's Digest	18,164,833	14,523,142
3	13	National Geographic	9,211,957	3,497,354
4	5	Family Circle	8,479,519	7,220,738
5	9	Woman's Day	8,164,817	6,444,437
6	10	Better Homes & Gardens	8,093,646	6,228,995
7	3	McCall's	6,511,891	8,220,798
8	7	Ladies' Home Journal	6,080,058	6,667,673
9	22	Playboy	5,405,443	1,772,777
10	11	Good Housekeeping	5,312,449	5,269,349
11	12	Redbook	4,574,495	3,699,457
12	16	Time	4,522,776	2,904,639
13	- -[a]	National Enquirer	4,502,730	- -[a]
14	- -	Penthouse	4,365,679	- -
15	23	Newsweek	3,012,945	1,600,948
16	17	American Legion	2,672,858	2,722,756
17	14	American Home	2,500,813	3,357,988
18	47	Sports Illustrated	2,310,879	1,036,154
19	54	Cosmopolitan	2,214,655	890,056
20	33	U. S. News & World Report	2,056,991	1,282,774
21	34	Field & Stream	2,000,073	1,273,986
22	19	Boys' Life	1,859,196	2,211,303
23	41	Glamour	1,855,835	1,137,878
24	32	Popular Science	1,822,736	1,286,772
25	36	The Workbasket	1,796,688	1,246,569
26	- -	Today's Education	1,791,878	- -
27	39	Outdoor Life	1,782,773	1,206,029
28	- -	People	1,776,953	- -
29	28	Popular Mechanics	1,671,216	1,334,420
30	20	True Story	1,632,502	2,098,270
31	44	V.F.W. Magazines	1,629,134	1,103,981
32	29	Elks Magazine	1,602,373	1,331,143
33	38	Mechanix Illustrated	1,586,331	1,212,173
34	15	Farm Journal	1,554,199	3,046,140
35	21	Parents' Magazine	1,506,103	1,917,969
36	43	Seventeen	1,450,105	1,110,712
37	- -	Hustler	1,448,815	- -
38	69	Sport	1,373,952	615,711
39	63	Sunset	1,366,043	733,304
40	- -	The Star	1,301,717	- -
41	58	Ebony	1,288,149	763,389
42	53	Grit	1,287,755	897,323
43	- -	Southern Living	1,279,645	- -
44	- -	Smithsonian	1,264,182	- -
45	- -	Oui	1,258,249	- -
46	31	Scouting	1,177,124	1,228,051
47	40	House & Garden	1,159,197	1,191,223
48	- -	Midnight	1,133,834	- -
49	37	Sports Afield	1,110,464	1,220,517
50	- -	Psychology Today	1,108,822	- -

Table 630–D. (Cont'd.)

1976 Rank	1963 Rank		1976 Circulation	1963 Circulation
51	55	Esquire	1,079,253	883,815
52	25	Junior Scholastic	1,065,154	1,402,401
53	59	Nation's Business	1,030,596	760,866
54	- -	Playgirl	1,006,755	- -
55	24	Photoplay	958,234	1,496,445
56	26	Progressive Farmer	936,162	1,401,749
57	76	'Teen	908,016	515,757
58	67	Co-ed	884,992	643,223
59	- -	Family Health	880,015	- -
60	71	Mademoiselle	873,686	596,331
61	68	Hot Rod	858,691	637,865
62	52	House Beautiful	840,629	911,998
63	- -	Golf Digest	834,208	- -
64	- -	Weight Watchers	792,648	- -
65	77	Vogue	770,954	498,272
66	87	Business Week	768,203	412,173
67	30	Successful Farming	764,322	1,329,684
68	- -	National Lampoon	763,935	- -
69	88	Popular Photography	750,085	406,469
70	64	TV Mirror	734,783	714,403
71	- -	Car & Driver	730,624	- -
72	75	Motor Trend	721,019	518,889
73	- -	Signature	718,410	- -
74	- -	Apartment Life	717,527	- -
75	- -	Gallery	713,857	- -
76	74	The Lion	697,753	542,651
77	- -	Decorating & Craft Ideas	672,353	- -
78	- -	Money	666,019	- -
79	98	Forbes	646,965	353,449
80	- -	Club	642,957	- -
81	99	Scientific American	642,282	352,792
82	93	Fortune	624,428	383,366
83	- -	Jet	623,933	- -
84	- -	Gourmet	616,347	- -
85	- -	Sphere	614,242	- -
86	- -	Golf	608,973	- -
87	57	American Girl	605,944	824,928
88	35	Argosy	603,618	1,254,657
89	18	True	585,890	2,414,266
90	61	Modern Screen	579,429	752,056
91	66	Modern Romances	569,935	700,561
92	- -	Carte Blanche	566,062	- -
93	- -	Penthouse Forum	556,885	- -
94	73	Flower & Garden	552,885	592,476
95	- -	The Lutheran	547,633	- -
96	82	Harper's Bazaar	540,339	463,058
97	- -	Modern Photography	537,912	- -
98	65	Catholic Digest	532,627	708,207
99	- -	Essence	500,035	- -
100	- -	Saturday Review	493,028	- -
		Total Circulation	**209,216,893**	- -[b]

Sources: 1963 data: Compaine (1974), pp. 57-58, citing Magazine Publishers Association data. 1976 data: Magazine Publishers Association.

Notes: Circulation data are estimates of annual circulation based on average circulation per issue for the first six months of each year. (a) Blanks indicate that these magazines were not in the top 100 ranking for that year. (b) Total cannot be calculated because of missing entries.

Table 631–A.
Distribution of Consumer Expenditures for Magazines in U.S., by Selected Family Characteristics, 1966

Family Characteristics	Percentage Distribution of All U. S. Families	Percentage Distribution of Expenditures on Magazines
Region		
Northeast	26.5%	30.5%
North Central	27.0	26.0
South	29.0	23.0
West	17.5	20.5
Race		
White	88.5	94.0
Nonwhite	11.5	6.0
Market Location		
Metropolitan Areas		
Central Cities	33.0	33.5
Urban Fringe	29.0	35.0
Other Areas	6.5	7.0
Outside Metropolitan Areas		
Urban	15.5	12.5
Rural	16.0	12.0
Education Level of Head of Household		
Grade School or less	29.5	13.5
Some High School	18.0	13.5
High School Graduate	29.0	30.0
Some College	10.0	15.5
College Graduate or higher	13.5	27.5
Family Income (before taxes)		
Under $3,000	16.0	3.5
$3,000 to $5,000	15.0	7.5
$5,000 to $7,500	21.0	15.5
$7,500 to $10,000	19.0	21.0
$10,000 and over	29.0	52.5
Occupation of Head of Household		
Professional/Technical	12.0	24.0
Managerial/Official	12.0	18.5
Clerical/Sales	11.5	12.5
Foreman/Craftsman	16.0	15.5
Operative	16.5	11.5
All other	32.0	18.0
Age of Head of Household		
Under 25	6.5	5.0
25 to 34	18.0	20.0
35 to 44	20.5	24.5
45 to 54	19.5	21.5
55 to 64	15.5	15.5
65 and over	20.0	13.5
Family Size		
One member	19.5	12.0
Two members	28.5	28.5
Three members	16.5	19.0
Four members	15.0	18.5
Five members or more	20.5	22.0

Source: National Industrial Conference Board (1967).

Table 631–B.
Estimated Percentages of Magazine Readership in U.S., by Type of Magazine and Selected Characteristics of the Readers, 1976

Note: All circulation figures are in thousands.

Magazines and National Newspapers	Total Circulation	Females			Males		
		Circulation as Percent of Female Population[a]	Number of Female Readers	Number of Female Readers per Copy	Circulation as Percent of Male Population[a]	Number of Male Readers	Number of Male Readers per Copy
	(48 states)						
American Baby	990	2.1%	1,604	1.62	.4%	257	.26
American Home	2,450	4.6	3,602	1.47	1.1	760	.31
Barron's	218	.3	262	1.20	1.0	726	3.33
Better Homes & Gardens	7,840	22.7	17,640	2.25	8.9	6,350	.81
Business Week	661	.9	721	1.09	4.1	2,895	4.38
Car & Driver	638	.7	510	.80	3.5	2,501	3.92
Cosmopolitan	1,547	7.2	5,616	3.63	2.3	1,655	1.07
Esquire	960	1.7	1,354	1.41	3.9	2,803	2.92
Family Circle	7,766	22.6	17,551	2.26	4.1	2,951	.38
Family Weekly	10,851	13.1	10,200	.94	11.7	8,355	.77
Field & Stream	1,940	3.5	2,697	1.39	9.9	7,062	3.64
Forbes	631	.6	448	.71	1.7	1,230	1.95
Fortune	531	.5	398	.75	1.7	1,211	2.28
Girl Talk	194	1.5	1,189	6.13	.2	124	.64
Glamour	1,745	8.3	6,457	3.70	1.0	681	.39
Golf	618	.6	482	.78	2.0	1,428	2.31
Golf Digest	808	.7	566	.70	2.1	1,527	1.89
Good Housekeeping	4,800	20.7	15,696	3.27	4.8	3,408	.71
Harper's/Atlantic/Natural History	973	1.8	1,382	1.42	2.3	1,625	1.67
House & Garden	930	6.6	5,115	5.50	2.4	1,739	1.87
House Beautiful	768	5.8	4,547	5.92	1.6	1,121	1.46
Ladies' Home Journal	5,820	17.1	13,328	2.29	3.3	2,328	.40
Mademoiselle	752	3.0	2,354	3.13	.3	211	.28
McCall's	6,305	21.2	16,519	2.62	4.6	3,279	.52
Mechanix Illustrated	1,380	1.2	938	.68	6.0	4,278	3.10
Money	637	.8	592	.93	1.6	1,121	1.76
Ms.	465	2.1	1,665	3.58	.6	391	.84
National Enquirer	4,136	8.8	6,866	1.66	7.2	5,129	1.24
National Geographic	7,920	13.5	10,534	1.33	18.1	12,910	1.63
National Observer	456	1.0	798	1.75	1.1	748	1.64

Table 631-B. (Cont'd.)

Magazines and National Newspapers	Total Circulation (48 states)	Females			Males		
		Circulation as Percent of Female Population[a]	Number of Female Readers	Number of Female Readers per Copy	Circulation as Percent of Male Population[a]	Number of Male Readers	Number of Male Readers per Copy
Newsweek	2,813	9.1	7,089	2.52	13.8	9,846	3.50
New York	371	1.0	805	2.17	1.0	738	1.99
New Yorker	419	1.6	1,240	2.96	2.3	1,605	3.83
New York Times	795	1.0	775	.95	2.0	1,391	1.75
New York Times Magazine	1,446	2.9	2,227	1.54	3.0	2,111	1.46
Oui	1,134	1.0	760	.67	5.2	3,708	3.24
Outdoor Life	1,669	2.3	1,803	1.08	7.2	5,107	3.06
Parade	19,537	23.8	18,560	.95	25.2	17,974	.92
Parents	1,440	4.5	3,528	2.45	1.0	734	.51
Penthouse	3,780	2.4	1,852	.49	11.6	8,240	2.18
People	1,656	8.6	6,723	4.06	6.7	4,786	2.89
Playboy	4,590	4.5	3,488	.76	16.6	11,842	2.58
Popular Mechanics	1,520	1.6	1,231	.81	7.1	5,077	3.34
Popular Science	1,652	1.2	942	.57	5.7	4,031	2.44
Psychology Today	1,070	3.0	2,397	2.24	2.7	1,937	1.81
Reader's Digest	17,218	27.9	21,695	1.26	24.9	17,735	1.03
Redbook	4,511	13.9	10,781	2.39	2.9	2,075	.46
Road and Track	435	.5	365	.84	4.8	3,397	7.81
Saturday Review	480	.6	494	1.03	1.1	768	1.60
Scientific American	510	.7	566	1.11	1.9	1,331	2.61
Sport	1,325	1.1	822	.62	5.1	3,604	2.72
Sports Afield	1,088	1.4	1,121	1.03	5.7	4,080	3.75
Sports Illustrated	2,160	3.6	2,786	1.29	12.3	8,791	4.07
Sunday	21,470	30.1	24,046	1.12	32.0	22,758	1.06
Time	4,208	11.0	8,500	2.02	14.9	10,604	2.52
TV Guide	17,100	27.5	21,375	1.25	24.5	17,442	1.02
U. S. News & World Report	1,960	3.9	3,018	1.54	7.0	4,978	2.54
Viva	370	1.2	918	2.48	1.3	958	2.59
Vogue	623	4.4	3,445	5.53	.5	336	.54
Wall St. Journal	1,451	1.9	1,509	1.04	4.7	3,337	2.30
Woman's Day	7,440	21.2	16,517	2.22	2.2	1,562	.21
Ziff Davis	3,074	4.6	3,627	1.18	15.8	11,220	3.65

Source: Batten, Barton, Durstine and Osborn Media Department (1977), pp. 30-31.
Note: (a) Based on W. R. Simmons estimated population for 48 states: 77,825,000 females and 71,232,000 males.

Interpretation of Tables

Table 631-A compares U.S. consumer expenditures for magazines according to selected characteristics of American households. An analysis of the table reveals that the population groups showing the highest percentage of expenditures for magazines—in proportion to the presence of these groups in the general population—are residents of the Northeast and West; suburbanites; people with more education and money; people in higher-status jobs; white people; and households with more than three members and a family head aged 25 to 54 years. The general association of magazine readership with the more affluent segments of the population is stronger than that for newspaper readership (see Section 621).

Table 631-B provides a list of the leading magazines and national-circulation daily newspapers and then breaks this list down according to the percentage of the population of both sexes which read the various magazines. Major differences in magazine preferences are evident between males and females. Men tend to read more magazines on business and finance, mechanics and science, sports and outdoor life, and "special-appeal" (*Esquire, Harpers, National Geographic, New Yorker, Scientific American,* etc.) and "men's" subjects (*Oui, Playboy, Road and Track,* and the Ziff-Davis network of *Boating, Cycle, Popular Photography, Stereo Review,* etc.). Women are the more frequent readers of "women's" magazines (*American Baby, Cosmopolitan, Ms., Redbook, Viva,* etc.); of fashion, beauty, and grooming magazines; of home service and home magazines; and of general-appeal magazines and national general-interest newspapers. Men and women devote about equal attention to newspaper-distributed magazines, such as *Sunday,* the *New York Times Magazine,* and *Parade.*

Note that a high number of readers per copy may cause the audience of a magazine to exceed its circulation, so that it ranks higher in overall audience than a magazine of larger circulation. Such a relationship between circulation and audience is evident in a comparison of *Road and Track* and *Car and Driver.* The former has only 68 percent of *Car and Driver's* 48-state circulation, but its audience is 36 percent larger.

Sources

The information in **Table 631-A** was originally collected in 1960-1961 by the U.S. Bureau of Labor Statistics as benchmark research for updating the Consumer Price Index. Analysts working for the National Industrial Conference Board then weighted the data to make them applicable to the U.S. population in 1966. A detailed description of this procedure can be found in the discussion of sources for **Table 610-B.**

Because of the updating procedures, this information can only be considered a reasonable estimate of magazine readership. But although the data are without a solid empirical basis, the overall patterns revealed in the table seem valid.

Table 631-B is a reworking of W. R. Simmons and Associates figures by the Media Department of Batten, Barton, Durstine, and Osborn (1977), an advertising agency. The circulation figures in the table come from the latest rate cards available from each publication at the time the table was originally printed, probably around mid-1977. These figures have been adjusted to correspond to the 48-state area covered by the Simmons survey. Since rate cards usually quote certified circulation figures, such as those audited by the Audit Bureau of Circulations, and since the rest of the information on the table is based on the Simmons work, the authors regard these data as valid and reliable. The two-*sigma* (approximately 95 percent) confidence intervals for each magazine's audience estimates are available from W. R. Simmons in its *Technical Guide* to the 1976-1977 study.

Further Information

A number of market research companies provide information about the magazine audience. A listing of these companies is available from the Magazine Publishers Association in its *Sources of Information about Magazines.* Media Decisions, Inc., *Encyclomedia,* includes extensive information on magazine circulation and readership.

Those periodicals which do not fall into the most widely circulated categories are not included in the information presented here. Little information is available on these house organs, small-circulation magazines, and scholarly publications, although two studies of scholarly publications are worth consulting: King et al. (1976) and Fry and White (1976). A bibliography for the study of magazines has been prepared by Schacht (1972).

Table 640–A.
Average Weekly Motion Picture Attendance in U.S., 1922–1965

Note: Weekly attendance figures are in thousands. Index figures are
calculated on a base of 100 for the years 1946-1948.

Year	Average Weekly Attendance	Attendance Index	5-Year Average Attendance per Household
1922	40,000	44	
1923	43,000	48	1.59
1924	46,000	51	
1925	46,000	51	
1926	50,000	56	
1927	57,000	63	2.08
1928	65,000	72	
1929	80,000	89	
1930	90,000	100	
1931	75,000	83	
1932	60,000	67	2.32
1933	60,000	67	
1934	70,000	78	
1935	80,000	89	
1936	88,000	98	
1937	88,000	98	2.57
1938	85,000	94	
1939	85,000	94	
1940	80,000	89	
1941	85,000	94	
1942	85,000	94	2.31
1943	85,000	94	
1944	85,000	94	
1945	85,000	94	
1946	90,000	100	
1947	90,000	100	2.15
1948	90,000	100	
1949	70,000	78	
1950	60,000	67	
1951	54,000	60	
1952	51,000	57	1.15
1953	46,000	51	
1954	49,000	54	
1955	46,000	51	
1956	47,000	52	
1957	45,000	50	.89
1958	40,000	44	
1959	42,000	47	
1960	40,000	44	
1961	42,000	47	
1962	43,000	47	.78
1963	42,000	47	
1964	44,000	49	
1965	44,000	49	

Source: *Historical Statistics* (1975), Series H-873, p. 400.

Table 640–B.
Distribution of Motion Picture Admissions in U.S., by Age Group, 1969–1976

Age Group	Percentage of Total Yearly Admissions						Percent of 1975 Resident U. S. Population
	1969	1970	1972	1973	1975	1976	
2 to 15 years	18%	16%	13%	14%	14%	14%	10%
16 to 20 years	31	27	30	29	32	31	12
21 to 29 years	28	29	30	30	28	31	19
Total, 12 to 29 years	77%	72%	73%	73%	74%	76%	41%
30 to 39 years	10%	12%	11%	13%	12%	13%	15%
40 to 49 years	6	8	10	8	8	5	13
50 to 59 years	3	6	4	4	3	3	13
60 years and older	4	2	2	2	3	3	18
Total, 30 years and older	23%	28%	27%	27%	26%	24%	59%

Sources: 1969-1970 data: *International Motion Picture Almanac* (1975), p. 19. 1972 data: Jowett (1976), p. 485. 1973-1975 data: National Association of Theater Owners (1976), p. 32. 1976 and basic population data: Motion Picture Association of American Research Department (October 1976).

Table 640–C.
Composition of the Motion Picture Audience in U.S., by Sex, Marital Status, Educational Level, and Number of Companions Attending Films, 1957

Characteristics of Audience	Percent of Week's Total Admissions	Four-Wall Theaters Only	Drive-In Theaters Only	Percent of U. S. Population
Sex				
Male	51%	N/A	N/A	49%
Female	49	N/A	N/A	51
Marital Status				
Single	51	N/A	N/A	27
Married, No Children under 15 years	17	N/A	N/A	34
Married, With Children under 15 years	32	N/A	N/A	39
Education Level				
8th Grade or less	18	N/A	N/A	29
Some High School	23	N/A	N/A	22
High School Graduate	37	N/A	N/A	28
Some College	21	N/A	N/A	19
Number of Companions in Attendance				
Total Group Attendance	87	81%	98%	- -
1 Companion	42	47	34	- -
2 Companions	14	15	12	- -
3 Companions	17	10	29	- -
4 or more Companions	10	7	16	- -
"Don't know"	4	2	7	- -
No Companions	13	19	2	- -

Source: Jowett (1976), pp. 477-478, citing data from Opinion Research Corporation, "The Public Appraises Movies"—done for the Motion Picture Association of America.

Table 640–D.
Results of Surveys Measuring Frequency
of Motion Picture Attendance in U.S., 1936–1957

Frequency of Attendance	1936	1946	1955	1957[a]
"More than once a week"	13%	37%	34%	15%
"Once a week"	25	- -	38	- -
"More than once a month"	12	27	14	26
"Once a month"	13	- -	8	- -
"Less than once a month"	21	25	6	31
"Never" (less than once a year)	16	11	- -	22

Sources: 1936 data: Jowett (1976), p. 285, based on a survey by *Fortune*. 1946 data: Handel (1950), p. 95, taken from Lazarsfeld (1947), pp. 161-168. 1955 data: Jowett (1976), p. 387, citing Smythe et al. in *Quarterly of Film, Radio and Television* (1955), p. 394. 1957 data: Jowett (1976), p. 478, citing Opinion Research Corporation, "The Public Appraises Movies," p. 9.

Note: (a) Excludes a 6 percent "no response" category.

Interpretation of Tables

While many studies have been done on the motion picture audience, very little of such information has been released to the public. Hollywood appears to distrust statistics—and to show an interest in them only when times are bad. The tables in this unit, some of them quite dated, are drawn from the information that is publicly available.

Table 640-A indicates that motion picture attendance, once a major pastime of millions, declined drastically from 1948 to 1965. This decline from the 1946-1948 peak level of 90 million weekly moviegoers is also illustrated by index figures based on the 1946-1948 attendance figures. The other column in the table provides the average number of motion picture attendances per U.S. household per week for each five-year period (data are available for only three years in the 1920s). Clearly, movie attendance has dropped sharply—both absolutely and relative to the population.

Table 640-B compares motion picture attendance by age group, showing that film audiences are far younger than the general population. Note that in 1976, persons in the 12-29 age group accounted for 76 percent of the admissions, although they made up only 41 percent of the population. This table refers to total *yearly* admissions.

Table 640-C examines 1957 film attendance according to audience characteristics, such as education, marital status, and number of companions in attendance. The figures clearly demonstrate that movie-going is primarily a group activity (two or more people) in both theaters and drive-ins.

Table 640-D, which focuses on the frequency of motion picture attendance, shows declining levels of attendance over the 20-year period from 1936 to 1957. The data for 1955 were based on a small sample of college-town moviegoers, which explains the higher level of interest in films.

Table 640-E provides fairly recent survey information on certain characteristics of filmgoers. Notice the sizeable percentages of people who claim they never attend films. Apparently, there is no information available on audiences under 12.

Sources

The attendance figures in Table 640-A are from *Historical Statistics* (1975). Using that information, the editors calculated the "attendance index." For more information on the average weekly attendance of films per U.S. household, the reader is referred to the base average household data in Unit 100.

The information in Table 640-B is taken from the *International Motion Picture Almanac* (1975), for the 1969-1970 data; from Jowett (1976), for the 1972 figures; and from the National Association of Theater Owners (NATO) (1976), for the 1973-1975 figures. The 1976 data and

Table 640-E.
Results of Surveys Measuring Frequency of Motion Picture Attendance in U.S., by Age, Marital Status, and Other Audience Characteristics, 1972–1975

Audience Characteristics	"At least one film per month"		"At least one film in 2 to 6 months"		"Less than one film in 6 months"		"Never attend films"	
	1972-73[a]	1975	1972-73[a]	1975	1972-73[a]	1975	1972	1975
Percent of Total Admissions	--	86%	--	12%	--	2%	--	--
Age								
12 to 17 years	39%	43	32%	34	13%	12	16%	11%
18 years and older	19	22	23	24	15	14	41	40
Marital Status[b]								
Single	26	32	22	19	10	9	--	--
Married	17	19	24	25	17	16	--	--
Married with Children under 13 years	--	26	--	33	--	17	--	--
Education Level								
Some College	35	36	29	30	16	13	20	--
High School Graduate	24	24	25	29	18	16	33	--
Some High School	10	11	11	13	13	12	66	--
Income Level								
$15,000 or more	31	30	32	--	16	--	21	--
$7,000 to $14,999	27	--	23	--	18	--	32	--
Under $7,000	15	16	15	--	10	--	60	--
Sex								
Female	22	23	22	--	16	--	40	--
Male	25	28	22	--	13	--	40	--

Sources: 1972 data in 1972-1973 columns and in the "never attend films" category: Jowett (1976), p. 485, citing Opinion Research Corporation data collected for the Motion Picture Association of America. 1973 data in 1972-1973 columns and 1975 data: National Association of Theater Owners (1976), pp. 32–33.

Notes: (a) These columns mix figures from two separate surveys—one in 1972, the other in 1973. (b) Includes only those respondents 18 years and older.

1975 basic population information came from the Research Department of the Motion Picture Association of America (MPAA) in a mimeo release (October 1976).

Table 640-C is based on data from the Opinion Research Corporation in its "The Public Appraises Movies"—a study sponsored by the Motion Picture Association of America. This information is cited in Jowett (1976).

Table 640-D combines information from four different surveys with different research approaches. The figures are therefore only roughly comparable. The data for 1936 are from Jowett

(1976), based on a *Fortune* magazine survey; the 1946 information is in Handel (1950), which reports Columbia University research done by Paul Lazarsfeld (1947); and the 1955 and 1957 data also are found in Jowett (1976). (The 1955 figures were taken by Jowett from a study by Dallas Smythe of Urbana, Illinois, and the 1957 data were based on an Opinion Research Corporation study.)

The figures in **Table 640**-E are the results of a survey for the MPAA by the Opinion Research Corporation. The data are reported in Jowett (1975), but no information is available on the approach of this research.

Further Information

The best description of film research at Hollywood's height is given in Handel (1950). Jowett (1975) and Jarvie (1970) include many examples of later research and cite others. Results of surveys of the motion picture audience are often published in *Variety*.

Disc/Tape Player Production and Disc/Tape Buyers 650

Table 650–A.
Number and Total Retail Value of Phonographs Manufactured in U.S., 1899–1972

Note: All unit and dollar figures are in thousands.

	Number of Units	Total Retail Value, Current Dollars	Total Retail Value, Constant (1972) Dollars
1899	151.4	$ 1,240.5	$ 6,202.5[a]
1904	N/A	2,966.3	13,796.7
1909	344.7	5,406.7	25,147.4
1914	514.2	15,290.5	63,710.4
1919	2,226.4	91,568.9	221,716.5
1921	596.0	38,604.7	90,197.9
1923	997.5	57,037.1	139,796.8
1925	642.0	22,613.9	53,971.1
1927	987.5	39,814.5	95,938.6
1931	48.4	2,499.8	6,867.6
1933	N/A	1,905.3	6,146.1
1935	N/A	2,106.6	6,422.6
1937	N/A	7,086.4	20,660.1
1939	N/A	22,506.0	67,789.2
1948	1,931.0	31,613.0	54,979.1
1954	3,264.0	70,544.0	109,881.6
1958	4,313.0	167,182.0	241,942.1
1963	3,700.0	320,100.0	437,295.1
1967	4,400.0	396,100.0	496,365.9
1972	3,900.0	373,400.0	373,400.0

Source: *Census of Manufactures.*

Notes: Unit and value figures prior to 1928 include office dictating machines, but these represent a small proportion of overall production in the industry. (a) Constant dollar figure is based on the Consumer Price Index for 1900.

Table 650–B.
Number and Total Retail Value of Phonographs Manufactured in U.S.,
and Number of Phonographs in Use in U.S., 1946–1976

Note: All unit and dollar figures are in thousands.

	Total Number of Units Manufactured	Current Dollar Value of Units	Constant (1972) Dollar Value of Units	Number of Phonographs in Use
1946	3,900	$216,000	$462,526	N/A
1947	4,200	300,000	561,798	N/A
1948	3,100	207,000	360,000	N/A
1949	2,000	115,000	201,754	N/A
1950	1,300	122,000	212,174	16,800
1951	1,500	65,000	104,670	18,000
1952	1,400	51,000	80,442	19,500
1953	1,600	58,000	90,767	20,800
1954	2,700	82,000	127,726	22,400
1955	2,600	99,000	154,688	24,000
1956	3,800	140,000	215,385	25,600
1957	4,700	240,000	356,612	27,100
1958	4,000	259,000	374,819	29,900
1959	4,300	339,000	486,370	32,000
1960	4,500	359,000	507,062	34,000
1961	4,000	304,000	425,175	35,700
1962	5,000	389,000	538,035	37,000
1963	5,100	421,000	575,137	39,000
1964	5,200	440,000	593,792	42,000
1965	6,100	505,000	678,763	45,000
1966	6,300	528,000	680,412	48,000
1967	6,600	480,000	601,504	51,000
1968	6,500	503,000	604,567	53,800
1969	6,300	490,000	559,350	58,700
1970	5,600	376,000	405,172	58,700
1971	6,000	425,000	632,231	61,200
1972	7,200	577,000	577,000	64,800
1973	6,100	502,000	472,693	68,600
1974	4,800	398,000	337,574	71,600
1975	3,200	265,000	205,905	73,100
1976	3,900	317,000	232,917	N/A

Sources: Electronic Industries Association, *Electronics Data Book* 1976) and *Consumer Electronics* (annual).

Interpretation of Tables

Tables 650-A and 650-B provide conflicting figures for the number of phonographs produced in the United States. Table 650-A provides data for a longer period of time, although the figures through 1927 include office dictating machines, which made up a small proportion of overall production. The peak in phonograph production in 1919 occurred just after World War I and just before radio broadcasting. The decline two years later was undoubtedly due mainly to radio's competition.

Tables 650-A and 650-B both trace the rapid production growth in this industry since World War II, but the actual figures in the tables vary substantially—casting doubt on the validity of both. The boom in phonograph production in the late 1950s is the result of the new disc-recording formats and the development of high-fidelity and stereo sound. The declines in the 1970s reflect the strong competition of Japanese imports.

Table 650-C provides the limited data available on the sales of home audio and videotape equipment. All of these machines were of the reel-to-reel variety until the early 1960s, when first

Table 650–C.
Number of Consumer Audio and Video Tape Recorders/Players Sold in U.S., 1954–1976

Note: All figures are in thousands.

	Number of Audio Tape Units	Number of Automobile Tape Player Units	Number of Videotape Units	Total Number of Tape Units Sold
1954	100	- -	- -	100
1955	360	- -	- -	360
1956	400	- -	- -	400
1957	500	- -	- -	500
1958	400	- -	- -	400
1959	400	- -	- -	400
1960	425	- -	- -	425
1961	1,166	- -	- -	1,166
1962	1,675	- -	- -	1,675
1963	2,841	- -	- -	2,841
1964	3,561	- -	- -	3,561
1965	3,445	N/A	N/A	3,445
1966	3,675	N/A	N/A	3,675
1967	4,581	N/A	N/A	4,581
1968[a]	6,168	1,224	9	7,401
1969	8,759	2,527	13	11,299
1970	11,733	2,779	24	14,536
1971	13,548	2,739	29	16,316
1972	18,136	3,641	42	21,819
1973	17,651	4,687	272	22,610
1974	13,575	4,983	138	18,696
1975	10,753	4,903	162	15,818
1976	16,807	9,136	291	26,234

Sources: Audio tape figures to 1960: estimates from *Electrical Merchandising Week* (now *Merchandising*), as reprinted in *Billboard Directory* (1963), © Billboard. All other data: *Electronics Data Book* (1976) and *Consumer Electronics* (annual).

Note: (a) All figures from 1968 on are for imports only.

the cartridge and then the cassette format appeared. The eight-track cartridge is currently the most popular tape system (see Unit 350).

Table 650-D is a 1976 measure of the characteristics and the purchases of the U.S. adult record-buying public (defined as persons buying at least one record or tape in the past year). The table indicates a strong consumer preference for popular and country music and shows that, like filmgoers, the recordings "audience" is a youthful one.

Sources

Table 650-A is taken from the *Census of Manufactures* for the years indicated. Table 650-B comes from the annual publication of the Electronic Industries Association (EIA), the *Electronic Market Data Book* (1976), and from a brief layman's summary of these data in *Consumer Electronics*. As noted earlier, the figures in both tables are, at best, "guesstimates"—although the Census Bureau data cover more of the industry and in a more reliable fashion.

Table 650-C is also entirely estimated and is at best an approximation of the actual production of tape equipment. Production figures on home audio-tape equipment to 1960 are reprinted from *Billboard Directory* (1963), which took the data from *Electrical Merchandising Week* (now *Merchandising*). No information is given in either source as to how these figures were derived. All other data in Table 650-C are from the EIA sources noted above. Information after 1968 refers *only* to imports, somewhat of a tacit admission of the impact of imports in this industry.

Table 650–D.

Results of a Survey Measuring the Type of Recordings Purchased by, and the Music Preferences of, U.S. Adults–by Sex, Age, and Marital Status of Respondents, 1976

| | All Respondents | "Purchased at least one recording in past year" Respondents Who Had Purchased a Recording | | | | | |
		Males	Females	25 to 34 Years	35 to 45 Years	Single	Married
Type of Recording Purchased							
LP	9%	11%	7%	19%	15%	14%	7%
Single	4	5	4	10	7	3	5
Tape	6	7	5	12	12	3	6
Type of Music Preferred							
Pop: Contemporary/Rock	33	44	25	44	17	43	32
Pop: Middle of the Road	16	9	21	5	29	6	18
Country	23	18	26	22	28	9	26
Classical	10	12	11	10	12	14	8
Jazz	5	9	2	5	6	17	3
Golden Oldies	2	3	1	1	1	- -	3
Soul	4	4	3	6	1	6	3
Gospel	3	1	6	3	5	3	4
Folk	1	1	1	2	- -	3	1
Other	3	- -	4	3	5	- -	4

Source: National Association of Record Merchandisers (NARM), citing a Home Testing Institute survey done for NARM.

Table 650-D is from unpublished research issued by the National Association of Record Merchandisers (NARM) and based on a national telephone survey by the Home Testing Institute under NARM researcher Jerry Cohen. Because further information was unavailable, it is hard to assess the value of this research. In addition, nonbuyer information is excluded from this buyer data, and sample sizes are not shown, making it difficult to combine or compare the two.

Further Information

The standard history of the phonograph is Read and Welch (1976), which details development of the cylinder and disc formats, as well as the later improvements, such as the new recording speeds and stereo options. The only regular reporting of the phonograph and tape market are the EIA's *Consumer Electronics* and the data appearing in *Merchandising*. For information on the record audience, see Denisoff (1975).

Table 660–A.
Number of Radio and Television Receivers Sold in U.S., 1922–1976

Note: All figures are in thousands.

Year	Radio Receivers Home	Radio Receivers Auto	Radio Receivers Total	Television Receivers B & W	Television Receivers Color	Television Receivers Total	Grand Total
1922	100	- -	100	- -	- -	- -	100
1923	550	- -	550	- -	- -	- -	550
1924	1,500	- -	1,500	- -	- -	- -	1,500
1925	2,000	- -	2,000	- -	- -	- -	2,000
1926	1,750	- -	1,750	- -	- -	- -	1,750
1927	1,350	- -	1,350	- -	- -	- -	1,350
1928	3,281	- -	3,281	- -	- -	- -	3,281
1929	4,428	- -	4,428	- -	- -	- -	4,428
1930	3,793	34	3,827	- -	- -	- -	3,827
1931	3,412	108	3,420	- -	- -	- -	3,420
1932	2,857	143	3,000	- -	- -	- -	3,000
1933	3,082	724	3,806	- -	- -	- -	3,806
1934	3,304	780	4,084	- -	- -	- -	4,084
1935	4,901	1,125	6,026	- -	- -	- -	6,026
1936	6,836	1,412	8,248	- -	- -	- -	8,248
1937	6,315	1,150	8,065	- -	- -	- -	8,065
1938	5,200	800	6,000	- -	- -	- -	6,000
1939	9,300	1,200	10,500	- -	- -	- -	10,500
1940	10,100	1,700	11,800	- -	- -	- -	11,800
1941	11,000	2,000	13,000	- -	- -	- -	13,000
1942	4,050	350	4,400	- -	- -	- -	4,400
1945	500	- -	500	- -	- -	- -	500
1946	12,800	1,200	14,000	6	- -	6	14,006
1947	13,800	3,200	17,000	179	- -	179	17,179
1948	9,900	4,100	14,000	970	- -	970	14,970
1949	6,500	3,500	10,000	2,970	- -	2,970	12,970
1950	9,218	4,740	13,958	7,355	- -	7,355	21,313
1951	6,445	4,544	10,989	5,312	- -	5,312	16,301
1952	7,232	3,243	10,475	6,194	- -	6,194	16,669
1953	7,283	5,183	12,466	6,870	- -	6,870	19,336
1954	6,119	4,124	10,243	7,405	5	7,410	17,653
1955	7,327	6,863	14,190	7,738	20	7,758	21,948
1956	8,951	5,057	14,008	7,351	100	7,451	21,459
1957	9,952	5,496	15,448	6,388	85	6,473	21,921
1958	10,797	3,715	14,512	5,051	80	5,131	19,643
1959	15,772	5,501	21,273	6,278	90	6,368	27,641
1960	18,031	6,432	24,463	5,709	120	5,829	30,292
1961	23,654	5,568	29,222	6,168	147	6,315	35,537
1962	24,781	7,249	32,030	6,696	438	7,134	39,164
1963	23,602	7,946	31,548	7,236	747	7,983	39,531
1964	23,558	8,313	31,871	8,360	1,404	9,764	41,635
1965	31,689	10,037	41,726	8,753	2,694	11,447	53,173
1966	34,779	9,394	44,173	7,702	5,012	12,714	56,887
1967	31,684	9,527	41,211	6,001	5,563	11,564	52,775
1968	34,322	12,510	46,832	6,996	6,215	13,211	60,043
1969	39,414	11,939	51,353	7,117	6,191	13,308	64,661
1970	34,049	10,378	44,427	6,900	5,320	12,220	56,647
1971	34,105	13,505	47,610	7,647	7,274	14,921	62,531
1972	42,149	13,162	55,311	8,239	8,845	17,084	72,395
1973	37,652	12,546	50,198	7,296	10,071	17,367	67,565
1974	33,231	10,762	43,993	6,868	8,411	15,279	59,272
1975	25,276	9,239	34,515	4,418	6,219	10,637	45,152
1976	31,656	12,445	44,101	5,937	8,194	14,131	58,232

Sources: *Broadcasting Yearbook 1977*, pp. B-175 (television) and C-310-11 (radio). 1922-1949 data for radio receivers originally supplied by Marketing World, Ltd. All other information provided to *Broadcasting Yearbook* by Electronic Industries Association.

Table 660-B.
Total Retail Value of Radio and Television Receivers Sold in U.S., 1922–1976

Note: All figures are in thousands of dollars.

	Radio Receivers			Television Receivers			Grand Total
	Home	Auto	Total	B&W	Color	Total	
1922	$ 5,000	- -	$ 5,000	- -	- -	- -	$ 5,000
1923	30,000	- -	30,000	- -	- -	- -	30,000
1924	100,000	- -	100,000	- -	- -	- -	100,000
1925	165,000	- -	165,000	- -	- -	- -	165,000
1926	200,000	- -	200,000	- -	- -	- -	200,000
1927	168,000	- -	168,000	- -	- -	- -	168,000
1928	400,000	- -	400,000	- -	- -	- -	400,000
1929	600,000	- -	600,000	- -	- -	- -	600,000
1930	297,000	$ 3,000	300,000	- -	- -	- -	300,000
1931	219,060	5,940	225,000	- -	- -	- -	225,000
1932	132,850	7,150	140,000	- -	- -	- -	140,000
1933	151,902	28,598	180,500	- -	- -	- -	180,500
1934	186,500	28,000	214,500	- -	- -	- -	214,500
1935	275,630	54,563	330,193	- -	- -	- -	330,193
1936	380,812	69,188	450,000	- -	- -	- -	450,000
1937	362,500	87,500	450,000	- -	- -	- -	450,000
1938	178,000	32,000	210,000	- -	- -	- -	210,000
1939	306,000	48,000	354,000	- -	- -	- -	354,000
1940	390,000	60,000	450,000	- -	- -	- -	450,000
1941	390,000	70,000	460,000	- -	- -	- -	460,000
1942	141,750	12,250	154,000	- -	- -	- -	154,000
1945	N/A	N/A	20,000	- -	- -	- -	20,000
1946	628,000	72,000	700,000	$ 1,000	- -	$ 1,000	701,000
1947	606,000	194,000	800,000	50,000	- -	50,000	850,000
1948	307,000	293,000	600,000	226,000	- -	226,000	826,000
1949	260,000	240,000	500,000	574,000	- -	574,000	1,074,000
1950	N/A	N/A	N/A	1,397,000	- -	1,397,000	N/A
1951	N/A	N/A	N/A	944,000	- -	944,000	N/A
1952	N/A	N/A	N/A	1,064,000	- -	1,064,000	N/A
1953	N/A	N/A	N/A	1,170,000	- -	1,170,000	N/A
1954	N/A	N/A	N/A	1,040,000	$ 2,000	1,042,000	N/A
1955	N/A	N/A	N/A	1,068,000	10,000	1,078,000	N/A
1956	N/A	N/A	N/A	934,000	46,000	980,000	N/A
1957	N/A	N/A	N/A	831,000	37,000	868,000	N/A
1958	159,000[a]	96,000	255,000	686,000	34,000	720,000	975,000
1959	192,000[a]	130,000	322,000	806,000	37,000	843,000	1,165,000
1960	190,000[a]	154,000	344,000	750,091	47,000	797,091	1,141,091
1961	190,000[a]	134,000	324,000	757,500	56,000	813,500	1,137,500
1962	207,000[a]	181,000	388,000	851,000	154,000	1,005,000	1,393,000
1963	179,000[a]	206,000	385,000	841,000	258,000	1,099,000	1,484,000
1964	267,000	205,000	472,000	896,000	488,000	1,384,000	1,856,000
1965	328,000	248,000	576,000	910,000	959,000	1,869,000	2,445,000
1966	346,000	267,000	613,000	756,000	1,861,000	2,617,000	3,230,000
1967	333,000	259,000	592,000	555,000	2,015,000	2,570,000	3,162,000
1968	371,000	330,000	701,000	591,000	2,086,000	2,677,000	3,378,000
1969	422,000	316,000	738,000	554,000	2,031,000	2,585,000	3,323,000

Interpretation of Tables

Tables 660-A and 660-B indicate that the changing patterns of the broadcast-receiver manufacturing industry generally conform to U.S. economic trends. The initial spurt of radio sales in the 1920s was followed by a decline in the Depression, a prewar rise of radios in cars, and a postwar explosion in the demand for both home and car radios. Comparison of the unit sales data

Table 660–B. (Cont'd.)

	Radio Receivers			Television Receivers			Grand Total
	Home	Auto	Total	B&W	Color	Total	
1970	$380,000	$271,000	$651,000	$518,000	$1,684,000	$2,202,000	$2,853,000
1971	487,000	315,000	802,000	621,000	2,355,000	2,976,000	3,778,000
1972	606,000	377,000	983,000	649,000	2,825,000	3,474,000	4,457,000
1973	572,000	391,000	963,000	560,000	3,097,000	3,657,000	4,620,000
1974	559,000	370,000	929,000	543,000	2,658,000	3,201,000	4,130,000
1975	369,000	355,000	724,000	371,000	2,121,000	2,492,000	3,216,000
1976	398,000	497,000	895,000	528,000	2,860,000	3,388,000	4,283,000

Sources: *Broadcasting Yearbook 1977*, pp. B-175 (television) and C-310-311 (radio). 1922-1949 data for radio receivers originally supplied by Marketing World, Ltd. All other information provided to *Broadcasting Yearbook* by Electronic Industries Association.

Note: (a) Imports are not included for these years.

Table 660–C.
Number of Radio-Television Stores and Repair Services in U.S., 1929–1972

	Radio-TV Stores	Repair Services	Total Number of Establishments
1929	16,037	N/A	N/A
1939	2,911	N/A	N/A
1948	7,231	12,558	19,789
1954	6,790	22,824	29,614
1958	16,761	37,884	54,645
1963	10,365	43,208	53,573
1967	9,701[a]	33,063[a]	42,764[a]
1972	12,711[a]	34,810[a]	47,521[a]

Sources: Radio-TV stores data: *Census of Business*. Repair services data: *Census of Selected Service Industries*.

Note: (a) Includes establishments with payrolls only.

(Table 660-A) with the retail price information (Table 660-B) shows that while radio unit sales continue to increase, the cost per receiver has declined significantly—in spite of inflation. A similar trend is evident with television (see average set prices cited in Units 670 and 680).

According to the July 28, 1975, *Electrical Merchandising Week* (now called *Merchandising*), most radios are purchased at discount stores (35 percent), with 25 percent from catalog and mail order, 15 percent from appliance and radio-TV stores, 10 percent from department stores, 3 percent from furniture outlets, and 12 percent from "other" places. The television pattern is quite different. Most television sets come from appliance and radio-TV stores (30 percent), 19 percent from department stores, 27 percent from discount outlets, only 4 percent from mail-order outlets, 15 percent from furniture stores, and 5 percent from "other" outlets.

Table 660-C provides a count of radio-TV stores and repair services. The larger number of repair services is mainly due to their smaller size. The abrupt decline in radio stores from 1929 to 1939 seems extreme and probably results from a change in the classification or data-collection procedures.

Table 660–D.
Total Number of Radio and Television Receivers in Use in U.S., 1922–1976

Note: All figures are in thousands.

Year[a]	Radio Receivers	Television Sets	Total Receivers
1922	400	--	400
1923	1,100	--	1,100
1924	3,000	--	3,000
1925	4,000	--	4,000
1926	5,700	--	5,700
1927	7,000	--	7,000
1928	8,500	--	8,500
1929	10,500	--	10,500
1930	13,000	--	13,000
1931	15,000	--	15,000
1932	18,000	--	18,000
1933	22,000	--	22,000
1934	26,000	--	26,000
1935	30,500	--	30,500
1936	33,000	--	33,000
1937	37,600	--	37,600
1938	40,800	--	40,800
1939	45,300	--	45,300
1940	51,000	--	51,000
1941	56,600	--	56,600
1942	59,300	--	59,300
1943	57,850	--	57,850
1944	55,000	--	55,000
1945	56,000	--	56,000
1946	60,000	10	60,010
1947	66,000	16	66,016
1948	74,000	190	74,190
1949	81,000	1,000	82,000
1950	85,200	4,000	89,200
1951	96,000	10,600	106,600
1952	105,300	15,800	121,100
1953	110,500	21,200	131,700
1954	117,500	27,300	144,800
1955	121,000	32,500	153,500
1956	123,900	37,600	161,500
1957	135,000	42,700	177,700
1958	139,500	47,000	186,500
1959	146,200	50,000	196,200
1960	156,400	53,300	209,700
1961	168,300	55,600	223,900
1962	183,800	58,175	241,975
1963	200,300	61,200	261,500
1964	214,100	64,175	278,275
1965	228,300	67,210	295,510
1966	242,000	70,560	312,560
1967	262,700	74,800	337,500
1968	281,800	79,000	360,800
1969	303,400	83,600	387,000

Table 660-D combines the information in the preceding tables to arrive at the cumulative number of radio and television receivers in use in the United States. The figures take into account the new sets purchased and the older sets scrapped. The declining labor costs shown in **Table 660-E** are the result of heavy imports of radio and television receivers after 1958 (see Units 770 and 780).

Table 660–D. (Cont'd.)

Year[a]	Radio Receivers	Television Sets	Total Receivers
1970	320,700	88,300	409,000
1971	336,000	93,200	429,200
1972	353,500	100,700	454,200
1973	383,400	109,800	493,200
1974	401,600	117,000	518,600
1975	413,100	121,100	534,200
1976	425,300	N/A	N/A

Sources: Radio data from Radio Advertising Bureau and television data from NBC Corporate Planning, as reprinted in *Television Factbook*.

Note: (a) Data as of December 31 for each year.

Table 660–E.
Total Receipts and Operating Expenses
of Radio-Television Receiver Manufacturers in U.S., 1958–1974

Note: All dollar figures are in millions.

	1958	1963	1967	1972	1974
Total Industry Receipts					
Current Dollars	$1,548.0	$2,254.9	$3,846.2	$4,440.1	$4,865.0
Constant (1972) Dollars	$2,345.5	$3,149.3	$4,868.6	$4,440.1	$4,179.6
Cost of Materials					
Current Dollars	$936.3	$1,389.4	$2,486.0	$2,715.4	$3,129.9
Percent of Total Receipts	*60%*	*62%*	*65%*	*61%*	*64%*
Total Payroll					
Current Dollars	$292.7	$411.9	$643.6	$651.4	$734.1
Percent of Total Receipts	*19%*	*18%*	*17%*	*15%*	*15%*
Production Payroll					
Current Dollars	$196.6	$289.3	$462.6	$453.6	$499.1
Percent of Total Receipts	*13%*	*13%*	*12%*	*10%*	*10%*
New Capital Expenditures					
Current Dollars	$13.3	$30.5	$86.1	$58.6	$104.5
Percent of Total Receipts	*1%*	*1%*	*2%*	*1%*	*2%*

Sources: 1958-1972 data: *Census of Manufactures*. 1974 data: *Annual Survey of Manufactures*.

Sources

Tables **660**-A and **660**-B have serious reliability limitations. All data are taken from *Broadcasting Yearbook 1977*. The radio information to 1949, from Marketing World, Ltd., appears to be estimated. Due to the wartime freeze in construction of consumer items, no radio sets were made in 1943-1944—hence, the omission of those years from the table.

Radio data after 1949 are from the Electronic Industries Association (EIA), which does not supply financial information from 1950 through 1957. Radio financial totals from 1958-1963 are low, and the sudden rise in 1964 is mainly due to the inclusion of the value of imports. The post-1963 figures can only be approximately compared to earlier totals. All the television information is also from the Electronic Industries Association.

For both radio and television, the data prior to 1971 reflect *factory sales* by U.S. manufacturers, plus products imported directly by U.S. distributors or dealers for resale. The post-1970 data differ, in that the figures showing factory sales are replaced by figures showing products produced or imports purchased by U.S. manufacturers. Complete financial data on imports are incorporated only after 1964—and the figures include import duties and freight. See Units 770 and 780 for details on radio-television imports and exports.

The final column in both tables is misleading in one important respect: It does *not* control for the overlap of radio-television console combinations. While it is difficult to estimate this overlap consistently, it appears to be two to three million units or more per year from the late 1950s to the present. All of the data are rounded estimates and, as suggested above, are not in reality as comparable as these tables make them appear.

Table 660-C is from the U.S. Census Bureau's *Census of Business* (for radio-TV stores) and the *Census of Selected Service Industries* (for repair services). The 1967 drop in the numbers of radio-TV stores and repair services is due to the exclusion of establishments without paid employees.

The information in **Table 660-D** was printed in various editions of *Television Factbook*, with television data from the NBC Corporate Planning office and radio data from the Radio Advertising Bureau. No information seems to be available on how these estimates were derived. As with **Tables 660-A** and **660-B**, the total column is a bit misleading, since a small proportion of radio and television sets are combined in consoles—and, therefore, would be double-counted in the last column.

The 1958-1972 data in **Table 660-E** come from the Census Bureau's *Census of Manufactures*. The 1974 figures are from the Bureau's *Annual Survey of Manufactures*.

Further Information

The standard information source for broadcast receivers is the major industry trade group— the Consumer Products Division of the Electronic Industries Association, which annually issues the *Electronic Market Data Book* and *Consumer Electronics*. Both volumes are based on regular, confidential sales reports to the EIA from several hundred companies in the field. Summary information from the EIA and other sources appears regularly in *Broadcasting Yearbook* and *Television Factbook*.

Another source for some of this information is the *Census of Manufactures* and the *Annual Survey of Manufactures*. However, the data aggregation in these volumes makes it difficult to "pull out" information specifically relating to broadcasting (see, for example, Unit 460).

Hours of Broadcast Listening/Viewing 661

Interpretation of Table

Table 661-A provides estimates of the average daily per-household hours of use of radio and television by the U.S. population. The data were taken from many different sources and are not strictly comparable. Also, the "total radio/television hours" column is misleading, in that it does not allow for the possibility that a typical household may have both a radio and a television playing at the same time in different rooms to different people. In that event, fewer actual clock hours would be consumed.

Despite these limitations, the table figures clearly indicate that radio use has declined since the advent of television, and that television use has reached higher levels than radio ever attained. The abrupt declines in average radio use in 1955 and 1960 are unlikely and are probably due to testing and sampling problems in *television* households.

Sources

The radio data presented here were drawn from diverse sources: Lumley (1934), for 1931; CBS (1937), for 1935; Sandage (1945), for 1943; Lichty and Topping (1975), for 1946 and 1965;

Table 661–A.
Average Daily Per-Household Hours of Radio
and Television Use in U.S., 1931–1975

| | Daily Hours per Household | | |
	Radio	Television	Total Radio/ TV Hours
1931	4:04	- -	4:04
1935	4:48	- -	4:48
1943	4:23	- -	4:23
1946	4:13	- -	4:13
1950	4:06	4:35	8:41
1955	2:12	4:51	7:03
1960	1:53	5:06	6:59
1965	2:27	5:29	7:56
1971	2:52	5:56	8:48
1975	N/A	6:07	N/A

Sources: Radio data: 1931: Lumley (1934), p. 196; 1935: Columbia Broadcasting System (1937), p. 30; 1943: Sandage (1945), p. 140; 1946 and 1965: Lichty and Topping (1975), p. 523; 1950 and 1955: Nielsen Television Index, A. C. Nielsen Co., *Radio and Television Audience 1956*, p. 4; Nielsen Television Index, A. C. Nielsen Co., *Nielsen Radio 1960*, p. 8; and 1971: CBS Radio (1973), p. 4. Television data: 1946: Lichty and Topping (1975), p. 523; all other years: *Broadcasting Basics II* (1976), p. 51. All television data are based on A. C. Nielsen Company ratings research.

A. C. Nielsen Company's *Radio and Television Audience 1956*, for 1950 and 1955; the Nielsen Company's *Nielsen Radio 1960*, for 1960; and CBS Radio (1973), for 1971.

    The television information is a bit more uniform. The 1945 figure was taken from Lichty and Topping (1975), while the figures for all other years came from *Broadcasting Basics II* (1976). All television data are based on A. C. Nielsen Company ratings research.

Further Information

    See the sources listed above for additional information on radio use. A. C. Nielsen Company publications provide the most comprehensive information on television use.

Distribution of Home and Automobile Radio Receivers 67

Interpretation of Tables

    As **Table 670**-A indicates, radio penetrated half of all U.S. households within a decade of its introduction. The number of homes with radio receivers increased despite the Depression and the construction freeze of World War II (during the war, those homes with more than one radio often loaned or sold their extra receivers to others). Only the number of car radios declined during the war years, and it was not until 1951 that half of the cars on the road were equipped with a radio.

    Average radio receiver costs dropped steadily as demand lowered the unit costs. In addition, such technological breakthroughs as plastic cases (just before and after World War II), transistors, and printed circuits (in the late 1960s) helped to lower the costs of receivers.

    Although **Table 670**-A covers AM radio only, it is also worth mentioning the progress of FM radio penetration into American households. For nearly 15 years, The Pulse, Inc., has provided approximate figures for FM receivers in a number of selected urban markets and throughout the entire nation. In 1966, Pulse estimated national FM penetration at 48 percent (figures were sub-

Table 670–A.
Number and Percentage of U.S. Households and Automobiles
with AM Radio Receivers, 1922–1977

	Households with Radio Receivers	Percent of All U. S. Households	Average Cost of Home Receivers	Automobiles with Radio Receivers	Percent of All U. S. Automobiles
1922[a]	60,000	0.2%	$50	- -	- -
1923	400,000	1.5	N/A	- -	- -
1924	1,250,000	4.7	N/A	- -	- -
1925	2,750,000	10.1	83	- -	- -
1926	4,500,000	16.0	N/A	- -	- -
1927	6,750,000	23.6	N/A	- -	- -
1928	8,000,000	27.5	N/A	- -	- -
1929	10,250,000	34.6	N/A	- -	- -
1930	13,750,000	45.8	78	80,000	.1%
1931	16,700,000	55.2	N/A	100,000	.4
1932	18,450,000	60.6	N/A	250,000	1.2
1933	19,250,000	62.5	N/A	500,000	2.4
1934	20,400,000	65.2	N/A	1,250,000	5.8
1935	21,456,000	67.3	55	2,000,000	8.9
1936	22,869,000	68.4	N/A	3,500,000	14.5
1937	24,500,000	74.0	N/A	5,000,000	19.7
1938	26,667,000	79.2	N/A	6,000,000	23.8
1939	27,500,000	79.9	N/A	6,500,000	24.9
1940	28,500,000	81.1	38	7,500,000	27.4
1941	29,300,000	81.5	N/A	8,750,000	29.6
1942	30,600,000	84.0	N/A	9,000,000	32.3
1943	30,800,000	83.6	N/A	8,000,000	30.9
1944	32,500,000	87.6	N/A	7,000,000	27.5
1945	33,100,000	88.0	40	6,000,000	23.4
1946	33,998,000	89.9	N/A	7,000,000	24.9
1947	35,900,000	93.1	N/A	9,000,000	29.3
1948	37,623,000	94.2	N/A	11,000,000	33.1
1949	39,300,000	94.8	N/A	14,000,000	38.6
1950	40,700,000	94.7	26	18,000,000	49.6
1951	41,900,000	95.5	N/A	21,000,000	52.3
1952	42,800,000	95.6	N/A	23,500,000	55.3
1953	44,800,000	98.2	N/A	25,000,000	57.3
1954	45,100,000	96.7	N/A	26,100,000	56.4
1955	45,900,000	96.4	20	29,000,000	60.0
1956	46,800,000	96.3	N/A	30,100,000	57.9
1957	47,600,000	96.2	N/A	35,000,000	64.6
1958	48,500,000	96.3	N/A	36,500,000	65.5
1959	49,450,000	96.7	N/A	37,200,000	65.7
1960	50,193,000	95.6	20	40,387,000	68.1
1961	50,695,000	95.3	N/A	42,616,000	69.5
1962	51,305,000	94.5	N/A	46,900,000	74.4
1963	52,300,000	94.9	N/A	49,948,000	75.9
1964	54,000,000	96.6	N/A	58,308,000	77.7

stantially higher in major cities). A decade later, this figure had grown to the near-saturation level of 94 percent. The following are the Pulse figures for the percentage of U.S. households with an FM radio receiver:

1966 — 48%		1972 — 85%	
1967 — 57		1973 — 89	
1968 — 65		1974 — 92	
1969 — 70		1975 — 93	
1970 — 74		1976 — 94	
1971 — 80		1977 — 95	

Table 670–A. (Cont'd.)

	Households with Radio Receivers	Percent of All U. S. Households	Average Cost of Home Receivers	Automobiles with Radio Receivers	Percent of All U. S. Automobiles
1965	55,200,000	98.6%	$10	56,871,000	79.1%
1966	57,000,000	98.6	N/A	60,000,000	79.9
1967	57,500,000	98.6	N/A	64,500,000	83.0
1968	58,500,000	98.6	N/A	69,000,000	85.8
1969	60,600,000	98.6	N/A	73,500,000	89.3
1970	62,000,000	98.6	11	80,500,000	92.5
1971	62,600,000	98.6	N/A	85,400,000	94.8
1972	64,100,000	98.6	N/A	91,700,000	95.0
1973	67,400,000	98.6	N/A	92,700,000	95.0
1974	68,500,000	98.6	N/A	94,500,000	95.0
1975	70,400,000	98.6	N/A	100,400,000	95.0
1976	71,400,000	98.6	N/A	N/A	N/A
1977	72,900,000	98.6	N/A	N/A	N/A

Sources: Radio households data: 1922-1950: National Broadcasting Company; 1951-1977: U. S. Bureau of the Census, as reissued by the Radio Advertising Bureau. Average cost data: Lichty and Topping (1975), p. 521, table 4. Automobile radio data: Radio Advertising Bureau.

Note: (a) Data as of January 1 of each year.

Sources

Table 670-A is reprinted from Sterling and Kittross (1978). All figures are estimates drawn from various original sources, including NBC (for the number of radio homes up to 1950); the Radio Advertising Bureau (for the number of radio homes since 1950, and for number and percent of cars with radios); and Lichty and Topping (1975) (for the average-cost data).

The percentages of U.S. automobiles with radios are based on U.S. Department of Transportation estimates for the number of cars in the United States compared with figures for car radio sales and scrappage. The Radio Advertising Bureau reports that 95 percent has been used as an arbitrary cut-off point for these percentages, since "there is no indication of ever reaching 100 percent."

Further Information

The standard source of information on broadcast receivers is the Electronic Industries Association and its annual volumes—*Electronic Market Data Book* and *Consumer Electronics*. Summary information from the EIA and other sources appears regularly in *Broadcasting Yearbook*.

Table 671–A.
Average Daily Hours of Radio Use by U.S. Population, by Sex, Age, and Other Characteristics of Audience, 1947–1968

Characteristics of Audience	Light Use of Radio		Moderate Use of Radio		Heavy Use of Radio	
	1947: Less than 1 hour	1968: Less than 2 hours	1947: 1 to 3 hours	1968: 2 to 4 hours	1947: 3 or more hours	1968: 4 or more hours
Sex						
Male	30%	40%	50%	29%	20%	30%
Female	20	28	49	31	31	40
Age						
21 to 29 years	20	- -	48	- -	32	- -
Under 34 years	- -	31	- -	29	- -	38
30 to 49 years	24	- -	49	- -	27	- -
34 to 49 years	- -	32	- -	29	- -	38
Over 50 years	27	39	45	30	28	31
Community Population						
1 million and more	24	33	48	31	28	35
50,000 to 1 million	22	30	48	33	30	37
2,500 to 50,000	26	40	52	27	22	33
Under 2,500	28	37	51	25	21	36
Education Level						
Grade School	N/A	41	N/A	27	N/A	32
High School	N/A	29	N/A	28	N/A	42
College	31	39	31	36	18	24
Race						
White	N/A	34	N/A	30	N/A	35
Black	N/A	30	N/A	24	N/A	46

Sources: 1947 data: Lazarsfeld and Kendall (1948), pp. 132-134. 1968 data: National Association of Broadcasters (1970), pp. 24-27.

Interpretation of Tables

Tables 671-A and 671-B analyze the characteristics and programming preferences of radio audiences in 1947, when network radio had reached its pre-television peak, and in 1968, when radio had been transformed by the competition of television into a very different service. Table 671-A is a profile of radio-audience characteristics, comparing light, moderate, and heavy listeners, by sex, age, population of home community, educational level, and race. Table 671-B compares listeners attitudes toward programs and finds similar patterns of preference, despite the changes made in radio during the 20-year gap.

Table 671-C provides more recent program preference data, from 1972 through 1976, by means of an analysis of station ratings and programming in the top 25 markets. The "middle-of-the-road" (MOR) format is a combination of various kinds of music, talk, news, and features which will appeal to a general (usually older) audience. The "other" category includes ethnic, religious, farm, and jazz formats, as well as stations outside metropolitan areas. Obvious trends in this table include increased audience preferences for country music, news stations, and progressive rock, and a declining interest in "talk" formats and in classical and "oldies" musical programming.

Table 671–B.
**Results of Surveys Measuring Program Preferences
of the Radio Audience in U.S., 1947 and 1968**

	1947	1968
Listeners' Attitudes/Complaints		
Have some complaints about radio commercials[a]	25%	29%
Responses to local news coverage:		
Too much time	2	2
About right amount	67	63
Not enough	24	25
Don't know/Not sure	7	10
Responses to national news coverage:		
Too much time	3	4[b]
About right amount	65	67
Not enough	26	21
Don't know/Not sure	6	8
Responses to international news coverage:		
Too much time	16	--[b]
About right amount	59	--
Not enough	16	--
Don't know/Not sure	9	--
Listeners' Program Preferences		
Public Affairs		
News	74	87
Talks or Discussion on Public Issues	44	31
Interviews with Interesting People	--	30
Telephone Interviews	--	19
Entertainment		
Comedy	59	--
Popular and Dance Music	49	77
Classical Music	30	--
Country/Western Music	26	--
Religion	21	26
Quiz and Audience Participation	56	--
Drama	46	--
Mystery	41	--
Sports	33	33
Programs that give advice	--	21
Miscellaneous (farm/weather/drama)	--	5

Sources: 1947 data: Lazarsfeld and Kendall (1948), pp. 119, 123. 1968 data: National Association of Broadcasters (1970), pp. 10, 35, 49-50.

Notes: The total sample in 1947 was 3,225; in 1968, 3,148. (a) These are aggregate figures which combine several specific categories of complaints about commercials. (b) The 1968 survey combined the categories of national and international news coverage.

Sources

The data in **Tables 671-A** and **671-B** were drawn from Lazarsfeld and Kendall (1948) and from the National Association of Broadcasters (NAB) (1970). The surveys which produced these data involved national interviews of 3,225 individuals (for 1947 data) and 3,148 individuals (for 1968 data). The two surveys also involved many parallel questions. Because the more recent survey was conducted under the auspices of the NAB, the reader should approach the reported results with some caution.

Table 671-C data are from a report in *Broadcasting*. The reader should consult that source for a full report of the methodology used to obtain these data. The total audience figures were based on Arbitron radio share reports of some 315 stations in the top 25 markets, while the breakdowns for men, women, and teenagers include a smaller number of stations (number not given) in the top 10 markets.

Table 671–C.
Programming Preferences of the Radio Audience in U.S., by Sex and Age, 1972 and 1976

Type of Programming	1972				1976				Percent Change, 1972-1976			
	Total Responses	Adult Men	Adult Women	All Teenagers	Total Responses	Adult Men	Adult Women	All Teenagers	Total Responses	Adult Men	Adult Women	All Teenagers
Beautiful Music	15.1%	15.5%	19.6%	3.5%	15.5%	15.9%	19.4%	1.8%	+2.6%	+2.6%	-1.0%	-48.6%
Country Music	4.4	3.3	3.1	0.7	6.7	6.6	5.3	1.8	+52.3	+100.0	+71.0	+157.0
News	3.2	7.6	5.6	0.7	5.2	9.8	7.6	0.7	+62.5	+28.9	+35.7	- -
Middle of the Road	19.7	17.7	17.5	5.7	17.4	14.4	13.9	4.8	-11.7	-18.6	-20.6	-15.8
Contemporary/Top 40	19.2	14.1	13.8	44.3	19.5	14.8	16.4	45.0	+1.5	+5.0	+18.8	+1.6
Progressive	4.8	6.3	3.7	12.9	7.7	9.5	5.9	18.2	+60.4	+50.8	+59.5	+41.1
Black	4.8	3.8	4.6	10.8	5.0	4.2	5.2	10.5	+4.2	+10.5	+13.0	-2.8
Talk	5.6	6.7	6.4	1.6	3.3	4.3	4.0	0.5	-41.1	-35.8	-37.5	-68.8
Classical	1.8	2.2	2.1	0.2	1.4	1.6	1.7	0.2	-22.2	-27.3	-19.1	- -
Oldies	1.4	1.9	1.9	1.7	1.2	2.7	3.1	2.7	-14.3	+42.1	+63.2	+58.8
Other	20.0	20.9	21.7	17.8	17.1	16.2	17.5	13.8	-14.5	-22.5	-19.4	-22.5

Source: *Broadcasting* (May 2, 1977), pp. 51-52.

Further Information

For information on the early development of radio research, the reader should see Lumley (1934), which contains an extensive bibliography of even earlier studies. Useful articles and statistics appear in Lichty and Topping (1975), and research methods are described in Chappell and Hooper (1944). See Sterling and Kittross (1978) for an historical review of broadcast audience research and findings. Current data on this subject appear in *Broadcasting* and *Variety*.

Table 680–A.
Number and Percentage of U.S. Homes with Television Receivers,
and Average Cost of Receivers, 1946–1977

Year	Homes with Television Receivers	Percent of All U. S. Homes	Percent with Two or More Receivers	Percent with UHF Receivers	Percent with Color Receivers	Average Cost of Receivers Black and White	Color
1946	8,000	.02%	- -	- -	- -		
1947	14,000	.04	- -	- -	- -	$279	- -
1948	172,000	.4	1%	- -	- -		
1949	940,000	2.3	1	- -	- -		
1950	3,875,000	9.0	1	- -	- -	190	- -
1951	10,320,000	23.5	2	- -	- -		
1952	15,300,000	34.2	2	- -	- -		
1953	20,400,000	44.7	3	- -	- -		
1954	26,000,000	55.7	3	- -	- -		
1955	30,700,000	64.5	3	- -	.02%	138	$500[a]
1956	34,900,000	71.8	5	- -	.05		
1957	38,900,000	78.6	6	9.2%	.2		
1958	41,925,000	83.2	8	8.1	.4		
1959	43,950,000	85.9	10	8.0	.6		
1960	45,750,000	87.1	13	7.0	.7	132	392
1961	47,200,000	88.8	13	7.1	.9	125	381
1962	48,855,000	90.0	14	7.3	1.2	128	352
1963	50,300,000	91.3	16	9.6	1.9	118	346
1964	51,600,000	92.3	19	15.8	3.1	109	348
1965	52,700,000	92.6	22	27.5	5.3	106	356
1966	53,850,000	93.0	25	38.0	9.7	98	371
1967	55,130,000	93.6	28	47.5	16.3	92	362
1968	56,670,000	94.6	29	57.0	24.2	74	336
1969	58,250,000	95.0	33	66.0	32.0	78	328
1970	59,700,000	95.2	34	73.0	39.2	75	317
1971	61,600,000	95.5	36	80.0	45.1	81	324
1972	63,500,000	95.8	38	81.0	52.8	79	319
1973	65,600,000	96.0	41	86.0	60.1	77	308
1974	66,800,000	96.1	42	89.0	67.3	79	316
1975	68,500,000	97.1	43	91.0	70.8	84	341
1976	70,500,000	97.3	45	N/A	73.3	89	349
1977	71,500,000	97.9	47	92.0	76.0	N/A	N/A

Sources: Sterling and Kittross (1978), p. 535. Original sources for the 1946-1959 data are as follows: Penetration and percentage figures: NBC Corporate Planning data as reprinted annually in *Television Factbook*. UHF figures: Advertising Research Foundation (to 1968) and U. S. Census reports. Cost figures: 1947-1959: Lichty and Topping (1975), p. 522, table 42; 1960-1977: *Television Digest* 17:27:9 (January 1977).

Note: (a) This cost figure is an estimate rather than an average.

Interpretation of Tables

The rapid growth of television is particularly remarkable when one considers that television sets in the early years were no small investment for a household, especially with the extra charges for antennas and installation. Yet, as **Table 680-A** reveals, more than half of all American households had at least one television set by 1954; and by 1969, that figure had risen to 95 percent. By

Table 680–B.
Percentage of U.S. Homes with Television Receivers,
by Region and Size of County, 1950–1975

	1950	1955	1960	1965	1970	1975
Region						
Northeast	24%	80%	92%	96%	96%	98%
East Central	8	72	90	96	97	98
West Central	7	60	87	95	96	98
South	2	46	79	90	94	97
Pacific	9	64	88	93	95	97
County Size[a]						
"A" counties	21%	82%	93%	96%	97%	98%
"B" counties	6	72	90	95	97	98
"C" and "D" counties	2	44	78	91	93	97

Sources: 1950-1970 data: Nielsen Television Index, A. C. Nielsen Company data, in Lichty and Topping (1975), p. 523, table 43. 1975 data: Nielsen Television Index, A. C. Nielsen Company (1976a), p. 8.

Note: (a) County-size categories from Nielsen Television Index, A. C. Nielsen Company (1976), p. 53: "A" counties: All counties in the 25 largest metropolitan areas. "B" counties: All counties not in "A" category with populations of over 150,000 or in metropolitan areas over 150,000. "C" counties: All counties not in "A" category with populations of over 35,000 or in metropolitan areas over 35,000. "D" counties: All other counties.

1970, one-third of the American households had two or more sets. Penetration by color television, with its far more expensive receivers, has been nearly as rapid.

Table 680-A also reveals that UHF made significant progress in reaching the American consumer only after Congress passed an all-channel receiver bill in 1962, with provisions for its enforcement after 1964. Not until the early 1970s did UHF penetration begin to approach national VHF levels—though in UHF markets, the penetration naturally took place at higher levels more rapidly. (The effect of these developments on the growth of UHF stations can be seen in Unit 180.)

In Table 680-B, the household penetration of television is broken down by region and size of county. Early television penetration levels were highest in the Northeast and in urban communities. Regional penetration levels evened out only after 1970, when the South and rural communities throughout the country began to approach the national averages.

Sources

All of the figures in Table 680-A are estimates gathered by the editors from a variety of sources. Most of these data also appear in *Television Factbook* tables, which are based on NBC Corporate Planning research, and in Sterling and Kittross (1978). The UHF figures were taken from the Advertising Research Foundation and from U.S. Census Bureau reports. Except for the 1955 color-receiver cost figure, which is an estimate by the editors, the cost averages are found in Lichty and Topping (1975), for the 1947-1959 figures, and from *Television Digest* (1977) for the 1960-1977 figures.

There are wide variations among sources for the "two or more receivers" data. The 1948-1963 estimates shown here are based on NBC Corporate Planning figures reported in *Television Factbook*. The remaining estimates came from the A. C. Nielsen Company. All of the figures are rounded. The Table 680-B data are also from the A. C. Nielsen Company.

Further Information

The Consumer Products Division of the Electronics Industry Association (EIA) is the primary source of information on the manufacture of television receivers. Two annual publications of the EIA, *Electronic Market Data Book* and *Consumer Electronics*, are useful sources. *Broadcasting Yearbook* and *Television Yearbook* are also useful general references, and the A. C. Nielsen Company is the best source of information on television penetration and on television audience characteristics and programming preferences.

Table 681–A.
Average Weekly Hours of Television Use by U.S. Population,
by Household Size, Number of Children, and Other Characteristics, 1960–1975

Characteristics of Audience	Average Viewing Hours per Week			
	1960	1965	1970	1975
Household Size				
1 to 2 members	33:01	32:50	36:31	37:26
3 to 4 members	39:20	45:13	49:03	50:36
5 or more members	49:49	52:09	59:03	56:46
Children under 18 years				
None	N/A	34:05	39:00	38:41
1 or more	N/A	49:08	55:46	53:12
Income Level				
$5,000 or less[a]	42:42	38:26	42:55	42:17
$5,000 to $15,000	44:36	44:27	45:35	48:03
$15,000 or more	41:12	40:44	43:20	46:52
Education Level				
Grade School	N/A	41:14	48:14	46:53
High School	N/A	43:03	49:50	48:21
1 or more years of College	N/A	39:33	40:22	40:27
County Size[b]				
Urban ("A" and "B" counties)	41:14	42:17	46:54	45:41
Rural ("C" and "D" counties)	37:31	40:53	42:58	43:56
National Average Viewing Hours	40:02	41:52	45:41	45:07

Sources: Data supplied to the editors by Nielsen Television Index, A. C. Nielsen Company.

Notes: All data are as of November of each year. (a) Income levels for 1975 were changed to $10,000 or less, $10,000 to $15,000, and $15,000 or more. (b) County-size categories are defined by A. C. Nielsen Company as follows:

"A" counties: All counties not in the 25 largest metropolitan areas. "B" counties: All counties not in the "A" category, with populations of over 150,000 or in metropolitan areas over 150,000. "C" counties: All counties not in "A" category, with populations of over 35,000 or in metropolitan areas over 35,000. "D" counties are all other counties.

Interpretation of Tables

Table 681-A presents various characteristics of television-owning households—household size, number of children under the age of 18, income and educational level, and urban or rural location—in relation to the average number of television-viewing hours per household per week. Throughout the 15-year period, from 1960 to 1975, the reader will note the generally increasing amounts of television viewing, especially in households with more children and with medium income and educational levels.

Table 681-B examines household uses of television, by the sex and age of viewers. Perhaps the most striking change which has taken place during the 20-year period (1955 through 1975) is the steady decline of children watching television. The general levels of television use have increased, however, and a much greater percentage of men are watching television prior to 8 p.m. Prime-time patterns of television use have not varied significantly during these two decades.

Table 681-C reports findings on viewer attitudes from two national studies conducted a decade apart (1960 and 1970). The data suggest that television has lost some of its hold on viewers.

Table 681–B.

Average Daily Household Use of Television in U.S., by Sex and Age of Viewers and Time of Day, 1955–1975

Time of Day and Viewer Characteristics	1955	1960	1965	1970	1975
Early Day (10 a.m. to 1 p.m.), Monday through Friday					
Households Using Television	16%	21%	19%	22%	21%
Men	12	14	15	16	19
Women	53	59	55	59	60
Teenagers	4	4	5	4	6
Children	31	23	25	21	15
Afternoon (1 to 4 p.m.), Monday through Friday					
Households Using Television	17	21	25	28	27
Men	14	18	16	16	17
Women	52	62	64	66	63
Teenagers	6	5	5	5	7
Children	28	15	15	13	13
Early Fringe (5 to 8 p.m.), Monday through Friday					
Households Using Television	42	48	42	52	52
Men	19	23	26	28	30
Women	27	34	36	38	39
Teenagers	13	12	10	10	10
Children	41	31	28	24	21
Prime (8 to 11 p.m.), Monday through Sunday					
Households Using Television	62	61	59	62	61
Men	32	32	32	32	34
Women	39	42	42	42	42
Teenagers	11	10	10	11	11
Children	18	16	16	15	13
Late Fringe (11 p.m. to 1 a.m.), Monday through Sunday					
Households Using Television	N/A	30[a]	31[a]	28	29
Men	N/A	37	39	39	41
Women	N/A	49	50	49	45
Teenagers	N/A	6	7	8	9
Children	N/A	8	4	4	5
Average Hours of Use per Day	4:51	5:06	5:29	6:32	6:26

Source: Data supplied to the editors by Nielsen Television Index, A. C. Nielsen Company.

Note: Data are as of November of each year. (a) 11 p.m. to midnight only.

The proportion of television viewers who describe themselves as "super-fans" has declined in all age groups since 1960. Viewers surveyed in 1970 also reacted with greater negativity to television advertising. (The rising percentage of viewers willing to pay to do without advertising may be an encouraging sign for pay-television systems.) Finally, although television's educational role (or, at least, potential) is still strongly endorsed by the public, its role as a "babysitter" has dropped sharply—or at least viewers are more reluctant to admit such a use of the television set. Concern about sex and bad language on the screen has increased more than 100 percent, while the concern about smoking, drinking, and other adult themes has increased more than 400 percent.

Table 681–C.
Results of Two Surveys (Steiner and Bower) Measuring Selected Viewer Attitudes about Television in U.S., 1960 and 1970

Viewer Attitudes	Steiner Study—1960	Bower Study—1970
Television Programming— Viewers who described themselves as "super-fans" of television:		
Sex		
Male	40%	24%
Female	41	31
Age		
18 to 19 years	44	25
20 to 29 years	33	29
30 to 39 years	39	24
40 to 49 years	38	23
50 to 59 years	44	27
60 years and older	50	33
Education Level		
Grade School	54	43
High School	42	28
College	20	15
Television Advertising:		
"Fair price to pay for entertainment"	75	70
"Most are too long"	63	65
"Some are very helpful"	58	54
"Some are more entertaining than program"	43	54
"Would prefer TV without ads"	43	48
"Ads are generally in poor taste and annoying"	40	43
"Would rather pay small amount to have TV without ads"	24	30
Television's Role with Children:		
Major Advantages:		
Education	65	80
Baby-sitting	28	16
Entertainment	19	22
Major Disadvantages:		
Violence/Horror	30	31
Crime/Gangsters	10	9
Sex/Bad Language	5	12
Smoking/Drinking/Adult Themes	4	18

Sources: Bower (1973), pp. 25, 84, 157, 161, which also cites data from Steiner (1963).

Sources

Of all mass media audiences, the television audience—especially at the national network level (see Unit 682)—has probably received the most attention from researchers. But because most audience data are gathered in an effort either to sell advertising time to more advertisers at higher prices or to convince funding sources of the worth of public television (see Unit 683), such data are necessarily somewhat suspect.

The most reliable source for national data on the television audience is the A. C. Nielsen Company, which provided the information for **Tables 681-A** and **681-B**, and which has been conducting national television program ratings since network television's beginnings in 1948. The precise figures in **Table 681-A** would suggest complete refinement, but all of the data in this unit (and all data on media audiences gathered by the sample process) are actually merely estimates. Nielsen Company ratings are usually given a 3 percent (plus or minus) margin of error.

Table 681-C data are estimates based on two nationwide, personal-interview surveys of large stratified sample populations. Both the Steiner (1960) and the Bower (1970) studies were financially supported by the CBS network, and the Bower study was also published by a CBS subsidiary. However, the researchers, and CBS as well, emphasize that the network did not enter into the process or results of the surveys in any way.

Further Information

Madow et al. (1961) remains the most exhaustive analysis and bibliography on the methods of television program ratings systems. The major ratings firms also regularly revise their booklets describing their methodologies. Readers interested in this field should consult A. C. Nielsen Company's *Reference Supplement* and Arbitron's *Description of Methodology*. Both publications are available from the companies.

Characteristics/Preferences of Network TV Audiences 682

Table 682–A.
Ranking and Average Audience Percentage of the Top 20 Network Television Entertainment Specials and Series in U.S., 1960–1977

Ranking	Date	Program	Network	Percent of Viewing Households
1	January 30, 1977	Roots, Part VIII	ABC	51.1%
2	November 7, 1976	Gone With the Wind, Part I	NBC	47.7
3	November 8, 1976	Gone With the Wind, Part II	NBC	47.4
4	January 15, 1970	Bob Hope Christmas Show	NBC	46.6
5	January 28, 1977	Roots, Part VI	ABC	45.9
6	August 29, 1967	The Fugitive (final episode of series)	ABC	45.9
7	January 27, 1977	Roots, Part V	ABC	45.7
8	January 14, 1971	Bob Hope Christmas Show	NBC	45.0
9	January 25, 1977	Roots, Part III	ABC	44.8
10	February 9, 1964	Ed Sullivan (first appearance of the Beatles)	CBS	44.6
11	January 9, 1977	Super Bowl XI	NBC	44.4
12	January 16, 1972	Super Bowl VI	CBS	44.2
13	January 24, 1977	Roots, Part II	ABC	44.1
14	January 8, 1964	Beverly Hillbillies	CBS	44.0
15	January 26, 1977	Roots, Part IV	ABC	43.8
16	April 7, 1970	Academy Awards	ABC	43.4
17	February 16, 1964	Ed Sullivan (second appearance of the Beatles)	CBS	43.2
18	January 15, 1964	Beverly Hillbillies	CBS	42.8
19	January 14, 1973	Super Bowl VII	NBC	42.7
20	January 12, 1975	Super Bowl IX	NBC	42.4

Source: Nielsen Television Index, A. C. Nielsen Company, *Nielsen Newscast* No. 1 (1977), p. 7.

Interpretation of Tables

Table 682-A lists the 20 most-watched entertainment programs and specials on network television from 1960 through 1977. All news events and all unsponsored or joint network broadcasts are excluded from the list. The January 30, 1977, episode of *Roots* drew the largest audience

Table 682–B.
Ranking and Number of Seasons of the Top 12 Network Television Entertainment Series in U.S., 1960–1976

Ranking	Series	Number of Episodes with 30 Percent or More of Viewing Households	Number of Seasons Aired
1	Bonanza	143	13
2	All in the Family	108	7[a]
3	Beverly Hillbillies	75	9
4	Andy Griffith Show	53	8
5	Gunsmoke	52	15
6	Wagon Train	52	5
7	Candid Camera	34	7
8	Dick Van Dyke Show	33	5
9	Red Skelton Hour	31	11
10	The Lucy Show and Here's Lucy	30	12
11	Sanford and Son	25	5
12	Bewitched	24	8

Source: Nielsen Television Index, A. C. Nielsen Company, *Television Audience 1976*, p. 71.

Note: (a) Still on the air as of the 1977-1978 season.

in television history—more than 36 million households. This list changes annually, of course, as new programs attain the top 20 list and as the national audience for television continues to grow.

Table 682-B lists those network entertainment series which have been major audience draws over extended periods from 1960 through 1976. Each series episode counted had achieved a 30-share rating or higher (30 percent of U.S. television households), which is considered a very good showing for most television programs. Since a television series typically presents 20 to 29 new episodes each year (though in recent years, fewer new episodes and more reruns are being shown in a season), it is evident that some of the programs on this list received very high ratings for many years. *All in the Family* is the only one of these programs which was still on the air with first-run episodes during the 1977-1978 season.

Table 682-C is a selective listing of the penetration and per-household viewing hours of one major news event for each of the 17 years between 1960 and 1976. Unlike the rating percentages in Tables 682-A and 682-B, Table 682-C lists the percentage of *all* U.S. households (not just TV households) which viewed each event. Of course, not all of the people in these households watched all of the event in question. Instead, these data show the cumulative audience over the duration of the program, and include many people who watched only a portion of the program (usually at least 10 or 15 minutes). The figures include all three commercial networks for each event.

Sources

Table 682-A data, from the A. C. Nielsen Company's *Nielsen Newscast* No. 1, are issued in revised form almost annually. Table 682-B, drawn from the Nielsen Company's *Television Audience 1976*, covers only those series programs which were on the air from September through August for the 1960-1976 television seasons. Table 682-C data were gathered by A. C. Nielsen Company and printed in Lichty and Topping (1975). The editors have added the data for 1960, 1970, 1972, 1975, and 1976 from various Nielsen publications, and all are limited by the Nielsen methodology, including a 3 percent (plus or minus) margin of error.

Further Information

The A. C. Nielsen Company is the chief source of network television audience information. Its annual publications, *Nielsen Television* and *Television Audience*, are the most readily available

Table 682–C.
Percentage of Audience and Per-Household Hours of Viewing
of Selected Network-Televised Special News Events, 1960–1976

Year	Selected News Event	Percent of All U. S. Households Viewing Event[a]	Average Hours of Viewing per Household
1960	Kennedy-Nixon Debates	89.8%	4:00
1960	Kennedy-Nixon Election Returns	91.8	4:30
1961	Kennedy Inaugural	59.5	- -
1962	John Glenn Orbital Mercury Flight	81.4	5:15
1963	Assassination of Kennedy	96.1	31:38
1964	Goldwater-Johnson Election Returns	90.6	2:51
1965	Gemini IV "Space Walk" Mission	92.1	4:47
1966	Congressional Election Returns	84.4	6:10
1967	Johnson State of the Union Address	59.6	- -
1968	Democratic Convention	90.1	9:28
1969	Apollo 11 Moon-Landing Mission	93.9	15:35
1970	Abortive Apollo 13 Mission	90.2	- -
1972	Democratic Convention	86.1	36:42
1974	Nixon Resignation Speech	60.3	:30
1975	Apollo-Soyuz Orbital Flight	71.3	- -
1976	Democratic Convention	88.5	30:48
1976	Ford-Carter Debates	90.0	5:45

Sources: Lichty and Topping (1975), p. 524, table 46, citing Nielsen Television Index, A. C. Nielsen Company data. Data on Kennedy-Nixon debates in 1960 and the special news events in 1970, 1972, 1975, and 1976 were added by the editors from other Nielsen publications.

Note: (a) Figures represent percentage of *all* U. S. households, rather than TV-households only.

sources of data. Furthermore, anyone may write to the Nielsen Company and ask to be placed on its mailing list for the quarterly *Nielsen Newscast* bulletins. The substantial *Television Audience*, issued each September since 1960, is a summation of special reports and data from regular ratings "sweeps." For general ratings data, see Unit 681. Data on the audience for crisis news events and political coverage appear in Greenberg and Parker (1965) and Kraus and Davis (1976).

Table 683–A.

Percentage and Number of U.S. Households Viewing Public Television, and Cumulative Ratings of Types of PTV Programming, 1970–1977

	Eight-Week Period			Four-Week Period				
	1970	1971	1972	1973	1974	1975	1976	1977
Prime-Time Hours Only								
Percent of PTV-Viewing Households	27.4%	30.2%	36.1%	32.8%	30.2%	32.6%	35.5%	39.4%
Number of PTV-Viewing Households	16,470	18,750	23,390	21,710	20,820	22,330	24,710	28,050
Average Number of PTV Telecasts Seen per Household	3.7	4.9	4.6	3.0	3.2	3.6	4.1	3.5
All Hours								
Percent of PTV-Viewing Households	N/A	N/A	N/A	48.9%	48.7%	49.2%	55.2%	60.1%
Number of PTV-Viewing Households	N/A	N/A	N/A	32,370	33,360	33,700	38,420	42,790
Average Number of PTV Telecasts Seen per Household	N/A	N/A	N/A	7.0	7.5	8.0	9.9	8.8
Cumulative Ratings by Type of PTV Programming								
Children's Shows	N/A	N/A	N/A	N/A	N/A	26.9%	26.1%	N/A
Arts/Humanities	18.1%	24.5%	25.4%	28.6%	22.4%	22.3	26.1	N/A
Science/Medicine	N/A	N/A	N/A	N/A	N/A	17.9	10.8	N/A
Public Affairs	13.9	12.7	19.1	14.1	12.8	12.8	19.2	N/A

Sources: Prime-time data based on Nielsen Television Index, A. C. Nielsen Company research for Public Broadcasting Corporation/Corporation for Public Broadcasting, as reported in CPB, *Status Report* (1973), p. 64, for the years 1970-1972, and *Status Report* (1977), p. 24, for the years 1973-1977. All-hours data from *Status Report* (1977), p. 24. Cumulative ratings from *Status Report* (1973), p. 64, for the years 1970-1973, from correspondence between CPB and the editors for the 1974 figures, and from *Status Report* (1977), p. 23, for the years 1975-1976.

Note: 1970 data are for October-December. 1971, 1972 data are for October-November. 1973, 1974 data are for November. 1975, 1976, 1977 data are for March.

Table 683–B.
Percentage of U.S. Households Viewing Public Television,
by Income, Education, and Occupation of Head of Household, 1973–1977

Head of Household Characteristics	November 1973 Prime-Time Hours	November 1973 All Hours	March 1975— All Hours	March 1976— All Hours	March 1977— All Hours
Income					
Under $10,000	33.2%	33.5%[a]	41.0%	43.8%	35%
$10,000 to $15,000	44.5	43.9	54.7	51.4	24
Over $15,000	51.9	47.5	55.7	69.7	41
Education Level					
Less than High School	31.6	30.4	40.3	45.5	28
High School Graduate	35.6	36.1	49.3	53.8	36
One Year of College or more	52.5	48.3	56.4	64.0	36
Occupation					
Professional/Managerial	48.5	45.0	N/A	67.7	N/A
Clerical/Sales	N/A	N/A	N/A	53.8	N/A
Blue Collar (skilled or semi-skilled)	34.6	31.6	N/A	51.0	N/A
Other (not in labor force)	38.0	38.1	N/A	N/A	N/A

Sources: 1973 prime-time data: Nielsen Television Index, A. C. Nielsen Company, *Television Audience 1974*, p. 119; 1973 all-hours data: Corporation for Public Broadcasting, *Status Report* (1973), p. 65. 1975-1976 data provided to editors by CPB Office of Communication Research. 1977 data from CPB, *Status Report* (1977), p. 25.

Note: (a) According to S. Young Lee of CPB, this figure should be between 30.4 and 33.5 percent.

Interpretation of Tables

Table 683-A traces the percentage and number of U.S. television households viewing public television programming during the eight-year period beginning in 1970, when consistent information on the national public television audience first became available through the Corporation for Public Broadcasting (CPB). The figures suggest a slowly growing audience for public television. In 1973, public television stations reached an estimated audience of about 78 percent of the nation's television households. By 1977, that estimate had grown to 87 percent.

Yet the number of public television telecasts seen per household, either during prime-time or total hours, still represents only a fraction of commercial television viewing. The cumulative ratings by program type reveal the greater popularity of children's and arts/humanities programming over science/medicine and public affairs programming (though it is worth noting the peaks which occurred in the viewing of public affairs programs during the presidential election years of 1972 and 1976).

Table 683-B provides the scattered information available on the characteristics of public television viewers—annual income, educational level, and occupational status—from 1973 through 1977. The data here suggest that the average public television viewer has a higher income, is better educated, and belongs to a higher socioeconomic status group than the average commercial television viewer.

The editors have not reported data on public *radio* audiences because: (1) the CPB has only recently begun to gather and analyze such information, and (2) the available data are currently restricted to CPB-qualified stations (representing only about 25 percent of all noncommercial AM/FM stations in operation).

Sources

Although data on public television are becoming more detailed and sophisticated, they still are limited in a number of ways: (1) They have been gathered for only a few years; (2) they are affected by ever-changing research approaches and definitions; and (3) they involve such small numbers of viewers. The average public television viewer would not even be counted in most commercial ratings. Indeed, in a single typical evening, commercial television viewers will watch the same number of shows as public television viewers watch during an entire week.

A. C. Nielsen Company research for the Public Broadcasting Service (PBS) and the Corporation for Public Broadcasting provided the information in **Table 683-A**. The information in **Table 683-B** comes from two different sources: A. C. Nielsen Company developed the 1973 and 1977 data, while the CPB Office of Communication Research provided the 1975 and 1976 data. The editors do not know what differences in research methods may have been involved, but the sharp declines in audience for 1977 suggest some problems with data inconsistency.

Further Information

An early, classic study of the public (formerly, educational) television audience is Schramm, Lyle, and Pool (1963). More recent discussions of public (and instructional) television audience research appear in Chu and Schramm (1968, 1974), and Lyle (1975), both of which reprint statistical information from a variety of surveys. The Office of Communication Research at CPB is the consistent source for data done by either CPB itself or by other organizations, such as the A. C. Nielsen Company. The reader will find the CPB's *Status Report* (1973) and *Status Report* (1977) most useful. Finally, Schramm (1977) assesses the instructional role of public television.

SECTION 7

U.S. Media Industries Abroad

Table 700–A.
**Number and Distribution of Foreign Correspondents Employed
by U. S. News Media, 1951–1975**

Number and Nationality of U. S. Foreign Correspondents						
	1951[a]	1963	1966	1969	1971	1975[b]
U. S. Citizens	N/A	515	836	724	738	N/A
Full-Time Correspondents	293	N/A	N/A	563	524	429
Part-Time Stringers	N/A	N/A	N/A	161	214	N/A
Foreign Nationals	N/A	718	540	738	601	N/A
Full-Time Correspondents	210	N/A	N/A	366	273	247
Part-Time Stringers	N/A	N/A	N/A	372	328	N/A
Total, All Foreign Correspondents	1,653	1,233	1,376	1,462	1,339	N/A
Full-Time Correspondents	503	924	838	929	797	676
Part-Time Stringers	1,150	309	538	533	542	N/A

Locations of U. S. Foreign Correspondents, by Percentage of Total Number			
	1963	1969	1975[b]
Asia/Australia	21%	23%	23%
Europe	51	54	51
Middle East	5	5	8
Africa	5	6	2
Latin America and Canada	19	12	16

Rankings of Eight Nations with Largest Number of U. S. Correspondents					
	1963	1966	1969	1972	1975
England	1	2	2	1	1
France	3	3	1	2	2
Japan	2	4 (tie)	6	6	3
Hong Kong	- -	7 (tie)	7	8	4
West Germany	5	6	5	5	5
Italy	4	1	4	4	6
USSR	- -	- -	8	7	7
Lebanon	- -	- -	- -	- -	8
South Vietnam	- -	4 (tie)	3	3	- -
Argentina	6	- -	- -	- -	- -
Brazil	7	- -	- -	- -	- -
Turkey	8	- -	- -	- -	- -
India	- -	7 (tie)	- -	- -	- -

Sources: 1951 data: Anderson (1951), pp. 10-12, 80-81. 1963 data: Wilhelm (1963), pp. 147 ff. 1966 data: Wilhelm (1966), pp. 42-43, 160, 180. 1969-1971 data: Wilhelm (1972). 1975 data: Kliesch (1976), pp. 18-19, 110 ff; except for ranking of nations, which was compiled by the editors from listings in appropriate issues of the *Directory of the Overseas Press Club of America.*

Notes: (a) Excludes Korean War correspondents. (b) Includes only full-time staff correspondents and a small number of full-time "heavy" stringers.

Table 700–B.
U. S. Network Television's Evening News Coverage of Events in 40 Countries, 1973–1976

CBS EVENING NEWS COVERAGE OF 40 COUNTRIES, 1972-1976

	1972 Stories Number	1972 Stories Percent	1973 Stories Number	1973 Stories Percent	1974 Stories Number	1974 Stories Percent	1975 Stories Number	1975 Stories Percent	1976 Stories Number	1976 Stories Percent	Total Stories Number	Total Stories Percent
United States	174	73%	128	66%	107	55%	162	62%	127	53%	698	61.6%
South Vietnam	96	40	43	22	5	3	52	20	11	5	207	18.3
U.S.S.R.	42	18	22	11	37	19	41	16	35	15	177	15.6
Israel	10	4	33	17	29	15	27	10	24	10	123	10.9
Great Britain	18	8	15	8	31	16	25	10	31	13	120	10.6
North Vietnam	69	29	30	15	0	0	7	3	1	0	107	9.4
France	31	13	19	10	16	8	14	5	18	8	98	8.6
People's Republic of China	21	9	5	3	7	4	11	4	17	7	61	5.4
Cambodia	7	3	27	14	2	1	22	8	0	0	58	5.1
Lebanon	2	1	4	2	5	3	13	5	32	13	56	4.9
Egypt	4	2	17	9	11	6	12	5	11	5	55	4.9
West Germany	8	3	10	5	10	5	11	4	11	5	50	4.4
Syria	0	0	12	6	15	8	6	2	17	7	50	4.4
Japan	9	4	10	5	8	4	7	3	8	3	42	3.7
Portugal	0	0	0	0	5	3	15	6	6	3	26	2.3
South Africa	0	0	0	0	2	1	4	2	19	8	25	2.2
Switzerland	4	2	2	1	6	3	5	2	7	3	24	2.1
Northern Ireland	8	3	2	1	7	4	1	0	6	3	24	2.1
Italy	2	1	2	1	5	3	8	3	6	3	23	2.0
Saudi Arabia	0	0	4	2	5	3	5	2	8	3	22	1.9
Spain	4	2	1	1	1	1	6	2	9	4	21	1.9
Turkey	0	0	0	0	12	6	5	2	4	2	21	1.9
Canada	4	2	2	1	4	2	3	1	8	3	21	1.9
Cuba	3	1	3	2	3	2	5	2	6	3	20	1.8
Greece	0	0	2	1	9	5	5	2	3	1	19	1.7
South Korea	2	1	2	1	2	1	7	3	5	2	18	1.6
Cyprus	0	0	0	0	15	8	2	1	0	0	17	1.5
Chile	3	1	8	4	1	1	3	1	1	0	16	1.4
Philippines	3	1	6	3	0	0	5	2	2	1	16	1.4
Angola	0	0	0	0	0	0	4	2	12	5	16	1.4
Iran	4	2	2	1	5	3	2	1	2	1	15	1.3
Jordan	2	1	3	2	5	3	3	1	2	1	15	1.3
Argentina	0	0	3	2	3	2	6	2	2	1	14	1.2
Rhodesia	1	0	0	0	0	0	0	0	13	5	14	1.2
Sweden	3	1	2	1	4	2	1	0	3	1	13	1.1
Mexico	3	1	0	0	1	1	2	1	7	3	13	1.1
Thailand	4	2	2	1	1	1	6	2	0	0	13	1.1
Netherlands	0	0	2	1	2	1	2	1	5	2	11	1.0
Algeria	1	0	3	2	1	1	3	1	3	1	11	1.0
Eire	1	0	2	1	1	1	4	2	2	1	10	0.9

Source: Larson, James (1978), pp. 75, 79, 80.

Interpretation of Tables

Although international news flow has only recently become a major interest to U.S. and foreign communications policymakers, communications scholars have been studying the subject for some time. The subject was clearly outlined as an international policy issue at least as early as 1953 (UNESCO, 1969), and its main issues were discussed by Schramm (1964). Over the past few years, policymakers too have begun to recognize international news flow as an important element in the general issue of North-South political and economic relations.

However, no organization has yet undertaken any comprehensive statistical measurement of the entire news flow situation. Instead, studies are being carried out on an ad hoc basis by individual researchers. The results of three such studies are presented in this unit. For other useful studies in this field, the reader is referred to the "Further Information" section at the end of this unit.

Table 700-A lists the number of foreign correspondents working for U.S. media, the percentage of these correspondents in various areas of the world, and the countries with the largest number of U.S. correspondents. The figures are not altogether historically comparable, in that only *full-time* correspondents were counted after 1971. Consequently, there are two series to interpret in **Table 700**-A: the total number of all U.S. foreign correspondents from 1951 to 1971, and the total number of full-time correspondents from 1951 to 1975.

Table 700–B. (Cont'd.)

ABC EVENING NEWS COVERAGE OF 40 COUNTRIES, 1972-1976

	1972 Stories		1973 Stories		1974 Stories		1975 Stories		1976 Stories		Total Stories	
	Number	Percent	Number	Percent	Number	Percent	Number	Percent	Number	Percent	Number	Percent
United States	171	64%	130	63%	81	52%	153	62%	109	52%	644	59.2%
South Vietnam	108	40	43	21	8	5	43	17	12	6	214	19.7
U.S.S.R.	36	13	18	9	34	22	40	16	39	19	167	15.3
Israel	24	9	37	18	28	18	38	15	16	8	143	13.1
North Vietnam	81	30	32	15	1	1	8	3	1	0	123	11.3
Great Britain	20	7	16	8	12	8	19	8	24	11	91	8.4
France	30	11	15	7	8	5	9	4	13	6	75	6.9
People's Republic of China	31	12	9	4	5	3	11	4	18	9	74	6.8
Egypt	3	1	16	8	14	9	25	10	3	1	61	5.6
Lebanon	5	2	5	2	6	4	13	5	27	13	56	5.1
Cambodia	4	1	28	14	3	2	17	7	1	0	53	4.9
Syria	4	1	12	6	16	10	11	4	10	5	53	4.9
Japan	13	5	15	7	6	4	3	1	12	6	49	4.5
Northern Ireland	11	4	5	2	5	3	3	1	6	3	30	2.8
West Germany	14	5	5	2	2	1	4	2	4	2	29	2.7
Turkey	0	0	0	0	17	11	6	2	4	2	27	2.5
Cuba	2	1	2	1	2	1	3	1	14	7	23	2.1
Italy	3	1	3	1	3	2	4	2	9	4	22	2.0
Cyprus	0	0	1	0	16	10	4	2	1	0	22	2.0
Canada	1	0	4	2	5	3	3	1	8	4	21	1.9
Greece	0	0	4	2	10	6	3	1	3	1	20	1.8
Laos	3	1	9	4	2	1	5	2	1	0	20	1.8
Philippines	7	3	3	1	2	1	4	2	3	1	19	1.7
Saudi Arabia	0	0	7	3	3	2	4	2	4	2	18	1.7
Portugal	0	0	0	0	3	2	12	5	2	1	17	1.6
Angola	0	0	0	0	0	0	2	1	14	7	16	1.5
Spain	2	1	0	0	2	1	6	2	5	2	15	1.4
Argentina	0	0	2	1	2	1	6	2	5	2	15	1.4
South Africa	0	0	0	0	0	0	1	0	14	7	15	1.4
Thailand	2	1	1	0	0	0	6	2	5	2	14	1.3
India	5	2	2	1	2	1	4	2	0	0	13	1.2
Jordan	2	1	0	0	3	2	7	3	1	0	13	1.2
Mexico	2	1	1	0	3	2	0	0	6	3	12	1.1
Netherlands	0	0	1	0	2	1	7	3	2	1	12	1.1
South Korea	6	2	0	0	0	0	3	1	2	1	11	1.0
Rhodesia	0	0	0	0	0	0	0	0	10	5	10	0.9
Sweden	3	1	1	0	1	1	2	1	3	1	10	0.9
Switzerland	1	0	1	0	2	1	3	1	3	1	10	0.9
Chile	1	0	2	1	2	1	2	1	2	1	9	0.8
Uganda	0	0	0	0	0	0	4	2	5	2	9	0.8

Source: Larson, James (1978), pp. 76, 81, 82.

The figures indicate that the total number of correspondents—full-time, part-time and stringers—decreased between 1951 and 1963, then increased steadily from 1963 to 1969, and, finally, decreased again by 8.4 percent between 1969 and 1971. The number of *full-time* foreign correspondents increased sharply between 1951 and 1963, declined between 1963 and 1966, rebounded to just above the 1963 level in 1969, and has declined in the years since. In 1975, the number of full-time correspondents was 27 percent below what it had been in 1969 and 15 percent below its 1971 level. It is not possible to tell from these figures whether part-time correspondents or stringers have been hired since 1969 to substitute for the declining numbers of full-time correspondents overseas.

The percentage distribution of U.S. foreign correspondents by location indicates that a fairly constant pattern has been in effect for many years. The majority of correspondents are stationed in Europe, and this has been the case since 1951, when Anderson (1951) counted the number of U.S. foreign correspondents abroad. Just under a quarter of this country's foreign correspondents have been stationed in Asia (largely in Hong Kong and Japan) and in Australia since 1963. The Western Hemisphere accounts for between 12 and 19 percent of all correspondents, with one-third of the full-time correspondents in 1975 on assignment in Canada.

The Middle East and Africa each have accounted for 5 to 8 percent of U.S. correspondents over this period. The drop to 2 percent for Africa in 1975 may be a statistical artifact, since examination of earlier data shows that the American media have traditionally relied heavily on stringers and part-time correspondents for their African coverage.

Table 700–B. (Cont'd.)

NBC EVENING NEWS COVERAGE OF 40 COUNTRIES, 1972-1976

	1972 Stories Number	Percent	1973 Stories Number	Percent	1974 Stories Number	Percent	1975 Stories Number	Percent	1976 Stories Number	Percent	Total Stories Number	Percent
United States	170	66%	135	65%	100	50%	142	59%	95	53%	642	59.0%
South Vietnam	106	41	44	21	5	2	39	16	9	5	203	18.7
U.S.S.R.	36	14	21	10	41	20	32	13	24	13	154	14.2
North Vietnam	81	31	30	14	0	0	13	5	0	0	124	11.4
Israel	11	4	36	17	36	18	28	12	13	7	124	11.4
Great Britain	18	7	12	6	26	13	17	7	20	11	93	8.5
France	36	14	18	9	14	7	11	5	12	7	91	8.4
Egypt	7	3	19	9	14	7	24	10	7	4	71	6.5
People's Republic of China	21	8	7	3	8	4	8	3	14	8	58	5.3
Cambodia	8	3	31	15	1	1	16	7	0	0	56	5.1
Syria	3	1	11	5	21	10	8	3	9	5	52	4.8
Lebanon	2	1	4	2	10	5	11	5	19	11	46	4.2
West Germany	10	4	8	4	7	3	8	3	10	6	43	4.0
Japan	12	5	10	5	10	5	4	2	5	3	41	3.8
Cuba	5	2	2	1	3	1	6	3	9	5	25	2.3
Northern Ireland	12	5	5	2	5	2	2	1	1	1	25	2.3
Italy	3	1	3	1	4	2	7	3	5	3	22	2.0
Greece	0	0	2	1	14	7	3	1	3	2	22	2.0
Thailand	4	2	4	2	1	1	10	4	3	2	22	2.0
Turkey	0	0	0	0	13	6	3	1	5	3	21	1.9
Canada	3	1	4	2	3	1	4	2	6	3	20	1.8
Portugal	0	0	0	0	3	1	13	5	4	2	20	1.8
Saudi Arabia	0	0	7	3	8	4	4	2	1	1	20	1.8
Spain	0	0	1	0	3	1	7	3	7	4	18	1.7
Laos	5	2	8	4	1	1	4	2	0	0	18	1.7
Cyprus	1	0	0	0	15	7	0	0	0	0	16	1.5
Switzerland	2	1	1	0	7	3	4	2	2	1	16	1.5
South Korea	4	2	2	1	1	1	6	3	3	2	16	1.5
Chile	6	2	2	1	5	2	1	0	1	1	15	1.4
Philippines	4	2	6	3	0	0	3	1	2	1	15	1.4
Angola	0	0	0	0	0	0	4	2	10	6	14	1.3
Jordan	1	0	2	1	7	3	3	1	1	1	14	1.3
South Africa	1	0	0	0	0	0	0	0	12	7	13	1.2
Belgium	4	2	0	0	2	1	4	2	2	1	12	1.1
Netherlands	2	1	3	1	3	1	3	1	1	1	12	1.1
Poland	4	2	4	2	0	0	2	1	2	1	12	1.1
Iran	3	1	3	1	1	1	1	0	4	2	12	1.1
India	7	3	1	0	1	1	3	1	0	0	12	1.1
Denmark	5	2	4	2	0	0	1	0	0	0	10	0.9
Sweden	2	1	4	2	1	1	1	0	1	1	9	0.8

Source: Larson, James (1978), pp. 77, 83, 84.

Examination of which nations have ranked highest in the number of U.S. correspondents reveals little change in the top five, with the obvious exception of South Vietnam. Kliesch (1975, p. 19) points out that there is a notable imbalance in the distribution of U.S. correspondents around the world. The 10 countries with the largest number of U.S. correspondents in 1975 (the eight nations listed in **Table 700-A**, plus Canada and Israel) account for 72 percent of the total number of correspondents. The concentration was even higher in 1969, when 77 percent of U.S. correspondents were located in 10 countries.

In **Table 700-B**, the focus shifts from the distribution of U.S. correspondents overseas to the distribution of international news stories on American television evening news programs. This table lists 40 nations and the number and percentage of television news stories that refer to each of the countries. The data were gathered in a random sample of network evening news broadcasts during the 1972-1976 period.

A thorough analysis of this information would require much time and attention, but several overall characteristics of this table can be noted. First, the countries receiving the most attention on U.S. television news shows are almost identical for all three networks. Second, while all of the news stories in this analysis are international in character—that is, the stories include the mention of at least one foreign country or international organization—the United States is also mentioned in nearly 60 percent of the stories. Third, it is clear that a few countries are mentioned much more often than the rest. In fact, only about 15 of the more than 200 countries and territories in the world are mentioned in more than 2 percent of all the international news stories sampled.

Table 700–C.
**News Agency and Newspaper Sources of the International News Items
in 16 Latin American Newspapers, 1975**

News Agency, Newspaper, etc.	Number of Items	Percentage
United Press International	506	39.0
Associated Press	270	21.0
Agence France-Presse	132	10.0
Reuter-Latin	123	9.0
EFE (Spain)	111	8.0
ANSA (Italy)	55	4.0
LATIN[a]	49	4.0
New York Times	31	2.0
Le Monde	12	1.0
Washington Post	7	0.5
Prensa Latina (Cuba)	4	0.3
Others	8	0.5
Total	1,308	100.0[b]

Source: Reyes Matta (1976), p. 32.

Notes: Samples were taken during a four-day period in November, 1975. (a) LATIN is an agency of large Latin American newspapers. (b) Percentages do not total 100 percent because of rounding.

Finally, while major world powers naturally make up a significant percentage of the most-mentioned nations on the list, a look at the year-to-year fluctuations recorded in **Table 700**-B is also revealing. For example, the reader will note the impact of the events of the Vietnam War, the flurry of interest in Cyprus and the surrounding area in 1974, and the rising coverage of southern African countries, such as Angola, Rhodesia, and South Africa. Portugal and Lebanon represent two other cases in which political crises attracted unusually high news coverage by the networks.

Tables 700-C and **700**-D turn the emphasis of the preceding table around by recording the sources and the sites of international news coverage in 16 Latin American newspapers over a four-day period in 1975. As **Table 700**-C demonstrates, more than 60 percent of the international news items in these Latin American newspapers came from U.S. news agencies. **Table 700**-D reveals the extent to which the United States and some U.S. cities receive coverage in Latin American newspapers.

All of the tables in this unit illustrate a problem that was expressed by a UNESCO report (1953, p. 200) 25 years ago:

With regard to the world news, the point to emphasize is that no truly international news agency has yet come into existence. . . . The six [major] world agencies are themselves, in reality, national in character. They have set up organizations which cover the entire globe, because the press and radio of the countries in which they have their headquarters are very highly developed and demand a world-wide news service. They have also undertaken distribution in a great number of countries, either directly or through national agencies. But their capital, their directors and chief executives, [and] the majority of the staff they employ are from the United States, Britain, France, or [the U.S.S.R.] . . . The news they collect and distribute is chosen, written up, and presented almost entirely by United States, British, French, or Russian journalists. No newspaper, no broadcasting station anywhere in the world, can obtain news on world events except as seen, selected, and edited by these men and women. And however impartial they may be—however strictly they may comply with the professional code of ethics—they will inevitably judge and present news from the viewpoint of the country of which they are citizens.

Table 700–D.
**Cities Receiving the Most Attention in the International News Items
in 16 Latin American Newspapers, 1975**

Note: Samples were taken during a four-day period in November 1975.

	Total News Coverage (column cm.)	Percentage of News Coverage		Number of News Items	Average Length of Item (column cm.)
		Including Madrid	Excluding Madrid		
United States, Total	4,427	19.0%	24.0%	157	28.2
Washington	2,462	11.0	13.0	89	27.6
New York	1,043	4.5	6.0	32	32.5
Detroit	472	2.0	2.5	16	29.5
California Cities	276	1.0	1.5	14	19.7
Dallas	174	1.0	1.0	6	29.0
Madrid	4,182	18.0	- -	103	40.6
Lisbon	2,538	1.0	14.0	54	47.0
Beirut	1,028	4.5	5.5	34	30.2
London	879	4.0	5.0	33	26.6
Buenos Aires	816	3.5	4.0	29	28.0
Moscow	656	3.0	3.5	25	26.2
Paramaribo	629	3.0	3.0	23	27.3
Rome	505	2.0	3.0	19	26.5
Santiago, Chile	500	1.0	3.0	21	23.8
UN, Geneva	474	2.0	2.5	22	21.5
Jerusalem/Tel Aviv	459	2.0	2.5	16	28.6
Bogota	431	2.0	2.0	20	21.5
Paris	429	2.0	2.0	16	26.8
Lima	369	1.5	2.0	14	26.3
La Paz	366	1.5	2.0	8	45.7
Hong Kong	185	1.0	1.0	8	23.1
Subtotal	18,873	82.5	79.0	602	31.4
Others	3,958	17.5	21.0	N/A	N/A
Total	22,831	100.0%	100.0%	N/A	N/A

Source: Reyes Matta (1976), p. 35.

Note: Madrid was the site of extraordinary events during the four-day period when the sample was taken—hence, the "including" and "excluding Madrid" columns. See text.

Sources

Table 700-A is a compilation of the work of three scholars who have attempted to record the nature and extent of this nation's overseas news corps. Up until 1975, the method for collecting these tallies was to obtain correspondent lists from U.S. embassies and Press Clubs abroad. The lists were then sent to senior correspondents in the countries in question for local verification. Yet, as Kliesch (1975, p. 18) points out: "The lists nevertheless were found on occasion to lack names and, at other times, to include names of nonjournalists or of newsmen no longer working in that country."

For 1975, and for a three-year update to be completed in 1978, a new method of estimating the number of foreign correspondents was used. Kliesch (p. 18) describes this new method:

It was decided this time to turn to media headquarters for names and locations of their personnel. Most major media were contacted in person. Virtually all others, including many minor organizations whose names surfaced as a result of the 1972 survey or perusals of *Editor and Publisher Yearbook* and other media lists, were queried by telephone or letter (with telephone followup). Although many of the smaller organizations reported only stringer use or no foreign-gathered content at all, there were virtually no nonrespondents.

This method of data-gathering still has its limitations, however. As noted earlier, the post-1971 figures omit stringers and part-time correspondents. Thus, whereas the earlier method of data-collection tended to overestimate the correspondent population, this new method does not report the full extent of news gathering by the U.S. media abroad.

The information in **Table 700-B** was collected by Larson (1978) as part of a doctoral dissertation completed at Stanford's Institute for Communication Research. The source of these data were the abstracts of evening network news shows contained in the *Television News Index and Abstracts*, published by the Vanderbilt Television News Archive. The researcher's method of coding began with a decision as to whether a story was "national" or "international." Stories that mentioned international organizations or countries and territories other than the United States were coded as "international" and are the only news stories counted for this table.

To determine the reliability of the *Television News Index and Abstracts*, the researcher compared audio tapes of a random sample of television newscasts with the abstracts of these newscasts. This test verified that the abstracts were a reliable measure of international news coverage. The editors therefore regard the data presented in **Table 700-B** as valid and reliable, but they also urge the reader to consult the original source, since space does not permit a detailed explication of the coding methods involved in the Larson study.

The Reyes Matta (1976) study, from which **Tables 700-C** and **700-D** are taken, was less formal than Larson, but typical of a great number of similar studies performed over the past several years. The Reyes Matta study's methodology was not fully explained with the results, but its coding methods were straightforward: The source of each story, in terms of news agency and city of origin, was counted for each story defined as "international." The study's major limitations are (1) its short time period (only four days), and (2) its restricted sample (a "representative selection" of South and Central American newspapers).

Further Information

Two bibliographies—Richstad and Bowen (1976) and Gerbner and Marvanyi (1977)—are of use in finding studies on international news flow and related subjects. The first of these sources is annotated; the other is not. Desmond (1978) provides a good integrated history of the early development of news communications and news agencies. General works dealing with this subject include Gerbner (1977), Oettinger et al. (1977), Richstad (1977), Read (1976), Schiller (1971, 1976), and Tunstall (1977).

In addition, Dr. Ralph E. Kliesch is continuing to update his series on the American overseas press corps. He welcomes inquiries and solicits corrections, additions, or deletions to the list of foreign correspondents which appears in Kliesch (1975). Dr. Kliesch's address is: School of Journalism, Ohio University, Athens, Ohio 45701. Dr. Kliesch and his associates are also at work on a project to measure the number of correspondents, from all countries, who are stationed in or covering news events in the Third World nations.

U.S. Government Media Activities Abroad 701

Interpretation of Tables

Table 701-A reflects changes in the appropriations, employment levels, and budgetary allocations of the United States Information Agency (USIA) from 1955 to 1975. The major portion of USIA funding has always supported various overseas missions, most of which are attached to the American embassies. Among the specific USIA media operations abroad, radio (Voice of America) has received the greatest share of funding. The reader will also note that although USIA appropriations have increased over the years, overall employment levels have declined from the peaks of the mid-1960s.

Table 701-B provides data on international broadcasting and the role of U.S. broadcasting outlets in this field. The data for 1945 are approximations and are therefore not directly comparable to the information for later years. With the exception of Cuba, which was included because of its proximity to the United States, all of the nations listed on this table were responsible for at least 350 hours per week of international broadcasts.

Table 701–A.
Summary of USIA Budgets, Employment Levels, and Budgetary Allocations, 1955–1975

	1955	1960	1965	1970	1975
Total Obligated Funds (millions)	$78,614	$104,880	$157,200	$189,174	$240,431
Number of Employees					
Domestic	944	2,678	3,448	3,243	3,142
Foreign					
U. S.	N/A	1,256	1,520	1,364	1,118
Locals	5,878	8,006	7,197	5,770	4,889
Total Number of Employees	6,822	11,940	12,165	10,377	9,149
Budget Allocations by Function					
Radio	24%	17%	18%	21%	24%
Press/Publications	6	9	8	8	5
Films/TV	- -[a]	6	7	6	4
Information Centers	5	5	4	4	3
Overseas Missions	44	42	42	41	54
General Support	21	21	20	20	11

Sources: *USIA Report to the Congress* (title has varied): 4th (1955), 14th (1960), 24th (1965), 34th (1970), and 43rd (1975).

Note: (a) Television and films for 1955 are included under the radio entry.

The overall trend in **Table 701-B** is unmistakable: Most of the 11 nations listed have increased their weekly international broadcast hours since the 1950s. Until 1970, the United States broadcast far more hours per week than any other nation, but this lead had been cut sharply by 1973.

Table 701-C examines the language and the target regions of Voice of America broadcasts over a 25-year period. These figures represent *approximate* hours of broadcast time per week, but the trend remains valid: Throughout the 25-year period, the Voice of America has focused on the Soviet Union, Eastern Europe, and the Far East. Africa and Latin America have received far less attention.

Table 701-D reveals the U.S. government's long-secret role in supporting Radio Liberty and Radio Free Europe—a role which was acknowledged only in the early 1970s. Support from private donations has always been insignificant and had declined to almost nothing in 1975.

Table 701-E provides a summary view of Radio Liberty and Radio Free Europe programming content in 1975. Radio Liberty directs its broadcasts to the Soviet Union, while Radio Free Europe broadcasts to the Eastern European communist nations.

Sources

Most of the data in **Table 701-A** and in **Tables 701-C** through **701-E** were reported by the USIA and Board for International Broadcasting (BIB) (for Radio Liberty and Radio Free Europe) during their annual treks to Congress for funding. In that sense, these data were released in the interest òf self-preservation. However, the data are also audited by various other governmental agencies and should therefore be considered reliable.

Except for the 1945 figures, the information on foreign broadcasting in **Table 701-B** was originally gathered by the British Broadcasting Corporation's External Broadcasting Audience Research division and reprinted in the Presidential Study Commission on International Radio (1974)—for the 1950-1970 data—and in Hale (1975) for the 1973 data. The 1945 figures were estimated by the editors from a chart, "Growth and Competition in International Broadcasting," in the *Foreign Service Journal* (1967).

Table 701–B.
Weekly Broadcast Hours of U. S. Radio Stations vs. International Stations of Other Nations, 1945–1973

Geographical Area	Number of Broadcast Hours Per Week						
	1945	1950	1955	1960	1965	1970	1973
United States	1,175	497	1,285	1,495	1,877	1,907	2,060
Voice of America	1,175	497	N/A	640	830	863	882
Radio Free Europe	- -	- -	N/A	444	1,077	547	576
Radio Liberty	- -	- -	N/A	411		497	602
USSR	550	533	656	1,015	1,417	1,908	1,952
People's Republic of China	- -	66	159	687	1,027	1,591	1,584
Warsaw Pact Nations (Except USSR)	- -	386	783	1,009	1,215	1,264	1,297
Cuba	- -	- -	- -	- -	325	320	327
BBC External Service	730	643	558	589	667	723	711
Federal Republic of Germany	- -	- -	105	315	671	779	806
Egypt	- -	- -	100	301	505	540	613
Albania	- -	26	47	63	153	487	490
Spain	- -	68	98	202	276	251	361
Netherlands	- -	127	120	178	235	335	370
11 Nation Total	N/A	2,346	3,911	5,854	8,368	10,105	10,571

Sources: 1945 data: *Foreign Service Journal* (February 1967), p. 21. 1950-1970 data: Presidential Study Commission on International Radio Broadcasting (1974), p. 13. 1973 data: Hale (1975), appendix B, p. 174.

Further Information

The best up-to-date discussion of the USIA and the BIB appears in the annual congressional budget hearings. These hearings offer a wealth of statistical information on current and past fiscal years, as well as insights into the rationale for the policies of these agencies.

The best current discussion of U.S. government broadcasting can be found in Abshire (1976) and Hale (1975), while the report of the Presidential Study Commission on International Radio Broadcasting (1973) provides interesting comparative statistics on Soviet broadcast efforts and the changes in U.S. policy. The reader should see the USIA annual reports for data on the Voice of America and other agency affairs, and the BIB annual reports for further information on Radio Liberty and Radio Free Europe. The most interesting and useful books on the USIA are those by Elder (1968) and Henderson (1969). Critical analyses of USIA and BIB activities are available in the reports by the GAO (1974, 1976). An overview of international propaganda can be found in Martin (1971).

Table 701–C.
Weekly Broadcast Hours of Voice of America, by Reception Area and Language of Broadcast, 1950–1975

Language and Target Region	1950	1955	Hours Broadcast Per Week[a] 1960	1965	1970	1975
English (both world-wide and specific regions/countries)	63:00	49:00	161:00	260:45	225:45	202:00
Vernacular Languages						
Eastern Europe and USSR	55:30	396:48	204:45	178:30	171:30	251:30
Middle East and North Africa	10:00		66:30	52:30	49:00	56:00
South Asia		87:30	24:30	21:00	21:00	28:00
Africa	26:15		3:30	31:30	42:30	51:00
Far East		197:45	140:00	175:00	248:30	143:00
Latin America	19:15	- -	14:00	85:30	71:30	49:00
Western Europe	26:15	- -	- -	- -	- -	- -
Total Weekly Broadcast Hours	**200:15**	**731:03**	**614:15**	**804:45**	**829:45**	**780:30**
Percent of English-Language Broadcasts	*31%*	*7%*	*26%*	*32%*	*27%*	*26%*

Sources: 1950 data: *The Voice of America, 1950-51*, p. 2. All other data from *USIA Reports to Congress* as follows: 1955: *4th Report*, pp. 28-29. 1960: *14th Report*, p. 25. 1965: *24th Report*, pp. 26-27. 1970: *34th Report*, p. 17. 1975: *43rd Report*, p. 94.

Note: (a) All data as of June 30th for year listed.

Table 701–D.
Sources of Financial Support for Radio Liberty and Radio Free Europe, 1950–1975

	Government Funding	Private Donations
1950	$ 3,108,969	- -
1956	16,937.731	$1,864,775
1960	21,785,979	1,613,574
1965	27,418,824	1,364,274
1970	32,844,535	1,277,280
1975[a]	49,550,000	181,392

Source: Board for International Broadcasting, *Third Annual Report, 1977*, p. 62.

Note: (a) Figures for 1975 do not include the operating expenses of the Board for International Broadcasting, which was formed in 1973.

Table 701–E.
Breakdown of Subject Matter of Broadcasts by Radio Free Europe and Radio Liberty, 1975

Subject Matter	Radio Liberty	Radio Free Europe[a]
Political, Economic, Social	41%	26%
News	31	32
Cultural	10	6
Music	- -	30
Documents	10	- -
Religion	1	2
Other	7	6

Source: Board for International Broadcasting, *Second Annual Report, 1975*, p. 45.

Note: (a) Figures do not add to 100 percent due to rounding.

Import and Export Trade in the U.S. Book Industry   710

Interpretation of Tables

Table 710-A details the growth, in current dollar values, of the import and export of books in the United States over the last 42 years. With the exception of a leveling-off of imports during World War II and a decline in exports during the 1948-1952 period, the general trend for both U.S. Census Bureau series has been upward, with accelerated growth in book imports and exports during the late 1950s and throughout the 1960s, followed by slower growth in more recent years. Note that World War II affected book imports and exports differently—imports declined, whereas exports increased rather dramatically during the war years.

Converting the Table 710-A figures to constant dollars reveals much the same pattern, except that the pattern becomes more extreme. Between 1935 and 1955, for example, the value of book imports remains almost unchanged, whereas from 1955 to 1965, the constant dollar value of book imports increases more than four-fold.

It is difficult to accurately interpret the figures in Table 710-A because of changes in the Census Bureau's accounting procedures in 1950 and again in 1969. These changes decreased the percentage of book imports and exports that were reported, but the amount of the percentage decrease remains uncertain (see the discussion of this problem in the "Sources" section below).

Table 710-B lists the top 25 importers of U.S. books at 10-year intervals for the last 40 years. Canada has remained the primary destination for U.S. printed matter during this period, but the rankings of the other importing countries have changed considerably. The data reveal that political changes, such as Philippine independence, World War II, and the Chinese and Cuban revolutions, have influenced the rankings. But beyond this observation, the information in Table 710-B is difficult to interpret without systematic study. Especially interesting would be a multiple-regression analysis of these data, predicting book sales to a country in terms of such characteristics as distance from New York City, per-capita income of the importing nation, English-speaking nations versus other languages, etc.

Table 710-C breaks down the U.S. book import-export figures for recent years by type of book. The greatest increases in both imports and exports appear to be among religious and children's books. Exports of encyclopedias have declined recently.

As a contrast to the Census Bureau figures in the above tables, Tables 710-D and 710-E present data from a different source, the annual surveys of the Association of American Publishers (AAP). Comparison of the figures in Tables 710-C and 710-D reveals a considerable difference

Table 710–A.
Value of Imports and Exports by U. S. Book Industry, 1935–1976

Year	Imports	Exports
1935	$ 3,697,852	$ 4,052,680
1936	3,465,554	4,297,136
1937	3,804,694	5,514,063
1938	3,574,102	5,543,646
1939	3,251,485	5,010,456
1940	2,444,786	4,495,950
1941	1,811,944	4,907,879
1942	1,331,417	5,080,131
1943	1,375,057	7,020,325
1944	1,595,805	8,913,049
1945	1,930,863	12,035,736
1946	3,700,529	19,406,151
1947	4,387,025	24,294,851
1948	5,644,285	20,271,324
1949	6,523,830	20,427,531
1950	7,153,793	16,100,785
1951	7,074,654	18,821,732
1952	8,460,531	20,490,736
1953	8,195,346	23,911,986
1954	8,461,097	25,378,455
1955	8,727,534	27,628,222
1956	11,355,353	30,871,227
1957	13,471,094	36,576,036
1958	14,867,540	39,003,227
1959	17,444,326	44,707,626
1960	20,749,821	51,232,037
1961	24,063,249	56,966,054
1962	31,904,301	65,113,619
1963	37,836,951	77,746,675
1964	42,999,284	88,642,210
1965	46,852,971	99,322,588
1966	59,738,609	120,803,303
1967	69,241,912	143,193,226
1968	68,391,884	151,623,195
1969	78,352,540	166,141,099
1970	92,022,837	174,936,928
1971	100,993,571	176,662,158
1972	136,936,899	172,114,797
1973	133,860,747	194,515,884
1974	150,737,313	242,692,633
1975	147,557,721	269,348,834
1976	157,949,973	298,780,694

Source: Bureau of the Census.

between the import-export book sales recorded by the federal government and those reported by the trade association. As noted below in the "Sources" section, the AAP information is probably more valid. However, the format of the AAP figures has changed recently, so it is difficult to chart trends.

According to the AAP in **Table 710-D**, foreign sales of all U.S. trade books in 1976 represented about 4.8 percent of all U.S. publishers' sales. **Table 710-D** also points up interesting differences in book exports by type of book and by the geographical area of the sales. For example, the percentage of technical/scientific and medical books sold abroad is much larger than for other kinds of books.

Table 710–B.
Top 25 Nations Importing Books from U. S., 1935–1975

Note: All dollar figures in thousands.

1935

Country	U. S. Book Exports	Percent of Total
Canada	$1,628.5	40.2%
Philippines	809.1	20.0
United Kingdom	699.5	17.3
Argentina	128.3	3.2
Australia	111.9	2.8
Japan	104.0	2.6
South Africa	74.5	1.8
Brazil	66.4	1.6
China	54.3	1.3
British India	54.2	1.3
Mexico	51.4	1.3
Panama	43.4	1.1
New Zealand	20.6	.5
Germany	16.1	.4
Cuba	14.0	.3
Palestine	11.4	.3
Colombia	11.1	.3
Newfoundland/Labrador	9.4	.2
Uruguay	9.2	.2
Netherlands	8.1	.2
France	7.7	.2
Denmark	7.3	.2
Chile	6.3	.2
Venezuela	5.2	.1
Siam	5.0	.1
Other Countries	95.5	2.4
Total	$4,052.7	100.0%

Table 710-E compares foreign and domestic sales of U.S. textbooks at the El-hi (elementary and secondary) and college levels. Unlike Table 710-D, the dollar values shown here represent the estimated textbook sales of the *entire* U.S. book publishing industry (Table 710-D figures include only the sales of publishers reporting to the AAP). Thus, Table 710-E indicates that about 4.4 percent of all U.S. El-hi textbook sales were made outside the United States, while around 9.7 percent of all sales of college texts were to foreign markets.

The index figures in Table 710-E, based on sales figures for the 1966-1968 period, reveal that El-hi textbook sales abroad in 1976 were up 60 percent from 1966-1968, compared to a 46 percent increase for that period in domestic El-hi textbook sales. Among college texts, the growth in sales during this period was virtually the same in the U.S. and foreign markets. However, some interesting variations can be seen in college textbook sales in the different foreign markets.

Table 710-F presents another way of measuring the impact of U.S. book exports on the world market. (Differences in classification account for the different dollar figures here and in Table 710-A). Compared with the figures for 13 other book-exporting countries, the U.S. share of the total world market has declined significantly over the last 10 years. However, the drop in the U.S. market share does not mean an absolute drop in U.S. exports. Between 1966 and 1975, for example, U.S. exports increased by a modest 13 percent, measured in constant dollars.

Children's picture and painting books are not included in the totals in Table 710-F. The figures for this category of book are as follows: In 1975, the U.S. exported $6,326,000 worth of children's books—26.5 percent of the 14-country total on Table 710-F, and up from the 20 percent U.S. share of this market in 1971. The 1975, 14-country total for children's books was $23,903,000, of which $1,548,000 was exported to the U.S. Thus, the U.S. percentage of the 14-country total for exports outside the U.S. was 28.3 percent in 1975, up from 24.3 percent in 1971.

Tables 710-G and 710-H list the U.S. book-import totals as recorded by another source—the "Weekly Record" column of *Publishers Weekly*. As with virtually all new American book titles,

Table 710–B. (Cont'd.)

1945

Country	U. S. Book Exports	Percent of Total
Canada	$6,089.0	50.6%
United Kingdom	1,096.3	9.1
Australia	909.2	7.6
Philippines	570.2	4.7
Brazil	514.7	4.3
South Africa	425.9	3.5
Mexico	217.7	1.8
India	205.1	1.7
New Zealand	178.2	1.5
Palestine/Trans-Jordan	121.1	1.0
U.S.S.R.	97.6	.8
Cuba	92.0	.8
Argentina	91.7	.8
Sweden	89.8	.7
Colombia	80.3	.7
Chile	68.8	.6
France	64.0	.5
China	57.2	.5
Egypt	53.4	.4
Canal Zone	52.1	.4
Jamaica	42.3	.4
Venezuela	39.5	.3
Curacao	37.5	.3
Portugal	36.0	.3
Belgium/Luxembourg	31.3	.3
Other Countries	774.6	6.4
Total	$12,035.7	100.0%

imported book titles are reported to the "Weekly Record" as a pro forma notice to the trade of the existence of the imported books on the U.S. market. *Publishers Weekly* has been collecting this information for a number of years and, since 1958, has presented it as part of its annual report of book-trade statistics.

As with the reporting of American book-title output (see Section 110), some textbooks and mass-market paperbacks are excluded from the *Publishers Weekly* import data. In addition, major changes in the definition of "imports" have so severely affected the early data in **Table 710-G** that it is impossible to identify any general trends for the full 20-year period represented on the table. (See the discussion of these limitations in the "Sources" section below.) Since 1967, however, the definitions have remained constant; and from the figures for this period, one can see that the over-all number of book titles imported into the United States has declined somewhat.

Table 710-H provides a breakdown of the 1974-1976 book-import figures by subject matter. These figures can be compared with the identical breakdown for new U.S. book titles in **Table 510-B**. The reader will note that a larger proportion of the imports are in the categories of sociology/economics, science, and medicine.

Sources

The data in **Tables 710-A, 710-B**, and **710-C** come from the U.S. Bureau of the Census, which compiles the information from records of the U.S. Customs Bureau. For exports, these Customs records consist of copies of the Shipper's Export Declaration, which must be prepared by the American exporter. Since 1975, the Census Bureau has been compiling complete figures for all export shipments of goods valued at $1,000 or more. Shipments valued between $251 and $999 are estimated by the Census Bureau from a 50 percent sample of the Export Declarations.

Table 710–B. (Cont'd.)

1955

Country	U. S. Book Exports	Percent of Total
Canada	$15,955	57.7%
United Kingdom	2,526	9.1
Brazil	1,290	4.7
Philippines	971	3.5
Australia	595	2.2
Japan	585	2.1
India	566	2.0
Mexico	397	1.4
South Africa	356	1.3
New Zealand	312	1.1
Colombia	233	.8
Netherlands	206	.7
Venezuela	180	.7
West Germany	168	.6
France	135	.5
Panama	89	.3
Sweden	82	.3
Belgium	78	.3
Peru	73	.3
Italy	66	.2
Indonesia	62	.2
Switzerland	62	.2
Chile	55	.2
Thailand	47	.2
Denmark	41	.1
Other Countries	2,498	9.0
Total	$27,628	100.0%

The large volume of U.S. exports to Canada has resulted in different standards for goods shipped to that neighboring nation. The Census Bureau compiles complete figures for shipments to Canada only when the exports are valued at $2,000 or more. U.S.-Canadian shipments valued between $251 and $1,999 are estimated from a 10 percent sample of the Export Declarations.

Neither export nor import shippers in the United States are required to report shipments of goods valued at $250 or less—thus, the Census Bureau data do not include this category of the U.S. import-export trade. This omission causes severe problems for the validity of the import-export statistics for the U.S. book industry, since a great many shipments of books overseas or from abroad are in amounts of $250 or less. Book-trade statisticians have estimated the Census Bureau's underreporting of U.S. book exports at between 50 and 70 percent (Grannis, 1972, p. 128). The situation for book-import figures is supposed to be somewhat better, with Census Bureau import totals estimated to be about 10 percent under the actual value of such shipments (Grannis). The rankings of U.S. book-importing countries in **Table 710-B** can still be considered valid, since the Census Bureau's underreporting of book exports apparently affects all foreign destinations uniformly.

The historical comparability of the book-export data is also affected by the $250 minimum for the filing of Shipper's Declarations for the Customs Bureau; for before 1950, most exports, regardless of value, were recorded by customs agents and the Census Bureau. Then, from 1950 until the third quarter of 1969, the Customs Bureau made $100 the required minimum reporting level. In the fourth quarter of 1969, the minimum was raised to $250, and all shipments valued between $251 and $500 were merely estimated by the Census Bureau from a 50 percent sample. The 1975 change mentioned earlier raised the range of the 50 percent sample to exports valued at $251-$999. Obviously, these changes have affected the comparability of the statistics to some degree.

Table 710–B. (Cont'd.)

1965

Country	U. S. Book Exports	Percent of Total
Canada	$43,480	43.8%
United Kingdom	11,929	12.0
Japan	8,576	8.6
Australia	7,243	7.3
Philippines	2,399	2.4
South Africa	2,306	2.3
Netherlands	1,837	1.8
Brazil	1,815	1.8
Indonesia	1,488	1.5
Mexico	1,416	1.4
Italy	1,399	1.4
Sweden	1,220	1.2
New Zealand	1,129	1.1
India	1,088	1.1
Chile	1,008	1.0
West Germany	849	.9
Argentina	699	.7
Venezuela	585	.6
France	582	.6
Belgium	469	.5
Malaysia	458	.5
Panama	436	.4
Denmark	397	.4
Peru	374	.4
Spain	331	.3
Other Countries	5,812	5.9
Total	$99,323	100.0%

Other changes and omissions in the Census Bureau's book import-export statistics make these data difficult to compare and to assess. For example, up until 1965, several changes were made in the product categories for book trade import-export figures. A number of pertinent statistics are also left out of the Census Bureau summaries, including foreign rights, royalty, and translation payments and foreign book-club sales. (U.S. book-club sales to Canada equal more than 3 percent of all U.S. book-club sales.) Although U.S. publishers' sales to foreign subsidiaries are included in the Census Bureau trade statistics, the sales by these foreign holdings themselves are not recorded.

With all of these limitations, these data are best used merely for a broad estimation of the growth of U.S. import-export trade in books and for a fairly accurate notion of the changing destinations for exported book products. With the exception of the revision years of 1950-1951 and 1969-1970, the year-to-year fluctuations in the U.S.-foreign book trade can also be used with caution.

Tables 710-D and 710-E come from the 1976 AAP report of book industry statistics. These data are estimates based on the AAP surveys, which are mailed to publishers and returned on a voluntary basis. In Table 710-D, the foreign and domestic sales of 32 trade and 21 professional book publishers are reported. This group of respondents represents about 62 percent of the estimated trade book sales, and about 30 percent of the professional book sales of the entire industry. Thus, the trade book figures can probably be considered the more valid.

It is also difficult to assess the validity of the estimates in Table 710-E, since the AAP survey includes miscellaneous educational materials as well as text books. Moreover, only 23 publishers responded to the survey. Finally, and most important, the precise method by which the AAP arrives at these estimates is not explained in the source. Thus, the editors must consider the Table 710-E figures as good trade estimates, but nothing more. (The reader should also note that the foreign sales figures in Table 710-E include shipments to the U.S. Armed Forces, a category which is excluded in both the AAP data in Table 710-D and the Census Bureau reports represented in Tables 710-A, 710-B, and 710-C.)

Table 710–B. (Cont'd.)

1975

Country	U. S. Book Exports	Percent of Total
Canada	$118,564	44.0 %
United Kingdom	34,245	12.7
Australia	27,936	10.4
Japan	14,296	5.3
Netherlands	7,968	3.0
Mexico	6,487	2.4
South Africa	4,198	1.6
Brazil	3,737	1.4
West Germany	3,736	1.4
Italy	3,113	1.2
Singapore	3,032	1.1
India	2,620	1.0
Philippines	2,573	1.0
New Zealand	2,541	.9
Venezuela	2,227	.8
France	2,133	.8
Jamaica	1,910	.7
Indonesia	1,518	.6
Iran	1,457	.5
Switzerland	1,309	.5
Saudi Arabia	1,183	.4
Panama	1,084	.4
Peru	1,056	.4
Spain	986	.4
Argentina	984	.4
Other Countries	18,456	6.9
Total	$269,349	100.0 %

Source: Bureau of the Census.

The information in **Table 710-F** was originally compiled by the U.N. on the basis of export statistics supplied by the 14 countries listed in the table note. The U.S. book-export statistics in **Table 710-F** do not match those reported by the Census Bureau in earlier tables because of differences in aggregating the various subcategories of books in the Standard International Trade Classification used by the U.N. agency. The U.S. Census Bureau includes the subcategories listed in **Table 710-C**, while the U.N. excludes children's picture and painting books but includes bound newspapers and periodicals.

Tables **710-G** and **710-H** come originally from the compilations of new imported book titles listed in the "Weekly Record" column of *Publishers Weekly*. The 1956-1959 data in **Table 710-G** were taken directly from summary January issues of *Publishers Weekly*. The 1960-1973 figures were taken from *The Bowker Annual*, and the 1974-1976 figures are found in Grannis (1977). All of the material in **Table 710-H** are found in Grannis (1977).

Publishers Weekly generally relies upon the information on a book's copyright page to identify the publication as an import. If the copyright information identifies a book as "printed abroad and distributed on an exclusive basis in the United States"—and if not more than one year has elapsed since the book's initial publication abroad—the book is counted as an import.

Prior to 1964, *Publishers Weekly* also required a study of the book's history in order to determine that it had been "conceived, manufactured and originally published abroad and distributed in the United States by exclusive agreement." As imports increased, however, this procedure was abandoned as too time-consuming and difficult. This change in 1964 created a major statistical discontinuity, as did the 1967 requirement that "no more than a year should elapse between the time a book is published abroad and the time it is available in this country."

Table 710–C.
Value and Number of Imports and Exports by U. S. Book Industry, by Type of Book, 1967–1976

Note: All figures are in thousands.

Exports

	Textbooks Value	Technical/Scientific /Professional Books Value	Number	Religious Books Value	Number	Dictionaries Value	Number	Encyclopedias Value	Number	Other Books Value	Number	Children's Picture/ Painting Books Value	Number
1967	$30,003	$24,539	13,108	$ 4,981	9,339	$3,941	1,441	$33,551	8,037	$ 46,178	69,906	N/A	N/A
1968	29,807	23,978	11,860	5,733	12,271	3,626	1,070	39,145	9,714	49,334	72,734	N/A	N/A
1969	36,835	24,640	12,474	6,277	22,555	3,347	785	42,371	11,069	52,671	85,750	N/A	N/A
1970	38,694	24,856	11,289	5,826	22,429	4,219	1,178	46,109	11,109	52,666	74,846	$2,566	4,804
1971	41,278	31,537	13,951	6,531	20,376	3,618	764	32,170	8,713	58,137	79,499	3,391	11,249
1972	40,560	30,161	12,507	8,247	28,409	2,873	678	24,395	7,643	61,534	77,568	4,346	11,171
1973	43,832	35,773	16,168	9,686	28,800	3,321	759	25,960	8,296	70,595	93,036	5,350	13,172
1974	53,782	42,454	16,755	12,006	45,918	6,143	1,269	33,383	10,027	88,438	109,201	6,488	15,908
1975	63,896	43,955	15,320	13,320	47,257	4,447	1,202	31,905	10,176	105,504	114,497	6,317	16,524
1976	70,356	47,062	16,020	15,339	35,526	4,455	1,324	28,581	9,321	126,131	130,446	6,857	17,394

Table 710–C. (Cont'd.)

Imports

| | Religious Books | | Non-English Language | | Books by U. S. Citizen or Resident | | Other Books | | Toy/ Coloring Books |
	Value	Number	Value	Number	Value	Number	Value	Number	Value
1967	$3,599	2,799	$10,774	21,624	$3,344	2,422	$ 51,351	70,026	$ 173
1968	3,028	3,441	11,261	13,794	3,197	1,779	50,589	76,776	318
1969	3,103	4,011	10,687	9,299	2,970	2,314	60,431	101,747	1,162
1970	4,023	4,872	11,803	13,011	4,344	3,953	71,070	121,586	783
1971	4,241	6,191	10,751	11,262	3,392	3,590	81,257	162,388	1,352
1972	6,508	18,802	12,415	12,690	2,148	2,104	113,262	188,815	2,604
1973	4,168	32,810	13,958	15,743	2,280	1,578	111,103	177,103	2,352
1974	3,594	24,749	14,314	12,009	4,462	4,245	125,793	174,226	2,574
1975	4,676	7,252	16,900	14,596	3,591	3,102	120,928	153,591	1,463
1976	6,109	5,416	19,624	15,227	3,753	2,393	127,427	146,460	1,036

Source: U. S. Department of Commerce, Bureau of Domestic Commerce.

Table 710–D.
Net Domestic and Foreign Sales of U. S. Trade and Professional Books, by Nation or Geopolitical Area, 1976

Note: All dollar figures are in thousands.

Net Sales of Trade Books[a]

	Total United States Sales	Foreign Sales								Total Foreign Sales	Total Sales
		Canada	Latin America	Australia/ New Zealand	Asia	United Kingdom	Continental Europe	Africa, Near/ Middle East	Unspecified[b]		
All Books											
Net Sales	$339,860	$9,040	$367	$823	$807	$884	$1,117	$292	$3,826	$17,156	$357,016
Percent of Total Sales	*95.2%*	*3.3%*	*0.1%*	*0.3%*	*0.3%*	*0.3%*	*0.4%*	*0.1%*	*- -*	*4.8%*	*100.0%*
Adult Hardbound											
Net Sales	$128,961	$2,166	$254	$315	$553	$450	$891	$89	$1,218	$6,036	$134,997
Percent of Total Sales	*95.5%*	*2.1%*	*0.2%*	*0.3%*	*0.5%*	*0.4%*	*0.8%*	*0.1%*	*- -*	*4.5%*	*100.0%*
Adult Paperbound											
Net Sales	$50,601	$1,276	$76	$161	$132	$258	$157	$145	$595	$2,800	$53,401
Percent of Total Sales	*94.8%*	*3.0%*	*0.2%*	*0.4%*	*0.3%*	*0.6%*	*0.4%*	*0.3%*	*- -*	*5.2%*	*100.0%*
Juvenile Hardbound											
Net Sales	$47,782	$2,155	$10	$210	$62	$68	$29	$14	$481	$3,029	$50,811
Percent of Total Sales	*94.0%*	*5.0%*	*0.0%*	*0.5%*	*0.1%*	*0.2%*	*0.1%*	*0.0%*	*- -*	*6.0%*	*100.0%*
Juvenile Paperbound											
Net Sales	$6,085	$283	$2	$15	$2	$1	$2	$1	$46	$352	$6,437
Percent of Total Sales	*94.5%*	*5.1%*	*0.0%*	*0.3%*	*0.0%*	*0.0%*	*0.0%*	*0.0%*	*- -*	*5.5%*	*100.0%*
Religious											
Net Sales	$14,855	$373	$22	$46	$37	$71	$32	$23	$0	$604	$15,459
Percent of Total Sales	*96.1%*	*2.4%*	*0.1%*	*0.3%*	*0.2%*	*0.5%*	*0.2%*	*0.1%*	*- -*	*3.9%*	*100.0%*

Table 710–D. (Cont'd.)

Net Sales of Professional Books[c]

	Total United States Sales	Foreign Sales								Total Foreign Sales	Total Sales
		Canada	Latin America	Australia/ New Zealand	Asia	United Kingdom	Continental Europe	Africa, Near/ Middle East	Unspecified[b]		
All Books											
Net Sales	$140,674	$4,471	$2,816	$1,506	$3,131	$4,780	$3,711	$1,481	$4,370	$26,266	$166,940
Percent of Total Sales	*84.3%*	*3.2%*	*2.0%*	*1.1%*	*2.2%*	*3.4%*	*2.7%*	*1.1%*	*- -*	*15.7%*	*100.0%*
Technical/Scientific											
Net Sales	$36,663	$874	$1,143	$424	$1,718	$1,655	$2,066	$908	$350	$9,138	$45,801
Percent of Total Sales	*80.0%*	*2.0%*	*2.6%*	*1.0%*	*3.9%*	*3.8%*	*4.7%*	*2.1%*	*- -*	*20.0%*	*100.0%*
Business/Other Professional											
Net Sales	$32,797	$793	$101	$107	$158	$464	$496	$67	$128	$2,314	$35,111
Percent of Total Sales	*93.4%*	*2.4%*	*0.3%*	*0.3%*	*0.5%*	*1.4%*	*1.5%*	*0.2%*	*- -*	*6.6%*	*100.0%*
Medical											
Net Sales	$32,630	$986	$547	$404	$1,255	$728	$1,149	$506	$1,755	$7,330	$39,960
Percent of Total Sales	*81.7%*	*3.2%*	*1.8%*	*1.3%*	*4.1%*	*2.4%*	*3.8%*	*1.7%*	*- -*	*18.3%*	*100.0%*

Source: Association of American Publishers (1977), pp. 28, 57.

Notes: (a) As reported by 32 publishers. (b) For the purposes of computing the percentage of sales, the unspecified foreign sales have been distributed proportionally among the geographical categories. (c) As reported by 21 publishers.

Table 710–E.
Average Domestic and Foreign Sales of U. S. El-Hi
and College Textbooks, 1966–1976

Note: All dollar figures are in thousands.
Index figures are calculated on a base of 100 for the years 1966-68.

El-Hi Textbooks

Geographical Location	1966-68[a] Sales	1975 Sales	1975 Index	1976 Sales	1976 Index
Total Domestic U. S.	$415,784	$612,610	147	$609,029	146
Puerto Rico/ Other U. S. Possessions	2,162	2,507	116	3,229	149
Canada	8,967	19,374	216	18,793	210
Europe	1,527	1,925	126	2,574	169
Other[b]	7,191	6,660	93	6,933	96
Total Foreign	17,685	27,959	158	28,300	160
Total, All Sales	$435,631	$643,076	148	$640,558	147

College Textbooks

Geographical Location	1966-68[a] Sales	1975 Sales	1975 Index	1976 Sales	1976 Index
Total Domestic U. S.	$260,959	$473,590	181	$504,160	193
Puerto Rico/ Other U. S. Possessions	1,044	4,831	462	4,879	467
Canada	11,518	18,110	157	19,667	171
Europe	6,252	14,623	234	14,620	234
Other[b]	10,393	19,433	168	20,638	199
Total Foreign	28,163	52,166	185	54,925	195
Total, All Sales	$290,166	$530,587	183	$563,964	194

Source: Association of American Publishers (1977), pp. 103, 128.

Notes. (a) Figures in this column, which provide the base (100%) for the Index, represent the average for the years 1966 through 1968. (b) Includes sales to the Armed Forces.

Within the limits of the above definitions, these import figures from *Publishers Weekly* are probably as accurate as the trade magazine's data for American book title output. But the historical discontinuities mentioned above make it impossible to determine trends prior to 1967.

In 1977, *Publishers Weekly* instituted a new system of counting, for both the American and the imported new-titles series. Grannis (1977b, p. 32) describes the situation which led to the change:

> A number of factors over the past five years have combined to bring about increasing delays in listing, so that 12 months of listings became insufficient to represent the output of a given year compared to the output of the preceding year.

Some (not all) of these factors were: the process of adapting to new Library of Congress procedures; adjustment to increasingly sophisticated computer operation; and some shifts in internal operations. The greatest factor, however, has been the immense

Table 710-F.
Value of Book and Pamphlet Exports by the U. S.
and 14 Other Nations, 1966-1975

Note: All dollar figures are in thousands.

	Exports From 14 Countries[a]	United States Exports	
		Value	Percent of Total
World Exports, 1966-75			
1966	$447,993	$147,738	33.0%
1967	491,882	166,042	33.8
1968	540,606	174,571	32.3
1969	593,730	182,838	30.8
1970	637,379	184,377	28.9
1971	707,062	185,223	26.2
1972	825,224	180,017	21.8
1973	976,261	200,459	20.5
1974	1,115,633	249,509	22.4
1975	1,253,064	277,068	22.1
World Exports, Excluding Those to the U. S., 1966-75			
1966	402,471	147,738	36.7
1967	436,409	166,042	38.0
1968	478,767	174,571	36.5
1969	524,258	182,838	34.9
1970	560,549	184,377	32.9
1971	623,046	185,223	29.7
1972	725,417	180,017	24.8
1973	868,370	200,459	23.1
1974	1,002,616	249,509	24.9
1975	1,147,090	277,068	24.2

Sources: 1966-1970: Lofquist (1972), p. 17. 1971-1975: Bureau of International Economic Policy and Research, U. S. Department of Commerce (1976a), p. 1.

Note: (a) United States, Austria, Belgium/Luxembourg, Canada, Denmark, France, Federal Republic of Germany, Italy, Spain, Netherlands, Norway, Sweden, Switzerland, and the United Kingdom. These totals include items classified as books and pamphlets under Standard International Trade Classification (SITC) number 892.11. Children's picture and painting books (SITC 892.12) are not included.

increase in the amount of data arising from the CIP (Cataloguing in Publication) system and—with that factor—the increased difficulty in establishing prices and publication dates. The "Weekly Record," in fact, verifies prices and publication dates to round out partial CIP listings.

In order to arrive at more comprehensive totals for 1976 book title output . . . Bowker decided to postpone publication of the figures . . . available—based on 12 months of listings—and to count, in addition, the 1976 books that could be listed during a further six months of 1977—18 months in all.

Obviously, the 1976 figures based on 18 months of listings are not really comparable with the previous 12 months of listings. *It must be assumed, therefore, that the final 1976 counts . . . begin a new statistical series. Bowker intends to use similar procedures for the publications of 1977, 1978, and so on, so that the yearly data will be reasonably comparable.*

Further Information

Both *Publishers Weekly* and *Printing and Publishing* magazines occasionally feature articles on the international book trade. Each issue of *Printing and Publishing* contains the U.S. import-

Table 710–G.
Number of New Book Titles Imported by the U.S., 1956–1976

	New Books	New Editions	Total
1956	1,569	270	1,839
1957	1,755	284	2,039
1958	1,773	246	2,019
1959	1,595	305	1,900
1960	1,854	304	2,158
1961	1,374	194	1,568
1962	1,691	360	2,051
1963	1,778	383	2,161
1964[a]	3,954	843	4,797
1965	4,042	628	4,670
1966	5,468	879	6,347
1967[b]	4,107	745	4,852
1968	3,734	573	4,307
1969	3,587	516	4,103
1970	3,902	557	4,459
1971	3,408	474	3,882
1972	3,329	521	3,850
1973	2,915	368	3,283
1974	3,088	390	3,478
1975	3,792	367	4,159
1976	3,507	485	3,992

Sources: 1956-1959 data: *Publishers Weekly*, annual statistical issues (January of each year). 1960-1973 data: *Bowker Annual*, appropriate issues. 1974-1976 data: Grannis (1977), p. 36.

Notes: (a) The definition of "imported" was changed. Thus, figures for 1964 and after are not comparable with those for preceding years. See text. (b) A new time restriction was put on books which were to be included in the tally. Figures for 1967 and after are therefore not comparable with those for preceding years. See text.

export figures for the most recent quarter, but annual summaries and interpretative articles are more rare. January issues of *Publishers Weekly* provide an annual summary of import-export figures, which are then reprinted in *The Bowker Annual*. The annual book-import figures of the "Weekly Record" also appear in *Publishers Weekly* and in *The Bowker Annual*.

Many nations keep better book publishing statistics than the United States, at least to the extent that different, more extensive breakdowns are reported to UNESCO. The *UNESCO Statistical Yearbook* contains a great deal of this comparative information, including estimated world book production (number of titles and copies) by country, subject, region, and language of publication; number of copies by country; number of copies of first editions by country; world production of school textbooks and children's books (number of titles and copies); and number of translations by subject, country of publication, and original language. UNESCO also presents a list of the authors most frequently translated. Some of the information in the *UNESCO Statistical Yearbook* also appears in the more general *United Nations Statistical Yearbook*.

Table 710-H.
Number of New Book Titles Imported by the U.S., by Subject Matter of Books, 1974-1976

Subject Matter	1974 New Books	1974 New Editions	1974 Total	1975 New Books	1975 New Editions	1975 Total	1976 New Books	1976 New Editions	1976 Total	1976[a] New Books	1976[a] New Editions	1976[a] Total
Agriculture	37	3	40	58	7	65	52	12	64	77	13	90
Art	96	17	113	133	9	142	103	13	116	134	15	149
Biography	78	22	100	88	8	96	88	14	102	120	19	139
Business	71	8	79	61	5	66	56	9	65	73	11	84
Education	107	5	112	119	4	123	112	7	119	148	8	156
Fiction	30	6	36	26	11	37	52	16	68	60	19	79
General Works	92	19	111	109	10	119	111	5	116	140	8	148
History	87	11	98	167	21	188	213	25	238	265	30	295
Home Economics	17	5	22	26	1	27	26	3	29	34	4	38
Juveniles	18	9	27	12	1	13	30	2	32	33	3	36
Language	58	11	69	114	11	125	78	12	90	113	14	127
Law	53	5	58	46	6	52	51	11	62	66	14	80
Literature	140	15	155	196	14	210	135	35	170	176	45	221
Medicine	273	67	340	347	74	421	317	99	416	417	114	531
Music	13	6	19	16	1	17	28	4	32	32	5	37
Philosophy, Psychology	105	9	114	116	6	122	102	8	110	142	10	152
Poetry, Drama	69	8	77	133	12	145	143	24	167	177	26	203
Religion	60	10	70	74	9	83	72	21	93	87	23	110
Science	691	56	747	764	53	817	629	56	685	802	63	865
Sociology, Economics	630	41	671	858	51	909	796	50	846	1,030	63	1,093
Sports, Recreation	40	9	49	64	6	70	81	13	94	110	14	124
Technology	149	24	173	178	33	211	168	30	198	234	38	272
Travel	174	24	198	87	14	101	64	16	80	78	19	97
Total	3,088	390	3,478	3,792	367	4,159	3,507	485	3,992	4,548	578	5,126

Source: Grannis (1977), p. 36, citing data from *Publishers Weekly.*

Note: (a) This second set of 1976 data are based on a new 18-month reporting period. Earlier data are on a 12-month basis.

Table 720–A.
Value of U. S. Newspaper and Periodical Exports and Imports, 1941–1976

Note: All figures are in thousands.

	Exports			Imports		
	Newspapers	Periodicals	Total	Newspapers	Periodicals	Total
1941	$1,452	$ 4,920	$ 6,372	N/A	N/A	N/A
1942	1,494	6,125	7,619	N/A	N/A	N/A
1943	1,550	6,343	7,893	N/A	N/A	N/A
1944	1,034	6,362	7,396	N/A	N/A	$ 460
1945	950	7,691	8,641	N/A	N/A	1,577
1946	1,512	12,932	14,444	N/A	N/A	1,809
1947	1,490	15,443	16,933	N/A	N/A	1,911
1948	1,793	13,371	15,164	N/A	N/A	1,948
1949	1,930	14,285	16,215	N/A	N/A	1,351
1950	1,878	15,859	17,737	N/A	N/A	973
1951	1,984	21,702	23,686	N/A	N/A	2,456
1952	2,419	24,495	26,914	N/A	N/A	2,846
1953	2,467	28,346	30,813	N/A	N/A	2,140
1954	2,703	28,774	31,477	N/A	N/A	2,358
1955	2,595	29,827	32,422	N/A	N/A	2,221
1956	2,709	31,152	33,861	N/A	N/A	2,207
1957	3,438	32,288	35,726	N/A	N/A	N/A
1958	3,932	32,043	35,975	N/A	N/A	N/A
1959	3,878	35,114	38,992	N/A	N/A	N/A
1960	3,602	39,538	43,140	N/A	N/A	N/A
1961	2,731	44,862	47,593	N/A	N/A	N/A
1962	2,326	45,851	48,177	N/A	N/A	2,723
1963	2,219	46,333	48,552	N/A	N/A	N/A
1964	2,331	54,451	56,782	$ 1,829	$ 4,545	6,374
1965	2,770	65,226	67,996	2,494	3,640	6,134
1966	3,142	74,166	77,308	2,869	3,366	6,235
1967	2,872	76,434	79,306	3,507	3,843	7,350
1968	2,926	78,089	81,015	4,778	5,697	10,475
1969	3,636	78,994	82,630	5,540	8,031	13,571
1970	2,837	83,675	86,512	6,788	16,895	23,683
1971	3,753	86,502	90,255	8,147	16,465	24,612
1972	2,365	97,814	100,179	11,753	19,091	30,844
1973	1,414	105,313	106,727	13,305	23,105	36,410
1974	2,011	130,971	132,982	21,370	26,551	47,921
1975	4,345	147,605	151,950	26,744	25,215	51,959
1976	5,263	158,265	163,528	25,823	25,647	51,470

Sources: Exports, 1941-1943: U. S. Bureau of the Census, *Foreign Commerce and Navigation of the United States* (1941, 1942, 1943); 1944-1976: U. S. Bureau of the Census, *U. S. Exports, Schedule B, Commodity by Country* (1944-1964, volume for calendar year; 1965-1976, December issue of appropriate year). Imports, 1944-1976: U. S. Bureau of the Census, *U. S. Imports, General* and *Consumption Schedule A, Commodity by Country*.

Interpretation of Tables

Table 720-A presents import-export figures for the newspaper and periodicals industries in the United States. U.S. periodical exports have exceeded those for newspaper exports by an enormous amount. In 1976, for example, the value of exported U.S. periodicals was more than 30 times the value of exported newspapers. The situation for imports of newspapers and periodicals into the United States is more balanced, with newspaper imports steadily gaining on periodicals and finally exceeding periodical imports for the first time in 1976.

Table 720–B.
Value of Newspaper and Periodical Exports by the U. S.
Compared with 14 Other Nations, 1966–1975

Note: All dollar figures are in thousands.

	Exports From 14 Countries[a]	United States Exports Value	United States Exports Percent of Total
World Exports, 1966-75			
1966	$227,867	$ 50,374	22.1 %
1967	257,362	56,459	21.9
1968	284,408	57,940	20.4
1969	335,565	65,920	19.6
1970	364,150	76,727	21.1
1971	393,877	79,086	20.1
1972	444,386	88,743	20.0
1973	543,202	97,180	17.9
1974	622,557	121,089	19.5
1975	710,676	140,234	19.7
World Exports, Excluding Those to the U. S., 1966-75			
1966	217,568	50,374	23.2
1967	245,515	56,459	23.0
1968	270,150	57,940	21.4
1969	319,151	65,920	20.7
1970	337,426	76,727	22.7
1971	367,221	79,086	21.5
1972	413,745	88,743	21.4
1973	503,506	97,180	19.3
1974	578,280	121,089	20.9
1975	665,637	140,234	21.1

Sources: 1966-1970: Lofquist (1972), p. 28. 1971-1975: Bureau of International Economic Policy and Research, U. S. Department of Commerce (1976b), p. 1.

Note: (a) United States, Austria, Belgium/Luxembourg, Canada, Denmark, France, Federal Republic of Germany, Italy, Japan, Netherlands, Norway, Sweden, Switzerland, and the United Kingdom. These totals include items classified as newspapers and periodicals under Standard International Trade Classification (SITC) number 892.2. Not included are bound newspapers and periodicals (SITC 892.116), which are included in the figures for books and pamphlets (SITC 892.11) in Table 710-F.

The United States has been a net exporter of periodicals for at least as long as these statistics have been recorded. However, the gap between exports and imports is narrowing. In 1967, the ratio of periodical exports to imports was about 20 to 1. By 1976, the ratio had diminished to just over 6 to 1.

The relative rise in newspaper imports into the United States has been even more startling. In 1967, U.S. newspaper imports exceeded exports by a ratio of 1.22 to 1, but by 1976, the United States had become a net importer of newspapers, with a 4.9 to 1 import-export ratio.

Periodical and newspaper exports, in combination, achieved their greatest rate of growth during the 1950s. This growth slowed during the 1960s, but has accelerated somewhat since 1970. Periodical and newspaper imports, on the other hand, have been doubling in constant dollar value about every five years since 1965.

Table 720-B compares newspaper-periodical export statistics for the United States alone and for the United States in combination with 13 other nations. The U.S. share of the world newspaper/periodicals market has declined slightly over the past decade; and since 1972, the United States has ceded the world lead to Germany. However, this decline is not so serious as the one affecting U.S. book exports (see **Table 710-F**), since the whole story of the U.S. periodicals industry overseas is probably not reflected in these figures (see the "Sources" section below).

Table 720-C presents the top 25 nations which import U.S. newspapers and periodicals, along with the percentage of total U.S. exports which each nation represents. The reasons for some changes on this list are obvious—for example, the disappearance of Cuba by 1965 (Cuba ranked

Table 720–C.
Value of U.S. Exports of Newspapers and Periodicals to Top 25 Importing Nations, 1945–1975

Note: All dollar figures are in thousands.

1945

Nation	Total Value of U. S. Exports	Percent of Total Exports
1. Canada	$6,640	76.8%
2. United Kingdom	350	4.0
3. Brazil	321	3.7
4. Mexico	216	2.5
5. Cuba	205	2.4
6. Argentina	132	1.5
7. USSR	121	1.4
8. South Africa	95	1.1
9. New Zealand	83	1.0
10. Venezuela	56	- -
11. Portugal	32	- -
12. Chile	31	- -
13. Australia	29	- -
14. Egypt	29	- -
15. Bermuda	26	- -
16. Iceland	25	- -
17. Panama	24	- -
18. Canal Zone	24	- -
19. Jamaica	23	- -
20. Colombia	22	- -
21. Sweden	20	- -
22. Curacao	18	- -
23. Newfoundland	16	- -
24. Philippines	14	- -
25. India	13	- -
All Other Nations	75	- -

fifth on the list in 1945 and fourth in 1955). Other fluctuations cannot be explained without additional data and research. Several factors would be of interest, including the language, political-economic system, per-capita income, and literacy level of the importing nations; the proximity of the nations to the United States; and the extent to which U.S. exports are depressed by the presence of U.S.-owned subsidiary firms in a nation.

Sources

The data for **Tables 720-A, 720-B,** and **720-C** were gathered from newspaper and periodical exporters in the United States and abroad by the U.S. Customs Bureau, and then aggregated by the U.S. Census Bureau. All of these figures are limited in a number of ways which severely affect meaningful interpretation.

For example, the annual totals for newspaper and periodical imports and exports in **Table 720-A** have limited value as indicators of historical trends because of changes (1) in the minimum-value reporting level for shippers to and from the United States, and (2) in the product categories from which the totals are compiled. Changes in the minimum values for Customs declarations are explained in Unit 710. The changes took place in 1950 and 1969 for exports, and in 1954 and 1969 for imports. Changes in product categorization occurred in 1965 for periodical exports and in 1967 for newspaper and periodical imports.

Another limiting factor for these data is the common practice of offering *individual* international subscriptions to newspapers or magazines. All such subscriptions are, of course, unrecorded by the Customs and Census Bureaus. Although there is no available estimate of the number of

Table 720–C. (Cont'd.)

| | 1955 | |
Nation	Total Value of U. S. Exports	Percent of Total Exports
1. Canada	$23,779	73.3%
2. United Kingdom	2,473	7.6
3. Mexico	870	2.7
4. Cuba	730	2.3
5. South Africa	577	1.8
6. Venezuela	487	1.5
7. France	287	- -
8. Brazil	278	- -
9. Italy	227	- -
10. Netherlands	174	- -
11. Sweden	171	- -
12. West Germany	160	- -
13. Japan	145	- -
14. New Zealand	122	- -
15. Belgium	115	- -
16. Israel	108	- -
17. Saudi Arabia	107	- -
18. British Malaya	102	- -
19. Philippines	101	- -
20. Norway	94	- -
21. Jamaica	92	- -
22. Colombia	91	- -
23. Bermuda	82	- -
24. Uruguay	70	- -
25. Ireland	68	- -
All Other Nations	911	2.8

U.S. newspaper and periodical exports which go unrecorded, book industry statisticians have suggested that as much as 70 percent of all book exports are not reported (Grannis, 1972, p. 128). It may well be that with individual international subscriptions, the underreporting of exported newspapers and periodicals is even more extensive.

Yet another problem is the different formulas used by different agencies for aggregating the same data. For example, the totals for U.S. exports of newspapers and periodicals vary from **Table 720-A** to **Table 720-B** because the Census Bureau (the source of **Table 720-A**) includes shipments of *bound* newspapers and periodicals in its newspaper-periodicals totals, whereas the Department of Commerce (the source of **Table 720-B**) uses the Standard International Trade Classifications (SITC) of the U.N. and therefore classifies bound periodicals and newspapers as "books" (see **Table 710-F**). In addition, some of the tallies for imports and exports are based on sample estimates, while others are exhaustive (see the "Sources" discussion in Unit 710).

At this point, the reader may question the value of any of the data on the international newspaper and periodical trade. But the problems with these data are even more extensive and complex. Lofquist (1969, p. 12) notes that the type of export figures given in **Tables 720-A, 720-B,** and **720-C** reflect sales from U.S. parent companies to their foreign subsidiaries, but do not include the sales by the subsidiaries themselves. In a parallel study, Hokkanen (1969) discovered that the total number of *international* editions of U.S. magazines and of independent foreign language magazines published abroad by U.S. companies increased by 88.2 percent during the nine-year period from 1961 to 1969. The circulation of these U.S.-based foreign periodicals went up 126.5 percent. The size of these increases suggests that such publications must be taken into account in any thorough examination of the U.S. print media overseas.

A final problem with the data in these three tables is the inclusion of Canada in the import-export tallies. Canada has consistently accounted for more than 60 percent of all recorded U.S.

Table 720–C. (Cont'd.)

| | 1965 | |
Nation	Total Value of U. S. Exports	Percent of Total Exports
1. Canada	$41,562	61.1%
2. United Kingdom	5,677	8.3
3. Australia	2,675	3.9
4. Mexico	2,260	3.3
5. Switzerland	1,233	1.8
6. Venezuela	1,213	1.8
7. West Germany	1,092	1.6
8. South Africa	950	1.4
9. Japan	838	1.2
10. France	775	1.1
11. India	771	1.1
12. Panama	715	1.1
13. New Zealand	671	1.0
14. Netherlands	563	- -
15. Colombia	515	- -
16. Argentina	482	- -
17. Sweden	478	- -
18. Peru	469	- -
19. Philippines	464	- -
20. Jamaica	383	- -
21. Belgium	374	- -
22. Malaysia	322	- -
23. Guatamala	243	- -
24. Italy	242	- -
25. Brazil	224	- -
All Other Nations	2,803	4.1

exports of publications. Consequently, that nation has a massive and rather misleading impact upon the total figures. In addition, these figures do not take into account the extensive Canadian publishing operations of some U.S. periodical companies which publish and print Canadian editions.

Further Information

The Standard Rate and Data Service's publications, *Consumer Magazine and Farm Publication Rates and Data* and *Business Publication Rates and Data*, list international editions of U.S. periodicals and foreign magazines owned by U.S. firms. Here, the reader will find circulation figures and other specific information of use to advertisers. However, with the exception of the article by Hokkanen (1969) described above, the editors are not aware of any analyses of these data.

The U.S. Department of Commerce magazine, *Printing and Publishing*, is the best single source of articles interpreting U.S. import-export statistics. Aside from this publication, the next best sources are private publications available from international advertising agencies.

Additional data are available when the search is broadened from U.S. newspapers and periodicals abroad to more general international information about newspapers and periodicals. For example, the *Editor and Publisher International Yearbook* lists newspapers published in most countries around the world. Related features include the number and circulation of Canadian dailies (similar to the data prepared for the United States), as well as a listing of group owners of newspapers in Canada. (Canadian entries may also be covered in directories of U.S. newspapers and periodicals. One example is the *Ayer Directory of Publications*.)

The United Nations presents various descriptions of newspaper and periodical publishing activity in the world. Its best publication is probably the *UNESCO Statistical Yearbook*, which

Table 720–C. (Cont'd.)

Nation	1975 Total Value of U. S. Exports	Percent of Total Exports
1. Canada	$102,334	67.3%
2. Australia	10,021	6.6
3. United Kingdom	6,966	4.6
4. Venezuela	3,623	2.4
5. Mexico	3,232	2.1
6. New Zealand	2,910	1.9
7. Netherlands	2,248	1.5
8. France	1,911	1.3
9. West Germany	1,689	1.1
10. Japan	1,484	1.0
11. South Africa	1,238	- -
12. Colombia	888	- -
13. Belgium	774	- -
14. Italy	694	- -
15. Peru	663	- -
16. Sweden	616	- -
17. Philippines	599	- -
18. Switzerland	519	- -
19. Israel	489	- -
20. Jamaica	456	- -
21. Dominican Republic	432	- -
22. Bermuda	305	- -
23. Brazil	297	- -
24. Saudi Arabia	277	- -
25. Guatamala	261	- -
All Other Nations	7,026	4.6

Sources: U. S. Bureau of the Census, *U. S. Exports, Commodity by Country* (1945), pp. 47-48; (1955), pp. 365-366; (December 1965), pp. 486-487; and (December 1975), pp. 2-456 and 2-457.

Note: Unspecified percentage figures are all less than one percent.

lists the number of dailies in each country, by circulation; the number, circulation, and circulation per 1,000 inhabitants of nondaily general-interest newspapers and other periodicals, by country; and the number and circulation of periodicals other than general-interest newspapers, by subject group and country. Further information on newspapers in other countries can be found in *World Communications* (UNESCO, 1975).

Table 721–A.
Value of U. S. Printing Machinery Exports, 1943–1976

Year	Total U. S. Exports (thousands)
1943	$ 1,191
1944	3,406
1945	5,542
1946	12,606
1947	33,107
1948	39,950
1949	44,866
1950	39,273
1951	35,823
1952	28,328
1953	29,761
1954	36,473
1955	40,562
1956	39,022
1957	40,059
1958	37,749
1959	35,884
1960	48,082
1961	57,629
1962	67,714
1963	72,905
1964	86,990
1965	77,360
1966	88,268
1967	98,366
1968	109,352
1969	124,113
1970	144,246
1971	136,091
1972	152,778
1973	216,832
1974	280,715
1975	308,179
1976	309,953

Source: U. S. Bureau of the Census, *U. S. Exports, Schedule B, Commodity by Country* (appropriate calendar years).

Interpretation of Tables

The printing and publishing industries are currently undergoing a technological revolution. Publishers around the world are converting their operations to photocomposition, offset printing, and integrated, automated printing and binding systems, as well as to a number of photographic and information-processing technologies which, previously, had no applications in the printing trades. As **Tables 721**-A and **721**-B reveal, the world market for new printing equipment has been growing very quickly in recent years. Between 1971 and 1975, the average annual rate of growth in this industry was approximately 15 percent.

Table 721–B.
Value of Printing Machinery Exports by the U. S.
Compared with 14 Other Nations, 1971–1975

Note: All dollar figures are in thousands.

	Exports From 14 Countries[a]	United States Exports	
		Value	Percent of Total
World Exports, 1971-75			
1971	$ 773,752	$137,286	17.7%
1972	876,579	160,155	18.3
1973	1,217,252	218,845	18.0
1974	1,421,129	283,107	19.9
1975	1,378,191	310,465	22.5
Exports to the U. S., 1971-75[b]			
1971	74,414	- -	0.0
1972	79,170	- -	0.0
1973	119,941	- -	0.0
1974	115,096	- -	0.0
1975	104,838	- -	0.0
World Exports, Excluding Those to the U. S., 1971-75[b]			
1971	699,338	137,286	19.6
1972	797,409	160,155	20.1
1973	1,097,311	218,845	19.9
1974	1,306,034	283,107	21.7
1975	1,273,352	310,465	24.4

Source: Data compiled by editors by totaling subcategories in Bureau of International Economic Policy and Research, U. S. Department of Commerce (1976c, p. 1; 1976d, p. 1; 1976e, p. 1).

Notes: (a) United States, Austria, Belgium/Luxembourg, Canada, Denmark, France, Federal Republic of Germany, Italy, Japan, Netherlands, Norway, Sweden, Switzerland, and the United Kingdom. The figures include totals for Standard International Trade Categories 718.21, Bookbinding Machinery; 718.22, Type-making and Type-setting Machinery; and 718.29, Other Printing Machinery, not elsewhere specified. (b) Totals of exports to the United States and exports to the world excluding the United States may not add to the world export total because of rounding.

The United States' share of this market has expanded as rapidly as the market itself. **Table 721-A** traces the U.S. export pattern for printing equipment over the past 34 years, from 1943 through 1976. Even with the current dollar figures provided in the table, it is evident that U.S. exports remained unchanged from about 1948 until 1959. (In constant dollars, the exports did not exceed their 1949 level until 1962.) Since the early 1960s, these exports have risen rapidly, and American producers of printing equipment now increasingly rely on exports to maintain their sales growth. At present, the United States is second only to Germany in printing equipment exports and the undisputed leader in the export of typemaking and typesetting machinery.

Table 721-B compares U.S. exports of printing equipment with those of 13 other exporting nations and shows that the U.S. percentage of total exports has grown in recent years. However, these aggregate figures were compiled from the totals of three subcategories, and these subcategories reveal mixed trends. Between 1971 and 1975, for example, the U.S. share of bookbinding machinery exports declined from 20.1 percent to 15.0 percent. On the other hand, figures for the general printing machinery category show the U.S. share of world sales rising from 15.0 percent in 1971 to 19.9 percent in 1975. The greatest increase in the world market share for the United States has been in the typemaking and typesetting machinery category, which rose from 25.5 to 34.2 percent over this same five-year period.

Sources

Table 721-A is based on declarations made by exporters to the U.S. Customs Bureau. The figures are then compiled by the U.S. Census Bureau. The validity problems of minimum reporting levels and percentage estimations of sales under $1,000—problems which limit the usefulness of book, newspaper, and periodical export figures (see Units 710 and 720)—are not a factor in the case of printing equipment, since such equipment is generally exported in fairly expensive shipments. The editors assume that the 3 percent error factor estimated for all U.S. exports would be appropriate or even a little high for this industry.

The editors compiled the totals for **Table 721-A** by combining the annual exports data listed for a number of international trade subclassifications. Since 1965, these subclassifications have included the following: bookbinding machines and parts; typesetting machines; electrotyping, stereotyping, and photoengraving machines; printing blocks, plates, etc., which are engraved, etched, or impressed (not textile, leather, or wallpaper); printing blocks, plates, etc., which are planed, grained, etc., and prepared for engraving or impressing; parts and accessories, not classified elsewhere, for typesetting, electrotyping, stereotyping, and other such machinery; printing presses, letterpress type; printing presses, offset type; printing presses, gravure type; printing presses which are not classified elsewhere; printing machines which are not classified elsewhere; and parts and accessories, not classified elsewhere, for printing machines and printing presses. Prior to 1965, these subcategories were somewhat different and less detailed.

Table 721-B comes from a United Nations compilation of the same data used in **Table 721-A**. The editors were unable to find the exact reason for the different figures reported for U.S. exports by the two sources. However, because differences in classification led to the discrepancies between figures for the export of books, newspapers, and periodicals (see Units 710 and 720), the editors suspect that the same problem may also be operating here.

The data used in **Tables 721-A** and **721-B** are also available in a breakdown by country of destination. **Table 721-B** data are also disaggregated by the major countries of origin.

Further Information

Aside from occasional articles in *Printing and Publishing*, a quarterly publication of the Construction and Forest Products Division of the U.S. Department of Commerce, very little has been done to record time-series trends in this field. The Bureau of International Commerce of the Commerce Department provides a number of services for potential exporters, including publication of market surveys of various countries.

UNESCO publishes occasional papers relevant to questions concerning the importation and exportation of print media technologies. One of these UNESCO publications, Smith (1977), provides insight into the implications of this technological revolution for developing nations and explains how the economies of a nation's printing and publishing operations change in relation to the availability of newer printing machinery.

Finally, the Domestic and International Business Administration of the U.S. Department of Commerce (1974) lists some of the forces which are responsible for the adoption of new technologies in the publishing industries.

Import/Export Trade in U.S. Motion Picture Industry 740

Interpretation of Tables

This unit provides the reader with different ways of analyzing the impact of both imported films on the American market and American films in overseas markets. In all cases, the discussion and data are limited to commercially produced feature films. For government film efforts, see Unit 701; for domestic nontheatrical films, see Unit 140.

Table 740-A illustrates the increasing reliance of American exhibitors on imported feature films. The table also shows that most of the imports have come from independent distribution firms rather than from the major Hollywood distributors. The reader should be warned that although the drop in the proportions of imports after 1968 would seem to indicate a trend, the change is actually due to variations in the reporting methods of the different sources of these data (see "Sources" section below).

Table 740-B ranks the top foreign markets for U.S. feature films in the past 15 years. The table raises the interesting question of which particular characteristics of a foreign country predispose it to rent more or fewer U.S. feature films. *Variety* estimates that over the 1963-1975 period, the top five film-importing nations accounted for 43 percent of overseas rentals of American films; the top 10 countries for 66 percent; and the top 15 for 75 percent.

Table 740–A.
Number, Percentage, and Distribution Source of Imported Feature Films Released in the U. S. Market, 1927–1972

Year	Number of Film Imports	Percent of All Releases in U. S.	Source of Imported Films Major U. S. Distributors	Independent U. S. Distributors
1927	65	8.7%	9	56
1928	193	21.8	83	160
1929	145	20.5	14	181
1930	86	14.5	6	86
1931	121	19.5	17	104
1932	196	28.6	18	178
1933	137	21.3	21	116
1934	182	27.5	11	171
1935	241	31.5	16	225
1936	213	29.0	14	199
1937	240	30.8	15	225
1938	314	40.8	16	298
1939	278	37.0	21	257
1940	196	29.1	15	181
1941	106	17.7	11	95
1942	45	8.4	12	33
1943	30	7.0	10	20
1944	41	9.3	8	33
1945	27	7.2	6	21
1946	89	19.1	13	76
1947	118	24.3	10	108
1948	93	20.3	23	70
1949	123	25.7	10	113
1950	239	38.1	21	218
1951	263	40.2	43	220
1952	139	34.5	26	113
1953	190	35.6	16	174
1954	174	40.7	28	146
1955	138	35.2	26	112
1956	207	43.2	27	180
1957	233	43.7	48	185
1958	266	52.5	63	203
1959	252	57.4	41	211
1960	233	60.2	65	168
1961	331	71.6	64	267
1962	280	65.6	60	220
1963	299	71.2	56	243
1964	361	71.9	58	303
1965	299	66.2	69	230
1966	295	65.4	56	239
1967	284	61.5	70	214
1968	274	60.4	79	195
1968[a]	123	--	--	--
1969	108	43.0	--	--
1970	99	32.4	--	--
1971	111	35.5	--	--
1972	103	33.0	--	--

Sources: 1927-1968 data: *Film Daily Yearbook 1969.* 1968 (second)-1972 data: *Variety* estimates, quoted in Office of Telecommunication Policy, *Analysis of the Causes and Effects of Increases in Same-Year Rerun Programming and Related Issues in Prime-Time Network Television* (1973), table 15.

Note: (a) The different sources for pre- and post-1968 data are the probable explanation for the marked drop in import totals beginning with the second set of 1968 figures.

Table 740–B.
U. S. Motion Picture Industry's 15 Largest Foreign Markets, 1963–1975

Country (listed in 1975 order)	Ranking in Order of Total Revenue for Year												
	1963	1964	1965	1966	1967	1968	1969	1970	1971	1972	1973	1974	1975
Canada	6	5	4	3	3	3	3	4	3	3	2	1	1
Japan	5	6	6	6	5	5	5	2	6	5	6	4	2
Italy	2	2	2	2	2	2	2	2	2	2	1	2	3
France	4	4	5	5	4	4	4	3	4	4	5	7	4
West Germany	3	3	3	4	4	6	6	5	5	6	3	6	5
United Kingdom	1	1	1	1	1	1	1	1	1	1	4	5	6
Australia	8	8	7	8	7	7	8	6	7	7	7	3	7
Spain	7	7	8	7	8	8	9	8	9	8	10	8	8
Brazil	10	10	11	10	8	9	7	7	8	9	9	10	9
South Africa	11	10	10	9	9	10	11	9	10	11	8	9	10
Mexico	9	9	9	11	10	11	10	10	11	10	11	11	11
Sweden	15	12	13	13	11	13	12	12	13	13	12	12	12
Switzerland	17	15	15	16	15	- -	16	14	16	15	- -	- -	13
Netherlands	22	17	19	18	19	20	19	15	19	14	16	15	14
Venezuela	14	14	16	15	16	16	15	13	12	12	14	14	15
Argentina	12	11	12	12	12	12	13	11	14	17	15	13	40

Sources: 1963, 1968 and 1973-1975 data: Tunstall (1977), p. 299, citing *Variety*. All other years: *Variety* (May 14, 1973).

Table 740–C.
U. S. Motion Picture Industry's Film Rental Income
from Domestic and Foreign Markets, 1963–1975

Note: All figures in millions of dollars.

	U. S. Rentals	Foreign Rentals	Total Rental Income
1963	$239.4	$293.0	$ 532.4
1968	372.0	339.0	711.0
1973	390.0	415.0	806.0
1974	545.9	494.8	1040.7
1975	628.0	592.0	1220.0

Sources: 1963, 1968, 1973, and 1975 data: Tunstall (1977), p. 299. 1974 data: *Variety* (September 1, 1976), p. 1.

The scattered financial information provided in **Table 740-C** demonstrates that foreign rentals of American films brought in more than half of the U.S. film industry's income until 1974, when a series of highly successful American-made films temporarily enhanced the domestic market.

Table 740-D provides further data on the export market for American feature films, with a calculation of the percentage of U.S. films among all of the films shown each year in selected foreign countries. The reader should note that with a declining Hollywood output, the proportions of American films shown abroad are also declining. Note also that the biggest film-*producing* countries in the world, Japan and India, import a substantially larger number of American films than other countries.

The **Table 740-D** data for 1960-1961 and 1970-1972 are not directly comparable to the earlier information, because the most current figures represent a comparison of imported U.S. films versus all *imported* films shown in a country. In many cases, of course, imported features are by no means even a majority of all exhibited films.

Sources

As noted on **Table 740-A**, the figures through 1968 are from the *Film Daily Yearbook 1969*, which was the final issue of that publication. The second set of 1968 figures and all subsequent annual figures are estimates drawn from *Variety* and reprinted in a report by the White House Office of Telecommunications Policy (OTP) (1973). The OTP publication provides an excellent analysis of the material and its source. The difference in the reporting methods of *Variety* and the *Film Daily Yearbook* is the likely cause of the apparent dramatic drop in the figures indicating the proportion of imported films shown in the United States in recent years.

All of the data in **Table 740-B** were originally reported in *Variety*. The figures for 1963, 1968, and 1973-1975 are reprinted and analyzed in Tunstall (1977); the data for all other years were taken directly from *Variety* by the editors, who converted the *Variety* rental figures to numerical rankings.

The **Table 740-C** source is Tunstall (1977), except for the 1974 data, which are drawn from *Variety*. All of the data were originally compiled by the Motion Picture Export Association of America and published in *Variety*.

The **Table 740-D** data for 1925, 1928, and 1937 come from Tunstall (1977), citing the *Harvard Business Review* for the first two years and the U.S. Department of Commerce, *Review of Foreign Film Markets*, for the 1937 figures. The 1948 figures are also found in Tunstall (1977), who summarizes data from UNESCO's *World Communications* (1950).

The data for 1960-1961 and 1970-1972 were extracted by the editors from UNESCO's *World Communications* (1964 and 1975). The editors arrived at the 1960-1961 and 1970-1972 figures by dividing the number of American-made imported films into the total number of films *imported* by each country during the sample periods. Thus, as noted earlier, the data for these last two columns are not directly comparable to those in the first four columns of **Table 740-D**. Moreover, the 1960-1961 and 1970-1972 data probably inflate the economic importance of U.S. films in some of these countries, such as Japan and India, in which there is a substantial amount of domestic film production.

Table 740–D.
U.S. Percentage of Foreign Feature Films Exhibited in Overseas Markets, 1925–1972

Country	1925	1928	1937	1948	1960-61	1970-72
Europe						
Austria	- -[a]	50%	- -	30%	38%	31%
Benelux nations	- -	- -	- -	74	34	31
Czechoslovakia	- -[a]	48	- -	18	- -	9
France	70%	63	45%	40	- -	- -
Germany	60	47	18	50[b]	36[b]	35[b]
Hungary	- -[a]	80	- -	25	- -	17
Italy	65	70	75	64	41	53
Scandinavia	85	65	- -	58	41	43
Spain/Portugal	90	85	- -	67[c]	40	36[c]
United Kingdom	95	81	65	68	49	52
Africa						
Egypt	- -	- -	76	35	72	46
Ethiopia	- -	- -	- -	90	90	39
Tunisia	- -	- -	- -	60	- -	48
North America						
Canada	95	95	75	77	47	40
Mexico	90	95	80	35	83	49
South America						
Argentina	90	90	70	50	56	60
Brazil	95	85	85	70	41	- -
Colombia	- -	- -	80	50	- -	- -
Asia						
India	- -	- -	46	5	90	69
Indonesia	- -	- -	- -	65	31	25
Israel	- -	- -	- -	55	39	28
Japan	30	22	34	30	56	49
Oceania						
Australia	} 95	82	75	85	- -	30
New Zealand		90	- -	83	46	43

Sources: 1925-1937 data: Tunstall (1977), p. 284, citing *Harvard Business Review* for 1925 and 1928, and *Review of Foreign Film Markets* for 1937. 1948 data: Tunstall (1977), pp. 289-292, summarizing data based on UNESCO's *World Communications* (1950). 1960-1961 data: *World Communications* (1964). 1970-1972 data: *World Communications* (1975).

Notes: (a) The figures for Austria, Czechoslovakia, and Hungary were combined in the 1925 report. In combination, the three countries took 25 percent of their 1925 feature films from the United States. (b) The 1948 figure is from the U.S.-occupied Zone only. The 1960-61 and 1970-72 figures represent West Germany only. (c) Portugal is not included in this figure.

Further Information

The best analysis of the international operations of American motion picture companies since World War II is by Guback (1969), although it is now a little dated. Nevertheless, the book provides a framework into which new data, gleaned from such trade sources as *Variety*, can be fit. Read (1976) and Tunstall (1977) also provide important information in the larger context of international news and entertainment.

Table 750–A.
U. S. Import/Export and Balance of Trade Values
for Electronics Industry Products, 1965–1975

Note: All dollar figures are in millions.

Product Group	1965			1970			1975		
	Value of U.S. Imports	Value of U.S. Exports	U.S. Balance of Trade	Value of U.S. Imports	Value of U.S. Exports	U.S. Balance of Trade	Value of U.S. Imports	Value of U.S. Exports	U.S. Balance of Trade
Consumer Electronics	$319	$ 55	-$264	$1,152	$ 77	-$1,075	$1,851	$ 517	-$1,334
Communications and Industrial Products	164	871	+707	514	2,439	+1,925	1,096	4,172	+3,076
Electron Tubes	35	60	+25	38	126	+88	69	216	+147
Solid State Products	24	82	+58	157	420	+263	803	1,054	+251
Electronic Parts	N/A	N/A	N/A	N/A	N/A	N/A	974	923	-51
Other Products	77	205	+128	328	463	+135	85	200	+115
Totals	$619	$1,273	+$654	$2,189	$3,525	+$1,336	$4,878	$7,082	+$2,204
Exports as Percentage of Imports	- -	- -	*206%*	- -	- -	*161%*	- -	- -	*145%*

Source: Electronic Industries Association, *Electronic Market Data Book* (1976), p. 105, and (1971), p. 83, reporting Bureau of the Census data.

Table 750–B.

U. S. Import/Export Values for Electronics Industry Consumer Products, 1958–1978

Note: All dollar figures are in millions.

	Current Dollar Values		Constant (1972) Dollar Values		
	Imports	Exports	Imports	Exports	Exports as Percent of Imports[a]
1958	21	74	32	112	350%
1959	78	72	116	107	92
1960	87	71	127	103	81
1961	121	80	175	115	66
1962	165	54	234	76	32
1963	158	54	221	75	34
1964	184	70	253	96	38
1965	264	80	355	108	30
1966	380	76	495	99	20
1967	562	98	942	139	17
1968	778	115	942	139	15
1969	893	135	1,030	156	15
1970	1,274	144	1,394	158	11
1971	1,487	169	1,549	176	11
1972	1,949	231	1,949	231	12
1973	2,203	318	2,082	301	14
1974	2,233	383	1,918	329	17
1975	1,783	392	1,401	308	22
1976[b]	2,931	498	2,189	372	17
1977[b]	3,400	420	N/A	N/A	N/A
1978[b]	3,800	430	N/A	N/A	N/A

Sources: *U. S. Industrial Outlook*, appropriate annual issues. Constant dollar figures were calculated by the editors.

Notes: (a) Percentages are based on the constant dollar figures. (b) The figures for these years are estimates.

Interpretation of Tables

Table 750-A outlines the import/export trade patterns of the U.S. electronics industry, from 1965 through 1975. The product categories in the table were established by the Electronic Industries Association (EIA). The figures indicate that the overall balance of trade in this industry remains favorable to the United States, even with a 25 percent decrease in export margins during the past decade. The consumer electronics segment of the industry has clearly been hurt by the predominance of imported products in the U.S. marketplace. However, the superiority of U.S.-made communications and industrial products—made up largely of computers and related equipment—has benefitted the United States balance of trade, since this nation still exports far more of these products than it imports.

Table 750-B provides a longer run of similar data for consumer electronics products only. The reader will note that the figures presented here do not match those given in **Table 750**-A. This is a common occurrence caused by differing definitions of "consumer electronics" (see "Sources" section below). **Table 750**-B indicates that American exports of consumer electronic products were showing strong growth during the 1970s, but then declined sharply in the estimates for 1977 and 1978. Based on the current dollar projections for 1977 and 1978, the U.S. exports would amount to only 12 percent of imports in 1977 and 11 percent in 1978.

The difficulties of the American consumer electronics industry are due primarily to the worldwide competition from Japanese products (see Unit 760). However, the American manufacturers' increasing uses of foreign locations, especially Mexico, for the assembly of consumer electronic devices (using U.S.-made components) has also had a negative effect on the export levels of the U.S. consumer electronics industry, as well as on the overall balance of trade for the United States.

Table 750-B also indicates a sharp rise in U.S. *imports* of consumer electronics products after 1959. This rise was due initially to the U.S. exportation of transistor technology. This new technology—combined with (1) lower wage rates overseas, (2) lighter components and, therefore, lower shipping costs, and (3) increasing automation of component assembly both here and abroad—resulted in nearly overwhelming foreign competition for American manufacturers of consumer electronics products. (See Table 460-E for the impact of this technological revolution on employment levels in the U.S. consumer electronics industry.)

The most important sources of imports in this industry are the countries of the Far East. In 1975, the U.S. import percentages for the *entire* electronics industry were divided among the following nations: Japan, 41 percent; Taiwan, 11 percent; Mexico, 12 percent; Singapore, 6 percent; and Hong Kong, Canada, and Korea, 5 percent each. In consumer electronics, the major import growth areas were video home systems (including videogames) and video cassettes.

The major destinations for U.S. electronics exports in 1975 were: Mexico, 12 percent; Canada, 11 percent; the U.K. and West Germany, 7 percent each; and Japan and Taiwan, 6 percent each. In many cases, these export figures represent U.S.-made components that later appear in completed equipment which is imported back into the United States.

Sources

All of the data in Table 750-A come from the U.S. Bureau of the Census. These data were arranged and presented by the Electronic Industries Association, the chief trade association of U.S. electronics manufacturers, in its annual *Electronic Market Data Book*. The editors have avoided unit information here in favor of dollar values, since the actual number of components is often impossible to determine.

The category of consumer electronics products in Table 750-A is defined by the EIA as including the following equipment: radio and television receivers, phonographs and other disc-recording equipment, audio tape equipment, home video systems, citizens band radios, personal calculators, and electronic watches (the latter two products are included only for the last three to five years). The category of communications and industrial products includes equipment for broadcast transmission and studios, navigation and guidance equipment, telephone and telegraph equipment, computers and related equipment, control and processing equipment, and other industrial products. The electron tubes category includes television picture tubes, receiving tubes, and power and microwave tubes.

According to the International Trade Commission, all of the statistics in Table 750-A are limited by problems of aggregation and classification and by imprecise trade records. Thus, the figures might best be termed "refined estimates" of actual practice.

In Table 750-B, taken from annual issues of the *U.S. Industrial Outlook*, the consumer electronics figures include radio and television receivers, phonographs and high-fidelity equipment, home video equipment (systems and games), and various accessories and combinations of the above. The differences between this definition and the definition of "consumer electronics" used in Table 750-A largely explain the differences in the totals for the two tables.

Further Information

The handiest compilation of annual data, with statistical tables for the past 5 to 20 years, is the EIA's *Electronic Market Data Book*. This volume, which has been published since about 1960, relies on information gathered by the industry and by the U.S. Census Bureau. For details on the original Census Bureau reports that supplied the EIA-reported data, the reader should turn to the table references in Unit 720, and especially the specific country-by-country breakdowns of U.S. imports and exports in two Census Bureau publications: *U.S. Exports, Commodity by Country* and *U.S. Imports, Commodity by Country*. The reader should also see the "consumer electronics" sections of the *U.S. Industrial Outlook*.

Table 760–A.
U.S. Import/Export Units and Values of Radio Receivers, 1950–1976

Note: All unit and dollar figures are in thousands.

	U.S. Imports, Total Units	Radio Receivers[a] Imports as Percent of Total U.S. Market	U.S. Exports, Total Units	Current Dollar Value of Imports	Current Dollar Value of Exports	Export Totals as Percent of Imports Units	Export Totals as Percent of Imports Value
1950	2	--	--	--	--	--	--
1951	5	--	--	--	--	--	--
1952	12	--	--	--	--	--	--
1953	25	--	--	--	--	--	--
1954	55	--	--	--	--	--	--
1955	141	.1%	--	--	--	--	--
1956	604	4.3	--	--	--	--	--
1957	1,011	7.0	--	--	--	--	--
1958	2,593	17.9	--	--	--	--	--
1959	5,876	27.6	--	--	--	--	--
1960	7,621	31.2	--	--	--	--	--
1961	12,359	42.3	--	--	--	--	--
1962	13,328	41.7	195	$ 88,463	$ 4,975	1%	6%
1963	13,783	43.7	212	86,431	5,279	2	6
1964	13,739	43.1	329	91,999	6,355	2	7
1965	19,637	47.1	352	125,103	8,667	2	7
1966	25,128	56.9	352	144,107	8,001	1	6
1967	24,200	58.7	438	171,110	9,409	2	5
1968	30,160	64.4	643	254,768	11,597	2	5
1969	36,396	70.9	770	336,136	15,258	2	5
1970	33,382	75.1	677	343,762	13,406	2	4
1971	34,138	71.7	719	358,088	16,171	2	5
1972	43,083	77.9	814	457,857	19,288	2	4
1973	45,366	90.4	754	540,007	19,950	2	4
1974	39,281	89.3	738	585,710	20,258	2	3
1975	31,941	92.5	654	477,347	21,375	2	4
1976	41,364	93.8	800	646,653	29,255	2	5

Sources: Electronic Industries Association: import data: *Consumer Electronics 1968*, p. 15, and *Consumer Electronics 1972*, p. 27, and *Consumer Electronics 1977*, p. 27; export data: *Consumer Electronics 1977*, p. 27.

Note: (a) Includes automobile radios.

Table 760-B.
U. S. Import/Export Units and Values of Television Receivers, 1960–1976

Note: All unit and dollar figures are in thousands.

	Black and White TV Receivers[a]			Color TV Receivers			Totals, U.S. TV Imports		Totals, U.S. TV Exports		Export Totals as Percent of Imports	
	U.S. Imports, Total Units	Imports as Percent of Total U.S. Market	U.S. Exports, Total Units	U.S. Imports, Total Units	Imports as Percent of Total U.S. Market	U.S. Exports, Total Units	B&W and Color Units	Current Dollar Value	B&W and Color Units	Current Dollar Value	Units	Value
1960	2	--	--	--	--	--	2	N/A	--	--	--	--
1961	13	--	--	--	--	--	13	N/A	--	--	--	--
1962	128	1.9%	140	--	--	--	128	$ 7,258	140	$18,099	109%	249%
1963	391	5.4	143	--	--	--	391	22,616	143	17,672	37	78
1964	661	7.9	202	--	--	--	661	39,261	202	23,293	31	59
1965	1,048	12.0	182	--	--	--	1,048	59,587	182	21,261	17	36
1966	1,519	19.7	168	--	--	--	1,519	114,520	168	26,291	11	23
1967	1,290	21.5	139	318	5.7%	--	1,608	123,837	139	23,559	9	19
1968	2,043	29.2	144	666	10.7	--	2,709	203,051	144	27,772	5	14
1969	3,121	43.9	99	912	14.7	58	4,033	295,777	157	33,339	4	11
1970	3,596	52.1	75	914	17.2	51	4,510	315,525	126	26,166	3	8
1971	4,166	54.5	74	1,281	17.6	88	5,447	413,316	162	37,146	3	9
1972	5,056	61.4	75	1,318	14.9	149	6,374	496,829	224	58,864	4	12
1973	4,999	68.5	99	1,399	13.9	215	6,398	531,253	314	83,618	5	16
1974	4,659	67.8	117	1,282	15.2	202	5,941	520,195	319	79,406	5	15
1975	2,975	67.3	91	1,215	19.5	141	4,190	401,490	232	59,504	6	15
1976	4,327	72.9	156	2,834	34.6	160	7,161	776,252	316	81,082	4	10

Sources: Electronic Industries Association: import data: *Consumer Electronics 1968*, p. 15, and *Consumer Electronics 1977*, p. 27; export data: *Consumer Electronics 1972*, p. 27, and *Consumer Electronics 1977*, p. 27.

Note: (a) The import figures include color television receivers through 1966, the export figures through 1967.

Interpretation of Tables

Tables **760**-A and **760**-B show that, with the exception of color television sets, broadcast receivers are predominantly an import product in the United States. Exactly the opposite is generally the case with station and studio equipment and other broadcast-related electronic equipment (see Unit 750).

Table **760**-A provides a 25-year time series on American imports and exports of radio receivers. The small number of radio imports into the United States in the early 1950s were primarily quality equipment from Europe, especially Germany. However, as transistor technology spread from the United States abroad in the late 1950s and into the 1960s, the import flow both expanded and shifted to the Far East—mainly Japan, Taiwan, and Hong Kong. By the mid-1970s, this import flow had nearly excluded all U.S.-made radios from the domestic market.

This situation has naturally had an effect on ownership concentrations in the U.S. radio manufacturing industry (see **Table 260**-D) and on domestic prices of radio receivers, which have not risen as rapidly as the prices for products in other media fields (see **Table 301**-A). The reader will note that even with the inflation rate over the past several years, the export percentages of import dollar values has remained at a constant two to three times the level of import *units*.

Table **760**-B provides parallel information for television receivers, both black-and-white and color units. The figures clearly demonstrate that as manufacturing companies in the United States became more involved in the production of color receivers during the mid-1960s, the black-and-white receiver market was left increasingly to the Far East manufacturers. Furthermore, although the majority of color receivers sold in this country are still made domestically, this state of affairs now appears to be changing as well—and rather rapidly. In 1977, the United States and Japan signed a new trade agreement in an attempt to limit the importation of several Japanese-built products, among them color television sets. U.S. manufacturers had accused the Japanese firms of "dumping" the television receivers (selling them at a price lower than the actual production-shipping costs) on the U.S. market.

Sources

All data in **Tables 760**-A and **760**-B come from the U.S. Department of Commerce and were printed and arranged by the Electronic Industries Association (EIA) in the following publications: *Consumer Electronics 1968* and *Consumer Electronics 1977*, for import data; and *Consumer Electronics 1972* and *Consumer Electronics 1977*, for export data. The editors calculated the "export as percentages of imports" and the "imports as percentages of total U.S. market" from the basic data in this unit and in Unit 660.

Although product classification is less a problem here than it is with recording equipment (see Unit 750) and nonconsumer electronics, there are often classification differences between import and export categories as reported by the Department of Commerce. As a rule, specific subcategories are identified by the editors only when a particular subcategory amounts to a substantial proportion of its larger category. For example, color television receivers are included with black-and-white receivers through 1966 for imports and through 1967 for exports. The editors separated color sets after these dates in order to point up the decline in black-and-white figures.

Further Information

Two annual source books—the EIA's *Electronic Market Data Book* and the *U.S. Industrial Outlook* (the consumer electronics sections)—contain useful data on international trade in the U.S. electronics industries. Two U.S. Census Bureau publications—*U.S. Exports, Commodity by Country* and *U.S. Imports, Commodity by Country*—provide specific country-by-country breakdowns of the U.S. import and export trade.

Annotation of Selected Government Statistical Publications

Much of the material in *The Mass Media* has been based upon, or has come directly from, government-gathered and -disseminated statistical reports. This appendix deals briefly with the more important of these publications, describing their background and intent, noting their terminology and definitions, and commenting on the reliability and limitations of their data. The year of publication is given only for those publications which are not annually or regularly issued.

The Office of Management and Budget (Executive Office of the President) has produced two publications which the editors found particularly useful: (1) Standard Industrial Classification Manual *(1972), and (2)* Statistical Services of the United States Government *(1975).*

The *Standard Industrial Classification Manual* (1972) describes the system of industrial classification developed over the years by experts in both government and private industry. In 1972, the system was extensively revised. This revision process seriously affected the historical comparability of some data, since the last major revision had been carried out in 1957. The *SIC Manual* divides all industries into several divisions: agriculture, mining, construction, manufacturing, transportation-communication-utilities, wholesale trade, retail trade, finance-insurance-real-estate, services, public administration (mainly government), and a miscellaneous category of nonclassifiable establishments. These divisions are subdivided into two-digit "major groups," and each major group is divided into three- or four-digit industries. Five- or seven-digit entries identify products or other outputs of the same industries.

The *SIC Manual* uses establishments, rather than companies, as the basis of its scheme: "For the purposes of this classification, an establishment is an economic unit, generally at a single physical location, where business is conducted or where services or industrial operations are performed" (p. 10). Distinct and separate economic activities performed at a single location are counted separately if the employment levels are significant in both, and if separate statistics can be compiled on important economic factors, such as employment, wages and salaries, and sales or receipts.

The *Statistical Services of the United States Government* (1975) is a regularly revised description of the programs and publications of independent and executive branch agencies. It reveals which agencies are responsible for what data, and it is also useful for its annotations on the content of the thousands of statistical publications issued by the U.S. government.

The Bureau of the Census (Department of Commerce) is the major publisher of regular census and survey-based economic information. Complete information regarding its many publications may be found in the latest annual issue of its Catalog of publications. *This appendix treats only eight Census Bureau publications which were used extensively throughout* The Mass Media: *(1)* Annual Survey of Manufactures, *(2)* Census of Manufactures, *(3)* Census of Retail Trade, *(4)* Census of Selected Service Industries, *(5)* Current Industrial Reports, *(6)* Historical Statistics *(1975), (7)* Social Indicators *(1973, 1976), and (8)* Statistical Abstract.

The *Annual Survey of Manufactures* has appeared since 1949, except during years ending in "2" or "7" (the *Census of Manufactures* years). It provides general statistics of manufacturing activity for industry groups, for important individual industries, and for geographic divisions of the country, including large Standard Metropolitan Statistical Areas (SMSAs). Beginning with 1960, figures are also provided for large industrial counties. Data include value added by manufacture, value of shipments, cost of materials, fuels and electric energy consumed, employment, man-hours and payrolls, capital expenditures, gross book value of assets, rental payments, and supplemental labor costs. According to the 1976 *Statistical Abstract*: "The most recent annual survey is based on a sample of about 70,000 of an approximate total of 320,000 manufacturing establishments. It comprises all large plants, which account for approximately two-thirds of total manufacturing employment in the United States, and a representative selection of the more numerous small plants. Government-owned and -operated establishments are excluded."

The *Census of Manufactures* first appeared in 1809. The 1972 census is the 29th and most recent in this series. Current legislation calls for the census to be held every five years, during years ending with "2" or "7". Census results for 1977 should begin to appear in 1979-1980.

Like other censuses conducted since 1947, the 1972 *Census of Manufactures* was primarily a mail canvass. The diversity of manufacturing activities made it necessary to use more than 200 different forms to collect data from the approximately 450 industries covered in the census. The 120,000 firms in the United States with less than 10 employees were not required to file reports. Estimates for these small establishments were mainly constructed from industry averages, although payroll and sales data were supplied by the Social Security Administration and the Internal Revenue Service. In most industries, these small establishments accounted for less than 3 percent of the payroll and value-added figures.

The census is conducted on the basis of "establishments," and an "industry" is generally defined as a group of establishments producing either a single product or a number of closely related products. The SIC system of industry definition is employed, and definitions become progressively narrower with the additions of numerical digits. There are 20 very broad two-digit major industry groups, approximately 150 three-digit groups, and 450 four-digit industries, while some 10,000 products have seven-digit codes and are grouped into 1,300 classes of products with five-digit codes. The seven- and five-digit products are considered the primary products of the industry with the same first four digits. Consequently, an establishment is classified in a particular industry if its production of the primary products of that industry exceeds the value of its production of the products of any other single industry.

The following industry groups appear in the *Census of Manufactures* and are of importance in *The Mass Media*. They are listed in ascending order of their SIC numbers. The reader should keep in mind that the definitions of various industries and products included in the censuses have often changed over time and that these changes have created difficulties in historical comparability.

Industry 2711: Newspapers (*Mass Media* 20 Series). These establishments carry on the various operations necessary for issuing newspapers, including the gathering of editorial content and advertisements. They may or may not perform their own printing. The code and definitions of the industry did not change between 1967 and 1972.

Industry 2721: Periodicals (*Mass Media* 30 Series). These establishments are engaged primarily in preparing, publishing, and printing periodicals. They may or may not do their own printing. Nonprofit organizations (religious, educational, social, charitable, etc.) have been included to the degree that the employees of such organizations are covered under Social Security. Publications are classified as periodicals rather than as newspapers if their news and editorial presentations do not appear to be directed to the public at large. Although sometimes considered to be newspapers, trade journals, house organs, local church or school papers, and similar publications with limited or specialized news treatment are treated as periodicals by the *Census of Manufactures*. Magazine and comic supplements for Sunday newspapers are also classified here as periodicals.

Industry 2731: Book Publishing (*Mass Media* 10 Series). These establishments are engaged in publishing and printing books and pamphlets. Nonprofit organizations are covered here if they are included under the Social Security system and able to report book publishing as a separate establishment. Census data refer to number of books sold (shipped and billed) during the census year, without regard to whether these books were actually published or printed in that year. The code and definitions were unchanged between 1967 and 1972.

Industry 2732: Book Printing (*Mass Media* 10 Series). These establishments are engaged in printing only, or in printing and binding books and pamphlets, but they are not engaged in publishing. They are similar in character to some establishments primarily engaged in commercial printing (Industries 2751, 2752, and 2754). The code and definitions here did not change between 1967 and 1972. In most cases, the editors have not included figures for these establishments in this volume's coverage of the book industry, in order to bring the relative size of book publishing into more direct comparison with periodical publishing.

Industry 2741: Miscellaneous Publishing (usually *Mass Media* 10 Series). These establishments are engaged primarily in miscellaneous publishing which is not classified elsewhere and may or may not involve printing. They generally offer financial, credit, or other business services, and may publish directories which are included in service industries. The code and definitions here did not change between 1967 and 1972.

Industry 3651: Radio and Television Receiving Sets (*Mass Media* 60, 70, and 80 Series). These establishments are engaged mainly in manufacturing electronic equipment for home entertainment. They also include those engaged in the manufacture of public address systems and music distribution apparatus, except records. Classification code and definitions were unchanged from 1967 to 1972.

Industry 3652: Phonograph Records and Prerecorded Magnetic Tape (*Mass Media* 50 Series). These establishments are engaged primarily in the manufacture of phonograph records and prerecorded magnetic tape. Blank tapes are included in Industry 3679. Although this category remained unchanged in number or definitions from 1967 through 1972, it was titled "Phonograph Records" prior to 1972.

Industry 3671: Electron Tubes, Receiving Type (*Mass Media* 60, 70, and 80 Series). These establishments are engaged primarily in the manufacture of radio and television receiving electron tubes, except cathode-ray tubes. No change in classification or definitions occurred between 1967 and 1972.

Industry 3672: Cathode-Ray Television Picture Tubes (*Mass Media* 60 and 80 Series). These establishments are engaged primarily in the manufacture of receiving-type cathode-ray tubes. No changes in classification or definitions were made between 1967 and 1972.

The *Census of Retail Trade* was classified as part of the *Census of Business* prior to 1972. The first economic census was conducted as a part of the 1810 population census; and prior to 1929, these censuses did not specifically cover wholesale and retail trade. After 1933, various services were also included. Business censuses were taken in 1935 and 1939, then resumed after the war in 1948 and continued in the same years as the manufacturing census: 1954, 1958, 1963, 1967, and 1972 (the ninth such census). Future censuses (divided in 1972 into separately titled sections on wholesale trade, retail trade, and selected service industries) will cover years ending in "2" and "7". Results for 1977 should begin to appear in the 1979-1980 period. The following industry groups, important to *The Mass Media*, appear in the *Census of Retail Trade*.

Industry 5732: Radio and Television Stores (*Mass Media* 60, 70, and 80 Series). These establishments are engaged primarily in the retail sale and installation of radios, televisions, record players, high-fidelity and sound-reproducing equipment. Such establishments may also sell additional products such as household appliances, musical instruments, or records.

Industry 5733: Music Stores (*Mass Media* 40 Series). These establishments are engaged primarily in the retail sale of musical instruments, phonograph records, sheet music, and similar musical supplies.

Industry 5942: Book Stores (*Mass Media* 10 Series). These establishments are engaged mainly in retail sale of new books and magazines.

Industry 5994: News Dealers and Newsstands (*Mass Media* 20 and 30 Series). The establishments in this industry are engaged mainly in the retail sale of newspapers, magazines, and other periodicals.

The *Census of Selected Service Industries* was part of the *Census of Business* prior to 1972, and its background is related to that of the retail trade census described above. A combination of Social Security and Internal Revenue Service information, along with a mail survey, produces the information it contains on location, kind of business, volume of receipts and payrolls, and number of employees. Firms with no paid employees during 1972, or firms with small payrolls below specific levels for various industries (generally one to three employees), were not included in the mail survey.

Historical comparability between this 1972 census and the 1967 census (part of the *Census of Business*) is harmed by some changes in classification, by changes in SMSA composition, and by lack of information on proprietors of unincorporated businesses in 1972. All forms of payroll (including salaried officers and executives of corporations who were on payroll for the entire year) are counted. The census reports employment for the pay period beginning March 12th and for the first quarter of the census year. (*The Mass Media* uses only the full-year figures.)

Receipts include total receipts from customers for services rendered and merchandise sold during 1972, whether or not payment was received in 1972. Receipts are net after deductions for refunds and returns, and include both local and state sales taxes. Excise taxes paid by the establishment are also included. Non-operating income, such as investments and rental of real estate, are not included. While the count of establishments given is for the end of the year, receipts are for all firms operating during the census year. The following service industries, important to *The Mass Media*, appear in the *Census of Selected Service Industries*.

Industry 7622: Radio and Television Repair Shops (*Mass Media* 50 and 60 Series). These establishments are engaged primarily in repairing radios, television sets, phonographs, high-fidelity or stereophonic equipment, and tape recorders. Also included are establishments which install and repair television sets, and amateur and citizens band antennaes—or those which install and service radio transmitting and receiving equipment in homes, offices, small boats, automobiles or other vehicles.

Industry 7813: Motion Picture Production, Except for Television (*Mass Media* 40 Series). These establishments are engaged mainly in the production of theatrical and nontheatrical motion pictures for exhibition, other than for films for television. Both production and distribution are covered here. Establishments which produce educational, industrial, and religious films are also included.

Industry 7814: Motion Picture and Tape Production for Television (*Mass Media* 40 and 80 Series). These establishments are engaged primarily in the production or distribution of theatrical and nontheatrical motion pictures and tape—including commercials—for television exhibition.

Industry 7819: Services Allied to Motion Picture Production (*Mass Media* 40 Series). These establishments are engaged mainly in performing services which are allied to, but independent of, motion picture production. Such services include film processing, editing, and titling, casting bureaus, wardrobe and studio property rental, television tape services, and stock-footage film libraries.

Industry 7823: Motion Picture Film Exchanges (*Mass Media* 40 Series). These establishments are engaged primarily in renting theatrical and nontheatrical film to exhibitors other than those in the field of television.

Industry 7824: Film or Tape Distribution for Television (*Mass Media* 40 Series). These establishments are engaged mainly in renting theatrical and nontheatrical film or tape to exhibitors in the field of television.

Industry 7829: Services Allied to Motion Picture Distribution (*Mass Media* 40 Series). These establishments are engaged primarily in performing auxiliary services to motion picture distribution. They include film delivery services, film purchasing and booking agencies, and film libraries.

Industry 7832: Motion Picture Theaters, Except Drive-Ins (*Mass Media* 40 Series). These establishments are commercially operated, conventional (or "four-wall") theaters primarily engaged in the indoor exhibition of motion pictures. Itinerant establishments with portable projection and sound equipment are also included.

Industry 7833: Drive-In Motion Picture Theaters (*Mass Media* 40 Series). These establishments are commercially operated outdoor theaters commonly known as "drive-ins" and primarily engaged in the outdoor exhibition of motion pictures.

Current Industrial Reports is a series of over 100 monthly, quarterly, and annual reports containing detailed statistics on some 5,000 manufactured products. Each report generally includes between two and eight tables concerning production, shipments, stocks and inventories, and foreign trade. Related titles include *Pulp, Paper and Board* (M26A), and *Radio Receivers and Television Sets; Phonographs and Record Players, Speakers and Related Equipment* (MA-36M). *Current Industrial Reports* also uses SIC product designations, allowing easy comparison of the data given here with those given in the *Annual Survey of Manufactures* and the *Census of Manufactures*. Each report typically provides data for the past three years or so (with revisions in earlier figures designated by notes), detailed definitions, and discussion of the limitations of the data. Prior to 1959, these reports were titled *Facts for Industry*.

Historical Statistics (1975) provides some 12,500 time-series concerning all aspects of American life, with supplementary text and notes. This two-volume work is a revision and expansion of a work which was first issued in 1949 (with 3,000 time-series carried to 1945) and later revised in 1960 (with 8,000 time-series carried to 1957), with shorter interim updates between editions. The present edition provides time-series to 1970, drawing data from both commercial and government sources.

The text information on source limitations and definitions is concise and generally excellent. As a general rule, data are presented for the nation as a whole, with few regional, state, or local breakdowns. Only annual or census year data are shown, and usually for periods no shorter than 20 years. Data are arranged in broad subject chapters with more specific subject subsections. A detailed 22-page index provides access to the two volumes.

Social Indicators (1973, 1976) are analytic reports on the state of the nation as viewed from the individual or family level. The emphasis throughout the text, charts, tables, and graphs is on results or outcomes rather than on various kinds of inputs. The 1976 report is divided into 11 major areas of social concern, and each area includes a brief text and color charts, statistical tables (providing details regarding the charts), and technical notes and definitions in support of the other materials.

Statistical Abstract, produced annually, is the official compendium of government and privately derived statistics concerning most aspects of American life. Issues since 1973 also serve as updates to *Historical Statistics*. The emphasis here is on current information with a minimum of descriptive text and discussion of statistical limitations. Since its first appearance in 1878, *Statistical Abstract* has become the single most important statistical compendium and reference issued by the government. In each of its sections, information is provided for the past three years or so, with several selected earlier benchmark years also included. Appendixes detail major sources and provide a cross-reference table with *Historical Statistics*. *Statistical Abstract* is published commercially as *The U.S. Factbook: The American Almanac*.

The Bureau of Domestic Commerce (Department of Commerce) has produced two works which the editors used in compiling The Mass Media: *(1)* Printing and Publishing, *and (2)* U.S. Industrial Outlook.

Printing and Publishing is published quarterly, and each issue of this magazine presents several articles on such topics as the growth, international business, employment, or finances of various parts of the printing and publishing industries. These articles usually are based on statistics from the U.S. Census Bureau, the Bureau of Labor Statistics, or other government sources, and the statistics are reproduced in intelligible tables. Also included in each issue are reports on imports and exports of printed materials. The editors found this source particularly valuable for its analysis of government statistics over long time-series, and for its reportage of changes in government data-collection procedures affecting the historical comparability of the statistics.

U.S. Industrial Outlook has been published since the early 1960s. It provides data on recent trends and the immediate outlook of some 200 industries with regard to changes in supply and demand, domestic and foreign markets, prices, employment and wages, and investment. The work is typically issued in January and contains hard data for the preceeding two years, as well as end-of-the-year estimates for the year prior to publication, and estimates for the cover-date year and the next several years to come. Industries are classified using the SIC system. A 50-page chapter in recent issues has dealt with communications—telecommunications, printing and publishing, and broadcasting—with a separate section on motion pictures.

Three works produced by the Bureau of Economic Analysis (Department of Commerce) are used throughout The Mass Media: (1) Survey of Current Business, (2) Business Statistics, and (3) The National Income and Product Accounts of the United States, 1929-74, Statistical Tables (1976).

The *Survey of Current Business* is the most important single current source of business and trade statistics. This monthly publication includes general business indicators and data on domestic and foreign trade, employment, and wages for specific industry groupings using the SIC scheme. The July issue provides cumulative data for the past three years on national income, with tables and supporting text on GNP, personal income and outlay, government receipts and expenditures, foreign transactions, savings and investment, production-income-employment by industry, implicit price deflators and indexes, and so forth. Several other special issues are produced, including the following two publications issued as supplements to the *Survey*.

Business Statistics (biennial) provides cumulative information from the *Survey of Current Business* from 1947 to date and is published in odd-numbered years. Explanatory notes and source references supplement the tables, which make up the bulk of *Business Statistics*. Some 2,500 series are included, with annual data in most cases and monthly figures for the most recent years.

The *National Income and Product Accounts of the United States, 1929-74, Statistical Tables* (1976) is issued irregularly—every 8 to 10 years—and cumulates the July sections of similar title from the monthly *Survey of Current Business*. It includes basically the same sections listed under the *Survey's* July issue. The first four pages provide detailed definitions underlying the tables. The publication of this volume often coincides with benchmark revisions in the historical series presented.

Four publications originating with the Bureau of Labor Statistics (Department of Labor) were particularly useful to the editors: (1) BLS Handbook of Methods for Surveys and Studies (1976), (2) Consumer Price Index Detailed Report, (3) Employment and Earnings, United States, 1909-1975 (1977), and (4) Handbook of Labor Statistics.

BLS Handbook of Methods for Surveys and Studies (1976) is a compilation of technical notes on the major BLS survey publications. The *Handbook* details the statistical methods of these surveys and discusses their limitations. Various sections deal with statistical series on such topics as current employment analysis, manpower structure and trends, prices and living conditions, wages and industrial relations, and productivity and technology.

The *Consumer Price Index Detailed Report* is a monthly publication which reveals average changes in prices of goods and services usually bought by urban wage earners and clerical workers. The Consumer Price Index (CPI) is based on prices of about 400 items selected to represent the movement of prices of all consumer goods and serivces. Prices for these items are collected from about 18,000 establishments in urban portions of 39 major statistical areas and 17 smaller cities. Each year, the December issue of *CPI Detailed Report* contains the annual average figures for the various CPIs, compared to the previous year. Notes in each issue detail methods of calculating index changes and the problem of seasonally adjusted data. The CPI uses 1967 as a base year, while the editors of this volume have generally employed a uniform base year of 1972.

Employment and Earnings, United States, 1909-1975 (1977) is the 11th comprehensive data book on national statistics to be released by the Bureau of Labor Statistics since 1961. Summary tables and charts included in past editions of this publication have been omitted from this edition. Data usually summarized in the analytical tables appear in detail within this publication. Charts containing related information are published each month in *Employment and Earnings*.

Detailed industry statistics on the nation's nonagricultural work force are presented in this volume, which includes monthly and annual employment averages for all employees, women, production workers in manufacturing and mining, construction workers in contract construction, and nonsupervisory workers in the remaining private nonmanufacturing industries. Also shown are average weekly and hourly earnings, average weekly and overtime hours, and labor turnover rates—with seasonally adjusted data for a number of these series. Each industry title in this work is identified by the appropriate SIC code. Only national data are presented in this work. A companion volume, *Employment and Earnings, States and Area, 1939-74*, provides similar information for all states, the District of Columbia, and more than 220 areas.

The *Handbook of Labor Statistics* provides some 400 pages of historical series—generally for the past decade—on the labor force, employment, unemployment, hours, productivity and unit labor costs, compensation, prices and living conditions, unions and industrial relations, occupational injuries and illnesses, foreign labor statistics, and general economic data. The data, supplied by the BLS and other departments, are accompanied by brief statements of the method and limitations of each series. Some 20 pages of "Technical Notes" begin the *Handbook* and deal with derivation and limits to the data presented on each topic.

Sources and References

U.S. Government Publications

Board for International Broadcasting. *Annual Report*. Washington: Government Printing Office, 1974 to date.

Bureau of the Census (Department of Commerce). *Annual Survey of Manufactures*. Washington: Government Printing Office, 1948 to date (annual, except not published 1954, 1958, 1963, 1967, 1972).

—————. *Census of Business*, 1929, 1933, 1935, 1939, 1948, 1954, 1958, 1963, 1967. (Washington: Government Printing Office (various dates).

—————. *Census of Manufactures*, 1899, 1914, 1919, 1921, 1923, 1925, 1927, 1929, 1931, 1933, 1935, 1937, 1939, 1947, 1954, 1958, 1963, 1967, 1972. Washington: Government Printing Office (various dates).

—————. *Census of Retail Trade*, 1972. Washington: Government Printing Office (various dates). (Earlier versions incorporated in *Census of Business*.)

—————. *Census of Selected Service Industries*, 1972. Washington: Government Printing Office (various dates). (Earlier versions incorporated in *Census of Business*.)

—————. *County Business Patterns*. Washington: Government Printing Office (annual).

—————. *Current Industrial Reports*. Washington: Government Printing Office (various dates, various subtitled series).

—————. *Current Population Reports*. Washington: Government Printing Office, August 1977.

—————. *Foreign Commerce and Navigation of the United States*. Washington: Government Printing Office (annual, then irregular). (Final issue for 1965 published in 1970.)

—————. *Foreign Trade Reports, FT410: U.S. Exports of Domestic and Foreign Merchandise, Commodity by Country of Destination. Part II: Commodity Groups 6-9. Calendar Year 1945*. Washington: Government Printing Office, 1945.

—————. *Historical Statistics of the United States, Colonial Times to 1970: Bicentennial Edition*. 2 vols. Washington: Government Printing Office, 1975.

—————. *Monthly Retail Trade: Sales and Accounts Receivable*. Washington: Government Printing Office (monthly).

—————. *Social Indicators 1976*. Washington: Government Printing Office, 1977.

—————. *The Statistical Abstract of the United States*. Washington: Government Printing Office, 1978 to date (annual). (Published commercially in the 1970s as *The U.S. Factbook: The American Almanac*.)

—————. *U.S. Exports, Commodity by Country* (see *Foreign Trade Reports, FT 410: U.S. Exports of Domestic and Foreign Merchandise, Commodity by Country of Destination. Part II: Commodity Groups 6-9. Calendar Year 1945*).

—————. *U.S. Exports, Schedule B, Commodity and Country* (FT 410). Washington: Government Printing Office (monthly).

—————. *U.S. General Imports, Schedule A, Commodity by Country* (FT 135). Washington: Government Printing Office (monthly).

—————. *U.S. Imports for Consumption and General Imports, SIC-Based Products and Area* (FT 210). Washington: Government Printing Office (annual).

—————. *1972 Survey of Minority-Owned Business Enterprises*. Washington: Government Printing Office, 1975.

Bureau of Domestic Commerce (Department of Commerce). *Printing and Publishing*. Washington: Government Printing Office (quarterly).

—————. *U.S. Industrial Outlook*. Washington: Government Printing Office, 1961 to date. (Title was *Current Industrial Outlook*.)

Bureau of Economic Analysis (Department of Commerce). *Business Statistics*. Washington: Government Printing Office, 1947 to date (biennial). (Supplement to *Survey of Current Business*.)

—————. *The National Income and Product Accounts of the United States, 1929-1974*. Washington: Government Printing Office, 1976.

—————. *Survey of Current Business*. Washington: Government Printing Office (monthly).

Bureau of Foreign and Domestic Commerce (Department of Commerce). *Review of Foreign Film Markets*, 1936, 1937, 1938. Washington: Government Printing Office, 1937 to 1939 (annual).

Bureau of International Commerce (Department of Commerce). *Global Market Survey: Export Opportunities for Printing and Graphic Arts Equipment*. Washington: Government Printing Office, 1974.

Bureau of International Economic Policy and Research (Department of Commerce). *Market Share Reports, Commodity Series, 1971-1975* (SITC Nos. 641.1 Newspapers and Periodicals, 718.21 Bookbinding Machinery, 718.22 Typemaking and Typesetting Machinery, 718.29 Other Printing Machinery N.E.S., 892.11 Printed Books and Pamphlets, 892.12 Children's Picture and Painting Books). Springfield, Va.: National Technical Information Service, 1976.

Bureau of Labor Statistics (Department of Labor). *Admission Price Index* (see *Consumer Price Index Detailed Report*).

—————. *BLS Handbook of Methods for Surveys and Studies* (Bulletin 1910). Washington: Government Printing Office, 1976b.

—————. *Consumer Price Index Detailed Report*. Washington: Government Printing Office (monthly).

—————. *Employment and Earnings, 1909-1975* (Bulletin 1312-10). Washington: Government Printing Office, 1976a.

—————. *Handbook of Labor Statistics*. (Bulletin 1966). Washington: Government Printing Office, 1977 (annual).

—————. *Occupational Employment: Industry Characteristics Surveys 1971*. Washington: Government Printing Office, 1974-1975. (This series of surveys consists of 104 pamphlets, each devoted to a specific industry.)

Bureau of Navigation (Department of Commerce). *Radio Service Bulletin No. 62*. Washington: Government Printing Office, June 1, 1922.

Commission on Civil Rights. *Window Dressing on the Set: Women and Minorities in Television*. Washington: Government Printing Office, 1977.

Corporation for Public Broadcasting. *Annual Report*. Washington: CPB, 1969 to date.

—————. *CPB-Qualified Public Radio Stations*. Washington: CPB, 1970 to date (annual, statistical reviews).

—————. *One Week of Educational Television*. Washington: CPB (series).

—————. *One Week of Public Radio, December 9-15, 1973*. Washington: CPB, 1974.

—————. *One Week of Public Television No. 7, April 1972*. Washington: CPB, 1973.

—————. "Preliminary Results of CPB/NCES Public Television Content Survey, January 1 to June 5, 1976." Washington: CPB (October 1976, advance edition).

—————. *Public Television Licensees Fiscal Year 1974*. Washington: CPB, 1970 to date (annual, statistical reviews).

—————' *Public Television Program Content: 1974*. Washington: CPB, 1975.

—————. *Public Television Programming by Category: 1976*. Washington: CPB, 1977.

—————. *Status Report on Public Broadcasting, 1973*. Washington: CPB, 1974.

—————. *Status Report of Public Broadcasting, 1977*. Washington: CPB, 1978.

—————. "Summary Financial Report of Public Television and Radio Licensees," *CPB Report* (October 25, 1976).

Domestic and International Business Administration (Department of Commerce). *The U.S. Consumer Electronics Industry*. By Stuart A. Pettingill, et al. Washington: Government Printing Office, September 1975.

Equal Employment Opportunity Commission. *Equal Opportunity Report No. 1: Job Patterns for Minorities and Women in Private Industry, Part 1*. Washington: Government Printing Office, 1968.

—————. *Equal Employment Opportunity Report, 1973: Job Patterns for Minorities and Women in Private Industry, Vol. I: United States*. Washington: Government Printing Office, 1975.

Federal Communications Commission. *AM and FM Broadcast Financial Data* (mimeo). Washington: FCC (annual).

—————. *Annual Report*. Washington: Government Printing Office, 1935 to date (issues for 1935-1955 reprinted by Arno Press, 1971).

—————. "Cable Industry EEO Study" (mimeo). Washington: FCC, 1975.

—————. "CATV Industry Financial Data for the Period Nov. 1975-Oct. 1976" (Mimeo No. 85210). Washington: FCC, June 10, 1977.

—————. *An Economic Study of Standard Broadcasting* (mimeo). Washington: FCC, October 31, 1947 (reprinted by Arno Press, 1974).

—————. *Network Broadcasting*, Report of the Network Study Staff to the Network Study Committee. House of Representatives Report 1297, 85th Congress, 2nd Session, 1958.

—————. *Report on Chain Broadcasting*. Washington: Government Printing Office, 1941 (reprinted by Arno Press, 1974).

—————. *Television Broadcast Programming Data* (mimeo). Washington: FCC, 1973 to date (annual).

—————. *TV Broadcast Financial Data* (mimeo). Washington: FCC (annual).

—————. "Use of Television Channels as of July 1, 1976" (Mimeo No. 72188). Washington: FCC, September 23, 1976.

Federal Radio Commission. "List of Licensed Broadcasting Stations by Call Letters" (mimeo). Washington: FRC, February 3, 1930.

General Accounting Office (U.S. Congress). *Suggestions to Improve Management of Radio Free Europe/Radio Liberty*. Washington: GAO Report ID-76-55, June 25, 1976 (for the Board for International Broadcasting).

————. *Telling America's Story to the World—Problems and Issues*. Washington: GAO Report B-118654, March 25, 1974 (for the United States Information Agency).

Information Agency. *Report to Congress* 5, 10-11, 38. Washington: Government Printing Office, 1955, 1958, 1972.

————. *Report to the Congress* 43 to date. Washington: Government Printing Office, 1974 to date.

————. *Review of Operations* 1-4, 6-9, 12-32, 35. Washington: Government Printing Office, 1953-1955, 1956-1957, 1959-1969, 1970.

————. *Semiannual Report to the Congress* 34, 36-37, 39-42. Washington: Government Printing Office, 1970, 1971, 1972-1974.

————. *Semiannual Review of Operations* 33. Washington: Government Printing Office, 1969.

International Information Program (Department of State). *The Voice of America: 1950-1951*. Washington: Department of State, 1951.

Library of Congress, Copyright Office (U.S. Congress). *Annual Report of the Register of Copyrights*. Washington: Government Printing Office (annual).

National Center for Educational Statistics (Department of Health, Education and Welfare). *Statistics for Public School Libraries' Media Centers, Fall 1974*. By Nicholas Osso. Washington: Government Printing Office, 1977.

National Commission on Libraries and Information Science. *National Information Policy: Report of the President of the United States*. Submitted by the Staff of the Domestic Council, Committee on the Right of Privacy. Washington: Government Printing Office, 1976.

Office of Education (Department of Health, Education and Welfare). *Library Statistics of Colleges and Universities, 1962-63*: Institutional Data (OE-15023-63). Washington: Government Printing Office, 1964.

————. *Public School Library Statistics*, 1962-63 (OE-15020-63). Washington: Government Printing Office, 1964.

————. *Statistics of Public Libraries, 1962. Part I: Selected Statistics of Public Libraries Serving Populations of 35,000 and Above*: Institutional Data. Washington: Government Printing Office, 1965.

Office of Management and Budget (Executive Office of the President). *Social Indicators 1973*. Washington: Government Printing Office, 1974.

————. *Standard Industrial Classification Manual 1972*. Washington: Government Printing Office, 1972.

————. *Statistical Services of the United States Government*. Washington: Government Printing Office, 1975 (frequently revised).

Office of Telecommunications Policy (Executive Office of the President). *Analysis of the Causes and Effects of Increases in Same-Year Rerun Programming and Related Issues in Prime-Time Network Television* (mimeo). Washington: OTP, March 1973.

Patent Office (Department of Commerce). *Annual Report of the Commissioner of Patents*. Washington: Government Printing Office (annual).

Presidential Study Commission on International Radio Broadcasting. *The Right to Know*. Washington: Government Printing Office, 1973.

Senate Finance Committee, Subcommittee on Foundations (U.S. Congress). *Role of Private Foundations in Public Broadcasting*, Hearings. 93rd Congress, 2nd Session, 1974.

Surgeon General's Scientific Advisory Committee on Television and Social Behavior. *Television and Growing Up: The Impact of Televised Violence*. Washington: Government Printing Office, 1972. (Supplemented with five vols. of research studies under the overall title of *Television and Social Behavior*.)

Temporary National Economic Committee (U.S. Congress). *Investigation of Concentration of Economic Power, Monograph No. 43: The Motion Picture Industry—A Pattern of Control*. By Daniel Bertrand, et al. Senate Committee Print, 76th Congress, 3rd Session, 1941.

Other Publications

Abshire, David M. *International Broadcasting: A New Dimension of Western Diplomacy*. Beverly Hills, Calif.: Sage Publications (Washington Papers No. 35), 1976.

Access (monthly).

Advertising Age (weekly).

Agee, Warren K. "Cross-Channel Ownership of Communication Media," *Journalism Quarterly* 26:410-416 (December 1949).

Albig, William. *Modern Public Opinion*. New York: McGraw-Hill, 1956.

Alexander, Herbert E. *Financing the 1968 Election*. Lexington, Mass.: Lexington Books, 1970.

—————. *Financing the 1972 Election*. Lexington, Mass.: Lexington Books, 1976.

American Book Trade Directory. New York: R. R. Bowker, 1958 to 1975.

American Film Institute. *Guide to College Courses in Film and Television*. 5th ed., 3rd ed., 1st ed. Washington: Acropolis Books, 1975, 1972, 1970.

American Library Directory. New York: R. R. Bowker (annual).

American Newspaper Publishers Association. *Comments of American Newspaper Publishers Association in Opposition (to FCC Docket No. 18110)*. 3 vols. New York: ANPA, 1971.

—————. *News and Editorial Content and Readership of the Daily Newspaper*. New York: ANPA, 1973.

—————. "Newspaper Readership and Circulation," *ANPA News Research Report No. 3* (May 27, 1977). Washington: ANPA.

—————. "Trend in 15-cent Dailies Continues," *ANPA General Bulletin No. 3* (January 21, 1976). Washington: ANPA.

Anderson, Charles B., ed. *Bookselling in America and the World*. New York: Quadrangle/The New York Times Book Co., 1975.

Anderson, Russell F. "News From Nowhere, Our Disappearing Foreign Correspondents," *The Saturday Review of Literature* 34:10-12, 80, 81 (November 17, 1951).

Arbitron Television. *ADI Book 1976-1977*. Beltsville, Md.: American Research Bureau, 1977.

—————. *Description of Methodology*. Beltsville, Md.: ARB (annual).

—————. *Syndicated Programming Analysis*. Beltsville, Md.: ARB (annual).

Association of American Publishers. *Annual Survey*. New York: AAP, 1977.

—————. *Industry Statistics, 1976*. New York: AAP.

—————. *1967 Industry Statistics*. New York: AAP.

Atkinson, Hugh C. "Prices of U.S. and Foreign Published Materials" in *The Bowker Annual of Library Book Trade Information*. 20th ed. New York: R. R. Bowker, 1975.

Audit Bureau of Circulations. *Daily Newspaper Circulation Rate Book*. Chicago: ABC.

Ayer Directory of Publications. Philadelphia: Ayer Press (annual).

Baer, Walter S., et al. *Concentration of Mass Media Ownership: Assessing the State of Current Knowledge* (R-1584-NSF). Santa Monica, Calif.: The Rand Corporation (September 1974).

Bagdikian, Ben H. *The Information Machines*. New York: Harper and Row, 1971.

—————. "Newspaper Mergers—the Final Phase," *Columbia Journalism Review, 15* (6):17-22 (March/April 1977).

—————. "Report of an Exaggerated Death: Daily Newspapers That Failed, 1961-1970," *Nieman Reports, 30* (4), *31*, (1):19-23 (Winter 1976, Spring 1977).

Bailey, Robert Lee. "The Content of Network Television Prime-Time Special Programming: 1948-1968," *Journal of Broadcasting* 14:325-336 (Summer 1970).

Barnouw, Erik. *Documentary: A History of the Non-Fiction Film*. New York: Oxford University Press, 1974.

—————. *Tube of Plenty: The Evolution of American Television*. New York: Oxford University Press, 1975.

Barrett, Marvin, ed. *The Alfred I. Dupont-Columbia University Survey of Broadcast Journalism*. New York: Grosset & Dunlap, 1968 to 1971 (annual); New York: Crowell, 1973 and 1975 (biennial).

Batscha, Robert M. *Foreign Affairs News and the Broadcast Journalist*. New York: Praeger Special Studies, 1975.

Batten, Barton, Durstine and Osborn. *BBDO Report on Prime-Time Network Television*, and *BBDO Report on Daytime Network Television*. New York: BBDO (annual).

Berelson, Bernard. *The Library's Public: A Report of the Public Library Inquiry of the Social Science Research Council*. New York: Columbia University Press, 1949.

Bertrand, Daniel. *Evidence Study No. 25 of the Motion Picture Industry* (preliminary draft). Washington: National Recovery Administration, Division of Review (November 1935).

Billboard (weekly). ©

Billboard International Buyer's Guide (title varies). Los Angeles: *Billboard* (annual). ☉

Blakely, Robert J. *The People's Instrument: A Philosophy of Programming for Public Television*. Washington: Public Affairs Press, 1971.

Bluem, A. William, and Jason E. Squire, eds. *The Movie Business: American Film Industry Practice*. New York: Hastings House, 1972.

Bogart, Leo. *The Age of Television*. 3rd ed. New York: Frederick Ungar, 1972.

Books in Print. New York: R. R. Bowker (annual).

Bottini, R. L. "Group Ownership of Newspapers," *Freedom of Information Center Report No. 190* (November 1967).

Bower, Robert T. *Television and the Public*. New York: Holt, Rinehart & Winston, 1973.

The Bowker Annual (title has varied). New York: R. R. Bowker, 1977.

The Bowker Annual of Library and Book Trade Information (title varies). New York: R. R. Bowker.

Boxoffice (weekly).

Braestrup, Peter. *Big Story: How the American Press and Television Reported and Interpreted the Crisis of Tet 1968 in Vietnam and Washington*. 2 vols. Boulder, Colo.: Westview Press, 1977.

Branscomb, Anne W. *The First Amendment as a Shield or a Sword: An Integrated Look at Regulation of Multi-Media Ownership* (P-5418). Santa Monica, Calif.: The Rand Corporation (April 1975).

Bratland, Rose Marie Zummo. "National and Regional Analysis of Daily Newspaper Growth," *Printing and Publishing 18* (2):9-13 (Spring 1977).

Broadcast Advertisers Reports. New York: Broadcast Advertising Research.

Broadcasting (weekly).

Broadcasting Yearbook (annual).

Brown, Richard. "Book Buying," *Publishers Weekly* (May 5, 1964), pp. 16-19.

Bunce, Richard. *Television in the Corporate Interest*. New York: Praeger Special Studies, 1976.

Cable Sourcebook. Washington: Broadcasting Publications, Inc. (annual).

Campbell, Augus, et al. "Television and the Election," *Scientific American* 188:5:46-48 (May 1953).

Carnegie Commission on Educational Television. *Public Television: A Program for Action*. New York: Harper and Row, 1967.

Carroll, C. Edward. *The Professionalization of Education for Librarianship, with Special Reference to the Years 1940-1960*. Metuchen, N.J.: Scarecrow Press, 1970.

Cash Box (weekly).

Cater, Douglass, and Michael J. Nyhan. *The Future of Public Broadcasting*. New York: Praeger Publishers, Inc.; Palo Alto, Calif.: Aspen Institute for Humanistic Studies (copublishers), 1976.

CATV and Station Coverage Atlas. Washington: *Television Digest* (annual).

CBS Records, Market Research Department. "Recorded Music Industry Sales, 1971-76." New York: CBS Records, 1977.

Chaffee, Steven H., ed. *Political Communication: Issues and Strategies for Research*. Beverly Hills, Calif.: Sage Publications, 1975.

Chapin, Richard E. *Mass Communications: A Statistical Analysis*. East Lansing: Michigan State University Press, 1957.

Chappell, Matthew N., and C. E. Hooper. *Radio Audience Measurement*. New York: Stephen Daye Press, 1944.

Chapple, Steve, and Reebee Garofolo. *Rock 'n' Roll is Here to Pay: The History and Politics of the Music Industry*. Chicago: Nelson-Hall, 1977.

Cheney, O. H. *Economic Survey of the Book Industry* (reprinted). New York: R. R. Bowker, 1960.

Cherington, Paul W., et al. *Television Station Ownership: A Case Study of Federal Agency Regulation*. New York: Hastings House, 1971.

Chester, Edward W. *Radio, Television and American Politics*. New York: Sheed and Ward, 1969.

Chu, Godwin C., and Wilbur Schramm. *Learning from Television: What the Research Says*. Washington: National Association of Educational Broadcasters, 1968 (revised 1974).

Cogley, John. *Report on Blacklisting: Movies*. New York: Fund for the Republic, 1956 (reprinted by Arno Press 1970).

Columbia Broadcasting System. *Radio in 1937*. New York: CBS, 1937.

Compaine, Benjamin M. *Book Distribution and Marketing, 1976-1980*. White Plains, N.Y.: Knowledge Industry Publications, 1976.

————. *Consumer Magazines at the Crossroads: A Study of General and Special Interest Magazines*. White Plains, N.Y.: Knowledge Industry Publications, 1974.

————. *Papers and Profits: A Special Report on the Newspaper Business*. White Plains, N.Y.: Knowledge Industry Publications, 1973, 1974.

Comstock, George, et al. *Television and Human Behavior* (bibliography). 3 vols. Santa Monica, Calif.: The Rand Corporation, 1975.

Conant, Michael. *Antitrust in the Motion Picture Industry: Economic and Legal Analysis (BBER)*. Berkeley: University of California Press, 1960.

Cook, Charles R. "Employment Patterns in Printing and Publishing," *Printing and Publishing, 14* (2):3-6 (April 1973).

—————. "Wages and Hours in the U.S. Printing Industry," *Printing and Publishing, 17* (2):3-9 (Spring 1976).

Cox Looks at FM Radio. Atlanta: Cox Broadcasting Corporation, 1976.

Crandall, Robert W. "The Postwar Performance of the Motion-Picture Industry," *The Antitrust Bulletin 20* (1):49-88 (Spring 1975).

Dale, Edgar. *The Content of Motion Pictures*. New York: The Macmillan Co., 1935 (reprinted by Arno Press, 1970).

Daniells, Lorna M. *Business Information Sources*. Berkeley: University of California Press, 1976.

David, Nina. *TV Season*. Phoenix, Ariz.: Oryx Press, 1976 to date (annual).

Davis, Donald G. "Education for Librarianship," *Library Trends* (July 1976), pp. 113-134.

de Lesseps, Suzanne. "News Media Ownership," *Editorial Research Reports 1* (10):185-202 (March 11, 1977).

Denisoff, R. Serge. *Solid Gold: The Popular Record Industry*. New Brunswick, N.J.: Transaction Books, 1975.

Desmond, Robert W. *The Information Process: World News Reporting to the 20th Century*. Iowa City: University of Iowa Press, 1978.

Dessauer, John P. *Book Publishing: What It Is, What It Does*. New York: R. R. Bowker, 1974.

—————. *Library Acquisitions: A Look into the Future*. New York: Book Industry Study Group, 1976.

—————. "U.S. Book Markets: Where They Have Been, Where They Are Going," *Publishers Weekly* (July 26, 1976), pp. 39-49.

—————. "Where the Book Buyers' Money Goes," *Publishers Weekly* 204(5):42-43 (July 30, 1973).

—————, Paul D. Doebler, and E. Wayne Nordberg. *Book Industry Trends, 1977*. Darien, Conn.: Book Industry Study Group, 1977.

Dissertation Abstracts. Ann Arbor, Mich.: University Microfilms, Inc. (monthly).

Editor and Publisher (weekly).

Editor and Publisher International Yearbook (title varies) (annual).

Educational Television and Radio Center. *Educational Television Program Survey*. Ann Arbor, Mich.: 1958.

Elder, Robert E. *The Information Machine: The United States Information Agency and American Foreign Policy*. Syracuse, N.Y.: Syracuse University Press, 1968.

Eldridge, Marie D. *National Center for Education Statistics Release No. 76-192* and *No. 76-193*. Washington: U.S. Department of Health, Education and Welfare (January 28, 1976).

Electrical Merchandising Week (see *Merchandising*).

Electronic Industries Association. *Consumer Electronics*. Washington: EIA (annual).

—————. *Consumer Electronics Annual Review*. Washington: EIA.

—————. *Electronics Data Book*. Washington: EIA, 1976 (annual).

—————. *Electronics Market Data Book: 1976 Edition* (title has varied). Washington: EIA.

Emery, Edwin. "Press Support for Johnson and Goldwater," *Journalism Quarterly* 41:485-488 (Autumn 1964).

Emery, Walter B. *Broadcasting and Government: Responsibilities and Regulations*. 2nd ed. East Lansing: Michigan State University Press, 1971.

Encyclomedia: 1977 Newspaper Edition. New York: *Media Decisions*.

Ennis, Philip H. "Who Reads?" in *The Metropolitan Library*. Edited by Ralph W. Conant and Kathleen Molz. Cambridge, Mass.: The M.I.T. Press, 1972.

Epstein, Edward Jay. *News from Nowhere: Television and the News*. New York: Random House, 1973.

Fielding, Raymond. *The American Newsreel, 1911-1967*. Norman: University of Oklahoma Press, 1972.

Film Daily.

Film Daily Yearbook (annual, no longer published).

Folio: The Magazine for Magazine Management. New Canaan, Conn.: Folio Magazine Publishing Co. (monthly).

The Ford Foundation. *Ford Foundation Activities in Noncommercial Broadcasting, 1951-1976.*
New York: The Ford Foundation, 1976.

Foreign Service Journal (monthly).

Fortune (monthly).

Fry, Bernard M., and Herbert S. White, with Marjorie Shepley. *Publishers and Libraries: A Study of Scholarly and Research Journals.* Lexington, Mass.: Lexington Books/D. C. Heath and Co., 1976.

Gelatt, Roland. *The Fabulous Phonograph, 1877-1977.* New York: Macmillan, 1977.

Gerbner, George. "The Violence Index: An Exchange of Views," *Journal of Broadcasting* 21: 273-303 (Summer 1977).

————, et al. *Violence Profile No. 7* and *Violence Profile No. 8.* Philadelphia: Annenberg School of Communications, University of Pennsylvania, 1976 and 1977.

————, and Larry Gross. "Living with Television: The Violence Profile," *Journal of Communication* 26:173-199 (Spring 1976).

————, and George Marvanyi. "The Many Worlds of the World's Press," *Journal of Communication* 27 (1):52-66 (Winter 1977).

Gormley, William T., Jr. *The Effects of Newspaper-Television Cross-Ownership on News Homogeneity.* Chapel Hill: Institute for Research in Social Science, University of North Carolina, 1976.

Grannis, Chandler B. "AAP 1975 Statistics: What the Figures Show," *Publishers Weekly* (June 28, 1976), pp. 44-46.

————. "American Imports and Exports: Informational Title Output," *Publishers Weekly* (September 19, 1977), pp. 93-96. (Grannis, 1977c)

————. "1977: The Year in Review," *Publishers Weekly* (February 20, 1978), pp. 51-71.

————. "Statistics—More or Less," *Publishers Weekly* (September 18, 1972), p. 128.

————. "Title Counts and Average Prices per Volume," *Publishers Weekly* (August 22, 1977), pp. 32-39. (Grannis, 1977b)

————. "U.S. Book Industry Statistics: Prices, Sales, Trends," *Publishers Weekly* (February 14, 1977), pp. 52-56. (Grannis, 1977a)

Greenberg, Bradley S., and Edwin B. Parker, eds. *The Kennedy Assassination and the American Public: Social Communication in Crisis.* Stanford, Calif.: Stanford University Press, 1965.

Guback, Thomas H. *The International Film Industry: Western Europe and America Since 1945.* Bloomington: Indiana University Press, 1969.

Hale, Julian. *Radio Power: Propaganda and International Broadcasting.* Philadelphia: Temple University Press, 1975.

Hall, Ben M. *The Best Remaining Seats: The Story of the Golden Age of the Movie Palace.* New York: Crown, 1961.

Handel, Leo. *Hollywood Looks at Its Audience.* Urbana: University of Illinois Press, 1950.

Hatcher, David M. *Syndication in American Television, 1950-1975* (unpublished MA thesis). Madison: University of Wisconsin, 1976.

Head, Sydney W. *Broadcasting in America: A Survey of Television and Radio.* 3rd ed. Boston: Houghton-Mifflin, 1976.

Heard, Alexander. *The Costs of Democracy.* Chapel Hill: University of North Carolina Press, 1960.

Heidbreder, M. Arin. "Research Needed in the Fields of Reading and Communications," *Library Trends* 22 (2): 239-251 (October 1973).

Henderson, John W. *The United States Information Agency.* New York: Praeger, 1969.

Hokkanen, Dorothy B. "American Book Title Output—A Ninety-Year Overview," *Printing and Publishing* 11 (3):25-28 (July 1970). (Hokkanen, 1970a)

————. "International Markets Draw U.S. Periodical Publishers," *Printing and Publishing* 10 (3):10-11 (July 1969).

————. "Thirty-five Years of International Book Trade," *Printing and Publishing* 11 (2):15-22 (April 1970). (Hokkanen, 1970b)

————. "Twenty Years of Periodical Growth," *Printing and Publishing* 12 (1):11-13 (January 1971).

Hollowell, Mary Louise, ed. *Cable Handbook 1975-76.* Washington: Communications Press, 1975.

Hope Reports. Rochester, N.Y.: Hope Reports, Inc. (monthly surveys and biennial compilations).

Howard, Herbert H. "The Contemporary Status of Television Group Ownership," *Journalism Quarterly* 53:399-405 (Autumn 1976). (Howard, 1976b)

————. "Recent Trends in Broadcast Multiple Ownership," *Client* 4:1:6-14 (Fall 1976). (Howard, 1976a)

Huettig, Mae D. *Economic Control of the Motion Picture Industry: A Study in Industrial Organization.* Philadelphia: University of Pennsylvania Press, 1944 (reprinted by Jerome Ozer, 1971).

University of Illinois, Graduate School of Library Science. *1962 Statistics of Public Libraries Serving Populations of Less than 35,000*. Urbana: University of Illinois Graduate School of Library Science, 1966.

International Motion Picture Almanac. New York: Quigley Publications, 1929 to date (annual).

Jarvie, I. C. *Movies and Society*. New York: Basic Books, 1970.

Johnstone, John W. C., et al. *The News People: A Sociological Portrait of American Journalists and Their Work*. Urbana: University of Illinois Press, 1976.

Joint Council on Educational Television. "The 1959 Educational Television Directory," *Educational Television Factsheet*. Washington: JCET (January 1959).

Journalism Educator (quarterly).

Journalism Quarterly.

Jowett, Garth. *Film: The Democratic Art*. Boston: Little, Brown, 1976.

Kahn, E. J. *The American People*. Baltimore: Penguin Books, 1975.

Karian, George Thomas. *The Directory of American Book Publishing*. New York: Simon and Schuster, 1975.

Katzen, May. *Mass Communication: Teaching and Studies at Universities*. Paris: UNESCO (New York: Unipub), 1975.

Katzman, Natan. *Program Decisions in Public Television*. Washington: Corporation for Public Broadcasting, and National Association of Educational Broadcasters, 1976.

King, D. W., D. D. McDonald, N. K. Roderer, and B. L. Wood. *Statistical Indicators of Scientific and Technical Communication 1960-1980, Volume 1*. Washington: U.S. Govt. Printing Office, 1976. (A summary report for National Science Foundation Division of Science Information.)

Kliesch, Ralph E. *Directory of the Overseas Press Club of America*. New York: Overseas Press Club of America, 1976.

—————. "A Vanishing Species: The American Newsman Abroad," *Directory of the Overseas Press Club of America*. New York: Overseas Press Club of America, 1975.

Knight, Douglas M., and E. Shepley Nourse, eds. *Libraries at Large*. New York: R. R. Bowker, 1969.

Koenig, Allen E., ed. *Broadcasting and Bargaining: Labor Relations in Radio and Television*. Madison: University of Wisconsin Press, 1970.

Kraus, Sidney, and Dennis Davis. *The Effects of Mass Communication on Political Behavior*. University Park: Pennsylvania State University Press, 1976.

Kroeger, A. R. "How Things Stand with the Groups," *Television* (March 1966), pp. 30-31ff.

Ladd, Boyd. *National Inventory of Library Needs, 1975: Resources Needed for Public and Academic Libraries and Public School Library/Media Centers. A Study Submitted to the National Commission on Libraries and Information Science (March 1977)*. Washington: U.S. Govt. Printing Office, 1977.

Land, Herbert W., Associates, Inc. *Television and the Wired City: A Study of the Implications of a Change in the Mode of Transmission*. Washington: National Association of Broadcasters, 1968.

Larson, James F. *International Affairs Coverage on U.S. Network Television Evening News Broadcasts, 1972-1976*. Stanford, Calif.: Institute for Communication Research, Stanford University, 1978.

Larson, Timothy L. "Concentration in the U.S. Television Industry and the Question of Network Divestiture of Owned and Operated Television Stations." (Paper delivered before the 1977 Annual Meeting of the Broadcast Education Association, Washington, D.C., 1977.)

Lashner, Marilyn A. "The Role of Foundations in Public Broadcasting, I: Development and Trends," *Journal of Broadcasting* 20:529-547 (Fall 1976).

—————. "The Role of Foundations in Public Broadcasting, II," *Journal of Broadcasting* 21:235-254 (Spring 1977).

Lavey, Warren G. *Toward a Quantification of the Information/Communication Industries*. Cambridge, Mass.: Harvard University, Program on Information Technologies and Public Policy (May 1974).

Lazarsfeld, Paul F. "Audience Research in the Movie Field," *Annals of the American Academy of Political and Social Science* (November 1947).

—————, and Patricia Kendall. *Radio Listening in America*. New York: Prentice-Hall, 1948.

Ledding, Mary S., and Walter Baer. *Minority Participation in Media Ownership: A Literature Study* (WN-8649-NSF). Santa Monica, Calif.: The Rand Corporation, 1973.

LeDuc, Don R. *Cable Television and the FCC: A Crisis in Media Control*. Philadelphia: Temple University Press, 1973.

Lee, Alfred M. *The Daily Newspaper in America*. New York: Macmillan, 1937.

Levin, Harvey J. *Broadcast Regulation and Joint Ownership of Media*. New York: New York University Press, 1960.

—————. "The Policy on Joint Ownership of Newspapers and Television Stations: Some Assumptions, Objectives, and Effects." New York: Center for Policy Research (April 1971). (Statement on Docket No. 18110 before the Federal Communications Commission.)

Lewis, Howard T. *The Motion Picture Industry*. New York: Van Nostrand, 1933 (reprinted by Jerome Ozer, 1971).

Library Journal (monthly).

Lichty, Lawrence W. *Broadcasting Yearbook*, 1936, 1945, 1960, 1971, 1976.

—————. "A History of Network Television Programming, 1948-1973." Madison: University of Wisconsin, Department of Communication Arts (mimeograph), n.d. (work in progress for eventual publication).

—————, and Malachi C. Topping, eds. *American Broadcasting: A Sourcebook on the History of Radio and Television*. New York: Hastings House, 1975.

—————, et al. "Political Programs on National Television Networks: 1960 and 1964," *Journal of Broadcasting* 9:217-229 (Summer 1965).

Literary Market Place, 1976-1977 edition. New York: R. R. Bowker, 1976.

A. D. Little Co. *Television Program Production, Procurement and Syndication*. 2 vols. Cambridge, Mass.: A. D. Little Co., 1966.

—————. *Television Program Production, Procurement, Distribution and Scheduling*. Cambridge, Mass.: A. D. Little Co., 1969 (with subsequent corrections issued by publisher).

Lofquist, William S. "Historical Analysis of U.S. Book Publishing Statistics," *Printing and Publishing* 11 (3):13-25 (July 1970).

—————. "Patterns of Concentration in the U.S. Graphic Arts Industries," *Printing and Publishing* 17 (1):12-27 (Winter 1976).

—————. "U.S. Bookstores Show Rapid Growth," *Printing and Publishing* 18 (1):14-19 (Winter 1976-1977).

—————. "U.S. Periodical Publishers Eye Foreign Markets," *Printing and Publishing* 10 (4):12-16 (October 1969).

—————. "Wages and Hours Worked in the U.S. Printing Industry," *Printing and Publishing* 13 (4):5-11 (October 1972).

Lumley, Frederick H. *Measurement in Radio*. Columbus: Ohio State University Press, 1934 (reprinted by Arno Press, 1972).

Lyle, Jack. *The People Look at Public Television: 1974*. Washington: Corporation for Public Broadcasting, 1975.

Machlup, Fritz. *The Production and Distribution of Knowledge in the United States*. Princeton, N.J.: Princeton University Press, 1962.

Madow, William G., et al. *Evaluation of Statistical Methods Used in Obtaining Broadcast Ratings*. House Report 193, 87th Congress, 1st Session (1961).

Magazine Editorial Reports. Greenwich, Conn.: R. Russell Hall Co. (monthly).

Magazine Publishers Association. *Sources of Information about Magazines*. New York: MPA, 1973.

Manvell, Roger, et al., eds. *The International Encyclopedia of Film*. New York: Crown, 1972.

"The Many Worlds of Radio." *Broadcasting* (September 27, 1976).

Marketing Communications (six times per year).

Martin, L. John, ed. "Propaganda in International Affairs," *The Annals No. 398*. Philadelphia: American Academy of Political and Social Science (November 1971), pp. 1-139.

Mathews, Virginia H. "Adult Reading Studies: Their Implications for Private, Professional and Public Policy," *Library Trends 22* (2):149-177 (October 1973).

McAlpine, Dennis B. *The Television Programming Industry*. New York: Tucker Anthony & R. L. Day (January 1975).

McCombs, Maxwell E. "Mass Media in the Marketplace," *Journalism Monographs* No. 24 (August 1972).

Media Decisions (monthly).

Merchandising (monthly). (This publication has had various titles and frequencies of appearance; see especially the annual sales report and projection published in the Spring.)

Merrill Lynch, Pierce, Fenner and Smith. *Broadcasting Basics II*. New York: Merrill Lynch, Pierce, Fenner and Smith, 1975 to date (irregular).

————. *Broadcasting Industry*. New York: Merrill Lynch, Pierce, Fenner and Smith, 1975 to date (irregular).

————. *Broadcasting Monthly*. New York: Merrill Lynch, Pierce, Fenner and Smith, 1975 to date (irregular).

Minow, Newton, et al. *Presidential Television*. New York: Basic Books, 1973.

Moody's Industrial Manual. New York: Moody's Investor's Service.

Motion Picture Association of America. *Annual Report*. Los Angeles: MPAA, 1930 to date.

————. "Incidence of Motion Picture Attendance, July-August 1976," New York: MPAA (October 1976, mimeo).

————. "The Public Appraises Movies" (see Jowett, 1976).

Mott, Frank Luther. *American Journalism: A History: 1690-1960*. 3rd ed. New York: Macmillan, 1962.

National Association of Broadcasters. *Radio Financial Report*. Washington: NAB, 1955 to date (annual).

————. *Radio in 1985*. Washington: NAB, 1977.

————. *Radio Today*. Washington: NAB, 1970.

————. *Television Financial Report*. Washington: NAB (annual).

National Association of Educational Broadcasters. *Directory of Public Telecommunications*. Washington: NAEB (annual).

————. *The Financial Status of Public Broadcasting Stations in the United States, 1968-69*. Washington: NAEB, 1969.

————. *Four Years of New York Television, 1951-1954*. Urbana, Ill.: NAEB, 1954.

————. *Los Angeles Television: May 23-29, 1951*. Urbana, Ill.: NAEB, 1951.

National Association of FM Broadcasters. *National FM Programming Trends*. New York: NAFMB, 1967.

National Association of Theatre Owners. *Encyclopedia of Exhibition*. New York: NATO, 1976.

National Newspaper Association. *National Directory of Weekly Newspapers*. Washington: NNA (annual).

New York Times (daily).

Nielsen Television Index, A. C. Nielsen Co. *Network Television Audiences to Primaries, Conventions, Elections*. Northbrook, Ill.: A. C. Nielsen Co., 1976.

————. *Nielsen Newscast* (quarterly).

————. *Nielsen Television*. Northbrook, Ill.: A. C. Nielsen Co., 1955 to date (annual).

————. *Radio and Television Audience 1956*. Northbrook, Ill.: A. C. Nielsen Co.

————. *Radio 1960*. Northbrook, Ill.: A. C. Nielsen Co.

————. *Reference Supplement*. Northbrook, Ill.: A. C. Nielsen Co. (annual).

————. *Report on Syndicated Programs*. Northbrook, Ill.: A. C. Nielsen Co.

————. *Television Audience*. Northbrook, Ill.: A. C. Nielsen Co., 1959 to date (annual).

Niven, Harold. *Broadcast Education*, Second Report (1956); Fifth Report (1960); Ninth Report (1965); Twelfth Report (1970); and Fourteenth Report (1975). Washington: National Association of Broadcasters, 1956 to date (approx. biennial).

————. "Fourteenth Survey of Colleges and Universities Offering Courses in Broadcasting," *Journal of Broadcasting* 19:453-495 (Fall 1975).

Nixon, Raymond B. "Number of Dailies in Groups Increased by 11% in Three Years," *Editor and Publisher* 107 (8):9 (February 23, 1974).

Noble, J. Kendrick. "AAP 1976 Statistics—Using the Figures," *Publishers Weekly* (July 4, 1977), pp. 41-43.

————. "Book Industry Stocks: Past, Present and Prospects," *Publishers Weekly* (July 26, 1976), pp. 49-50.

Noll, Roger, et al. *Economic Aspects of Television Regulation*. Washington: Brookings Institution, 1973.

Nordberg, E. Wayne. "Economic Events in 1975 and Their Impact on Book Demand," *Publishers Weekly* (July 26, 1976), pp. 36-39.

Oettinger, Anthony G. *Elements of Information Resources Policy: Library and Other Information Services*. Cambridge, Mass.: Harvard University Program on Information Technologies and Public Policy, 1976 (revised edition).

————, Paul J. Berman, and William H. Read. *High and Low Politics: Information Resources for the 1980's*. Cambridge, Mass.: Ballinger Publishing Co., 1977.

Ogan, Christine, et al. "The Changing Front Page of the New York Times, 1900-1970," *Journalism Quarterly* 52:340-344 (Summer 1975).

Olson, Edwin. *Survey of Federal Libraries, 1972*. Washington: U.S. Department of Health, Education and Welfare (National Center for Education Statistics), 1975.

One Week of Educational Television No. 3, April 19-25, 1964. Waltham, Mass.: Morse Communication Research Center, Brandeis University, 1965.

—————. *No. 4, April 17-23, 1966*. Bloomington, Ind.: National Center for School and College Television, 1966.

—————. *No. 5, May 6-12, 1968*. 2 vols. Bloomington, Ind.: National Instructional Television Center, 1969.

—————. *No. 6, March 9-15, 1970*. Bloomington, Ind.: National Instructional Television Center, 1971.

Opinion Research Corporation. "The Public Appraises Movies" (see Jowett, 1976).

Origination Directory. Washington: National Cable Television Association (annual).

Owen, Bruce. *Economics and Freedom of Expression: Media Structure and the First Amendment*. Cambridge, Mass.: Ballinger Publishing, 1975.

—————, et al. *Television Economics*. Lexington, Mass.: Lexington Books, 1974.

Park, R. E. *New Television Networks* (R-1408-MF). Santa Monica, Calif.: The Rand Corporation (December 1973).

Pavlakis, Christopher. *The American Music Handbook*. New York: The Free Press, 1974.

Pay TV Newsletter. Rockville Centre, N.Y.: Paul Kagan Associates (weekly).

Penkert, Bill, ed. *Gebbie House Magazine Directory*. 7th ed. Sioux City, Iowa: House Magazine Publishing Co., 1971.

Perry, Martin. "Recent Trends in the Structure of the Cable Television Industry." Stanford, Calif.: Stanford University Department of Economics (May 1974, discussion paper).

Peter, ———. "The American Listener in 1940," *Annals* (January 1941).

Peterson, Paul. *Journalism Quarterly*, 1960 to 1970 (first yearly issues).

Peterson, Theodore. *Magazines in the Twentieth Century*. 2nd ed. Urbana: University of Illinois Press, 1964.

Phillips, Kevin. "Busting the Media Trusts," *Harper's* (July 1977), pp. 23-34.

Porat, Marc Uri. *The Information Economy, Volume I*. Stanford, Calif.: Program in Information Technology and Telecommunications, Center for Interdisciplinary Research, Stanford University, Report No. 27 (August 1976).

—————, and Michael Rubin. *The Information Economy*. 9 vols. Washington: U.S. Department of Commerce, Office of Telecommunications, OT Special Publication 77-12 (May 1977).

Predicasts Basebook. Cleveland: Predicasts, Inc. (annual).

Printer's Ink (biweekly, no longer published).

Printing and Publishing (quarterly).

Public Telecommunications Review (bimonthly).

Publishers Weekly.

Read, Oliver, and Walter L. Welch. *From Tin Foil to Stereo: Evolution of the Phonograph*. 2nd ed. Indianapolis: Howard W. Sams, 1976.

Read, William H. *America's Mass Media Merchants*. Baltimore: The Johns Hopkins University Press, 1977.

Reeves, Michael G., and Tom W. Hoffer. "The Safe, Cheap and Known: A Content Analysis of the First (1974) PBS Program Cooperative," *Journal of Broadcasting* 20:549-565 (Fall 1976).

Reyes Matta, Fernando. "The Information Bedazzlement of Latin America," *Development Dialogue*. (Sweden) 1976 (2):29-42 (1976).

Richstad, Jim, ed. *New Perspectives in International Communication*. Honolulu: East-West Communication Institute, East-West Center, 1977.

—————, and Jackie Bowen. *International Communication Policy and Flow: A Selected Annotated Bibliography*. Honolulu: East-West Communication Institute, East-West Center, 1976.

Rivers, William L., and David M. Rubin. *A Region's Press: Anatomy of Newspapers in the San Francisco Bay Area*. Berkeley: Institute of Governmental Studies, University of California, 1971.

Rogers, Charles E. "Quantitative Survey of AASDJ Schools and Departments of Journalism," *Journalism Quarterly* 22:317-329 (December 1945).

Rogers, Everett M., ed. *Communication and Development: Critical Perspectives*. Beverly Hills, Calif.: Sage Publications, 1976.

—————, and Rekha Agarwala-Rogers. *Communication in Organizations*. New York: Free Press, 1976.

Roper Organization. *Changing Public Attitudes Toward Television and other Mass Media: 1959-1976*. New York: Television Information Office, 1976. (This is the 10th report in a series dating back to 1959, most of the data cumulating in later reports.)

Ross, Leonard. *Economic and Legal Foundations of Cable Television*. Beverly Hills, Calif.: Sage (Publications in the Social Sciences No. 90-012), 1974.

Rosse, James N., Bruce M. Owen, and James Dertouzos. "Trends in the Daily Newspaper Industry 1923-1973," *Studies in Industry Economics No. 57*. Stanford, Calif.: Department of Economics, Stanford University (May 1975).

Routt, Edd. *Dimensions of Broadcast Editorializing*. Blue Ridge Summit, Penn.: TAB Books, 1974.

Rucker, Bryce W. *The First Freedom*. Carbondale: Southern Illinois University Press, 1968.

Sandage, C. H. *Radio Advertising for Retailers*. Cambridge, Mass.: Harvard University Press, 1945.

Schacht, J. H. *A Bibliography for the Study of Magazines*. Urbana: College of Communications, University of Illinois, 1972.

Schick, Frank L., and William H. Kurth. *Library Statistics: The Cost of Library Materials; Price Trends of Publications*. Washington: U.S. Office of Education, Publication No. OE-15029A (October 1961).

Schiller, Herbert I. *Mass Communications and American Empire*. Boston: Beacon Press, 1971.

Schmookler, Jacob. *Invention and Economic Growth*. Cambridge, Mass.: Harvard University Press, 1966.

Schnapper, Amy. *The Distribution of Theatrical Feature Films to Television* (unpublished dissertation). Madison: University of Wisconsin, 1976.

Schramm, Wilbur. *Big Media, Little Media: Tools and Technologies for Instruction*. Beverly Hills, Calif.: Sage Publications, 1977.

—————. *Mass Media and National Development: The Role of Information in the Developing Countries*. Stanford, Calif.: Stanford University Press, 1964.

—————, Jack Lyle, and Edwin B. Parker. *Television in the Lives of our Children*. Stanford, Calif.: Stanford University Press, 1961.

—————, Jack Lyle, and Ithiel de Sola Pool. *The People Look at Educational Television*. Stanford, Calif.: Stanford University Press, 1963.

—————, and Lyle Nelson. *The Financing of Public Television*. Palo Alto, Calif.: Aspen Program on Communications and Society, 1972.

Scott, James D. *Cable Television: Strategy for Penetrating Key Urban Markets*. Ann Arbor: Graduate School of Business, University of Michigan (Michigan Business Reports No. 58), 1976.

Seiden, Martin H. *Cable Television U.S.A.: An Analysis of Government Policy*. New York: Praeger Special Studies, 1972.

—————. *Who Controls the Mass Media? Popular Myths and Economics Realities*. New York: Basic Books, 1975.

Shemel, Sidney. *This Business of Music*. New York: Billboard Publications, Inc., 1977.

W. R. Simmons and Associates Research. *Simmons Media Studies*. New York: W. R. Simmons and Associates, 1976, 1977.

—————. *Study of Selective Markets and the Media Reaching Them*. New York: W. R. Simmons and Associates, 1977.

Slanker, Barbara O. "The Need for Further Research," in John P. Dessauer et al., *Book Industry Trends 1977*. Darien, Conn.: Book Industry Study Group, Inc., 1977.

Smith, Datus C., Jr. *The Economics of Book Publishing in Developing Countries*. Paris: UNESCO Reports and Papers on Mass Communication (No. 79), 1977.

—————. *Guide to Book-Publishing*. New York: R. R. Bowker, 1966.

Smythe, Dallas W., et al. "Portrait of a First-Run Audience," *Quarterly of Film, Radio and Television* 9:394 (1955).

Sponsor Basics (annual, title varies, no longer published).

Standard and Poor's Corporation. *Standard and Poor's Directory of Corporations*. New York: S & P (annual).

—————. *Standard and Poor's Index of Corporations*. New York: S & P (annual).

—————. *Standard and Poor's Industry Surveys*. New York: S & P (quarterly and annual surveys of 36 industries). (Of special value here are the following annuals: *Amusements* to 1973, *Leisure Time* since 1973, and *Communication* since 1973.)

—————. *Standard and Poor's Standard Corporation Descriptions*. New York: S & P (weekly, with a daily news section).

Standard Rate and Data Service, Inc. *Business Publication Rates and Data*. Skokie, Ill.: SRDS (monthly).

—————. *Consumer Magazine and Farm Publication Rates and Data*. Skokie, Ill.: SRDS (monthly).

—————. *Daily Newspapers*. Skokie, Ill.: SRDS (biannual).

—————. "Multiple Business Publication Publishers Index," *Business Publication Rates and Data, 59* (11):1360-1364 (November 23, 1977). Skokie, Ill.: SRDS.

—————. "Multiple Consumer Magazine (Incl. International) and Farm Publishers," *Consumer Magazine and Farm Publication Rates and Data, 59* (10):606-608 (October 27, 1977). Skokie, Ill.: SRDS.

Statistical Trends in Broadcasting. New York: John Blair Co., 1964 to date (annual).

Steiner, Gary A. *The People Look at Television*. New York: Knopf, 1963.

Sterling, Christopher H. "Broadcast Education: Status and Trends," *Educational Media Yearbook 1977*. Edited by James W. Brown. New York: R. R. Bowker, 1977, pp. 56-63.

—————. "Newspaper Ownership of Broadcast Stations, 1920-68," *Journalism Quarterly* 46: 227-236, 254 (Summer 1969).

—————. *Ownership Characteristics of Broadcasting Stations and Newspapers in the Top 100 Markets, 1922-1967*. Washington: National Association of Broadcasters (March 5, 1971). (Filed with FCC concerning Docket 18110.)

—————. "Supplement to National Association of Broadcasters' Exhibit C Regarding Cross-Ownership of Broadcasting Stations and Newspapers" (May 1974). (Docket No. 18110, before the Federal Communications Commission—adds information to study above.)

—————. "Trends in Daily Newspaper and Broadcast Ownership, 1922-1970," *Journalism Quarterly* 52:247-256, 320 (Summer 1975).

—————, and John M. Kittross. *Stay Tuned: A Concise History of American Broadcasting*. Belmont, Calif.: Wadsworth Publishing Co., 1978.

Stevenson, Tom. "The Profitable Nonprofit Press," *Folio: The Magazine for Magazine Management*, 38-47 (October 1976).

Summers, Harrison B. *A Thirty Year History of Programs Carried on National Radio Networks in the United States, 1926-1956*. Columbus: Ohio State University Department of Speech, 1958 (reprinted by Arno Press, 1972).

Tebell, John. *The American Magazine: A Compact History*. New York: Hawthorne Books, 1969.

Telefilm (monthly, no longer published).

Television Digest (weekly).

Television Factbook. 2 vols. Washington: *Television Digest* (annual).

Television News Index and Abstracts. Nashville: Vanderbilt Television News Archive (monthly).

Terrace, Vincent. *The Complete Encyclopedia of Television Programs, 1947-1976*. 2 vols. South Brunswick, N.J.: A. S. Barnes, 1976.

Tunstall, Jeremy. *The Media Are American*. New York: Columbia University Press, 1977.

Udell, Jon G. "Dynamics of U.S. Daily Newspapers and Newsprint Consumption: Recent Developments and the Future Outlook," *American Newspaper Publishers Association Newsprint and Traffic Bulletin No. 2* (January 21, 1976).

—————. *The Economics of the American Newspaper*. New York: Hastings House, 1978.

—————. *Economic Trends in the Daily Newspaper Business*. Madison: Bureau of Research and Service, University of Wisconsin (December 1970).

—————. "U.S. Economic Growth and Newspaper Consumption," *American Newspaper Publishers Association Newsprint and Traffic Bulletin No. 1* (January 5, 1977).

UNESCO. *News Agencies: Their Structure and Operation*. New York: Greenwood Press, 1969. (Reprint of 1953 UNESCO publication.)

—————. *Press Film Radio, Volume IV*. Paris: UNESCO, 1950 (includes United States).

—————. *UNESCO Statistical Yearbook*. Paris: UNESCO, 1968, 1971, 1974.

—————. *World Communications*. 1st ed., 2nd ed., 4th ed., 5th ed. Paris: UNESCO, 1950, 1951, 1964, 1975.

University Microfilms, Inc. *Dissertation Abstracts*. Ann Arbor, Mich.: University Microfilms (monthly).

United Church of Christ, Office of Communication. *Television Station Employment Practices: The Status of Minorities and Women*. New York: United Church of Christ, Office of Communication, 1973 to date (annual).

United Nations Statistical Yearbook. New York: United Nations.

Vanier, Dinoo J. *Market Structure and the Business of Book Publishing*. New York: Pitman Publishing Co., 1973.

Variety (weekly).

"Violence Ratings: A Dialogue," *Journal of Broadcasting* 17:3-35 (Winter 1972-1973).

Wagner, Paul H. "The Evolution of Newspaper Interest in Radio," *Journalism Quarterly* 23:182-188 (June 1976).

Watkins, Gordon S., ed. "The Motion Picture Industry," *Annals of the American Academy of Political and Social Science* No. 254 (November 1947) (reprinted by Arno Press, 1970).

Weintraub, D. Kathryn, and Sarah R. Reed, eds. *North American Library Education: Directory and Statistics, 1971-73*. Bloomington: Indiana University Graduate Library School, 1974.

Welles, Chris. "Do Most People Depend on TV for News?" *Columbia Journalism Review* 16 (5): 12-14 (January/February 1978).

Wilhelm, John R. *1966 Directory of the Overseas Press Club of America*. New York: OPC.

—————. "The Overseas Correspondent," *Journalism Quarterly* 40:147-168 (Spring 1963).

—————. "The World Press Corps Dwindles: A Fifth World Survey of Foreign Correspondents." (Paper read at the International Division Session of the Annual Convention of the Association for Education in Journalism, Carbondale, Ill., August 22, 1972.)

Willey, Malcolm M., and Stuart A. Rice. *Communication Agencies and Social Life*. New York: McGraw-Hill, 1933.

Wolf, Frank. *Television Programming for News and Public Affairs: A Quantitative Analysis of Networks and Stations*. New York: Praeger Special Studies, 1972.

Wolseley, Roland E. *The Changing Magazine: Trends in Readership and Management*. New York: Hastings House, 1973.

—————. *Understanding Magazines*. 2nd ed. Ames: Iowa State University Press, 1969.

Wood, Donald N., and Donald G. Wylie. *Educational Telecommunications*. Belmont, Calif.: Wadsworth, 1977.

Wood, James P. *Magazines in the United States*. 3rd ed. New York: Ronald Press, 1971.

Organizations

ABC, Inc. (American Broadcasting Company). New York.
Academy for Educational Development. New York and Washington, D.C.
Advertising Research Foundation. New York.
American Federation of Television and Radio Artists (AFTRA). New York.
American Film Institute (AFI). Washington, D.C.
American Library Association (ALA). Chicago.
American Newspaper Publishers Association (ANPA). Washington, D.C.
American Newspaper Representatives, Inc. Brooklyn.
ANPA News Research Center. Syracuse University.
Arbitron Television (ARB). Beltsville, Md.
Association for Education in Journalism (AEJ). DeKalb, Ill.
Association of American Publishers (AAP). New York.
Association of American University Presses (AAUP). New York.
Association of Independent Television Stations, Inc. New York.
Association of Research Libraries. Washington, D.C.
Audit Bureau of Circulations (ABC). Chicago.
Audits and Surveys, Co., Inc. New York.
Axiom Market Research Bureau, Inc. New York.
Ted Bates & Co. New York.
Batten, Barton, Durstine and Osborn, Inc. (BBD&O). New York.
John Blair and Company. New York.
Broadcast Advertising Research (BAR). New York.
Broadcast Education Association. Washington, D.C.
Business Publications Audit of Circulation, Inc. New York.
Cable Television Information Center. Washington, D.C.
Carnegie Commission on Educational Television. New York.
CBS Records, Market Research Department. New York.
Children's Television Workshop (CTW). New York.
Citizens Research Foundation. Princeton, N.J.
Columbia Broadcasting System (CBS). New York.
Communications Resource Center (formerly Cablecommunications Resource Center). Washington, D.C.
The Conference Board. New York.
Corporation for Public Broadcasting (CPB). Washington, D.C.
Cox Broadcasting Corporation. Atlanta.
CTW (formerly Children's Television Workshop). New York.
Educational Television and Radio Center. Ann Arbor, Mich.
Electronic Industries Association (EIA). Washington, D.C.
Evangelical Christian Publishers Association.
The Ford Foundation. New York.
Freedom of Information (FOI) Center. Columbia, Mo.
The Gallup Organization. Princeton, N.J.
GOP National Committee. Washington, D.C.
Group W. New York.
R. Russell Hall Co. Greenwich, Conn.
Home Testing Institute, Inc. New York.
Hope Reports, Inc. Rochester, N.Y.
Joint Council on Educational Television (JECT). Washington, D.C.
Paul Kagan Associates. Rockville Centre, N.Y.
Herman W. Land Associates. Washington, D.C.
A. D. Little Company. Cambridge, Mass.
Magazine Advertising Bureau (see Magazine Publishers Association).
Magazine Publishers Association (MPA). New York.
McCann-Erickson, Inc. New York.
Media Records, Inc. New York.
Medical Library Association. Chicago.
Merrill Lynch, Pierce, Fenner & Smith, Inc., Securities Research Division. New York.
Moody's Investor's Service. New York.
Morse Communication Research Center. Brandeis University. Waltham, Mass.
Motion Picture Association of America (MPAA). New York.
National Association of Broadcasters (NAB). Washington, D.C.

National Association of College Bookstores. Oberlin, Ohio.
National Association of Educational Broadcasters (NAEB). Washington, D.C.
National Association of FM Broadcasters (NAFMB). New York.
National Association of Record Merchandisers (NARM). Cherry Hill, N.J.
National Association of Theatre Owners (NATO). New York.
National Broadcasting Corporation (NBC). New York.
National Cable Television Association (NCTA). Washington, D.C.
National Center for School and College Television (see National Instructional Television Center).
National Industrial Conference Board (see The Conference Board).
National Instructional Television Center. Bloomington, Ind.
National Newspaper Association. Washington, D.C.
National Opinion Research Center. University of Chicago.
National Public Radio. Washington, D.C.
National Radio Broadcasters Association. Washington, D.C.
National Science Foundation (NSF). Washington, D.C.
Newspaper Advertising Bureau. New York.
Newspaper Analysis Service. Cincinnati.
The Newspaper Fund. Princeton, N.J.
The Newspaper Guild. Washington, D.C.
Nielsen Television Index, A. C. Nielsen Company. Northbrook, Ill.
Opinion Research Corporation. Washington, D.C.
Overseas Press Club. New York.
Predicasts, Inc. Cleveland.
Public Broadcasting Service (PBS). Washington, D.C.
Publishers Information Bureau. New York.
Pulse, Inc. New York.
Radio Advertising Bureau. New York.
Recording Industry Association of America (RIAA). New York.
The Roper Organization. New York.
Screen Actors Guild (SAG). Hollywood.
Screen Writers Guild (see Writers Guild of America West).
W. R. Simmons and Associates Research. New York.
Standard and Poor's Corporation. New York.
Standard Rate and Data Service. Skokie, Ill.
Television Bureau of Advertising. New York.
Television Information Office (TIO). New York.
J. Walter Thompson Co. New York.
UNESCO. Paris.
United Church of Christ, Office of Communication. New York.
Warner Communications, Inc. New York.
Writers Guild of America West. Los Angeles.

Subject Index

Evangelical Christian Publishers Association, 142
exports
See import/export trade.

F

Fairness Doctrine, Communications Act, 279
FCC
    regulations, 44-49, 56, 58, 91, 93, 96, 99, 210, 279-81, 306, 321
    survey, 270
Federal Election Committee, 280
Federal Radio Commission, 45
"first-run" TV shows, 307, 378
film rental revenues, 87-88, 421
films
    See motion picture industry.
Ford Foundation, 194, 197, 200-1, 310
foreign correspondents, 386-88

G

Gallup Polls, 273-75
Gerbner violence profile, 319-21
Gold Records, 39
Gross National Product (GNP), 111-14, 138
group ownership, TV stations, 99-102
Group W (Westinghouse), 97-98, 213

H

Hall, R. Russell, 292-93
hardcover books, 149-51
Hollywood craft unions, 265, 267
Hollywood "majors", 87, 183-85
Home Testing Institute, 359

I

import/export trade
    books, 12, 395-409
    consumer electronics, 423-25
    motion picture, 418-22
    periodicals, 410-15
    print media technology, 416-18
    radio-TV, 92-93, 364-65, 426-27
    recordings, 90, 357-58
Institute for Communication Research, 391
international news, 385-91
International Trade Commission, 425
intra-market ownership, 91, 93

J

Joint Council on Educational Television, 104
journalism
    broadcast, 300-4
    educational programs, 231-34
    job characteristics, 236-38

K

Kagan Associates, Paul, 59, 215

L

libraries, 15-18, 153-56, 177-78, 180, 222, 231
licensing
 radio, 46
 television, 52, 59
Lichty, L. W., 213-14
Little Company, A. D., 55, 214

M

McCann-Erickson, Inc., 124, 127, 129
made-for-television films, 32-33, 307
Magazine Advertising Bureau, 125
magazine industry
 circulation, 325-26, 341-47
 finances, 170-80
 publishers, 27-29
 readership, 348-51
 See also advertising, consumer expenditures, employment, imports, news, political campaigns,
  subject matter.
Magazine Publishers Association (MPA), 128, 172, 174, 176, 180, 292-93, 341
mail-order houses, 14, 39, 42, 362
market concentrations, motion picture, 87-90
media centers, 17, 18, 155
Media Records, Inc., 293
mergers, book industry, 75, 77
Medical Library Association, 18, 156
minority
 employment, 223-31, 259
 -interest programming, radio, 306
 media ownership, 73-75
monopoly, newspaper, 82
Motion Picture Association of America (MPAA), 34-37, 293-95, 355-56
motion picture industry
 audience, 352-56
 educational programs, 231-32, 235
 finances, 181-89
 production and distribution, 29-34, 325-26
 theaters, 29, 34-37, 88-90
 See also consumer expenditures, employment, imports, occupations, ownership, subject matter.
multi-media firms, 65-72
Multiple System Operators (MSOs), 106-7
musical compositions
 consumer expenditures for, 115
 copyrights, 6
Mutual Network, 45, 303

P

paperbacks, 12, 14, 149-50
patents, 5-8
pay-television, 33, 58-59, 107, 375
periodicals
 See magazines.
personal consumption expenditures, 114, 138

style categories, 299-300
See also consumer expenditures, employment, ownership concentrations.
regulations
Cable TV, 56, 58
employment, 230
See also FCC.
re-runs, 307
RKO Corporation, 87-89, 99
Roots, 377-78
Roper Organization, 273, 275, 280

S

sales concentrations
book, 75, 77
newspaper, 81
satellite-affiliate TV stations, 55
Screen Actors Guild (SAG), 260, 263-64, 267
Simmons and Associates Research, W. R., 331
specials, television, 317, 377-78
spot advertising, 121, 125-27
Standard International Trade Classification (SITC), 401, 413
Standard Metropolitan Statistical Areas (SMSA), 63-64, 96-97, 231
Standard Rate and Data Service (SRDS), 336
Station Program Cooperative (SPC), 311-13
subject matter
book, 283-87
magazine, 291-93
motion picture, 293-98
newspaper, 288-90
subsidiaries, 72, 85
Subsidiary Communications Authorizations, 46
Supreme Court decisions, 45, 96
Surveys
news media, 273-276
political campaigns, 280
See also survey organizations, by name.

T

technology, printing and publishing, 416-18
television
audiences, 365-66, 374-82
educational programs, 77, 231-32, 235
finances, 206-15
networks, 53-55, 301, 307-8
programming, 306-24
receivers, 325-26, 360-65, 372-73
stations, 48-55, 91-94
See also advertising, consumer expenditures, cable television, employment, news, occupations, ownership, pay-television, presidential campaigns, public television, rankings, specials.
Television Information Office (TIO), 273, 275
Temporary National Economic Committee, 33
theaters
See motion picture industry.
Thompson Co., J. Walter, 125, 128

U

UHF stations, 48-51, 74, 97, 99, 206, 210, 307, 373

UNESCO, 10, 12, 389, 401, 408, 418
United Network, 54
United States Information Agency (USIA), 391, 393
U.S. Equal Employment Opportunity Commission (EEOC), 230-31, 260

V

Vanderbilt Television News Archives, 391
VHF stations, 48-52, 74, 91, 206, 373
violence on television, 319-21
Voice of America, 391-94

W

Warner Brothers, 89-90, 183-84
wholesaling, book, 141, 143
Wilson Company, H. W., 180
Writers Guild, 260, 265

ABOUT THE AUTHORS

Christopher H. Sterling is a member of the faculty of the School of Communications and Theater at Temple University, where he has been teaching since 1970. His interest in descriptive media statistics began in the late 1960s, while he was working on his doctorate at the University of Wisconsin-Madison. He is the co-author of *Stay Tuned: A Concise History of American Broadcasting* and is editor/publisher of *Mass Media Booknotes*. He edited the *Journal of Broadcasting* from 1972 through 1976 and was co-editor of *Mass News: Practices, Controversies, and Alternatives*. In addition, he is the author of numerous articles and editor of several reprint book collections on mass communications. He has also had on-the-air experience in both commercial and educational radio and television.

Timothy R. Haight completes work on his doctorate at Stanford University as this book is published and will begin teaching as an Assistant Professor in the Department of Communication Arts at the University of Wisconsin-Madison in August, 1978. After he completed his undergraduate education at Stanford he worked as a freelance newspaper and radio reporter and as a photographer.